THE INDEPENDENT SCHOOLS GUIDE 2009 – 2010

THE INDEPENDENT SCHOOLS GUIDE 2009 – 2010

A fully comprehensive guide to independent education in the United Kingdom

15th edition

OVER A CENTURY OF SUCCESS STORIES

KOGAN PAGE

London and Philadelphia

First published in 1995
This fifteenth edition published in 2009

Kogan Page Ltd
120 Pentonville Road
London N1 9JN
United Kingdom
www.koganpage.com

Kogan Page US
525 South 4th Street, #241
Philadelphia PA 19147
USA

© Gabbitas and Kogan Page, 2009

British Library Cataloguing in Publication Data

A CIP record for this book is available from the British Library

ISBN   978 0 7494 5516 3
ISSN   1478 6893

Typeset by AJS Solutions, Dundee & Huddersfield
Printed and bound in Great Britain by MPG Books Ltd, Bodmin, Cornwall

Contents

PART 1:
THE INDEPENDENT SECTOR

PART 2:
GEOGRAPHICAL DIRECTORY

PART 3:
SCHOOL PROFILES

Acknowledgements

This Guide is the product of many hours of data collection and meticulous proof-reading by staff at Gabbitas and Kogan Page, together with cooperation and contributions from a wide-ranging team of experts. Gabbitas would like to thank all those who have helped in the preparation of this Guide, in particular Towry Law Financial Services Ltd; Sevenoaks School, CATS Cambridge and Lord Wandsworth College for kind permission to reproduce photographs; and the educational associations, Heads and schools that have so promptly provided the information required for publication.

Gabbitas Educational Consultants Ltd
February 2009

Foreword

Gabbitas Educational Consultants

Welcome to the 15th edition of *The Independent Schools Guide*, the most comprehensive directory of independent schools in the UK. Compiled from our unique database and fully updated every year, the Guide includes nearly 2,000 schools as well as practical advice from the Gabbitas team for parents about to start their search for the right school.

The Guide's accompanying website pages offer an online school search to help you identify schools suited to your requirements as well as direct links to school websites.

Established for over 130 years, Gabbitas is uniquely placed to offer parents expert advice. Each year we help thousands of parents and students in the UK and abroad who seek personal guidance at all stages of education:

- choosing the right independent school or college;

- educational assessment;

- sixth form options – including A levels, International Baccalaureate and vocational courses;

- university and degree choices and UCAS applications;

- alternatives to university;

- careers assessment and guidance, job searching and interview techniques.

Gabbitas also advises on transfer into the British educational system and provides guardianship services for children from overseas attending boarding schools in the UK. To find out more about Gabbitas, visit our website at www.gabbitas.co.uk or contact us at:

Gabbitas Educational Consultants
Carrington House, 126–130 Regent Street, London W1B 5EE
Tel: +44 (0)20 7734 0161 Fax: +44 (0)20 7437 1764
E-mail: admin@gabbitas.co.uk

How to Use the Guide

About independent schools

The first part of this Guide offers extensive information about independent schools, examinations, fee-planning, scholarships and bursaries as well as guidance on choosing a school.

Researching individual schools

The main index at the back gives all page references for each school.

Selecting schools

If you are looking for a school in a specific area, turn to the directory section (Part Two), which is arranged geographically by town and county. Schools in London are listed under their postal areas. Each entry gives the name, postal address, telephone and fax numbers and e-mail address of the school, together with the name of the Head, details of the type and age range of pupils accepted, the number of pupils, number of boarders (where applicable) and the annual fees.

Schools which have an asterisk also appear in the School Profiles section (Part Three), where advertisers provide more detailed information. These schools also have a map reference to show their exact location.

The Schools by Category section contains a number of advertising schools listed with details of their particular charactersitics.

For further references, for example to find out whether a school offers scholarships, turn to the appropriate index at the back.

Scholarships, bursaries and reserved entrance awards

Many schools offer scholarships for children with a particular talent, bursaries where there is financial hardship or reserved entrance awards for children with a parent in a specific profession such as the clergy or HM Forces. Part Four contains a complete list of schools, by county, which offer such awards.

This section is necessarily only a brief guide to awards available. More specific information can be obtained from individual schools.

Religious affiliation

The index in Part Four provides a full list of schools under appropriate headings.

Single-sex schools

For a complete list of single-sex schools, turn to Part Five.

Boarding schools

Schools with boarding provision generally offer full, weekly or flexi-boarding options. Some Sixth Form colleges, with no residential facilities, may offer accommodation with host families. The number of boarders is shown in the entries in Part Two. For an index of boarding provision by county, see Part Five.

Dyslexia

Most schools offer help, in varying degrees, for pupils with dyslexia. A list of schools registered with CReSTeD (Council for the Registration of Schools Teaching Dyslexic Pupils) appears in Part Five.

English as a foreign language

Most independent schools offer assistance to overseas pupils who require special English language tuition. A list of schools, arranged by county, appears in Part Five.

Schools accredited by the Independent Schools Council

Part Four contains an index of schools in membership of the associations listed below, which together form the Independent Schools Council (ISC). A satisfactory inspection report by the Independent Schools Inspectorate is a requirement for any school wishing to join one of these associations and for its continued accreditation as a member. For more information on the inspection of independent schools, see Part 1.1.

- Headmasters' and Headmistresses' Conference (HMC)

- Girls' Schools Association (GSA) (including the Girls' Day School Trust GDST)

- Society of Headmasters and Headmistresses of Independent Schools (SHMIS)

- Independent Association of Prep Schools (IAPS)

- Independent Schools Association (ISA).

Other associations which are constituent members of ISC but are not covered by the index are the Association of Governing Bodies of Independent Schools (AGBIS) and the Independent Schools Bursars' Association (ISBA).

School search online

Remember that you can search for schools at www.gabbitas.co.uk.

Part 1

The Independent Sector

1.1
What is an Independent School?

Independent schools educate about 7 per cent of the whole school population. Under the Education Act 2002 all independent schools must be registered with the Department for Children, Schools and Families (DCSF) and must meet certain regulations set by the DCSF (in Wales the Welsh Office Education Department – WOED). However, independent schools are largely self-governing and are not required to comply with all legislation covering schools maintained by the State.

There is sometimes confusion over the terms used to describe independent schools. 'Public schools' generally refers to old-established schools in membership of the Headmasters' and Headmistresses' Conference (HMC). Because many of these schools date back to the days when education was a luxury, received chiefly through private tutors, the term 'public school' indicated a school which the public could attend. Most schools are now described as independent. A 'private school' simply means a school which charges fees.

How are independent schools funded?

Independent schools are usually funded by fees charged to parents. Some have generous endowments that enable them to keep fees at a lower level than might otherwise be possible. Most independent schools are run as charitable trusts under a Board of Governors. Schools with charitable status are effectively non-profit-making concerns; surplus funds are allocated at the discretion of the Governors. Often they are invested in new facilities or in scholarships or bursaries. A few schools are still privately owned.

Who is responsible for the management of an independent school?

The Board of Governors is the policy-making body for the school. It is responsible for the appointment of the Head, allocation of finances and major decisions affecting the school and its development. Governors give their time voluntarily. Often they can contribute professional expertise in education, business, finance, marketing or other areas relevant to the management of the school. The Board often includes a number of parent-governors who have children at the school.

Day-to-day responsibility for the running of the school is delegated to the Head, who is accountable to the Board of Governors and who is supported by one or more Deputy Heads. Other key figures include the Bursar, who is responsible for the school's financial management, the Director of Studies, who manages the curriculum, timetable, examinations and other academic matters, and the Registrar, who is responsible for admissions and arrangements for parents to visit the school. Many schools also have a Development Director, who is responsible for marketing and presentation.

Academic staff in independent schools are not legally required to hold teaching qualifications, but schools almost always insist on a first degree in a subject which normally forms a part of the secondary school curriculum and a Postgraduate Certificate in Education (PGCE). All schools look for enthusiastic and committed staff with flair and ability. Salary scales at independent schools tend to reflect the depth of commitment expected of staff and are often more generous than those in the maintained sector, enabling schools to attract higher-calibre teachers. Further information on teaching in the independent sector can be found on the Gabbitas website at www.gabbitas.co.uk.

Do independent schools have to follow the National Curriculum?

Although not bound to follow the National Curriculum, most independent schools choose to do so. Almost all prepare pupils for GCSE and A level examinations (or in Scotland, for Scottish National Qualifications). An increasing number also prepare students for the International Baccalaureate Diploma and some now offer the Cambridge Pre-University Diploma. There is no requirement for independent schools to set pupils the National Tests used in the maintained sector. In practice, most schools have regular assessments throughout the year and set formal, internal exams two or three times a year, the results of which are included in the end-of-term report.

Who inspects independent schools?

While the performance of maintained schools is monitored by the Office for Standards in Education (OFSTED), most independent schools in England and Wales are inspected by the Independent Schools Inspectorate (ISI), which was established in April 2000 and works closely with OFSTED and the DCSF.

The ISI is responsible for the inspection of independent schools which are members of the school associations that form the Independent Schools Council (ISC). These are: the Headmasters' and Headmistresses' Conference (HMC); the Girls' Schools Association (GSA), including the Girls' Day School Trust (GDST); the Society of Headmasters and Headmistresses of Independent Schools (SHMIS); the Independent Association of Prep Schools (IAPS); and the Independent Schools Association (ISA).

A satisfactory ISI report is a requirement for any school wishing to join one of the above associations and for its continued accreditation as a member.

Inspection of ISC schools in Scotland and Northern Ireland is the responsibility of the appropriate national bodies.

How often are schools inspected, and what does an inspection cover?

ISC schools are normally inspected by the ISI every six years. The aims, as published by the ISI, are to improve the quality of education provided, to raise levels of achievement by pupils and to confirm whether or not schools comply with the registration standards set by the DCSF.

ISI inspections provide a comprehensive assessment of: the quality of education offered by the school, including educational experience provided, pupil's learning and achievement, spiritual, moral, social and cultural development of pupils and quality of teaching; the quality of care and relationships, including pastoral care, welfare, health and safety of pupils, quality of links with parents and the community and quality of boarding education; and the effectiveness of governance and management. Inspections usually last three or four days.

The views of parents are also assessed using a confidential questionnaire. The school receives only a statistical summary. Inspectors investigate concerns which are significant and, if they feel it appropriate to do so, make recommendations in their final report. However, they do not enter into individual correspondence with parents.

Inspection of boarding provision

ISI works in partnership with OFSTED for the inspection of national boarding standards. ISI inspections always include consideration for the impact of boarding on pupils' educational development. However, detailed inspection of boarding provision is carried out by OFSTED inspectors. Where possible ISI and OFSTED inspections are conducted together. Each team produces its own report, which is sent to all parents.

Who are the inspectors?

Inspection teams are led by a Reporting Inspector, who must be an OFSTED Registered Inspector, a recently retired Her Majesty's Inspector (HMI), a recently retired independent school Head or a highly experienced serving independent school Head. Other members of the team must also fulfil one of the above criteria or be a senior independent school teacher. All ISI inspectors must have satisfactorily completed training courses based on OFSTED principles.

What is done about the findings of the inspection?
Can parents get a copy?

As stated above, a satisfactory report is required in order for a school to take up membership of one of the associations that form the ISC or to be re-accredited for continued membership, and the ISI therefore also advises the relevant association accordingly. All parents of children at the school receive a free summary of the inspection findings and may obtain the full report free of charge on request. Reports can also be found on the ISI website at www.isinspect.org.uk.

Schools must submit a plan to their sssociation to remedy any deficiencies highlighted by the inspectors. The association reviews the inspection findings and the proposed action plan and may wish to arrange a further visit to the school to assess progress or offer guidance. The association may also require a follow-up inspection before membership can be confirmed or renewed.

ISI also advises the DCSF whether the school meets statutory requirements, and the DCSF will ask the school to submit an action plan to address any shortcomings. In cases where inspectors report that a school is failing to provide an acceptable standard of education or where the safety and welfare of pupils is in question, the DCSF may ask HMI to visit the school and to monitor the situation until the concerns are resolved.

Whom do I contact if I have a complaint about my child's school?

In the first instance complaints should be referred to the Head. Parents who feel thereafter that their concerns have still not been adequately addressed can refer the matter to the Board of Governors. The ISI inspection system also allows parents to express concerns in confidence to the inspection team. If an inspection is due within the next two terms, complaints about the quality of education or safety and welfare of pupils can be addressed in writing to Durell Barns, Head of Communications, Independent Schools Inspectorate, CAP House, 9–12 Long Lane, London EC1A 9HA, e-mail: durrell@ isinspect.org.uk. At other times, concerns may be sent to Julia Armstrong, DCSF, Mowden Hall, Staindrop Road, Darlington DL3 9BG (tel: 01325 392164; e-mail: julia.armstrong@dcsf.gsi.gov.uk). All such correspondence is treated in the strictest confidence.

Who inspects independent schools which are not members of one of the ISC constituent associations?

These schools are inspected by OFSTED at least every six years. Findings are published in a report which is available to the school, parents and wider community. Schools are given copies for distribution. Reports are also available via the OFSTED website at www.ofsted.gov.uk. The DCSF may ask OFSTED to revisit a school within the six-year period to review progress on any action points drawn up following the first inspection in areas where regulatory requirements had not been met. Parents' views, which are treated in confidence, also form part of the inspection. Reports refer only to the view of parents generally.

New schools must comply with the regulations before they are allowed to open. Information on the registration of new schools is available on the DCSF website at www.dcsf.gov.uk.

Accreditation and inspection of independent colleges

A number of independent colleges are accredited by the British Accreditation Council (BAC) (see below). Some independent Sixth Form and tutorial colleges are also in membership of the Council for Independent Further Education (CIFE) (see below). All colleges taking five or more students below the age of 16 are inspected by OFSTED on behalf of the DCSF.

The British Accreditation Council (BAC)

The BAC is the main inspection and accreditation body for independent colleges accepting pupils over the age of 16. Inspections cover: premises and health and safety; administration and staffing; quality management; student welfare; and teaching and learning: delivery and resources. Accredited colleges are re-inspected every five years, with an interim visit during the intervening period. Accreditation may be refused or withdrawn if any aspect of the college does not meet the required standards for accreditation. For further information visit the website at www.the-bac.org.

Council for Independent Further Education (CIFE)

There are 14 independent Sixth Form and tutorial colleges in membership of CIFE. Member colleges offer one- and two-year A level and GCSE courses, retake courses, revision courses and also one-year foundation courses for students who wish to enter a UK university but have been educated outside the British system. CIFE members are required to hold accreditation from either the BAC or ISC.

Council of International Schools (CIS)

Some international schools in the UK are accredited by CIS, a membership organization comprising international schools in all parts of the world. As part of a range of services offered to its member schools, CIS offers regular and associate schools a programme of evaluation and accreditation specially developed for international schools. Those schools that meet the standards for accreditation are given accredited status and in addition to regular monitoring must undergo a full re-evaluation every ten years.

Useful addresses

Independent Schools Inspectorate (ISI)
CAP House
9–12 Long Lane
London EC1A 9HA
Tel: (020) 7600 0100
Fax: (020) 7776 8849
E-mail: info@isinspect.org.uk
Website: www.isinspect.org.uk

The Chief Executive
The British Accreditation Council
44 Bedford Row
London WC1R 4LL
Tel: (020) 7447 2584
Fax: (020) 7447 2585
E-mail: info@the-bac.org
Website: www.the-bac.org

Council for Independent Further Education
1 Knightsbridge Green
London SW1X 7NN
Tel: (020) 8767 8666
Fax: (020) 8767 9444
E-mail: enquiries@cife.org.uk
Website: www.cife.org.uk

Council of International Schools (UK office)
21A Lavant Street
Petersfield
Hampshire GU32 3EL
Tel: (01730) 263131
Fax: (01730) 268913
E-mail: cois@cois.org
Website: www.cois.org

Office for Standards in Education (OFSTED)
Alexandra House
33 Kingsway
London WC2B 6SE
Tel: (020) 7421 6800
Website: www.ofsted.gov.uk

1.2
The Independent Sector

Why choose independent education?

Variety and choice

The independent sector includes schools of many different styles and philosophies, including both the traditional and the more liberal. Each school has its own ethos and atmosphere. Schools also vary widely in size. Some are based in towns and cities. Most boarding schools have more rural locations. Some are co-educational, others are single-sex, although many boys' schools now have co-educational Sixth Forms.

A school to suit your child

Your child's academic needs are the top priority. Not all independent schools educate highly academic children, but there is always some form of selection. While some schools will only accept pupils able to keep pace with a fast-moving curriculum, there are many others which cater for a wider spectrum of ability and some which specialize in helping those in need of more individual attention in a less academic environment.

Academic success

Good independent schools enable pupils, whatever their academic ability, to achieve their best. Their success in helping children to fulfil their potential is reflected in the exam results both of highly selective schools and of schools with less competitive entry requirements where children may need more individual support and encouragement.

An all-round education

Independent schools encourage pupils to develop their strengths outside as well as inside the classroom, ensuring that special talents, in music, drama, art or sport, are nurtured and providing a range of extra-curricular activities which inspire enthusiasm for a great many wider interests.

Small classes and individual attention

Class size at the lower end of the age range normally averages 15 to 20, GCSE groups about 12 to 18 and A level between 4 and 12, although this varies from one school to another and according to subject. Most independent schools have a staff:pupil ratio which ensures that pupils receive plenty of individual attention in accordance with their needs.

St Teresa's School, Surrey p. 368

Pastoral care

Independent schools generally place great emphasis on the traditional values of tolerance and consideration for others and on personal development within a secure but disciplined environment. Pupils normally have a personal tutor who, as part of an experienced team, monitors progress and emotional welfare throughout their school career.

Excellent facilities

Many schools offer first-class facilities for teaching, accommodation, sports and all aspects of school life.

Maintaining high standards

Independent schools must meet rigorous inspection criteria. Schools in membership of any of the associations which form the Independent Schools Council must conform to strict accreditation requirements and are inspected every six years by the Independent Schools Inspectorate. Other independent schools in England and Wales are inspected by Her Majesty's Inspectorate for OFSTED (see Section 1.1).

The boarding option

About 13 per cent of all independent school pupils are boarders. Research has shown that boarders enjoy school life and welcome the special opportunities which boarding offers, including long-lasting friendships, self-reliance and immediate access to help with studies and to a full range of facilities and activities.

While traditional full boarding has declined in popularity, interest is growing in more flexible boarding arrangements. Flexi- and weekly boarding are now much more widely available, enabling pupils to spend more time with their families, while still enjoying all the benefits of boarding life. Flexi-boarding generally means an arrangement that enables pupils to board for half the week and attend as day pupils for the remainder. Most schools can also offer a bed on an occasional basis, for example before a school trip or in the event of an emergency at home.

Full boarders normally enjoy busy weekends which offer access to a range of activities. A few schools timetable lessons on Saturday mornings, although this is becoming much less common as weekly boarding becomes more popular. Schools often arrange weekend trips away, for example to centres of cultural or historical interest or for activities such as walking or sailing. Otherwise pupils may be occupied with sports fixtures, musical or theatre performances or favourite hobbies. Most attend chapel on Sundays and have free time in which to study or relax.

Accommodation in boarding schools is often of an exceptionally high standard. Pupils share well-decorated bedrooms for small groups and are encouraged to bring comforts from home such as their own duvet covers, toys and posters. Sixth Form students often have single-study bedrooms in their own accommodation block and are allowed a greater degree of freedom. Houseparents provide constant care and supervision and are there to help with any problems arising. The Housemaster or Housemistress is normally assisted by a qualified Matron and one or two assistants, depending on the number of children in the House.

About 700 schools, including single-sex and co-educational schools, offer boarding places. Very few schools are for boarders only. Most also admit a significant number of day pupils. Whether you are looking for a boarding or a day place, it is wise to check the proportions of boarding and day pupils, since these will influence the overall ethos and character of a school. Numbers of boarders at each school are shown in Part Two. An index of boarding provision by county appears in Part Five.

Prior's Field School, Surrey p. 365

State-maintained and grant-maintained boarding schools

There are 35 state-maintained schools which accept boarding pupils, although day pupils are usually in the majority. UK and EU nationals and children from outside the EU who have the right of residence in the UK can be accepted as boarders. They pay only for the cost of boarding at these schools and are not charged for tuition. This means that fees, which are generally around £2,000 a term, are much lower than those charged by independent boarding schools. For further information see the school profiles beginning on page 253 or contact the Boarding Schools' Association (see page 499).

Types of independent schools

Independent schools in the UK cover all age ranges; some offer education from nursery level through to 18, others are junior or senior only. Most are day schools, but a large number offer both boarding and day places. There is a variety of co-educational and single-sex schools; many of the latter, particularly boys' schools, offer co-education at Sixth Form level.

Age range	Type of establishment
2–7/8	**Nursery or Pre-Preparatory School**
7/8–13	**Preparatory School**
11/13–16/18	**Senior School**
16–18	**Sixth Form**

Nursery and pre-preparatory schools

Nursery education refers to schools for pupils under the age of 5, pre-preparatory education for pupils aged 5–7/8. Many preparatory schools have their own nursery and pre-prep departments.

Pupils under the age of 5 are rarely required to meet more than the very basic practical requirements for entry, although the Head will wish to meet the child in advance. Some schools also set relatively simple tests. Most schools offer entry at the beginning of each term.

The youngest children attend either mornings or afternoons only, before progressing to a full day. Emphasis is given to the development of academic, social, language and aesthetic skills through play, music, drama and handicrafts. Children may cover basic letter and number work, handwriting and spelling. Approaches vary, from traditional teaching styles to more modern methods. Montessori schools teach according to a series of principles which centre on observation of the individual needs of each child and provision of appropriate stimuli and tasks accordingly.

Francis Holland School, London p. 331

Preparatory schools

Many prep schools accept pupils from the age of 3 upwards. Entry is usually dependent upon an interview with the Head and a satisfactory report from the previous school. Some schools also set verbal or written entrance tests in English and Mathematics, although pupils entering the preparatory department of a pre-preparatory school which they already attend may be exempted from such tests. It may be difficult to join a school for the final one or two years of preparatory education when pupils are approaching Common Entrance and other entrance examinations. Schools which prepare pupils primarily for Common Entrance may test older entrants more rigorously to ensure that they have the capacity to pass at 11, 12 or 13.

When single-sex education was more common, it was usual for girls to remain at their prep school until the age of 11 and for boys to remain until 13. However, with the growth of co-education the options are now more flexible.

Most preparatory schools are preparing pupils for the Common Entrance examination, taken at 11+, 12+ or 13+ for entry to senior boarding or day schools, although some schools, particularly city day schools, set their own entrance examinations. Some parts of the country retain the old examinations for entry to local grammar schools, which require no formal preparation. The destination of school leavers and the main

Dean Close Preparatory School, Gloucestershire p. 279

academic thrust of the school may well be influenced by available provision at senior level. The Head of your child's school will want to know which senior school you have chosen when he or she reaches the last two years of prep school. Further information about Common Entrance is given on page 41.

Pupils are normally taught by class teachers until the age of about 8. After this they may be grouped according to ability. By the age of 9 or 10 there is increasing emphasis on subject teaching by specialists and close attention to the requirements of the National Curriculum, which may be complemented by other elements such as current affairs and topical studies, group projects and field trips.

Formal assessments of academic progress and achievements as well as performance in sports and other activities are made regularly. Examinations are normally held twice a year or at the end of each term. Grades are entered in the termly report for parents.

Senior schools

Senior schools generally admit pupils from 11 to 18, although some boys' schools still maintain the traditional age of entry at 13. Schools with their own preparatory department may offer a straightforward transfer into the senior school, but most demand successful completion of entrance tests. Some schools set their own entrance tests in English, Mathematics and a general paper. Many use the Common Entrance examination.

Many senior schools also offer a range of scholarships for pupils demonstrating exceptional talent and potential in academic studies, music or art. Examinations are normally held in February and March for entry in September. Changing

Bromsgrove School, Worcestershire p. 289

St Margaret's School, London p. 344

schools at 15 or 17 is not generally recommended because of the likely disruption to GCSE or A level studies, particularly if the move means a change to a different examination syllabus. If a move has to be made after age 13, it may be best to wait until after GCSEs or their equivalent have been completed.

Changing schools at 16 is quite common. Entry to the Sixth Form of most schools is dependent upon interview, together with specified results at GCSE, which will vary from one school to another. Some schools also offer scholarships at this level. Entry requirements for independent Sixth Form colleges tend to be more flexible than in schools.

Independent schools in England and Wales are not required to teach the National Curriculum or to use the National Tests, which are compulsory for state-maintained schools. However, since most are preparing students for public examinations, they generally follow the National Curriculum, complementing it with additional options or areas of study as desired. Independent schools in Scotland are free to form their own curriculum policy, but, like maintained schools in Scotland, they are normally preparing pupils for Standard and Higher examinations.

Most senior schools in England and Wales are preparing pupils for the General Certificate of Secondary Education (GCSEs), taken at 16, the Advanced Subsidiary (AS) and Advanced GCE (A2). In Scotland pupils are prepared for the Scottish National Qualifications.

Pupils at the lower end of the age range are often taught in sets, a method which groups children for each subject according to their ability in that subject. Streaming, which groups children according to ability on a cross-curricular basis, is used in a smaller number of schools.

Kingswood School, Bath p. 393

The two-year GCSE course begins at 14. Most pupils take eight or nine subjects. In some cases very able children may take certain GCSE examinations after one year rather than two. In Scotland pupils normally take seven to eight Standard Grade subjects.

Assessments or examinations in each subject may take place each term. Many schools operate a tutorial system under which a House tutor is assigned to each pupil to monitor social and personal development as well as academic progress. Parents receive a full report at the end of each term. In some schools, mock examinations (in preparation for GCSE, AS/A2 or Scottish equivalents) are held in the spring preceding the real examinations. These are marked internally by the school and give an indication of likely performance in the summer.

Most Sixth Form students study a combination of up to four AS levels in the first year, which are normally reduced to three subjects in the final year (A2). Many schools also offer Applied A levels. For further details see page 43.

A few schools offer the International Baccalaureate (IB) and a small number now offer the recently introduced, Cambridge Pre-University Diploma (Pre-U). Both are demanding two-year courses with the capacity to assess achievement at the highest ability levels. All British universities currently accept the IB as an alternative means of entry and most have confirmed that the Pre-U will be accepted in 2010, when it is first awarded.

Some schools also run one-year courses for students who do not wish to take a full Sixth Form examination course but may wish to take a general course which includes the opportunity to take additional GCSEs, supplemented by vocational options.

Boarding schools in Scotland usually follow the English examination system, though many also offer Scottish qualifications. Higher examinations form the basis for entry to Higher Education and are offered in a wide range of subjects. Some schools also offer vocational programmes. See page 45 for details.

Pupils at Sixth Form level are encouraged to develop a more independent approach to their studies, to learn how to determine priorities and manage their time wisely. As well as timetabled lessons they normally have periods set aside for private study.

All-round education

Aside from academic studies, independent schools place great emphasis on wider activities. Many excel in areas such as sport, where pupils can develop their talents through fixtures against other schools as well as county or national school championships. Most schools recognize, however, that not all pupils enjoy team games. Many offer more individual sports, including, for example, squash, horse-riding, sailing and golf. Music, art and drama are also important aspects of the curriculum and extra-curricular activities. Many schools offer individual music lessons on a range of instruments and encourage students to play in the school orchestra or other

Merchiston Castle School, Edinburgh p. 402

music groups or to sing in the choir. Drama is often taught to a very high standard, with performances staged for public festivals as well as in school. Many schools offer preparation for examinations set by the Associated Board of the Royal Schools of Music and the London Academy of Music and Dramatic Art (LAMDA) and there may be regular trips to galleries, concerts, the theatre or the ballet.

Independent Sixth Form colleges

Many students remain in the same school for A level studies, which offers the benefits of continuity and familiarity at a crucial stage of education. Others choose to move to a different school or college, for example if their preferred combination of subjects is not available or if a different type of environment is sought. Independent Sixth Form (tutorial) colleges offer an alternative option for students who are seeking a different style of education, for whom entry to a school Sixth Form is not appropriate or in situations where a mid-course transfer to an alternative mainstream school is not possible. Most colleges offer resit and short revision courses as well as full-time one-year and two-year GCSE and AS/A2 courses. Tuition is in small groups, with special emphasis given to exam technique and study skills. Attendance at lessons and coverage of academic work are strictly monitored, although the overall atmosphere within a college is usually less formal than that in schools.

Cambridge Centre for Sixth Form Studies, Cambridgeshire p. 268

Most independent colleges are located in major cities, including London, Oxford, Cambridge, Birmingham and Manchester. Most are day colleges but some offer accommodation in their own halls of residence or with local families. Some colleges provide a range of sports and extra-curricular activities, but few can offer the campus-style environment and full range of on-site facilities and activities offered by some schools.

For students who wish to pursue a more vocational route there are a variety of independent further education colleges. These tend to be much smaller than state-maintained further education colleges and specialize in specific areas such as Business, Secretarial Training, Computing or Beauty Therapy.

Pastoral care and discipline

Many independent schools, whether boarding or day, operate a House system, which divides pupils into smaller communities to ensure a good staff:pupil ratio for pastoral care. Boarders are often accommodated in small groups with resident House staff. The Housemaster or Housemistress is in charge of pastoral care and will also go through the school report with each child at the end of term. House staff monitor overall progress, keep the Head informed about each child and, in boarding schools, may be the first point of contact for parents. Many schools also allocate each pupil a personal tutor, who assists with educational guidance, keeps progress and welfare under constant review and can deal with issues arising on a day-to-day basis. All schools are legally obliged to provide a statement of the policy and system of care in place for pupils. They are also required to have a published policy on bullying.

Most schools keep rules simple, encouraging self-discipline and common sense in their pupils and giving praise for good behaviour. Sometimes children may contribute to a

House points system, being awarded points for good work, thoughtful behaviour and for showing initiative or making a particular effort. Points might be deducted for bad behaviour. Other sanctions imposed might include limitations on leaving school premises or detention. A breach of school rules with regard to smoking or alcohol may mean suspension. Breaches involving illegal drugs may mean immediate permanent exclusion. Corporal punishment is illegal in all schools.

Religion

Spiritual growth is an important aspect of life in most independent schools, whatever their affiliation. The range includes Church of England, Roman Catholic, Quaker, Methodist, Jewish and others. Most adopt an inter-denominational approach and are happy to accept children of other faiths, but parents should check with individual schools the extent to which their child, if of a faith other than the majority of pupils, would be expected to participate in school worship. An index of schools by religious affiliation starts on page 464.

Contact with parents

Every child receives a termly report which is sent home to parents. Schools also hold parents' evenings at regular intervals to allow parents to discuss with teaching and pastoral staff any issues of concern and to be fully briefed on their child's progress. The school report will also contain results of any internal exams held during the term. Parents are often invited to attend school sporting, musical or theatrical events, whether or not their child is taking part, and sometimes to help with school projects such as fundraising activities.

Educational guidance and careers assessment

The value of good educational guidance cannot be overestimated, particularly in view of the complexity and variety of options now available to school leavers and the importance of making the right choice. Some schools have a well-stocked, permanently staffed careers department and a full programme of careers guidance which includes formal assessment, talks from visiting speakers and work experience opportunities. Others may have more limited resources. For parents seeking specialist guidance from an independent source, Gabbitas offers extensive one-to-one careers assessment and advice for students aged 15+.

Special educational needs

Parents of children in need of extensive individual attention, usually those with specific learning difficulties such as dyslexia, will find that there are a large number of mainstream independent schools which offer facilities and tuition in varying degrees. Some schools may bring in a specialist teacher to assist pupils at set times during the week. Some may have specialist teachers permanently on the staff. Others may run a specially staffed department or unit. Parents interested in schools which offer provision in some form will find a number of these profiled in Part Three. More detailed information is available from Dyslexia Action, the British Dyslexia Association and CReSTeD (see Part Five). Many schools also offer English as a Foreign Language (EFL) support to students coming from overseas, although in most cases pupils will be expected to have a certain level of English on arrival. A list of schools offering EFL support appears in Part Five. More detailed information on special needs provision and special schools may be found in a separate Gabbitas publication, *Schools for Special Needs – A Complete Guide*, available in bookshops or direct from Gabbitas. To search for special schools online, visit www.gabbitas.co.uk.

Extra-curricular activities

Many schools offer an impressive range of options, from art appreciation to abseiling, from fencing to fishing, often at very high standards. Most schools have a range of musical activities – orchestras, choir, madrigal groups, wind ensembles, to name but a few – and offer wide-ranging opportunities for individual music tuition. Most sports form part of extra-curricular activities as well as time-tabled lessons. Other activities might include chess, badminton, canoeing, Duke of Edinburgh's Award, horse-riding, Brownies and Scout groups, ballet, cookery, gardening, trampolining, rowing, golf, billiards, furniture restoration, stamps, sailing, carpentry, model-making, DT, pottery, drama, French clubs, community service and outward bound activities. Individual schools should be happy to supply parents with a list of their activities.

Kent College, Kent p. 354

School staff – who's who?

The Board of Governors

The Board of Governors is the planning and policy-making body which controls the administration and finance of the school. Some may also be parents of children at the school. The Governors are responsible for the appointment of the Head and for all major decisions affecting the school. Governors give their time voluntarily. Many are individuals with expertise in their professional lives, for example in law or accountancy, who can contribute their knowledge for the benefit of the school.

Head

Accountable to the Governors for the safety and welfare of pupils and the competence of staff, the Head is responsible for all aspects of the day-to-day management of the school, including appointment of staff, pupil admission policy and pupil recruitment, staffing and administrative structure, curriculum content and management. As figureheads for their schools, many Heads also regard the marketing of their school as a key part of their role, although some schools now employ a Development Director specifically for the purpose. Most Heads also include several hours' teaching in the week, which helps them to keep in touch and get to know pupils individually.

Bursar

The Bursar, in conjunction with the Governors, is responsible for financial matters within the school. The Bursar also takes charge of maintenance of the grounds, premises and buildings as well as catering arrangements.

Director of Studies

Many schools have a Director of Studies, who is responsible for day-to-day curriculum matters and timetabling and for ensuring that staff are kept informed of new developments.

Registrar/Admissions Secretary

The Registrar is responsible for the admission of pupils and making arrangements for parents to visit the school and meet the Head. He or she also takes care of the practical aspects of registration and joining.

Housemaster/Housemistress

The Housemaster or Housemistress takes care of the welfare and overall progress of children in the House and is normally the first point of contact for parents. He or she will keep the Head informed of each child's progress and may often be the first to hear of any problems. Serious issues are always referred to the Head.

Subject teachers

Subject teachers are responsible for the academic progress of pupils and will produce a termly report for those taking their subject. Open evenings offer parents the opportunity to discuss any matters of concern with subject teachers.

Chaplain

The Chaplain has a special role within school. Independent of academic or disciplinary considerations, the Chaplain is responsible for the spiritual development of pupils and can often provide a sympathetic ear to children who seek guidance on issues of concern.

Matron

The Matron looks after the practical aspects of boarding life, supervising and arranging laundry. Separate Houses normally have their own Matron. She often knows children individually and can provide sympathy and support for those who feel homesick or upset.

Sister

The Sister is a qualified nurse responsible for medical arrangements. She looks after pupils who may be admitted into the sanatorium with minor ailments and may require a few days in bed. Within a boarding school, serious medical matters are always referred to the school doctor and where necessary children will be taken to hospital.

Students

Independent schools encourage their pupils to take on positions of responsibility as part of school life. Senior pupils who show good sense and have contributed to the school by their achievements in academic work, musical or sporting activities for example, may be granted suitable senior positions in recognition of their efforts. Hence an excellent sportsman may be made Games Captain or an outstanding chorister Head of Choir. Pupils with an excellent academic record or who deserve merit for other contributions may be given the post of Head Boy or Girl. Prefects have responsibility for some of the daily routines in school and are encouraged to set a good example to younger pupils.

What will it cost?

Fees vary widely, but as a general guide, in 2009/2010 parents can expect to pay annual fees of between £4,000 and £12,000 at a day preparatory school or £12,000 to £19,000 for boarding. At senior level fees range from about £8,000 to £17,000 at day schools, or £18,000 to £24,000+ for a boarding place. Fees at girls' schools tend to be marginally lower than those at boys' and co-educational schools.

Fees in independent Sixth Form colleges are usually charged per subject, with accommodation charged separately. The overall costs of tuition and accommodation for a student studying three subjects at A level are broadly in line with those charged at a senior boarding school.

Parents are normally asked to pay fees in three termly instalments, one at the start of each term, although some schools may offer a choice of payment methods. If you wish to move your child to another school, the present school will normally require a full term's notice in writing. Otherwise you may find that you are charged an additional term's fees in lieu.

Many schools also encourage parents to take out insurance against the risk of their child not being able to attend school, for example in the event of illness.

Parents may be asked to meet additional costs during the school year for school lunches, school trips, sports kit, music lessons and similar items, so it is important to check what is and what is not included in the basic termly fee and to take account of other essentials when estimating the overall costs. Boarders will also require additional items such as bedlinen and weekend wear.

If you live overseas, bear in mind that there will be other costs associated with a boarding education in the UK. These include the costs of guardianship, discussed in Part 1.4, travel and any specialist dental treatment, eye tests or spectacles which your child may need while he or she is in the UK. Your child will also need a regular supply of pocket money. Schools discourage pupils from carrying large amounts of cash, but your child will probably want to buy music or clothes as well as small treats.

Scholarships and bursaries

If your child is exceptionally talented in a specific area, there may well be scholarship opportunities which could reduce the fees by as much as 50 per cent or possibly more. If financial hardship is an issue, bursaries may be available to help top up the shortfall. The decision to grant a bursary will be taken according to individual circumstances.

Further information about planning for school fees begins on page 33. Information on scholarship and bursary opportunities begins on page 37 and a full list of schools offering scholarships and bursaries appears in Part Five (pp. 421–46).

1.3
Choosing your School

'Which is the best school?'

There is no one school which can provide the best possible education for every child. Begin by working out your child's needs, then look for schools which meet these requirements. You will undoubtedly hear differing views about individual schools but remember that you are the best judge of your own child's needs. The question to ask is 'Which school will suit my child best?'

Avoid drawing up your shortlist on the basis of published league tables. These are an unreliable guide to the suitability of schools for your child and can be misleading. Finding the right school requires a much wider approach.

When to start

For entry to preparatory school at 7 or 8, you should be thinking about your choice once your child reaches the age of about 4. This allows you to be clearer about his or her academic potential, while allowing plenty of time for your research. For entry to senior schools, most parents start to look at the options two to three years ahead.

If you are thinking about a change of school at 16, remember that your child will be expected to sit an entrance exam. These often take place in October or November for entry the following September, with the offer of a place normally conditional upon GCSE results. It is therefore important to begin your search during Year 10, ie, the first year of your child's GCSE course.

Similarly, for entry to schools in Year 10 there is normally some form of entrance exam during the preceding year, so it is wise to allow plenty of time beforehand to consider the options.

What type of school will be appropriate?

- **Single sex or co-educational:** This is really a matter of personal preference; some argue that single-sex education enables pupils to achieve at a higher level without the distraction of the opposite sex. Others believe that co-education offers a more natural environment. An index of single-sex schools appears in Part Five.

- **Day or boarding:** Boarding does not suit all children, but for those who enjoy it there are many benefits. For some children it may be a necessity. Ensure that your knowledge is up to date: most boarding schools today offer flexi-boarding or weekly boarding options, which enable pupils to spend more time with their families. Some schools offer 'taster' days and weekends which enable prospective pupils to sample boarding life in advance.
- **Location:** Remember to consider the likely travelling time, particularly by car, during the morning and evening rush hours. Travel to and from school will also be required for parents' evenings, sports days and other school events. If public transport is to be used, how easy is the journey? Schools in more rural areas often offer a minibus service. Many parents of boarders, who today generally have many opportunities to go home during the term, choose schools within about two hours' drive.
- **Religious affiliation:** Would you prefer a school of a particular denomination or are you willing to include others in your choice?

Your child's needs

Academic needs are the first priority. Be realistic about your child's potential and avoid trying to gain a place at a very academic school unless you are confident of your child's ability to cope. Consider also any other interests your child may have, for example in music or sport, as well as your child's overall personality. Some children thrive in a highly active environment offering a multitude of stimuli and the company of other lively and confident youngsters. Others may benefit from being a part of a smaller school community.

Finding out

The Head of your child's present school can probably recommend suitable options, but you may also find it helpful to obtain an independent viewpoint from an educational consultant. Ask those schools which interest you to send you a prospectus. Most schools also have a website, which often has more recent news of activities and developments. Website addresses appear in Part Three of this Guide, or you can access sites for all these schools at www.gabbitas.co.uk. If you would like independent recommendations in line with your needs, contact Gabbitas.

Visiting schools

A personal visit is the only way to find out whether or not you like a particular school and will allow you to meet staff and pupils and experience the overall atmosphere. If possible, try to visit more than one school, so that you have a means of comparison. You may be invited to an Open Day, but the best time to visit is on a normal day during term time. That way you can see the day-to-day routine in place and the children at their usual activities. In most cases you will meet the Head, who will want to interview your child, following which a member of staff or senior pupil may give you a tour of the school.

In a boarding school you should also be able to meet the Housemaster or House-mistress. Each House has its own style and it is important to find out which will suit you best. As the House will be a home-from-home during term time, consider whether your child will be most comfortable in a structured environment or a more relaxed one. It is also important that you feel comfortable with the Head and other staff who will be responsible for your child.

There are a number of areas you may wish to enquire about during your visit.

Academic policy and destination of leavers

- At prep level, is the school's policy appropriate for your longer-term plans? Some schools may be preparing pupils primarily for entry to senior indepen-dent schools; others may have significant numbers whose parents are interested in good local state schools. Scholarship examinations also vary in syllabus from one school to another. Since some prep schools prepare pupils for a limited range of senior schools, you may wish to find out which ones are covered.
- At secondary level, what is the school's academic pace and focus?
- Ask about subjects in which your child has a particular interest or strength. How are these taught? Are pupils encouraged to develop their knowledge and interest through special projects, trips or events?
- How many children take GCSEs and AS/A2 levels, or their equivalents?
- How many GCSE and AS/A2 level subjects are offered?
- How big is the Sixth Form?
- How many pupils stay on into the Sixth Form? If a large proportion of pupils leave after GCSE, why is this and where do they go?
- Is there any evident bias in the numbers taking certain subjects?
- What other courses are offered in the Sixth Form?
- Ask about the destinations of Sixth Form leavers. What proportion go on to university or other forms of higher education or training? In which subject areas?

Exam results

- Exam results, if you can compare them with results in previous years, are a useful measure of the school's academic performance and any trends, but take care when interpreting the figures. A 100 per cent pass rate seems impressive, but how many pupils took the exam? Some schools pre-select candidates, which inevitably improves the pass rate statistics.

Testing and assessment

- What systems are in place to monitor performance?
- How much communication is there between staff and parents?

Educational and careers guidance

- What guidance is offered to pupils choosing subjects for examination study, higher education and career options? At what stage does this begin? How is it developed as pupils progress through school?
- What experience do advisers have?
- What facilities are available? Is there a dedicated careers unit with specialist staff?
- Are there any work experience programmes in place?

Special needs

- If your child has special educational needs, exactly how will the school provide for these? What experience do staff have of meeting these needs? The same applies if your child has any special medical or dietary requirements.

Pastoral care and boarders

- How is the welfare of students monitored? How will you be kept in touch?
- If your child is to be a day pupil in a boarding school, you may wish to know whether day pupils can join in with evening and weekend activities at school.
- Many working parents may find before- and after-school care facilities attractive. Some schools, particularly city day schools, offer this service.
- Parents of boarders must have complete confidence in those who will be responsible for their child's welfare. Ask about the school's policy for the care and supervision of boarders.
- What is the routine at weekends? May pupils leave the premises?
- Who is on duty in the evenings, at night and at weekends? Are they suitably qualified and experienced?
- What happens in the event of an emergency? What is the school's responsibility?
- Do boarders receive regular medical and dental checks?
- Make sure that you are shown the boarding accommodation. Is it clean, warm and welcoming? Is there plenty of space for your child's clothes and personal effects? Is there a secure area for valuables?
- What are boarders permitted to bring to school? Some schools allow small pets.

Teaching staff

- Are staff appropriately qualified? Are they specialists in the subjects they teach?
- How many are full-time?
- Is there a high staff turnover? If so, why?
- How is teaching organized?

Extra-curricular activities

- If your child has a particular interest or strength, will the school encourage and develop it?

Discipline

- Be sure that you agree with the school's policies. How do they deal with incidents involving smoking, alcohol or drugs?
- Will you be informed of any disciplinary matter which involves your child?

Seeing the school

- What do your first impressions tell you? Are staff and pupils polite and welcoming? Is the Reception area easy to find? Are the buildings and grounds neat and well kept?
- Is there a sense of order and purpose? What are the noise levels like?
- Do the noticeboards suggest an active, enthusiastic school?
- How do pupils respond to you? Are they articulate and confident? How do they respond to teachers in class?
- How do staff respond to the Head?

Registration and confirmation

Registering your child commits neither you nor the school. Schools normally charge a non-refundable registration fee, which may be anything up to £100 for a senior school. It is wise to have your child registered at more than one school in case no place is offered or available at your first choice. You will need to make up your mind about a year before your child is due to start. Once you have formally accepted a place there is a contract between you and the school. Should you change your mind, your deposit may or may not be refundable, depending upon the terms set by the school. As with any contractual arrangement, ensure that you understand and accept the school's published terms and conditions before going ahead.

The final choice

After your visits, check the schools' performance against your original criteria. Each school will have its own strengths. Which are most important to you? Your child must also be happy with the final choice, but the decision must be yours. If you have difficulty deciding between two schools, the answer is to trust your instincts. The right school is the one which will allow your child to develop his or her full potential in the company of liked and trusted staff and pupils in an environment where he or she feels happy and at home.

1.4
Coming from Overseas

If you live overseas, the best advice is to plan ahead as far as possible and at least a year in advance. This will give you a wider choice of school and allow you time to research all the options properly and make an informed choice. Parents may find it helpful to bear in mind the following aspects.

Level of English

Most independent schools will expect your child to speak some English on arrival, although additional tuition is often available in school to improve fluency and accuracy and to ensure that your child can cope with a normal curriculum.

If your child is to board in the UK but speaks only a little or no English, he or she may benefit from a short period in one of the specialist boarding schools (often called international study centres) which prepare overseas pupils for entry into mainstream boarding schools at secondary level. A list of international study centres is given at the end of this section.

Alternatively, you may wish to arrange for your child to spend the summer at one of the UK's many language schools before joining a boarding school in September. Details of suitable courses can be obtained from reputable consultants such as Gabbitas.

Academic background

If your child has been educated within the British system, it should not be difficult to join a school in the UK, although care should be taken to avoid changing schools while a student is in the middle of GCSE or A level studies. However, if your child has not been following a British curriculum, entry to a mainstream independent school may be less straightforward. The younger your child, the easier it is likely to be for him or her to adapt to a new school environment. Prep schools may accept overseas pupils at any stage up to the final two years, when pupils are prepared for Common Entrance exams and entry may be more difficult. Senior schools, in particular, will normally look for evidence of ability and achievement comparable with pupils educated in the British system and will probably wish to test your child in English, Maths and Science before deciding whether to offer a place. Students wishing to enter the Sixth Form will probably be tested in the subjects they wish to study. Recent reports and transcripts, in translation, should also be made available to schools.

If your child has been following the International Baccalaureate (IB) programme overseas, you will find a number of schools and colleges in the UK, both state and independent, which offer the IB. Details of the IB and the independent schools and colleges offering it are given on pages 51–57.

Length of stay

If you are planning to live in the UK for a relatively short period, perhaps no more than a year, you may find it more appropriate for your child to attend an international school. These schools specialize in educating children whose stay is limited and who regularly move around the world with their parents. Most are day schools, though some also offer boarding provision. These schools tend to have a broad mix of nationalities and offer a curriculum, normally based either on the British or the American system, sufficiently flexible to allow a smooth transition afterwards into international schools elsewhere in the world. Many also offer the IB, as described above.

If your stay is relatively short and you plan to return home afterwards, you may be able to enter your child in one of the schools in the UK specifically for nationals of other countries who are based in the UK. France, Germany, Sweden, Norway, Greece and Japan are all represented. Your own embassy in London should be able to provide further details.

Location

If you are looking for a boarding school, try not to focus your search too narrowly. Most schools, including those in the most beautiful and rural parts of the UK, are within easy reach of major transport links and the UK is well served by air, rail and road routes. In addition, most schools will make arrangements to have your child escorted between school and the airport and vice versa.

Visiting schools

Once you have decided on the most suitable type of school, you can obtain information on specific schools. Gabbitas can identify schools likely to meet your requirements, and arrange for you to receive prospectuses. It is essential that you visit schools before making a choice. Try to plan your visits to schools during term time. The school year in the UK begins in September and comprises three terms: early September to mid-December, early January to mid-March and early April to early July. There are also three half-term breaks, normally from two days to a week, at the end of October, in mid- to late February and at the end of May. Gabbitas can arrange a schedule of visits for you to ensure that you make the best use of your time in the UK.

Questions to ask

English language support

What level of English does the school expect? Is additional support available at school? How is this organized? Is there a qualified teacher?

Pupil mix

International schools naturally have pupils of many different nationalities at any one time. However, if you are looking to enter your child into a mainstream independent school, you may wish to find out how many other pupils of your nationality attend the school and what arrangements are made to encourage them to mix with English pupils.

Pastoral care

If your child has special dietary needs or is required to observe specific religious principles, is the school willing and able to cope? Would your child also be expected to take part in the school's normal worship?

If your child speaks little English, it can be very comforting during the early days when homesickness and minor worries arise, or in the event of an emergency, to have a member of staff on hand to whom the child can speak in his or her own language. Bear in mind, however, that fewer schools are likely to have staff who speak non-European languages.

Ask about arrangements for escorting your child to and from school at the beginning and end of term. Some schools have a minibus service to take children to railway stations and airports or will arrange a taxi where appropriate.

Guardianship

Most schools insist that boarding pupils whose parents live overseas have an appointed guardian living near the school who can offer a home for 'exeats' (weekends out of school), half-term breaks and at the beginning and end of term in case flights do not coincide exactly with school dates. A guardian may be a relative or friend appointed by parents, but it should be remembered that the arrangement may need to continue for some years and that guardianship is a substantial commitment.

For parents with no suitable contacts in the UK, schools may be able to assist in making arrangements. Alternatively there are independent organizations, including

Gabbitas, which specialize in the provision of guardianship services. Good guardian families should offer a 'home from home', looking after the interests and welfare of your child as they would their own, providing a separate room and space for study, attending school events and parents' evenings, involving your child in all aspects of family life and encouraging him or her to feel comfortable and relaxed while away from school. Some guardianship organizations are very experienced in selecting suitable families who will offer a safe and happy home to students a long way from their own parents. The range of services offered and fees charged by different providers will vary, but you should certainly look for a service which:

- personally ensures that families are visited in their homes by an experienced member of staff and that all appropriate checks are made;
- takes a genuine interest in your child's educational and social welfare and progress;
- keeps in touch with you, your child, the school and the guardian family to ensure that all is running smoothly;
- provides, as required, administrative support and assistance with visa and travel requirements, medical and dental checks and insurance, and any other matters such as the purchase of school uniform, sports kit and casual clothes.

Parents seeking a guardianship provider may like to contact AEGIS (the Association for the Education and Guardianship of International Students), of which Gabbitas is a founder member. The purpose of AEGIS is to promote best practice in all areas of guardianship and to safeguard the welfare and happiness of overseas children attending educational institutions in the UK. AEGIS aims to provide accreditation for all reputable guardianship organizations. Applicants for membership are required to undergo assessment and inspection to ensure that they are adhering to the AEGIS Code of Practice and fulfilling the Membership Criteria before full membership can be granted. For further details of the Gabbitas Guardianship Service, contact Catherine Stoker on +44 (0)20 7734 0161 or visit www.gabbitas.co.uk. For further information about AEGIS, visit the website at www.aegisuk.net.

Preparing your child to come to the UK

Coming to school in a different country is an enriching and exciting experience. You can help your child to settle in more quickly by encouraging him or her to take a positive approach and to try to absorb the traditions and social customs of school and family life in the UK. After the first year, most children begin to feel more confident and comfortable in their surroundings, both at school and with their guardian family. A good guardianship organization will ensure that you and your child know what to expect from life in the UK, and that you are aware of the kind of behaviour and approach which the school and guardian family will expect from your child. They will also be able to advise on aspects such as appropriate clothes to bring for a UK climate, which may be very different from that at home. Similarly, they should be able to advise on visas, UK entry requirements and related matters.

Where to go for help

You may be able to obtain information about schools from official sources in your own country. For detailed guidance and assistance in the UK you may wish to contact an independent educational consultancy such as Gabbitas which can advise you on all aspects of education in the UK and transferring into the British system.

International study centres

For contact details, please refer to the entries in Part Two.

- Bedford School Study Centre, Bedfordshire
- Box Hill International Study Centre, Surrey
- Diana, Princess of Wales Study Centre, Riddlesworth Hall, Norfolk
- Dover College, International Study Centre, Kent
- The International Centre, Ackworth School, West Yorkshire
- International College, Sherborne School, Dorset
- International Study Centre at Kent College, Canterbury, Kent
- International Study Centre at The Royal School, Haslemere, Surrey
- King's International Study Centre, The King's School, Ely, Cambridgeshire
- Millfield English Language School, Millfield School, Somerset
- Rossall School International Study Centre, Lancashire
- Sidcot Academic English School, Sidcot School, North Somerset
- Taunton International Study Centre, Somerset

1.5
Finding the Fees

Towry Law Financial Services Limited

How much will it cost?

Your first decision is what fees you are planning to meet. Do you have a specific school or schools in mind and if so what are the fees? Hopefully you have started planning early, which means that you are unlikely to have made a final choice of school. In this case you need to work on the average or typical fees for the type of school. This can range from day preparatory to senior boarding school. If your child was born in the latter part of the year, check that you are planning for the right period, ie don't plan to provide funds a year early, leaving a gap year at the end.

Next, you need to allow for inflation. A school's major cost is teacher and other salaries, which tend to increase in line with earnings rather than prices. Historically, earnings rise faster than prices so inflation is not something you can ignore.

The distinctive feature of planning for educational costs

This lies in the fact that you are planning for a 'known commitment'. You know that at the beginning of each term or school year you will have a bill to pay and will need to draw on your investments.

This is where the 'reward–risk' spectrum comes in. At one end, asset-backed investments offer a higher potential reward but also a degree of investment risk and potential volatility. In the longer term, such investments have been the way to achieve real growth and outpace inflation (though the past is not necessarily a guide to future performance). On the other hand, you do not want to rely on such investments if it means encashing them at the worst possible time, just after a stock market setback. Remember, because of the nature of educational planning you probably do not have any choice about when you need funds to pay a bill.

At the other end of the reward–risk spectrum are deposit accounts; just about as safe as safe can be (so long as the institution is safe), but will they keep up with inflation?

You do not need to plump for either extreme. The answer partly depends on the period over which you are investing. If you are starting soon after birth, asset-backed investment can play a larger role, giving greater potential for real growth. Nearer the time, your holdings can be switched on a phased basis into more secure investment vehicles to lock in any gains and from which you can draw during the schooling period.

An alternative approach is 'mix and match'. A mixture of asset-backed investments and more secure ones will allow you to draw from the former in years when their values are high. In other years, you can draw from the more secure investments.

Existing investments

Your strategy should take into account any existing investments or savings that may be suitable. These may not have been taken out with school fees in mind. For example, you may have started a mortgage endowment some years ago and changed to a repayment mortgage. This would free up the endowment, which could be used for school fees.

Tax-efficient investments

You can invest regular contributions or a lump sum into Individual Savings Accounts (ISAs). They are generally a good idea, especially for a higher-rate taxpayer, because the tax benefits should enhance returns. You can use ISAs for cash deposits, equities, fixed interest and commercial property investments. There is a limit on the contributions that can be made in each year, but both husband and wife can take out an ISA.

Rather than investing in individual shares, investors nowadays more commonly use 'collective' investments like unit trusts (or Open Ended Investment Companies – OEICs) or investment trusts. Collective funds give access to the benefits of equity investments without the investment risk inherent in investing in one or a small number of individual shares. Collective funds are a low-cost way of spreading risk by investing in a portfolio of shares, with the added advantage of professional fund management.

Investment services are now available that offer diversification across a wider range of asset classes than just equities and bonds. The allocation between asset classes should also be maintained to keep the investment in line with your objectives of meeting as much of the fees as possible without undue risk. Together, this very broad diversification and ongoing oversight of the investment should achieve an effective form of risk management.

Any existing ISAs could, of course, be used as part of your planning. Not everyone is aware that you can transfer existing ISAs from one manager to another if appropriate, so that they will better meet your current objectives. (PEPs are now classified as ISAs.)

Other investment options

A range of other investment options are available. For instance, if you will be over 50 (rising to 55 in 2010) when fees (or university expenses) are required, you may be eligible to contribute more to a pension and use the benefits towards the bills (although this will reduce the amount available to provide retirement income).

Once you have used your ISA entitlement, you can still invest in the same underlying funds and benefit from the manager's expertise, but without the tax advantages of an ISA.

Insurance companies also offer a number of lump-sum investment options with a range of underlying investments and risk ratings.

Expatriate parents

If you are an expatriate or offshore investor, there are offshore versions of most of the investments described above. Important considerations are your tax position while you are offshore and, if you will be returning to the UK during the schooling period, your UK tax position.

Late planning

If you have left it late to start planning, say within five years, you could consider the following:

- Check the school's terms for payment in advance (sometimes called composition fees schemes) as these can be attractive. Ask what happens if, for whatever reason, you switch to another school.
- Consider deposit-based schemes. Tax-efficient investments may play a part (cash ISAs).
- For other deposit accounts, consider internet or postal accounts, as they often offer better rates.
- National Savings, gilts and fixed-interest securities could also be considered.
- Loan schemes may be available whereby you arrange a 'drawdown' facility secured on your house. This assumes you have some 'free equity' (the difference between the value of the house and your mortgage) and is usually set up as a second mortgage. You can then 'drawdown' from the facility as and when you need to pay fees. Hence, you do not start paying interest sooner than necessary, keeping down the total cost. However, you should think carefully before securing other debts against your home. Your home may be repossessed if you do not keep up repayments on your mortgage.
- Because of the interest payments, loan schemes are costly, so they should be regarded as a last resort and only after you have reviewed your finances to check that there is no alternative.

The need for protection

For most families, the major resource for educational expenses is the parents' earnings. Death or prolonged illness could destroy a well-laid plan and have a terrible effect on a family's standard of living and a child's education. You should therefore review your existing arrangements (whether from a company or private scheme) and make sure you are sufficiently protected.

University expenses

Although many of the same investment considerations apply, planning needs to cover living expenses and the appropriate fees. There is a system of student loans.

Although university expenses are generally not as high as school fees, they have become more onerous in recent years, a trend that is likely to continue.

Seeking advice

Whatever your circumstances, it is sensible to take professional advice to ensure you are headed in the right direction; making inappropriate investment decisions can be very costly. You should seek an independent Wealth Adviser, able to advise on all investment products, who is not paid solely by commissions from sales.

'Golden' rules of educational planning

- Plan as early in the child's life as possible.
- Set out what funds you need and when you need them, and plan accordingly.
- Mitigate tax on the investments wherever possible.
- Use capital if available, particularly from grandparents.
- Take professional financial advice.

This article briefly outlines some of the considerations and investment opportunities and does not make specific or individual recommendations. There is no one answer to suit everyone as solutions depend on a number of considerations. For a strategy tailored to your individual circumstances, seek professional advice.

TOWRY LAW FINANCIAL SERVICES LIMITED
Towry Law House,
Western Road,
Bracknell RG12 1TL
Tel: 0845 788 9933
E-mail: info@towrylaw.com
Website: www.towrylaw.com

1.6
Scholarships, Bursaries and Other Awards

In addition to the many financial planning schemes available, assistance with the payment of fees may be obtainable from a variety of other sources.

Scholarships

Many senior schools offer scholarship opportunities. These are awarded, at the discretion of the school, to pupils displaying particular ability or promise, either in academic subjects, as an all-rounder or in specific areas such as music or art. Candidates are normally assessed on the basis of their performance in an examination or audition. Scholarship examinations are normally held in the February or March preceding September entry. Pupils awarded scholarships in, for example, music or art, may be required to sit the Common Entrance examination to ensure that they meet the normal academic requirements of the awarding school.

Scholarships are normally offered upon the usual age of entry to the school. Some schools also offer awards for Sixth Form entry, for example for students who have performed particularly well in the GCSE examinations. These awards may be restricted to pupils already attending the school or may also be open to prospective entrants coming from other schools.

Scholarships vary in value, although full-fee scholarships are now rarely available. Scholarships are awarded as a percentage of the full tuition fee to allow for inflation.

Fewer scholarships are available at preparatory school level. Choristers, however, are a special category. Choir schools generally offer much reduced fees for Choristers, well below the normal day fee. Help may also be available at senior schools, although in practice it is common for Choristers to gain music scholarships at their senior schools. A list of schools belonging to the Choir Schools Association appears on pp. 501–02. Details of schools specializing in the arts, dance and music appear on page 447.

Information about other music awards at independent schools is available from the Music Masters' and Mistresses' Association (MMA) at www.mma-online.org.uk. The site includes a searchable database of music awards offered by individual schools. The

MMA's annual guide to 'Music Awards at Independent Schools' is also available in printed form in music shops and libraries or by mail order from the MMA.

For a general guide to scholarships offered by individual schools, turn to the Scholarships index in Part Five.

Bursaries

Bursaries are intended primarily to ensure that children obtain provision suited to their needs and ability in cases where parents cannot afford the normal fees. They are awarded on the basis of financial hardship, rather than particular ability. All pupils applying for a bursary, however, will be required to show that they meet academic requirements, normally by passing Common Entrance or the school's own entry tests. The size of the award is entirely at the discretion of the school.

A list of schools that offer bursaries is given in Part Five.

Reserved entrance awards

Some schools reserve awards for children with parents in a specific profession, for example in HM Forces, the clergy or in teaching. These are similar to bursaries in that the child must meet the normal entry requirements of the school, but eligibility for the award will be dependent upon fulfilment of one of the criteria stated above. Normally schools will reserve only a few places on this basis. Once a place for a specific award has been filled, it will not become available again until the pupil currently in receipt leaves the school. Hence the award may be available only once every five years or so.

A list of schools and brief summary of the reserved entrance awards offered by each is given in Part Four. The awards covered include those offered to children with one or both parents working in any of HM Forces, the Foreign Office, the medical profession, teaching, the clergy or as Christian missionaries.

Other awards

Schools may also offer concessions for brothers and sisters or for the children of former pupils.

If you are interested in the possibility of a scholarship or bursary or in other awards which might be available from schools in which you are interested, it is a good idea to advise schools accordingly when you first contact them.

The GDST Scholarship and Bursary Scheme

The GDST (Girls' Day School Trust), which comprises 29 independent girls' schools educating over 20,000 girls, has traditionally aimed to make its schools accessible to bright, motivated girls from families who could not afford a place at a GDST school without financial assistance. It has a Scholarship and Bursary Scheme specifically designed for low-income families. Grants are only awarded at GDST schools.

Most bursaries under the Scheme are awarded to girls from families with a total annual income of under £17,250, and it is unlikely that a bursary would be awarded in cases where total gross income exceeds £49,000. Bursaries are means-tested and may cover up to full fees. Scholarships, which are not means-tested, are awarded on merit and may cover up to half the fees. Most awards are available either on entry at 11 or for girls entering the Sixth Form. The Scheme is also designed to assist pupils already attending a GDST school whose parents face unexpected financial difficulties which could mean having to remove their daughter from the school and disrupt her education.

Awards are made at the discretion of individual school Heads rather than the Trust and requests for further information should therefore be directed to the Head of the school at which parents wish to apply for a place. A full list of GDST schools appears on page 505.

Other government grants

Assistance with the payment of fees is also offered to personnel employed by the Foreign and Commonwealth Office and by the Ministry of Defence, where a boarding education may be the only feasible option for parents whose professional lives demand frequent moves or postings overseas.

The FCO termly boarding allowance is available to FCO parents on request and is reviewed annually. Parents in need of further information should contact the FCO Personnel Services Department on 020 7238 4357.

Services personnel may seek guidance from the Service Children's Education Advisory Service, which can advise on choosing a boarding school and on the Continuity of Education Allowance (formerly boarding allowance). The Continuity of Education Allowance is about £4,000 per term for junior boarding pupils and £5,000 per term for senior boarding pupils. An allowance is also available for children with special educational needs. Further information may be obtained from Children's Education Advisory Service, Trenchard Lines, Upavon, Pewsey, Wiltshire SN9 6BE; Tel: 01980 618244. You may also find it helpful to visit www.army.mod.uk and www.sceschools.com.

Parents may also find it helpful to consult the list of schools offering reserved entrance awards. Some schools may be able to supplement allowances offered by employers through a reserved entrance award offered to pupils who meet the relevant criteria, eg with a parent in HM Forces.

Grant-giving Trusts

There are various educational and charitable Trusts which exist to provide help with the payment of independent school fees. Usually the criteria restrict eligibility to particular groups, for example orphans, or to cases of sudden and unforeseen financial hardship. In many cases a grant may be given only to enable a child to complete the present stage of education, eg to finish a GCSE or A Level course. Applications are normally considered on an individual basis by an appointed committee. The criteria for eligibility and for the award of a grant will vary according to individual policy. In some cases several Trusts may each contribute an agreed sum towards one individual case in order to make up the fees required. It should be noted that such Trusts receive many more applications for grants than can possibly be issued and competition is fierce. Applications for financial help purely on the grounds that parents would like an independent education for their child but cannot afford it from their own resources will be rejected. Parents are advised to consider carefully before applying for an independent school place and entering a child for the entrance examination if they cannot meet the fees unaided nor demonstrate a genuine need, as defined by the criteria published by the awarding Trusts, for an independent school education. Parents may find it helpful to consult the *Educational Grants Directory*, published by the Directory of Social Change. For further information about charitable funding contact ISC Educational Grants Advisory Service, Joint Educational Trust, 6–8 Fenchurch Buildings, London EC3M 5HT; Tel: 020 3217 1100.

Local Authority grants

Grants from Local Authorities are sometimes available where a need for a child to board can be demonstrated, for example where the child has special educational needs which cannot be met in a day school environment or where travel on a daily basis is not feasible. Such grants are few in number. Awards for boarding fees at an independent school may not be granted unless it can be shown that there is no boarding place available at one of the state boarding schools, of which there are 35 nationwide.

Awards from Local Authorities are a complex issue. Parents wishing to find out more should contact the Director of Education for the Authority in which they live.

1.7
Examinations and Qualifications in the UK

Common Entrance

The Common Entrance examination forms the basis of entry to most independent senior schools, although some schools set their own entrance exams. Traditionally it is taken by boys at the age of 13 and by girls at the age of 11. However, with the growth of co-education at senior level the divisions have become less sharply defined and the examinations are open to both boys and girls.

The Common Entrance papers are set centrally by the Independent Schools Examinations Board, which comprises members of the Headmasters' and Headmistresses' Conference (HMC), the Girls' Schools Association (GSA) and the Independent Association of Prep Schools (IAPS). The papers are marked, however, by the individual schools, which have their own marking schemes and set their own entry standards. Common Entrance is not an exam which candidates pass by reaching a national standard.

The content of the Common Entrance papers has undergone regular review and the Independent Schools Examinations Board has adapted syllabuses to bring them into line with National Curriculum requirements.

Candidates are entered for Independent Schools Examinations by their junior or preparatory schools. Parents whose children attend state primary schools should apply to the Independent School Examinations Board direct, ideally four months before the scheduled examination date. Some pupils may need additional coaching for the exam if they are not attending an independent preparatory school. To be eligible, pupils must normally have been offered a place by a senior school subject to their performance in the exam. Pupils applying for scholarships may be required to pass Common Entrance before sitting the scholarship exam. Candidates normally take the exam in their own junior or preparatory school.

At 11+ the Common Entrance exam consists of papers in English, Mathematics and Science, and is designed to be suitable for all pupils, whether they attend an independent or a state school. Most pupils who take the exam at 13+ come from independent preparatory schools. Subjects are English, Mathematics, Science (these are compulsory);

French, History, Geography, Religious Studies, German, Spanish, Latin and Greek (these are optional).

The examination for 13+ entry takes place in January and May/June. For entry at 11+ the exam is held in January. For further information on Common Entrance, contact: The General Secretary, Independent Schools Examinations Board, Jordan House, Christchurch Road, New Milton, Hampshire BH25 6QJ; Tel: 01425 621111; fax: 01425 620044; E-mail: ce@iseb.co.uk.

General Certificate of Secondary Education (GCSE)

The GCSE forms the principal means assessing Key Stage Four of the National Curriculum. Pupils are generally required to choose GCSE subjects in year nine before commencing their studies in year ten at age 14. Most pupils of average ability take eight or nine GCSEs including Mathematics, English and Science, although some may take ten or eleven. Most GCSE courses are taught over two years but very able pupils may take some GCSE examinations after one year. GCSE (Short Course) qualifications are also available, which are designed to take only half the study time of a full GCSE and are the equivalent of half a GCSE. They are graded on the same scale as a full GCSE but cover fewer topics. The GCSE (Short Course) can be used in various ways: to offer able students additional choices such as a second modern language or to offer a subject which could not otherwise be studied as a full GCSE because of other subject choices. It may also be attractive to students who need extra time in their studies and would be better suited to a two-year course devoted to a GCSE (Short Course) rather than a full GCSE.

All results for GCSE are graded on a scale from A* to G. Examinations generally have differentiated or tiered papers that target different ability ranges within the A*–G grade range. Nearly all large-entry GCSE subjects are examined through a foundation tier covering grades C–G and a higher tier covering grades A*–D.

A review of the GCSE has led to changes in the assessment system, which affect both course work and examinations. Course work is replaced by *controlled assessment* in most subjects and external examination questions are revised. Controlled assessment is being introduced to provide greater control in three areas: *setting of tasks, task taking* and *task marking*. Assessed *task taking*, for example, is carried out in a supervised environment such as the classroom to safeguard against plagiarism and undue assistance. External examinations now incorporate a number of different question styles to enable students to better demonstrate their knowledge, understanding and ability.

International General Certificate of Secondary Education (IGCSE)

The International General Certificate of Secondary Education (IGCSE) was originally developed for use by international schools. However, IGCSEs have since been adopted by some independent schools in the UK because they are thought to afford greater flexibility and rigour in assessment, including the capacity to stretch the more able candidates.

Since the IGCSE is not approved by the Secretary of State under Section 96 of the Education Act 1, state-maintained schools cannot run courses leading to the qualifications for pupils aged up to 16 years. As a result the qualifications do not contribute to Achievement and Attainment Tables. However, this situation may change in light of government consultations regarding the possibility of including the IGCSE in the national curriculum assessment framework for 14–16 year-olds.

The IGCSE, which is marked on the same A*–G scale as the GCSE, is widely recognized by schools, universities and employers as equivalent, and provides progression to AS and A level study in the same way. There are, however, differences in the content and examination of the two qualifications, which vary by subject.

It has been reported that the IGCSE covers certain subject areas in greater depth than the GCSE; this has been particularly noted in Science and Mathematics. Examination of the IGCSE generally has either an optional coursework component with terminal examination – or examination only assessment.

There are two awarding bodies for IGCSEs: University of Cambridge International Examinations (CIE), which has been awarding the qualifications for over 20 years; and Edexcel which began to award IGCSEs more recently. In addition to the differences between the IGCSE and GCSE, the content and assessment structure of the CIE and Edexel IGCSE also vary by subject. Please contact these organizations for further information.

University of Cambridge International Examinations
1 Hills Road
Cambridge
CB1 2EU
United Kingdom
Tel: +44 1223 553554
Fax: +44 (0)1223 553558

Edexcel International
One90 High Holborn
London WC1V 7BH
United Kingdom
Tel: +44 (0) 1204 770696
Fax: +44 (0) 207 190 5700

GCE A levels and GCE AS levels

Following a review of the A level curriculum a number of changes have been introduced. The majority of six unit subjects have, or will soon be, reduced to four, with the exception of Biology, Chemistry, Electronics, Geology, Human Biology, Music, Physics and Science. Course work has been removed from some A levels and only remains in practical or expressive subjects such as Art, Computing, Chemistry, Physics and Music. The synoptic assessment component of A level, which focuses on students' understanding of a course as a whole and the connections between its different elements, has been addressed to make it more effective. An extended assignment, which promotes independent study and research skills, has been introduced as an option that students can take with A levels. Moreover, the external examination component has been revised to include a variety of different question styles to provide better scope for the demonstration of understanding.

For each of the new four unit subjects, two units form an Advanced Subsidiary (AS) course and represent the first half of the Advanced GCE (A level) course. The remaining two units (known as A2) represent the final year's study. Completion of all four units is required for the award of an A level. An A level grade is reached by combining AS and A2 grades. AS and A levels have UCAS (University and Colleges Admission Service) point scores for the purposes of university entry. Students who do not pursue a subject beyond the first year but who successfully complete the first year units will be awarded an AS level; a qualification in its own right. However, completion of the A2 units alone does not represent a qualification.

There are a few free-standing AS subjects where no corresponding A level is available. AS is designed to provide extra breadth to Sixth Form studies. Students may take four or five AS subjects in the first year of Sixth Form, but they may narrow down to three A2 units in the second year.

AS units focus on material appropriate for the first year of an A level course and are assessed accordingly. A2 is more demanding and is assessed as full A level standard. Overall assessment is based on examinations and/or coursework and may be made at the end of the course (linear) or at stages during the course (modular). The AS and A levels are initially graded on a scale of A to E for passes with U (unclassified) indicating a fail. For students beginning A level courses from September 2008, an A* grade will be awarded for the achievement of an A grade overall and a score of 90 per cent or more on the Uniform Mark Scale. Restriction on resitting individual units were dropped from January 2004 and students are therefore able to resit units more than once. When a request is made for certification, the best attempt will count towards an award.

There is a programme of Key Skills qualifications. The first three, covering Communication, Application of Number and Information Technology, are separate qualifications in their own right and are usually taken alongside other qualifications and groups of qualifications. They are offered at Levels 1 to 4 and the assessment consists of a portfolio of evidence. Many A level subjects offer opportunities for students to provide evidence for their Key Skills portfolio. Key Skills qualifications also attract UCAS points; for example a Level 3 in all three skills qualifications is worth 60 tariff points, the same value as an A grade at AS level.

An optional extended project has also been available since 2008. Schools may offer students the opportunity to undertake an extended project, on a subject of their own choosing, in addition to their A level courses. The extended project is a single piece of work, which requires a high degree of planning, preparation, research and autonomous working. It is taught at the same level as A level but is equivalent to half. Like A levels the extended project is graded from A* to E and for university entrance attracts half the UCAS points of an A level.

The advanced extension is available in 18 subjects including Business, Chemistry, Latin, Mathematics and Spanish. The qualification is taught at a level beyond A level, to challenge the most able students and to ensure they are tested against standards comparable with the most demanding worldwide. The qualification is included in the UCAS points tariff for university entry in 2009, with a Distinction providing 40 points and a Merit 20.

Vocational education and training

There are 116 awarding bodies. Many of these are sector-based and provide specific qualifications for their particular industry. However, there are also a number of key awarding bodies that provide a wide range of vocational qualifications across sectors and subjects. These include:

- Edexcel (offers BTEC qualifications);
- City & Guilds;
- Cambridge International Examinations;
- Oxford, Cambridge and RSA Examinations;
- AQA;
- Education Development International (formerly known as LCCIEB).

Many vocational qualifications come within the National Qualifications Framework, falling into one of two broad categories, namely Vocationally-Related Qualifications and National Vocational Qualifications (NVQs). The latter are competence-based occupational qualifications and are generally taken while the candidate is in employment. The body responsible for the overall framework is the Qualifications and Curriculum Authority. In Scotland the equivalent bodies, for the Scottish Vocational Qualifications framework (SVQ) and (GSVQ), is the Scottish Qualifications Authority.

GCSEs in Applied Subjects

These qualifications are designed for students who seek a course that gives a general introduction to a broad vocational area. Most GCSEs in applied subjects are available as single and double awards. Double award GCSEs are graded from A*A* to GG.

The following nine Applied GCSE subjects are currently available: Applied Art and Design; Applied Business; Applied ICT; Applied Performing Arts; Applied Science; Engineering; Health and Social Care; Leisure and Tourism; and Manufacturing. However, the range of subjects available is likely to be extended to include Construction and the Built Environment; Hospitality and Catering; Media; and Applied PE.

GCEs in Applied Subjects

Applied A levels were designed as Level 3 general qualifications set in the context of a broad vocational area. Like other A levels, they are usually taken over two years and students are normally expected to have achieved at least four or five GCSEs at grades A* to C. Like all A levels, the applied A levels provide a preparation for both higher education and employment. Applied A levels assess students' abilities to apply their skills and understanding in a vocational context. Assessment is one-third external and two-thirds internal. From September 2005 the VCEs were redesigned with an AS/A2 structure and the title VCE was changed to GCE. VCE subject titles such as Art and Design, Business, ICT and Science (which were offered as VCE and GCE) are now known as 'GCE in Applied Art and Design' and so on.

In Scotland, General Scottish Vocational Qualifications (GSVQs) have been brought under the new National Qualifications framework. Applied A levels and GSVQs are recognized by universities as a basis for entry to Higher Education.

As well as qualifications within the vocational framework, the Awarding Bodies offer a range of other qualifications. Further guidance may be obtained from schools, colleges and careers advisers. Alternatively, contact a reputable independent consultancy such as Gabbitas.

Scottish National Qualifications

Most schools in Scotland prepare students for Standard Grade examinations taken at 16. All students who stay on in education after Standard Grade follow a qualifications system which begins at one of five levels, depending on their examination results.

Access, Intermediate 1 and Intermediate 2 are progressive levels which a student might take to gain a better grounding in a subject before going on to take one of two higher levels: Higher and Advanced Higher. The lower three levels are not compulsory for students with aptitude, who may move straight on to study one of the Higher level courses. With the exception of Standard Grade, each National Qualification is built on units, courses and group awards:

- National Units – these are the smallest elements of a qualification and are internally assessed; most require 40 hours of study.
- Courses – National Courses are usually taken in S5 or S6 and at college. They are made up of three units each, and are assessed internally and by examination for which grades A–C are awarded.
- Scottish Group Awards (SGAs) – these are programmes of courses and units that cover 16 broad subject areas. An SGA can be obtained within one year, or worked towards over a longer period.

There are 75 subjects available, including Philosophy, Politics, Care; job-orientated subjects such as Travel and Tourism, and traditional ones such as Maths and English. All National Qualifications have core skills embedded in them, although it is possible to take stand-alone units, for example Problem Solving, Communication, Numeracy and Information Technology.

For further information contact the Scottish Qualifications Authority – www.sqa. org.uk.

Cambridge Pre-University Diploma

The Cambridge Pre-U Diploma is a new post-16 qualification developed by University of Cambridge International Examinations in coordination with schools and universities. The qualification is designed to prepare students with the skills and knowledge required for successful progression to higher education.

Recently accredited by the Qualifications and Curriculum Authority, the Cambridge Pre-U is expected to be available at over 100 schools in the next two–three years. Schools will initially offer the Cambridge Pre-U alongside A levels. Within the structure of the qualification it is possible to exchange up to two A levels for corresponding Principal Subjects.

The Cambridge Pre-U Diploma offers opportunities for interdisciplinary study, includes independent research that builds on individual subject specialisms and is informed by an international perspective. Students choose from a total of 26 Principal Subjects. To qualify for the Cambridge Pre-U Diploma, students must study at least three Principal Subjects and complete an Independent Research Report and a Global Perspectives portfolio.

Cambridge Pre-U is underpinned by the following educational aims:

- Encouraging the development of well-informed, open and independent-minded individuals.
- Promoting deep understanding through subject specialization, with a depth and rigour appropriate to progression to higher education.
- Helping learners to acquire specific skills of problem-solving, critical thinking, creativity, team-working, independent learning and effective communication.
- Recognizing a wide range of individual talents and interests.
- Promoting an international outlook and cross-cultural awareness.

Unlike the modular format of the A level, the Cambridge Pre-U follows a linear structure with one set of examinations at the end of the two-year course. Achievement is reported on a scale of nine grades: D1 (Distinction 1), D2, D3, M1 (Merit 1), M2, M3, P1 (Pass 1), P2, P3. The grade D1 reports achievement above the A level A* grade (see GCE A levels and GCE Advanced Subsidiary). The intention is to enable greater differentiation between students, especially at the higher end of the grading scale.

Many universities have formally notified University of Cambridge International Examinations that they will accept applications from candidates with the Cambridge Pre-U. Moreover, Wendy Piatt, Director-General of the Russell Group, comprising 20 major research-focused universities in the United Kingdom, has indicated that they welcome the 'linear structure' and 'retention of subject specialism' provided by the qualification.

For more information about Cambridge Pre-U diploma please contact:

University of Cambridge International Examinations
1 Hills Road
Cambridge
CB1 2EU
Tel: 01223 553554
E-mail: international@cie.org.uk

The International Baccalaureate
(Information supplied by the International Baccalaureate)

The International Baccalaureate is a non-profit, international educational foundation registered in Switzerland that was established in 1968. The Diploma Programme, for which the IB is best known, was developed by a group of schools seeking to establish a common curriculum and a university-entry credential for geographically mobile students. They believed that an education that emphasized critical thinking and exposure to a variety of points of view would encourage inter-cultural understanding and acceptance of others by young people. They designed a comprehensive curriculum for the last two years of secondary school that could be administered in any country and that would be recognized by universities worldwide.

Today the IB offers three programmes to schools. The Diploma Programme is for students aged 16 to 19 in the final two years of secondary school. The Middle Years Programme, adopted in 1994, is for students aged 11 to 16. The Primary Years Programme, adopted in 1997, is for students aged 3 to 12. The IB has 2,400 authorized schools in 129 countries. This number is fairly evenly divided between state schools and private (including international) schools.

The Diploma Programme

The Diploma Programme (DP), for students aged 16 to 19, is a two-year course of study. Recognized internationally as a qualification for university entrance, it also allows students to fulfil the requirements of their national education system. Students share an educational experience that emphasizes critical thinking as well as inter-cultural understanding and respect for others in the global community.

The DP offers a broad and balanced curriculum in which students are encouraged to apply what they learn in the classroom to real-world issues and problems. Wherever possible, subjects are taught from an international perspective. In economics, for example, students look at economic systems from around the world. Students study six courses (including both the sciences and the humanities) selected from the following six subject groups:

Group 1   language A1
Group 2   (second language) language *ab initio*, language B, language A2, classical languages
Group 3   individuals and societies
Group 4   experimental sciences
Group 5   mathematics and computer science
Group 6   the arts

Students must also submit an extended essay, follow a course in theory of knowledge (TOK) and take part in activities to complete the creativity, action and service (CAS) requirement.

The assessment of student work in the DP is largely external. At the end of the course, students take examinations that are marked by external examiners who work closely with the IB. The types of questions asked in the examination papers include multiple-choice questions, essay questions, data-analysis questions and case studies. Students are also graded on the extended essay and on an essay and oral presentation for the TOK course.

A smaller part of the assessment of student work is carried out within schools by DP teachers. The work that is assessed includes oral commentaries in the languages, practical experimental work in the sciences, fieldwork and investigations in the humanities, and exhibitions and performances in the arts. Examiners check the assessment of samples of work from each school to ensure that IB standards are consistently applied. For each examination session, approximately 80 per cent of DP students are awarded the Diploma. The majority of students register for the Diploma, but students may also register for a limited number of Diploma subjects, for each of which they are awarded a certificate with the final grade.

The Middle Years Programme (MYP)

The Middle Years Programme (MYP), for students aged 11 to 16, recognizes that students in this age group are particularly sensitive to social and cultural influences and are struggling to define themselves and their relationships to others. The programme helps students develop the skills to cope with this period of uncertainty. It encourages them to think critically and independently, to work collaboratively and to take a disciplined approach to studying.

The aim of the MYP is to give students an international perspective to help them become informed about the experiences of people and cultures throughout the world. It also fosters a commitment to help others and to act as a responsible member of the community at the local, national and international levels.

Students in the MYP study all the major disciplines, including languages, humanities, sciences, mathematics, arts, technology and physical education. Each of the disciplines or 'subject groups' is studied through *five areas of interaction*:

- approaches to learning;
- community and service;
- human ingenuity;
- environment;
- health and social education.

The framework is flexible enough to allow a school to include subjects that are not part of the MYP curriculum but that might be required by local authorities. While the courses provide students with a strong knowledge base, they emphasize the principles and concepts of the subject and approach topics from a variety of points of view, including the perspectives of other cultures.

MYP teachers use a variety of tools to assess student progress, including oral presentations, tests, essays and projects, and they apply the assessment criteria established by the IB to students' work. Schools may opt for official IB certification by asking the IB to validate their internal assessment. This is often referred to as the 'moderation system'. In this process, the IB reviews samples of the schools' assessment of student work and checks that schools are correctly applying the MYP assessment criteria. The IB offers guidance for teachers in the form of published examples of assessment.

The Primary Years Programme

The Primary Years Programme (PYP), for students aged 3 to 12, focuses on the development of the whole child, addressing social, physical, emotional and cultural needs. At the same time, it gives students a strong foundation in all the major areas of knowledge: mathematics, social studies, drama, language, music, visual arts, science, personal and social education, and physical education. The PYP aims to help students develop an international perspective – to become aware of and sensitive to the points of view of people in other parts of the world.

The PYP curriculum is organized around six themes:

- who we are
- where we are in place and time
- how we express ourselves
- how the world works
- how we organize ourselves
- sharing the planet.

These themes are intended to help students make sense of themselves, of other people and of the physical environment, and to give them different ways of looking at the world.

Assessment is used for two purposes: to guide teaching and to give students an opportunity to show, in a variety of ways, what they know and what they can do. In the PYP, assessment takes many forms. It ranges from completing checklists to monitor progress to compiling a portfolio of a student's work. The IB offers schools substantial guidance for conducting assessment, including a detailed handbook and professional development workshops. Student portfolios and records of PYP exhibitions are reviewed on a regular basis by the IB as part of programme evaluation.

For further information about the IB programmes, please contact:

International Baccalaureate Programme
Route des Morillons 15
CH-1218 Grand-Saconnex
Geneva
Switzerland
Tel: +41 22 791 7740
Fax: + 41 22 791 0277
E-mail: ibhq@ibo.org
Website: www.ibo.org

Independent schools authorized to offer the International Baccalaureate's Diploma Programme in the United Kingdom

ENGLAND

Bedfordshire

Bedford High School
Bromham Road
Bedford MK40 2BS
Tel: 01234 360221
Fax: 01234 353552
E-mail: ph@bedfordhigh.co.uk
IB Co-ordinator: Mr Philip Herrick

Bedford School
De Parys Avenue
Bedford MK40 7TU
Tel: 01234 362200
Fax: 01234 362283
E-mail: ib@bedfordschool.org.uk
IB Co-ordinator: Mr Adrian Johnson

Berkshire

The Abbey School
17 Kendrick Road
Reading RG1 5DZ
Tel: 01189 872 256
E-mail: schooloffice@theabbey.co.uk
IB Co-ordinator: Mrs Rachel Dent

Wellington College
Crowthorne RG45 7PU
Tel: 01344 444 000
E-mail: info@wellingtoncollege.org.uk
IB Co-ordinator: Mr David James

Cambridgeshire

The Stephen Perse Sixth Form College
Union Road
Cambridge CB2 1HF
Tel: 01223 454700
E-mail: office@perse.cambs.sch.uk
IB Co-ordinator: Mr Simon D Armitage

Cornwall

The Bolitho School
Polwithen
Penzance TR18 4JR
Tel: 01736 363271
Fax: 01736 330960
E-mail:
  enquiries@bolitho.cornwall.sch.uk
IB Co-ordinator: Mr Patrick Ian Minm

Cumbria

Windermere St Anne's School
Patterdale Road
Windermere
Cumbria CA23 1NW
Tel: 01539 446164
Fax: 01539 488414
E-mail: admissions@wsasschool.com
IB Co-ordinator: Mrs Jenny Davey

Dorset

Sherborne School
Abbey Road
Sherborne DT9 3AP
Tel: 01935 812 249
E-mail: enquiries@sherborne.org
IB Co-ordinator: Dr Peter Such

Sherborne School for Girls
Bradford Road
Sherborne
Dorset DT9 3QN
Tel: 01935 812245
Fax: 01935 889445
E-mail: enquiry@sherborne.com
IB Co-ordinator: Ms Sue Moody

Essex

Brentwood School
Ingrave Road
Brentwood
Essex CM15 8AS
Tel: 01277 243243
IB Co-ordinator: Mr Timothy Woffenden

Felstead School
Dunmow
Essex CM6 3LL
Tel: 01371 822600
IB Co-ordinator: Mr Paul Clark

Gloucestershire

Cheltenham Ladies' College
Bayshill Road
Cheltenham GL50 3EP
Tel: 01242 520691
E-mail: enquiries@cheltladiescollege.org
IB Co-ordinator: Mrs Julie Keylock

Greater Manchester

The Manchester Grammar School
Old Hall Lane
Manchester M13 0XT
Tel: 0161 224 7201
E-mail: general@mgs.org
IB Co-ordinator: Mr Chris Buckley

Hertfordshire

Haileybury
Hertford
Hertfordshire SG13 7NU
Tel: 01992 706205
Fax: 01992 706276
E-mail: jameshk@haileybury.com
IB Co-ordinator: Mr James Kazi

Stanborough School
Stanborough Park
Watford
Hertfordshire WD25 9JT
Tel: 01923 673268
IB Co-ordinator: Mr Peter Martin

Isle of Man

King William's College
Castletown
Isle of Man IM9 1TP
Tel: 01624 822551
Fax: 01624 824207
E-mail: rene.filho@kwc.sch.im
IB Co-ordinator: Dr Rene Filho

Kent

Sevenoaks School
Sevenoaks
Kent TN13 1HU
Tel: 01732 455133
Fax: 01732 456143
E-mail: sma@sevenoaksschool.org
IB Co-ordinator: Sue Austin

Lancashire

Rossall School
Broadway
Fleetwood
Lancashire FY7 8JW
Tel: 01253 774201
Fax: 01253 772052
E-mail: ibatrossall@hotmail.com
IB Co-ordinator: Dr Doris Dohmen

London

The Godolphin and Latymer School
Iffley Road
Hammersmith
London W6 0PG
Tel: 020 8741 1936
Fax: 020 8746 3352
E-mail: ctrimming@
  godolphinandlatymer.com
IB Co-ordinator: Mrs Caroline Trimming

Highlands School
148 Worlds End Lane
London N21 1QQ
Tel: 020 8370 1100
Fax: 020 8370 1110
E-mail: tutonk@highlands.enfield.sch.uk
IB Co-ordinator: Mr Karl Tuton

International School of London
139 Gunnersbury Avenue
London W3 8LG
Tel: 020 8992 5823
Fax: 020 8993 7012
E-mail: huwbach@btopenworld.com
IB Co-ordinator: Mr Huw Davies

King's College School
Wimbledon
Southside
Wimbledon Common
London SW19 4TT
Tel: 020 8255 5300
IB Co-ordinator: Mr Neil Tetley

North London International School
Friern Barnet Road
Friern Barnet
London N11 3DR
Tel: 020 8368 3777
Fax: 020 8368 3220
E-mail: acobbin@wpis.org
IB Co-ordinator: Ms Alison Cobbin

St Dunstan's College
Stanstead Road
London SE6 4TY
Tel: 020 8516 7200
Fax: 020 8516 7300
E-mail: salgeo@sdmail.co.uk
IB Co-ordinator: Sue Algeo

Southbank International School
63–65 Portland Place
London W1B 1QR
Tel: 020 7436 9699
IB Co-ordinator: Ms Lori Fritz

Merseyside

Liverpool College
Queen's Drive
Mossley Hill
Liverpool L18 8BG
Tel: 01517 244000
E-mail: admin@liverpoolcollege.org.uk
IB Co-ordinator: Mr Harry Lock

Middlesex

ACS Hillingdon International School
108 Vine Lane
Hillingdon
Uxbridge
Middlesex UB10 0BE
Tel: 01895 259771
Fax: 01895 256974
E-mail: dwynne-jones@acs-england.co.uk
IB Co-ordinator: Mr David Wynne-Jones

North London Collegiate School
Canons
Edgware
Middlesex HA8 7RJ
Tel: 020 8952 0912
Fax: 020 8951 1391
E-mail: mburke@nlcs.org.uk
IB Co-ordinator: Mr Michael Burke

St Helen's School
Eastbury Road
Northwood
Middlesex HA6 3AS
Tel: 01923 843210
Fax: 01923 843211
E-mail: mbowman@
  sthelensnorthwood.co.uk
IB Co-ordinator: Mrs Mary Bowman

Norfolk

Gresham's School
Cromer Road
Holt NR25 6EA
Tel: 0126 371 4515
E-mail: reception@greshams.com
IB Co-ordinator: Mr Mark Russell Abbott

Oxfordshire

St Clare's
139 Banbury Road
Oxford OX2 7AL
Tel: 01865 517332
Fax: 01865 310002
E-mail: nick.lee@stclares.ac.uk
IB Co-ordinator: Mr Nick Lee

St Edward's, Oxford
Woodstock Road
Oxford OX2 7NN
Tel: 01865 319 204
E-mail: registrar@stedwards.oxon.sch.uk
IB Co-ordinator: Mr Jesse Elzinga

Rutland

Oakham School
Chapel Close
Oakham
Rutland LE15 6DT
Tel: 01572 758698
Fax: 01572 758623
E-mail: jr@oakham.rutland.sch.uk
IB Co-ordinator: Dr Jill Rutherford

Shropshire

Ellesmere College
Ellesmere
Shropshire SY12 9AB
Tel: 01691 622321
IB Co-ordinator: Mrs HT Scanisbrick

Somerset

Taunton School
Taunton
Somerset TA2 6AD
Tel: 01823 349200/349223
Fax: 01823 349201
E-mail: enquiries@tauntonschool.co.uk
IB Co-ordinator: Mr Martin Blumel

North Somerset

Sidcot School
Oakridge Lane
Wiscombe
North Somerset BS25 1PD
Tel: 01934 843102
Fax: 01934 844181
E-mail: admissions@sidcot.org.uk
IB Co-ordinator: Mr Philip Pertens

Surrey

ACS Cobham International School
Portsmouth Road
Cobham
Surrey KT11 1BL
Tel: 01932 867251
Fax: 01932 869791
E-mail: cworthington@acs-england.co.uk
IB Co-ordinator: Mr Craig Worthington

ACS Egham International School
London Road
Egham
Surrey TW20 0HS
Tel: 01784 430800
Fax: 01784 430153
IB Co-ordinator: Mr Colin Sercombe

King Edward's School
Witley
Godalming
Surrey GU8 5SG
Tel: 01428 686700
Fax: 01428 682850
E-mail: mehargc@kesw.surrey.sch.uk
IB Co-ordinator: Ms Christine Meharg

Marymount International School
George Road
Kingston upon Thames
Surrey KT2 7PE
Tel: 020 8949 0571
Fax: 020 8336 2485
E-mail: acdean@
*   marymount.kingston.sch.uk*
IB Co-ordinator: Dr Brian Johnson

TASIS The American School in England
Coldharbour Lane
Thorpe
Egham
Surrey TW20 8TE
Tel: 01932 565252
Fax: 01932 564644
E-mail: cgoldon@tasis.com
IB Co-ordinator: Mrs Chantal Goldon

Whitgift School
Haling Park
South Croydon
Surrey CR2 6YT
Tel: 020 8688 9222
Fax: 020 8760 0682
E-mail: stewartcook@totalise.co.uk
IB Co-ordinator: Mr Stewart Cook

Sussex

Ardingly College
College Road
Ardingly
Haywards Heath
West Sussex RH17 6SQ
Tel: 01444 893000
Fax: 01444 893001
E-mail: widgetcat@hotmail.com
IB Co-ordinator: Mr John Langford

Worth School
Paddockhurst Road
Turners Hill
West Sussex RH10 4SD
Tel: 01342 710222
Fax: 01342 710230
E-mail: nconnolly@worth.org.uk
IB Co-ordinator: Mr Nicholas Connolly

Wiltshire

Warminster School
Church Street
Warminster
Wiltshire BD12 8PS
Tel: 01985 210100
IB Co-ordinator: Ms Olivia Bolline

Worcestershire

Malvern College
College Road
Malvern
Worcestershire WR14 3DF
Tel: 01684 581500
Fax: 01684 581617
E-mail: jpk@malcol.org
IB Co-ordinator: Mr John Knee

North Yorkshire

Queen Ethelburga's College
Thorpe Underwood Hall
Ouseburn
York YO26 9SS
Tel: 01423 333 300
E-mail: info@queenethelburgas.edu
IB Co-ordinator: Mr Daniel Machin

Scarborough College
Filey Road
Scarborough
Yorkshire YO11 3BA
Tel: 01723 360620
IB Co-ordinator: Mrs Amanda Evinger

West Yorkshire

The Grammar School at Leeds
Alwoodley Gates
Harrogate Rd
Leeds LS17 8GS
Tel: 0113 274 4000
E-mail: info@lgs.leeds.sch.uk
IB Co-ordinator: Mr Mark Humphries

SCOTLAND

Aberdeenshire

The International School of Aberdeen
'Fairgirth'
296 North Deeside Road
Milltimber
Aberdeen AB13 0AB
Tel: 01224 732267
Fax: 01224 734879
E-mail: marybeth.kiley@
  isa.aberdeen.sch.uk
IB Co-ordinator: Mrs Beth Kiley

Edinburgh

Fettes College
Carrington Road
Edinburgh EH4 1QX
Tel: 0131 332 2281
IB Co-ordinator: Mr John Fern

Fife

St Leonards School
St Andrews
Fife KY16 9QJ
Tel: 01334 472126
IB Co-ordinator: Mrs Ann Scot

WALES

Conwy

Rydal Penrhos
Pwllycrochan Avenue
Colwyn Bay
Conwy LL29 7BT
Tel: 01492 530155
Fax: 01492 531872
E-mail: wynniewil@hotmail.com
IB Co-ordinator: Mr Wyn Williams

South Glamorgan

United World College of the Atlantic
St Donat's Castle
Llantwit Major
Vale of Glamorgan
CF6 7WF
Tel: 01446 799002
Fax: 01446 799013
E-mail: gareth.rees@uwc.net
IB Co-ordinator: Mr Gareth Rees

Examining and awarding bodies: useful addresses

Assessment and Qualifications Alliance (AQA)
Devas Street
Manchester M15 6EX
Tel: 0161 953 1180
Fax: 0161 273 7572
E-mail: mailbox@aqa.org.uk
Website: www.aqa.org.uk

Stag Hill House
Guildford
Surrey GU2 7XJ
Tel: 01483 506506
Fax: 01483 300152
E-mail: postmaster@aqa.org.uk
Website: www.aqa.org.uk

Unit 10
City Business Park
Easton Road
Bristol BS5 0SP
Tel: 0117 927 3434
Fax: 0117 929 0268

31–33 Springfield Avenue
Harrogate
North Yorkshire HG1 2HW
Tel: 01423 840015
Fax: 01423 523678

City & Guilds
1 Giltspur Street
London EC1A 9DD
Tel: 020 7294 2800
Fax: 020 7294 2400
E-mail: enquiry@city-and-guilds.co.uk
Website: www.city-and-guilds.co.uk

University of Cambridge International Examinations
1 Hills Road
Cambridge CB1 2EU
Tel: 01223 553558
Fax: 01223 553554
E-mail: international@cie.org.uk
Website: www.cie.org.uk

Edexcel Foundation
One90 High Holborn
London WC1V 7BH
Tel: 0870 240 9800
Fax: 020 7190 5700
E-mail: enquiries@edexcel.org.uk
Website: www.edexcel.org.uk

OCR (Oxford, Cambridge and RSA Examinations)
1 Hills Road
Cambridge CB2 2EU
Tel: 01223 553998
Fax: 01223 552627
E-mail: general.qualifications@ocr.org.uk
Website: www.ocr.org.uk

Qualifications and Curriculum Authority
Customer Relations
83 Piccadilly
London W1J 8QA
Tel: 020 7509 5555
Fax: 020 7509 6666
E-mail: info@qca.org.uk
Website: www.qca.org.uk

Scottish Qualifications Authority
The Optima Building
58 Robertson Street
Glasgow G2 8DQ
Tel: 0845 279 1000
Fax: 0845 213 5000
E-mail: customer@sqa.org.uk
Website: www.sqa.org.uk

Welsh Joint Education Committee
245 Western Avenue
Cardiff CF5 2YX
Tel: 029 2026 5000
Fax: 029 2057 5994
E-mail: info@wjec.co.uk
Website: www.wjec.co.uk

1.8

The Sixth Form and Beyond – a Parents' Guide

If you have a son or daughter studying for GCSEs or the equivalent, he or she, like most 15 and 16 year olds, is probably still some way from decisions about higher education and careers. At this stage there is, of course, plenty of room for the development of ideas and interests, and it is important to have an open mind about all the options. Some preliminary planning, however, is essential.

Choosing the right Sixth Form course is becoming increasingly important as the options at 18 become more complex. Students who have given some thought to their future plans, to their own strengths and personal qualities, will find it easier to identify broad potential career areas. This in turn will enable them to choose suitable Sixth Form and higher education options which still allow flexibility for the development of their skills and personality over the next few years. At the same time, extra-curricular activities, relevant work experience and other research will help to build up the essential personal and practical skills sought by today's employers.

Good advice is essential. Some schools have excellent careers guidance programmes and materials and may also arrange talks from visiting speakers and work experience opportunities. Others may have more limited resources. Computerized careers assessments are often used in schools. These are not designed to provide all the answers, and it is vital that they should form part of a much more extensive discussion that includes consideration of academic achievements and aspirations, attitudes, interests and any special needs.

Your son or daughter may also find it helpful to speak to an independent consultant, who can offer an objective view and perhaps a wider perspective of the possibilities.

Choosing Sixth Form options

The main options available after GCSE are: Advanced Subsidiary GCE (AS) and Advanced GCE (A2); in Scotland, National Qualifications (Highers); the International Baccalaureate (IB); and Applied A levels; although the Cambridge Pre-U is now available at some schools. The basic structure of these courses is covered in Part 1.7.

All can be used as a means of entry to British universities. The IB, as its name implies, is an international qualification and is also recognized for admission purposes by many universities worldwide. Unlike the other options above, however, the IB Diploma course is not widely available in the UK. A list of UK schools and colleges authorized to run the IB Diploma course is given on pages 51–57.

Before making a choice, students may find it helpful to consider the following.

Subjects or areas of study

Is depth or breadth the most important factor? A levels offer a high degree of specialization. The IB is a demanding academic qualification but covers a wider range of subjects in less depth. A vocational course will probably have a focus on a particular career area such as Business, Leisure & Tourism or Information Technology.

Course load

Most students take four AS subjects in the Lower Sixth and continue three of these as A2s in the Upper Sixth, thus emerging from school with three full A levels and one AS in a fourth subject. Because of the diversity of the current Sixth Form programme, entry requirements vary significantly between one course and another. The equivalent of three A level passes is the core requirement. However, in some cases universities may ask for specific grades in certain subjects and in others they may seek an overall number of UCAS points. In this relatively uncertain climate, sixth formers should appreciate that quality is more important than quantity – in other words additional courses should not be taken if this would jeopardize the grades obtained in core subjects. If they are in any doubt about the combination of A/AS levels and grades which will be acceptable to a university, they should not hesitate to contact admissions staff or seek other forms of professional advice.

Availability

Is the required course available at your child's present school or, if not, at another school or college locally? Is living away from home an option? Applied A level courses are widely available in maintained colleges. Some vocational courses are also offered by a much smaller number of independent schools.

Assessment method and course structure

Some students prefer regular assessment through submission of coursework or projects rather than exam-based assessment. Many A level courses, traditionally assessed through a final exam, now include coursework as part of the assessment. The IB is assessed chiefly by examinations. Applied A levels are assessed largely on coursework.

Academic ability

A level courses often demand a good deal of reading and the ability to write well-argued essays. In science-based subjects, abstract thinking and in some cases strong mathematical skills are important.

Future plans

Students aiming for a specific career should check whether their preferred options are suitable. Those still undecided should choose a programme which allows some flexibility.

Which A levels?

It is natural for students to want to continue with subjects they enjoy. Clearly, a high GCSE result suggests that a similar result may be expected at A level. This is important, of course, but students must also consider whether or not their preferred combination of subjects is suitable for their higher education or career plans. It is also possible to take certain A level courses in subjects not previously studied.

Career choice

Some careers, for example engineering, medicine and architecture, demand a specific degree. This may limit, or sometimes dictate, the choice of A level subjects and students must be confident that they can do well in these. If career plans are undecided, it is wise to choose subjects which will leave a number of options open.

Ability

It is advisable to have achieved at least a grade B at GCSE in any subjects being considered for A level (ideally grade A in Maths, Science and Modern Languages). Some A level subjects such as Economics can be taken without any previous knowledge, but students should consider what skills are required, eg numerical, analytical or essay-writing, and whether or not it will suit them.

Different examining bodies may assess the same subject in different ways. If your son or daughter has concerns about a final exam-based assessment, he or she might consider a syllabus which offers a modular structure and a higher degree of assessment through coursework. Remember, however, that if all the subjects chosen are assessed on this basis, the workload and the pressure to meet deadlines during the course could be very heavy.

Interest

Genuine interest is essential if a student is to feel motivated throughout the two-year course and achieve high grades. Students in a dilemma over the choice between a subject they enjoy and a subject which they feel they ought to do might be well advised to opt for the former, but should check that this is suitable for their future plans. Students who are thinking of taking up a new subject, for example Psychology, may find it helpful to read a few books on the subject to test their interest before making any decisions.

Which subject combinations?

If no specific combination is demanded, how can students ensure a suitable choice? At least two subjects should be complementary, ie two arts/social sciences or two sciences. It is quite common for students to combine arts and sciences. It should be remembered that even those career areas which do not demand specific degree courses may still require certain skills, which some A level subjects will develop better than others.

If a particular degree course does not require an A level in the subject, eg Psychology, it may be better to choose a different A level subject or perhaps a complementary vocational option and so demonstrate a wider knowledge/skills base to university admissions tutors. This also avoids the risk of repeating the A level syllabus in the first year at university.

Other matters to consider include the timetabling constraints at school, which may make a certain combination impossible, in which case students may have to compromise or change to a school or college with greater flexibility.

Where shall I study?

Staying on into the Sixth Form of the present school does have advantages, including continuity and familiarity with surroundings, staff and fellow students. It is not unusual, however, for students to change schools at 16. Some may be looking for a course, subjects or combination of subjects not available at their present school; others may simply want a change of atmosphere or a different style of education.

If a change to a different school is sought, consider the school's academic pace and examination results, its university entry record, the criteria for entry to the Sixth Form and the availability of places, the size of the Sixth Form and of the teaching groups and, where appropriate, the opportunities to develop skills or pursue interests aside from A level studies.

Independent Sixth Form or tutorial colleges offer an alternative environment and are described on page 16. There are also specialist independent colleges which focus on specific vocational areas such as business, accountancy or computing.

Maintained Sixth Form colleges offer a wide range of A levels and, increasingly, vocational options such as Vocational A levels. They may have between 500 and 1,000 students and because of their size can normally offer quite extensive facilities. However, teaching groups may be much larger than those in the independent sector.

Maintained further education colleges are located in all parts of the country and offer a vast range of A levels and vocational courses to students of all ages, many on a part-time basis. Colleges can be huge in size and may occupy several sites. Some also offer degree and diploma courses and may therefore be able to offer extensive facilities and resources, particularly for vocational studies. The age range of such colleges is much wider than in the independent sector, so it is also important to check that there is a suitable system of pastoral care for 16–18 year olds.

There are also Apprenticeship schemes, which incorporate employment with part-time study. The best source of information on these is usually the local careers office or Connexions Service. Such programmes have a national NVQ rating equivalent to GCSE or Sixth Form studies, depending on the level and the content.

The university challenge

Access to degree courses in the UK is now wider than ever before. Despite continuing pressures on graduate employment opportunities and the introduction of tuition fees, students entering higher education have reached record numbers.

Higher education offers a unique range of academic, career and social opportunities. However, poor preparation for university can prove disastrous. There are growing concerns about the rising number of students – currently nearly one in five – who do not complete their degree courses. The sense of having made the wrong choice is an often-cited factor.

Why does your son or daughter want to go to university? Is he or she genuinely motivated and keen to study a particular subject in depth, to qualify for a specific career, and to take advantage of all the benefits which university life offers? All these reasons are valid, but some students may apply to university largely because they feel under pressure at home and/or at school to do so. Timing is also important. Students still unsure what to study should not rush into a decision. It may be better to take a year out and to use the additional time constructively before making a choice.

Most schools encourage students to begin thinking seriously about higher education soon after entering the Sixth Form. During the spring and summer terms of the Lower Sixth, students should be doing their research. Information is available from reference guides, from the internet and from university prospectuses. Most universities organize open days, when students can visit and talk to staff and students. This means that students should be well prepared for the autumn when application forms should be sent to UCAS (the Universities and Colleges Admissions Service): by 15 October for applications that include Oxford, Cambridge or Medicine and by 15 January for all other applications (with the exception of some for Art and Design).

Support and guidance from school, from external advisers and from parents is essential throughout this period, but the final choice of course and university lies with the student, and he or she should be taking an active part in the process. So what are the key points to consider?

Which course?

Is a specific degree necessary for a specific career? In some cases, typically Medicine, yes. In many cases, however, including Law, students have more flexibility. If there are no specific requirements, prospective employers will often take account of the quality of degree obtained and the reputation of the university as much as the subject studied, and will look for other skills and qualities which match their requirements. This means that students should take a subject in which they expect to do well rather than something which they may, perhaps wrongly, believe to be 'the right thing'. It is also important to demonstrate a breadth of knowledge and skills, for example interpersonal skills, language skills, commercial awareness or an understanding of science or information technology, in addition to the subject studied. There are differing views over the importance of taking some career-related degree subjects, for example, Business Studies or Media/Communication Studies. Some employers may prefer to employ graduates with a wider education background and train them in-house. Others may prefer applicants to be able to demonstrate practical knowledge and interest. Taking the above examples, this might include work experience with a company or involvement with the university newspaper or radio station.

Sandwich courses, offered mainly in science, engineering and social sciences, include work experience as part of the programme. This can help employment prospects, enhance practical skills and allow students to test their interest in a particular career before committing themselves. In some cases placements may turn into permanent positions with the same employer after graduation. Some students, however, may not want to delay graduation (a sandwich course may take an extra year), and may dislike the disruption between work and study. Many universities also offer students (and not only those taking modern language degrees) the opportunity to study abroad as part of their course.

Foundation degrees

Foundation degrees are vocational in content and focus, and offer a qualification below the level of an Honours degree. Foundation degrees take two years' full-time study, but they can also be studied part time. They often combine work experience with the traditional academic structure of a degree course and are intended to equip students with the skills required by today's employers and to enable them to go straight into their chosen career upon successful completion of the course. Each Foundation degree is usually linked with at least one Honours degree in the same subject area, which means that those who wish to further their qualification can go on to a BA/BSc (Hons) qualification if they choose to do so. Entry to Foundation degrees is flexible in order to attract not just school leavers but also those who are already in employment and who have the right level of ability.

Specialization

Students have a choice of studying one subject (single honours) or a combination (joint honours or a modular degree). A combined course offers more breadth and the opportunity to follow complementary studies, but almost always means a heavier workload.

For students unsure about taking a subject not studied at school or going directly into a specialized field, for example Civil Engineering, a more general foundation year may be helpful in providing essential core skills before deciding on a specialization.

Checking course content

Courses with the same name may be very different in content, so it is essential to read the prospectus for details. Modern language degrees, for example, vary widely in focus. Some place particular emphasis on practical language skills and an understanding of current affairs; others may have a more traditional emphasis on literature. Course titles like Communication Studies can also mean a wide variety of things.

Entry requirements

What subjects and grades does the course specify? Is the student likely to achieve these grades or should he or she look for a course with less stringent entry requirements? Remember that published grades are given only as a guide and may be adjusted upwards or downwards when offers are made to individual students. With the variety of Sixth Form programmes being taken, Gabbitas strongly recommends students contact universities direct to find out what they may be expected to achieve. For arts A level students who wish to take a degree in a science-based subject such as Medicine or Engineering, one-year conversion courses are available, but students will be expected to have good GCSE grades in Maths and Science. Many modern language courses do not require previous knowledge, although evidence of competency in another foreign language is usually essential.

Remember too that as the A level pass rate rises, admissions tutors increasingly use GCSE results as well as A level grades as an indicator of ability.

Which university?

Quality and reputation are as important for the individual course and department as for the institution as a whole. Beware of published league tables, which will not necessarily answer your questions. Find out about the career or employment destinations of recent graduates. This information may be available direct from the university or in one of the many published handbooks. If you have in mind a particular career or employer, it may be useful to contact the recruitment department or an appropriate professional body to find out their views on specific universities or degree courses. You may also want to ask the university about the teaching styles, methods of assessment and the level of supervision available.

There is, of course, much more to finding the right university than simply the course. Aspects such as accommodation (both on and off campus), location or social atmosphere can generate just as much anxiety and dissatisfaction if things go wrong and may just as likely lead to abandonment of the course.

Some students may be attracted to a collegiate style university such as Oxford, Cambridge or London. Others may prefer a self-contained campus where all academic, social and other facilities are available on-site. Some may prefer a big city environment; others a smaller, more rural location. Living costs are a further important but often neglected issue. What is the quality and frequency of local transport? Is a car necessary? How safe is the area after dark? How important is the distance from home? What other facilities are offered to cater for individual hobbies and interests?

Alternatives to university entry

Students who are not attracted by the idea of full-time study at university will find that there are a number of alternatives available. It is possible to study for a degree part time by distance learning through private institutions, or if practical skills are sought there are many short courses available in areas such as business, computer skills, marketing and PR, and languages.

There are companies and other organizations which take on young people with A levels or the equivalent and which offer them part-time academic training leading to relevant professional qualifications, some of which are regarded as the equivalent of a first degree. Examples include the Armed Forces and Emergency Services, the Merchant Navy, retail, hotel and catering, IT, accountancy, estate agency, and certain branches of the Law.

Finding out more

There are, of course, many other options and issues which your son or daughter may want to discuss. These might include the pros and cons of taking a year out after school and how to make the best use of it, sponsorship to help finance a degree course, presenting a well-structured and effective UCAS application, interview techniques, CV writing and job applications.

Advice should be available from your child's school. Expert, independent guidance is available from Gabbitas, who also advise students who are unhappy at university as well as recent graduates and those looking for a career move in later life. If you would like to know more about the Gabbitas Advisory and Careers Assessment Services, please telephone Catherine Walters on 020 7734 0161 or e-mail catherine.walters@ gabbitas.co.uk.

Part 2

Geographical Directory

2.1
Notes on Information given in the Directory Section

Type of school

The directory comprises schools listed within the Department for Children, Schools and Families register of Independent schools. Maintained schools, foundation schools, special schools, independent further education colleges and overseas schools are not included, unless they have a profile in Part Three.

Each school is given a brief description, which explains whether the school is single-sex or co-educational. In some cases single-sex schools take small numbers of the opposite sex within a specified age range. These are indicated where appropriate, eg: Boys boarding and day 3–18 (Day girls 16–18).

Schools are described as 'boarding' (which indicates boarding pupils only), 'boarding and day', 'day and boarding' (indicating a predominance of day pupils) or 'day' only.

Number of boarders

Where appropriate these are divided into full boarders (F) and weekly boarders (W). Weekly boarding arrangements vary according to individual school policy.

Fees

All fees are given annually from September 2008 unless otherwise stated. It should be remembered, however, that some schools increase fees during the year and the figures shown may therefore be subject to change after September 2008. Where fees from September 2008 aren't available those from September 2007 are shown. Otherwise fees are available on request. Figures are shown for full boarding (FB), weekly boarding (WB) and day fees. In some instances the fees for full and weekly boarding are the same (F/WB £). A minimum and a maximum fee are given for each range. These figures are intended as a guide only. For more precise information schools should be contacted direct.

Key

* denotes that the school has a profile in Part Three;

† denotes that the school is registered with the Council for the Registration of Schools Teaching Dyslexic Pupils.

2.2
England

BEDFORDSHIRE

BEDFORD

ACORN SCHOOL
15 St Andrews Road, Bedford,
Bedfordshire MK40 2LL
Tel: (01234) 343449
Fax: (01234) 343449
Email: acornschool@
  btinternet.com
Head: Mrs M Mason
Type: Co-educational Day 2–8
No of pupils: 130
Fees: On application

BEDFORD HIGH SCHOOL
FOR GIRLS
Bromham Road, Bedford,
Bedfordshire MK40 2BS
Tel: (01234) 360221
Fax: (01234) 353552
Email: admissions@
  bedfordhigh.co.uk
Head: Mrs J Eldridge
Type: Girls Day and Boarding
7–18
No of pupils: 800
No of boarders: F135
Fees: (September 07) FB £18864
Day £7203–£10158

BEDFORD MODERN
SCHOOL
Manton Lane, Bedford,
Bedfordshire MK41 7NT
Tel: (01234) 332500
Fax: (01234) 332550
Email: info@bedmod.co.uk
Head: Mr S Smith
Type: Co-educational Day 7–18
No of pupils: B958 G221
Fees: (September 07)
Day £6777–£9498

BEDFORD PREPARATORY
SCHOOL
De Parys Avenue, Bedford,
Bedfordshire MK40 2TU
Tel: (01234) 362274
Fax: (01234) 362285
Email: prepinfo@
  bedfordschool.org.uk
Head: Mr C Godwin
Type: Boys Boarding and Day
7–13
No of pupils: 452
No of boarders: F23 W6
Fees: On application

BEDFORD SCHOOL
De Parys Avenue, Bedford,
Bedfordshire MK40 2TU
Tel: (01234) 362200
Fax: (01234) 362283
Email: registrar@
  bedfordschool.org.uk
Head: Mr J S Moule
Type: Boys Boarding and Day
7–18
No of pupils: 1102
No of boarders: F191 W70
Fees: (September 08)
FB £15414–£22608
WB £14694–£21861
Day £9312–£14367

BEDFORD SCHOOL STUDY
CENTRE
67 De Parys Avenue, Bedford,
Bedfordshire MK40 2TR
Tel: (01234) 362300
Fax: (01234) 362305
Email: bssc@bedfordschool.org.uk
Head: Mrs O Heffill
Type: Co-educational Boarding
10–17
No of pupils: B20 G10
No of boarders: F30
Fees: (September 07) FB £27075

DAME ALICE HARPUR SCHOOL
Cardington Road, Bedford,
Bedfordshire MK42 0BX
Tel: (01234) 340871
Fax: (01234) 344125
Email: admissions@dahs.co.uk
Head: Mrs J Berry
Type: Girls Day 7–18
No of pupils: 910
Fees: On application

PILGRIMS PRE-PREPARATORY SCHOOL
Brickhill Drive, Bedford,
Bedfordshire MK41 7QZ
Tel: (01234) 369555
Fax: (01234) 359556
Email: pilgrims@
   harpur-trust.org.uk
Head: Mrs M Shaw
Type: Co-educational Day 0–8
No of pupils: B144 G134
Fees: On application

POLAM SCHOOL
45 Lansdowne Road, Bedford,
Bedfordshire MK40 2BU
Tel: (01234) 261864
Fax: (01234) 261194
Email: info@polamschool.co.uk
Head: Miss D Parton
Type: Co-educational Day 2–9
No of pupils: B80 G80
Fees: (September 07)
Day £5235–£5235

RUSHMOOR SCHOOL
58–60 Shakespeare Road,
Bedford, Bedfordshire MK40 2DL
Tel: (01234) 352031
Fax: (01234) 348395
Email: office@
   rushmoorschool.co.uk
Head: Mr K M Knight
Type: Co-educational Day
Boys 4–16 Girls 4–10
No of pupils: B293 G9
Fees: On application

ST ANDREW'S SCHOOL
78 Kimbolton Road, Bedford,
Bedfordshire MK40 2PA
Tel: (01234) 267272
Fax: (01234) 355105
Email: standrews@
   standrewsschoolbedford.com
Head: Mrs J Marsland
Type: Girls Day 3–16 (Boys 3–7)
No of pupils: B38 G295
Fees: On application

DUNSTABLE

ST GEORGE'S
28 Priory Road, Dunstable,
Bedfordshire LU5 4HR
Tel: (01582) 661471
Fax: (01582) 663605
Email: info@
   stgeorgesdunstable.co.uk
Head: Mrs P Plater
Type: Co-educational Day 2–11
No of pupils: B65 G65
Fees: On application

SCEPTRE SCHOOL
Ridgeway Avenue, Dunstable,
Bedfordshire LU5 4QL
Tel: (01582) 665676
Head: Mr Simon Wells
Type: Co-educational Day
Boys 11–17 Girls 11–18
No of pupils: B40 G66
Fees: On application

LUTON

MOORLANDS SCHOOL
Leagrave Hall, Luton, Bedfordshire
LU4 9LE
Tel: (01582) 573376
Fax: (01582) 509008
Email: moorlands@
   moorlandsprepschool.co.uk
Head: Mrs D K Attias
Type: Co-educational Day 2–11
No of pupils: B142 G131
Fees: (September 07)
Day £5211–£5640

SANDY

CHILDREN'S MONTESSORI SCHOOL
Green End, Gamlingay, Sandy,
Bedfordshire SG19 3LB
Tel: (01767) 650645
Email: patriciajenkins_151@
   hotmail.com
Head: Mrs P L Jenkins
Type: Co-educational Day 4–9
(Nursery)
Fees: On application

BERKSHIRE

ALDERMASTON

CEDARS SCHOOL
Church Road, Aldermaston,
Berkshire RG7 4LR
Tel: (0118) 971 4251
Email: enquiries@
   thecedarsschool.co.uk
Head: Mrs J O'Halloran
Type: Co-educational Day 4–11
No of pupils: B25 G25
Fees: On application

ASCOT

HEATHFIELD ST MARY'S SCHOOL*
London Road, Ascot, Berkshire
SL5 8BQ
Tel: (01344) 898342
Fax: (01344) 890689
Email: registrar@
   heathfieldstmarys.net
Head: Mrs M McSwiggan
Type: Girls Boarding 11–18
No of pupils: 220
No of boarders: F220
Fees: (September 08)
FB £24300–£26094

HURST LODGE SCHOOL
Bagshot Road, Ascot, Berkshire
SL5 9JU
Tel: (01344) 622154
Fax: (01344) 627049
Email: admissions@
   hurstlodgesch.co.uk
Head: Miss V Smit
Type: Co-educational Day and
Boarding Boys 3–11
Girls 3–18(Boys 3–7)
No of pupils: B20 G192
No of boarders: W20
Fees: (September 08) WB £19740
Day £6975–£12075

LICENSED VICTUALLERS' SCHOOL*

London Road, Ascot, Berkshire
SL5 8DR
Tel: (01344) 882770
Fax: (01344) 890648
Email: registrar@lvs.ascot.sch.uk
Head: Mr I A Mullins and
Mr G Best
Type: Co-educational Boarding
and Day 4–18
No of pupils: B525 G370
No of boarders: F140 W31
Fees: (September 08)
F/WB £18330–£21735
Day £7155–£12375

THE MARIST PREPARATORY SCHOOL*

Kings Road, Sunninghill, Ascot,
Berkshire SL5 7PS
Tel: (01344) 626137
Fax: (01344) 621566
Email: head@marist-prep.windsor-
maidenhead.sch.uk
Head: Mrs J A Peachey
Type: Girls Day 3–11
No of pupils: 247
Fees: (September 08) Day £7050

THE MARIST SENIOR SCHOOL*

Kings Road, Sunninghill, Ascot,
Berkshire SL5 7PS
Tel: (01344) 624291
Fax: (01344) 874963
Email: pa2head@
marist.ascot.org.uk
Head: Mr K McCloskey
Type: Girls Day 11–18
No of pupils: 315
Fees: (September 08) Day £9660

PAPPLEWICK SCHOOL*

Windsor Road, Ascot, Berkshire
SL5 7LH
Tel: (01344) 621488
Fax: (01344) 874639
Email: hm@papplewick.org.uk
Head: Mr T W Bunbury
Type: Boys Boarding and Day
7–13
No of pupils: 190
No of boarders: F101
Fees: (September 07) FB £21150
Day £16245

ST GEORGE'S SCHOOL*

Ascot, Berkshire SL5 7DZ
Tel: (01344) 629900
Fax: (01344) 629901
Email: office@
stgeorges-ascot.org.uk
Head: Mrs C Jordan
Type: Girls Boarding and Day
11–18
No of pupils: 270
No of boarders: F117
Fees: (September 08) FB £25350
Day £16640

ST MARY'S SCHOOL, ASCOT*

St Mary's Road, Ascot, Berkshire
SL5 9JF
Tel: (01344) 623721
Fax: (01344) 873281
Email: admissions@
st-marys-ascot.co.uk
Head: Mrs M Breen
Type: Girls Boarding and Day
11–18
No of pupils: 371
No of boarders: F355
Fees: (September 08) FB £26610
Day £18930

BRACKNELL

LAMBROOK HAILEYBURY

Winkfield Row, Bracknell,
Berkshire RG42 6LU
Tel: (01344) 882717
Fax: (01344) 891114
Email: info@
lambrook.berks.sch.uk
Head: Mr J E A Barnes
Type: Co-educational Boarding
and Day 3–13
No of pupils: B288 G147
No of boarders: W18
Fees: (September 08)
FB £16845–£18825
Day £7562–£13800

MEADOWBROOK MONTESSORI SCHOOL

Malt Hill, Warfield, Bracknell,
Berkshire RG42 6JQ
Tel: (01344) 890869
Fax: (01344) 890869
Email: mbrookuk@aol.com
Head: Mrs S Gunn and
Miss B O'Sullivan
Type: Co-educational Day 3–11
No of pupils: B50 G50
Fees: (September 08)
Day £6495–£8025

NEWBOLD SCHOOL

Popeswood Road, Binfield,
Bracknell, Berkshire RG42 4AH
Tel: (01344) 421088
Email: newboldschool@
hotmail.co.uk
Head: Mrs V Chilvers
Type: Co-educational Day 3–11
Fees: (September 08) Day £3030

CROWTHORNE

OUR LADY'S PREPARATORY SCHOOL

The Avenue, Crowthorne,
Berkshire RG45 6PB
Tel: (01344) 773394
Fax: (01344) 773394
Email: office@olps.co.uk
Head: Mrs H Robinson
Type: Co-educational Day 1–11
No of pupils: B50 G50
Fees: On application

WELLINGTON COLLEGE*

Duke's Ride, Crowthorne,
Berkshire RG45 7PU
Tel: (01344) 444013
Fax: (01344) 444115
Email: admissions@
wellingtoncollege.org.uk
Head: Dr A F Seldon
Type: Co-educational Boarding
and Day 13–18 (Co-ed VIth Form,
fully co-ed from 09/06)
No of pupils: B626 G218
No of boarders: F689
Fees: (September 08) FB £26925
Day £19215–£20175

MAIDENHEAD

CLAIRES COURT SCHOOL

Ray Mill Road East, Maidenhead,
Berkshire SL6 8TE
Tel: (01628) 411470
Fax: (01628) 411466
Email: Head@clairescourt.co.uk
Head: Mr J T Wilding
Type: Boys Day 11–16 (Co-ed VIth
Form)
No of pupils: 300
Fees: (September 08)
Day £8325–£10935

England – Berkshire

CLAIRES COURT SCHOOLS, RIDGEWAY
Maidenhead Thicket,
Maidenhead, Berkshire SL6 3QE
Tel: (01628) 411490
Fax: (01628) 411465
Email: registrar@clairescourt.com
Head: Mrs K M Rogg
Type: Boys Day 4–11
No of pupils: 234
Fees: (September 08)
Day £6435–£9360

CLAIRES COURT SCHOOLS, THE COLLEGE
1 College Avenue, Maidenhead,
Berkshire SL6 6AW
Tel: (01628) 411480
Fax: (01628) 411467
Email: registrar@clairescourt.com
Head: Mrs L Green
Type: Girls Day 3–16 (Boys 3–5,
co-ed VIth Form)
No of pupils: B48 G278
Fees: (September 08)
Day £6435–£10935

HERRIES SCHOOL
Dean Lane, Cookham Dean,
Maidenhead, Berkshire SL6 9BD
Tel: (01628) 483350
Fax: (01628) 483329
Email: office@herries.ws
Head: Mrs A M Bradberry
Type: Co-educational Day 3–11
No of pupils: B35 G57
Fees: (September 08)
Day £5595–£7620

HIGHFIELD SCHOOL
2 West Road, Maidenhead,
Berkshire SL6 1PD
Tel: (01628) 624918
Fax: (01628) 635747
Email: office@
   highfield.berks.sch.uk
Head: Mrs C M A Lane
Type: Girls Day 3–11
No of pupils: 170
Fees: On application

REDROOFS THEATRE SCHOOL
Littlewick Green, Maidenhead,
Berkshire SL6 3QY
Tel: (01628) 822461
Email: sam@redroofs.co.uk
Head: Mrs Helen Cocksedge and
Ms June Rose
Type: Co-educational Day 9–16
No of pupils: 65
Fees: (September 08)
Day £6900–£9800

ST PIRAN'S PREPARATORY SCHOOL*
Gringer Hill, Maidenhead,
Berkshire SL6 7LZ
Tel: (01628) 594302
Fax: (01628) 594301
Email: registrar@stpirans.co.uk
Head: Mr J Carroll
Type: Co-educational Day 3–13
No of pupils: B225 G150
Fees: (September 08)
Day £2850–£10560

WINBURY SCHOOL
Braywick Park, Hibbert Road,
Bray, Maidenhead, Berkshire
SL6 1UU
Tel: (01628) 627412
Fax: (01628) 627412
Email: info@winburyschool.co.uk
Head: Mrs P L Prewett
Type: Co-educational Day 2–8
No of pupils: B50 G50
Fees: (September 08)
Day £3300–£5715

NEWBURY

BROCKHURST AND MARLSTON HOUSE SCHOOLS
Hermitage, Newbury, Berkshire
RG18 9UL
Tel: (01635) 200293
Fax: (01635) 200190
Email: info@brockmarl.org.uk
Head: Mr D J W Fleming and Mrs
C E Riley
Type: Co-educational Boarding
and Day 3–13
No of pupils: B155 G146
No of boarders: F6 W70
Fees: (September 08) F/WB £17355
Day £7800–£13080

CHEAM SCHOOL*
Headley, Newbury, Berkshire
RG19 8LD
Tel: (01635) 268381
Fax: (01635) 269345
Email: registrar@
   cheamschool.co.uk
Head: Mr M R Johnson
Type: Co-educational Boarding
and Day 3–13
No of pupils: B226 G174
No of boarders: F2 W65
Fees: (September 08) F/WB £20535
Day £3990–£15210

HORRIS HILL SCHOOL
Newtown, Newbury, Berkshire
RG20 9DJ
Tel: (01635) 40594
Email: enquiries@horrishill.com
Head: Mr J H L Phillips
Type: Boys Boarding and Day
7–13
No of pupils: 115
No of boarders: F115
Fees: On application

ST GABRIEL'S
Sandleford Priory, Newbury,
Berkshire RG20 9BD
Tel: (01635) 555680
Fax: (01635) 555698
Email: info@stgabriels.co.uk
Head: Mr A Jones
Type: Girls Day 3–18 (Boys 3–7)
No of pupils: 500
Fees: (September 07)
Day £8055–£11490

ST MICHAELS SCHOOL
Harts Lane, Burghclere, Newbury,
Berkshire RG20 9JW
Tel: (01635) 278137
Fax: (01635) 278601
Head: Father J Dreher
Type: Co-educational Boarding
and Day 7–18 (Single-sex ed
13–18)
No of pupils: B37 G35
No of boarders: F20 W33
Fees: On application

THORNGROVE SCHOOL
The Mount, Highclere, Newbury,
Berkshire RG20 9PS
Tel: (01635) 253172
Fax: (01635) 254135
Email: admin@
   thorngroveschool.co.uk
Head: Mr N J Broughton and Mrs
C B Broughton
Type: Co-educational Day 2–13
No of pupils: B140 G97
Fees: (September 08)
Day £8640–£10590

PANGBOURNE

PANGBOURNE COLLEGE
Pangbourne, Berkshire RG8 8LA
Tel: (0118) 984 2101
Fax: (0118) 984 5443
Email: registrar@pangcoll.co.uk
Head: Mr T J Garnier
Type: Co-educational Boarding
and Day 11–18
No of pupils: B294 G100
No of boarders: F193
Fees: (September 08)
FB £18129–£24951
WB £15990–£21951
Day £12753–£17460

READING

THE ABBEY SCHOOL
Kendrick Road, Reading, Berkshire
RG1 5DZ
Tel: (0118) 987 2256
Fax: (0118) 987 1478
Email: schooloffice@
theabbey.co.uk
Head: Mrs B E Stanley
Type: Girls Day 3–18
No of pupils: 1030
Fees: (September 08)
Day £6990–£10980

ALDER BRIDGE SCHOOL
Bridge House, Mill Lane,
Padworth, Reading, Berkshire
RG7 4JU
Tel: (0118) 971 4471
Fax: (07092) 042631
Email: info@
alderbridge.w-berks.sch.uk
Type: Co-educational Day 3–11
No of pupils: B32 G29
Fees: (September 08)
Day £3450–£6195

THE ARK SCHOOL
School Road, Padworth, Reading,
Berkshire RG7 4JA
Tel: (0118) 983 4802
Fax: (0118) 983 6894
Email: office@
arkschool.fsnet.co.uk
Head: Mrs P A Oakley
Type: Co-educational Day 0–11
No of pupils: B53 G58
Fees: On application

BRADFIELD COLLEGE*
Bradfield, Reading, Berkshire
RG7 6AU
Tel: (0118) 964 4510
Fax: (0118) 964 4513
Email: headmaster@
bradfieldcollege.org.uk
Head: Mr P J M Roberts
Type: Co-educational Boarding
and Day 13–18
No of pupils: B466 G237
No of boarders: F589
Fees: (September 08) FB £26100
Day £20880

CHILTERN COLLEGE SCHOOL
16 Peppard Road, Caversham,
Reading, Berkshire RG4 8JZ
Tel: (0118) 947 1847
Fax: (0118) 946 3218
Email: info@chilterncollege.com
Head: Mrs J Halliday
Type: Co-educational Day 4–11
No of pupils: 80
Fees: (September 08) Day £5925

CROSFIELDS SCHOOL
Shinfield, Reading, Berkshire
RG2 9BL
Tel: (0118) 987 1810
Fax: (0118) 931 0806
Email: office@crosfields.com
Head: Mr J Wansey
Type: Boys Day 4–13
No of pupils: 466
Fees: On application

DOLPHIN SCHOOL
Waltham Road, Hurst, Reading,
Berkshire RG10 0FR
Tel: (0118) 934 1277
Fax: (0118) 934 4110
Email: omnes@dolphinschool.com
Head: Mrs V Gibbs
Type: Co-educational Day 3–13
No of pupils: B153 G138
Fees: (September 08)
Day £7185–£9855

ELSTREE SCHOOL
Woolhampton, Reading, Berkshire
RG7 5TD
Tel: (0118) 971 3302
Fax: (0118) 971 4280
Email: secretary@
elstreeschool.org.uk
Head: Mr S M Hill
Type: Boys Boarding and Day
3–13 (Girls 3–7)
No of pupils: B240 G20
No of boarders: F50 W10
Fees: (September 07) FB £18150
Day £13100–£13650

THE ELVIAN SCHOOL
61 Bath Road, Reading, Berkshire
RG30 2BB
Tel: (0118) 957 2861
Fax: (0118) 957 2220
Email: mansers@
elvian.reading.sch.uk
Head: Mrs S Manser
Type: Co-educational Day 3–18
No of pupils: B151 G25
Fees: On application

HEMDEAN HOUSE SCHOOL
Hemdean Road, Caversham,
Reading, Berkshire RG4 7SD
Tel: (0118) 947 2590
Fax: (0118) 946 4474
Email: office@
hemdeanhouse.co.uk
Head: Mrs J Harris
Type: Co-educational Day
Boys 3–11 Girls 3–16
No of pupils: B50 G130
Fees: (September 08)
Day £4680–£6540

THE HIGHLANDS SCHOOL
Wardle Avenue, Tilehurst,
Reading, Berkshire RG31 6JR
Tel: (0118) 942 7186
Fax: (0118) 945 4953
Email: enquiries@
highlandsschool.co.uk
Head: Mrs C A Bennett
Type: Co-educational Day
Boys 2–7 Girls 2–11
No of pupils: B39 G100
Fees: On application

LEIGHTON PARK SCHOOL
Shinfield Road, Reading, Berkshire
RG2 7ED
Tel: (0118) 987 9600
Fax: (0118) 987 9589
Email: admissions@
leightonpark.com
Head: Mr J Dunston
Type: Co-educational Boarding
and Day 11–18
No of pupils: B302 G173
No of boarders: F75 W71
Fees: On application

England – Berkshire

**THE ORATORY
PREPARATORY SCHOOL***
Goring Heath, Reading RG8 7SF
Tel: (0118) 984 4511
Fax: (0118) 984 4806
Email: office@oratoryprep.co.uk
Head: Dr R J Hillier
Type: Co-educational Day and
Boarding 3–13
No of pupils: B250 G150
No of boarders: F20 W10
Fees: (September 08) FB £15135
WB £13935 Day £3285–£10980

THE ORATORY SCHOOL
Woodcote, Reading, Berkshire
RG8 0PJ
Tel: (01491) 683500
Fax: (01491) 680020
Email: enquiries@oratory.co.uk
Head: Mr C I Dytor
Type: Boys Day and Boarding
11–18
No of pupils: 400
No of boarders: F220
Fees: On application

PADWORTH COLLEGE*
Padworth, Reading, Berkshire
RG7 4NR
Tel: (0118) 983 2644
Fax: (0118) 983 4515
Email: info@padworth.com
Head: Mrs L Melhuish
Type: Co-educational Boarding
and Day 13–19
No of pupils: B59 G51
No of boarders: F79 W4
Fees: (September 08) FB £20850
WB £15900 Day £9000

QUEEN ANNE'S SCHOOL*
6 Henley Road, Caversham,
Reading, Berkshire RG4 6DX
Tel: (0118) 918 7333
Fax: (0118) 918 7310
Email: admissions@qas.org.uk
Head: Mrs J Harrington
Type: Girls Boarding and Day
11–18
No of pupils: 320
No of boarders: F140
Fees: (September 08) FB £24585
Day £16680

**READING BLUE COAT
SCHOOL***
Holme Park, Sonning-on-Thames,
Reading, Berkshire RG4 6SU
Tel: (0118) 944 1005
Fax: (0118) 944 2690
Email: vmf@
   blue-coat.reading.sch.uk
Head: Mr M J Windsor
Type: Boys Day 11–18 (Co-ed VIth
Form)
No of pupils: B677 G61
Fees: On application

ST ANDREW'S SCHOOL
Buckhold, Pangbourne, Reading,
Berkshire RG8 8QA
Tel: (0118) 974 4276
Fax: (0118) 974 5049
Email: registrar@
   standrewspangbourne.co.uk
Head: Mr J M Snow
Type: Co-educational Day and
Boarding 3–13
No of pupils: B162 G116
Fees: (September 08) WB £14850
Day £3450–£12450

ST EDWARD'S SCHOOL
64 Tilehurst Road, Reading,
Berkshire RG30 2JH
Tel: (0118) 957 4342
Fax: (0118) 950 3736
Email: admin@stedwards.org.uk
Head: Mr G Mottram and
Mr D Cumming
Type: Boys Day 4–13
No of pupils: 160
Fees: (September 08)
Day £6435–£8265

**ST JOSEPH'S CONVENT
SCHOOL**
Upper Redlands Road, Reading,
Berkshire RG1 5JT
Tel: (0118) 966 1000
Fax: (0118) 926 9932
Email: mailbox@
   st-josephs.reading.sch.uk
Head: Mrs M T Sheridan
Type: Girls Day 3–18
No of pupils: B10 G309
Fees: (September 08)
Day £4965–£10500

SANDHURST

EAGLE HOUSE*
Crowthorne Road, Sandhurst,
Berkshire GU47 8PH
Tel: (01344) 772134
Fax: (01344) 779039
Email: info@
   eaglehouseschool.com
Head: Mr Andrew Barnard
Type: Co-educational Day and
Boarding 3–13
No of pupils: B201 G119
No of boarders: F14 W13
Fees: (September 08) F/WB £17400
Day £12975

SLOUGH

ETON END PNEU
35 Eton Road, Datchet, Slough,
Berkshire SL3 9AX
Tel: (01753) 541075
Fax: (01753) 541123
Email: admin@etonend.org
Head: Mrs V M Pilgerstorfer
Type: Co-educational Day
Boys 3–7 Girls 3–11(Boys 3–7)
No of pupils: B50 G200
Fees: (September 08)
Day £4770–£8790

LANGLEY MANOR SCHOOL
St Marys Road, Langley, Slough,
Berkshire SL3 6BZ
Tel: (01753) 825368
Fax: (01753) 821451
Email: ldurell@cfbt.com
Head: Mr Nicholas Owlett
Type: Co-educational Day 3–11
No of pupils: B140 G123
Fees: On application

LONG CLOSE SCHOOL
Upton Court Road, Slough,
Berkshire SL3 7LU
Tel: (01753) 520095
Fax: (01753) 821463
Email: info@
   longcloseschool.co.uk
Head: Mr D Brazier
Type: Co-educational Day 2–16
Fees: (September 08)
Day £5715–£10080

**ST BERNARD'S
PREPARATORY SCHOOL**
Hawtrey Close, Slough, Berkshire
SL1 1TB
Tel: (01753) 521821
Fax: (01753) 552364
Email: info@stbernardsprep.org
Head: Mrs M B Smith
Type: Co-educational Day 3–11
No of pupils: B138 G78
Fees: On application

SUNNINGDALE

SUNNINGDALE SCHOOL*
Dry Arch Road, Sunningdale,
Berkshire SL5 9PY
Tel: (01344) 620159
Fax: (01344) 873304
Email: headmaster@
   sunningdaleschool.co.uk
Head: Mr T A C N Dawson
Type: Boys Boarding 8–13
No of pupils: 100
No of boarders: F95
Fees: (September 08) FB £16470
Day £12690

THATCHAM

**BROCKHURST & MARLSTON
HOUSE PRE-PREPARATORY
SCHOOL**
Hermitage, Thatcham, Berkshire
RG18 9UL
Tel: (01635) 200293
Fax: (01635) 200190
Email: info@brockmarl.org.uk
Head: Mrs C Riley
Type: Co-educational Day 3–6
No of pupils: B25 G22
Fees: On application

DOWNE HOUSE*
Cold Ash, Thatcham, Berkshire
RG18 9JJ
Tel: (01635) 200286
Fax: (01635) 202026
Email: correspondence@
   downehouse.net
Head: Mrs E McKendrick
Type: Girls Boarding and Day
11–18
No of pupils: 567
No of boarders: F550
Fees: (September 07) FB £25968
Day £18801

WINDSOR

**BRIGIDINE SCHOOL
WINDSOR**
Queensmead, Kings Road,
Windsor, Berkshire SL4 2AX
Tel: (01753) 863779
Fax: (01753) 850278
Email: mail@brigidine.org.uk
Head: Ms Elizabeth Robinson
Type: Girls Day 3–18 (Boys 3–7)
No of pupils: B4 G248
Fees: On application

ETON COLLEGE
Windsor, Berkshire SL4 6DW
Tel: (01753) 671249
Fax: (01753) 671248
Email: admissions@
   etoncollege.org.uk
Head: Mr A R M Little
Type: Boys Boarding 13–18
No of pupils: 1304
No of boarders: F1304
Fees: On application

ST GEORGE'S SCHOOL
Windsor Castle, Windsor,
Berkshire SL4 1QF
Tel: (01753) 865553
Fax: (01753) 842093
Email: enqs@stgwindsor.co.uk
Head: Mr J R Jones
Type: Co-educational Boarding
and Day 3–13
No of pupils: B362 G120
No of boarders: F23 W9
Fees: (September 08) FB £16812
WB £16374 Day £3114–£11007

ST JOHN'S BEAUMONT*
Priest Hill, Old Windsor, Windsor,
Berkshire SL4 2JN
Tel: (01784) 432428
Fax: (01784) 494048
Email: admissions@
   stjohnsbeaumont.co.uk
Head: Mr G Delaney
Type: Boys Boarding and Day
4–13
No of pupils: 325
No of boarders: F30 W30
Fees: (September 08) FB £19550
WB £16920 Day £6900–£12870

UPTON HOUSE SCHOOL*
115 St Leonard's Road, Windsor,
Berkshire SL4 3DF
Tel: (01753) 862610
Fax: (01753) 621950
Email: info@uptonhouse.org.uk
Head: Mrs M Collins
Type: Co-educational Day
Boys 2–7 Girls 2–11
No of pupils: B80 G170
Fees: (September 07)
Day £3900–£10425

WOKINGHAM

BEARWOOD COLLEGE*
Bearwood Road, Wokingham,
Berkshire RG41 5BG
Tel: (0118) 974 8300
Fax: (0118) 977 3186
Email: headmaster@
   bearwoodcollege.co.uk
Head: Mr S Aiano
Type: Co-educational Boarding
and Day 11–18 (3–18 Preparatory
and Senior School)
No of pupils: B355 G135
No of boarders: F71 W20
Fees: (September 08)
FB £22020–£25380
WB £22020–£25830
Day £12555–£14790

HOLME GRANGE SCHOOL
Heathlands Road, Wokingham,
Berkshire RG40 3AL
Tel: (0118) 978 1566
Fax: (0118) 977 0810
Email: school@holmegrange.org
Head: Mr N J Brodrick
Type: Co-educational Day 3–13
No of pupils: B150 G134
Fees: On application

**LUCKLEY-OAKFIELD
SCHOOL***
Luckley Road, Wokingham,
Berkshire RG40 3EU
Tel: (0118) 978 4175
Fax: (0118) 977 0305
Email: registrar@
   luckley.wokingham.sch.uk
Head: Miss V A Davis
Type: Girls Boarding and Day
11–18
No of pupils: 304
No of boarders: F30 W10
Fees: (September 08) FB £20964
WB £19428 Day £12303

England – Berkshire

LUDGROVE
Wokingham, Berkshire RG40 3AB
Tel: (0118) 978 9881
Fax: (0118) 979 2973
Email: office@
  ludgroveschool.co.uk
Head: Mr S W T Barber and
Mr A C T Inglis
Type: Boys Boarding 8–13
No of pupils:
No of boarders: F191
Fees: (September 08) FB £19500

WAVERLEY SCHOOL
Waverley Way, Finchampstead,
Wokingham, Berkshire RG40 4YD
Tel: (0118) 973 1121
Fax: (0118) 973 1131
Email: waverleyschool@
  waverley.wokingham.sch.uk
Head: Mr S G Melton
Type: Co-educational Day 3–11
No of pupils: B65 G63
Fees: On application

**WHITE HOUSE
PREPARATORY SCHOOL**
Finchampstead Road,
Wokingham, Berkshire RG40 3HD
Tel: (0118) 978 5151
Fax: (0118) 979 4716
Email: office@
  whitehouse.wokingham.sch.uk
Head: Mrs S J Gillam
Type: Girls Day 2–11 (Boys 2–4)
No of pupils: B5 G116
Fees: (September 08)
Day £2271–£8175

BRISTOL

BACKWELL

FAIRFIELD SCHOOL
Fairfield Way, Backwell, Bristol
BS48 3PD
Tel: (01275) 462743
Fax: (01275) 464347
Email: secretary@
  fairfieldschool.org.uk
Head: Mrs L Barton
Type: Co-educational Day 3–11
No of pupils: B62 G72
Fees: (September 08)
Day £6000–£6585

BRISTOL

BADMINTON SCHOOL*
Westbury Road, Bristol BS9 3BA
Tel: (0117) 905 5271
Fax: (0117) 962 8963
Email: admissions@
  badminton.bristol.sch.uk
Head: Mrs J Scarrow
Type: Girls Boarding and Day
4–18
No of pupils: 420
No of boarders: F166 W15
Fees: (September 08)
F/WB £16928–£25530
Day £6690–£14370

**BRISTOL CATHEDRAL
SCHOOL**
College Square, Bristol BS1 5TS
Tel: (0117) 929 1872
Fax: (0117) 930 4219
Email: info@
  bristolcathedral.org.uk
Head: Mrs Anne Davey
Type: Co-educational Day 10–18
(Co-ed VIth Form)
No of pupils: B313 G72
Fees: On application

**BRISTOL GRAMMAR
SCHOOL**
University Road, Bristol BS8 1SR
Tel: (0117) 973 6006
Fax: (0117) 946 7485
Email: headmaster@
  bgs.bristol.sch.uk
Head: Mr R I MacKinnon
Type: Co-educational Day 7–18
No of pupils: B753 G420
Fees: (September 07)
FB £5970–£9297

BRISTOL STEINER SCHOOL
Redland Hill House, Redland Hill,
Bristol BS6 6UX
Tel: (0117) 933 9990
Fax: (0117) 933 9999
Email: office@
  steiner.bristol.sch.uk
Head: Mr C Nelson
Type: Co-educational Day 3–14
Fees: On application

**CARMEL CHRISTIAN
SCHOOL**
817A Bath Road, Brislington,
Bristol BS4 5NL
Tel: (0117) 9775535
Fax: (0117) 9775678
Email: info@carmelcentre.org
Head: Miss S Watt
Type: Co-educational Day 4–17
No of pupils: B13 G15
Fees: On application

CLEVE HOUSE SCHOOL
254 Wells Road, Bristol BS4 2PN
Tel: (0117) 977 7218
Fax: (0117) 977 3915
Email: clevehouseschool@
  btconnect.com
Head: Mr D Lawson and
Mrs E Lawson
Type: Co-educational Day 3–11
No of pupils: B56 G65
Fees: On application

CLIFTON COLLEGE*
32 College Road, Clifton, Bristol
BS8 3JH
Tel: (0117) 315 7000
Fax: (0117) 315 7101
Email: admissions@
  clifton-college.avon.sch.uk
Head: Mr Mark Moore
Type: Co-educational Boarding
and Day 13–18
No of pupils: B440 G270
No of boarders: F280
Fees: (September 07) FB £25530
Day £17220

CLIFTON COLLEGE PRE-PREP–BUTCOMBE
Guthrie Road, Bristol BS8 3EZ
Tel: (0117) 315 7591
Fax: (0117) 315 7592
Email: wbowring@
clifton-college.avon.sch.uk
Head: Dr W E Bowring
Type: Co-educational Day 3–8
No of pupils: B138 G80
Fees: On application

CLIFTON COLLEGE PREPARATORY SCHOOL[†]
32 College Road, Clifton, Bristol
BS8 3JH
Tel: (0117) 315 7501
Fax: (0117) 315 7504
Email: lturley@
clifton-college.avon.sch.uk
Head: Dr R J Acheson
Type: Co-educational Boarding
and Day 3–13
No of pupils: B377 G213
No of boarders: F38 W8
Fees: (September 07)
FB £17070–£17700
WB £16305–£16920
Day £8130–£11700

CLIFTON HIGH SCHOOL
College Road, Clifton, Bristol
BS8 3JD
Tel: (0117) 973 0201
Fax: (0117) 923 8962
Email: admissions@
cliftonhigh.bristol.sch.uk
Head: Dr Alison Neil
Type: Co-educational Day and
Boarding Boys 3–11 Girls 3–18
No of pupils: B81 G423
Fees: (September 08)
Day £3645–£9600

COLSTON'S COLLEGIATE SCHOOL
Stapleton, Bristol BS16 1BJ
Tel: (0117) 965 5207
Fax: (0117) 958 5652
Email: enquiries@
colstons.bristol.sch.uk
Head: Mr D G Crawford
Type: Co-educational Boarding
and Day 3–18
No of pupils: B611 G257
No of boarders: F20 W40
Fees: On application

COLSTON'S GIRLS' SCHOOL
Cheltenham Road, Bristol BS6 5RD
Tel: (0117) 942 4328
Fax: (0117) 942 1052
Email: admin@
colstonsgirls.bristol.sch.uk
Head: Mrs L A Jones
Type: Girls Day 10–18
No of pupils: 450
Fees: On application

COLSTON'S LOWER SCHOOL
Park Road, Bristol BS16 1BA
Tel: (0117) 965 5297
Fax: (0117) 965 6330
Email: schooladmin@
colstons.bristol.sch.uk
Head: Mrs C A Aspden
Type: Co-educational Day 3–11
No of pupils: B156 G74
Fees: (September 09)
Day £4749–£7800

PROSPECT SCHOOL
1 Tramway Road, Brislington,
Bristol BS4 3DS
Tel: (0117) 977 2271
Head: Mrs Lucy Sherrin
Type: Co-educational Day 11–17
No of pupils: B21 G20
Fees: On application

QUEEN ELIZABETH'S HOSPITAL
Berkeley Place, Clifton, Bristol
BS8 1JX
Tel: (0117) 930 3040
Fax: (0117) 929 3106
Email: headmaster@
qehbristol.co.uk
Head: Mr S W Holliday
Type: Boys Day 7–18
No of pupils: 640
Fees: (September 08)
Day £5985–£9552

THE RED MAIDS' SCHOOL
Westbury-on-Trym, Bristol
BS9 3AW
Tel: (0117) 962 2641
Fax: (0117) 962 1687
Email: admissions@
redmaids.bristol.sch.uk
Head: Mrs I Tobias
Type: Girls Day 11–18
No of pupils: 450
Fees: (September 08) Day £9015

REDLAND HIGH SCHOOL
Redland Court, Bristol BS6 7EF
Tel: (0117) 924 5796
Fax: (0117) 924 1127
Email: admissions@
redland.bristol.sch.uk
Head: Dr R Weeks
Type: Girls Day 3–18
No of pupils: 672
Fees: (September 08)
Day £5310–£6270

TORWOOD HOUSE SCHOOL
27–29 Durdham Park, Redland,
Bristol BS6 6XE
Tel: (0117) 973 6620
Fax: (0117) 973 6620
Email: emailus@
torwoodhouse.bristol.sch.uk
Head: Mrs D Seagrove
Type: Co-educational Day 0–11
No of pupils: B100 G102
Fees: On application

FISHPONDS

GRACEFIELD PREPARATORY SCHOOL
266 Overndale Road, Fishponds,
Bristol BS16 2RG
Tel: (0117) 956 7977
Fax: (0117) 956 3397
Email: enquiries@
gracefieldschool.co.uk
Head: Mrs E Morgan
Type: Co-educational Day 4–11
No of pupils: B45 G45
Fees: On application

OLD SODBURY

OVERNDALE SCHOOL
Chapel Lane, Old Sodbury, Bristol
BS37 6NQ
Tel: (01454) 310332
Fax: (01454) 310022
Email: info@
overndaleschool.co.uk
Head: Mrs K Winstanley
Type: Co-educational Day 1–11
No of pupils: B55 G45
Fees: On application

England – Bristol

TOCKINGTON

TOCKINGTON MANOR SCHOOL
Tockington, Bristol BS32 4NY
Tel: (01454) 613229
Fax: (01454) 613676
Email: admin@
  tockington.bristol.sch.uk
Head: Mr R G Tovey
Type: Co-educational Day and
Boarding 2–14
No of pupils: B168 G87
No of boarders: F14
Fees: (September 07) FB £14400
Day £6360–£10590

WESTBURY-ON-TRYM

ST URSULA'S HIGH SCHOOL
Brecon Road, Westbury-on-Trym,
Bristol BS9 4DT
Tel: (0117) 962 2616
Fax: (0117) 962 2616
Email: office@
  st-ursulas.bristol.sch.uk
Head: Mrs L Carter
Type: Co-educational Day 3–16
No of pupils: B160 G96
Fees: On application

WRAXALL

THE DOWNS SCHOOL
Wraxall, Bristol BS48 1PF
Tel: (01275) 852008
Fax: (01275) 855840
Email: office@
  thedownsschool.co.uk
Head: Mr M A Gunn
Type: Co-educational Day and
Boarding 4–13
No of pupils: B152 G67
No of boarders: W6
Fees: On application

BUCKINGHAMSHIRE

AMERSHAM

THE BEACON SCHOOL
Chesham Bois, Amersham,
Buckinghamshire HP6 5PF
Tel: (01494) 433654
Fax: (01494) 727849
Email: enquiries@
  beaconschool.co.uk
Head: Mr M W Spinney
Type: Boys Day 3–13
No of pupils: 430
Fees: (September 08)
Day £4260–£11460

HEATHERTON HOUSE SCHOOL
Copperkins Lane, Chesham Bois,
Amersham, Buckinghamshire
HP6 5QB
Tel: (01494) 726433
Fax: (01494) 729628
Email: admissions@
  heathertonhouse.co.uk
Head: Mr P Rushforth
Type: Girls Day 3–11 (Boys 2–5)
No of pupils: 175
Fees: (September 08)
Day £1185–£9450

AYLESBURY

ASHFOLD SCHOOL
Dorton, Aylesbury,
Buckinghamshire HP18 9NG
Tel: (01844) 238237
Fax: (01844) 238505
Email: katrina.hartley@
  ashfoldschool.co.uk
Head: Mr M O M Chitty
Type: Co-educational Day and
Boarding 3–13
No of pupils: B177 G109
No of boarders: W25
Fees: (September 08) WB £14745
Day £3210–£12615

LADYMEDE
Little Kimble, Aylesbury,
Buckinghamshire HP17 0XP
Tel: (01844) 346154
Fax: (01844) 275660
Email: office@ladymede.com
Head: Mrs C Hawkins
Type: Co-educational Day 3–11
No of pupils: B54 G60
Fees: (September 07)
Day £1261–£6993

BEACONSFIELD

DAVENIES SCHOOL
Beaconsfield, Buckinghamshire
HP9 1AA
Tel: (01494) 685400
Fax: (01494) 685408
Email: office@davenies.co.uk
Head: Mr C Watson
Type: Boys Day 4–13
No of pupils: 325
Fees: On application

HIGH MARCH SCHOOL
23 Ledborough Lane,
Beaconsfield, Buckinghamshire
HP9 2PZ
Tel: (01494) 675186
Fax: (01494) 675377
Email: head@
  highmarch.bucks.sch.uk
Head: Mrs S J Clifford
Type: Girls Day 3–11 (Boys 3–5)
No of pupils: B4 G254
Fees: (September 08)
Day £1440–£9900

BUCKINGHAM

AKELEY WOOD LOWER SCHOOL
Lillingstone Dayrell, Buckingham,
Buckinghamshire MK18 5AN
Tel: (01280) 860182
Fax: (01280) 860194
Email: enquiries@
  akeleywoodschool.co.uk
Head: Mrs A Taylor
Type: Co-educational Day 9–11
No of pupils: B72 G83
Fees: On application

AKELEY WOOD SCHOOL
Akeley Wood, Buckingham,
Buckinghamshire MK18 5AE
Tel: (01280) 812000
Fax: (01280) 822945
Email: enquiries@
  akeleywoodschool.co.uk
Head: Dr J Grundy
Type: Co-educational Day 3–18
No of pupils: B521 G367
Fees: On application

STOWE SCHOOL
Stowe, Buckingham,
Buckinghamshire MK18 5EH
Tel: (01280) 818323 / 818205
Fax: (01280) 818181
Email: admissions@stowe.co.uk
Head: Dr A K Wallersteiner
Type: Co-educational Boarding
and Day 13–18
No of pupils: B495 G229
No of boarders: F628
Fees: (September 08) FB £26850
Day £19860

CHESHAM

CHESHAM PREPARATORY SCHOOL
Orchard Leigh, Chesham,
Buckinghamshire HP5 3QF
Tel: (01494) 782619
Fax: (01494) 791645
Email: secretary@
  chesham-prep.bucks.sch.uk
Head: Mr J Marjoribanks
Type: Co-educational Day 4–13
No of pupils: B212 G148
Fees: On application

FARNHAM ROYAL

CALDICOTT SCHOOL
Crown Lane, Farnham Royal,
Buckinghamshire SL2 3SL
Tel: (01753) 649300
Fax: (01753) 649325
Email: office@caldicott.com
Head: Mr S J G Doggart
Type: Boys Boarding and Day
7–13
No of pupils: 240
No of boarders: F116 W126
Fees: (September 08) FB £18480
Day £12570–£13596

DAIR HOUSE SCHOOL TRUST LTD
Bishops Blake, Beaconsfield Road,
Farnham Royal, Buckinghamshire
SL2 3BY
Tel: (01753) 643964
Fax: (01753) 642376
Email: info@dairhouse.co.uk
Head: Mr T C Wintle
Type: Co-educational Day 3–11
No of pupils: B66 G40
Fees: (September 08)
Day £8226–£8526

GERRARDS CROSS

GAYHURST SCHOOL
Bull Lane, Gerrards Cross,
Buckinghamshire SL9 8RJ
Tel: (01753) 882690
Fax: (01753) 887451
Email: gayhurst@
  gayhurst.bucks.sch.uk
Head: Mr A J Sims
Type: Boys Day 4–13
Fees: (September 08)
Day £7929–£10074

KINGSCOTE PRE-PREPARATORY SCHOOL
Oval Way, Gerrards Cross,
Buckinghamshire SL9 8PZ
Tel: (01753) 885535
Fax: (01753) 891783
Email: office@
  kingscoteschool.info
Head: Mrs S A Tunstall
Type: Boys Day 3–7
No of pupils: 130
Fees: (September 08)
Day £5055–£7578

MALTMAN'S GREEN SCHOOL
Maltmans Lane, Gerrards Cross,
Buckinghamshire SL9 8RR
Tel: (01753) 883022
Fax: (01753) 891237
Email: registrar@
  maltmansgreen.com
Head: Mrs J R Pardon
Type: Girls Day 3–11
No of pupils: 400
Fees: (September 08)
Day £6780–£9945

ST MARY'S SCHOOL
94 Packhorse Road, Gerrards
Cross, Buckinghamshire SL9 8JQ
Tel: (01753) 883370
Fax: (01753) 890966
Email: registrar@
  st-marys.bucks.sch.uk
Head: Mrs F A Balcombe
Type: Girls Day 3–18
No of pupils: 325
Fees: (September 08)
Day £3195–£11475

THORPE HOUSE SCHOOL
Oval Way, Gerrards Cross,
Buckinghamshire SL9 8QA
Tel: (01753) 882474
Fax: (01753) 889755
Email: office@
  thorpehouse.bucks.sch.uk
Head: Mr A F Lock
Type: Boys Day 3–16
No of pupils: 280
Fees: (September 08)
Day £9915–£11880

GREAT MISSENDEN

GATEWAY SCHOOL
1 High Street, Great Missenden,
Buckinghamshire HP16 9AA
Tel: (01494) 862407
Fax: (01494) 865787
Email: headteacher@
  gateway.bucks.sch.uk
Head: Mr S Wade
Type: Co-educational Day 2–12
No of pupils: B172 G110
Fees: On application

England – Buckinghamshire

HIGH WYCOMBE

CROWN HOUSE SCHOOL
19 London Road, High Wycombe,
Buckinghamshire HP11 1BJ
Tel: (01494) 529927
Fax: (01494) 525693
Email: education@
crownhouseschool.co.uk
Head: Mr L Clark
Type: Co-educational Day 4–11
No of pupils: B78 G59
Fees: (September 08)
Day £6540–£7440

GODSTOWE PREPARATORY SCHOOL
Shrubbery Road, High Wycombe,
Buckinghamshire HP13 6PR
Tel: (01494) 529273
Fax: (01494) 429009
Email: head@godstowe.org
Head: Mr D St C Gainer
Type: Girls Day and Boarding
3–13 (Boys 3–8)
No of pupils: B27 G350
No of boarders: F60 W21
Fees: (September 08) F/WB £18330
Day £3630–£12480

PIPERS CORNER SCHOOL*
Pipers Lane, Great Kingshill, High
Wycombe, Buckinghamshire
HP15 6LP
Tel: (01494) 718255
Fax: (01494) 719806
Email: theschool@
piperscorner.co.uk
Head: Mrs H J Ness-Gifford
Type: Girls Day and Boarding
3–18
No of pupils: 514
No of boarders: F25 W9
Fees: (September 08)
FB £16200–£19650
WB £15960–£19410
Day £6150–£11925

WYCOMBE ABBEY SCHOOL
High Wycombe, Buckinghamshire
HP11 1PE
Tel: (01494) 520381
Fax: (01494) 473836
Email: schoolsecretary@
wycombeabbey.com
Head: Mrs C L Hall
Type: Girls Boarding and Day
11–18
No of pupils: 561
No of boarders: F530
Fees: (September 08) FB £27300
Day £20475

MILTON KEYNES

BURY LAWN SCHOOL
Soskin Drive, Stantonbury Fields,
Milton Keynes, Buckinghamshire
MK14 6DP
Tel: (01908) 574740
Fax: (01908) 574741
Email: registrar@
burylawnschool.co.uk
Head: Mr J Moreland
Type: Co-educational Day 2–18
No of pupils: B184 G122
Fees: (September 07)
Day £5859–£8652

GROVE INDEPENDENT SCHOOL
Redland Drive, Loughton, Milton
Keynes, Buckinghamshire
MK5 8HD
Tel: (01908) 690590
Fax: (01908) 649043
Email: office@
groveindependentschool.co.uk
Head: Mrs D M Berkin
Type: Co-educational Day 2–13
Fees: On application

MILTON KEYNES PREPARATORY SCHOOL
Tattenhoe Lane, Milton Keynes,
Buckinghamshire MK3 7EG
Tel: (01908) 642111
Fax: (01908) 366365
Email: info@mkps.co.uk
Head: Mrs H A Pauley
Type: Co-educational Day 0–11
No of pupils: B250 G250
Fees: (September 08)
Day £10020–£115320

SWANBOURNE HOUSE SCHOOL*
Swanbourne, Milton Keynes,
Buckinghamshire MK17 0HZ
Tel: (01296) 720264
Fax: (01296) 728089
Email: office@swanbourne.org
Head: Mr S D Goodhart and
Mrs J S Goodhart
Type: Co-educational Boarding
and Day 3–13
No of pupils: B225 G188
No of boarders: F28 W21
Fees: (September 08) F/WB £16785
Day £6150–£13095

THORNTON COLLEGE CONVENT OF JESUS AND MARY
Thornton, Milton Keynes,
Buckinghamshire MK17 0HJ
Tel: (01280) 812610
Fax: (01280) 824042
Email: registrar@
thorntoncollege.com
Head: Miss A Williams
Type: Girls Day and Boarding
2–16 (Boys 2–4)
No of pupils: 358
No of boarders: F30 W15
Fees: (September 08)
FB £12450–£15450
WB £9750–£12420
Day £5880–£9390

NEWPORT PAGNELL

FILGRAVE SCHOOL
Filgrave, Newport Pagnell,
Buckinghamshire MK16 9ET
Tel: (01234) 711534
Email: enquiries@
filgraveschool.org.uk
Head: Mrs D Smith
Type: Co-educational Day 3–9
No of pupils: B20 G21
Fees: On application

PRINCES RISBOROUGH

ST TERESA'S CATHOLIC INDEPENDENT & NURSERY SCHOOL
Aylesbury Road, Princes
Risborough, Buckinghamshire
HP27 0JW
Tel: (01844) 345005
Fax: (01844) 345131
Email: office@
   st-teresas.bucks.sch.uk
Head: Mr R P Duigan
Type: Co-educational Day 3–11
No of pupils: B70 G68
Fees: (September 08)
Day £265–£6486

STOKE POGES

SEFTON PARK SCHOOL
School Lane, Stoke Poges,
Buckinghamshire SL2 4QA
Tel: (01753) 662482
Fax: (01753) 662168
Head: Mr M Hockley
Type: Co-educational Day 11–18
No of pupils: B63 G45
Fees: On application

CAMBRIDGESHIRE

CAMBRIDGE

BELLERBYS COLLEGE & EMBASSY CES CAMBRIDGE
Queens Campus, Bateman Street,
Cambridge, Cambridgeshire
CB2 1LU
Tel: (01223) 363159
Fax: (01223) 307425
Email: cambridge@bellerbys.com
Head: Mr J Rushton
Type: Co-educational Boarding
14–25
No of pupils: B250 G250
No of boarders: F500
Fees: (September 07)
FB £10710–£22740

CAMBRIDGE CENTRE FOR SIXTH-FORM STUDIES*
1 Salisbury Villas, Station Road,
Cambridge, Cambridgeshire
CB1 2JF
Tel: (01223) 716890
Fax: (01223) 517530
Email: enquiries@ccss.co.uk
Head: Mr N Roskilly
Type: Co-educational Day and
Boarding 15–19
No of pupils: B113 G87
No of boarders: F116 W4
Fees: (September 08)
FB £15762–£26091
Day £6285–£16614

CATS CAMBRIDGE*
13–14 Round Church Street,
Cambridge, Cambridgeshire
CB5 8AD
Tel: (01223) 314431
Fax: (01223) 467773
Email: enquiries@
   catscambridge.com
Head: Dr G Hawkins and
Mr J Ullmer
Type: Co-educational Boarding
and Day 14–19
No of pupils: B181 G131
No of boarders: F279
Fees: (September 08)
FB £20850–£32625
Day £15000–£23475

THE LEYS SCHOOL*
Trumpington Road, Cambridge,
Cambridgeshire CB2 7AD
Tel: (01223) 508900
Fax: (01223) 505303
Email: office@theleys.net
Head: Mr Mark Slater
Type: Co-educational Boarding
and Day 11–18
No of pupils: B324 G202
No of boarders: F280
Fees: (September 08)
FB £17250–£23940
Day £11145–£15630

MADINGLEY PRE-PREPARATORY SCHOOL
Cambridge Road, Madingley,
Cambridge, Cambridgeshire
CB23 8AH
Tel: (01954) 210309
Fax: (01233) 264169
Email: admin@
   madingleyschool.co.uk
Head: Mrs P Evans
Type: Co-educational Day 3–8
No of pupils: B30 G30
Fees: (September 08) Day £8550

MPW (MANDER PORTMAN WOODWARD)
3/4 Brookside, Cambridge,
Cambridgeshire CB2 1JE
Tel: (01223) 350158
Fax: (01223) 366429
Email: enquiries@
   cambridge.mpw.co.uk
Head: Dr N Marriott
Type: Co-educational Day and
Boarding 15–21
No of pupils: B60 G60
No of boarders: F20 W20
Fees: On application

THE PERSE SCHOOL
Hills Road, Cambridge,
Cambridgeshire CB2 8QF
Tel: (01223) 403800
Fax: (01223) 403810
Email: office@perse.co.uk
Head: Mr Edward Elliott
Type: Co-educational Day
Boys 11–18 Girls 16–18
No of pupils: B590 G86
Fees: (September 07)
Day £11724–£12216

THE PERSE SCHOOL FOR GIRLS
Union Road, Cambridge,
Cambridgeshire CB2 1HF
Tel: (01223) 454700
Fax: (01223) 467420
Email: office@
    admin.perse.cambs.sch.uk
Head: Miss P M Kelleher
Type: Girls Day 7–18
No of pupils: 668
Fees: On application

ST ANDREW'S
13 Station Road, Cambridge,
Cambridgeshire CB1 2JB
Tel: (01223) 360040
Fax: (01223) 467150
Email: registrar@
    standrewscambridge.co.uk
Head: Mrs C Williams
Type: Co-educational Boarding
and Day 14–18
No of pupils: B67 G53
No of boarders: F120
Fees: (September 07)
Day £11100–£14790

ST COLETTE'S SCHOOL
Tenison Road, Cambridge,
Cambridgeshire CB1 2DP
Tel: (01223) 353696
Fax: (01223) 517784
Email: info@stcolettes.com
Head: Mrs A C Wilson
Type: Co-educational Day 2–7
No of pupils: B60 G60
Fees: (September 08)
Day £5913–£6732

ST FAITH'S
Trumpington Road, Cambridge,
Cambridgeshire CB2 2AG
Tel: (01223) 352073
Fax: (01223) 314757
Email: admissions@stfaiths.co.uk
Head: Mr C S S Drew
Type: Co-educational Day 4–13
No of pupils: B318 G196
Fees: (September 08)
Day £8685–£10950

ST JOHN'S COLLEGE SCHOOL
73 Grange Road, Cambridge,
Cambridgeshire CB3 9AB
Tel: (01223) 353532
Fax: (01223) 355846
Email: admissions@sjcs.co.uk
Head: Mr K L Jones
Type: Co-educational Day and
Boarding 4–13
No of pupils: B248 G213
No of boarders: F40
Fees: (September 08)
FB £5914–£17742
Day £6705–£11232

ST MARY'S JUNIOR SCHOOL
2 Brookside, Cambridge,
Cambridgeshire CB2 1JE
Tel: (01223) 311666
Fax: (01223) 472168
Email: juniorschool@
    stmaryscambridge.co.uk
Head: Mrs D O'Sullivan
Type: Girls Day 4–11
No of pupils: 163
Fees: (September 07)
Day £6675–£7680

ST MARY'S SCHOOL*
Bateman Street, Cambridge,
Cambridgeshire CB2 1LY
Tel: (01223) 353253
Fax: (01223) 357451
Email: enquiries@
    stmaryscambridge.co.uk
Head: Miss C Avery
Type: Girls Day and Boarding
4–18
No of pupils: 669
No of boarders: F53 W7
Fees: (September 08) FB £23310
WB £20475 Day £11625

SANCTON WOOD SCHOOL
2 St Paul's Road, Cambridge,
Cambridgeshire CB1 2EZ
Tel: (01223) 359488
Fax: (01223) 359488
Email: sturdy@sturdy.demon.co.uk
Head: Rev J McDonald
Type: Co-educational Day 1–16
No of pupils: B105 G69
Fees: On application

ELY

THE KING'S SCHOOL ELY
Ely, Cambridgeshire CB7 4DB
Tel: (01353) 660702
Fax: (01353) 667485
Email: admissions@
    kings-ely.cambs.sch.uk
Head: Mrs S E Freestone
Type: Co-educational Boarding
and Day 2–18
No of pupils: B518 G385
No of boarders: F194
Fees: On application

HUNTINGDON

KIMBOLTON SCHOOL
Kimbolton, Huntingdon,
Cambridgeshire PE28 0EA
Tel: (01480) 860505
Fax: (01480) 860386
Email: registrar@
    kimbolton.cambs.sch.uk
Head: Mr J Belbin
Type: Co-educational Boarding
and Day 4–18 (Boarders from 11)
No of pupils: B462 G400
No of boarders: F54
Fees: On application

WHITEHALL SCHOOL
117 High Street, Somersham,
Huntingdon, Cambridgeshire
PE28 3EH
Tel: (01487) 840966
Email: office@
    whitehallschool.com
Head: Mr S Peace
Type: Co-educational Day 3–11
No of pupils: B50 G50
Fees: (September 08)
Day £4530–£5859

MARCH

STATION SCHOOL
5 Station Approach, March,
Cambridgeshire PE15 8SJ
Tel: (01354) 659968
Fax: (01354) 659964
Head: Mr W Parbi
Type: Co-educational Day 11–16
No of pupils: B1 G4
Fees: On application

PETERBOROUGH

**PETERBOROUGH HIGH
SCHOOL***
Thorpe Road, Peterborough,
Cambridgeshire PE3 6JF
Tel: (01733) 343357
Fax: (01733) 355710
Email: phs@
    peterboroughhigh.co.uk
Head: Mr A D Meadows
Type: Girls Day and Boarding
3–18 (Boys 3–11)
No of pupils: B70 G285
No of boarders: F16 W14
Fees: (September 07)
FB £17909–£19371
WB £15756–£16719
Day £7428–£10491

WISBECH

**WISBECH GRAMMAR
SCHOOL**
North Brink, Wisbech,
Cambridgeshire PE13 1JX
Tel: (01945) 583631
Fax: (01945) 476746
Email: hmsecretary@
    wisbechgs.demon.co.uk
Head: Mr N J G Hammond
Type: Co-educational Day 4–18
No of pupils: B366 G321
Fees: (September 08)
Day £6600–£9600

CHANNEL ISLANDS

ALDERNEY

**ORMER HOUSE
PREPARATORY SCHOOL**
La Vallee, Alderney, Channel
Islands GY9 3XA
Tel: (01481) 823287
Fax: (01481) 824053
Email: ormerhouse@cwgsy.net
Head: Mrs M Burridge
Type: Co-educational Day 2–13
No of pupils: B28 G24
Fees: On application

GUERNSEY

CONVENT OF MERCY
Cordier Hill, St Peter Port,
Guernsey, Channel Islands
GY1 1JH
Tel: (01481) 720729
Fax: (01481) 716339
Head: Sister C Blackburn
Type: Co-educational Day 3–7
No of pupils: B57 G46
Fees: On application

ELIZABETH COLLEGE
Guernsey, Channel Islands
GY1 2PY
Tel: (01481) 726544
Fax: (01481) 714839
Email: secretary@
    elizabethcollege.guernsey.net
Head: Dr N Argent
Type: Boys Day 2–18 (Co-ed VIth
Form)
No of pupils: 740
Fees: (September 08)
Day £6234–£6933

THE LADIES' COLLEGE
Les Gravees, St Peter Port,
Guernsey, Channel Islands
GY1 1RW
Tel: (01481) 721602
Fax: (01481) 724209
Email: secretary@
    ladiescollege.education.gg
Head: Ms J Riches
Type: Girls Day 4–18
No of pupils: 541
Fees: (September 08)
Day £5385–£5964

JERSEY

**BEAULIEU CONVENT
SCHOOL**
Wellington Road, Saint Helier,
Jersey, Channel Islands JE2 4RJ
Tel: (01534) 731280
Fax: (01534) 888607
Email: secondaryadmin@
    beaulieu.sch.je
Head: Mr C Beirne
Type: Girls Day 4–18
No of pupils: 623
Fees: On application

FCJ PRIMARY SCHOOL
Deloraine Road, St Saviour, Jersey,
Channel Islands JE2 7XB
Tel: (01534) 723063
Fax: (01534) 880353
Email: admin@fcj.sch.je
Head: Ms M Doyle
Type: Co-educational Day 4–11
No of pupils: B113 G180
Fees: On application

England – Cambridgeshire/Channel Islands

ST GEORGE'S PREPARATORY SCHOOL
La Hague Manor, Rue de la Hague, St Peter, Jersey, Channel Islands JE3 7DB
Tel: (01534) 481593
Fax: (01534) 484304
Email: admin@
    stgeorgesprep.co.uk
Head: Mr Colin Moore
Type: Co-educational Day 3–13
No of pupils: B106 G91
Fees: On application

ST MICHAEL'S PREPARATORY SCHOOL
La Rue de la Houguette, St Saviour, Jersey, Channel Islands JE2 7UG
Tel: (01534) 856904
Fax: (01534) 856620
Email: tm@stmichaels.je
Head: Mr R De Figueiredo
Type: Co-educational Day 3–13
No of pupils: B197 G138
Fees: (September 08)
Day £7545–£11601

VICTORIA COLLEGE
Jersey, Channel Islands JE1 4HT
Tel: (01534) 638200
Fax: (01534) 727448
Email: admin@vcj.sch.je
Head: Mr R G Cook
Type: Boys Day 11–19
No of pupils: 650
Fees: On application

VICTORIA COLLEGE PREPARATORY SCHOOL
Pleasant Street, St Helier, Jersey, Channel Islands
Tel: (01534) 723468
Fax: (01534) 780596
Email: admin@vcp.sch.je
Head: Mr P Stevenson
Type: Boys Day 7–11
No of pupils: 280
Fees: On application

CHESHIRE

ALDERLEY EDGE

ALDERLEY EDGE SCHOOL FOR GIRLS
Wilmslow Road, Alderley Edge, Cheshire SK9 7QE
Tel: (01625) 583028
Fax: (01625) 590271
Email: schoolmail@aesg.co.uk
Head: Mrs K Mills
Type: Girls Day 3–18
No of pupils: 600
Fees: (September 08)
Day £5487–£8277

THE RYLEYS
Ryleys Lane, Alderley Edge, Cheshire SK9 7UY
Tel: (01625) 583241
Fax: (01625) 581900
Email: headmaster@
    ryleys.cheshire.sch.uk
Head: Mr P G Barrett
Type: Boys Day 3–13
No of pupils: 236
Fees: On application

ALTRINCHAM

ALTRINCHAM PREPARATORY SCHOOL
Marlborough Road, Bowdon, Altrincham, Cheshire WA14 2RR
Tel: (0161) 928 3366
Fax: (0161) 929 6747
Email: admin@altprep.co.uk
Head: Mr A Potts
Type: Boys Day 4–11
No of pupils: 310
Fees: On application

BOWDON PREPARATORY SCHOOL FOR GIRLS
48 Stamford Road, Bowdon, Altrincham, Cheshire WA14 2JP
Tel: (0161) 928 0678
Email: bps@bowdonprep.org.uk
Head: Mrs J H Tan
Type: Girls Day 2–12
No of pupils: 220
Fees: On application

CULCHETH HALL
Ashley Road, Altrincham, Cheshire WA14 2LT
Tel: (0161) 928 1862
Fax: (0161) 929 6893
Email: admin@
    culcheth-hall.org.uk
Head: Miss M A Stockwell
Type: Girls Day 2–16 (Boys 2–4)
No of pupils: B12 G203
Fees: On application

FOREST SCHOOL
Moss Lane, Timperley, Altrincham, Cheshire WA15 6LJ
Tel: (0161) 980 4075
Fax: (0161) 903 9275
Email: headteacher@
    forestschool.co.uk
Head: Mrs E A Irons
Type: Co-educational Day 2–11
No of pupils: B86 G81
Fees: On application

HALE PREPARATORY SCHOOL
Broomfield Lane, Hale,
Altrincham, Cheshire WA15 9AS
Tel: (0161) 928 2386
Fax: (0161) 941 7934
Email: johnconnor9@
    btinternet.com
Head: Mr J Connor
Type: Co-educational Day 4–11
No of pupils: B99 G83
Fees: On application

LORETO PREPARATORY SCHOOL
Dunham Road, Altrincham,
Cheshire WA14 4GZ
Tel: (0161) 928 8310
Fax: (0161) 929 5801
Email: info.loretoprep@
    btconnect.com
Head: Mrs R A Hedger
Type: Girls Day 3–11 (Boys 4–7)
No of pupils: 163
Fees: (September 08) Day £4410

NORTH CESTRIAN GRAMMAR SCHOOL
Dunham Road, Altrincham,
Cheshire WA14 4AJ
Tel: (0161) 928 1856
Fax: (0161) 929 8657
Email: office@ncgs.co.uk
Head: Mr D G Vanstone
Type: Co-educational Day 11–18
No of pupils: B300 G30
Fees: (September 08) Day £7470

ST AMBROSE PREPARATORY SCHOOL
Hale Barns, Altrincham, Cheshire
WA15 0HE
Tel: (0161) 903 9193
Fax: (0161) 903 8138
Email: stambroseprep.admin@
    traffordlearning.org
Head: Mr M J Lochery
Type: Boys Day 4–11
No of pupils: 191
Fees: (September 08)
Day £5121–£5334

CHEADLE

CHEADLE HULME SCHOOL
Claremont Road, Cheadle Hulme,
Cheadle, Cheshire SK8 6EF
Tel: (0161) 488 3330
Fax: (0161) 488 3344
Email: headmaster@
    chschool.co.uk
Head: Mr P V Dixon
Type: Co-educational Day 4–18
No of pupils: B706 G612
Fees: On application

GREENBANK
Heathbank Road, Cheadle Hulme,
Cheadle, Cheshire SK8 6HU
Tel: (0161) 485 3724
Fax: (0161) 485 5519
Email: kevinphillips@
    greenbank.stockport.sch.uk
Head: Mr K Phillips
Type: Co-educational Day 3–11
No of pupils: B98 G62
Fees: On application

HULME HALL SCHOOLS
75 Hulme Hall Road, Cheadle
Hulme, Cheadle, Cheshire
SK8 6LA
Tel: (0161) 485 4638/3524
Fax: (0161) 485 5966
Email: secretary@
    hulmehallschool.co.uk
Head: Mr P Marland
Type: Co-educational Day 2–16
No of pupils: B255 G130
Fees: On application

HULME HALL SCHOOLS (JUNIOR DIVISION)
75 Hulme Hall Road, Cheadle
Hulme, Cheadle, Cheshire
SK8 6LA
Tel: (0161) 486 9970
Fax: (0161) 485 5966
Email: secretary@
    hulmehallschool.co.uk
Head: Mr P Marland
Type: Co-educational Day 3–11
No of pupils: B58 G32
Fees: On application

LADY BARN HOUSE SCHOOL
Langlands, Schools Hill, Cheadle
Hulme, Cheadle, Cheshire SK8 1JE
Tel: (0161) 428 2912
Fax: (0161) 428 5798
Email: info@
    ladybarnhouse.stockport.sch.uk
Head: Mrs S Yule
Type: Co-educational Day 3–11
No of pupils: B280 G187
Fees: On application

RAMILLIES HALL SCHOOL[†]
Ramillies Avenue, Cheadle
Hulme, Cheadle, Cheshire SK8 7AJ
Tel: (0161) 485 3804
Fax: (0161) 486 6021
Email: info@ramillieshall.co.uk
Head: Miss D M Patterson and
Mrs A L Poole
Type: Co-educational Day 0–16
No of pupils: B114 G69
Fees: On application

CHESTER

ABBEY GATE COLLEGE
Saighton Grange, Saighton,
Chester, Cheshire CH3 6EN
Tel: (01244) 332077
Fax: (01244) 335510
Email: bursar@
    abbeygatecollege.co.uk
Head: Mrs L M Horner
Type: Co-educational Day 4–18
No of pupils: B241 G194
Fees: (September 07)
Day £5130–£8745

ABBEY GATE SCHOOL
Clare Avenue, Hoole, Chester,
Cheshire CH2 3HR
Tel: (01244) 319649
Email: abbeygateschool@
    talk21.com
Head: Mrs SM Fisher
Type: Co-educational Day
Boys 30–11 Girls 35–11
No of pupils: 33
Fees: (September 08)
Day £5250–£5685

England – Cheshire

THE FIRS SCHOOL
45 Newton Lane, Chester,
Cheshire CH2 2HJ
Tel: (01244) 322443
Fax: (01244) 400450
Email: firsschool.admin@
    btopenworld.com
Head: Mrs M Denton
Type: Co-educational Day 4–11
No of pupils: B134 G81
Fees: (September 08) Day £6180

HAMMOND SCHOOL
Hoole Bank House, Mannings
Lane, Chester, Cheshire CH2 4ES
Tel: (01244) 305350
Fax: (01244) 305351
Email: enquiries@
    thehammondschool.co.uk
Head: Mrs M P Dangerfield
Type: Co-educational Day and
Boarding 11–18
No of pupils: B50 G170
No of boarders: F59
Fees: On application

THE KING'S SCHOOL
Wrexham Road, Chester, Cheshire
CH4 7QL
Tel: (01244) 689500
Fax: (01244) 689501
Email: admissions@
    kingschester.co.uk
Head: Mr C Ramsey
Type: Co-educational Day 7–18
No of pupils: B699 G117
Fees: (September 08)
Day £7251–£9462

MERTON HOUSE
Abbot's Park, Off Liverpool Road,
Chester, Cheshire CH1 4BD
Tel: (01244) 377165
Fax: (01244) 374569
Email: secretary@
    mertonhousechester.co.uk
Head: Mr S White
Type: Co-educational Day 3–11
No of pupils: B58 G65
Fees: (September 08) Day £6180

THE QUEEN'S SCHOOL
City Walls Road, Chester,
Cheshire CH1 2NN
Tel: (01244) 312078
Fax: (01244) 321507
Email: secretary@
    queens.cheshire.sch.uk
Head: Mrs C M Buckley
Type: Girls Day 4–18
No of pupils: 591
Fees: (September 08)
Day £6600–£9420

HOLMES CHAPEL

TERRA NOVA SCHOOL
Jodrell Bank, Holmes Chapel,
Cheshire CW4 8BT
Tel: (01477) 571251
Fax: (01477) 571646
Email: enquiries@
    terranovaschool.co uk
Head: Mr N Johnson
Type: Co-educational Day and
Boarding 3–13
No of pupils: B139 G124
No of boarders: F6 W20
Fees: (September 08) WB £13800
Day £6300–£11130

KNUTSFORD

YORSTON LODGE SCHOOL
18 St John's Road, Knutsford,
Cheshire WA16 0DP
Tel: (01565) 633177
Fax: (01565) 632484
Email: headmistress@
    yorstonlodge.com
Head: Mrs J Dallimore
Type: Co-educational Day 3–11
No of pupils: B63 G61
Fees: (September 08) Day £5000

MACCLESFIELD

BEECH HALL SCHOOL
Beech Hall Drive, Tytherington,
Macclesfield, Cheshire SK10 2EG
Tel: (01625) 422192
Fax: (01625) 502424
Email: secretary@
    beechhallschool.freeserve.co.uk
Head: Mr TJG Scott
Type: Co-educational Day 4–16
(Kindergarten 1–5)
No of pupils: B110 G72
Fees: (September 08)
Day £5685–£8340

THE KING'S SCHOOL
Macclesfield, Cheshire SK10 1DA
Tel: (01625) 260000
Fax: (01625) 260022
Email: mail@kingsmac.co.uk
Head: Dr S Coyne
Type: Co-educational Day 3–18
(Single-sex ed 11–16)
No of pupils: B800 G600
Fees: (September 08)
Day £5790–£8355

NORTHWICH

CRANSLEY SCHOOL
Belmont Hall, Great Budworth,
Northwich, Cheshire CW9 6HN
Tel: (01606) 891747
Fax: (01606) 892122
Email: admin.cransleyschool@
    btinternet.com
Head: Mrs G Gaunt
Type: Co-educational Day
Boys 3–11 Girls 3–16(Boys 3–11)
No of pupils: B23 G154
Fees: On application

THE GRANGE SCHOOL
Bradburns Lane, Hartford,
Northwich, Cheshire CW8 1LU
Tel: (01606) 74007
Fax: (01606) 784581
Email: office@grange.org.uk
Head: Mr C P Jeffery
Type: Co-educational Day 4–18
No of pupils: B606 G528
Fees: On application

SALE

CHRIST THE KING SCHOOL
The King's Centre, Raglan Road,
Sale, Cheshire M33 4AQ
Tel: (0161) 969 1906
Fax: (0161) 905 1586
Email: info@ctks.org.uk
Head: Mr D Baynes
Type: Co-educational Day 5–16
No of pupils: B25 G27
Fees: On application

FOREST PARK SCHOOL
Lauriston House, 27 Oakfield,
Sale, Cheshire M33 6NB
Tel: (0161) 973 4835
Fax: (0161) 282 9021
Email: post@
    forestparkschool.freeserve.co.uk
Head: Mr L B R Groves
Type: Co-educational Day 3–11
No of pupils: B80 G60
Fees: (September 08)
Day £4740–£5190

SANDBACH

NORFOLK HOUSE PREPARATORY & KIDS CORNER NURSERY
Norfolk House, 120 Congleton Road, Sandbach, Cheshire CW11 1HF
Tel: (01270) 759257
Fax: (01270) 753519
Email: post@norfolkhouse.net
Head: Mrs P M Jones
Type: Co-educational Day 0–11
No of pupils: B42 G43
Fees: On application

SOUTH WIRRAL

MOSTYN HOUSE SCHOOL[†]
Parkgate, Neston, South Wirral, Cheshire CH64 6SG
Tel: (0151) 336 1010
Fax: (0151) 353 1040
Email: enquiries@ mostynhouse.co.uk
Head: Miss S M T Grenfell
Type: Co-educational Day 4–18
No of pupils: B116 G72
Fees: On application

STALYBRIDGE

TRINITY SCHOOL
Birbeck Street, Stalybridge, Cheshire SK15 1SH
Tel: (0161) 303 0674
Email: office@trinityschool.org.uk
Head: Mr W R Evans
Type: Co-educational Day 4–18
No of pupils: B67 G64
Fees: On application

STOCKPORT

BRABYNS SCHOOL
34–36 Arkwright Road, Marple, Stockport, Cheshire SK6 7DB
Tel: (0161) 427 2395
Fax: (0161) 449 0704
Email: brabyns@indschool.org
Head: Mr L Sanders
Type: Co-educational Day 2–11
No of pupils: B57 G59
Fees: (September 08)
Day £3939–£5337

HILLCREST GRAMMAR SCHOOL
Beech Avenue, Cale Green, Stockport, Cheshire SK3 8HB
Tel: (0161) 480 0329
Fax: (0161) 476 2814
Email: headmaster@ hillcrest.stockport.sch.uk
Head: Mr D J Eversley
Type: Co-educational Day 3–16
No of pupils: B198 G145
Fees: (September 08)
Day £4326–£6996

ST CATHERINE'S PREPARATORY SCHOOL
Hollins Lane, Marple Bridge, Stockport, Cheshire SK6 5BB
Tel: (0161) 449 8800
Fax: (0161) 449 8181
Email: info@stcatherinesprep. stockport.sch.uk
Head: Mrs R A Brierley
Type: Co-educational Day 3–11
No of pupils: B61 G88
Fees: On application

STELLA MARIS JUNIOR SCHOOL
St John's Road, Heaton Mersey, Stockport, Cheshire SK4 3BR
Tel: (0161) 432 0532
Fax: (0161) 432 9440
Email: office@ stellamarisschool.co.uk
Head: Mr A Whittell
Type: Co-educational Day 3–11
No of pupils: B40 G40
Fees: (September 08) Day £4980

STOCKPORT GRAMMAR SCHOOL
Buxton Road, Stockport, Cheshire SK2 7AF
Tel: (0161) 456 9000
Fax: (0161) 419 2407
Email: sgs@ stockportgrammar.co.uk
Head: Mr A H Chicken
Type: Co-educational Day 3–18
No of pupils: B792 G668
Fees: (September 08)
Day £6336–£8226

WILMSLOW

POWNALL HALL SCHOOL
Carrwood Road, Wilmslow, Cheshire SK9 5DW
Tel: (01625) 523141
Fax: (01625) 525209
Email: genoffice@ pownallhall.cheshire.sch.uk
Head: Mr J J Meadmore
Type: Co-educational Day 2–11
No of pupils: B134 G65
Fees: (September 07)
Day £3570–£7680

WILMSLOW PREPARATORY SCHOOL
Grove Avenue, Wilmslow, Cheshire SK9 5EG
Tel: (01625) 524246
Fax: (01625) 536660
Email: secretary@ wilmslowprep.co.uk
Head: Mrs H J Shaw
Type: Girls Day 2–11
No of pupils: 160
Fees: (September 08)
Day £2070–£7650

England – Cheshire

CORNWALL

BUDE

ST PETROC'S SCHOOL
Ocean View Road, Bude,
Cornwall EX23 8NJ
Tel: (01288) 352876
Fax: (01288) 352876
Email: office@stpetrocs.com
Head: Dr I T Whitehurst
Type: Co-educational Day 3–11
(Nursery from 3 mths)
No of pupils: B48 G42
Fees: On application

HAYLE

ST PIRAN'S PREPARATORY SCHOOL
14 Trelissick Road, Hayle,
Cornwall TR27 4HY
Tel: (01736) 752612
Fax: (01736) 759446
Email: office@
  stpirans.fsbusiness.co.uk
Head: Mrs C A de Labat
Type: Co-educational Day 3–16
No of pupils: B26 G26
Fees: (September 08) Day £3995

LAUNCESTON

ST JOSEPH'S SCHOOL
St Stephen's Hill, Launceston,
Cornwall PL15 8HN
Tel: (01566) 772580
Fax: (01566) 775902
Email: registrar@
  stjosephs.eclipse.co.uk
Head: Mr Graeme Garrett and
Mrs E Mann
Type: Co-educational Day
Boys 3–11 Girls 3–16(Boys 3–11)
No of pupils: B27 G154
Fees: (September 07)
Day £5259–£8355

PAR

ROSELYON
St Blazey Road, Par, Cornwall
PL24 2HZ
Tel: (01726) 812110
Fax: (01726) 812110
Email: roselyonsch@
  btconnect.com
Head: Mr S C Bradley
Type: Co-educational Day 2–11
No of pupils: B38 G45
Fees: On application

PENZANCE

THE BOLITHO SCHOOL
Polwithen, Penzance, Cornwall
TR18 4JR
Tel: (01736) 363271
Fax: (01736) 330960
Email: tthomas@
  bolitho.cornwall.sch.uk
Head: Mr D Dobson
Type: Co-educational Day and
Boarding 4–18
No of pupils: B195 G172
No of boarders: F59 W46
Fees: (September 08)
FB £5600–£6800
WB £4900–£6100
Day £1825–£3800

REDRUTH

HIGHFIELDS PRIVATE SCHOOL
Lower Cardrew Lane, Redruth,
Cornwall TR15 1SY
Tel: (01209) 210665
Fax: (01209) 210667
Email: highfieldschool@aol.com
Head: Mrs M D Haddy
Type: Co-educational Day 4–16
No of pupils: B34 G30
Fees: (September 08) Day £5400

ST IVES

ST IA SCHOOL
St Ives Road, Carbis Bay, St Ives,
Cornwall TR26 2SF
Tel: (01736) 796963
Email: betsan@
  hill3129.freeserve.co.uk
Head: Miss B R Hill
Type: Co-educational Day
Boys 3–9 Girls 3–11
No of pupils: B10 G12
Fees: (September 08)
Day £1590–£1650

TRURO

POLWHELE HOUSE SCHOOL
Newquay Road, Truro, Cornwall
TR4 9AE
Tel: (01872) 273011
Fax: (01872) 273011
Email: polwhele@talk21.com
Head: Mr J Mason
Type: Co-educational Day and
Boarding 3–13
No of pupils: B96 G84
No of boarders: W15
Fees: On application

TRURO HIGH SCHOOL
Falmouth Road, Truro, Cornwall
TR1 2HU
Tel: (01872) 272830
Fax: (01872) 279393
Email: admin@trurohigh.co.uk
Head: Mr M McDowell
Type: Girls Boarding and Day
3–18 (Boys 3–5)
No of pupils: B2 G463
No of boarders: F38 W10
Fees: (September 08)
FB £12693–£18375
WB £12468–£18150
Day £4060–£9750

TRURO SCHOOL PREPARATORY SCHOOL
Highertown, Truro, Cornwall
TR1 3QN
Tel: (01872) 243120
Fax: (01872) 222377
Email: enquiries@truroprep.com
Head: Mr M Lovett
Type: Co-educational Day 3–11
No of pupils: B128 G97
Fees: (September 08)
Day £6450–£9135

TRURO SCHOOL
Trennick Lane, Truro, Cornwall
TR1 1TH
Tel: (01872) 272763
Fax: (01872) 223431
Email: enquiries@truroschool.com
Head: Mr P K Smith
Type: Co-educational Day and
Boarding 11–18
No of pupils: B533 G293
No of boarders: F45
Fees: (September 08) FB £19380
Day £10080

CUMBRIA

BARROW-IN-FURNESS

CHETWYNDE SCHOOL*
Croslands, Rating Lane, Barrow-in-
Furness, Cumbria LA13 0NY
Tel: (01229) 824210
Fax: (01229) 871440
Email: info@
  chetwynde.cumbria.sch.uk
Head: Mrs I Nixon
Type: Co-educational Day 3–18
Fees: (September 08)
Day £5994–£6996

CARLISLE

**AUSTIN FRIARS ST
MONICA'S SCHOOL**
Etterby Scaur, Carlisle, Cumbria
CA3 9PB
Tel: (01228) 528042
Fax: (01228) 810327
Email: office@
  austinfriars.cumbria.sch.uk
Head: Mr C J Lumb
Type: Co-educational Day 3–18
No of pupils: B301 G205
Fees: On application

LIME HOUSE SCHOOL*†
Holm Hill, Dalston, Carlisle,
Cumbria CA5 7BX
Tel: (01228) 710225
Fax: (01228) 710508
Email: lhsoffice@aol.com
Head: Mr N A Rice
Type: Co-educational Boarding
and Day 4–18
No of pupils: B115 G86
No of boarders: F110 W4
Fees: (September 08)
F/WB £9000–£16500
Day £3000–£7350

KENDAL

HOLME PARK SCHOOL
Hill Top, New Hutton, Kendal,
Cumbria LA8 0AE
Tel: (01539) 721245
Fax: (01539) 721245
Email: holmeparkschool@
  hotmail.com
Head: Ms V Curry
Type: Co-educational Day and
Boarding 2–12
No of pupils: B50 G15
Fees: On application

KIRKBY LONSDALE

CASTERTON SCHOOL
Kirkby Lonsdale, Cumbria LA6 2SG
Tel: (01524) 279200
Fax: (01524) 279208
Email: admissions@
  castertonschool.co.uk
Head: Dr P McLaughlin
Type: Girls Boarding and Day
3–18 (Day boys 3–11)
No of pupils: B15 G355
No of boarders: F281
Fees: (September 08)
FB £16035–£21633
Day £6027–£12945

PENRITH

HUNTER HALL SCHOOL
Frenchfield, Penrith, Cumbria
CA11 8UA
Tel: (01768) 891291
Fax: (01768) 899161
Email: office@
  hunterhall.cumbria.sch.uk
Head: Mr A J Short
Type: Co-educational Day 3–11
No of pupils: B68 G80
Fees: On application

England – Cornwall/Cumbria

SEASCALE

HARECROFT HALL SCHOOL
Gosforth, Seascale, Cumbria
CA20 1HS
Tel: (01946) 725220
Fax: (01946) 725885
Email: harecroft.hall@
    btopenworld.com
Head: Mr P Block
Type: Co-educational Boarding
and Day 3–16
No of pupils: B51 G28
No of boarders: F11
Fees: On application

SEDBERGH

SEDBERGH JUNIOR SCHOOL
Sedbergh, Cumbria LA10 5HG
Tel: (015396) 20535
Fax: (015396) 21301
Email: hmsjs@
    sedberghjuniorschool.org
Head: Mr P Reynolds
Type: Co-educational Boarding
and Day 4–13
No of pupils: B79 G29
No of boarders: F27 W19
Fees: On application

SEDBERGH SCHOOL*
Sedbergh, Cumbria LA10 5HG
Tel: (015396) 20535
Fax: (015396) 21301
Email: hm@sedberghschool.org
Head: Mr C H Hirst
Type: Co-educational Boarding
and Day 13–18
No of pupils: B345 G135
No of boarders: F465
Fees: (September 08) FB £8250

ST BEES

ST BEES SCHOOL†
St Bees, Cumbria CA27 0DS
Tel: (01946) 828010
Fax: (01946) 828011
Email: helen.miller@
    st-bees-school.co.uk
Head: Mr P J Capes
Type: Co-educational Boarding
and Day 11–18
No of pupils: B172 G118
No of boarders: F95 W24
Fees: (September 08)
FB £16785–£23145
WB £13776–£19746
Day £10743–£13872

WIGTON

ST URSULAS CONVENT SCHOOL
Burnfoot, Wigton, Cumbria
CA7 9HL
Tel: (01697) 344359
Fax: (01697) 344420
Email: stursula@btconnect.com
Head: Mrs J Monkhouse
Type: Co-educational Day 2–11
No of pupils: B20 G31
Fees: On application

WINDERMERE

WINDERMERE ST ANNE'S
Patterdale Road, Windermere,
Cumbria LA23 1NW
Tel: (01539) 446164
Fax: (01539) 488414
Email: admissions@
    wsaschool.com
Head: Mr A Graham
Type: Co-educational Boarding
and Day 2–18
No of pupils: B180 G200
No of boarders: F83 W44
Fees: (September 07) FB £22005
WB £19860 Day £11580

DERBYSHIRE

BAKEWELL

S ANSELM'S SCHOOL
Bakewell, Derbyshire DE45 1DP
Tel: (01629) 812734
Fax: (01629) 812742
Email: headmaster@anselms.co.uk
Head: Mr Simon Northcott
Type: Co-educational Boarding
and Day 3–13
No of pupils: B160 G120
No of boarders: F94
Fees: (September 08) FB £17130
Day £11610–£14580

CHESTERFIELD

BARLBOROUGH HALL SCHOOL*
Barlborough, Chesterfield,
Derbyshire S43 4TJ
Tel: (01246) 810511
Fax: (01246) 570605
Email: barlborough.hall@
    virgin.net
Head: Mrs W E Parkinson
Type: Co-educational Day 3–11
No of pupils: B122 G138
Fees: £5250–£7500

ST JOSEPH'S CONVENT
42 Newbold Road, Chesterfield,
Derbyshire S41 7PL
Tel: (01246) 232392
Fax: (01246) 201965
Email: info@
    st-josephs-convent-sch.org.uk
Head: Mrs B Deane
Type: Co-educational Day 2–11
No of pupils: B69 G66
Fees: On application

ST PETER & ST PAUL SCHOOL
Brambling House, Hady Hill,
Chesterfield, Derbyshire S41 0EF
Tel: (01246) 278522
Fax: (01246) 273861
Email: head@spsp.org.uk
Head: Mr A Lamb
Type: Co-educational Day 4–11
No of pupils: B73 G59
Fees: (September 08)
Day £1975–£2095

DERBY

DERBY GRAMMAR SCHOOL
Rykneld Road, Littleover, Derby,
Derbyshire DE23 4BX
Tel: (01332) 523027
Fax: (01332) 518670
Email: headmaster@
derbygrammar.co.uk
Head: Mr R D Waller
Type: Co-educational Day
Boys 7–18 Girls 16–18
No of pupils: B303 G8
Fees: (September 07)
Day £7053–£9531

DERBY HIGH SCHOOL
Hillsway, Littleover, Derby,
Derbyshire DE23 3DT
Tel: (01332) 514267
Fax: (01332) 516085
Email: headsecretary@
derbyhigh.derby.sch.uk
Head: Mr C T Callaghan
Type: Co-educational Day
Boys 3–11 Girls 3–18
No of pupils: B90 G500
Fees: (September 08)
Day £6540–£8730

EMMANUEL SCHOOL
Juniper Lodge, 43 Kedleston Road,
Derby, Derbyshire DE22 1FP
Tel: (01332) 340505
Fax: (01332) 299168
Email: emmanuelschool@emcf.net
Head: Mr A Townsend
Type: Co-educational Day 3–11
No of pupils: B33 G30
Fees: (September 07)
Day £1572–£2532

FOREMARKE HALL SCHOOL
Milton, Derby, Derbyshire
DE65 6EJ
Tel: (01283) 703269
Fax: (01283) 701185
Email: office@foremarke.org.uk
Head: Mr P Watson
Type: Co-educational Day and
Boarding 3–13
No of pupils: B267 G173
No of boarders: F59 W20
Fees: (September 08) F/WB £16890
Day £6570–£12720

MORLEY HALL PREPARATORY SCHOOL
Hill House, Morley Road,
Oakwood, Derby, Derbyshire
DE21 4QZ
Tel: (01332) 674501
Email: julie.lee@
morleyhall-school.co.uk
Head: Mrs R N Hassell
Type: Co-educational Day 3–11
No of pupils: B35 G37
Fees: On application

OCKBROOK SCHOOL
The Settlement, Ockbrook, Derby,
Derbyshire DE72 3RJ
Tel: (01332) 673532
Fax: (01332) 665184
Email: enquiries@
ockbrook.derby.sch.uk
Head: Ms Alison Steele
Type: Girls Day and Boarding
3–18
No of pupils: B40 G460
No of boarders: F18
Fees: (September 08) F/WB £15195
Day £5670–£8340

THE OLD VICARAGE SCHOOL
11 Church Lane, Darley Abbey,
Derby, Derbyshire DE22 1EW
Tel: (01332) 557130
Email: office@
oldvicarageschool.co.uk
Head: Mr M Adshead
Type: Co-educational Day 3–11
No of pupils: B44 G44
Fees: (September 08)
Day £5142–£5460

REPTON SCHOOL
Repton, Derby, Derbyshire
DE65 6FH
Tel: (01283) 559222
Fax: (01283) 559223
Email: registrar@repton.org.uk
Head: Mr R Holroyd
Type: Co-educational Boarding
and Day 13–18
No of pupils: B362 G277
No of boarders: F464
Fees: (September 08) FB £25125
Day £18645

HEANOR

MICHAEL HOUSE STEINER SCHOOL
The Field, Shipley, Heanor,
Derbyshire DE75 7JH
Tel: (01773) 718050
Fax: (01773) 711784
Email: admin@
michaelhouseschool.co.uk
Head: Ms D Eccott
Type: Co-educational Day 4–16
No of pupils: B85 G80
Fees: On application

ILKESTON

GATEWAY CHRISTIAN SCHOOL
Moor Lane, Dale Abbey, Ilkeston,
Derbyshire DE7 4PP
Tel: (0115) 944 0609
Fax: (0115) 944 0622
Email: admin@
gatewayschool.org.uk
Head: Mrs C Fergus
Type: Co-educational Day 3–11
No of pupils: B18 G16
Fees: (September 08) Day £2400

REPTON

ST WYSTAN'S SCHOOL
High Street, Repton, Derbyshire
DE65 6GE
Tel: (01283) 703258
Fax: (01283) 703258
Email: head@stwystans.org.uk
Head: Mr P Soutar
Type: Co-educational Day 2–11
No of pupils: B54 G59
Fees: (September 08)
Day £2955–£6225

England – Derbyshire

SPINKHILL

MOUNT ST MARY'S COLLEGE*
Spinkhill, Derbyshire S21 3YL
Tel: (01246) 433388
Fax: (01246) 435511
Email: info@msmcollege.com
Head: Mr L McKell
Type: Co-educational Boarding and Day 11–18
No of pupils: B252 G153
No of boarders: F51 W18
Fees: (September 08)
FB £14160–£18690
WB £12000–£16140
Day £8445–£9780

DEVON

ASHBURTON

SANDS SCHOOL
Greylands, 48 East Street,
Ashburton, Devon TQ13 7AX
Tel: (01364) 653666
Fax: (01364) 653666
Email: enquiry@
sandsschool.demon.co.uk
Head: Mr S Bellamy
Type: Co-educational Day 11–17
No of pupils: B36 G34
Fees: On application

BARNSTAPLE

ST MICHAEL'S
Tawstock Court, Barnstaple,
Devon EX31 3HY
Tel: (01271) 343242
Fax: (01271) 346771
Email: mail@
st-michaels-school.com
Head: Mr J W Pratt
Type: Co-educational Day 0–13
No of pupils: B114 G86
Fees: On application

WEST BUCKLAND PREPARATORY SCHOOL
West Buckland, Barnstaple, Devon
EX32 0SX
Tel: (01598) 760629
Fax: (01598) 760546
Email: prephm@
westbuckland.devon.sch.uk
Head: Mr J Vick
Type: Co-educational Day and Boarding 3–11
No of pupils: B120 G110
No of boarders: F8
Fees: (September 08)
FB £12795–£18675
Day £5910–£10800

WEST BUCKLAND SCHOOL
Barnstaple, Devon EX32 0SX
Tel: (01598) 760281
Fax: (01598) 760546
Email: headmaster@
westbuckland.devon.sch.uk
Head: Mr J F Vick
Type: Co-educational Boarding and Day 3–18
No of pupils: B363 G319
No of boarders: F92 W4
Fees: (September 08)
F/WB £13875–£18675
Day £5910–£10800

BEAWORTHY

SHEBBEAR COLLEGE
Shebbear, Beaworthy, Devon
EX21 5HJ
Tel: (01409) 282000
Fax: (01409) 281784
Email: info@
shebbearcollege.co.uk
Head: Mr R S Barnes
Type: Co-educational Boarding and Day 3–18
No of pupils: B195 G124
No of boarders: F73 W39
Fees: On application

BIDEFORD

EDGEHILL COLLEGE
Northdown Road, Bideford,
Devon EX39 3LY
Tel: (01237) 471701
Fax: (01237) 425981
Email: edgehill@btconnect.com
Head: Mr S Nicholson
Type: Co-educational Boarding and Day 2–18
No of pupils: B100 G100
No of boarders: F50 W3
Fees: On application

GRENVILLE COLLEGE[†]
Belvoir Road, Bideford, Devon
EX39 3JP
Tel: (01237) 472212
Fax: (01237) 477020
Email: registrar@
   grenvillecollege.co.uk
Head: Mr Andy Waters
Type: Co-educational Boarding
and Day 3–19
No of pupils: B225 G137
No of boarders: F59 W15
Fees: (September 08)
FB £16650–£20655
WB £13305–£16650
Day £4845–£10575

DARTINGTON

RUDOLF STEINER SCHOOL
Hood Manor, Dartington, Devon
TQ9 6AB
Tel: (01803) 762528
Fax: (01803) 762528
Email: enquiries@
   steiner-south-devon.org
Head: Mr M Whitlock
Type: Co-educational Day 3–16
No of pupils: B139 G145
Fees: On application

EXETER

BENDARROCH SCHOOL
Aylesbeare, Exeter, Devon
EX5 2BY
Tel: (01395) 233553
Email: info@bendarroch.co.uk
Head: Mr N R Home
Type: Co-educational Day 5–13
No of pupils: B25 G25
Fees: (September 08)
Day £4725–£5175

BRAMDEAN SCHOOL*
Richmond Lodge, Homefield
Road, Heavitree, Exeter, Devon
EX1 2QR
Tel: (01392) 273387
Fax: (01392) 439330
Email: info@bramdeanschool.com
Head: Ms D Stoneman
Type: Co-educational Day 3–18
No of pupils: B110 G90
Fees: (September 08) WB £10662
Day £4740–£7875

EMMANUEL SCHOOL
36–38 Blackboy Road, Exeter,
Devon EX4 6SZ
Tel: (01392) 258150
Fax: (01392) 258150
Email: emmanuelschool@
   tiscali.co.uk
Head: Mr D Rust
Type: Co-educational Day 5–16
No of pupils: B24 G27
Fees: On application

EXETER CATHEDRAL SCHOOL
The Chantry, Palace Gate, Exeter,
Devon EX1 1HX
Tel: (01392) 255298
Fax: (01392) 422718
Email: admin@exetercs.org
Head: Mr B J McDowell
Type: Co-educational Day and
Boarding 3–13
No of pupils: B103 G90
No of boarders: F14 W1
Fees: (September 08)
FB £13698–£14010
WB £13092–£13404
Day £5064–£8568

EXETER JUNIOR SCHOOL
Victoria Park Road, Exeter, Devon
EX2 4NS
Tel: (01392) 273679
Fax: (01392) 498144
Email: admissions@
   exeterschool.org.uk
Head: Mrs A J Turner
Type: Co-educational Day 7–11
No of pupils: B109 G73
Fees: (September 08) Day £8400

EXETER SCHOOL
Victoria Park Road, Exeter, Devon
EX2 4NS
Tel: (01392) 273679
Fax: (01392) 498144
Email: admissions@
   exeterschool.org.uk
Head: Mr R Griffin
Type: Co-educational Day 7–18
No of pupils: B542 G300
Fees: (September 08)
Day £8400–£9300

EXETER TUTORIAL COLLEGE
44/46 Magdalen Road, Exeter,
Devon EX2 4TE
Tel: (01392) 278101
Fax: (01392) 494853
Email: info@tutorialcollege.com
Head: Ms J Burghes and Mr K Jack
Type: Co-educational Day 15+
No of pupils: B30 G30
Fees: (September 08)
Day £2955–£8865

MAGDALEN COURT SCHOOL
Mulberry House, Victoria Park
Road, Exeter, Devon EX2 4NU
Tel: (01392) 494919
Fax: (01392) 494919
Email: admin@mcs-exeter.co.uk
Head: Mr J G Bushrod
Type: Co-educational Day 2–18
No of pupils: B85 G80
Fees: On application

MARIA MONTESSORI SCHOOL
3 St Leonards Place, Exeter, Devon
EX2 4LZ
Tel: (01392) 201303
Email: mmontexe@aol.com
Head: Ms Ruth Bloomfield
Type: Co-educational Day 3–7
No of pupils: B26 G37
Fees: On application

THE MAYNARD SCHOOL
Denmark Road, Exeter, Devon
EX1 1SJ
Tel: (01392) 273417
Fax: (01392) 355999
Email: office@maynard.co.uk
Head: Ms B Hughes
Type: Girls Day 7–18
No of pupils: 475
Fees: (September 08)
Day £7566–£9465

NEW SCHOOL
The Avenue, Exminster, Exeter,
Devon EX6 8AT
Tel: (01392) 496122
Fax: (01392) 496122
Email: thenewschool@
   supanet.com
Head: Mrs M Taylor
Type: Co-educational Day 3–8
No of pupils: B32 G31
Fees: On application

England – Devon

ST MARGARET'S SCHOOL
147 Magdalen Road, Exeter,
Devon EX2 4TS
Tel: (01392) 273197
Fax: (01392) 251402
Email: mail@
    stmargarets-school.co.uk
Head: Miss R Edbrooke
Type: Girls Day 7–18
No of pupils: 289
Fees: (September 07)
Day £7110–£8580

ST WILFRID'S SCHOOL
29 St David's Hill, Exeter, Devon
EX4 4DA
Tel: (01392) 276171
Fax: (01392) 438666
Email: office@
    stwilfrids.devon.sch.uk
Head: Mrs A E M Macdonald-Dent
Type: Co-educational Day 5–16
No of pupils: B75 G70
Fees: (September 08)
Day £4500–£7849

EXMOUTH

THE DOLPHIN SCHOOL
Raddenstile Lane, Exmouth,
Devon EX8 2JH
Tel: (01395) 272418
Email: dolphinschool@aol.com
Head: Mr Bill Gott
Type: Co-educational Day 3–11
No of pupils: B11 G28
Fees: On application

ST PETER'S SCHOOL
Harefield, Lympstone, Exmouth,
Devon EX8 5AU
Tel: (01395) 272148
Fax: (01395) 222410
Email: hmoffice@
    stpetersprep.co.uk
Head: Mr R J Williams
Type: Co-educational Day and
Boarding 3–13
No of pupils: B177 G87
No of boarders: W17
Fees: (September 08) WB £14070
Day £5460–£9330

HONITON

MANOR HOUSE SCHOOL
Springfield House, Honiton,
Devon EX14 9TL
Tel: (01404) 42026
Fax: (01404) 41153
Email: office@
    manorhouseschoolhoniton.
    co.uk
Head: Mr A Gibson
Type: Co-educational Day 3–11
No of pupils: B85 G85
Fees: On application

NEWTON ABBOT

ABBOTSBURY SCHOOL
90 Torquay Road, Newton Abbot,
Devon TQ12 2JD
Tel: (01626) 352164
Email: abbotsbury.school@
    tesco.net
Head: Mr R J Manley
Type: Co-educational Day 2–7
No of pupils: B50 G50
Fees: On application

STOVER SCHOOL
Newton Abbot, Devon TQ12 6QG
Tel: (01626) 354505
Fax: (01626) 361475
Email: mail@stover.co.uk
Head: Mrs S Bradley
Type: Co-educational Day and
Boarding 3–18
No of pupils: B145 G328
No of boarders: F40 W38
Fees: (September 07)
FB £4875–£6195
WB £4337–£5250
Day £1900–£2995

PAIGNTON

TOWER HOUSE SCHOOL
Fisher Street, Paignton, Devon
TQ4 5EW
Tel: (01803) 557077
Fax: (01803) 557077
Email: twrhouse@aol.com
Head: Mr W M Miller
Type: Co-educational Day 2–16
No of pupils: B148 G135
Fees: (September 08)
Day £5640–£8900

PLYMOUTH

FLETEWOOD SCHOOL
88 North Road East, Plymouth,
Devon PL4 6AN
Tel: (01752) 663782
Fax: (01752) 663782
Email: headteacher@
    fletewoodschool.co.uk
Head: Mr J Martin
Type: Co-educational Day 3–11
No of pupils: B35 G35
Fees: On application

KING'S SCHOOL
Hartley Road, Mannamead,
Plymouth, Devon PL3 5LW
Tel: (01752) 771789
Fax: (01752) 770826
Email: school.secretary@
    kingsschool-plymouth.co.uk
Head: Mrs J Lee
Type: Co-educational Day 3–11
No of pupils: B75 G72
Fees: On application

PLYMOUTH COLLEGE
Ford Park, Plymouth, Devon
PL4 6RN
Tel: (01752) 203300
Fax: (01752) 203246
Email: mail@
    plymouthcollege.com
Head: Mr S J Wormleighton
Type: Co-educational Day and
Boarding 11–18
No of pupils: B354 G258
No of boarders: F89 W10
Fees: On application

PLYMOUTH COLLEGE
JUNIOR SCHOOL
St Dunstan's Abbey,
The Millfields, Plymouth, Devon
PL1 3JL
Tel: (01752) 201352
Fax: (01752) 201351
Email: juniorschool@
    plymouthcollege.com
Head: Mr R P Jeynes
Type: Co-educational Day 3–11
No of pupils: B142 G130
Fees: (September 07)
Day £4776–£7215

TAVISTOCK

KELLY COLLEGE
Parkwood Road, Tavistock, Devon
PL19 0HZ
Tel: (01822) 813100
Fax: (01822) 612050
Email: registrar@kellycollege.com
Head: Mr M S Steed
Type: Co-educational Boarding
and Day 11–18
No of pupils: B217 G142
No of boarders: F86 W56
Fees: On application

KELLY COLLEGE PREPARATORY SCHOOL
Hazeldon House, Parkwood Road,
Tavistock, Devon PL19 0JS
Tel: (01822) 612919
Fax: (01822) 612919
Email: admin@
  kellycollegeprep.com
Head: Mr R Stevenson
Type: Co-educational Day and
Boarding 2–11
No of pupils: B105 G95
No of boarders: W9
Fees: On application

MOUNT HOUSE SCHOOL
Tavistock, Devon PL19 9JL
Tel: (01822) 612244
Fax: (01822) 610042
Email: office@mounthouse.com
Head: Mr J R O Massey
Type: Co-educational Boarding
and Day 3–13
No of pupils: B144 G96
No of boarders: F80 W7
Fees: (September 08)
FB £15330–£17340
WB £14880–£14880
Day £8895–£13005

TEIGNMOUTH

TRINITY SCHOOL
Buckeridge Road, Teignmouth,
Devon TQ14 8LY
Tel: (01626) 774138
Fax: (01626) 771541
Email: enquiries@
  trinityschool.co.uk
Head: Mr Tim Waters and
Mr D Milnes
Type: Co-educational Day and
Boarding 3–19
No of pupils: B329 G206
No of boarders: F130 W10
Fees: (September 08)
FB £17310–£19800
WB £17010–£19500
Day £6945–£9435

TIVERTON

BLUNDELL'S PREPARATORY SCHOOL
Milestones House, Blundell's
Road, Tiverton, Devon EX16 4NA
Tel: (01884) 252393
Fax: (01884) 232333
Email: prep@blundells.org
Head: Mr N A Folland
Type: Co-educational Day 3–11
No of pupils: B138 G112
Fees: (September 08)
Day £1638–£8325

BLUNDELL'S SCHOOL*
Tiverton, Devon EX16 4DN
Tel: (01884) 252543
Fax: (01884) 243232
Email: registrars@blundells.org
Head: Mr I R Davenport
Type: Co-educational Boarding
and Day 11–18
No of pupils: B335 G235
No of boarders: F130 W260
Fees: (September 08)
FB £16365–£24255
WB £14790–£21345
Day £9750–£15645

TORQUAY

THE ABBEY SCHOOL
Hampton Court, St Marychurch,
Torquay, Devon TQ1 4PR
Tel: (01803) 327868
Fax: (01803) 327868
Email: mail@abbeyschool.co.uk
Head: Mrs J Joyce
Type: Co-educational Day 0–11
No of pupils: B84 G67
Fees: On application

STOODLEY KNOWLE SCHOOL
Ansteys Cove Road, Torquay,
Devon TQ1 2JB
Tel: (01803) 293160
Fax: (01803) 214757
Email: headoffice@
  stoodleyknowle.fsnet.co.uk
Head: Sister Perpetua
Type: Girls Day 2–18
No of pupils: 301
Fees: On application

TOTNES

PARK SCHOOL
Park Road, Dartington, Totnes,
Devon TQ9 6EQ
Tel: (01803) 864588
Fax: (01803) 864588
Email: park@schooldartington.
  freeserve.co.uk
Head: Mrs A Bellamy
Type: Co-educational Day 3–11
No of pupils: B39 G28
Fees: (September 08)
Day £473–£5496

ST CHRISTOPHERS SCHOOL
Mount Barton, Staverton, Totnes,
Devon TQ9 6PF
Tel: (01803) 762202
Fax: (01803) 762202
Email: office@
  st-christophers.devon.sch.uk
Head: Mrs J E Kenyon
Type: Co-educational Day 3–11
No of pupils: B60 G40
Fees: (September 07)
Day £3390–£5250

England – Devon

DORSET

BLANDFORD FORUM

BRYANSTON SCHOOL*
Blandford Forum, Dorset
DT11 0PX
Tel: (01258) 452411
Fax: (01258) 484661
Email: admissions@
  bryanston.co.uk
Head: Ms S J Thomas
Type: Co-educational Boarding
and Day 13–18
No of pupils: B380 G282
No of boarders: F580
Fees: (September 08) FB £26985
Day £21588

CLAYESMORE
PREPARATORY SCHOOL†
Iwerne Minster, Blandford Forum,
Dorset DT11 8PH
Tel: (01747) 811707
Fax: (01747) 811692
Email: prepsec@clayesmore.com
Head: Mr R Geffen
Type: Co-educational Boarding
and Day 2–13
No of pupils: B140 G89
No of boarders: F50
Fees: (September 08)
F/WB £5615–£6154
Day £2247–£4570

CLAYESMORE*†
Iwerne Minster, Blandford Forum,
Dorset DT11 8LL
Tel: (01747) 812122
Fax: (01747) 813187
Email: admissions@
  clayesmore.com
Head: Mr M G Cooke
Type: Co-educational Boarding
and Day 2–18
No of pupils: B268 G142
No of boarders: F283
Fees: (September 08)
FB £16845–£25392
Day £12843–£18579

HANFORD SCHOOL
Childe Okeford, Blandford Forum,
Dorset DT11 8HL
Tel: (01258) 860219
Fax: (01258) 861255
Email: hanfordsch@aol.com
Head: Mr N S Mackay
Type: Girls Boarding and Day
7–13
No of pupils: 100
No of boarders: F80
Fees: On application

KNIGHTON HOUSE
Durweston, Blandford Forum,
Dorset DT11 0PY
Tel: (01258) 452065
Fax: (01258) 450744
Email: enquiries@
  knighton-house.co.uk
Head: Mrs C L Renton Bourne
Type: Girls Day and Boarding
2–13 (Day boys 4–7)
No of pupils: B3 G129
No of boarders: F25 W31
Fees: (September 08) F/WB £18735
Day £7125–£14070

MILTON ABBEY SCHOOL*†
Blandford Forum, Dorset
DT11 0BZ
Tel: (01258) 880484
Fax: (01258) 881194
Email: info@miltonabbey.co.uk
Head: Mr W J Hughes-D'Aeth
Type: Co-educational Boarding
and Day Boys 13–18 Girls 16–18
No of boarders: F210
Fees: (September 08) FB £9060
Day £6800

BOURNEMOUTH

THE PARK SCHOOL
Queen's Park South Drive,
Bournemouth, Dorset BH8 9BJ
Tel: (01202) 396640
Fax: (01202) 392705
Email: headmaster.parkschool@
  virgin.net
Head: Mr C Cole
Type: Co-educational Day 4–11
No of pupils: B156 G116
Fees: On application

ST MARTIN'S SCHOOL
15 Stokewood Road,
Bournemouth, Dorset BH3 7NA
Tel: (01202) 760744
Head: Mr T B T Shenton
Type: Co-educational Day 4–12
No of pupils: B50 G50
Fees: (September 08)
Day £3150–£5250

ST THOMAS GARNET'S
SCHOOL
Parkwood Road, Boscombe,
Bournemouth, Dorset BH5 2BH
Tel: (01202) 420172 /
Pre-school: 01202 431286
Fax: (01202) 773060
Email: enquiries@
  thomasgamets.com
Head: Mr P R Gillings
Type: Co-educational Day 0–11
No of pupils: B75 G80
Fees: (September 07)
Day £4650–£6150

TALBOT HEATH
Rothesay Road, Bournemouth,
Dorset BH4 9NJ
Tel: (01202) 761881
Fax: (01202) 768155
Email: admissions@
  talbotheath.org
Head: Mrs C Dipple
Type: Girls Day and Boarding
3–18 (Boys 3–7)
No of pupils: B6 G628
No of boarders: F26 W6
Fees: On application

TALBOT HOUSE
PREPARATORY SCHOOL
8 Firs Glen Road, Bournemouth,
Dorset BH9 2LR
Tel: (01202) 510348
Fax: (01202) 775904
Email: admin.talbot@
  ntlworld.com
Head: Mrs C Oosthuizen and
Mr M Broadway
Type: Co-educational Day 3–12
No of pupils: B66 G49
Fees: On application

WENTWORTH COLLEGE*
College Road, Bournemouth,
Dorset BH5 2DY
Tel: (01202) 423266
Fax: (01202) 418030
Email: enquiries@
   wentworthcollege.com
Head: Mr H MacDonald
Type: Co-educational Boarding
and Day 11–18
No of pupils: B20 G130
No of boarders: F30 W10
Fees: (September 08) F/WB £5975
Day £3645

DORCHESTER

**SUNNINGHILL
PREPARATORY SCHOOL**
South Court, South Walks,
Dorchester, Dorset DT1 1EB
Tel: (01305) 262306
Fax: (01305) 261254
Email: sunninghillschool@
   lineone.net
Head: Mr A Roberts-Wray
Type: Co-educational Day 3–13
No of pupils: B97 G94
Fees: On application

POOLE

BUCKHOLME TOWERS
18 Commercial Road, Parkstone,
Poole, Dorset BH14 0JW
Tel: (01202) 742871
Fax: (01202) 740754
Email: office@
   buckholme.dorset.sch.uk
Head: Mrs S Mercer
Type: Co-educational Day 3–12
No of pupils: B70 G70
Fees: (September 08)
Day £4638–£5457

UPLANDS SCHOOL
40 St Osmund's Road, Parkstone,
Poole, Dorset BH14 9JY
Tel: (01202) 742626
Fax: (01202) 731037
Email: headteacher@
   uplands.poole.sch.uk
Head: Mrs S Mercer
Type: Co-educational Day 2–16
No of pupils: B182 G102
Fees: On application

YARRELLS SCHOOL
Yarrells House, Upton, Poole,
Dorset BH16 5EU
Tel: (01202) 622229
Fax: (01202) 620870
Email: enquiries@yarrells.co.uk
Head: Mrs N A Covell
Type: Co-educational Day 2–13
No of pupils: B87 G111
Fees: On application

SHAFTESBURY

PORT REGIS SCHOOL
Motcombe Park, Shaftesbury,
Dorset SP7 9QA
Tel: (01747) 857800
Fax: (01747) 857810
Email: office@portregis.com
Head: Mr P A E Dix
Type: Co-educational Boarding
and Day 3–13
No of pupils: B210 G186
No of boarders: F130 W100
Fees: (September 08) F/WB £6995
Day £2265–£5494

ST MARY'S SCHOOL
Shaftesbury, Dorset SP7 9LP
Tel: (01747) 854005
Fax: (01747) 851557
Email: head@
   st-marys-shaftesbury.co.uk
Head: Mr R James
Type: Girls Boarding and Day
9–18
No of pupils: 309
No of boarders: F181
Fees: (September 08)
FB £20730–£21780
Day £14250–£14970

SHERBORNE

**INTERNATIONAL COLLEGE,
SHERBORNE SCHOOL***
Newell Grange, Sherborne, Dorset
DT9 4EZ
Tel: (01935) 814743
Fax: (01935) 816863
Email: reception@sherborne-ic.net
Head: Dr C J Greenfield
Type: Co-educational Boarding
11–17
No of pupils: B95 G50
No of boarders: F145
Fees: (September 08)
FB £29100–£31500

LEWESTON SCHOOL
Sherborne, Dorset DT9 6EN
Tel: (01963) 211010
Fax: (01963) 211080
Email: admissions@
   leweston.dorset.sch.uk
Head: Mr A Aylward
Type: Girls Boarding and Day
2–18 (Boys 2–11)
No of pupils: B6 G315
No of boarders: F66 W18
Fees: (September 07)
FB £14085–£20985
WB £12285–£17985
Day £9585–£13695

**SHERBORNE PREPARATORY
SCHOOL**
Acreman Street, Sherborne, Dorset
DT9 3NY
Tel: (01935) 812097
Fax: (01935) 813948
Email: sh@sherborneprep.org
Head: Mr P S Tait
Type: Co-educational Day and
Boarding 3–13
No of pupils: B166 G82
No of boarders: F34 W25
Fees: (September 08)
F/WB £5810–£6075
Day £2295–£4250

SHERBORNE SCHOOL
Abbey Road, Sherborne, Dorset
DT9 3AP
Tel: (01935) 812249
Fax: (01935) 810426
Email: enquiries@sherborne.org
Head: Mr S F Eliot
Type: Boys Boarding and Day
13–18
No of pupils: 574
No of boarders: F530
Fees: (September 08) FB £26580
Day £21525

SHERBORNE GIRLS
Bradford Road, Sherborne, Dorset
DT9 3QN
Tel: (01935) 812245
Fax: (01935) 389445
Email: enquiry@sherborne.com
Head: Mrs J Dwyer
Type: Girls Boarding and Day
11–18
No of pupils: 380
No of boarders: F350
Fees: On application

England – Dorset

WEYMOUTH

THORNLOW PREPARATORY SCHOOL
Connaught Road, Weymouth, Dorset DT4 0SA
Tel: (01305) 785703
Fax: (01305) 780976
Email: admin@thornlow.co.uk
Head: Mr R A Fowke
Type: Co-educational Day 3–13
No of pupils: B43 G35
Fees: (September 08)
Day £1953–£6510

WIMBORNE

CANFORD SCHOOL
Wimborne, Dorset BH21 3AD
Tel: (01202) 847207
Fax: (01202) 881723
Email: admissions@canford.com
Head: Mr J D Lever
Type: Co-educational Boarding and Day 13–18
No of pupils: B359 G264
No of boarders: F418
Fees: (September 08) FB £8190
Day £6306

CASTLE COURT PREPARATORY SCHOOL
The Knoll House, Knoll Lane, Corfe Mullen, Wimborne, Dorset BH21 3RF
Tel: (01202) 694438
Fax: (01202) 659063
Email: office@castlecourt.com
Head: Mr R E T Nicholl
Type: Co-educational Day 3–13
No of pupils: B214 G129
Fees: (September 07)
Day £5610–£12450

DUMPTON SCHOOL
Deans Grove House, Wimborne, Dorset BH21 7AF
Tel: (01202) 883818
Fax: (01202) 848760
Email: secretary@dumpton.com
Head: Mr A W Browning
Type: Co-educational Day 2–13
No of pupils: B192 G115
Fees: On application

COUNTY DURHAM

BARNARD CASTLE

BARNARD CASTLE SCHOOL
Barnard Castle, County Durham DL12 8UN
Tel: (01833) 690222
Fax: (01833) 638985
Email: secretary@
  barneyschool.org.uk
Head: Mr D H Ewart
Type: Co-educational Boarding and Day 4–18
No of pupils: B484 G273
No of boarders: F192
Fees: (September 08)
F/WB £12993–£17274
Day £4476–£9996

DARLINGTON

HURWORTH HOUSE SCHOOL
The Green, Hurworth-on-Tees, Darlington, County Durham DL2 2AD
Tel: (01325) 720645
Fax: (01325) 720122
Email: info@hurworthhouse.co.uk
Head: Mr C R T Fenwick
Type: Boys Day 3–18
No of pupils: B193 G22
Fees: On application

POLAM HALL
Grange Road, Darlington, County Durham DL1 5PA
Tel: (01325) 463383
Fax: (01325) 383539
Email: information@
  polamhall.com
Head: Miss M Green
Type: Girls Boarding and Day 4–18
No of pupils: B8 G400
No of boarders: F41 W12
Fees: (September 08)
FB £15975–£19710
WB £15375–£19110
Day £5775–£10560

YARM AT RAVENTHORPE SCHOOL
96 Carmel Road North, Darlington, County Durham DL3 8JB
Tel: (01325) 463373
Fax: (01325) 353086
Email: yar@yarmschool.org
Head: Mrs W Young
Type: Co-educational Day 3–11
No of pupils: B39 G35
Fees: (September 08)
Day £3243–£5802

DURHAM

THE CHORISTER SCHOOL
The College, Durham, County Durham DH1 3EL
Tel: (0191) 384 2935
Fax: (0191) 383 1275
Email: head@
  choristers.durham.sch.uk
Head: Mr I Hawksby
Type: Co-educational Day and Boarding 4–13
No of pupils: B121 G56
No of boarders: F27 W3
Fees: On application

DURHAM HIGH SCHOOL FOR GIRLS

Farewell Hall, Durham, County Durham DH1 3TB
Tel: (0191) 384 3226
Fax: (0191) 386 7381
Email: headmistress@dhsfg.org.uk
Head: Mrs A J Templeman
Type: Girls Day 3–18
No of pupils: 600
Fees: (September 08)
Day £5640–£8940

DURHAM SCHOOL

Quarryheads Lane, Durham, County Durham DH1 4SZ
Tel: (0191) 386 4783
Fax: (0191) 383 1025
Email: enquiries@ durhamschool.co.uk
Head: Mr N G Kern
Type: Co-educational Day and Boarding 3–18
No of pupils: B307 G124
No of boarders: F35 W41
Fees: On application

ESSEX

BILLERICAY

ST JOHN'S SCHOOL

Stock Road, Billericay, Essex CM12 0AR
Tel: (01277) 623070
Fax: (01277) 651288
Email: registrar@stjohnsschool.net
Head: Mrs F Armour
Type: Co-educational Day 3–16
No of pupils: B244 G191
Fees: (September 08)
Day £4863–£9195

BRENTWOOD

BRENTWOOD SCHOOL

Ingrave Road, Brentwood, Essex CM15 8AS
Tel: (01277) 243243
Fax: (01277) 243299
Email: headmaster@ brentwood.essex.sch.uk
Head: Mr D J Davies
Type: Co-educational Day and Boarding 3–18 (Single-sex ed 11–16)
No of pupils: B889 G601
No of boarders: F52 W18
Fees: (September 07) F/WB £21426
Day £12144

HERINGTON HOUSE SCHOOL

Mount Avenue, Hutton, Brentwood, Essex CM13 2NS
Tel: (01277) 211595
Fax: (01277) 200404
Email: principal@ herringtonhouseschool.co.uk
Head: Mr R Dudley-Cooke
Type: Co-educational Day 3–11
No of pupils: B43 G92
Fees: On application

URSULINE PREPARATORY SCHOOL

Old Great Ropers, Great Ropers Lane, Warley, Brentwood, Essex CM13 3HR
Tel: (01277) 227152
Fax: (01277) 202559
Email: rozdownes@ ursulineprepwarley.co.uk
Head: Mrs PM Wilson
Type: Co-educational Day 3–11
No of pupils: B74 G81
Fees: On application

WOODLANDS SCHOOLS

Warley Street, Great Warley, Brentwood, Essex CM13 3LA
Tel: (01277) 233 288
Fax: (01277) 232 715
Email: ukinfo@ woodlandsschools.co.uk
Head: Mr R O'Doherty
Type: Co-educational Day 3–11
No of pupils: B147 G134
Fees: On application

BUCKHURST HILL

BRAESIDE SCHOOL FOR GIRLS

130 High Road, Buckhurst Hill, Essex IG9 5SD
Tel: (020) 8504 1133
Fax: (020) 8505 6675
Email: enquiries@ braesideschool.co.uk
Head: Mrs G Haddon
Type: Girls Day 3–16
No of pupils: 210
Fees: (September 08)
Day £5265–£8550

THE DAIGLEN SCHOOL

68 Palmerston Road, Buckhurst Hill, Essex IG9 5LG
Tel: (020) 8504 7108
Fax: (020) 8502 9608
Email: admin@ daiglenschool.co.uk
Head: Mrs M Bradfield
Type: Co-educational Day Boys 3–11
Fees: On application

LOYOLA PREPARATORY SCHOOL

103 Palmerston Road, Buckhurst Hill, Essex IG9 5NH
Tel: (020) 8504 7372
Fax: (020) 8504 7372
Email: enquiries@ loyola.essex.sch.uk
Head: Mr P G Nicholson
Type: Boys Day 3–11
No of pupils: 184
Fees: (September 08)
Day £4356–£7260

England – County Durham/Essex

CHELMSFORD

ELM GREEN PREPARATORY SCHOOL

Parsonage Lane, Little Baddow, Chelmsford, Essex CM3 4SU
Tel: (01245) 225230
Fax: (01245) 226008
Email: admin@
    elmgreen.essex.sch.uk
Head: Ms A Milner
Type: Co-educational Day 4–11
No of pupils: B110 G110
Fees: On application

HEATHCOTE SCHOOL

Eves Corner, Danbury, Chelmsford, Essex CM3 4QB
Tel: (01245) 223131
Fax: (01245) 224568
Email: enquiries@heathcote.co.uk
Head: Mrs J Carn
Type: Co-educational Day 2–11
No of pupils: B96 G88
Fees: (September 08) Day £6390

NEW HALL SCHOOL

Boreham, Chelmsford, Essex CM3 3HS
Tel: (01245) 467588
Fax: (01245) 464348
Email: admin@
    newhallschool.co.uk
Head: Mrs K Jeffrey
Type: Co-educational Boarding and Day 4–18 (Boys day 4–11)
No of pupils: B96 G624
No of boarders: F120
Fees: On application

ST ANNE'S PREPARATORY SCHOOL

154 New London Road, Chelmsford, Essex CM2 0AW
Tel: (01245) 353488
Fax: (01245) 353488
Email: headmistress@
    stannesprep.essex.sch.uk
Head: Mrs F Pirrie
Type: Co-educational Day 3–11
No of pupils: B70 G90
Fees: On application

ST CEDD'S SCHOOL

Maltese Road, Chelmsford, Essex CM1 2PB
Tel: (01245) 354380
Fax: (01245) 348635
Email: tthorogood@stcedds.org.uk
Head: Mrs B A Windley
Type: Co-educational Day 4–11
No of pupils: B155 G177
Fees: (September 07)
Day £6300–£6750

WIDFORD LODGE

Widford Road, Chelmsford, Essex CM2 9AN
Tel: (01245) 352581
Fax: (01245) 281329
Email: admin@
    widfordlodge.org.uk
Head: Mr S C Trowell
Type: Co-educational Day 2–11
No of pupils: B77 G45
Fees: On application

CHIGWELL

CHIGWELL SCHOOL*

High Road, Chigwell, Essex IG7 6QF
Tel: (020) 8501 5700
Fax: (020) 8500 6232
Email: hm@chigwell-school.org
Head: Mr M.E. Punt
Type: Co-educational Day and Boarding 7–18
No of pupils: B405 G330
No of boarders: F45
Fees: (September 08)
FB £19611–£19611
WB £17493–£18567
Day £8391–£12903

COLCHESTER

COLCHESTER HIGH SCHOOL

Wellesley Road, Colchester, Essex CO3 3HD
Tel: (01206) 573389
Fax: (01206) 573114
Email: info@
    colchesterhighschool.co.uk
Head: Mr D E Wood
Type: Co-educational Day 3–16
No of pupils: B338 G79
Fees: (September 07)
Day £5190–£8030

HOLMWOOD HOUSE[†]

Chitts Hill, Lexden, Colchester, Essex CO3 9ST
Tel: (01206) 574305
Fax: (01206) 768269
Email: hst@
    holmwood.essex.sch.uk
Head: Mr H S Thackrah
Type: Co-educational Day and Boarding 4–13
No of pupils: B228 G128
No of boarders: W25
Fees: (September 08) WB £16644
Day £7224–£12870

LITTLEGARTH SCHOOL

Horkesley Park, Nayland, Colchester, Essex CO6 4JR
Tel: (01206) 262332
Fax: (01206) 263101
Email: office@
    littlegarth.essex.sch.uk
Head: Mr P H Jones
Type: Co-educational Day 2–11
No of pupils: B170 G150
Fees: (September 08)
Day £1710–£7590

OXFORD HOUSE SCHOOL

2 Lexden Road, Colchester, Essex CO3 3NE
Tel: (01206) 576686
Fax: (01206) 577670
Email: ohs@supanet.com
Head: Mr D Wood
Type: Co-educational Day 2–11
No of pupils: B65 G65
Fees: (September 08)
Day £3420–£6810

ST MARY'S SCHOOL

91 Lexden Road, Colchester, Essex CO3 3RB
Tel: (01206) 572544
Fax: (01206) 576437
Email: stmaryschoolcol@
    tinyonline.co.uk
Head: Mrs H K Vipond
Type: Girls Day 4–16
No of pupils: 450
Fees: On application

EPPING

COOPERSALE HALL SCHOOL
Flux's Lane, off Steward's Green Road, Epping, Essex CM16 7PE
Tel: (01992) 577133
Fax: (01992) 571544
Email: info@
coopersalehallschool.co.uk
Head: Mr R Probyn
Type: Co-educational Day 3–11
No of pupils: B150 G110
Fees: On application

FELSTED

FELSTED PREPARATORY SCHOOL
Braintree Road, Felsted, Essex CM6 3JL
Tel: (01371) 822610
Fax: (01371) 822617
Email: info@felstedprep.org
Head: Mrs J M Burrett
Type: Co-educational Boarding and Day 4–13
No of pupils: B248 G153
No of boarders: W18
Fees: On application

FELSTED SCHOOL
Felsted, Essex CM6 3LL
Tel: (01371) 822605
Fax: (01371) 822607
Email: ado@felsted.org
Head: Dr M Walker
Type: Co-educational Boarding and Day 13–18
No of pupils: B281 G188
No of boarders: F254 W159
Fees: (September 07) FB £22431 WB £20412 Day £16788

FRINTON-ON-SEA

ST PHILOMENA'S PREPARATORY SCHOOL
Hadleigh Road, Frinton-on-Sea, Essex CO13 9HQ
Tel: (01255) 674492
Fax: (01255) 674459
Email: admin@stphilomenas.com
Head: Mrs B Buck
Type: Co-educational Day 3–11
No of pupils: B67 G71
Fees: (September 08) Day £4320–£5100

HALSTEAD

GOSFIELD SCHOOL
Halstead Road, Gosfield, Halstead, Essex CO9 1PF
Tel: (01787) 474040
Fax: (01787) 478228
Email: principal@
gosfieldschool.org.uk
Head: Mrs C Goodchild
Type: Co-educational Day and Boarding 2–18
No of pupils: B124 G71
No of boarders: F13 W13
Fees: On application

ST MARGARET'S SCHOOL
Gosfield Hall Park, Gosfield, Halstead, Essex CO9 1SE
Tel: (01787) 472134
Fax: (01787) 478207
Email: admin@
stmargaretsprep.com
Head: Mrs B Y Boyton-Corbett
Type: Co-educational Day 2–11
No of pupils: B140 G130
Fees: On application

HARLOW

ST NICHOLAS SCHOOL
Hillingdon House, Hobbs Cross Road, Harlow, Essex CM17 0NJ
Tel: (01279) 429910
Fax: (01279) 450224
Email: office@
saintnicholasschool.net
Head: Mr R Cusworth
Type: Co-educational Day 4–16
No of pupils: B180 G180
Fees: On application

HORNCHURCH

GOODRINGTON SCHOOL
17 Walden Road, Emerson Park, Hornchurch, Essex RM11 2JT
Tel: (01708) 448349
Email: info@goodrington.org
Head: Mrs R Ellenby
Type: Co-educational Day 3–11
No of pupils: B37 G42
Fees: (September 08) Day £3900

RAPHAEL INDEPENDENT SCHOOL
Park Lane, Hornchurch, Essex RM11 1XY
Tel: (01708) 744735
Fax: (01708) 722432
Email: admin@raphaelschool.com
Head: Mrs J C Lawrence
Type: Co-educational Day 4–16
No of pupils: B81 G62
Fees: (September 08)
Day £4350–£7500

ILFORD

BEEHIVE PREPARATORY SCHOOL
233 Beehive Lane, Redbridge, Ilford, Essex IG4 5ED
Tel: (020) 8550 3224
Head: Mr C J Beasant
Type: Co-educational Day 4–11
No of pupils: B50 G45
Fees: On application

CRANBROOK COLLEGE
34 Mansfield Road, Ilford, Essex IG1 3BD
Tel: (020) 8554 1757
Fax: (020) 8518 0317
Email: info@
cranbrookcollege.org.uk
Head: Mr A Moss
Type: Boys Day 4–16
No of pupils: 210
Fees: (September 08)
Day £6405–£8235

EASTCOURT INDEPENDENT SCHOOL
1 Eastwood Road, Goodmayes, Ilford, Essex IG3 8UW
Tel: (020) 8590 5472
Fax: (020) 8597 8313
Email: eastcourtschool@
talk21.com
Head: Mrs C Redgrave
Type: Co-educational Day 4–11
No of pupils: B163 G177
Fees: On application

GLENARM COLLEGE
20 Coventry Road, Ilford, Essex IG1 4QR
Tel: (020) 8554 1760
Email: head@glenarmcollege.com
Head: Mr C Perkins
Type: Co-educational Day 3–11
No of pupils: B53 G80
Fees: On application

England – Essex

ILFORD PREPARATORY SCHOOL

Carnegie Buildings, 785 High Road, Ilford, Essex IG3 8RW
Tel: (020) 8599 8822
Fax: (020) 8597 2797
Email: head@ilfprep.demon.co.uk
Head: Mrs B P M Wiggs
Type: Co-educational Day 3–11
No of pupils: B100 G92
Fees: (September 08)
Day £4950–£7050

ILFORD URSULINE PREPARATORY SCHOOL

2 Coventry Road, Ilford, Essex IG1 4QR
Tel: (020) 8518 4050
Fax: (020) 8518 2060
Email: iups@ilfordursuline-prep.redbridge.sch.uk
Head: Mrs C Spinner
Type: Girls Day 3–11
No of pupils: 154
Fees: On application

PARK SCHOOL FOR GIRLS

20–22 Park Avenue, Ilford, Essex IG1 4RS
Tel: (020) 8554 2466
Fax: (020) 8554 3003
Email: admin@parkschool.org.uk
Head: Mrs N O'Brien
Type: Girls Day 7–18
No of pupils: 186
Fees: (September 08)
Day £6060–£8010

LEIGH-ON-SEA

COLLEGE SAINT-PIERRE

16 Leigh Road, Leigh-on-Sea, Essex SS9 1LE
Tel: (01702) 474164
Fax: (01702) 474164
Email: college@saintpierre.fsnet.co.uk
Head: Mr K Davies
Type: Co-educational Day 2–11
No of pupils: B60 G40
Fees: On application

ST MICHAEL'S SCHOOL

198 Hadleigh Road, Leigh-on-Sea, Essex SS9 2LP
Tel: (01702) 478719
Fax: (01702) 710183
Email: info@stmichaelsschool.com
Head: Mrs L Morshead
Type: Co-educational Day 3–11
No of pupils: B143 G122
Fees: (September 08)
Day £3330–£6630

LOUGHTON

OAKLANDS SCHOOL

8 Albion Hill, Loughton, Essex IG10 4RA
Tel: (020) 8508 3517
Fax: (020) 8508 4454
Email: info@oaklandsschool.co.uk
Head: Mrs P Simmonds
Type: Co-educational Day
Boys 2–7 Girls 2–11
No of pupils: B62 G185
Fees: (September 07)
Day £3795–£7650

MALDON

MALDON COURT PREPARATORY SCHOOL

Silver Street, Maldon, Essex CM9 4QE
Tel: (01621) 853529
Fax: (01621) 874606
Email: enquiries@maldoncourtschool.org
Head: Mrs L F Coyle
Type: Co-educational Day 3–11
No of pupils: B66 G57
Fees: On application

ROCHFORD

CROWSTONE PREPARATORY SCHOOL (SUTTON ANNEXE)

Fleethall Lane, Shopland Road, Rochford, Essex SS4 1LL
Tel: (01702) 540629
Email: info@crowstoneprepschool.com
Head: Mr J P Thayer
Type: Co-educational Day 2–11
No of pupils: 110
Fees: On application

ROMFORD

GIDEA PARK COLLEGE

Balgores House, 2 Balgores Lane, Romford, Essex RM2 5JR
Tel: (01708) 740381
Fax: (01708) 740381
Email: office@gideaparkcollege.co.uk
Head: Mrs V S Lee
Type: Co-educational Day 2–11
No of pupils: B86 G100
Fees: On application

IMMANUEL SCHOOL

Havering Grange Centre, Havering Road, Romford, Essex RM1 4HR
Tel: (01708) 764449
Head: Miss F Norcross
Type: Co-educational Day 3–16
No of pupils: B71 G54
Fees: On application

ST MARY'S HARE PARK SCHOOL

South Drive, Gidea Park, Romford, Essex RM2 6HH
Tel: (01708) 761220
Fax: (01708) 380255
Email: harepark@btconnect.com
Head: Mrs K Karwacinski
Type: Co-educational Day 2–11
No of pupils: B70 G84
Fees: On application

SAFFRON WALDEN

DAME BRADBURY'S SCHOOL

Ashdon Road, Saffron Walden, Essex CB10 2AL
Tel: (01799) 522348
Fax: (01799) 516762
Email: info@damebradburys.com
Head: Mrs Jane Crouch
Type: Co-educational Day 3–11
No of pupils: B144 G155
Fees: (September 07)
Day £5295–£7800

FRIENDS' SCHOOL

Mount Pleasant Road, Saffron Walden, Essex CB11 3EB
Tel: (01799) 525351
Fax: (01799) 523808
Email: admin@friends.org.uk
Head: Mr G Wigley
Type: Boarding and Day
No of pupils: B210 G160
No of boarders: F34 W30
Fees: On application

SOUTHEND-ON-SEA

ALLEYN COURT PREPARATORY SCHOOL

Wakering Road, Great Wakering, Southend-on-Sea, Essex SS3 0PW
Tel: (01702) 582553
Fax: (01702) 584574
Email: acitsuite@tiscali.co.uk
Head: Mr R Chandler
Type: Co-educational Day 2–11
No of pupils: B175 G126
Fees: On application

THORPE HALL SCHOOL
Wakering Road, Southend-on-Sea,
Essex SS1 3RD
Tel: (01702) 582340
Fax: (01702) 587070
Email: sec@
   thorpehall.southend.sch.uk
Head: Mr A Hampton
Type: Co-educational Day 2–16
No of pupils: B226 G139
Fees: (September 08)
Day £3231–£7455

UPMINSTER

OAKFIELDS MONTESSORI SCHOOLS LTD
Harwood Hall, Harwood Hall
Lane, Corbets Tey, Upminster,
Essex RM14 2YG
Tel: (01708) 220117
Fax: (01708) 227911
Email: office@
   oakfieldsmontessorischool.
   org.uk
Head: Mrs E Hill
Type: Co-educational Day 2–11
No of pupils: B82 G90
Fees: On application

WESTCLIFF-ON-SEA

CROWSTONE PREPARATORY SCHOOL
121–123 Crowstone Road,
Westcliff-on-Sea, Essex SS0 8LH
Tel: (01702) 346758
Fax: (01702) 390632
Email: info@
   crowstone.southend.sch.uk
Head: Mr J P Thayer
Type: Co-educational Day 2–11
No of pupils: B120 G110
Fees: On application

ST HILDA'S SCHOOL
15 Imperial Avenue,
Westcliff-on-Sea, Essex SS0 8NE
Tel: (01702) 344542
Fax: (01702)344547
Email: sthilda15@aol.com
Head: Mrs S O'Riordan
Type: Girls Day 2–16 (Boys 2–7)
No of pupils: 180
Fees: On application

WOODFORD GREEN

AVON HOUSE[†]
490 High Road, Woodford Green,
Essex IG8 0PN
Tel: (020) 8504 1749
Email: info@avonhouse.org
Head: Mrs S Ferrari
Type: Co-educational Day 3–11
No of pupils: B100 G95
Fees: (September 07)
Day £5760–£6930

BANCROFT'S SCHOOL
Woodford Green, Essex IG8 0RF
Tel: (020) 8505 4821
Fax: (020) 8559 0032
Email: office@bancrofts.org
Head: Mrs M E Ireland
Type: Co-educational Day 7–18
No of pupils: B538 G465
Fees: (September 08)
Day £8760–£11550

ST AUBYN'S SCHOOL
Bunces Lane, Woodford Green,
Essex IG8 9DU
Tel: (020) 8504 1577
Fax: (020) 8504 2053
Email: registrar@staubyns.com
Head: Mr G James
Type: Co-educational Day 3–13
No of pupils: B290 G210
Fees: (September 07)
Day £3165–£8355

WOODFORD GREEN PREPARATORY SCHOOL
Glengall Road, Woodford Green,
Essex IG8 0BZ
Tel: (020) 8504 5045
Fax: (020) 8505 0639
Email: admin@wgps.co.uk
Head: Mr A J Blackhurst
Type: Co-educational Day 3–11
No of pupils: B202 G181
Fees: (September 08) Day £6210

GLOUCESTERSHIRE

CHELTENHAM

AIRTHRIE SCHOOL*
27–29 Christchurch Road,
Cheltenham, Gloucestershire
GL50 2NY
Tel: (01242) 512837
Fax: (01242) 579583
Email: mail@airthrie-school.co.uk
Head: Mrs A E Sullivan
Type: Co-educational Day 3–11
No of pupils: B80 G86
Fees: (September 08)
Day £4935–£6894

BERKHAMPSTEAD SCHOOL
Pittville Circus Road, Cheltenham,
Gloucestershire GL52 2QA
Tel: (01242) 523263
Fax: (01242) 514114
Email: headberky@aol.com
Head: Mr T Owen
Type: Co-educational Day 3–11
No of pupils: B129 G128
Fees: On application

CHELTENHAM COLLEGE
Bath Road, Cheltenham,
Gloucestershire GL53 7LD
Tel: (01242) 265600
Fax: (01242) 265630
Email: admissions@
   cheltcoll.gloucs.sch.uk
Head: Mr J S Richardson
Type: Co-educational Boarding
and Day 13–18
No of pupils: B391 G212
No of boarders: F472
Fees: (September 07) FB £25845
Day £19365

England – Essex/Gloucestershire

**CHELTENHAM COLLEGE
JUNIOR SCHOOL**
Thirlestaine Road, Cheltenham,
Gloucestershire GL53 7AB
Tel: (01242) 522697
Fax: (01242) 265620
Email: ccjs@
  cheltcoll.gloucs.sch.uk
Head: Mr N I Archdale
Type: Co-educational Boarding
and Day 3–13
No of pupils: B222 G161
No of boarders: F50 W10
Fees: (September 07)
FB £13800–£17940
Day £8835–£13815

**THE CHELTENHAM LADIES'
COLLEGE**
Bayshill Road, Cheltenham,
Gloucestershire GL50 3EP
Tel: (01242) 520691
Fax: (01242) 227882
Email: enquiries@
  cheltladiescollege.org
Head: Mrs V Tuck
Type: Girls Boarding and Day
11–18
No of pupils: 870
No of boarders: F647
Fees: (September 08) FB £25509
Day £17130

**DEAN CLOSE PREPARATORY
SCHOOL***
Lansdown Road, Cheltenham,
Gloucestershire GL51 6QS
Tel: (01242) 512217
Fax: (01242) 258005
Email: dcpsoffice@
  deanclose.org.uk
Head: Rev L Browne
Type: Co-educational Boarding
and Day 2–13
No of pupils: B220 G208
No of boarders: F60
Fees: (September 08)
FB £14610–£18495
Day £8760–£12930

DEAN CLOSE SCHOOL*
Shelburne Road, Cheltenham,
Gloucestershire GL51 6HE
Tel: (01242) 258044
Fax: (01242) 258003
Email: registrar@deanclose.org.uk
Head: J Lancashire
Type: Co-educational Boarding
and Day 13–18
No of pupils: B285 G207
No of boarders: F289
Fees: (September 08) FB £26160
Day £18480

**THE RICHARD PATE
SCHOOL**
Southern Road, Leckhampton,
Cheltenham, Gloucestershire
GL53 9RP
Tel: (01242) 522086
Fax: (01242) 584035
Email: hm@richardpate.co.uk
Head: Mr R A MacDonald
Type: Co-educational Day 3–11
No of pupils: B143 G150
Fees: (September 08)
Day £3315–£7785

**ST EDWARD'S SCHOOL
CHELTENHAM**
Cirencester Road, Cheltenham,
Gloucestershire GL53 8EY
Tel: (01242) 538600
Fax: (01242) 538160
Email: headmaster@
  stedwards.co.uk
Head: Dr A J Nash
Type: Co-educational Day 11–18
No of pupils: B258 G211
Fees: (September 08)
Day £5085–£7875

CINDERFORD

ST ANTHONYS SCHOOL
93 Bellevue Road, Cinderford,
Gloucestershire GL14 2AA
Tel: (01594) 823558
Fax: (01594) 824799
Email: sister@gl142aafsnet.co.uk
Head: Sister M C McKenna
Type: Co-educational Day 3–11
No of pupils: B61 G61
Fees: (September 08) Day £4140

CIRENCESTER

**HATHEROP CASTLE
SCHOOL**
Hatherop, Cirencester,
Gloucestershire GL7 3NB
Tel: (01285) 750206
Fax: (01285) 750430
Email: admissions@
  hatheropcastle.co.uk
Head: Mr P Easterbrook
Type: Co-educational Boarding
and Day 2–13
No of pupils: B98 G94
No of boarders: F22 W5
Fees: (September 08)
FB £13980–£14760
Day £5760–£9570

RENDCOMB COLLEGE
Rendcomb, Cirencester,
Gloucestershire GL7 7HA
Tel: (01285) 831213
Fax: (01285) 831121
Email: info@
  rendcomb.gloucs.sch.uk
Head: Mr Gerry Holden and
Mr Martin Watson
Type: Co-educational Boarding
and Day 3–18
No of pupils: B215 G209
No of boarders: F148
Fees: (September 08)
F/WB £17544–£23199
Day £12570–£17280

GLOUCESTER

**GLOUCESTERSHIRE ISLAMIC
SECONDARY SCHOOL FOR
GIRLS**
Sinope Street, off Widden Street,
Gloucester, Gloucestershire
GL1 4AW
Tel: (01452) 300465
Email: iacademy@yahoo.co.uk
Head: Mrs C Sandall
Type: Girls Day 11–16
No of pupils: 90
Fees: On application

THE KING'S SCHOOL
Gloucester, Gloucestershire
GL1 2BG
Tel: (01452) 337337
Fax: (01452) 337314
Email: office@
  thekingsschool.co.uk
Head: Mr A K J Macnaughton
Type: Co-educational Day 3–18
No of pupils: B272 G209
Fees: (September 08)
Day £5985–£14340

THE SCHOOL OF THE LION
Beauchamp House, Churcham,
Gloucester, Gloucestershire
GL2 8AA
Tel: (01452) 750253
Fax: (01452) 750253
Email: office@
  schoolofthelion.org.uk
Head: Mr N Steele
Type: Co-educational Day 4–18
No of pupils: B9 G11
Fees: On application

WYNSTONES SCHOOL
Church Lane, Whaddon,
Gloucester, Gloucestershire
GL4 0UF
Tel: (01452) 429220
Fax: (01452) 429221
Email: info@wynstones.com
Head: Ms H Duffield
Type: Co-educational Day and
Boarding 3–19
No of pupils: B151 G159
No of boarders: F5 W2
Fees: On application

MORETON-IN-MARSH

THE DORMER HOUSE PNEU SCHOOL
High Street, Moreton-in-Marsh,
Gloucestershire GL56 0AD
Tel: (01608) 650758
Fax: (01608) 652238
Email: office@dormerhouse.co.uk
Head: Mrs A D Thomas
Type: Co-educational Day 2–11
No of pupils: B54 G58
Fees: (September 07) Day £5376

NAILSWORTH

ACORN SCHOOL
Church Street, Nailsworth,
Gloucestershire GL6 0BP
Tel: (01453) 836508
Fax: (01453) 836508
Email: info@theacornschool.com
Head: Mr G E B Whiting
Type: Co-educational Day 3–19
Fees: (September 08)
Day £4170–£6300

STONEHOUSE

HOPELANDS SCHOOL
38 Regent Street, Stonehouse,
Gloucestershire GL10 2AD
Tel: (01453) 822164
Fax: (01453) 827288
Email: enquiries@
hopelands.org.uk
Head: Mrs S Bradburn
Type: Co-educational Day 3–11
No of pupils: B20 G42
Fees: On application

WYCLIFFE*
Bath Road, Stonehouse,
Gloucestershire GL10 2JQ
Tel: (01453) 822432
Fax: (01453) 827634
Email: senior@wycliffe.co.uk
Head: Mrs M E Burnet Ward
Type: Co-educational Boarding
and Day 13–18
No of pupils: B278 G141
No of boarders: F233
Fees: (September 08)
FB £23235–£28335
Day £14145–£15465

WYCLIFFE PREPARATORY SCHOOL*[†]
Ryeford Hall, Stonehouse,
Gloucestershire GL10 2LD
Tel: (01453) 820471
Fax: (01453) 825604
Email: prep@wycliffe.co.uk
Head: Mr A Palmer
Type: Co-educational Boarding
and Day 2–13
No of pupils: B201 G151
No of boarders: F67
Fees: (September 08)
F/WB £13230–£16965
Day £5160–£10680

STROUD

BEAUDESERT PARK SCHOOL
Minchinhampton, Stroud,
Gloucestershire GL6 9AF
Tel: (01453) 832072
Fax: (01453) 836040
Email: office@
beaudesert.gloucs.sch.uk
Head: Mr J P R Womersley
Type: Co-educational Boarding
and Day 4–13
No of pupils: B232 G176
No of boarders: W40
Fees: (September 08)
WB £14700–£16860
Day £6600–£12885

TETBURY

QUERNS WESTONBIRT SCHOOL
Tetbury, Gloucestershire GL8 8QG
Tel: (01666) 881390
Fax: (01666) 881391
Email: querns@
westonbirt.gloucs.sch.uk
Head: Miss V James
Type: Co-educational Day 4–11
No of pupils: B35 G45
Fees: On application

WESTONBIRT SCHOOL
Tetbury, Gloucestershire GL8 8QG
Tel: (01666) 880333
Fax: (01666) 880364
Email: office@
westonbirt.gloucs.sch.uk
Head: Mrs M Henderson
Type: Girls Boarding and Day
11–18
No of pupils: 250
No of boarders: F125 W37
Fees: (September 08)
F/WB £21678–£24900
Day £14820–£17280

TEWKESBURY

BREDON SCHOOL[†]
Pull Court, Bushley, Tewkesbury,
Gloucestershire GL20 6AH
Tel: (01684) 293156
Fax: (01684) 276392
Email: enquiries@
bredonschool.co.uk
Head: Mr D J Keyte
Type: Co-educational Boarding
and Day 7–18
No of pupils: B171 G59
No of boarders: F81 W41
Fees: (September 08)
FB £16245–£22959
WB £15825–£22575
Day £6375–£14655

WOTTON-UNDER-EDGE

ROSE HILL SCHOOL
Alderley, Wotton-under-Edge,
Gloucestershire GL12 7QT
Tel: (01453) 843196
Fax: (01453) 846126
Email: office@rosehillschool.com
Head: Mr P Cawley- Wakefield
Type: Co-educational Day 3–13
No of pupils: B70 G60
Fees: On application

England – Gloucestershire

SOUTH GLOUCESTERSHIRE

WINTERBOURNE

SILVERHILL SCHOOL
Swan Lane, Winterbourne,
South Gloucestershire BS36 1RL
Tel: (01454) 772156
Fax: (01454) 777141
Email: silverhill@btconnect.com
Head: Mrs J Capper and Mr P J
Capper
Type: Co-educational Day 2–11
No of pupils: B98 G87
Fees: (September 08)
Day £100–£6135

HAMPSHIRE

ALTON

ALTON CONVENT SCHOOL
Anstey Lane, Alton, Hampshire
GU34 2NG
Tel: (01420) 82070
Fax: (01420) 541711
Email: enquiries@
  alton-convent.com
Head: Mrs S Kirkham
Type: Girls Day 2–18 (Co-ed
2–11)
No of pupils: B75 G380
Fees: (September 08)
Day £5850–£9465

ANDOVER

FARLEIGH SCHOOL
Red Rice, Andover, Hampshire
SP11 7PW
Tel: (01264) 710766
Fax: (01264) 710070
Email: office@farleighschool.co.uk
Head: S Everson
Type: Co-educational Boarding
and Day 3–13
No of pupils: B236 G177
No of boarders: F131
Fees: (September 07)
F/WB £15645–£17385
Day £3675–£13350

ROOKWOOD SCHOOL*
Weyhill Road, Andover,
Hampshire SP10 3AL
Tel: (01264) 325900
Fax: (01264) 325909
Email: office@
  rookwood.hants.sch.uk
Head: Mrs M P Langley
Type: Co-educational Day and
Boarding 3–16 (Boy boarders from
age 8)
No of pupils: B172 G188
No of boarders: F31
Fees: (September 08)
FB £16500–£19320
Day £6555–£10800

BASINGSTOKE

DANESHILL SCHOOL
Stratfield Turgis, Basingstoke,
Hampshire RG27 0AR
Tel: (01256) 882707
Fax: (01256) 882007
Email: office@
  daneshill.hants.sch.uk
Head: Mr S V Spencer
Type: Co-educational Day 2–13
No of pupils: B124 G137
Fees: On application

THE KING'S SCHOOL
Basingstoke Community Church,
Sarum Hill, Basingstoke,
Hampshire RG21 8SR
Tel: (01256) 467092
Fax: (01256) 473605
Head: Mr Paul Davis
Type: Co-educational Day 7–16
No of pupils: B99 G73
Fees: On application

BRAMDEAN

**BROCKWOOD PARK
SCHOOL**
Bramdean, Hampshire SO24 0LQ
Tel: (01962) 771744
Fax: (01962) 771875
Email: enquiry@brockwood.org.uk
Head: Mr B Taylor and Mr Adrian
Sydenham
Type: Co-educational Boarding
14–19
No of pupils: B31 G36
No of boarders: F67
Fees: (September 08) FB £14200

CATHERINGTON

KINGSCOURT SCHOOL
Catherington House, 182 Five
Meads Road, Catherington,
Hampshire PO8 9NJ
Tel: (023) 9259 3251
Fax: (023) 9259 7481
Email: office@kingscourt.org.uk
Head: Jacky Easton
Type: Co-educational 2–11
Fees: On application

CHANDLER'S FORD

WOODHILL SCHOOL
61 Brownhill Road, Chandler's
Ford, Hampshire SO53 2EH
Tel: (023) 8026 8012
Fax: (023) 8026 8012
Email: Office-CF@
    Woodhill.hants.sch.uk
Head: Mrs M Dacombe
Type: Co-educational Day 3–11
No of pupils: B60 G60
Fees: On application

EASTLEIGH

THE KING'S SCHOOL SENIOR
Lakesmere House, Allington Lane,
Fair Oak, Eastleigh, Hampshire
SO50 7DB
Tel: (023) 8060 0956
Fax: (023) 8060 0956
Email: office@
    kingssenior.hants.sch.uk
Head: Mrs R Pierson
Type: Co-educational Day 11–16
No of pupils: B62 G43
Fees: On application

SHERBORNE HOUSE SCHOOL
Lakewood Road, Chandler's Ford,
Eastleigh, Hampshire SO53 1EU
Tel: (023) 8025 2440
Fax: (023) 8025 2553
Email: info@sherbornehouse.co.uk
Head: Mrs H Hopson-Hill
Type: Co-educational Day 2–11
No of pupils: B139 G138
Fees: On application

FAREHAM

BOUNDARY OAK SCHOOL
Roche Court, Wickham Road,
Fareham, Hampshire PO17 5BL
Tel: (01329) 280955
Fax: (01329) 827656
Email: secretary@
    boundaryoak.co.uk
Head: Mr Stephen Symonds
Type: Co-educational Boarding
and Day 3–13
No of pupils: 143
No of boarders: W20
Fees: (September 08)
WB £11310–£15390
Day £3240–£10800

MEONCROSS SCHOOL
Burnt House Lane, Stubbington,
Fareham, Hampshire PO14 2EF
Tel: (01329) 662182
Fax: (01329) 664680
Email: meoncross@aol.com
Head: Mr C J Ford
Type: Co-educational Day 3–16
No of pupils: B225 G180
Fees: On application

WYKEHAM HOUSE SCHOOL
East Street, Fareham, Hampshire
PO16 0BW
Tel: (01329) 280178
Fax: (01329) 823964
Email: office@
    wykehamhouse.com
Head: Mrs L Clarke
Type: Girls Day 2–16
No of pupils: 250
Fees: (September 08)
Day £3600–£8985

FARNBOROUGH

FARNBOROUGH HILL
Farnborough, Hampshire
GU14 8AT
Tel: (01252) 545197
Fax: (01252) 513037
Email: devdir@
    farnborough-hill.org.uk
Head: Mrs S Buckle
Type: Girls Day 11–18
No of pupils: 500
Fees: (September 07) Day £9390

SALESIAN COLLEGE
Reading Road, Farnborough,
Hampshire GU14 6PA
Tel: (01252) 893000
Fax: (01252) 893032
Email: office@
    salesian.hants.sch.uk
Head: Mr P A Wilson
Type: Boys Day 11–18
Fees: On application

FLEET

ST NICHOLAS' SCHOOL*
Redfields House, Redfields Lane,
Church Crookham, Fleet,
Hampshire GU52 0RF
Tel: (01252) 850121
Fax: (01252) 850718
Email: registrar@
    st-nicholas.hants.sch.uk
Head: Mrs A V Whatmough
Type: Girls Day 3–16 (Boys 3–7)
No of pupils: B14 G389
Fees: (September 08)
Day £3696–£10038

STOCKTON HOUSE SCHOOL
Stockton Avenue, Fleet,
Hampshire GU51 4NS
Tel: (01252) 616323
Fax: (01252) 627011
Email: stocktonialtd@
    waitrose.com
Head: Mrs S Forrest
Type: Co-educational Day 2–6
No of pupils: B45 G37
Fees: (September 07)
Day £1192–£3900

FORDINGBRIDGE

FORRES SANDLE MANOR
Fordingbridge, Hampshire
SP6 1NS
Tel: (01425) 653181
Fax: (01425) 655676
Email: office@fsmschool.com
Head: Mr R P J Moore
Type: Co-educational Boarding
and Day 3–13
No of pupils: B147 G127
No of boarders: F61 W35
Fees: On application

England – Hampshire

GOSPORT

MARYCOURT SCHOOL
27 Crescent Road, Alverstoke,
Gosport, Hampshire PO12 2DJ
Tel: (023) 9258 1766
Fax: (023) 9258 1766
Email: admin@
   marycourt.hants.sch.uk
Head: Mrs J Norman
Type: Co-educational Day 2–9
No of pupils: B35 G30
Fees: (September 08)
Day £2550–£4657

HAVANT

GLENHURST SCHOOL
16 Beechworth Road, Havant,
Hampshire PO9 1AX
Tel: (023) 9248 4054
Fax: (023) 9248 4054
Email: office@
   glenhurstschool.co.uk
Head: Mrs E Haines
Type: Co-educational Day 2–9
No of pupils: B40 G40
Fees: On application

HOOK

GREY HOUSE PREPARATORY SCHOOL
Mount Pleasant Road, Hartley
Wintney, Hook, Hampshire
RG27 8PW
Tel: (01252) 842353
Fax: (01252) 845527
Email: schooloffice@
   grey-house.co.uk
Head: Mrs C Allen
Type: Co-educational Day 4–11
No of pupils: B96 G45
Fees: (September 08)
Day £5967–£7485

LORD WANDSWORTH COLLEGE*
Long Sutton, Hook, Hampshire
RG29 1TB
Tel: (01256) 862201
Fax: (01256) 860363
Email: info@lordwandsworth.org
Head: Mr I G Power
Type: Co-educational Boarding
and Day 11–18
No of pupils: B377 G171
No of boarders: F55 W200
Fees: (September 08)
FB £21426–£23754
WB £21426–£22614
Day £15999–£16854

ST NEOT'S SCHOOL
St Neots Road, Eversley, Hook,
Hampshire RG27 0PN
Tel: (0118) 973 2118
Fax: (0118) 973 9949
Email: office@st-neots-prep.co.uk
Head: Mr R J Thorp
Type: Co-educational Day and
Boarding 1–13
No of pupils: B180 G130
No of boarders: W26
Fees: (September 08) WB £15390
Day £7500–£12450

SHERFIELD SCHOOL
Reading Road, Sherfield-on-
Loddon, Hook, Hampshire
RG27 0HT
Tel: (01256) 884800
Fax: (01256) 883172
Email: info@sherfieldschool.co.uk
Head: Mr J Murphy-O'Connor and
Professor P Preedy
Type: Co-educational Day 0–18
(Upper age increased to 18)
No of pupils: B217 G190
Fees: (September 07)
Day £6120–£10917

LEE-ON-THE-SOLENT

ST ANNE'S PRE-SCHOOL
13 Milvil Road, Lee-on-the-Solent,
Hampshire PO13 9LU
Tel: (023) 9255 0820
Email: st_annes_school@
   yahoo.co.uk
Head: Mrs A M Whitting
Type: Co-educational Day 2–8
No of pupils: B15 G15
Fees: On application

LIPHOOK

CHURCHERS COLLEGE JUNIOR SCHOOL
Midhurst Road, Liphook,
Hampshire GU30 7HT
Tel: (01730) 236870
Fax: (01428) 722550
Email: ccjsoffice@
   churcherscollege.com
Head: Mrs S Rivett
Type: Co-educational Day 4–11
No of pupils: B114 G109
Fees: (September 08)
Day £6585–£7020

HIGHFIELD SCHOOL
Highfield Lane, Liphook,
Hampshire GU30 7LQ
Tel: (01428) 728000
Fax: (01428) 728001
Email: office@
   highfieldschool.org.uk
Head: Mr P G S Evitt
Type: Co-educational Boarding
and Day 8–13
No of pupils: B125 G115
No of boarders: F100
Fees: (September 07)
FB £15600–£17256
Day £11850–£15150

LYMINGTON

HORDLE WALHAMPTON SCHOOL†
Lymington, Hampshire SO41 5ZG
Tel: (01590) 672013
Fax: (01590) 678498
Email: registrar@
   hordlewalhampton.co.uk
Head: Mr R H C Phillips
Type: Co-educational Boarding
and Day 2–13
No of pupils: B183 G143
No of boarders: F41
Fees: (September 08)
Day £9015–£16665

NEW MILTON

BALLARD SCHOOL
Fernhill Lane, New Milton,
Hampshire BH25 5SU
Tel: (01425) 611153
Fax: (01425) 622099
Email: admissions@
  ballardschool.co.uk
Head: Mr S P Duckitt
Type: Co-educational Day 2–16
No of pupils: B318 G296
Fees: (September 08)
Day £5607–£10758

DURLSTON COURT
Becton Lane, Barton-on-Sea,
New Milton, Hampshire
BH25 7AQ
Tel: (01425) 610010
Fax: (01425) 622731
Email: secretary@
  durlstoncourt.co.uk
Head: Mr D C Wansey
Type: Co-educational Day 2–13
No of pupils: B182 G138
Fees: (September 08)
Day £3435–£11895

PETERSFIELD

BEDALES SCHOOL*
Petersfield, Hampshire GU32 2DG
Tel: (01730) 300100
Fax: (01730) 300500
Email: admissions@bedales.org.uk
Head: Mr K Budge
Type: Co-educational Boarding
and Day 3–18
No of pupils: B350 G382
No of boarders: 373
Fees: (September 08)
FB £18327–£26664
Day £3567–£20976

CHURCHERS COLLEGE
Portsmouth Road, Petersfield,
Hampshire GU31 4AS
Tel: (01730) 263033
Fax: (01730) 231437
Email: enquiries@
  churcherscollege.com
Head: Mr S H Williams
Type: Co-educational Day 4–18
No of pupils: B475 G360
Fees: On application

DITCHAM PARK SCHOOL
Ditcham Park, Petersfield,
Hampshire GU31 5RN
Tel: (01730) 825659
Fax: (01730) 825070
Email: info@ditchampark.com
Head: Mrs K S Morton
Type: Co-educational Day 4–16
No of pupils: B192 G156
Fees: On application

DUNHURST (BEDALES JUNIOR SCHOOL)
Petersfield, Hampshire GU32 2DP
Tel: (01730) 300200
Fax: (01730) 300600
Email: dunhurst@bedales.org.uk
Head: Mrs P Watkins
Type: Co-educational Boarding
and Day 8–13
No of pupils: B90 G94
No of boarders: F53
Fees: (September 08) FB £18327
Day £14346

PORTSMOUTH

THE PORTSMOUTH GRAMMAR SCHOOL
High Street, Portsmouth,
Hampshire PO1 2LN
Tel: (023) 9236 0036
Fax: (023) 9236 4202
Email: admissions@pgs.org.uk
Head: Mr J E Priory
Type: Co-educational Day 2–18
No of pupils: B1030 G617
Fees: (September 07)
Day £6285–£9801

ROOKESBURY PARK SCHOOL
Southwick Road, Wickham,
Portsmouth, Hampshire PO17 6HT
Tel: (01329) 833108
Fax: (01329) 835090
Email: enquiries@
  rookesburypark.co.uk
Head: Mrs Pippa Harris-Burland
Type: Co-educational Boarding
and Day 3–13
No of pupils: B41 G59
No of boarders: F8 W5
Fees: (September 08)
F/WB £12537–£16410
Day £5607–£11055

RINGWOOD

MOYLES COURT SCHOOL†
Moyles Court, Ringwood,
Hampshire BH24 3NF
Tel: (01425) 472 856
Fax: (01425) 474 715
Email: info@moylescourt.co.uk
Head: Mr Greg Meakin
Type: Co-educational Day and
Boarding 3–16
No of pupils: B84 G67
No of boarders: F44
Fees: (September 08)
FB £13887–£18837
Day £4965–£10755

RINGWOOD WALDORF SCHOOL
Ashley, Ringwood, Hampshire
BH24 2NN
Tel: (01425) 472664
Email: mail@ringwood-waldorf-
  school.fsnet.co.uk
Type: Co-educational Day 4–14
No of pupils: B100 G100
Fees: On application

ROMSEY

HAMPSHIRE COLLEGIATE SCHOOL, UCST*
Embley Park, Romsey, Hampshire
SO51 6ZE
Tel: (01794) 512206
Fax: (01794) 518737
Email: info@hampshirecs.org.uk
Head: Mr H S MacDonald
Type: Co-educational Boarding
and Day 3–18
No of pupils: B400 G367
No of boarders: F30 W46
Fees: (September 08)
FB £19869–£20271
Day £7434–£12252

STANBRIDGE EARLS SCHOOL
Stanbridge Lane, Romsey,
Hampshire SO51 0ZS
Tel: (01794) 529400
Fax: (01794) 511201
Email: admin@
  stanbridgeearls.co.uk
Head: Mr G P Link
Type: Co-educational Boarding
and Day 10–19
No of pupils: B147 G29
No of boarders: F135
Fees: (September 07)
FB £20265–£22602
Day £15201–£16800

England – Hampshire

THE STROUD SCHOOL
Highwood House, Highwood
Lane, Romsey, Hampshire
SO51 9ZH
Tel: (01794) 513231
Fax: (01794) 514432
Email: secretary@
    stroud-romsey-sch.co.uk
Head: Mr A J Dodds
Type: Co-educational Day 3–13
No of pupils: B188 G127
Fees: (September 07)
Day £6750–£11070

SOUTHAMPTON

THE GREGG SCHOOL
Townhill Park House, Cutbush
Lane, Southampton, Hampshire
SO18 2GF
Tel: (023) 8047 2133
Fax: (023) 8047 1080
Email: office@
    gregg.southampton.sch.uk
Head: Mr R D Hart
Type: Co-educational Day 11–16
No of pupils: B187 G133
Fees: (September 07) Day £8610

KING EDWARD VI SCHOOL
Wilton Road, Southampton,
Hampshire SO15 5UQ
Tel: (023) 8070 4561
Fax: (023) 8070 5937
Email: registrar@kes.hants.sch.uk
Head: Mr A J Thould
Type: Co-educational Day 11–18
No of pupils: B604 G704
Fees: (September 08) Day £10485

KINGS PRIMARY SCHOOL
26 Quob Lane, West End,
Southampton, Hampshire
SO30 3HN
Tel: (023) 8047 2266
Fax: (023) 8047 2282
Email: kingschool@lineone.net
Head: Mr K Ford
Type: Co-educational Day 5–11
No of pupils: 120
Fees: (September 08) Day £4140

ST MARY'S COLLEGE
57 Midanbury Lane, Bitterne Park,
Southampton, Hampshire
SO18 4DJ
Tel: (023) 8067 1267
Fax: (023) 8067 7575
Email: stmarysoffice@aol.com
Head: Rev J J Davis
Type: Co-educational Day 3–18
Fees: On application

ST WINIFRED'S SCHOOL
17–19 Winn Road, Southampton,
Hampshire SO17 1EJ
Tel: (023) 8055 7352
Fax: (023) 80679055
Email: office@
    stwinifreds.southampton.sch.uk
Head: Mrs C A Pearcey
Type: Co-educational Day 2–11
Fees: (September 08)
Day £4230–£5910

WOODHILL PREPARATORY SCHOOL
Brook Lane, Botley, Southampton,
Hampshire SO30 2ER
Tel: (01489) 781112
Fax: (01489) 799362
Email: m.dacombe@
    woodhill.hants.sch.uk
Head: Mrs M Dacombe
Type: Co-educational Day 3–11
No of pupils: B62 G48
Fees: On application

SOUTHSEA

MAYVILLE HIGH SCHOOL[†]
35 St Simon's Road, Southsea,
Hampshire PO5 2PE
Tel: (023) 9273 4847
Fax: (023) 9229 3649
Email: mayvillehighschoolpr@
    talk21.com
Head: Mrs L Owens and
Mr M Castle
Type: Co-educational Day 0–16
No of pupils: B236 G238
Fees: On application

PORTSMOUTH HIGH SCHOOL GDST
Kent Road, Southsea, Hampshire
PO5 3EQ
Tel: (023) 9282 6714
Fax: (023) 9281 4814
Email: headsec@por.gdst.net
Head: Mrs J J Clough
Type: Girls Day 3–18
No of pupils: 550
Fees: (September 08)
Day £5328–£8898

ST JOHN'S COLLEGE
Grove Road South, Southsea,
Hampshire PO5 3QW
Tel: (023) 9281 5118
Fax: (023) 9287 3603
Email: info@stjohnscollege.co.uk
Head: Mr N W Thorne
Type: Co-educational Boarding
and Day 2–18
No of pupils: B378 G178
No of boarders: F114
Fees: On application

WINCHESTER

THE PILGRIMS' SCHOOL
3 The Close, Winchester,
Hampshire SO23 9LT
Tel: (01962) 854189
Fax: (01962) 843610
Email: info@pilgrims-school.co.uk
Head: Dr B A Rees
Type: Boys Boarding and Day
7–13
No of pupils: 200
No of boarders: F40 W25
Fees: (September 08) FB £17445
Day £7920–£13785

PRINCE'S MEAD SCHOOL
Worthy Park House, Kingsworthy,
Winchester, Hampshire SO21 1AN
Tel: (01962) 888000
Fax: (01962) 886888
Email: admin@
    princesmeadschool.org.uk
Head: Miss P Kirk
Type: Co-educational Day 3–11
No of pupils: B74 G153
Fees: On application

ST SWITHUN'S SCHOOL
Alresford Road, Winchester,
Hampshire SO21 1HA
Tel: (01962) 835700
Fax: (01962) 835779
Email: office@stswithuns.com
Head: Dr H L Harvey
Type: Girls Boarding and Day
11–18
No of pupils: 480
No of boarders: F62 W165
Fees: (September 08) F/WB £22950
Day £13920–£13920

ST SWITHUN'S JUNIOR SCHOOL
Alresford Road, Winchester, Hampshire SO21 1HA
Tel: (44 (0) 01962 835750
Fax: (44 (0) 01962 835781
Email: office.juniorschool@ stswithuns.com
Head: Mrs Pim Grimes
Type: Co-educational Day Boys 3–7 Girls 3–11(Accepts Boys 3–6)
No of pupils: B20 G164
Fees: On application

TWYFORD SCHOOL
Twyford, Winchester, Hampshire SO21 1NW
Tel: (01962) 712269
Fax: (01962) 712100
Email: registrar@ twyfordschool.com
Head: Dr D Livingstone
Type: Co-educational Day and Boarding 3–13
No of pupils: B181 G111
No of boarders: W24
Fees: On application

WINCHESTER COLLEGE*
College Street, Winchester, Hampshire SO23 9NA
Tel: (01962) 621247
Fax: (01962) 621106
Email: admissions@wincoll.ac.uk
Head: Dr R D Townsend
Type: Boys Boarding and Day 13–18
No of pupils: 685
No of boarders: F681
Fees: (September 08) FB £27870 Day £26475

YATELEY

YATELEY MANOR PREPARATORY SCHOOL
51 Reading Road, Yateley, Hampshire GU46 7UQ
Tel: (01252) 405500
Fax: (01252) 405504
Email: office@yateleymanor.com
Head: Mr F G Howard
Type: Co-educational Day 3–13
No of pupils: B311 G178
Fees: (September 08) Day £3795–£10491

HEREFORDSHIRE

BROMYARD

ST RICHARD'S
Bredenbury Court, Bromyard, Herefordshire HR7 4TD
Tel: (01885) 482491
Fax: (01885) 488982
Email: schooloffice@ st-richards.org.uk
Head: Mr N Cheesman
Type: Co-educational Boarding and Day 3–13
No of pupils: B54 G70
No of boarders: F20 W35
Fees: (September 08) FB £15420 WB £14640 Day £3870–£10665

HEREFORD

THE HEREFORD CATHEDRAL JUNIOR SCHOOL
28 Castle Street, Hereford, Herefordshire HR1 2NW
Tel: (01432) 363511
Fax: (01432) 363515
Email: secretary@hcjs.co.uk
Head: Mr T Wheeler
Type: Co-educational Day 3–11
No of pupils: B190 G137
Fees: (September 08) Day £6111–£7596

THE HEREFORD CATHEDRAL SCHOOL
Old Deanery, Cathedral Close, Hereford, Herefordshire HR1 2NG
Tel: (01432) 363522
Fax: (01432) 363525
Email: enquiry@hcsch.org
Head: Mr P A Smith
Type: Co-educational Day 11–18
No of pupils: B322 G272
Fees: (September 08) Day £9100

LEOMINSTER

LUCTON SCHOOL
Leominster, Herefordshire HR6 9PN
Tel: (01568) 782000
Fax: (01568) 782001
Email: enquiries@luctonschool.org
Head: Mrs G Thorne
Type: Co-educational Boarding and Day 0–16 (VIth Form from Sept 2005)
No of pupils: B80 G72
No of boarders: F38 W15
Fees: On application

HERTFORDSHIRE

ALDENHAM

EDGE GROVE
Aldenham Village, Aldenham,
Hertfordshire WD25 8NL
Tel: (01923) 855724
Fax: (01923) 859920
Email: enquiries@
   edgegrove.indschools.co.uk
Head: Mr M T Wilson
Type: Co-educational Boarding
and Day 3–13
No of pupils: B234 G100
No of boarders: F50 W40
Fees: On application

BARNET

LYONSDOWN SCHOOL TRUST LTD
3 Richmond Road, New Barnet,
Barnet, Hertfordshire EN5 1SA
Tel: (020) 8449 0225
Fax: (020) 8441 4690
Email: enquiries@
   lyonsdownschool.co.uk
Head: Mrs L Maggs-Wellings
Type: Co-educational Day
Boys 3–7 Girls 3–11
No of pupils: B54 G158
Fees: On application

NORFOLK LODGE MONTESSORI NURSERY
Dancers Hill Road, Barnet,
Hertfordshire EN5 4RP
Tel: (020) 8447 1565
Fax: (020) 8447 1833
Email: NorfolkLodgeHQ@aol.com
Head: Mrs K Conroy
Type: Co-educational Day 3–4
Fees: On application

ST MARTHA'S SENIOR SCHOOL
Camlet Way, Hadley, Barnet,
Hertfordshire EN4 0NJ
Tel: (020) 8449 6889
Fax: (020) 8441 5632
Email: office@st-marthas.org.uk
Head: Mr J Sheridan
Type: Girls Day 11–18
No of pupils: 320
Fees: On application

SUSI EARNSHAW THEATRE SCHOOL
The Bull Theatre, 68 High Street,
Barnet, Hertfordshire EN5 5SJ
Tel: (020) 8441 5010
Fax: (020) 8364 9618
Email: info@sets.org.uk
Head: Mr D Earnshaw
Type: Co-educational Day 11–16
No of pupils: B33 G42
Fees: (September 08)
Day £6175–£6750

BERKHAMSTED

BERKHAMSTED COLLEGIATE PREPARATORY SCHOOL
Kings Road, Berkhamsted,
Hertfordshire HP4 3YP
Tel: (01442) 358201/2
Fax: (01442) 358203
Email: prepadmin@bcschool.org
Head: Mr A J Taylor
Type: Co-educational Day 3–11
No of pupils: B229 G234
Fees: (September 08)
Day £2190–£4947

BERKHAMSTED COLLEGIATE SCHOOL
Castle Street, Berkhamsted,
Hertfordshire HP4 2BB
Tel: (01442) 358000
Fax: (01442) 358040
Email: info@bcschool.org
Head: Mr M Steed
Type: Co-educational Day and
Boarding 11–18 (Single-sex ed
11–16)
No of pupils: B620 G418
No of boarders: F43 W4
Fees: (September 07)
F/WB £20121–£22227
Day £11964–£14070

EGERTON ROTHESAY SCHOOL
Durrants Lane, Berkhamsted,
Hertfordshire HP4 3UJ
Tel: (01442) 865275
Fax: (01442) 864977
Email: admin.dl@eger-roth.co.uk
Head: Mrs N Boddam-Whetham
Type: Co-educational Day 5–16
No of pupils: B176 G71
Fees: (September 08) Day £8553

HARESFOOT PREPARATORY SCHOOL*
Chesham Road, Berkhamsted,
Hertfordshire HP4 2SZ
Tel: (01442) 872742
Fax: (01442) 872742
Email: haresfootschool@
   btconnect.com
Head: Mrs S Jaspal
Type: Co-educational Day 0–11
No of pupils: B77 G65
Fees: (September 08)
Day £1524–£8070

BISHOP'S STORTFORD

BISHOP'S STORTFORD COLLEGE
Maze Green Road, Bishop's
Stortford, Hertfordshire CM23 2PJ
Tel: (01279) 838575
Fax: (01279) 836570
Email: admissions@bsc.biblio.net
Head: Mr J G Trotman
Type: Co-educational Boarding
and Day 13–18
No of pupils: B297 G213
No of boarders: F90 W90
Fees: (September 08) FB £18843
WB £18654 Day £13551

BISHOP'S STORTFORD COLLEGE JUNIOR SCHOOL
Maze Green Road, Bishop's
Stortford, Hertfordshire CM23 2PH
Tel: (01279) 838607
Fax: (01279) 306110
Email: jsadmissions@
   bsc.biblio.net
Head: Mr J A Greathead
Type: Co-educational Boarding
and Day 4–13
No of pupils: B298 G248
No of boarders: F13 W29
Fees: (September 08)
FB £13128–£14283
WB £12996–£14139
Day £6336–£10839

HOWE GREEN HOUSE SCHOOL
Great Hallingbury, Bishop's Stortford, Hertfordshire CM22 7UF
Tel: (01279) 657706
Fax: (01279) 501333
Email: info@
  howegreenhouseschool.co.uk
Head: Mr G R Gorton
Type: Co-educational Day 2–11
No of pupils: B101 G88
Fees: (September 08)
Day £5280–£8391

BUSHEY

IMMANUEL COLLEGE
87/91 Elstree Road, Bushey, Hertfordshire WD23 4EB
Tel: (020) 8950 0604
Fax: (020) 8950 8687
Email: enquiries@
  immanuel.herts.sch.uk
Head: Mr P Skelker
Type: Co-educational Day 11–18
No of pupils: B262 G256
Fees: On application

LITTLE ACORNS MONTESSORI SCHOOL
Lincolnsfields Centre, Bushey Hall Drive, Bushey, Hertfordshire WD2 2ER
Tel: (01923) 230705
Fax: (01923) 230705
Head: Ms J Nugent and Ms R Lau
Type: Co-educational Day 2–7
No of pupils: 24
Fees: On application

LONGWOOD SCHOOL
Bushey Hall Drive, Bushey, Hertfordshire WD23 2QG
Tel: (01923) 253715
Fax: (01923) 222760
Email: info@
  longwoodschool.co.uk
Head: Mrs M Garman
Type: Co-educational Day 3–11
No of pupils: B74 G66
Fees: On application

THE PURCELL SCHOOL
Aldenham Road, Bushey, Hertfordshire WD23 2TS
Tel: (01923) 331100
Fax: (01923) 331166
Email: info@purcell-school.org
Head: Mr A P Crook
Type: Co-educational Day and Boarding 8–18
No of pupils: B59 G109
No of boarders: F100
Fees: On application

ST HILDA'S SCHOOL
High Street, Bushey, Hertfordshire WD23 3DA
Tel: (020) 8950 1751
Fax: (020) 8420 4523
Email: registrar@
  sthildasbushey.co.uk
Head: Mrs L Cavanagh
Type: Girls Day 3–11 (Boys 3–5)
No of pupils: B5 G120
Fees: (September 07)
Day £4455–£8355

ST MARGARET'S SCHOOL*
Merry Hill Road, Bushey, Hertfordshire WD23 1DT
Tel: (020) 8901 0870
Fax: (020) 8950 1677
Email: admissions@
  stmargarets.herts.sch.uk
Head: Mrs Lynne Crighton
Type: Girls Boarding and Day 4–18
No of pupils: 443
No of boarders: F48 W10
Fees: (September 08) FB £22035 WB £18885 Day £8130–£12240

BUSHEY HEATH

WESTWOOD
6 Hartsbourne Road, Bushey Heath, Hertfordshire WD23 1JH
Tel: (020) 8950 1138
Email: westwood.school@
  virgin.net
Head: Mrs J Hill
Type: Co-educational Day 4–8
No of pupils: B36 G36
Fees: On application

ELSTREE

ALDENHAM SCHOOL*
Elstree, Hertfordshire WD6 3AJ
Tel: (01923) 858122
Fax: (01923) 854410
Email: enquiries@aldenham.com
Head: Mr J C Fowler
Type: Co-educational Boarding and Day 3–18
No of pupils: B551 G149
No of boarders: F100 W27
Fees: (September 08)
Boarding £17436–£24351
Day £11643–£16752

HABERDASHERS' ASKE'S BOYS' SCHOOL
Butterfly Lane, Elstree, Hertfordshire WD6 3AF
Tel: (020) 8266 1700
Fax: (020) 8266 1800
Email: office@habsboys.org.uk
Head: Mr P B Hamilton
Type: Boys Day 5–18
No of pupils: 1400
Fees: (September 08)
Day £9675–£12885

HABERDASHERS' ASKE'S SCHOOL FOR GIRLS
Aldenham Road, Elstree, Hertfordshire WD6 3BT
Tel: (020) 8266 2302
Fax: (020) 8266 2303
Email: theschool@habsgirls.org.uk
Head: Mrs E J Radice
Type: Girls Day 4–18
Fees: (September 08)
Day £8802–£10686

HARPENDEN

ALDWICKBURY SCHOOL
Wheathampstead Road, Harpenden, Hertfordshire AL5 1AD
Tel: (01582) 713022
Fax: (01582) 767696
Email: registrar@
  aldwickbury.org.uk
Head: Mr V W Hales
Type: Boys Day and Boarding 4–13
No of pupils: 295
No of boarders: W35
Fees: (September 08) WB £13050
Day £8895–£10350

England – Hertfordshire

THE KING'S SCHOOL
Elmfield, Ambrose Lane,
Harpenden, Hertfordshire
AL5 4DU
Tel: (01582) 767566
Fax: (01582) 765406
Email: office@thekingsschool.com
Head: Mr C J Case
Type: Co-educational Day 4–16
No of pupils: B101 G95
Fees: (September 08) Day £4380

ST HILDA'S SCHOOL
28 Douglas Road, Harpenden,
Hertfordshire AL5 2ES
Tel: (01582) 712307
Fax: (01582) 763892
Email: office@
   st-hildasschool.herts.sch.uk
Head: Mrs C Godlee
Type: Girls Day 2–11
No of pupils: 180
Fees: (September 08)
Day £1272–£7425

HATFIELD

QUEENSWOOD*
Shepherds Way, Brookmans Park,
Hatfield, Hertfordshire AL9 6NS
Tel: (01707) 602500
Fax: (01707) 602597
Email: registry@queenswood.org
Head: Mrs P Edgar
Type: Girls Boarding and Day
11–18
No of pupils: 411
No of boarders: F206
Fees: (September 08)
FB £23370–£25485
Day £18015–£19680

HEMEL HEMPSTEAD

ABBOT'S HILL SCHOOL*
Bunkers Lane, Hemel Hempstead,
Hertfordshire HP3 8RP
Tel: (01442) 240333
Fax: (01442) 269981
Email: registrar@
   abbotshill.herts.sch.uk
Head: Mrs K Lewis
Type: Girls Day 3–16 (Boys 3–5)
No of pupils: 482
Fees: (September 08)
Day £1200–£12990

LOCKERS PARK
Lockers Park Lane, Hemel
Hempstead, Hertfordshire HP1 1TL
Tel: (01442) 251712
Fax: (01442) 234150
Email: secretary@
   lockerspark.herts.sch.uk
Head: Mr H J Wickham
Type: Boys Boarding and Day
5–13
No of pupils: 144
No of boarders: F20 W29
Fees: (September 08) FB £17190
Day £7500–£13890

WESTBROOK HAY PREPARATORY SCHOOL
London Road, Westbrook Hay,
Hemel Hempstead, Hertfordshire
HP1 2RF
Tel: (01442) 256143
Fax: (01442) 232076
Email: admin@
   westbrookhay.co.uk
Head: Mr K Young
Type: Co-educational Day
Boys 2–13 Girls 2–11
No of pupils: B200 G90
Fees: (September 07)
Day £6000–£10650

HERTFORD

DUNCOMBE SCHOOL
4 Warren Park Road, Bengeo,
Hertford, Hertfordshire SG14 3JA
Tel: (01992) 414100
Fax: (01992) 414111
Email: admissions@
   duncombe-school.co.uk
Head: Mrs V White
Type: Co-educational Day 2–11
No of pupils: B156 G149
Fees: (September 07)
Day £6726–£9171

HAILEYBURY*
Hertford, Hertfordshire SG13 7NU
Tel: (01992) 463353
Fax: (01992) 470663
Email: registrar@haileybury.com
Head: Mr J S Davies
Type: Co-educational Boarding
and Day 11–18
No of pupils: B442 G309
No of boarders: F500
Fees: (September 08)
FB £16050–£25305
Day £12630–£19005

HEATH MOUNT SCHOOL
Woodhall Park, Watton-at-Stone,
Hertford, Hertfordshire SG14 3NG
Tel: (01920) 830230
Fax: (01920) 830357
Email: office@heathmount.org
Head: Mr H J Matthews
Type: Co-educational Boarding
and Day 3–13
No of pupils: B207 G150
No of boarders: W15
Fees: (September 08)

ST JOSEPH'S IN THE PARK
St Mary's Lane, Hertingfordbury,
Hertford, Hertfordshire SG14 2LX
Tel: (01992) 581378
Fax: (01992) 505202
Email: admissions@
   stjosephsinthepark.co.uk
Head: Mrs W Heath-Clarke
Type: Co-educational Day 3–11
No of pupils: B100 G75
Fees: (September 07)
Day £4071–£12384

HITCHIN

KINGSHOTT SCHOOL
St Ippolyts, Hitchin, Hertfordshire
SG4 7JX
Tel: (01462) 432009
Fax: (01462) 421652
Email: pi@kingshott.herts.sch.uk
Head: Mr P R Ilott
Type: Co-educational Day 4–13
No of pupils: B236 G110
Fees: (September 07)
Day £7350–£8985

THE PRINCESS HELENA COLLEGE
Preston, Hitchin, Hertfordshire
SG4 7RT
Tel: (01462) 432100
Fax: (01462) 443871
Email: head@phc.herts.sch.uk
Head: Mrs J Duncan
Type: Girls Day and Boarding
11–18
No of pupils: 215
No of boarders: F25 W60
Fees: (September 08)
F/WB £17235–£22035
Day £12060–£15240

KINGS LANGLEY

RUDOLF STEINER SCHOOL
Langley Hill, Kings Langley,
Hertfordshire WD4 9HG
Tel: (01923) 262505
Fax: (01923) 270958
Email: info@rsskl.org.uk
Type: Co-educational Day 3–19
No of pupils: B224 G189
Fees: On application

LETCHWORTH

ST CHRISTOPHER SCHOOL
Barrington Road, Letchworth,
Hertfordshire SG6 3JZ
Tel: (01462) 650850
Fax: (01462) 481578
Email: admissions@stchris.co.uk
Head: Mr R Palmer
Type: Co-educational Boarding
and Day 2–18
No of pupils: B332 G202
No of boarders: F50
Fees: (September 08)
FB £18375–£23700
Day £3150–£13500

LETCHWORTH GARDEN CITY

ST FRANCIS' COLLEGE*
The Broadway, Letchworth
Garden City, Hertfordshire SG6 3PJ
Tel: (01462) 670511
Fax: (01462) 682361
Email: enquiries@
st-francis.herts.sch.uk
Head: Mrs D MacGinty
Type: Girls Boarding and Day
3–18
No of pupils: 450
No of boarders: F25 W3
Fees: (September 08)
FB £17865–£20685
WB £14520–£17400
Day £2040–£10515

POTTERS BAR

LOCHINVER HOUSE SCHOOL
Heath Road, Little Heath, Potters
Bar, Hertfordshire EN6 1LW
Tel: (01707) 653064
Fax: (01707) 620030
Email: registrar@
lochinverhouse.herts.sch.uk
Head: Mr J Gear
Type: Boys Day 4–13
No of pupils: 343
Fees: On application

ST JOHN'S PREPARATORY SCHOOL
Brownlowes, The Ridgeway,
Potters Bar, Hertfordshire EN6 5QT
Tel: (01707) 657294
Fax: (020) 8363 4439
Email: stjohnssc@aol.com
Head: Mrs C Tardios
Type: Co-educational Day 4–11
No of pupils: B101 G94
Fees: (September 08)
Day £7140–£7680

STORMONT
The Causeway, Potters Bar,
Hertfordshire EN6 5HA
Tel: (01707) 654037
Fax: (01707) 663295
Email: admin@
stormont.herts.sch.uk
Head: Mrs M E Johnston
Type: Girls Day 4–11
No of pupils: 168
Fees: (September 08)
Day £8760–£9210

RADLETT

RADLETT PREPARATORY SCHOOL
Kendal Hall, Watling Street,
Radlett, Hertfordshire WD7 7LY
Tel: (01923) 856812
Fax: (01923) 855880
Email: admin@
radlett-prep.herts.sch.uk
Head: Mr W N Warren
Type: Co-educational Day 4–11
No of pupils: B265 G225
Fees: On application

RICKMANSWORTH

NORTHWOOD PREPARATORY SCHOOL
Moor Farm, Sandy Lodge Road,
Rickmansworth, Hertfordshire
WD3 1LW
Tel: (01923) 825648
Fax: (01923) 835802
Email: office@
northwoodprep.co.uk
Head: Mr T Lee
Type: Boys Day 4–13 (Girls 3–4)
No of pupils: 300
Fees: (September 08)
Day £10188–£10734

RICKMANSWORTH PNEU SCHOOL
88 The Drive, Rickmansworth,
Hertfordshire WD3 4DU
Tel: (01923) 772101
Fax: (01923) 776268
Email: office@
rickmansworthpneu.co.uk
Head: Mrs S J Hayes
Type: Girls Day 3–11
No of pupils: 150
Fees: On application

THE ROYAL MASONIC SCHOOL FOR GIRLS*
Rickmansworth Park,
Rickmansworth, Hertfordshire
WD3 4HF
Tel: (01923) 773168
Fax: (01923) 896729
Email: admissions@
royalmasonic.herts.sch.uk
Head: Mrs D Rose
Type: Girls Day and Boarding
4–18
No of pupils: 786
No of boarders: F82 W46
Fees: (September 08)
FB £12150–£20415
WB £11940–£19920
Day £6840–£12780

YORK HOUSE SCHOOL*
Redheath, Sarratt Road, Croxley
Green, Rickmansworth,
Hertfordshire WD3 4LW
Tel: (01923) 772395
Fax: (01923) 779231
Email: yhsoffice@aol.com
Head: Mr P R MacDougall
Type: Boys Day 3–13 (Co-ed 2–5)
No of pupils: B280 G15
Fees: (September 08) Day £9720

England – Hertfordshire

SHENLEY

MANOR LODGE SCHOOL
Rectory Lane, Ridge Hill, Shenley,
Hertfordshire WD7 9BG
Tel: (01707) 642424
Fax: (01707) 645206
Email: prospectus@
  manorlodgeschool.com
Head: Mrs J M Smart
Type: Co-educational Day 3–11
No of pupils: B215 G205
Fees: (September 08)
Day £6930–£8820

ST ALBANS

BEECHWOOD PARK SCHOOL
Markyate, St Albans, Hertfordshire
AL3 8AW
Tel: (01582) 840333
Fax: (01582) 842372
Email: admissions@
  beechwoodpark.herts.sch.uk
Head: Mr P C E Atkinson
Type: Co-educational Day and
Boarding 4–13
No of pupils: B300 G160
No of boarders: W50
Fees: (September 08)
WB £11427–£14493
Day £8337–£11403

HOMEWOOD PRE-PREPARATORY SCHOOL
Hazel Road, Park Street, St Albans,
Hertfordshire AL2 2AH
Tel: (01727) 873542
Email: homewood@chalkface.net
Head: Mr B Cooper
Type: Co-educational Day 3–8
No of pupils: B37 G41
Fees: On application

ST ALBANS HIGH SCHOOL FOR GIRLS*
Townsend Avenue, St Albans,
Hertfordshire AL1 3SJ
Tel: (01727) 853800
Fax: (01727) 792516
Email: info@
  stalbans-high.herts.sch.uk
Head: Ms J C Pain
Type: Girls Day 4–18
No of pupils: 950
Fees: (September 08)
Day £8745–£11115

ST ALBANS SCHOOL*
Abbey Gateway, St Albans,
Hertfordshire AL3 4HB
Tel: (01727) 855521
Fax: (01727) 843447
Email: hm@
  st-albans-school.org.uk
Head: Mr A R Grant
Type: Boys Day 11–18 (Co-ed VIth
Form)
No of pupils: B772 G34
Fees: (September 08) Day £12405

ST COLUMBA'S COLLEGE*
King Harry Lane, St Albans,
Hertfordshire AL3 4AW
Tel: (01727) 855185
Fax: (01727) 892024
Email: admissions@
  st-columbas.herts.sch.uk
Head: Mr D Buxton
Type: Boys Day 4–18
No of pupils: 850
Fees: (September 08)
Day £7920–£10017

STEVENAGE

REDEMPTION ACADEMY
PO BOX 352, Stevenage,
Hertfordshire SG1 9AG
Tel: (01438) 727370
Email: info@
  redemption-church.org.uk
Head: Rev M Neale
Type: Co-educational Day 3–18
No of pupils: B16 G26
Fees: (September 08)
Day £3600–£5400

TRING

ARTS EDUCATIONAL SCHOOL, TRING PARK*
Tring Park, Tring, Hertfordshire
HP23 5LX
Tel: (01442) 824255
Fax: (01442) 891069
Email: info@aes-tring.com
Head: Mr S Anderson
Type: Co-educational Boarding
and Day 8–19
No of pupils: B72 G222
No of boarders: F213
Fees: (September 08)
FB £19005–£26850
Day £12600–£19710

FRANCIS HOUSE PREPARATORY SCHOOL
Aylesbury Road, Tring,
Hertfordshire HP23 4DL
Tel: (01442) 822315
Fax: (01442) 827080
Email: info@
  francishouseschool.co.uk
Head: Mrs Janice Hiley
Type: Co-educational Day 2–11
No of pupils: B68 G63
Fees: On application

WARE

ST EDMUND'S COLLEGE AND ST HUGH'S SCHOOL*
Old Hall Green, Ware,
Hertfordshire SG11 1DS
Tel: (01920) 821504
Fax: (01920) 823011
Email: admissions@
  stedmundscollege.org
Head: Mr C P Long
Type: Co-educational Day and
Boarding 3–18
No of pupils: B525 G305
No of boarders: F97 W20
Fees: (September 08)
FB £18945–£21660
WB £17190–£19575
Day £8430–£13350

WATFORD

ST ANDREW'S MONTESSORI SCHOOL*
High Elms Lane, Watford,
Hertfordshire WD25 0JX
Tel: (01923) 681103/663875
Fax: (01923) 681103
Email: standrewsmont@
  hotmail.com
Head: Mrs S R M O'Neill
Type: Co-educational Day 0–11
No of pupils: B40 G30
Fees: (September 08)
Day £1749–£7466

STANBOROUGH SCHOOL
Stanborough Park, Garston,
Watford, Hertfordshire WD25 9JT
Tel: (01923) 673268
Fax: (01923) 893943
Email: director@spsch.org
Head: Mr S Rivers
Type: Co-educational Day and
Boarding 3–16
No of pupils: B150 G150
No of boarders: F30 W20
Fees: On application

WELWYN

**SHERRARDSWOOD
SCHOOL**
Lockleys, Welwyn, Hertfordshire
AL6 0BJ
Tel: (01438) 714282
Fax: (01438) 840616
Email: mimram@
  sherrardswood.herts.sch.uk
Head: Mrs L E Corry
Type: Co-educational Day 2–18
Fees: (September 08)
Day £6720–£12120

ISLE OF MAN

CASTLETOWN

THE BUCHAN SCHOOL
Arbory Road, West Hill,
Castletown, Isle of Man IM9 1RD
Tel: (01624) 820481
Fax: (01624) 820403
Email: head@buchan.sch.im
Head: Mrs Alison Hope–Hedley
Type: Co-educational Day 4–11
No of pupils: B108 G90
Fees: On application

KING WILLIAM'S COLLEGE
Castletown, Isle of Man IM9 1TP
Tel: (01624) 820110
Fax: (01624) 820401
Email: registrar@kwc.sch.im
Head: Dr S J Welch
Type: Co-educational Boarding
and Day 11–18
No of pupils: B205 G189
No of boarders: F85 W5
Fees: (September 08)
FB £19323–£24264
Day £11717–£16659

ISLE OF WIGHT

RYDE

RYDE SCHOOL
Queen's Road, Ryde, Isle of Wight
PO33 3BE
Tel: (01983) 562229
Fax: (01983) 564714
Email: school.office@
  rydeschool.org.uk
Head: Dr N J England
Type: Co-educational Day and
Boarding 3–18
No of pupils: B391 G382
No of boarders: F30 W7
Fees: On application

SHANKLIN

PRIORY SCHOOL
Alverstone Manor, Luccombe
Road, Shanklin, Isle of Wight
PO37 7JB
Tel: (01983) 861222
Email: info@prioryschool.gov.uk
Head: Mrs K D'Costa
Type: Co-educational Day 2–18
No of pupils: B56 G53
Fees: On application

KENT

ASHFORD

ASHFORD SCHOOL*
East Hill, Ashford, Kent TN24 8PB
Tel: (01233) 739030
Fax: (01233) 665215
Email: registrar@
  ashfordschool.co.uk
Head: Mr M R Buchanan
Type: Co-educational Day and
Boarding 3–18 (Co-ed 3–11)
No of pupils: B231 G475
No of boarders: F115 W20
Fees: (September 08)
FB £23226–£23823 WB £21099
Day £5640–£13104

SPRING GROVE SCHOOL
Harville Road, Wye, Ashford, Kent
TN25 5EZ
Tel: (01233) 812337
Fax: (01233) 813390
Email: office@
  springgroveschool.co.uk
Head: Mr B Jones
Type: Co-educational Day 2–13
No of pupils: B110 G117
Fees: (September 08)
Day £6810–£8985

BECKENHAM

ST CHRISTOPHER'S SCHOOL
49 Bromley Road, Beckenham,
Kent BR3 5PA
Tel: (020) 8650 2200
Fax: (020) 8650 1031
Email: secretary@
  stchristophersthehall.co.uk
Head: Mr A Velasco
Type: Co-educational Day 3–11
No of pupils: B142 G126
Fees: On application

BROADSTAIRS

HADDON DENE SCHOOL
57 Gladstone Road, Broadstairs,
Kent CT10 2HY
Tel: (01843) 861176
Email: secretary@
  haddondene.co.uk
Head: Mr N Armstrong
Type: Co-educational Day 3–11
No of pupils: 150
Fees: (September 08)
Day £4500–£5025

WELLESLEY HOUSE SCHOOL
Broadstairs, Kent CT10 2DG
Tel: (01843) 862991
Fax: (01843) 602068
Email: office@wellesleyhouse.org
Head: Mr S.T.P. O'Malley
Type: Co-educational Boarding
and Day 7–13
No of pupils: B85 G44
No of boarders: F53 W59
Fees: (September 08) F/WB £18195
Day £15000

BROMLEY

ASHGROVE SCHOOL
116 Widmore Road, Bromley,
Kent BR1 3BE
Tel: (020) 8460 4143
Email: enquiries@ashgrove.org.uk
Head: Dr P Ash
Type: Co-educational Day 3–11
No of pupils: B62 G52
Fees: (September 08) Day £6855

BASTON SCHOOL
Baston Road, Hayes, Bromley,
Kent BR2 7AB
Tel: (020) 8462 1010
Fax: (020) 8462 0438
Email: admissions@
  bastonschool.org.uk
Head: Mrs A-M Jefferys
Type: Girls Day 2–16
No of pupils: 150
Fees: (September 07)
Day £7155–£9090

BICKLEY PARK SCHOOL
14/24 Page Heath Lane, Bickley,
Bromley, Kent BR1 2DS
Tel: (020) 8467 2195
Fax: (020) 8325 5511
Email: info@
  bickleyparkschool.co.uk
Head: Mr P Ashley
Type: Boys Day 3–13
No of pupils: B380 G20
Fees: (September 07)
Day £3840–£10995

BISHOP CHALLONER RC SCHOOL
228 Bromley Road, Shortlands,
Bromley, Kent BR2 0BS
Tel: (020) 8460 3546
Fax: (020) 8466 8885
Email: office@
  bishopchallonerschool.com
Head: Ms Karen Barry
Type: Co-educational Day 3–18
No of pupils: B271 G139
Fees: (September 08)
Day £5850–£8235

BREASIDE PREPARATORY SCHOOL
41 Orchard Road, Bromley, Kent
BR1 2PR
Tel: (020) 8460 0916
Fax: (020) 8466 5664
Email: info@breaside.co.uk
Head: Mrs K A Nicholson
Type: Co-educational Day 3–11
No of pupils: B137 G96
Fees: (September 08)
Day £4314–£8595

BROMLEY HIGH SCHOOL GDST
Blackbrook Lane, Bickley,
Bromley, Kent BR1 2TW
Tel: (020) 8468 7981
Fax: (020) 8295 1062
Email: bhs@bro.gdst.net
Head: Mrs L Duggleby
Type: Girls Day 4–18
No of pupils: 912
Fees: (September 08)
Day £8637–£11100

CANTERBURY

CANTERBURY STEINER SCHOOL
Garlinge Green, Chartham,
Canterbury, Kent CT4 5RU
Tel: (01227) 738285
Fax: (01227) 731158
Email: info@
  canterburysteiner.co.uk
Head: Mrs M McIntee
Type: Co-educational Day 4–17
No of pupils: 250
Fees: On application

CATS CANTERBURY*
68 New Dover Road, Stafford
House, Canterbury, Kent CT1 3LQ
Tel: (01227) 866540
Fax: (01227) 866550
Email: admissions@
 catscanterbury.com
Head: Ms M L Banning
Type: Co-educational Boarding
and Day Boys 15–28 Girls 15–26
No of pupils: B105 G75
No of boarders: F166
Fees: (September 08)
FB £18495–£27300
Day £14400–£18000

JUNIOR KING'S SCHOOL*
Milner Court, Sturry, Canterbury,
Kent CT2 0AY
Tel: (01227) 714000
Fax: (01227) 713171
Email: head@junior-kings.co.uk
Head: Mr P M Wells
Type: Co-educational Day and
Boarding 3–13
No of pupils: B226 G177
No of boarders: F54 W20
Fees: (September 08) F/WB £18780
Day £12450–£13780

KENT COLLEGE*
Whitstable Road, Canterbury, Kent
CT2 9DT
Tel: (01227) 763231
Fax: (01227) 787450
Email: registrar@kentcollege.co.uk
Head: Dr D J Lamper
Type: Co-educational Boarding
and Day 3–18
No of pupils: B373 G272
No of boarders: F151 W2
Fees: (September 08)
FB £17169–£23949
WB £22620–£22941
Day £6405–£14187

KENT COLLEGE INFANT &
JUNIOR SCHOOL
Vernon Holme, Harbledown,
Canterbury, Kent CT2 9AQ
Tel: (01227) 762436
Fax: (01227) 763880
Email: info@vernonholme.co.uk
Head: Mr A Carter
Type: Co-educational Day and
Boarding 3–11
No of pupils: B106 G94
No of boarders: F9
Fees: On application

THE KING'S SCHOOL
Canterbury, Kent CT1 2ES
Tel: (01227) 595501
Fax: (01227) 595595
Email: headmaster@
 kings-school.co.uk
Head: Rev Canon K H Wilkinson
Type: Co-educational Boarding
and Day 13–18
No of pupils: B434 G364
No of boarders: F639
Fees: On application

ST CHRISTOPHER'S SCHOOL
New Dover Road, Canterbury,
Kent CT1 3DT
Tel: (01227) 462960
Fax: (01227) 478220
Email: enquiries@
 stchristopherscanterbury.org.uk
Head: Mr D Evans
Type: Co-educational Day 3–11
No of pupils: B60 G70
Fees: On application

ST EDMUNDS JUNIOR
SCHOOL
St Thomas Hill, Canterbury, Kent
CT2 8HU
Tel: (01227) 475600
Fax: (01227) 471083
Email: info@stedmunds.org.uk
Head: Mr R G Bacon
Type: Co-educational Day and
Boarding 7–13
No of pupils: B110 G85
No of boarders: F40 W5
Fees: (September 08) FB £17424
WB £15300 Day £11841

ST EDMUND'S SCHOOL
CANTERBURY*
St Thomas Hill, Canterbury, Kent
CT2 8HU
Tel: (01227) 475600
Fax: (01227) 471083
Email: seniorschool@
 stedmunds.org.uk;
 juniorschool@stedmunds.org.uk
Head: Mr J M Gladwin
Type: Co-educational Day and
Boarding 3–18
No of pupils: B318 G215
No of boarders: F113
Fees: (September 08)
FB £16818–£24057 WB £15324
Day £11841–£15534

ST FAITH'S AT ASH SCHOOL
5 The Street, Ash, Canterbury,
Kent CT3 2HH
Tel: (01304) 813409
Fax: (01304) 813235
Email: st-faithsatash@
 tinyworld.co.uk
Head: Mr S G I Kerruish
Type: Co-educational Day 3–11
No of pupils: B109 G91
Fees: On application

STAFFORD HOUSE SCHOOL
OF ENGLISH
19 New Dover Road, Canterbury,
Kent CT1 3AH
Tel: (01227) 453237
Fax: (01227) 787740
Email: info@staffordhouse.com
Head: Ms Pat O'Donoghue
Type:
Fees: On application

CHISLEHURST

BABINGTON HOUSE
SCHOOL
Grange Drive, Chislehurst, Kent
BR7 5ES
Tel: (020) 8467 5537
Fax: (020) 8295 1175
Email: enquiries@
 babingtonhouse.com
Head: Miss D Odysseas-Bailey
Type: Girls Day 3–16 (Boys 3–7)
No of pupils: B65 G165
Fees: On application

DARUL ULOOM LONDON
Foxbury Avenue, Perry Street,
Chislehurst, Kent BR7 6SD
Tel: (020) 8295 0637
Fax: (020) 8467 0655
Email: info@
 darululoomlondon.co.uk
Head: Mr M Musa
Type: Boys Boarding 11–18
No of pupils: 160
No of boarders: F160
Fees: On application

England – Kent

FARRINGTONS SCHOOL*
Perry Street, Chislehurst, Kent
BR7 6LR
Tel: (020) 8467 0256
Fax: (020) 8467 5442
Email: admissions@
  farringtons.kent.sch.uk
Head: Mrs C E James
Type: Girls Day and Boarding
3–19
No of pupils: B40 G470
No of boarders: F46 W2
Fees: (September 08) FB £19800
WB £18600 Day £7830–£10830

CRANBROOK

BEDGEBURY SCHOOL
Bedgebury Park, Goudhurst,
Cranbrook, Kent TN17 2SH
Tel: (01580) 879100
Fax: (01580) 879102
Email: registrar@
  bedgeburyschool.co.uk
Head: Mrs H Moriarty and
Mr J Lambert
Type: Girls Boarding and Day
2–18 (Boys day 2–7)
No of pupils: B4 G293
No of boarders: F96 W49
Fees: On application

**BELL BEDGEBURY
INTERNATIONAL SCHOOL***
Goudhurst, Cranbrook, Kent
TN17 2SH
Tel: (01580) 879100
Fax: (01580) 879102
Email: bedgebury@
  bell-centres.com
Head: Mr E J Squires
Type: Co-educational Boarding
and Day 12–17
No of pupils: B30 G13
No of boarders: F40
Fees: (September 08) FB £22965

BENENDEN SCHOOL
Cranbrook, Kent TN17 4AA
Tel: (01580) 240592
Fax: (01580) 240280
Email: registry@
  benenden.kent.sch.uk
Head: Mrs C M Oulton
Type: Girls Boarding 11–18
No of pupils: 503
No of boarders: F503
Fees: On application

BETHANY SCHOOL[†]
Goudhurst, Curtisden Green,
Cranbrook, Kent TN17 1LB
Tel: (01580) 211273
Fax: (01580) 211151
Email: registrar@
  bethanyschool.org.uk
Head: Mr N.D.B. Dorey
Type: Co-educational Boarding
and Day 11–18
No of pupils: B289 G133
No of boarders: F60 W60
Fees: (September 08)
FB £21498–£22953
WB £29877–£22332
Day £13770–£15228

CRANBROOK SCHOOL*
Cranbrook, Kent TN17 3JD
Tel: (01580) 711800
Fax: (01580) 711828
Email: registrar@
  cranbrook.kent.sch.uk
Head: Mrs A S Daly
Type: Co-educational Day and
Boarding 13–18
No of pupils: B402 G354
No of boarders: F236
Fees: (September 07)
FB £8850–£9525

**DULWICH PREPARATORY
SCHOOL, CRANBROOK**
Coursehorn, Cranbrook, Kent
TN17 3NP
Tel: (01580) 712179
Fax: (01580) 715322
Email: registrar@dcpskent.org
Head: Mr S Duckitt
Type: Co-educational Day and
Boarding 3–13
No of pupils: B292 G232
No of boarders: W4
Fees: On application

DEAL

**NORTHBOURNE PARK
SCHOOL**
Betteshanger, Deal, Kent
CT14 0NW
Tel: (01304) 611215/8
Fax: (01304) 619020
Email: office@
  northbourne.kent.sch.uk
Head: Mr E Balfour
Type: Co-educational Day and
Boarding 3–13
No of pupils: B100 G82
No of boarders: F43
Fees: (September 08)
FB £15948–£18048
WB £14910–£17010
Day £7050–£12510

DOVER

DOVER COLLEGE[†]
Effingham Crescent, Dover, Kent
CT17 9RH
Tel: (01304) 205969
Fax: (01304) 242208
Email: registrar@
  dovercollege.org.uk
Head: Mr Stephen Jones
Type: Co-educational Boarding
and Day 4–18
No of pupils: B206 G154
No of boarders: F120 W13
Fees: (September 07)
FB £15630–£21570
WB £14670–£17160
Day £5250–£10770

**DUKE OF YORK'S ROYAL
MILITARY SCHOOL**
Dover, Kent CT15 5EQ
Tel: (01304) 245024
Fax: (01304) 245019
Email: headmaster@doyrms.com
Head: Mr C H Johnson
Type: Co-educational Boarding
11–18
No of pupils: B270 G230
No of boarders: F500
Fees: (September 08)
FB £1650–£7323

FAVERSHAM

LORENDEN PREPARATORY SCHOOL
Painter's Forstal, Faversham, Kent ME13 0EN
Tel: (01795) 590030
Fax: (01795) 538002
Email: admin@lorenden.org.uk
Head: Mrs P Tebbit
Type: Co-educational Day 3–11
No of pupils: B60 G60
Fees: (September 08)
Day £3060–£8142

GILLINGHAM

BRYONY SCHOOL
Marshall Road, Rainham, Gillingham, Kent ME8 0AJ
Tel: (01634) 231511
Fax: (01634) 311746
Head: Mr D E Edmunds and Mrs M P Edmunds
Type: Co-educational Day 2–11
No of pupils: B124 G118
Fees: On application

GRAVESEND

BRONTE SCHOOL
7 Pelham Road, Gravesend, Kent DA11 0HN
Tel: (01474) 533805
Fax: (01474) 352003
Email: enquiry@
 bronteschool.co.uk
Head: Mr R A Dyson
Type: Co-educational Day 3–11
No of pupils: B72 G54
Fees: (September 07)
Day £3675–£5775

COBHAM HALL*†
Cobham, Gravesend, Kent DA12 3BL
Tel: (01474) 823371
Fax: (01474) 825906
Email: enquiries@
 cobhamhall.com
Head: Mr P Mitchell
Type: Girls Boarding and Day 11–18
No of pupils: 200
No of boarders: F80 W20
Fees: (September 08)
F/WB £19800–£24900
Day £13200–£16500

CONVENT PREPARATORY SCHOOL
46 Old Road East, Gravesend, Kent DA12 1NR
Tel: (01474) 533012
Fax: (01474) 533012
Email: sisteranne@sjcps.org
Head: Sister A C O'Connell
Type: Co-educational Day 3–11
No of pupils: B110 G105
Fees: On application

ST JOSEPH'S CONVENT PREPARATORY SCHOOL
46 Old Road East, Gravesend, Kent DA12 1NR
Tel: 01474 533012
Email: headteacher@sjcps.org
Head: C Timney
Type: Co-educational
Fees: On application

HAWKHURST

MARLBOROUGH HOUSE SCHOOL
High Street, Hawkhurst, Kent TN18 4PY
Tel: (01580) 753555
Fax: (01580) 754281
Email: registrar@
 marlboroughhouse.kent.sch.uk
Head: Mr D N Hopkins
Type: Co-educational Day and Boarding 3–13
No of pupils: B192 G144
Fees: (September 08)
Day £3735–£12960

ST RONAN'S SCHOOL
Water Lane, Hawkhurst, Kent TN18 5DJ
Tel: (01580) 752271
Fax: (01580) 754882
Email: info@stronans.kent.sch.uk
Head: Mr W Trelawny-Vernon
Type: Co-educational Boarding and Day 3–13
No of pupils: B180 G120
No of boarders: W4
Fees: On application

LONGFIELD

STEEPHILL INDEPENDENT SCHOOL*
Castle Hill, Fawkham, Longfield, Kent DA3 7BG
Tel: (01474) 702107
Fax: (01474) 706011
Email: secretary@steephill.co.uk
Head: Mrs C Birtwell
Type: Co-educational Day 3–11
No of pupils: B60 G58
Fees: (September 08) Day £6735

MAIDSTONE

SHERNOLD SCHOOL
Hill Place, Queens Avenue, Maidstone, Kent ME16 0ER
Tel: (01622) 752868
Fax: (01622) 752868
Email: Shernold@
 shernold.plus.com
Head: Mrs L Dack
Type: Day
No of pupils: B52 G96
Fees: On application

SUTTON VALENCE PREPARATORY SCHOOL*
Church Road, Chart Sutton, Maidstone, Kent ME17 3RF
Tel: (01622) 842117
Fax: (01622) 844201
Email: enquiries@
 svprep.svs.org.uk
Head: Mr C A Gibbs
Type: Co-educational Day 3–11
No of pupils: B365 G166
Fees: (September 08)
Day £3495–£10080

SUTTON VALENCE SCHOOL*
Sutton Valence, Maidstone, Kent ME17 3HL
Tel: (01622) 845200
Fax: (01622) 844103
Email: enquiries@svs.org.uk
Head: Mr J S Davies
Type: Co-educational Boarding and Day 3–18
No of pupils: B565 G350
No of boarders: F47 W90
Fees: (September 08)
F/WB £18960–£24960
Day £6990–£15780

England – Kent

RAMSGATE

ST LAWRENCE COLLEGE JUNIOR SCHOOL
College Road, Ramsgate, Kent
CT11 7AF
Tel: (01843) 572912
Fax: (01843) 572913
Email: hjs@slcuk.com
Head: Mr S J E Whittle
Type: Co-educational Boarding and Day 3–11
No of pupils: B98 G92
No of boarders: F9
Fees: (September 08) F/WB £17505
Day £5406–£8700

ST LAWRENCE COLLEGE*
College Road, Ramsgate, Kent
CT11 7AE
Tel: (01843) 572931
Fax: (01843) 572901
Email: ah@slcuk.com
Head: Rev C W M Aitken
Type: Co-educational Boarding and Day 3–18
No of pupils: B300 G220
No of boarders: F214
Fees: (September 08)
F/WB £17505–£23292
Day £5406–£13641

ROCHESTER

GAD'S HILL SCHOOL
Higham, Rochester, Kent ME3 7PA
Tel: (01474) 822366
Fax: (01474) 822977
Email: admissions@
  gadshillschool.co.uk
Head: Mr D G Craggs
Type: Co-educational Day 3–16
No of pupils: B180 G180
Fees: On application

KING'S PREPARATORY SCHOOL
King Edward Road, Rochester,
Kent ME1 1UB
Tel: (01634) 888577
Fax: (01634) 888507
Email: walker@
  kings-school-rochester.co.uk
Head: Mr R Overend
Type: Co-educational Day and Boarding 8–13
No of pupils: B140 G70
No of boarders: F5
Fees: On application

KING'S SCHOOL ROCHESTER
Satis House, Boley Hill, Rochester,
Kent ME1 1TE
Tel: (01634) 888555
Fax: (01634) 888505
Email: walker@
  kings-school-rochester.co.uk
Head: Dr I R Walker
Type: Co-educational Day and Boarding 3–18
No of pupils: B413 G227
No of boarders: F49 W5
Fees: (September 08)
F/WB £17970–£25380
Day £6520–£15090

ROCHESTER INDEPENDENT COLLEGE*
Star Hill, Rochester, Kent ME1 1XF
Tel: (01634) 828115
Fax: (01634) 405667
Email: admissions@
  rochester-college.org
Head: Mr A Brownlow and Mr B Pain
Type: Co-educational Day and Boarding 11–21
No of pupils: B110 G110
No of boarders: F60
Fees: (September 08) FB £24426
Day £9450–£12750

ST ANDREW'S SCHOOL
24–28 Watts Avenue, Rochester,
Kent ME1 1SA
Tel: (01634) 843479
Fax: (01634) 840789
Email: jjabbour@cfbt.com
Head: Mrs J Jabbour
Type: Co-educational Day 3–11
No of pupils: B197 G186
Fees: (September 08)
Day £4813–£5090

SEVENOAKS

COMBE BANK SCHOOL
Combe Bank Drive, Sundridge,
Nr Sevenoaks, Kent TN14 6AE
Tel: (01959) 567166
Fax: (01959) 561997
Email: registrar@
  combebank.kent.sch.uk
Head: Mrs J Abbotts
Type: Girls Day 3–18
No of pupils: B13 G390
Fees: (September 08)
Day £7455–£13350

THE GRANVILLE SCHOOL
2 Bradbourne Park Road,
Sevenoaks, Kent TN13 3LJ
Tel: (01732) 453039
Fax: (01732) 743634
Email: granvilleschool@
  tiscali.co.uk
Head: Mrs Jane Scott
Type: Girls Day 3–11 (Boys 3–5)
No of pupils: B10 G190
Fees: (September 08)
Day £3945–£10200

THE NEW BEACON
Brittains Lane, Sevenoaks, Kent
TN13 2PB
Tel: (01732) 452131
Fax: (01732) 459509
Email: admin@
  newbeacon.kent.sch.uk
Head: Mr M Piercy
Type: Boys Day 4–13
No of pupils: 400
Fees: On application

RUSSELL HOUSE SCHOOL
Station Road, Otford, Sevenoaks,
Kent TN14 5QU
Tel: (01959) 522352
Fax: (01959) 524913
Email: head@
  russellhouse.kent.sch.uk
Head: Mrs A Cooke
Type: Co-educational Day 2–11
No of pupils: B100 G100
Fees: On application

ST MICHAEL'S SCHOOL
Otford Court, Otford, Sevenoaks,
Kent TN14 5SA
Tel: (01959) 522137
Fax: (01959) 526044
Email: office@
  stmichaels.kent.sch.uk
Head: Mr K S Crombie
Type: Co-educational Day 2–13
No of pupils: B260 G181
Fees: (September 07)
Day £1506–£9870

SEVENOAKS PREPARATORY SCHOOL
Godden Green, Sevenoaks, Kent
TN15 0JU
Tel: (01732) 762336
Fax: (01732) 764279
Email: admin@
  sevenoaksprep.kent.sch.uk
Head: Mr P J Oldroyd
Type: Co-educational Day 2–13
No of pupils: B230 G136
Fees: (September 08) Day £9840

SEVENOAKS SCHOOL*
Sevenoaks, Kent TN13 1HU
Tel: (01732) 455133
Fax: (01732) 456143
Email: regist@sevenoaksschool.org
Head: Mrs C L Ricks
Type: Co-educational Day and
Boarding 11–18
No of pupils: B473 G517
No of boarders: F342
Fees: (September 08)
FB £25554–£27720
Day £15936–£18102

SOLEFIELD SCHOOL
Solefields Road, Sevenoaks, Kent
TN13 1PH
Tel: (01732) 452142
Fax: (01732) 740388
Email: solefield.school@
btinternet.com
Head: Mr D Philps
Type: Boys Day 4–13
No of pupils: 160
Fees: On application

WALTHAMSTOW HALL
Hollybush Lane, Sevenoaks, Kent
TN13 3UL
Tel: (01732) 451334
Fax: (01732) 740439
Email: registrar@
walthamstowhall.kent.sch.uk
Head: Mrs J Milner
Type: Girls Day 0–18
No of pupils: 520
Fees: On application

SHEERNESS

ELLIOTT PARK SCHOOL
18–20 Marina Drive, Minster, Isle
of Sheppey, Sheerness, Kent
ME12 2DP
Tel: (01795) 873372
Fax: (01795) 873372
Email: elliottparkschool@
tiscali.co.uk
Head: Mr R Barson
Type: Co-educational Day 4–11
No of pupils: B30 G28
Fees: On application

SIDCUP

BENEDICT HOUSE PREPARATORY SCHOOL
1–5 Victoria Road, Sidcup, Kent
DA15 7HD
Tel: (020) 8300 7206
Fax: (020) 8309 6014
Email: office@
benedicthouseprepschool.co.uk
Head: Ms R Harries
Type: Co-educational Day 3–11
No of pupils: B70 G70
Fees: (September 07)
Day £3135–£7185

HARENC SCHOOL TRUST
167 Rectory Lane, Footscray,
Sidcup, Kent DA14 5BU
Tel: (020) 8309 0619
Fax: (020) 8309 5051
Email: info@harencschool.co.uk
Head: Miss S Woodward
Type: Boys Day 3–11
No of pupils: 160
Fees: (September 07)
Day £5616–£7362

MERTON COURT PREPARATORY SCHOOL
38 Knoll Road, Sidcup, Kent
DA14 4QU
Tel: (020) 8300 2112
Fax: (020) 8300 2112
Email: office@
mertoncourt.kent.sch.uk
Head: Mr D Price
Type: Co-educational Day 2–11
No of pupils: B180 G152
Fees: (September 08)
Day £5910–£8550

WEST LODGE PREPARATORY SCHOOL
36 Station Road, Sidcup, Kent
DA15 7DU
Tel: (020) 8300 2489
Fax: (020) 8308 1905
Email: info@westlodge.org.uk
Head: Mrs S Webb
Type: Co-educational Day 3–11
No of pupils: B56 G104
Fees: (September 08)
Day £4230–£7050

TONBRIDGE

DERWENT LODGE SCHOOL FOR GIRLS
Somerhill, Tonbridge, Kent
TN11 0NJ
Tel: (01732) 352124
Fax: (01732) 363381
Email: office@
schoolsatsomerhill.com
Head: Mrs E Hill
Type: Girls Day 7–11
No of pupils: 144
Fees: (September 08) Day £11115

FOSSE BANK SCHOOL
Mountains Country House, Noble
Tree Road, Hildenborough,
Tonbridge, Kent TN11 8ND
Tel: (01732) 834212
Fax: (01732) 834884
Email: office@
fossebankschool.co.uk
Head: Mrs G Lovatt-Young
Type: Co-educational Day 3–11
No of pupils: B67 G45
Fees: (September 07)
Day £2397–£8241

HILDEN GRANGE SCHOOL
62 Dry Hill Park Road, Tonbridge,
Kent TN10 3BX
Tel: (01732) 352706
Fax: (01732) 773360
Email: office@
hildengrange.gdst.net
Head: Mr J Withers
Type: Co-educational Day 3–13
No of pupils: B204 G100
Fees: (September 08)
Day £8586–£10413

HILDEN OAKS SCHOOL
38 Dry Hill Park Road, Tonbridge,
Kent TN10 3BU
Tel: (01732) 353941
Fax: (01732) 353942
Email: secretary@hildenoaks.co.uk
Head: Mrs S A Sunderland
Type: Co-educational Day
Boys 0–7 Girls 0–11
No of pupils: B16 G124
Fees: (September 08)
Day £6300–£8580

England – Kent

SACKVILLE SCHOOL
Tonbridge Road, Hildenborough,
Tonbridge, Kent TN11 9HN
Tel: (01732) 838888
Fax: (01732) 836404
Email: office@sackvilleschool.com
Head: Mr Philip Humphreys
Type: Co-educational Day 11–18
No of pupils: B181 G38
Fees: (September 08) Day £11070

**SOMERHILL
PRE-PREPARATORY SCHOOL**
Somerhill, Tonbridge, Kent
TN11 0NJ
Tel: (01732) 352124
Fax: (01732) 363381
Email: office@
    schoolsatsomerhill.com
Head: Mrs J R Sorensen
Type: Co-educational Day 3–7
No of pupils: 271
Fees: (September 08)
Day £3690–£8550

TONBRIDGE SCHOOL*
Tonbridge, Kent TN9 1JP
Tel: (01732) 304297
Fax: (01732) 363424
Email: admissions@
    tonbridge-school.org
Head: Mr T H P Haynes
Type: Boys Boarding and Day
13–18
No of pupils: 769
No of boarders: F441
Fees: (September 08) F/WB £28140
Day £20910

**YARDLEY COURT
PREPARATORY SCHOOL**
Somerhill, Tonbridge, Kent
TN11 0NJ
Tel: (01732) 352124
Fax: (01732) 363381
Email: office@
    schoolsatsomerhill.com
Head: Mr J T Coakley
Type: Boys Day 7–13
No of pupils: 231
Fees: (September 08) Day £11370

TUNBRIDGE WELLS

**BEECHWOOD SACRED
HEART SCHOOL***
Pembury Road, Tunbridge Wells,
Kent TN2 3QD
Tel: (01892) 532747
Fax: (01892) 536164
Email: registrar@
    beechwood.org.uk
Head: Mr N R Beesley
Type: Co-educational Boarding
and Day 3–18 (Boarding for Girls
only – from 11)
No of pupils: B87 G313
No of boarders: F60 W20
Fees: (September 08) FB £21945
WB £19380 Day £6285–£12945

HOLMEWOOD HOUSE*
Langton Green, Tunbridge Wells,
Kent TN3 0EB
Tel: (01892) 860006
Fax: (01892) 863970
Email: registrar@
    holmewood.kent.sch.uk
Head: Mr A S R Corbett
Type: Co-educational Day 3–13
No of pupils: B281 G193
Fees: (September 08)
Day £5165–£15165

KENT COLLEGE PEMBURY
Old Church Road, Tunbridge
Wells, Kent TN2 4AX
Tel: (01892) 822006
Fax: (01892) 820221
Email: admissions@
    kentcollege.kent.sch.uk
Head: Mrs Sally-Anne Huang
Type: Girls Boarding and Day
3–18
No of pupils: 550
No of boarders: F80 W10
Fees: (September 07)
F/WB £17220–£22395
Day £6330–£13890

THE MEAD SCHOOL
16 Frant Road, Tunbridge Wells,
Kent TN2 5SN
Tel: (01892) 525837
Fax: (01892) 525837
Email: meadschool@hotmail.co.uk
Head: Mrs A Culley
Type: Co-educational Day 3–11
No of pupils: B85 G85
Fees: (September 08)
Day £850–£2880

WEST WICKHAM

ST DAVID'S COLLEGE
Justin Hall, Beckenham Road,
West Wickham, Kent BR4 0QS
Tel: (020) 8777 5852
Fax: (020) 8777 9549
Email: stdavids@dial.pipex.com
Head: Mrs A Wagstaff and
Mrs S Adams
Type: Co-educational Day 4–11
No of pupils: B80 G63
Fees: On application

WICKHAM COURT SCHOOL
Layhams Road, West Wickham,
Kent BR4 9HW
Tel: (020) 8777 2942
Fax: (020) 8777 4276
Email: wickham@
    schillerintschool.com
Head: Ms B Hunter
Type: Co-educational Day 2–12
No of pupils: B76 G45
Fees: On application

WESTGATE-ON-SEA

CHARTFIELD SCHOOL
45 Minster Road, Westgate-on-
Sea, Kent CT8 8DA
Tel: (01843) 831716
Fax: (01843)221973
Email: chartfield1@btclick.com
Head: Mrs J L Prebble
Type: Co-educational Day 4–11
No of pupils: B39 G36
Fees: On application

LANCASHIRE

ACCRINGTON

HEATHLAND COLLEGE
Broadoak, Sandy Lane,
Accrington, Lancashire BB5 2AN
Tel: (01254) 234284
Fax: (01254) 235398
Email: bursar@
    heathlandcollege.co.uk
Head: Mrs J Harrison
Type: Co-educational Day 0–11
No of pupils: B30 G25
Fees: (September 08)
Day £4785–£6042

BLACKBURN

AL-ISLAH SCHOOL
108 Audley Range, Blackburn,
Lancashire BB1 1TF
Tel: (01254) 261573
Fax: (01254) 671604
Email: allslahschool@hotmail.com
Head: Ms F Patel
Type: Co-educational Day 5–16
No of pupils: B32 G213
Fees: (September 08) Day £1100

ISLAMIYAH SCHOOL
Willow Street, Little Harwood,
Blackburn, Lancashire BB1 5NQ
Tel: 01254 661259
Fax: 01254 661259
Email: z.seedat@
    blackburnmail.com
Head: Mrs Zarina Seedat
Type: Girls Day 11–16
No of pupils: 250
Fees: On application

MARKAZUL ULOOM
Park Lee Road, Blackburn,
Lancashire BB2 3NY
Tel: 01254 660026
Fax: 01254 279406
Head: Mrs Asiya Gajaria
Type: Girls Day 11–19
No of pupils: 220
Fees: On application

QUEEN ELIZABETH'S GRAMMAR SCHOOL
West Park Road, Blackburn,
Lancashire BB2 6DF
Tel: (01254) 686300
Fax: (01254) 692314
Email: headmaster@
    qegs.blackburn.sch.uk
Head: Mr S A Corns
Type: Co-educational Day 3–18
No of pupils: B592 G110
Fees: (September 08)
Day £5001–£8829

RAWDHA TUL ULOOM
19 Dock Street, Blackburn,
Lancashire BB1 3AT
Tel: 01254 670017
Email: info@
    gardenofknowledge.org
Head: Mr A W Waswany
Type: Co-educational Day 4–11
No of pupils: B49 G44
Fees: On application

TAUHEEDUL ISLAM GIRLS HIGH SCHOOL
31 Bicknell Street, Blackburn,
Lancashire BB1 7EY
Tel: (01254) 54021
Fax: (01254) 54021
Email: admin@tighs.com
Head: Mr I Patel
Type: Girls Day 11–16
No of pupils: 265
Fees: On application

WESTHOLME SCHOOL
Wilmar Lodge, Meins Road,
Blackburn, Lancashire BB2 6QU
Tel: (01254) 506070
Fax: (01254) 506080
Email: principal@
    westholmeschool.com
Head: Mrs L Croston
Type: Girls Day 3–18 (Boys 3–7)
No of pupils: B102 G987
Fees: (September 08)
Day £4740–£7530

BLACKPOOL

ARNOLD SCHOOL
Lytham Road, Blackpool,
Lancashire FY4 1JG
Tel: (01253) 346391
Fax: (01253) 336250
Email: Admissions.Arnold@
    church-schools.com
Head: Mr B M Hughes
Type: Co-educational Day 2–18
No of pupils: B420 G417
Fees: (September 08)
Day £6387–£8334

EMMANUEL CHRISTIAN SCHOOL
Fylde Community, Blackpool,
Lancashire FY3 0BE
Tel: (01253) 882873
Fax: (01253) 892022
Email: office@ecs@yahoo.co.uk
Head: Mr M Derry and
Mrs P Derry
Type: Co-educational Day 5–16
No of pupils: 71
Fees: On application

LANGDALE PREPARATORY SCHOOL
95 Warbreck Drive, Blackpool,
Lancashire FY2 9RZ
Tel: (01253) 354812
Fax: (01253) 354812
Email: langdaleschool@
    btconnect.com
Head: Miss M J Hayes and
Mr P G E Clay
Type: Co-educational Day 3–11
No of pupils: B46 G46
Fees: (September 08)
Day £3000–£3700

BOLTON

BOLTON MUSLIM GIRLS SCHOOL
Swan Lane, Bolton, Lancashire
BL3 6TQ
Tel: (01204) 361103
Fax: (01204) 533220
Email: idrish.patel@bmgs.uk
Head: Mr I A Patel
Type: Girls Day 11–16
No of pupils: 374
Fees: On application

BOLTON SCHOOL (BOYS' DIVISION)
Chorley New Road, Bolton,
Lancashire BL1 4PA
Tel: (01204) 840201
Fax: (01204) 849477
Email: hm@boys.bolton.sch.uk
Head: Mr M E W Brooker
Type: Boys Day 7–18
No of pupils: 1106
Fees: (September 08)
Day £6243–£8331

BOLTON SCHOOL (GIRLS' DIVISION)
Chorley New Road, Bolton,
Lancashire BL1 4PB
Tel: (01204) 840201
Fax: (01204) 434710
Email: info@girls.bolton.sch.uk
Head: Mrs G Richards
Type: Girls Day 4–18 (Boys 4–7)
No of pupils: B99 G1117
Fees: On application

CLEVELANDS PREPARATORY SCHOOL
Chorley New Road, Bolton,
Lancashire BL1 5DH
Tel: (01204) 843898
Fax: (01204) 848007
Email: clevelands@indschool.org
Head: Mrs L Parlane
Type: Co-educational Day 2–11
No of pupils: B90 G90
Fees: (September 07) Day £5148

LORD'S COLLEGE
53 Manchester Road, Bolton,
Lancashire BL2 1ES
Tel: (01204) 523731
Head: Mrs H Seager
Type: Co-educational Day 10–17
No of pupils: B40 G35
Fees: On application

BURNLEY

ST JOSEPH'S SCHOOL, PARK HILL
Park Hill, Padiham Road, Burnley,
Lancashire BB12 6TG
Tel: (01282) 455622
Fax: (01282) 435375
Email: parkhillschool@aol.com
Type: Co-educational Day 3–11
No of pupils: B54 G55
Fees: (September 08) Day £4320

BURY

BURY CATHOLIC PREPARATORY SCHOOL
Arden House, 172 Manchester
Road, Bury, Lancashire BL9 9BH
Tel: (0161) 764 2346
Fax: (0161) 764 2346
Email: admin@
   burycatholicprepschool.co.uk
Head: Mrs A C Dean
Type: Co-educational Day 3–11
No of pupils: B73 G61
Fees: On application

BURY GRAMMAR SCHOOL BOYS
Tenterden Street, Bury, Lancashire
BL9 0HN
Tel: (0161) 797 2700
Fax: (0161) 763 4655
Email: info@bgsboys.co.uk
Head: Rev S C Harvey
Type: Boys Day 7–18
No of pupils: 765
Fees: On application

BURY GRAMMAR SCHOOL GIRLS
Bridge Road, Bury, Lancashire
BL9 0HH
Tel: (0161) 797 2808
Fax: (0161) 763 4658
Email: info@bgsg.bury.sch.uk
Head: Mrs R S Georghiou
Type: Girls Day 3–18 (Boys 4–7)
No of pupils: B88 G912
Fees: On application

THE POTTERS HOUSE SCHOOL
6 Arley Avenue, Bury, Lancashire
BL9 5HD
Tel: (0161) 7051885
Fax: (0161) 7051885
Head: Mrs Catherine M Mitchell
Type: Co-educational Day 5–10
No of pupils: B6 G3
Fees: On application

CHORLEY

THE BENNETT HOUSE SCHOOL
332 Eaves Lane, Chorley,
Lancashire PR6 0DX
Tel: (01257) 267393
Fax: (01257) 262838
Email: catherine@
   bennetthouse332.fsnet.co.uk
Head: Mrs C A Mills
Type: Co-educational Day 0–11
No of pupils: B18 G17
Fees: (September 07)
Day £1500–£10000

CLITHEROE

MOORLAND SCHOOL
Ribblesdale Avenue, Clitheroe,
Lancashire BB7 2JA
Tel: (01200) 423833
Fax: (01200) 429339
Email: bursar@
   moorlandschool.co.uk
Head: Mr P Smith
Type: Co-educational Boarding
and Day 1–16
No of pupils: B150 G150
No of boarders: F58 W4
Fees: (September 07)
FB £13000–£16200
WB £12600–£15300
Day £4620–£6225

OAKHILL COLLEGE
Wiswell Lane, Whalley, Clitheroe,
Lancashire BB7 9AF
Tel: (01254) 823546
Fax: (01254) 822662
Email: enquiries@
   oakhillcollege.co.uk
Head: Mr M Kennedy
Type: Co-educational Day 2–16
No of pupils: B143 G137
Fees: On application

STONYHURST COLLEGE*
Stonyhurst, Clitheroe, Lancashire
BB7 9PZ
Tel: (01254) 827073
Fax: (01254) 827135
Email: admissions@
   stonyhurst.ac.uk
Head: Mr A R Johnson
Type: Co-educational Boarding
and Day 13–18
No of pupils: B309 G154
No of boarders: F242 W50
Fees: (September 08) FB £24192
WB £20700 Day £14142

FLEETWOOD

ROSSALL JUNIOR SCHOOL
Fleetwood, Lancashire FY7 8JW
Tel: (01253) 774222
Fax: (01253) 774222
Email: enquiries@
  rossallcorporation.co.uk
Head: Mr S Winkley
Type: Co-educational Day and
Boarding 2–11
No of pupils: B71 G67
No of boarders: F3
Fees: (September 08)
Day £14910–£26490

ROSSALL SCHOOL
Fleetwood, Lancashire FY7 8JW
Tel: (01253) 774201
Fax: (01253) 772052
Email: enquiries@
  rossallcorporation.co.uk
Head: Dr S Winkley
Type: Co-educational Boarding
and Day 11–18
No of pupils: B242 G184
No of boarders: F180
Fees: On application

ROSSALL SCHOOL
INTERNATIONAL STUDY
CENTRE
Rossall School, Broadway,
Fleetwood, Lancashire FY7 8JW
Tel: (01253) 774204
Fax: (01253) 779415
Email: isc@
  rossallcorporation.co.uk
Head: Mr D Rose
Type: Co-educational Boarding
11–16
No of pupils: B60 G20
No of boarders: F80
Fees: On application

HORWICH

RIVINGTON PARK
INDEPENDENT SCHOOL
Knowle House, Rivington Lane,
Rivington, Horwich, Lancashire
BL6 7RX
Tel: (01204) 669332
Fax: (01204) 696891
Email: info@
  rivingtonparkschool.co.uk
Head: Mr Michael Ruaux
Type: Co-educational Day 1–16
No of pupils: B49 G43
Fees: On application

LANCASTER

JAMEA AL KAUTHAR
Ashton Road, Lancaster,
Lancashire LA1 5AJ
Tel: (01524) 389898
Fax: (01524) 389333
Head: Ms Aneesa Sajid
Type: Girls Boarding 11–19
No of pupils: 392
No of boarders: F392
Fees: On application

LANCASTER STEINER
SCHOOL
Lune Road, Lancaster, Lancashire
LA1 5QU
Tel: 01524 841351
Email: lancastersteinerschool@
  yahoo.co.uk
Head: Mr Mark Bamford
Type: Co-educational Day 5–14
No of pupils: B24 G24
Fees: On application

LEYLAND

STONEHOUSE NURSERY
SCHOOL
90 School Lane, Leyland,
Lancashire PR25 2TU
Tel: (01772) 435529
Fax: (01772) 622093
Email: welcome.stonehouse@
  fsmail.net
Head: Mrs Linda Williams
Type: Co-educational Day 0–5
No of pupils: B14 G13
Fees: (September 08)
Day £5625–£5925

LYTHAM ST ANNES

KING EDWARD VII AND
QUEEN MARY SCHOOL
Clifton Drive South, Lytham St
Annes, Lancashire FY8 1DT
Tel: (01253) 784100
Fax: (01253) 784150
Email: admin@keqms.co.uk
Head: Mr R J Karling
Type: Co-educational Day 2–18
No of pupils: B366 G315
Fees: On application

ST ANNE'S COLLEGE
GRAMMAR SCHOOL
293 Clifton Drive South, St Annes-
on-Sea, Lytham St Annes,
Lancashire FY8 1HN
Tel: (01253) 725815
Fax: (01253) 782250
Email: principal@
  collgram.u-net.com
Head: Mr S R Welsby
Type: Co-educational Day and
Boarding 3–18
No of pupils: B109 G111
No of boarders: F11 W2
Fees: On application

OLDHAM

FARROWDALE HOUSE
PREPARATORY SCHOOL
Farrow Street, Shaw, Oldham,
Lancashire OL2 7AD
Tel: (01706) 844533
Email: farrowdale@aol.com
Head: Mr F G Wilkinson
Type: Co-educational Day 3–11
No of pupils: B56 G57
Fees: On application

FIRWOOD MANOR PREP
SCHOOL
Broadway, Chadderton, Oldham,
Lancashire OL9 0AD
Tel: (0161) 620 6570
Fax: (0161) 626 3550
Email: admin@
  firwoodmanor.org.uk
Head: Mrs P M Wild
Type: Co-educational Day 2–11
No of pupils: B79 G62
Fees: On application

GRASSCROFT
INDEPENDENT SCHOOL
Lydgate Parish Hall, Stockport
Road, Lydgate, Oldham,
Lancashire OL4 4JJ
Tel: (01457) 820485
Head: Mrs J O'Hara
Type: Co-educational Day 2–7
No of pupils: 45
Fees: On application

THE HULME GRAMMAR SCHOOL FOR GIRLS
Chamber Road, Oldham,
Lancashire OL8 4BX
Tel: (0161) 624 2523
Fax: (0161) 620 0234
Email: girlsinfo@
  hulmegrammarschools.org.uk
Head: Dr P G Neeson
Type: Girls Day 3–18
No of pupils: 571
Fees: (September 08)
Day £5013–£7866

THE OLDHAM HULME GRAMMAR SCHOOL
Chamber Road, Oldham,
Lancashire OL8 4BX
Tel: (0161) 624 4497
Fax: (0161) 652 4107
Email: boysenq@
  hulmegrammarschool.org.uk
Head: Dr P G Neeson
Type: Boys Day 7–18
No of pupils: 719
Fees: (September 08)
Day £5649–£7866

OLDHAM HULME KINDERGARTEN
Plum Street, Oldham, Lancashire
OL8 1TJ
Tel: (0161) 624 2947
Fax: (0161) 628 9756
Email: admin@
  hulmekindergarten.co.uk
Head: Mrs A S Richards
Type: Co-educational Day 3–7
No of pupils: B46 G53
Fees: On application

SADDLEWORTH PREPARATORY SCHOOL
Huddersfield Road, Scouthead,
Oldham, Lancashire OL4 4AG
Tel: (01457) 877442
Email: info@
  saddleworthpreparatoryschool.
  org.uk
Head: Mrs L W K Hirst
Type: Co-educational Day 4–7
No of pupils: B27 G29
Fees: On application

ORMSKIRK

KINGSWOOD COLLEGE TRUST[†]
Southport Road, Ormskirk,
Lancashire L40 9RQ
Tel: (01704) 880200
Fax: (01704) 880032
Email: admin@
  kingswoodcollege.co.uk
Head: Mr E J Borowski
Type: Co-educational Day 2–16
No of pupils: B182 G196
Fees: (September 08)
Day £4140–£7920

MAHARISHI SCHOOL
Ashtons Farm, Cobbs Brow Lane,
Lathom, Ormskirk, Lancashire
L40 6JJ
Tel: 01695 729912
Fax: 01695 729030
Email: enquiries@
  maharishischool.com
Type: Co-educational 4–16
No of pupils: 78
Fees: On application

PRESTON

ASHBRIDGE INDEPENDENT SCHOOL
Lindle Lane, Hutton, Preston,
Lancashire PR4 4AQ
Tel: 01772 619900
Fax: 01772 610894
Email: info@
  ashbridgeschool.co.uk
Head: Mrs Hilary Sharples
Type: Co-educational Day 2–11
No of pupils: B154 G129
Fees: On application

HIGHFIELD PRIORY SCHOOL
Fulwood Row, Fulwood, Preston,
Lancashire PR2 6SL
Tel: (01772) 709624
Fax: (01772) 655621
Email: info@highfieldpriory.co.uk
Head: Mr D Williams
Type: Co-educational Day 2–11
No of pupils: B134 G139
Fees: On application

KIRKHAM GRAMMAR SCHOOL
Ribby Road, Kirkham, Preston,
Lancashire PR4 2BH
Tel: (01772) 671079
Fax: (01772) 672747
Email: info@
  kirkhamgrammar.co.uk
Head: Mr D R Walker
Type: Co-educational Boarding
and Day 3–18
No of pupils: B492 G459
No of boarders: F67 W5
Fees: (September 07) FB £14349
WB £14017 Day £7704

ST PIUS X PREPARATORY SCHOOL
200 Garstang Road, Fulwood,
Preston, Lancashire PR2 8RD
Tel: (01772) 719937
Fax: (01772) 787535
Email: st-pius-x@supanet.com
Head: Miss B Banks
Type: Co-educational Day 2–11
No of pupils: B136 G151
Fees: (September 08) Day £5700

ROCHDALE

BEECH HOUSE SCHOOL
184 Manchester Road, Rochdale,
Lancashire OL11 4JQ
Tel: (01706) 646309
Fax: (01706) 860685
Email: bschool119@aol.com
Head: Mr K Sartain
Type: Co-educational Day 3–16
No of pupils: B135 G140
Fees: (September 08)
Day £2100–£4938

ROCHDALE GIRLS SCHOOL
36 Taylor Street, Rochdale,
Lancashire OL12 0HX
Fax: (01706) 646642
Head: Mr A Razzak
Type: Girls Day 11–16
No of pupils: 120
Fees: On application

SALFORD

TASHBAR SCHOOL
20 Upper Park Road, Salford,
Lancashire M7 4HL
Tel: (0161) 7208254
Fax: (0161) 7208146
Head: Mr A Pinczewski
Type: Boys Day 2–11
No of pupils: 325
Fees: On application

STONYHURST

ST MARY'S HALL*
Stonyhurst, Lancashire BB7 9PU
Tel: (01254) 826242
Fax: (01254) 827316
Email: t.ashton@stonyhurst.ac.uk
Head: Mr L A Crouch
Type: Co-educational Boarding
and Day 3–13
No of pupils: B157 G112
No of boarders: F43 W9
Fees: (September 08) FB £17049
WB £14997 Day £5934–£11832

LEICESTERSHIRE

ASHBY-DE-LA-ZOUCH

MANOR HOUSE SCHOOL
South Street, Ashby-de-la-Zouch,
Leicestershire LE65 1BR
Tel: (01530) 412932
Fax: (01530) 417435
Email: enquiries@
manorhouseashby.co.uk
Head: Mr I R Clews
Type: Co-educational Day 4–16
No of pupils: B72 G78
Fees: (September 08)
Day £5232–£7614

LEICESTER

AL-AQSA PRIMARY SCHOOL
The Wayne Way, Leicester,
Leicestershire LE5 4PP
Tel: (0116) 276 0953
Fax: (0116) 276 9791
Email: alaqsa@tiscali.co.uk
Head: Mr Ibrahim Hewitt
Type: Co-educational Day 3–11
Fees: On application

**GRACE DIEU MANOR
SCHOOL**
Grace Dieu, Thringstone,
Leicester, Leicestershire LE67 5UG
Tel: (01530) 222276
Fax: (01530) 223184
Email: registrar@gracedieu.com
Head: Mr C E Foulds
Type: Co-educational Day 3–13
No of pupils: B173 G146
Fees: (September 08)
Day £6315–£9456

IRWIN COLLEGE
164 London Road, Leicester,
Leicestershire LE2 1ND
Tel: (0116) 255 2648
Fax: (0116) 285 4935
Email: registrar@
irwincollege.wireless.pipex.net
Head: Mrs L G Tonks
Type: Co-educational Boarding
and Day 14–25
No of pupils: B110 G70
No of boarders: F160
Fees: On application

**LEICESTER GRAMMAR
JUNIOR SCHOOL**
Evington Hall, Spencefield Lane,
Leicester, Leicestershire LE5 6HN
Tel: (0116) 210 1299
Fax: (0116) 210 0432
Email: redfearnm@
leicestergrammar.org.uk
Head: Mrs M Redfearn
Type: Co-educational Day 3–11
No of pupils: B131 G117
Fees: On application

**LEICESTER GRAMMAR
SCHOOL**
8 Peacock Lane, Leicester,
Leicestershire LE1 5PX
Tel: (0116) 222 0400
Fax: (0116) 291 0505
Email: admissions@
leicestergrammar.org.uk
Head: Mr C P M King
Type: Co-educational Day 10–18
No of pupils: B383 G305
Fees: On application

**LEICESTER HIGH SCHOOL
FOR GIRLS**
454 London Road, Leicester,
Leicestershire LE2 2PP
Tel: (0116) 270 5338
Fax: (0116) 2448823
Email: enquiries@
leicesterhigh.co.uk
Head: Mrs J Burns
Type: Girls Day 3–18
No of pupils: 435
Fees: (September 08)
Day £5925–£8700

**LEICESTER MONTESSORI
GRAMMAR SCHOOL**
58 Stoneygate Road, Leicester,
Leicestershire LE2 2BN
Tel: (0116) 255 4441
Email: office@
montessorigroup.com
Head: Mrs D Bailey
Type: Co-educational Day 3–18
No of pupils: 300
Fees: On application

**LEICESTER MONTESSORI
SCHOOL**
194 London Road, Leicester,
Leicestershire LE1 1ND
Tel: (0116) 270 6667
Fax: (0116) 255 4440
Email: office@
montessorigroup.com
Head: Mrs D Bailey
Type: Co-educational Day 0–18
No of pupils: B90 G100
Fees: On application

RATCLIFFE COLLEGE*
Fosse Way, Ratcliffe on the
Wreake, Leicester, Leicestershire
LE7 4SG
Tel: (01509) 817000
Fax: (01509) 817004
Email: registrar@
    ratcliffe.leics.sch.uk
Head: Mr G Lloyd
Type: Co-educational Boarding
and Day 3–18
No of pupils: B388 G289
No of boarders: F94 W1
Fees: (September 08) FB £18846
WB £15198 Day £6690–£12498

ST CRISPIN'S SCHOOL[†]
6 St Mary's Road, Leicester,
Leicestershire LE2 1XA
Tel: (0116) 270 7648
Email: enquiries@stcrispins.co.uk
Head: Mrs D Lofthouse and
Mr J Lofthouse
Type: Co-educational Day 3–16
No of pupils: B75 G25
Fees: On application

STONEYGATE COLLEGE
2 Albert Road, Stoneygate,
Leicester, Leicestershire LE2 2AA
Tel: (0116) 270 7414
Fax: (0116) 270 7414
Email: office@
    stoneygatecollege.co.uk
Head: Dr S Cooper
Type: Co-educational Day 3–11
No of pupils: B61 G70
Fees: (September 08)
Day £4530–£5820

STONEYGATE SCHOOL
London Road, Great Glen,
Leicester, Leicestershire LE8 9DJ
Tel: (0116) 259 2282
Fax: (0116) 259 2176
Email: school@
    stoneygateschool.co.uk
Head: Mr J H Morris
Type: Co-educational Day 3–13
No of pupils: B180 G160
Fees: On application

TINY TOTS PRE- SCHOOL
16–20 Beal Street, Leicester,
Leicestershire LE2 0AA
Tel: (0116) 2515345
Head: Mr N Hussein
Type: Co-educational Day 5–7
No of pupils: B21 G27
Fees: On application

LOUGHBOROUGH

**ARLEY HOUSE PNEU
SCHOOL**
8 Station Road, East Leake,
Loughborough, Leicestershire
LE12 6LQ
Tel: (01509) 852229
Fax: (01509) 852229
Email: office@
    arley-pneu.eastleake.sch.uk
Head: Mrs C M Anderton
Type: Co-educational Day 3–11
No of pupils: B30 G26
Fees: (September 07)
Day £6555–£6975

**FAIRFIELD PREPARATORY
SCHOOL**
Leicester Road, Loughborough,
Leicestershire LE11 2AE
Tel: (01509) 215172
Fax: (01509) 238648
Email: admin@lesfairfield.org
Head: Mr R Outwin-Flinders
Type: Co-educational Day 4–11
No of pupils: B256 G250
Fees: On application

**LOUGHBOROUGH
GRAMMAR SCHOOL**
Burton Walks, Loughborough,
Leicestershire LE11 2DU
Tel: (01509) 233233
Fax: (01509) 218436
Email: registrar@
    loughgs.leics.sch.uk
Head: Mr P B Fisher
Type: Boys Day and Boarding
10–18
No of pupils: 1010
No of boarders: F38 W10
Fees: On application

**LOUGHBOROUGH HIGH
SCHOOL**
Burton Walks, Loughborough,
Leicestershire LE11 2DU
Tel: (01509) 212348
Fax: (01509) 215720
Email: admin@leshigh.org
Head: Miss B O'Connor
Type: Girls Day 11–18
No of pupils: 600
Fees: (September 08) Day £8793

**OUR LADY'S CONVENT
SCHOOL**
Burton Street, Loughborough,
Leicestershire LE11 2DT
Tel: (01509) 263901
Fax: (01509) 236193
Email: office@olcs.leics.sch.uk
Head: Mrs P Hawley
Type: Co-educational Day
Boys 3–11 Girls 3–18
No of pupils: B7 G500
Fees: (September 07)
Day £5925–£8280

MARKET BOSWORTH

**THE DIXIE GRAMMAR
SCHOOL**
Station Road, Market Bosworth,
Leicestershire CV13 0LE
Tel: (01455) 292244
Fax: (01455) 292151
Email: info@dixie.org.uk
Head: Mr J Wood
Type: Co-educational Day 3–18
No of pupils: B280 G272
Fees: (September 08)
Day £6015–£8280

MARKET HARBOROUGH

BROOKE HOUSE COLLEGE*
Leicester Road, Market
Harborough, Leicestershire
LE16 7AU
Tel: (01858) 462452
Fax: (01858) 462487
Email: enquiries@
    brookehouse.com
Head: Mr G E I Williams
Type: Co-educational Boarding
and Day 14–19
No of pupils: B100 G80
No of boarders: F175
Fees: (September 08) FB £19350
WB £10900 Day £10900

LINCOLNSHIRE

ALFORD

MAYPOLE HOUSE SCHOOL
Well Vale Hall, Alford,
Lincolnshire LN13 0ET
Tel: (01507) 462764
Fax: (01507) 462681
Email: info@
  maypolehouseschool.co.uk
Head: Mrs A White
Type: Co-educational Day 3–16
No of pupils: B20 G20
Fees: On application

BOSTON

BICKER PREPARATORY SCHOOL
School Lane, Bicker, Boston,
Lincolnshire PE20 3DW
Tel: (01775) 821786
Fax: (01775) 821786
Head: Mrs S A Page
Type: Co-educational Day 3–11
No of pupils: B40 G40
Fees: (September 08)
Day £3975–£4095

CONWAY PREPARATORY SCHOOL
Tunnard Street, Boston,
Lincolnshire PE21 6PL
Tel: (01205) 363150/355539
Fax: (01205) 363150
Email: conway@
  conwayschool.demon.co.uk
Head: Mr D A Wilson
Type: Co-educational Day 2–11
No of pupils: B30 G30
Fees: On application

FRISKNEY PRIVATE SCHOOL
Church Lane, Friskney, Boston,
Lincolnshire PE22 8NA
Tel: 01754 820970
Fax: 01754 820970
Head: Mrs D Wilcox
Type: Co-educational Day 5–10
No of pupils: B12 G7
Fees: On application

BOURNE

KIRKSTONE HOUSE SCHOOL
Main Street, Baston,
PETERBOROUGH, Bourne,
Lincolnshire PE6 9PA
Tel: (01778) 560350
Fax: (01778) 560547
Email: info@
  kirkstonehouseschool.co.uk
Head: Miss M Pepper
Type: Co-educational Day 4–16
No of pupils: B139 G73
Fees: (September 08)
Day £4401–£8115

WITHAM HALL
Witham-on-the-Hill, Bourne,
Lincolnshire PE10 0JJ
Tel: (01778) 590222
Fax: (01778) 590606
Email: heads@withamhall.com
Head: Mr D Telfer and Mrs S A Telfer
Type: Co-educational Boarding and Day 4–13
No of pupils: B120 G115
No of boarders: W40
Fees: (September 08) F/WB £14850
Day £6645–£10875

GAINSBOROUGH

HANDEL HOUSE PREPARATORY SCHOOL
Northolme, Gainsborough,
Lincolnshire DN21 2JB
Tel: (01427) 612426
Fax: (01427) 612426
Email:
  handelhouseschoolheadteacher@btinternet.com
Head: Mrs V C Haigh
Type: Co-educational Day 2–11
No of pupils: B30 G29
Fees: (September 08)
Day £2580–£3075

GRANTHAM

DUDLEY HOUSE SCHOOL
1 Dudley Road, Grantham,
Lincolnshire NG31 9AA
Tel: (01476) 400184
Fax: (01476) 400184
Email: headteacher@
  dudleyhouseschool.co.uk
Head: Mrs JH Johnson
Type: Co-educational Day 3–11
No of pupils: B38 G22
Fees: (September 08) Day £3660

THE GRANTHAM PREPARATORY SCHOOL
Gorse Lane, Grantham,
Lincolnshire NG31 7UF
Tel: (01476) 593293
Fax: (01476) 593293
Email: admin@
  granthamprep.co.uk
Head: Mrs K A Korcz
Type: Co-educational Day 3–11
No of pupils: B53 G51
Fees: (September 08)
Day £4548–£6600

LINCOLN

LINCOLN MINSTER SCHOOL*
The Prior Building, Upper Lindum Street, Lincoln, Lincolnshire LN2 5RW
Tel: (01522) 551300
Fax: (01522) 551310
Email: enquiries.lincoln@
  church-schools.com
Head: Mr C Rickart
Type: Co-educational Day and Boarding 2–18
No of pupils: 802
Fees: (September 07)
FB £16266–£18867
WB £15075–£17457
Day £6834–£9969

ST MARY'S PREPARATORY SCHOOL
5 Pottergate, Lincoln, Lincolnshire LN2 1PH
Tel: (01522) 524622
Fax: (01522) 523637
Email: office@
    st-marys-prep.lincs.sch.uk
Head: Mr A A Salmond Smith
Type: Co-educational Day 2–11
No of pupils: B112 G108
Fees: On application

LOUTH

GREENWICH HOUSE INDEPENDENT SCHOOL
106 High Holme Road, Louth, Lincolnshire LN11 0HE
Tel: (01507) 609252
Fax: (01507) 606294
Head: Mrs J M Brindle
Type: Co-educational Day 0–11
No of pupils: 150
Fees: On application

MANBY

LOCKSLEY CHRISTIAN SCHOOL
Bilney Block, Manby Park, Manby, Lincolnshire LN11 8UT
Tel: 01507 327859
Fax: 01507 328512
Email: locksleychristianschool@
    hotmail.com
Head: Mrs A P Franklin
Type: Co-educational Day 3–19
No of pupils: B31 G33
Fees: On application

SKEGNESS

VIKING SCHOOL
140 Church Road North, Skegness, Lincolnshire PE25 2QJ
Tel: 01754 765749
Fax: 01754 765749
Head: Mrs S Barker
Type: Co-educational Day 2–11
No of pupils: B65 G60
Fees: On application

SLEAFORD

FEN SCHOOL
Side Bar Lane, Heckington Fen, Sleaford, Lincolnshire NG34 9LY
Tel: (01529) 460966
Head: Mrs J M Dunkley
Type: Co-educational Day 2–16
No of pupils: B14 G16
Fees: On application

SPALDING

AYSCOUGHFEE HALL SCHOOL
Welland Hall, London Road, Spalding, Lincolnshire PE11 2TE
Tel: (01775) 724733
Fax: (01775) 769669
Email: admin@ahs.me.uk
Head: Mr B Chittick
Type: Co-educational Day 3–11
No of pupils: B70 G83
Fees: (September 07)
Day £3840–£4680

STAMFORD

COPTHILL SCHOOL
Barnack Road, Uffington, Stamford, Lincolnshire PE9 4TD
Tel: (01780) 757506
Fax: (01780) 482938
Email: copthill@btinternet.com
Head: Mr J A Teesdale
Type: Co-educational Day 2–11
No of pupils: B149 G140
Fees: On application

STAMFORD HIGH SCHOOL
St Martin's, Stamford, Lincolnshire PE9 2LL
Tel: (01780) 484200
Fax: (01780) 484201
Email: headshs@ses.lincs.sch.uk
Head: Mrs Y L Powell
Type: Girls Day and Boarding 11–18
No of pupils: 633
No of boarders: F41 W5
Fees: (September 08) FB £20304
WB £20196 Day £10848

STAMFORD JUNIOR SCHOOL
Stamford, Lincolnshire PE9 2LR
Tel: (01780) 484400
Fax: (01780) 484401
Email: headjs@ses.lincs.sch.uk
Head: Miss E M Craig
Type: Co-educational Boarding and Day 2–11
No of pupils: B169 G172
No of boarders: F2 W6
Fees: (September 07) FB £16416
WB £16322 Day £8028

STAMFORD SCHOOL
St Paul's Street, Stamford, Lincolnshire PE9 2BQ
Tel: (01780) 750300/1
Fax: (01780) 750336
Email: headss@ses.lincs.sch.uk
Head: Dr P R Mason
Type: Boys Day and Boarding 11–18
No of pupils:
No of boarders: F75 W10
Fees: On application

WOODHALL SPA

ST HUGH'S SCHOOL
Cromwell Avenue, Woodhall Spa, Lincolnshire LN10 6TQ
Tel: (01526) 352169
Fax: (01526) 351520
Email: sthughs-schooloffice@
    btconnect.com
Head: Mr S G Greenish
Type: Co-educational Boarding and Day 2–13
No of pupils: B111 G92
No of boarders: F46
Fees: (September 08)
F/WB £14010–£14250
Day £5775–£10680

NORTH EAST LINCOLNSHIRE

GRIMSBY

ST JAMES' SCHOOL
22 Bargate, Grimsby, North East
Lincolnshire DN34 4SY
Tel: (01472) 503260
Fax: (01472) 503275
Email: enquiries@
  saintjamesschool.co.uk
Head: Mrs S M Isaac
Type: Co-educational Day and
Boarding 2–18
No of pupils: B128 G108
No of boarders: F30
Fees: On application

ST MARTIN'S PREPARATORY SCHOOL
63 Bargate, Grimsby, North East
Lincolnshire DN34 5AA
Tel: (01472) 878907
Email: info@stmartinsprep.com
Head: Mr S Thompson
Type: Co-educational Day 3–11
Fees: On application

NORTH LINCOLNSHIRE

BRIGG

BRIGG PREPARATORY SCHOOL
Bigby Street, Brigg, North
Lincolnshire DN20 8EF
Tel: (01652) 653237
Fax: (01652) 658879
Email: info@
  briggprepschool.co.uk
Head: Mrs P Newman
Type: Co-educational Day 3–11
No of pupils: B57 G66
Fees: On application

KEADBY

TRENTVALE PREPARATORY SCHOOL
Trentside, Keadby, North
Lincolnshire DN17 3EF
Tel: (01724) 782904
Email: trentvale@btconnect.com
Head: Mr P Wright
Type: Co-educational Day 3–11
No of pupils: B40 G40
Fees: On application

LONDON

E1

AL-MIZAN PRIMARY & LONDON EAST ACADEMY SECONDARY & SIXTH FORM
82–92 Whitechapel Road, London E1 1JX
Tel: (0207) 650 3070
Fax: (0207) 650 3071
Email: admin@leacademy.com
Head: Mr Faradhi
Type: Boys Day 7–18
No of pupils: 180
Fees: (September 08)
Day £2100–£2850

GREEN GABLES MONTESSORI PRIMARY SCHOOL
The Institute, 302 The Highway, Wapping, London E1W 3DH
Tel: (020) 7488 2374
Fax: (020) 7488 2376
Email: info@greengables.org.uk
Head: Mrs J Brierley
Type: Co-educational Day 0–8
No of pupils: B24 G25
Fees: (September 08)
Day £8400–£10800

LONDON EAST ACADEMY
46 Whitechapel Road, London E1 1JX
Tel: (020) 7650 3070
Fax: (020) 7650 3071
Email: admin@leacademy.com
Head: Mr A M Faradhi
Type: Boys Day 7–16
No of pupils: 124
Fees: On application

LONDON ISLAMIC SCHOOL
18–22 Damien Street, London E1 2HX
Tel: 020 7265 9667
Fax: 020 7790 5536
Head: Mr A Rouf
Type: Boys Day 11–16
No of pupils: 140
Fees: On application

MADNI GIRLS SCHOOL
Myrdle Street, London E1 1HL
Tel: (020) 377 1992
Fax: (020) 377 1424
Email: madni_school@hotmail.com
Head: Mrs F R Liyawdeen
Type: Girls Day 12–18
No of pupils: 215
Fees: On application

E2

DARUL HADIS LATIFIAH
1 Cornwall Avenue, London E2 0HW
Tel: 020 8980 2673
Fax: 020 8983 7942
Email: darulhadis@hotmail.co.uk
Head: Maulana M Hussain
Type: Boys Day 11–19
No of pupils: 120
Fees: On application

GATEHOUSE SCHOOL*
Sewardstone Road, Victoria Park, London E2 9JG
Tel: (020) 8980 2978
Fax: (020) 8983 1642
Email: admin@gatehouseschool.co.uk
Head: Mrs Belinda Canham
Type: Co-educational Day 3–11
No of pupils: B150 G150
Fees: (September 08)
Day £6300–£7740

E4

NORMANHURST SCHOOL
68/74 Station Road, Chingford, London E4 7BA
Tel: (020) 8529 4307
Fax: (020) 8524 7737
Email: info@normanhurstschool.co.uk
Head: Mr P J Williams
Type: Co-educational Day 3–16
Fees: On application

E5

LUBAVITCH HOUSE SCHOOL (JUNIOR BOYS)
135 Clapton Common, London E5 9AE
Tel: 020 88001044
Fax: 020 88802707
Email: boysprimary@luabvitchuk.com
Head: Rabbi D Karnowsky
Type: Boys Day 5–13
No of pupils: 131
Fees: On application

PARAGON CHRISTIAN ACADEMY
233–241 Glyn Road, London E5 0JP
Tel: (020) 8985 1119
Head: Mr G Olson
Type: Co-educational Day 3–11
No of pupils: B17 G14
Fees: On application

E7

GRANGEWOOD INDEPENDENT SCHOOL
Chester Road, Forest Gate, London E7 8QT
Tel: (020) 8472 3552
Fax: (020) 8552 8817
Email: admin@grangewoodschool.com
Head: Mrs C A Adams
Type: Co-educational Day 4–11
No of pupils: B42 G33
Fees: (September 08)
Day £3480–£4485

QUWWATT UL ISLAM GIRLS SCHOOL
16 Chaucer Road, Forest Gate, London E7 9NB
Tel: 020 8548 4736
Fax: 020 8472 4411
Email: info@quwwatulislam.com
Head: Mrs B Khan
Type: Girls Day 4–13
No of pupils: 193
Fees: On application

E8

EAST LONDON CHRISTIAN CHOIR SCHOOL
St. Mark's Community Halls, Colvestone Crescent, Dalston, London E8 2NL
Tel: (07918) 75086
Fax: (020) 7254 5760
Email: online@ elccs.hcconline.org.uk
Head: Mr F Tobun
Type: Co-educational Day 2–16
No of pupils: B17 G18
Fees: On application

E10

NOOR UL ISLAM PRIMARY SCHOOL
135 Dawlish Road, Leyton, London E10 6QW
Tel: (020) 85588765
Fax: (020) 85585235
Email: primary@noorulislam.co.uk
Head: Mr Aslam Hansa
Type: Co-educational Day 4–11
No of pupils: B85 G80
Fees: (September 08)
Day £2200–£2400

E11

ST JOSEPH'S CONVENT SCHOOL
59 Cambridge Park, London E11 2PR
Tel: (020) 8989 4700
Fax: (020) 8989 4700
Email: stjosephswanstead@ btconnect.com
Head: Ms C Glover
Type: Girls Day 3–11
No of pupils: 161
Fees: On application

E14

RIVER HOUSE MONTESSORI SCHOOL
15/16 Heron Quay, London E14 4JB
Tel: (020) 7538 9886
Fax: (020) 7538 9886
Email: website@river-house.co.uk
Head: Ms S Greenwood
Type: Co-educational Day 2–11
No of pupils: B90 G70
Fees: (September 07)
Day £3825–£11980

E17

FOREST SCHOOL
College Place, Snaresbrook, London E17 3PY
Tel: (020) 8520 1744
Fax: (020) 8520 3656
Email: info@forest.org.uk
Head: Mr A G Boggis
Type: Co-educational Day 4–18 (Single-sex ed 7–16)
No of pupils: B600 G600
Fees: (September 08)
Day £8070–£12405

HYLAND HOUSE
896 Forest Road, Walthamstow, London E17 4AE
Tel: (020) 8520 4186
Fax: (020) 8520 1549
Email: hylandhouseschool@ btconnect.com
Head: Mrs Abbequaye
Type: Co-educational Day 3–11
No of pupils: B55 G40
Fees: On application

WALTHAMSTOW MONTESSORI SCHOOL
Penryhn Hall, Penryhn Avenue, Walthamstow, London E17 5DA
Tel: 020 85232968
Email: e17montessori@aol.com
Head: Mrs Lorna Mahoney
Type: Co-educational Day 3–11
Fees: On application

E18

SNARESBROOK COLLEGE PREPARATORY SCHOOL
75 Woodford Road, South Woodford, London E18 2EA
Tel: (020) 8989 2394
Fax: (020) 8989 4379
Email: office@ snaresbrookcollege.org.uk
Head: Mrs L J Chiverrell
Type: Co-educational Day 3–11
No of pupils: B76 G84
Fees: On application

EC1

CHARTERHOUSE SQUARE SCHOOL
40 Charterhouse Square, London EC1M 6EA
Tel: (020) 7600 3805
Fax: (020) 7600 3805
Email: cssch@gotadsl.co.uk
Head: Mrs J Malden
Type: Co-educational Day Boys 3–11 Girls 4–11
No of pupils: B90 G80
Fees: (September 08) Day £11550

DALLINGTON SCHOOL
8 Dallington Street, London EC1V 0BW
Tel: (020) 7251 2284
Fax: (020) 7336 0972
Email: postmaster@ dallingtonschool.co.uk
Head: Mrs M C Hercules
Type: Co-educational Day 3–11
No of pupils: B102 G110
Fees: (September 07)
Day £6200–£7650

THE ITALIA CONTI ACADEMY OF THEATRE ARTS
23 Goswell Road, London EC1M 7AJ
Tel: (020) 7608 0047
Email: acting@lsbu.ac.uk
Head: Mr C Vote
Type: Co-educational Day 9–21
No of pupils: B45 G200
Fees: On application

THE URDANG ACADEMY OF BALLET
The Old Finsbury Town Hall, Roseberry Avenue, London EC1R 4RP
Tel: (0)207 713 7710
Fax: (0)207 278 6727
Email: info@ theurdangacademy.com
Head: Miss S Goumain
Type: Co-educational Day 16–23
No of pupils: B27 G114
Fees: On application

EC2

CITY OF LONDON SCHOOL FOR GIRLS*
St Giles' Terrace, Barbican,
London EC2Y 8BB
Tel: (020) 7847 5500
Fax: (020) 7638 3212
Email: info@clsg.org.uk
Head: Miss D Vernon
Type: Girls Day 7–18
No of pupils: 683
Fees: (September 08) Day £12375

EC4

ST PAUL'S CATHEDRAL SCHOOL*
2 New Change, London
EC4M 9AD
Tel: (020) 7248 5156
Fax: (020) 7329 6568
Email: admissions@
  spcs.london.sch.uk
Head: Mr A H Dobbin
Type: Co-educational Boarding
and Day 4–13
No of pupils:
No of boarders: F31
Fees: (September 08) FB £6336
Day £10170

CITY OF LONDON SCHOOL*
Queen Victoria Street, London
EC4V 3AL
Tel: (020) 7489 0291
Fax: (020) 7329 6887
Email: headmaster@clsb.org.uk
Head: Mr D Levin
Type: Boys Day 10–18
No of pupils: 871
Fees: (September 08) Day £12267

N2

ANNEMOUNT SCHOOL
18 Holne Chase, Hampstead
Garden Suburb, London N2 0QN
Tel: (020) 8455 2132
Fax: (020) 8381 4010
Email: headteacher@
  annemount.co.uk
Head: Mrs G Maidment
Type: Co-educational Day 2–7
No of pupils: B50 G50
Fees: On application

KEREM SCHOOL
Norrice Lea, London N2 0RE
Tel: (020) 8455 0909
Fax: (020) 8209 0726
Email: admin@kerem.org.uk
Head: Mrs R Goulden
Type: Co-educational Day 4–11
No of pupils: B97 G98
Fees: (September 08)
Day £7155–£7350

N3

AKIVA SCHOOL
Levy House, The Sternberg Centre,
80 East End Road, London N3 2SY
Tel: (020) 8349 4980
Fax: (020) 8349 4959
Email: admin@akivaschool.org
Head: Mrs S de Botton
Type: Co-educational Day 4–11
No of pupils: B81 G73
Fees: On application

PARDES GRAMMAR BOYS' SCHOOL
Hendon Lane, London N3 1SA
Tel: (020) 8343 3568
Fax: (020) 8343 4804
Email: admin@phgrammar.co.uk
Head: Rabbi D Dunner
Type: Boys Day 11–17
No of pupils: 250
Fees: On application

N4

BEIS CHINUCH LEBANOS GIRLS SCHOOL
Woodberry Down Centre,
Woodberry Down, London
N4 2SH
Tel: (020) 88097737
Fax: (020) 88027996
Email: info@bclschool.co.uk
Head: Mrs R Springer
Type: Girls Day 2–16
No of pupils: 419
Fees: On application

HOLLY PARK MONTESSORI SCHOOL
The Holly Park, Methodist Church,
Crouch Hill, London N4 4BY
Tel: (020) 7435 3646
Fax: (020) 7431 8096
Email: schools@
  mariamontessori.org
Head: Ms K Pearce
Type: Co-educational Day 2–7
No of pupils: B30 G30
Fees: (September 08)
Day £1550–£2510

N5

PRIMROSE INDEPENDENT SCHOOL
Congregational Church, Highbury
Quadrant, Highbury, London
N5 2TE
Tel: (020) 74245741
Fax: (020) 74245741
Email: primroseschool_1984@
  yahoo.co.uk
Head: Mrs L Grandson
Type: Co-educational Day 2–11
No of pupils: B30 G25
Fees: On application

N6

CHANNING JUNIOR SCHOOL
Fairseat, 1 Highgate High Street,
London N6 5JR
Tel: (020) 8342 9862
Fax: (020) 8348 3122
Email: fairseat@channing.co.uk
Head: Mrs J Todd
Type: Girls Day 4–11
No of pupils: 167
Fees: On application

CHANNING SCHOOL*
Highgate, London N6 5HF
Tel: (020) 8340 2328
Fax: (020) 8341 5698
Email: info@channing.co.uk
Head: Mrs B Elliott
Type: Girls Day 4–18
No of pupils: 590
Fees: (September 08)
Day £11430–£12390

HIGHGATE SCHOOL
North Road, London N6 4AY
Tel: (020) 8340 1524
Fax: (020) 8340 7674
Email: admissions@
  highgateschool.org.uk
Head: Mr A S Pettitt
Type: Co-educational Day 3–18
No of pupils: B1009 G179
Fees: (September 08)
Day £12294–£14190

N10

THE MONTESSORI HOUSE
5 Princes Avenue, Muswell Hill,
London N10 3LS
Tel: (020) 8444 4399
Fax: (020) 8444 4399
Email: mail@
  montessori-house.co.uk
Head: Mrs L Christoforou
Type: Co-educational Day 1–6
No of pupils: B42 G43
Fees: (September 08)
Day £5205–£9270

NORFOLK HOUSE SCHOOL
10 Muswell Avenue, Muswell Hill,
London N10 2EG
Tel: (020) 8883 4584
Fax: (020) 8815 5654
Email: office@
  norfolkhouseschool.org
Head: Mr M Malley
Type: Co-educational Day 4–11
No of pupils: B65 G65
Fees: (September 08) Day £3025

N11

NORTH LONDON
INTERNATIONAL SCHOOL*†
6 Friern Barnet Lane, London
N11 3LX
Tel: (020) 8920 0600
Fax: (020) 8211 4605
Email: admissions@wpis.org
Head: Mr D P Rose
Type: Co-educational Day 2–19
No of pupils: B261 G144
Fees: (September 07)
Day £2820–£13500

N14

SALCOMBE PREPARATORY
SCHOOL
224–226 Chase Side, Southgate,
London N14 4PL
Tel: (020) 8441 5282 / 5356
Fax: (020) 8441 5282
Email: info@salcombeprep.co.uk
Head: Mr F Steadman
Type: Co-educational Day 4–11
No of pupils: B185 G115
Fees: (September 07) Day £7446

VITA ET PAX SCHOOL
Priory Close, Green Road,
Southgate, London N14 4AT
Tel: (020) 8449 8336
Fax: (020) 8440 0483
Email: vitaetpax@lineone.net
Head: Mrs M O'Connor
Type: Co-educational Day 3–11
No of pupils: B90 G90
Fees: On application

N15

ISLAMIC SHAKHSIYAH
FOUNDATION
1st Floor {Suffolk Road Entrance},
277 St Ann's Road, London
N15 5RG
Tel: (020) 8802 8651
Email: mail@isfnet.org.uk
Head: Mrs F Reddy
Type: Co-educational Day 5–11
Fees: On application

N16

BEIS ROCHEL D'SATMAR
GIRLS SCHOOL
51–57 Amhurst Park, London
N16 5DL
Tel: (020) 8800 9060
Fax: (020) 8809 7069
Head: Ms Gita Ruth Smus
Type: Girls Day 2–17
No of pupils: 831
Fees: On application

LUBAVITCH HOUSE SENIOR
SCHOOL FOR GIRLS
107–115 Stamford Hill, Hackney,
London N16 5RP
Tel: (020) 8800 0022
Fax: (020) 8809 7324
Head: Rabbi S Lew
Type: Girls Day 11–18
Fees: On application

MECHINAH LIYESHIVAH
ZICHRON MOSHE
86 Amhurst Park, London N16 5AR
Tel: (020) 8800 5892
Head: Rabbi M Halpern
Type: Boys Day 11–16
No of pupils: 60
Fees: On application

TALMUD TORAH BOBOV
PRIMARY SCHOOL
87 Egerton Road, London N16 6UE
Tel: 020 88091025
Head: Rabbi A Just
Type: Boys Day 2–13
No of pupils: 302
Fees: On application

TAWHID BOYS SCHOOL,
TAWHID EDUCATIONAL
TRUST
21 Cazenove Road, London
N16 6PA
Tel: 020 88062999
Email: tawhid@onetel.com
Head: Mr Usman Mapara
Type: Boys Day 9–16
No of pupils: 129
Fees: On application

TAYYIBAH GIRLS SCHOOL
88 Filey Avenue, Stamford Hill,
London N16 6JJ
Tel: (020) 8880 0085
Fax: (020) 8249 1767
Email: tayyibahschool@
  hotmail.com
Head: Mrs N B Qureshi
Type: Girls Day 5–18
No of pupils: 247
Fees: On application

YESODEY HATORAH JEWISH
SCHOOL
2–4 Amhurst Park, London
N16 5AE
Tel: (020) 8800 8612
Email: yeshatorah@aol.com
Head: Rabbi Abraham Pinter
Type: Co-educational Day 3–16
No of pupils: B250 G710
Fees: On application

YETEV LEV DAY SCHOOL
FOR BOYS
111–115 Cazenove Road, London
N16 6AX
Tel: (020) 8806 3834
Head: Mr Delange
Type: Boys Day 3–11
No of pupils: 320
Fees: On application

England – London

N17

EXCEL PREPARATORY SCHOOL
The Annex, Selby Centre, Off Whitehart Lane, Tottenham, London N17 8JL
Tel: 020 83651734
Head: Mrs M Jean-Marie
Type: Co-educational Day 2–12
No of pupils: B21 G17
Fees: On application

EXCELSIOR COLLEGE
Selby Centre, Selby Road, Tottenham, London N17 8JN
Tel: 0208 365 1153
Head: Mr G Gilfillian
Type: Co-educational Day 3–11
No of pupils: B9 G3
Fees: On application

PARKSIDE PREPARATORY SCHOOL
Church Lane, Bruce Grove, Tottenham, London N17 7AA
Tel: (020) 8808 1451
Fax: (020) 8808 1451
Email: parksideprep2002@ aol.com
Head: Mrs M Langford
Type: Co-educational Day 3–11
No of pupils: B27 G28
Fees: On application

N21

GRANGE PARK PREPARATORY SCHOOL
13 The Chine, Grange Park, London N21 2EA
Tel: (020) 8360 1469
Fax: (020) 8360 4869
Email: office@gpps.org.uk
Head: Mr A Martin
Type: Girls Day 4–11
No of pupils: 109
Fees: (September 08) Day £7425

KEBLE PREPARATORY SCHOOL
Wades Hill, Winchmore Hill, London N21 1BG
Tel: (020) 8360 3359
Fax: (020) 8360 4000
Email: office@kebleprep.co.uk
Head: Mr J McCarthy
Type: Boys Day 4–13
No of pupils: 220
Fees: On application

PALMERS GREEN HIGH SCHOOL
104 Hoppers Road, Winchmore Hill, London N21 3LJ
Tel: (020) 8886 1135
Fax: (020) 8882 9473
Email: office@ palmersgreen.enfield.sch.uk
Head: Mrs J C Edmundson
Type: Girls Day 3–16
No of pupils: 320
Fees: (September 07) Day £3300–£9795

NW1

THE CAVENDISH SCHOOL*
31 Inverness Street, London NW1 7HB
Tel: (020) 7485 1958
Fax: (020) 7267 0098
Email: admissions@ cavendish-school.co.uk
Head: Mrs T Dunbar
Type: Girls Day 2½–11 (Boys 2½–7)
No of pupils: B5 G165
Fees: (September 08) Day £5400–£10650

FRANCIS HOLLAND SCHOOL, REGENT'S PARK, NW1*
Clarence Gate, Ivor Place, London NW1 6XR
Tel: (020) 7723 0176
Fax: (020) 7706 1522
Email: registrar@fhs-nw1.org.uk
Head: Mrs V M Durham
Type: Girls Day 11–18
No of pupils: 433
Fees: (September 08) Day £12900

INTERNATIONAL COMMUNITY SCHOOL*
4 York Terrace East, Regents Park, London NW1 4PT
Tel: (020) 7935 1206
Fax: (020) 7935 7915
Email: admissions@ics.uk.net
Head: Mr P Hurd
Type: Co-educational Day 3–18
No of pupils: B120 G120
Fees: (September 08) Day £12240–£16740

NORTH BRIDGE HOUSE LOWER PREP SCHOOL
1 Gloucester Avenue, London NW1 7AB
Tel: (020) 7485 0661
Fax: (020) 7284 2508
Email: lowerprep@ northbridgehouse.com
Head: Mr B Bibby
Type: Co-educational Day 8–11
No of pupils: B72 G107
Fees: On application

NORTH BRIDGE HOUSE SENIOR SCHOOL*
1 Gloucester Avenue, London NW1 7AB
Tel: (020) 7267 6266
Fax: (020) 7284 2508
Email: seniorschool@ northbridgehouse.com
Head: Ms A Ayre
Type: Co-educational Day 11–16
No of pupils: B85 G85
Fees: (September 08) Day £3225–£11865

NORTH BRIDGE HOUSE UPPER PREP SCHOOL
1 Gloucester Avenue, London NW1 7AB
Tel: (020) 7485 9495
Fax: (020) 7284 2508
Email: upperprep@ northbridgehouse.com
Head: Mr B Bibby
Type: Boys Day 10–13
No of pupils: 94
Fees: On application

SYLVIA YOUNG THEATRE SCHOOL
Rossmore Road, Marylebone, London NW1 6NJ
Tel: (020) 7402 0673
Fax: (020) 7723 1040
Email: info@ sylviayoungtheatreschool.co.uk
Head: Ms F E Chave
Type: Co-educational Day and Boarding 10–16
No of pupils: B61 G101
No of boarders: W16
Fees: (September 08)
FB £15366–£16455
WB £12792–£13350
Day £6930–£9630

NW2

THE MULBERRY HOUSE SCHOOL*

7 Minster Road, West Hampstead, London NW2 3SD
Tel: (020) 8452 7340
Fax: (020) 8830 7015
Email: info@
mulberryhouseschool.com
Head: Ms B Lewis-Powell
Type: Co-educational Day 2–8
Fees: (September 08)
Day £7050–£13160

NW3

THE ACADEMY SCHOOL

2 Pilgrims Place, Rosslyn Hill, Hampstead, London NW3 1NG
Tel: (020) 7435 6621
Head: Mr Evans
Type: Co-educational Day 6–12
No of pupils: B40 G22
Fees: On application

DEVONSHIRE HOUSE PREPARATORY SCHOOL*

2 Arkwright Road, Hampstead, London NW3 6AE
Tel: (020) 7435 1916
Fax: (020) 7431 4787
Email: enquiries@
devonshirehouseprepschool.co.uk
Head: Mrs S Alexander
Type: Co-educational Day
Boys 2–13 Girls 2–11
No of pupils: B301 G220
Fees: (September 08)
Day £6450–£12450

FINE ARTS COLLEGE HAMPSTEAD*

24 Lambolle Place, Hampstead, London NW3 4PG
Tel: (020) 7586 0312
Fax: (020) 7483 0355
Email: mail@
hampsteadfinearts.com
Head: Mr N Cochrane
Type: Co-educational Day 14–19
No of pupils: B55 G65
Fees: (September 08)
Day £5400–£14550

THE HALL SCHOOL

23 Crossfield Road, Hampstead, London NW3 4NU
Tel: (020) 7722 1700
Fax: (020) 7483 0181
Email: office@hallschool.co.uk
Head: Mr Philip Lough
Type: Boys Day 4–13
No of pupils: 440
Fees: (September 08)
Day £10350–£12570

HAMPSTEAD HILL PRE-PREPARATORY & NURSERY SCHOOL

St Stephen's Hall, Pond Street, Hampstead, London NW3 2PP
Tel: (020) 7435 6262
Fax: (020) 7433 1272
Email: hampsteadhill@aol.com
Head: Mrs A Taylor
Type: Co-educational Day
Boys 2–8 Girls 2–7
No of pupils: B190 G110
Fees: On application

HEATHSIDE PREPARATORY SCHOOL

16 New End, Hampstead, London NW3 1JA
Tel: (020) 7794 5857
Fax: (020) 7435 6434
Email: info@heathside.net
Head: Ms J White and Ms M Remus
Type: Co-educational Day 3–11
No of pupils: B87 G78
Fees: (September 08)
Day £6450–£9300

HEREWARD HOUSE SCHOOL

14 Strathray Gardens, Hampstead, London NW3 4NY
Tel: (020) 7794 4820
Fax: (020) 7794 2024
Email: herewardhouse@
btconnect.com
Head: Mrs L Sampson
Type: Boys Day 4–13
No of pupils: 175
Fees: On application

LYNDHURST HOUSE PREPARATORY SCHOOL*

24 Lyndhurst Gardens, Hampstead, London NW3 5NW
Tel: (020) 7435 4936
Email: pmg@lyndhursthouse.co.uk
Head: Mr A J C Reid
Type: Boys Day 4–13
No of pupils: 150
Fees: (September 08)
Day £12330–£13740

MARIA MONTESSORI SCHOOL HAMPSTEAD

26 Lyndhurst Gardens, Hampstead, London NW3 5NW
Tel: (020) 7435 3646
Fax: (020) 7431 8096
Email: info@mariamontessori.org
Head: Mrs L Lawrence
Type: Co-educational Day 2–11
No of pupils: B30 G30
Fees: On application

NORTH BRIDGE HOUSE JUNIOR SCHOOL

8 Netherhall Gardens, London NW3 5RR
Tel: (020) 7435 2884
Fax: (020) 7794 1337
Email: junior@
northbridgehouse.com
Head: Mrs R Allsopp
Type: Co-educational Day 6–8
No of pupils: B95 G91
Fees: (September 08) Day £11865

NORTH BRIDGE HOUSE NURSERY SCHOOL

33 Fitzjohn's Avenue, London NW3 5JY
Tel: (020) 7435 9641
Fax: (020) 7431 7930
Email: nursery@
northbridgehouse.com
Head: Mrs R Allsopp
Type: Co-educational Day 3–6
Fees: (September 07)
Day £3060–£11250

THE PHOENIX SCHOOL

36 College Crescent, London NW3 5LF
Tel: (020) 7722 4433
Fax: (020) 7722 4601
Email: thephoenix@ucs.org.uk
Head: Mrs Lisa Mason-Jones
Type: Co-educational Day 3–7
No of pupils: B65 G65
Fees: (September 07)
Day £5000–£10850

England – London

THE ROYAL SCHOOL, HAMPSTEAD*

65 Rosslyn Hill, Hampstead, London NW3 5UD
Tel: (020) 7794 7708
Fax: (020) 7431 6741
Email: enquiries@
   royalschoolhampstead.net
Head: Ms J Ebner
Type: Girls Day and Boarding
3–16
No of pupils: 220
No of boarders: F10 W9
Fees: (September 08) FB £19080
WB £15870 Day £7680–£9600

ST ANTHONY'S PREPARATORY SCHOOL

90 Fitzjohns Avenue, Hampstead, London NW3 6NP
Tel: (020) 7431 1066
Fax: (020) 7435 9223
Email: gill@stanthonysprep.org.uk
Head: Mr C J M McGovern
Type: Boys Day 5–13
No of pupils: 280
Fees: (September 08)
Day £11985–£12315

ST CHRISTOPHER'S SCHOOL

32 Belsize Lane, London NW3 5AE
Tel: (020) 7435 1521
Fax: (020) 7431 6694
Email: admissions@st-
   christophers.hampstead.sch.uk
Head: Mrs F Cook
Type: Girls Day 4–11
No of pupils: 234
Fees: On application

ST MARGARET'S SCHOOL*

18 Kidderpore Gardens, London NW3 7SR
Tel: (020) 7435 2439
Fax: (020) 7431 1308
Email: principal@
   st-margarets.co.uk
Head: Mr MRT Webster
Type: Girls Day 4–16
No of pupils: 137
Fees: (September 08)
Day £8778–£10116

ST MARY'S SCHOOL HAMPSTEAD

47 Fitzjohn's Avenue, London NW3 6PG
Tel: (020) 7435 1868
Fax: (020) 7794 7922
Email: headmistress@stmh.co.uk
Head: Miss A Rawlinson
Type: Co-educational Day
Boys 2–7 Girls 2–11(Boys 2–7)
No of pupils: B41 G244
Fees: On application

SARUM HALL

15 Eton Avenue, London NW3 3EL
Tel: (020) 7794 2261
Fax: (020) 7431 7501
Email: office@
   sarumhallschool.co.uk
Head: Mrs C Smith
Type: Girls Day 3–11
No of pupils: 166
Fees: (September 08)
Day £8090–£10994

SOUTH HAMPSTEAD HIGH SCHOOL

3 Maresfield Gardens, London NW3 5SS
Tel: (020) 7435 2899
Fax: (020) 7431 8022
Email: senior@shhs.gdst.net
Head: Mrs J Stephen
Type: Girls Day 4–18
No of pupils: 823
Fees: (September 08)
Day £8637–£11100

SOUTHBANK INTERNATIONAL SCHOOL, HAMPSTEAD

16 Netherhall Gardens, Hampstead, London NW3 5TH
Tel: (020) 7243 3803
Fax: (020) 7727 3290
Email: admissions@southbank.org
Head: Mrs J Treftz
Type: Co-educational Day 3–11
No of pupils: B91 G102
Fees: (September 07)
Day £14100–£16500

TREVOR ROBERTS SCHOOL

57 Eton Avenue, London NW3 3ET
Tel: (020) 7586 1444
Fax: (020) 7722 0114
Email: trsenior@btconnect.com
Head: Mr S Trevor-Roberts
Type: Co-educational Day 5–13
No of pupils: B98 G80
Fees: (September 08)
Day £9900–£12000

UNIVERSITY COLLEGE SCHOOL

Frognal, Hampstead, London NW3 6XH
Tel: (020) 7435 2215
Fax: (020) 7433 2111
Email: seniorschool@ucs.org.uk
Head: Mr K J Durham
Type: Co-educational Day
Boys 11–18 Girls 16–18
No of pupils: B735 G35
Fees: (September 07) Day £13900

UNIVERSITY COLLEGE SCHOOL JUNIOR BRANCH

11 Holly Hill, Hampstead, London NW3 6QN
Tel: (020) 7435 3068
Fax: (020) 7435 7332
Email: juniorbranch@ucs.org.uk
Head: Mr K J Douglas
Type: Boys Day 7–11
No of pupils: 240
Fees: (September 07) Day £12810

THE VILLAGE SCHOOL

2 Parkhill Road, Belsize Park, London NW3 2YN
Tel: (020) 7485 4673
Fax: (020) 7267 8462
Email: admin@
   thevillageschool.co.uk
Head: Miss C Gay
Type: Girls Day 4–11
No of pupils: 110
Fees: (September 08) Day £11430

NW4

BETH JACOB GRAMMAR FOR GIRLS

Stratford Road, Hendon, London NW4 2AT
Tel: 020 82034322
Fax: 020 82028480
Head: Mrs D Steinberg
Type: Girls Day 10–16
No of pupils: 264
Fees: On application

BRAMPTON COLLEGE

Lodge House, Lodge Road, London NW4 4DQ
Tel: (020) 8203 5025
Fax: (020) 8203 0052
Email: enqs@
   bramptoncollege.com
Head: Mr B Canetti
Type: Co-educational Day 15–19
No of pupils: B131 G111
Fees: On application

HENDON PREPARATORY SCHOOL
20 Tenterden Grove, Hendon, London NW4 1TD
Tel: (020) 8203 7727
Fax: (020) 8203 3465
Email: info@hendonprep.co.uk
Head: Mr D Baldwin
Type: Co-educational Day 4–13
No of pupils: B90 G40
Fees: On application

LONDON JEWISH GIRLS' HIGH SCHOOL
18 Raleigh Close, Hendon, London NW4 2TA
Tel: 020 82038618
Fax: 020 82038618
Email: tiferes@onetel.com
Head: Mr Joel Rabinowitz
Type: Girls Day 11–16
No of pupils: 91
Fees: On application

OYH PRIMARY SCHOOL
Finchley Lane, Hendon, London NW4 1DJ
Tel: 020 82025646
Fax: 020 82037568
Email: office@nrps.co.uk
Head: Mr D A David
Type: Co-educational Day 3–11
No of pupils: B89 G91
Fees: On application

NW5

L'ILE AUX ENFANTS
22 Vicar's Road, London NW5 4NL
Tel: (020) 7267 7119
Email: secretaire@ ileauxenfants.co.uk
Head: Mr A Hadjadj
Type: Co-educational Day 3–11
No of pupils: 200
Fees: On application

NW6

AL-SADIQ AND AL-ZAHRA SCHOOLS
134 Salusbury Road, London NW6 6PF
Tel: (020) 7372 6760
Fax: (020) 7372 2752
Email: alsadiq@btconnect.com
Head: Dr M Movahedi
Type: Co-educational Day 4–16
No of pupils: B181 G201
Fees: On application

BROADHURST SCHOOL
19 Greencroft Gardens, London NW6 3LP
Tel: (020) 7328 4280
Fax: (020) 7328 9370
Email: office@ broadhurstschool.com
Head: Miss D Berkery
Type: Co-educational Day 2–5
No of pupils: B70 G70
Fees: (September 08) Day £7500

BRONDESBURY COLLEGE FOR BOYS
8 Brondesbury Park, London NW6 7BT
Tel: (020) 8830 4522
Fax: (020) 8830 4523
Email: brondesburycollege@ hotmail.com
Head: Dr N Butt
Type: Boys Day 11–16
No of pupils: 119
Fees: On application

ISLAMIA GIRLS' SCHOOL
129 Salusbury Road, London NW6 6PE
Tel: (020) 7372 3472
Fax: (020) 7604 4061
Email: headteacher@ islamiaschools.com
Head: Ms A Ali
Type: Girls Day 11–16
No of pupils: 125
Fees: (September 08) Day £6100–£6100

NAIMA JEWISH PREPARATORY SCHOOL
21 Andover Place, London NW6 5ED
Tel: (020) 7328 2802
Fax: (020) 7624 0161
Email: secretary@naimajps.co.uk
Head: Rabbi Dr A Levy and Mrs K Peters
Type: Co-educational Day 3–11
No of pupils: B86 G90
Fees: (September 08) Day £6750–£8400

RAINBOW MONTESSORI JUNIOR SCHOOL
13 Woodchurch Road, West Hampstead, London NW6 3PL
Tel: (020) 7328 8986
Fax: (020) 7624 4046
Email: rms@ rainbowmontessori.co.uk
Head: Mrs L Madden
Type: Co-educational Day 5–12
No of pupils: B25 G29
Fees: (September 08) Day £8160–£8280

NW7

BELMONT (MILL HILL PREPARATORY SCHOOL)
The Ridgeway, Mill Hill, London NW7 4ED
Tel: (020) 8906 7270
Fax: (020) 8906 3519
Email: registrar@ belmontschool.com
Head: Mrs L C Duncan
Type: Co-educational Day 7–13
No of pupils: B237 G148
Fees: (September 08) Day £13014

GOODWYN SCHOOL
Hammers Lane, Mill Hill, London NW7 4DB
Tel: (020) 8959 3756
Fax: (020) 8906 8961
Email: admin@ goodwyn.barnet.sch.uk
Head: Mr S W E Robertson
Type: Co-educational Day 3–11
No of pupils: B107 G118
Fees: (September 07) Day £3410–£7232

MILL HILL SCHOOL
The Ridgeway, Mill Hill, London NW7 1QS
Tel: (020) 8959 1176
Fax: (020) 8201 0663
Email: registrations@ millhill.org.uk
Head: Dr D A Luckett
Type: Co-educational Boarding and Day 13–18
No of pupils: B512 G190
No of boarders: F140
Fees: (September 07) FB £22983 Day £14547

England – London

THE MOUNT SCHOOL
Milespit Hill, Mill Hill, London
NW7 2RX
Tel: (020) 8959 3403
Fax: (020) 8959 1503
Email: admin@mountschool.com
Head: Mrs J K Jackson
Type: Girls Day 4–18
No of pupils: 400
Fees: On application

ST MARTIN'S
22 Goodwyn Avenue, Mill Hill,
London NW7 3RG
Tel: (020) 8959 1965
Fax: (020) 8959 9065
Email: info@
     stmartinsmillhill.co.uk
Head: Mrs A Wilson
Type: Co-educational Day 3–11
No of pupils: B50 G75
Fees: (September 07) Day £5610

NW8

ABERCORN SCHOOL
28 Abercorn Place, London
NW8 9XP
Tel: (020) 7286 4785
Fax: (020) 7266 0219
Email: admin@
     abercornschool.com
Head: Mrs A S Greystoke
Type: Co-educational Day 2–13
No of pupils: B180 G180
Fees: (September 08)
Day £7035–£13035

THE AMERICAN SCHOOL IN LONDON*
1 Waverley Place, London
NW8 0NP
Tel: (020) 7449 1200
Fax: (020) 7449 1350
Email: admissions@asl.org
Head: Mrs C R Hester
Type: Co-educational Day 4–18
No of pupils: B670 G653
Fees: (September 08)
Day £17100–£20920

ARNOLD HOUSE SCHOOL
1, Loudoun Road, St John's Wood,
London NW8 0LH
Tel: (020) 7266 4840
Fax: (020) 7266 6994
Email: registrar@
     arnoldhouse.co.uk
Head: Mr V W P Thomas
Type: Boys Day 5–13
No of pupils: 250
Fees: On application

ST CHRISTINA'S RC PREPARATORY SCHOOL
25 St Edmunds Terrace, Regents
Park, London NW8 7PY
Tel: (020) 7722 8784
Fax: (020) 7586 3454
Email: vanda@
     stchristinasschool.co.uk
Head: Miss N Clyne Wilson
Type: Co-educational Day
Boys 3–7 Girls 3–11(Boys 3–7)
No of pupils: B40 G180
Fees: (September 08)
Day £7935–£7935

ST JOHNS WOOD PRE-PREPARATORY SCHOOL
St Johns Hall, Lords Roundabout,
London NW8 7NE
Tel: (020) 7722 7149
Fax: (020) 7586 6093
Email: school@dircon.co.uk
Head: Mr A Ellis and
Ms D Louskas
Type: Co-educational Day 3–7
No of pupils: B40 G40
Fees: On application

NW9

GOWER HOUSE SCHOOL
Blackbird Hill, London NW9 8RR
Tel: (020) 8205 2509
Fax: (020) 8200 6491
Email: admin@
     gowerhouseschool.co.uk
Head: Mr M Keane
Type: Co-educational Day 2–11
No of pupils: B120 G110
Fees: On application

ST NICHOLAS SCHOOL
22 Salmon Street, London
NW9 8PN
Tel: (020) 8205 7153
Fax: (020) 8205 9744
Email: stnich@happychild.co.uk
Head: Mrs A Gregory
Type: Co-educational Day 2–11
No of pupils: B40 G40
Fees: On application

NW10

WELSH SCHOOL OF LONDON
Welsh School of London, c/o
Stonebridge Primary School,
Shakespeare Avenue, London
NW10 8NG
Tel: (020) 8965 3585
Email: cymraeg@
     llundain.freeserve.co.uk
Head: Mr M H Davies
Type: Co-educational Day 3–11
No of pupils: B9 G8
Fees: On application

NW11

BEIS HAMEDRASH ELYON
211 Golders Green Rd, London
NW11 9BY
Tel: 0208 2018668
Fax: 0208 2018769
Email: headteacher211@
     gmail.com
Head: Mr Clifford Walker
Type: Boys Day 11–14
No of pupils: 45
Fees: On application

GOLDERS HILL SCHOOL
666 Finchley Road, London
NW11 7NT
Tel: (020) 8455 2589
Fax: (020) 8209 0905
Email: admin@
     goldershillschool.co.uk
Head: Mrs A Eglash
Type: Co-educational Day 2–7
No of pupils: B110 G80
Fees: On application

THE KING ALFRED SCHOOL
149 North End Road, London
NW11 7HY
Tel: (020) 8457 5200
Fax: (020) 8457 5264
Email: KAS@kingalfred.org uk
Head: Mrs D Moore
Type: Co-educational Day 4–18
No of pupils: B300 G300
Fees: (September 08)
Day £10350–£12450

SE3

**BLACKHEATH HIGH
SCHOOL GDST**
Vanbrugh Park, Blackheath,
London SE3 7AG
Tel: (020) 8853 2929
Fax: (020) 8853 3663
Email: info@bla.gdst.net
Head: Mrs E Laws
Type: Girls Day 3–18
No of pupils: 600
Fees: (September 08)
Day £6285–£10470

**BLACKHEATH
PREPARATORY SCHOOL**
4 St Germans Place, Blackheath,
London SE3 0NJ
Tel: (020) 8858 0692
Fax: (020) 8858 7778
Email: info@
    blackheathprepschool.com
Head: Mrs P Thompson
Type: Co-educational Day 3–11
No of pupils: B162 G171
Fees: (September 08)
Day £4200–£8820

**HEATH HOUSE
PREPARATORY SCHOOL**
37 Wemyss Road, Blackheath,
London SE3 0TG
Tel: (020) 8297 1900
Fax: (020) 8297 1550
Email: info@
    heathhouseprepschool.com
Head: Mr I R Laslett
Type: Co-educational Day 4–11
No of pupils: B44 G38
Fees: (September 08)
Day £9300–£9900

THE POINTER SCHOOL
19 Stratheden Road, Blackheath,
London SE3 7TH
Tel: (020) 8293 1331
Fax: (020) 8293 1331
Email: secretary@
    pointers-school.co.uk
Head: Mr R J S Higgins
Type: Co-educational Day 3–11
No of pupils: B110 G110
Fees: (September 07)
Day £2898–£9292

SE6

ST DUNSTAN'S COLLEGE
Stanstead Road, London SE6 4TY
Tel: (020) 8516 7200
Fax: (020) 8516 7300
Email: admissions@sdmail.org.uk
Head: Mrs Jane Davies
Type: Co-educational Day 3–18
No of pupils: B540 G345
Fees: (September 08)
Day £6918–£12174

**SPRINGFIELD CHRISTIAN
SCHOOL**
145 Perry Hill, Catford, London
SE6 4LP
Tel: 020 82914433
Fax: 020 83144283
Email: info@springfieldsch.co.uk
Head: Mr Babs Oludimu
Type: Co-educational Day
No of pupils: B45 G46
Fees: On application

SE9

**ST OLAVE'S PREPARATORY
SCHOOL**
106–110 Southwood Road, New
Eltham, London SE9 3QS
Tel: (020) 8294 8930
Fax: (020) 8294 8939
Email: office@stolaves.org.uk
Head: Mrs C P Fisher
Type: Co-educational Day 3–11
No of pupils: B141 G99
Fees: (September 08)
Day £4920–£7800

SE12

COLFE'S SCHOOL
Horn Park Lane, London
SE12 8AW
Tel: (020) 8852 2283
Fax: (020) 8297 1216
Email: head@colfes.com
Head: Mr R F Russell
Type: Co-educational Day 3–18
No of pupils: B677 G395
Fees: (September 08)
Day £8235–£11781

RIVERSTON SCHOOL
63–69 Eltham Road, London
SE12 8UF
Tel: (020) 8318 4327
Fax: (020) 8297 0514
Email: info@
    riverston.greenwich.sch.uk
Head: Mrs S E Salathiel
Type: Co-educational Day 1–16
No of pupils: B245 G130
Fees: On application

SE15

**THE VILLA
PRE-PREPARATORY SCHOOL**
54 Lyndhurst Grove, London
SE15 5AH
Tel: (0207) 7036216
Fax: (0207) 2526536
Email: enquiries@
    thevillaschoolandnursery.com
Head: Mrs G Quinn
Type: Co-educational Day 4–7
No of pupils: B24 G24
Fees: (September 08) Day £7995

SE16

CAVENDISH SCHOOL
Lady Gomm House, 58
Hawkstone Road, London
SE16 2PA
Tel: (020) 7349 0088
Fax: (020) 7394 1015
Email: sara_cavendish@
    hotmail.co.uk
Head: Mrs S D Craggs
Type: Co-educational Day 11–16
No of pupils: B40 G2
Fees: (September 07) Day £22000

England – London

SE19

VIRGO FIDELIS
147 Central Hill, Upper Norwood,
London SE19 1RS
Tel: (020) 8653 2169
Fax: (020) 8766 8802
Email: office@vfps.co.uk
Head: Mrs J M Noronha
Type: Co-educational Day 3–11
No of pupils: B121 G142
Fees: On application

SE21

DULWICH COLLEGE
Dulwich Common, London
SE21 7LD
Tel: (020) 8693 3601
Fax: (020) 8693 6319
Email: info@dulwich.org.uk
Head: Mr G G Able
Type: Boys Day and Boarding
7–18
No of pupils: 1468
No of boarders: F114 W11
Fees: (September 08) FB £26532
WB £25494 Day £13176

DULWICH COLLEGE
PREPARATORY SCHOOL
42 Alleyn Park, Dulwich, London
SE21 7AA
Tel: (020) 8670 3217
Fax: (020) 8766 7586
Email: registrar@dcpslondon.org
Head: Mr G Marsh
Type: Boys Day and Boarding
3–13 (Girls 3–5)
No of pupils: B796 G30
No of boarders: W30
Fees: On application

OAKFIELD PREPARATORY
SCHOOL
125–128 Thurlow Park Road,
Dulwich, London SE21 8HP
Tel: (020) 8670 4206
Fax: (020) 8766 6744
Email: cdecisneros@cfbt.com
Head: Mr J Gibson
Type: Co-educational Day 2–11
No of pupils: B244 G186
Fees: (September 08) Day £7335

ROSEMEAD PREPARATORY
SCHOOL
70 Thurlow Park Road, London
SE21 8HZ
Tel: (020) 8670 5865
Fax: (020) 8761 9159
Email: admin@
    rosemeadprepschool.org.uk
Head: Mrs C Brown
Type: Co-educational Day 3–11
No of pupils: B151 G189
Fees: (September 07)
Day £6750–£7200

SE22

ALLEYN'S SCHOOL*
Townley Road, Dulwich, London
SE22 8SU
Tel: (020) 8557 1500
Fax: (020) 8557 1462
Email: registrar@alleyns.org.uk
Head: Dr C Diggory
Type: Co-educational Day 4–18
No of pupils: B580 G601
Fees: (September 08)
Day £10701–£12996

JAMES ALLEN'S GIRLS'
SCHOOL
East Dulwich Grove, London
SE22 8TE
Tel: (020) 8693 1181
Fax: (020) 8693 7842
Email: enquiries@jags.org.uk
Head: Mrs M Gibbs
Type: Girls Day 11–18
No of pupils: 770
Fees: (September 08) Day £12285

JAMES ALLEN'S
PREPARATORY SCHOOL
East Dulwich Grove, London
SE22 8TE
Tel: (020) 8693 0374
Fax: (020) 8693 8031
Email: debbie.hewlett@jags.org.uk
Head: Miss F Stack
Type: Co-educational Day
Boys 4–7 Girls 4–11
No of pupils: B9 G291
Fees: (September 08) Day £10848

THEODORE MCLEARY
PRIMARY SCHOOL
31 East Dulwich Grove, Clapham,
London SE22 8PW
Tel: 020 86934200
Fax: 020 86934200
Head: Mr C D Thompson
Type: Co-educational Day 5–10
No of pupils: B17 G4
Fees: On application

SE24

HERNE HILL SCHOOL
The Old Vicarage, 127 Herne Hill,
London SE24 9LY
Tel: (020) 7274 6336
Fax: (020) 7924 9510
Email: enquiries@
    hernehillschool.co.uk
Head: Mrs V Tabone
Type: Co-educational Day 3–7
No of pupils: B125 G125
Fees: (September 08)
Day £4245–£7665

SE26

SYDENHAM HIGH SCHOOL
GDST
19 Westwood Hill, London
SE26 6BL
Tel: (020) 8768 8000
Fax: (020) 8768 8002
Email: info@syd.gdst.net
Head: Mrs K Pullen
Type: Girls Day 4–18
No of pupils: 678
Fees: (September 08)
Day £8637–£11100

SW1

EATON HOUSE SCHOOL
BELGRAVIA
3–5 Eaton Gate, Eaton Square,
London SW1W 9BA
Tel: (020) 7730 9343
Fax: (020) 7730 1798
Email: admin@
    eatonhouseschools.com
Head: Miss L Watts
Type: Boys Day 4–8
No of pupils: 250
Fees: (September 08) Day £11085

EATON SQUARE SCHOOL
79 Eccleston Square, London
SW1V 1PP
Tel: (020) 7931 9469
Fax: (020) 7828 0164
Email: admissions@
eatonsquare.westminster.sch.uk
Head: Mr Paul David
Type: Co-educational Day
Boys 2–13 Girls 2–11
No of pupils: B256 G236
Fees: On application

FRANCIS HOLLAND SCHOOL, SW1
39 Graham Terrace, London
SW1W 8JF
Tel: (020) 7730 2971
Fax: (020) 7823 4066
Email: office@fhs-sw1.org.uk
Head: Miss S Pattenden
Type: Girls Day 4–18
No of pupils: 450
Fees: (September 08)
Day £11160–£13155

HILL HOUSE INTERNATIONAL JUNIOR SCHOOL
17 Hans Place, London SW1X 0EP
Tel: (020) 7584 1331
Fax: (020) 7591 3938
Email: r.townend@btconnect.com
Head: Mr R Townend
Type: Co-educational Day 4–13
No of pupils: B610 G395
Fees: (September 07)
Day £7400–£9000

KNIGHTSBRIDGE SCHOOL
67 Pont Street, Knightsbridge,
London SW1X 0BD
Tel: (020) 7590 9000
Email: info@
knightsbridgeschool.com
Head: Mr M Giles
Type: Co-educational Day 3–16
No of pupils: B49 G45
Fees: On application

MORE HOUSE*
22–24 Pont Street, Chelsea,
London SW1X 0AA
Tel: (020) 7235 2855
Fax: (020) 7259 6782
Email: office@morehouse.org.uk
Head: Mr R Carlysle
Type: Girls Day 11–18
No of pupils: 200
Fees: (September 08) Day £13497

SUSSEX HOUSE SCHOOL
68 Cadogan Square, Chelsea,
London SW1X 0EA
Tel: (020) 7584 1741
Fax: (020) 7589 2300
Email: schoolsecretary@
sussexhouseschool.co.uk
Head: Mr N P Kaye
Type: Boys Day 8–13
No of pupils: 180
Fees: (September 08) Day £12855

THOMAS'S KINDERGARTEN
14 Ranelagh Grove, London
SW1W 8PD
Tel: (020) 7730 3596
Fax: (020) 7730 3596
Email: tspierenburg@
thomas-s.co.uk
Head: Miss T Spierenburg
Type: Co-educational Day 2–4
No of pupils: B27 G27
Fees: (September 08)
Day £12480–£15045

WESTMINSTER ABBEY CHOIR SCHOOL
Dean's Yard, London SW1P 3NY
Tel: (020) 7222 6151
Fax: (020) 7222 1548
Email: headmaster@
westminster-abbey.org
Head: Mr J Milton
Type: Boys Boarding 8–13
No of pupils: 34
No of boarders: F34
Fees: (September 08) FB £5607

WESTMINSTER CATHEDRAL CHOIR SCHOOL
Ambrosden Avenue, London
SW1P 1QH
Tel: (020) 7798 9081
Fax: (020) 7630 7209
Email: office@choirschool.com
Head: Mr J Browne
Type: Boys Boarding and Day
8–13
No of pupils: 109
No of boarders: F31
Fees: (September 08) FB £20601
Day £13656

WESTMINSTER SCHOOL*
17 Dean's Yard, Westminster,
London SW1P 3PB
Tel: (020) 7963 1003
Fax: (020) 7963 1002
Email: registrar@
westminster.org.uk
Head: Dr S Spurr
Type: Co-educational Boarding
and Day Boys 13–18 Girls 16–18
No of pupils: B607 G126
No of boarders: F5 W166
Fees: (September 08) F/WB £27516
Day £19056–£20664

WESTMINSTER UNDER SCHOOL
Adrian House, 27 Vincent Square,
London SW1P 2NN
Tel: (020) 7821 5788
Fax: (020) 7821 0458
Email: under.school@
westminster.org.uk
Head: Mr J P Edwards
Type: Boys Day 7–13
No of pupils: 267
Fees: (September 08) Day £13236

SW3

CAMERON HOUSE SCHOOL*
4 The Vale, Chelsea, London
SW3 6AH
Tel: (020) 7352 4040
Fax: (020) 7352 2349
Email: info@
cameronhouseschool.org
Head: Mrs Lucie Moore
Type: Co-educational Day 4–11
No of pupils: B50 G66
Fees: (September 08) Day £13170

GARDEN HOUSE SCHOOL
Turks Row, London SW3 4TW
Tel: (020) 7730 1652
Fax: (020) 7730 0470
Email: info@
gardenhouseschool.co.uk
Head: Mrs W Challen and
Mrs J Webb
Type: Co-educational Day
Boys 3–8 Girls 3–11 (Co-ed
nursery)
No of pupils: B170 G282
Fees: (September 08)
Day £9100–£15885

England – London

THE HAMPSHIRE SCHOOL*
15 Manresa Road, London
SW3 6LR
Tel: (020) 7584 3297
Fax: (020) 7584 9733
Email: hampshire@indschool.org
Head: Mr A G Bray
Type: Co-educational Day 3–13
No of pupils: B110 G110
Fees: (September 08)
Day £7950–£11535

JAMAHIRIYA SCHOOL
Glebe Place, London SW3 5JP
Tel: (020) 7352 6642
Fax: (020) 7352 6642
Head: Mr Alkawash
Type: Co-educational Day 5–17
No of pupils: B200 G200
Fees: On application

SW4

EATON HOUSE THE MANOR GIRLS' SCHOOL
58 Clapham Common Northside,
London SW4 9RU
Tel: (020) 7924 6000
Fax: (020) 7924 1530
Email: admin@
   eatonhouseschools.com
Head: Mrs S Lang
Type: Girls Day 4–11
No of pupils: 140
Fees: (September 08) Day £11085

EATON HOUSE THE MANOR
58 Clapham Common Northside,
London SW4 9RU
Tel: (020) 7924 6000
Fax: (020) 7924 1530
Email: admin@
   eatonhouseschools.com
Head: Mr S Hepher and Mrs P
Cawthorne (Pre-Prep)
Type: Boys Day 2–13
No of pupils: B495 G70
Fees: (September 08)
Day £11085–£13410

PARKGATE HOUSE SCHOOL*
80 Clapham Common North Side,
London SW4 9SD
Tel: (020) 7350 2461
Fax: (020) 7738 1633
Email: office@
   parkgate-school.co.uk
Head: Ms C Shanley and
Mrs T Masterson
Type: Co-educational Day 2–11
No of pupils: B100 G120
Fees: (September 08)
Day £3855–£10650

SW5

COLLINGHAM INDEPENDENT GCSE AND SIXTH FORM COLLEGE*
23 Collingham Gardens, London
SW5 0HL
Tel: (020) 7244 7414
Fax: (020) 7370 7312
Email: london@collingham.co.uk
Head: Mr G Hattee
Type: Co-educational Day 14–20
No of pupils: B115 G105
Fees: (September 08) Day £15400

SW6

AL-MUNTADA ISLAMIC SCHOOL
7 Bridges Place, Parsons Green,
London SW6 4HW
Tel: (020) 7471 8283
Fax: (020) 7371 7318
Email: muntadaschool@
   yahoo.co.uk
Head: Mr Z Chehimi
Type: Co-educational Day 4–11
No of pupils: B83 G93
Fees: On application

CHELSEA INDEPENDENT COLLEGE
517–523 Fulham Road, London
SW6 1HD
Tel: (020) 7610 1114
Fax: (020) 7610 3404
Email: enqs@cic.ac
Head: Mr Paul Hunt
Type: Co-educational Day 14–22
No of pupils: B65 G65
Fees: (September 08)
Day £2520–£14700

ERIDGE HOUSE PREPARATORY
1 Fulham Park Road, Fulham,
London SW6 4LJ
Tel: (020) 7471 4816
Email: office@eridgehouse.co.uk
Head: Mrs L Waring
Type: Co-educational Day 2–11
No of pupils: B50 G50
Fees: On application

FULHAM PREP SCHOOL (PRE-PREP)
47A Fulham High Street, London
SW6 3JJ
Tel: (020) 7371 9911
Fax: (020) 7371 9922
Email: admin@fulhamprep.co.uk
Head: Ms Di Steven
Type: Co-educational Day 4–7
No of pupils: B109 G98
Fees: On application

KENSINGTON PREP SCHOOL
596 Fulham Road, London
SW6 5PA
Tel: (020) 7731 9300
Fax: (020) 7731 9301
Email: enquiries@kenprep.gdst.net
Head: Mrs P J F Lynch
Type: Girls Day 4–11
No of pupils: 275
Fees: On application

L'ECOLE DES PETITS
2 Hazlebury Road, London
SW6 2NB
Tel: (020) 7371 8350
Fax: (020) 7736 9522
Email: admin@
   lecoledespetits.co.uk
Head: Mrs M Otten and
Mrs F Brisset
Type: Co-educational Day 2–6
(Bilingual)
No of pupils: B65 G75
Fees: On application

SINCLAIR HOUSE SCHOOL
159 Munster Road, Fulham,
London SW6 6AD
Tel: (020) 7736 9182
Fax: (020) 7371 0295
Email: info@
   sinclairhouseschool.co.uk
Head: Mrs C T M O'Sullivan
Type: Co-educational Day 2–8
No of pupils: B28 G23
Fees: (September 08)
Day £3105–£8805

THOMAS'S FULHAM
Hugon Road, London Fulham,
London SW6 3ES
Tel: (020) 7751 8200
Fax: (020) 7751 8201
Email: fulham@thomas-s.co.uk
Head: Miss Annette Dobson
Type: Co-educational Day 4–11
No of pupils: B95 G93
Fees: On application

SW7

DUFF MILLER*
59 Queen's Gate, London SW7 5JP
Tel: (020) 7225 0577
Fax: (020) 7589 5155
Email: enqs@duffmiller.com
Head: Mr C Denning
Type: Co-educational Day 14–19
No of pupils: B110 G110
Fees: (September 08)
Day £4675–£15435

EATON HOUSE THE VALE
2 Elvaston Place, London
SW7 5QH
Tel: (020) 7584 9515
Fax: (020) 7584 8368
Email: admin@
    eatonhouseschools.com
Head: Mr R Greenwood
Type: Co-educational Day
Boys 4–8 Girls 4–11
No of pupils: B40 G60
Fees: (September 08) Day £11085

FALKNER HOUSE
19 Brechin Place, London
SW7 4QB
Tel: (020) 7373 4501
Fax: (020) 7835 0073
Email: office@falknerhouse.co.uk
Head: A Griggs
Type: Girls Day 3–11 (Co-ed 3–4)
No of pupils: B10 G170
Fees: (September 08)
Day £6300–£12600

**GLENDOWER
PREPARATORY SCHOOL***
87 Queen's Gate, South
Kensington, London SW7 5JX
Tel: (020) 7370 1927
Fax: (020) 7244 8308
Email: office@
    glendower.kensington.sch.uk
Head: Mrs R Bowman
Type: Girls Day 4–11
No of pupils: 182
Fees: (September 08) Day £11850

**THE HAMPSHIRE SCHOOLS
(THE EARLY YEARS SECTION)**
5 Wetherby Place, London
SW7 4NX
Tel: (020) 7584 3297
Fax: (020) 7584 9733
Email: hampshire@indschool.org
Head: Mr A G Bray
Type: Day
No of pupils: B45 G45
Fees: On application

**LYCEE FRANCAIS CHARLES
DE GAULLE**
35 Cromwell Road, London
SW7 2DG
Tel: (020) 7584 6322
Fax: (020) 7823 7684
Email: proviseur@
    lyceefrancais.org.uk
Head: Mr A Becherand
Type: Co-educational Day 4–19
No of pupils: B1684 G1718
Fees: On application

**MANDER PORTMAN
WOODWARD**
90–92 Queen's Gate, London
SW7 5AB
Tel: (020) 7835 1355
Fax: (020) 7259 2705
Email: london@mpw.co.uk
Head: Mr M Judd
Type: Co-educational Day 14+
No of pupils: B207 G170
Fees: On application

QUEEN'S GATE SCHOOL*
133 Queen's Gate, Kensington,
London SW7 5LE
Tel: (020) 7589 3587
Fax: (020) 7584 7691
Email: registrar@
    queensgate.org.uk
Head: Mrs R M Kamaryc
Type: Girls Day 4–18
Fees: (September 08)
Day £10995–£13455

**ST NICHOLAS
PREPARATORY SCHOOL***
23 Prince's Gate, London SW7 1PT
Tel: (020) 7225 1277
Fax: (020) 7823 7557
Email: info@stnicholasprep.co.uk
Head: Mr D Wilson
Type: Co-educational Day 3–11
No of pupils: B125 G125
Fees: (September 08)
Day £7575–£12150

ST PHILIP'S SCHOOL
6 Wetherby Place, London
SW7 4ND
Tel: (020) 7373 3944
Fax: (020) 7244 9766
Email: info@stphilipschool.co.uk
Head: Mr H Biggs-Davison
Type: Boys Day 7–13
No of pupils: 111
Fees: (September 08) Day £11160

WESTMINSTER TUTORS*
86 Old Brompton Road, London
SW7 3LQ
Tel: (020) 7584 1288
Fax: (020) 7584 2637
Email: info@
    westminstertutors.co.uk
Head: Ms V H Q L Maguire
Type: Co-educational Day 11–25
No of pupils: B20 G20
Fees: (September 08)
Day £15000–£18600

SW8

NEWTON PREP SCHOOL
149 Battersea Park Road, London
SW8 4BX
Tel: (020) 7720 4091
Fax: (020) 7498 9052
Email: registrar@
    newtonprep.co.uk
Head: Mr N Allen
Type: Co-educational Day 3–13
No of pupils: B290 G282
Fees: (September 08)
Day £6210–£12540

England – London

SW10

REDCLIFFE SCHOOL*
47 Redcliffe Gardens, London
SW10 9JH
Tel: (020) 7352 9247
Fax: (020) 7352 6936
Email: admissions@
  redcliffeschool.com
Head: Mrs S Bourne
Type: Co-educational Day
Boys 3–8 Girls 3–11
No of pupils: B38 G84
Fees: (September 08) Day £10950

SW11

DOLPHIN SCHOOL (INCLUDING NOAH'S ARK NURSERY SCHOOL)*
106 Northcote Road, Battersea,
London SW11 6QW
Tel: (020) 7924 3472
Fax: (020) 8265 8700
Email: admissions@
  dolphinschool.org.uk
Head: Mrs J Glen
Type: Co-educational Day
Boys 2–11 Girls 2–11
No of pupils: B125 G109
Fees: (September 08)
Day £4290–£8070

THE DOMINIE†
55 Warriner Gardens, Battersea,
London SW11 4DX
Tel: (020) 7720 8783
Fax: (020) 7622 4357
Email: aodoherty@
  thedominie.co.uk
Head: Miss A O'Doherty
Type: Co-educational Day 6–12
No of pupils: B16 G16
Fees: (September 08) Day £18900

EMANUEL SCHOOL
Battersea Rise, London SW11 1HS
Tel: (020) 8870 4171
Fax: (020) 8877 1424
Email: enquiries@emanuel.org.uk
Head: Mr M D Hanley-Browne
Type: Co-educational Day 10–18
No of pupils: B475 G230
Fees: (September 08) Day £13230

NORTHCOTE LODGE SCHOOL
26 Bolingbroke Grove, London
SW11 6EL
Tel: (020) 8682 8888
Fax: (020) 8682 8879
Email: northcote@
  northwoodschools.com
Head: Mr J Hansford
Type: Boys Day 8–13
No of pupils: 195
Fees: (September 08) Day £13485

THAMES CHRISTIAN COLLEGE†
Wye Street, Battersea, London
SW11 2HB
Tel: (020) 7228 3933
Fax: (020) 7924 1112
Email: info@
  thameschristiancollege.org.uk
Head: Dr S Holsgrove
Type: Co-educational Day 11–16
No of pupils: B55 G45
Fees: (September 08) Day £8850

THOMAS'S KINDERGARTEN, BATTERSEA
The Crypt, Saint Mary's Church,
Battersea Church Road, London
SW11 3NA
Tel: (020) 7738 0400
Head: Miss I Jennings
Type: Co-educational Day 2–5
No of pupils: B24 G24
Fees: On application

THOMAS'S PREPARATORY SCHOOL
28–40 Battersea High Street,
London SW11 3JB
Tel: (020) 7978 0900
Fax: (020) 7978 0901
Email: Battersea@thomas-s.co.uk
Head: Mr B V R Thomas
Type: Co-educational Day 4–13
No of pupils: B270 G215
Fees: (September 08) Day £12480

THOMAS'S PREPARATORY SCHOOL CLAPHAM
Broomwood Road, London
SW11 6JZ
Tel: (020) 7326 9300
Fax: (020) 7326 9301
Email: clapham@thomas-s.co.uk
Head: Mrs P Evelegh
Type: Co-educational Day 4–13
No of pupils: B245 G276
Fees: (September 08)
Day £11655–£13185

SW12

BALHAM PREPARATORY SCHOOL
47a Balham High Road, London
SW12 9AW
Tel: (020) 8675 7747
Fax: (020) 8675 7912
Head: Mr K Bahauddin
Type: Co-educational Day 3–16
No of pupils: 500
Fees: On application

BROOMWOOD HALL SCHOOL
68–74 Nightingale Lane, London
SW12 8NR
Tel: (020) 8682 8830
Fax: (020) 8682 8805
Email: broomwood@
  northwoodschools.com
Head: Lady K A H Colquhoun and
Mrs C Jenkinson
Type: Co-educational Day
Boys 4–8 Girls 4–13
No of pupils: B182 G399
Fees: (September 08)
Day £10950–£13350

HORNSBY HOUSE SCHOOL
Hearnville Road, London
SW12 8RS
Tel: (020) 8673 7573
Fax: (020) 8673 6722
Email: school@
  hornsby-house.co.uk
Head: Mrs J Strong
Type: Co-educational Day 4–11
No of pupils: B161 G128
Fees: (September 08)
Day £10056–£10830

THE WHITE HOUSE PREP & WOODENTOPS KINDERGARTEN
24 Thornton Road, Clapham Park,
London SW12 0LF
Tel: (020) 8674 9514
Email: office@
  whitehouseschool.com
Head: Mrs E Davies
Type: Co-educational Day
Boys 2–11 Girls 3–11
No of pupils: B75 G75
Fees: (September 08)
Day £3495–£10050

SW13

THE HARRODIAN
Lonsdale Road, London
SW13 9QN
Tel: (020) 8748 6117
Fax: (020) 8563 7327
Email: admin@harrodian.com
Head: Mr J R Hooke
Type: Co-educational Day 5–18
No of pupils: B450 G400
Fees: On application

ST PAUL'S PREPARATORY SCHOOL
Colet Court, Lonsdale Road,
London SW13 9JT
Tel: (020) 8748 3461
Fax: (020) 8563 7361
Email: HMCC@
   stpaulsschool.org.uk
Head: Mr T A Meunier
Type: Boys Day 7–13
No of pupils: 437
Fees: (September 08) Day £13089

ST PAUL'S SCHOOL
Lonsdale Road, Barnes, London
SW13 9JT
Tel: (020) 8748 9162
Fax: (020) 8746 5353
Email: hmcc@stpaulsschool.org.uk
Head: Dr Martin Stephen
Type: Boys Day and Boarding
13–18
No of pupils:
No of boarders: F40 W40
Fees: On application

SW14

TOWER HOUSE SCHOOL
188 Sheen Lane, East Sheen,
London SW14 8LF
Tel: (020) 8876 3323
Fax: (020) 8876 3321
Email: head@
   towerhouse.richmond.sch.uk
Head: Mrs J Compton-Howlett
Type: Boys Day 4–13
No of pupils: 186
Fees: (September 08)
Day £9507–£10764

SW15

THE HURLINGHAM SCHOOL
122 Putney Bridge Road, Putney,
London SW15 2NQ
Tel: (020) 8874 7186
Fax: (020) 8875 0372
Email: admissions@
   hurlinghamschool.co.uk
Head: Mrs Val Willmott
Type: Co-educational Day 4–11
No of pupils: B95 G135
Fees: (September 08)
Day £10200–£10800

IBSTOCK PLACE SCHOOL
Clarence Lane, Roehampton,
London SW15 5PY
Tel: (020) 8876 9991
Fax: (020) 8878 4897
Email: registrar@
   ibstockplaceschool.co.uk
Head: Mrs A Sylvester-Johnson
Type: Co-educational Day 3–18
No of pupils: B452 G410
Fees: (September 08)
Day £5370–£13725

LION HOUSE SCHOOL
The Old Methodist Hall,
Gwendolen Avenue, London
SW15 6EH
Tel: (020) 8780 9446
Fax: (020) 8789 3331
Email: office@
   lionhouseschool.co.uk
Head: Miss H J Luard
Type: Co-educational Day 3–8
No of pupils: B63 G38
Fees: (September 07)
Day £3555–£9630

THE MERLIN SCHOOL
4 Carlton Drive, Putney, London
SW15 2BZ
Tel: (020) 8788 2769
Fax: (020) 8789 5227
Email: secretary@merlinschool.net
Head: Mrs K Prest
Type: Co-educational Day 4–8
No of pupils: B100 G60
Fees: (September 07)
Day £9066–£9600

PROSPECT HOUSE SCHOOL*
75 Putney Hill, London SW15 3NT
Tel: (020) 8780 0456
Fax: (020) 8780 3010
Email: info@prospecths.org.uk
Head: Mrs D Barratt
Type: Co-educational Day 3–11
No of pupils: B100 G100
Fees: (September 08)
Day £5640–£11694

PUTNEY HIGH SCHOOL GDST
35 Putney Hill, London SW15 6BH
Tel: (020) 8788 4886
Fax: (020) 8789 8068
Email: putneyhigh@put.gdst.net
Head: Dr D V Lodge
Type: Girls Day 4–18
No of pupils: 870
Fees: (September 08)
Day £8637–£11100

PUTNEY PARK SCHOOL*
11 Woodborough Road, Putney,
London SW15 6PY
Tel: (020) 8788 8316
Fax: (020) 8780 2376
Email: office@
   putneypark.london.sch.uk
Head: Mrs Ruth Mann
Type: Co-educational Day
Boys 4–8 Girls 4–16
No of pupils: B42 G227
Fees: (September 07)

SW16

STREATHAM AND CLAPHAM HIGH SCHOOL
42 Abbotswood Road, London
SW16 1AW
Tel: (020) 8677 8400
Fax: (020) 8677 2001
Email: enquiry@shc.gdst-net
Head: Mrs S Mitchell
Type: Girls Day 3–18 (Boys 3–5)
No of pupils: B1 G840
Fees: On application

WALDORF SCHOOL OF SOUTH WEST LONDON
Woodfields, Abbotswood Road,
London SW16 1AP
Tel: (020) 8769 6587
Fax: (020) 8677 5334
Email: info@waldorf-swlondon.org
Head: Ms T COUTINHO
Type: Co-educational Day 4–14
No of pupils: B55 G45
Fees: On application

England – London

SW17

EVELINE DAY SCHOOL
14 Trinity Crescent, Upper
Tooting, London SW17 7AE
Tel: (020) 8672 4673
Fax: (020) 8672 7259
Email: eveline@
  evelinedayschool.com
Head: Ms E Drut
Type: Co-educational Day 3–11
No of pupils: B34 G41
Fees: On application

FINTON HOUSE SCHOOL
171 Trinity Road, London
SW17 7HL
Tel: (020) 8682 0921
Fax: (020) 8767 5017
Email: admissions@
  fintonhouse.org.uk
Head: Mr A Floyd
Type: Co-educational Day 4–11
No of pupils: B130 G180
Fees: On application

SW18

THE ROCHE SCHOOL
11 Frogmore, Wandsworth,
London SW18 1HW
Tel: (020) 8877 0823
Fax: (020) 8875 1156
Email: office@
  therocheschool.co.uk
Head: Dr J Roche
Type: Co-educational Day 3–11
No of pupils: B88 G86
Fees: On application

SW19

DONHEAD PREP SCHOOL
33 Edge Hill, Wimbledon, London
SW19 4NP
Tel: (020) 8946 7000
Fax: (020) 8947 1219
Email: office@donhead.org.uk
Head: Mr G C McGrath
Type: Boys Day 4–11
No of pupils: 193
Fees: On application

KING'S COLLEGE JUNIOR SCHOOL
Southside, Wimbledon Common,
London SW19 4TT
Tel: (020) 8255 5335
Fax: (020) 8255 5339
Email: jsadmissions@kcs.org.uk
Head: Dr G A Silverlock
Type: Boys Day 7–13
No of pupils: 460
Fees: (September 08)
Day £11445–£12900

KING'S COLLEGE SCHOOL
Wimbledon Common, London
SW19 4TT
Tel: (020) 8255 5352
Fax: (020) 8255 5357
Email: admissions@kcs.org.uk
Head: Mr A C V Evans
Type: Boys Day 13–18
No of pupils: 752
Fees: (September 07) Day £14325

THE STUDY PREPARATORY SCHOOL
Wilberforce House, Camp Road,
Wimbledon Common, London
SW19 4UN
Tel: (020) 8947 6969
Fax: (020) 8944 5975
Email: wilberforce@
  thestudyprep.co.uk
Head: Mrs J Nicol
Type: Girls Day 4–11
No of pupils: 320
Fees: On application

WILLINGTON SCHOOL
Worcester Road, Wimbledon,
London SW19 7QQ
Tel: (020) 8944 7020
Fax: (020) 8944 9596
Email: office@
  willingtonschool.co.uk
Head: Mr Graham Hill
Type: Boys Day 4–13
No of pupils: 240
Fees: (September 08)
Day £2650–£3150

WIMBLEDON COMMON PREPARATORY SCHOOL
113 Ridgway, Wimbledon,
London SW19 4TA
Tel: (020) 8946 1001
Fax: (020) 8946 1001
Email: info@
  wimbledoncommonprep.co.uk
Head: Mr N J Worsey
Type: Boys Day 4–8
No of pupils: 143
Fees: (September 07)
Day £5580–£6105

WIMBLEDON HIGH SCHOOL GDST
Mansel Road, London SW19 4AB
Tel: (020) 8971 0900
Fax: (020) 8971 0901
Email: info@wim.gdst.net
Head: Ms Heather Hanbury
Type: Day
No of pupils: 900
Fees: (September 08)
Day £8637–£11100

SW20

HALL SCHOOL WIMBLEDON
17 The Downs (Senior School),
Wimbledon, London SW20 8HF
Tel: (020) 8879 9200
Fax: (020) 8946 0864
Email: enquiries@
  hallschoolwimbledon.co.uk
Head: Mr T Hobbs and Mr J Hobbs
Type: Co-educational Day 4–16
No of pupils: B320 G280
Fees: On application

THE NORWEGIAN SCHOOL
28 Arterberry Road, Wimbledon,
London SW20 8AH
Tel: (020) 8947 6617/6627
Fax: (020) 8944 7345
Email: dnslondon@aol.com
Head: Mr A Larsen
Type: Co-educational Day 3–16
No of pupils: 101
Fees: On application

THE ROWANS SCHOOL
19 Drax Avenue, Wimbledon,
London SW20 0EG
Tel: (020) 8946 8220
Fax: (020) 8944 0822
Email: therowansschool@
    btinternet.com
Head: Mrs E Tyrrell
Type: Co-educational Day 3–8
No of pupils: B75 G50
Fees: On application

URSULINE PREPARATORY SCHOOL
18 The Downs, London SW20 8HR
Tel: (020) 8947 0859
Fax: (020) 8947 0885
Email: info@
    ursuline-prep.merton.sch.uk
Head: Mrs C Grogan
Type: Girls Day 3–11 (Boys 3–7)
No of pupils: B76 G172
Fees: On application

W1

ALBEMARLE INDEPENDENT COLLEGE
18 Dunraven Street, London
W1K 7FE
Tel: (020) 7409 7273
Fax: (020) 7629 9146
Email: admin@albemarle.org.uk
Head: Mr J Eytle and Miss B
Mellon
Type: Co-educational Day 14–19
No of pupils: B82 G73
Fees: (September 07)
Day £3150–£13950

DAVIES LAING AND DICK*
100 Marylebone Lane, London
W1U 2QB
Tel: (020) 7935 8411
Fax: (020) 7935 0755
Email: dld@dld.org
Head: Mr D Lowe
Type: Co-educational Day 14–25
No of pupils: B162 G138
Fees: (September 08)
Day £2680–£18000

GREAT BEGINNINGS MONTESSORI SCHOOL
39 Brendon Street, Marylebone,
Westminster, London W1H 5JE
Tel: (020) 7258 1066
Email: wendyinnes@
    greatbeginningsnursery.com
Head: Mrs W Innes
Type: Co-educational Day 2–6
No of pupils: B30 G30
Fees: (September 08)
Day £1695–£2565

PORTLAND PLACE SCHOOL
56–58 Portland Place, London
W1B 1NJ
Tel: (020) 7307 8700
Fax: (020) 7436 2676
Email: admin@
    portland-place.co.uk
Head: Mr R Walker
Type: Co-educational Day 11–18
No of pupils: B258 G90
Fees: (September 07) Day £12585

QUEEN'S COLLEGE
43–49 Harley Street, London
W1G 8BT
Tel: (020) 7291 7000
Fax: (020) 7291 7099
Email: queens@qcl.org.uk
Head: Miss M M Connell
Type: Girls Day 11–18
No of pupils: 372
Fees: On application

QUEEN'S COLLEGE PREP SCHOOL
61 Portland Place, London
W1B 1QP
Tel: (0207) 2910660
Fax: (0207) 2910669
Email: tbrook@qcps.org.uk
Head: Mrs J Davies
Type: Girls Day 3–11
No of pupils: 200
Fees: (September 07)
Day £6075–£11610

SOUTHBANK INTERNATIONAL SCHOOL, WESTMINSTER
63–65 Portland Place, London
W1B 1QR
Tel: (020) 7243 3803
Fax: (020) 7727 3290
Email: admissions@southbank.org
Head: Mr T Hedger
Type: Co-educational Day 11–18
No of pupils: B153 G177
Fees: (September 07)
Day £17700–£19590

W2

CONNAUGHT HOUSE
47 Connaught Square, London
W2 2HL
Tel: (020) 7262 8830
Fax: (020) 7262 0781
Email: office@
    connaughthouseschool.co.uk
Head: F Hampton
Type: Co-educational Day
Boys 4–8 Girls 4–11
No of pupils: B35 G35
Fees: (September 08)
Day £8700–£11700

LANSDOWNE COLLEGE*
40–44 Bark Place, London W2 4AT
Tel: (020) 7616 4400
Fax: (020) 7616 4401
Email: education@
    lansdownecollege.com
Head: Mr H Templeton
Type: Co-educational Day 14–19
No of pupils: B112 G108
Fees: (September 08)
Day £2900–£15500

PEMBRIDGE HALL
18 Pembridge Square, London
W2 4EH
Tel: (020) 7229 0121
Fax: (020) 7792 1086
Email: contact@
    pembridgehall.co.uk
Head: Mrs E Marsden
Type: Girls Day 4–11
No of pupils: 403
Fees: (September 08) Day £13260

RAVENSTONE HOUSE PRE-PREPARATORY AND NURSERY
The Long Garden, Albion Street,
Marble Arch, London W2 2AX
Tel: (020) 7262 1190
Fax: (020) 7724 6980
Email: info@
    ravenstonehouse.co.uk
Head: Mrs A Saunders
Type: Co-educational Day 0–5
No of pupils: B50 G50
Fees: On application

England – London

WETHERBY SCHOOL*
11 Pembridge Square, London
W2 4ED
Tel: (020) 7727 9581
Fax: (020) 7221 8827
Email: learn@
    WetherbySchool.co.uk
Head: Mr MWE Snell
Type: Boys Day 4–8
No of pupils: 240
Fees: (September 08) Day £12975

W3

**BARBARA SPEAKE STAGE
SCHOOL**
East Acton Lane, London W3 7EG
Tel: (020) 8743 1306
Fax: (020) 8743 1306
Email: cpuk@aol.com
Head: Miss B M Speake and Mr D
R Speake
Type: Co-educational Day 3–16
No of pupils: B45 G91
Fees: (September 07)
Day £4500–£4800

**INTERNATIONAL SCHOOL
OF LONDON***
139 Gunnersbury Avenue, London
W3 8LG
Tel: (020) 8992 5823
Fax: (020) 8993 7012
Email: mail@islondon.com
Head: Mr A Makarem
Type: Co-educational Day
Boys 3–19 Girls 3–18
No of pupils: B193 G149
Fees: (September 08)
Day £13000–£18250

THE JAPANESE SCHOOL
87 Creffield Road, Acton, London
W3 9PU
Tel: (020) 8993 7145
Fax: (020) 8992 1224
Head: Mr F Fudo
Type: Co-educational Day 6–15
No of pupils: B320 G260
Fees: On application

KING FAHAD ACADEMY
Bromyard Avenue, East Acton,
London W3 7HD
Tel: (020) 8743 0131
Fax: (020) 8749 7085
Email: academy@thekfa.org.uk
Head: Mr Mansour Ghazali
Type: Co-educational Day 5–18
No of pupils: B300 G350
Fees: On application

W4

**ARTS EDUCATIONAL
SCHOOLS LONDON***
Cone Ripman House, 14 Bath
Road, Chiswick, London W4 1LY
Tel: (020) 8987 6600
Fax: (020) 8987 6601
Email: pupils@artsed.co.uk
Head: Mr O Price
Type: Co-educational Day 11–18
No of pupils: B39 G113
Fees: (September 07)
Day £9840–£10494

**CHISWICK AND BEDFORD
PARK PREPARATORY
SCHOOL**
Priory House, Priory Avenue,
Bedford Park, London W4 1TX
Tel: (020) 8994 1804
Fax: (020) 8995 3603
Email: cbpschool@aol.com
Head: Mrs C A Sunderland
Type: Co-educational Day
Boys 4–8 Girls 4–11
No of pupils: B70 G115
Fees: On application

**THE FALCONS SCHOOL FOR
BOYS**
2 Burnaby Gardens, Chiswick,
London W4 3DT
Tel: (020) 8747 8393
Fax: (020) 8752 1653
Email: admin@falconsgirls.co.uk
Head: Mr B H Evans
Type: Boys Day 3–8
No of pupils: 200
Fees: On application

**HEATHFIELD HOUSE
SCHOOL**
Turnham Green Church Hall,
Chiswick, London W4 4JU
Tel: 020 89943385
Fax: 020 89950255
Email: enquiries@
    heathfieldhouse.co.uk
Head: Mrs Caroline Goodsman
Type: Co-educational Day 4–11
Fees: On application

**ORCHARD HOUSE
SCHOOL***
16 Newton Grove, Bedford Park,
London W4 1LB
Tel: (020) 8742 8544
Fax: (020) 8742 8522
Email: info@orchardhs.org.uk
Head: Mrs S A B Hobbs
Type: Co-educational Day
Boys 3–8 Girls 3–11
No of pupils: B80 G140
Fees: (September 08)
Day £5820–£12006

W5

ASTON HOUSE SCHOOL
1 Aston Road, Ealing, London
W5 2RL
Tel: (020) 8566 7300
Fax: (020) 8566 7499
Email: ahs@happychild.co.uk
Head: Mrs P Seabrook
Type: Co-educational Day 2–11
No of pupils: B75 G75
Fees: On application

**CLIFTON LODGE
PREPARATORY SCHOOL**
8 Mattock Lane, Ealing, London
W5 5BG
Tel: (020) 8579 3662
Fax: (020) 8810 1332
Email: info@
    cliftonlodgeschool.co.uk
Head: Mr A Gibson
Type: Boys Day 4–13
No of pupils: 180
Fees: (September 08)
Day £8994–£9759

DURSTON HOUSE
12–14 & 26 Castlebar Road,
Ealing, London W5 2DR
Tel: (020) 8991 6532
Fax: (020) 8991 6547
Email: info@durstonhouse.org
Head: Mr N I Kendrick
Type: Boys Day 4–13
No of pupils: 380
Fees: (September 08)
Day £8550–£11490

EALING INDEPENDENT COLLEGE
83 New Broadway, Ealing, London W5 5AL
Tel: (020) 8579 6668
Fax: (020) 8567 8688
Email: ealingcollege@
 btconnect.com
Head: Dr I Moores
Type: Co-educational Day 13–20
No of pupils: B48 G47
Fees: (September 08)
Day £5500–£11810

THE FALCONS SCHOOL FOR GIRLS
15 Gunnersbury Avenue, Ealing, London W5 3XD
Tel: (020) 8992 5189
Fax: (020) 8752 1635
Email: admin@falconsgirls.co.uk
Head: Mr B H Evans
Type: Girls Day 4–11
No of pupils: 120
Fees: On application

HARVINGTON SCHOOL
20 Castlebar Road, Ealing, London W5 2DS
Tel: (020) 8997 1583
Fax: (020) 8810 4756
Email: admin@
 harvingtonschool.com
Head: Dr F Meek
Type: Girls Day 3–16 (Boys 3–5)
No of pupils: B14 G210
Fees: On application

ST AUGUSTINE'S PRIORY
Hillcrest Road, Ealing, London W5 2JL
Tel: (020) 8997 2022
Fax: (020) 8810 6501
Email: registrar@
 staugustinespriory.org.uk
Head: Mrs F J Gumley-Mason
Type: Girls Day 4–18
No of pupils: 500
Fees: (September 08)
Day £7095–£9900

ST BENEDICT'S JUNIOR SCHOOL
5 Montpelier Avenue, Ealing, London W5 2XP
Tel: (020) 8862 2050
Fax: (020) 8862 2058
Email: jssecretary@
 stbenedicts.org.uk
Head: Mr R G Simmons
Type: Co-educational Day 3–11
No of pupils: B243 G58
Fees: (September 08) Day £10080

ST BENEDICT'S SCHOOL*
54 Eaton Rise, Ealing, London W5 2ES
Tel: (020) 8862 2254
Fax: (020) 8862 2199
Email: enquiries@
 stbenedicts.org.uk
Head: Mr C J Cleugh
Type: Co-educational Day 3–18
No of pupils: B815 G135
Fees: (September 08)
Day £10080–£11460

W6

BUTE HOUSE PREPARATORY SCHOOL FOR GIRLS
Luxemburg Gardens, London W6 7EA
Tel: (020) 7603 7381
Fax: (020) 7371 3446
Email: mail@butehouse.co.uk
Head: Mrs S Salvidant
Type: Girls Day 4–11
Fees: (September 08) Day £10755

ECOLE FRANCAISE JACQUES PREVERT
59 Brook Green, London W6 7BE
Tel: (020) 7602 6871
Fax: (020) 7602 3162
Email: info@ecoleprevert.org.uk
Head: Mr R Salva
Type: Co-educational Day 4–11
No of pupils: B136 G128
Fees: On application

THE GODOLPHIN AND LATYMER SCHOOL
Iffley Road, Hammersmith, London W6 0PG
Tel: (020) 8741 1936
Fax: (020) 8746 3352
Email: registrar@
 godolphinandlatymer.com
Head: Miss M Rudland
Type: Girls Day 11–18
No of pupils: 707
Fees: (September 08) Day £14346

LATYMER PREP SCHOOL*
36 Upper Mall, Hammersmith, London W6 9TA
Tel: (0845) 638 5700
Fax: (0845) 638 5732
Email: mlp@latymerprep.org
Head: Mr S P Dorrian
Type: Co-educational Day 7–11
Fees: (September 08) Day £12105

LATYMER UPPER SCHOOL*
King Street, Hammersmith, London W6 9LR
Tel: (0845) 638 5800
Fax: (020) 8748 5212
Email: registrar@
 latymer-upper.org
Head: Mr P J Winter
Type: Co-educational Day 11–18
No of pupils: B681 G406
Fees: (September 08) Day £13470

LE HERISSON
c/o The Methodist Church, Rivercourt Road, Hammersmith, London W6 9JT
Tel: (020) 8563 7664
Fax: (020) 8563 7664
Email: administration@
 leherissonschool.co.uk
Head: Ms B Rios
Type: Co-educational Day 2–6
No of pupils: B30 G34
Fees: On application

RAVENSCOURT PARK PREPARATORY SCHOOL*
16 Ravenscourt Avenue, London W6 0SL
Tel: (020) 8846 9153
Fax: (020) 8846 9413
Email: secretary@rpps.co.uk
Head: Mr R Relton
Type: Co-educational Day 4–11
No of pupils: B127 G134
Fees: (September 08) Day £11907

RAVENSCOURT THEATRE SCHOOL
8–30 Galena Road, London W6 0LT
Tel: (020) 8741 0707
Fax: (020) 8741 1786
Head: Miss Judi Swinney
Type: Co-educational Day 8–16
No of pupils: 72
Fees: (September 08) Day £8100

ST PAUL'S GIRLS' SCHOOL
Brook Green, London W6 7BS
Tel: (020) 7603 2288
Fax: (020) 7602 9932
Email: admissions@spgs.org
Head: Ms C Faarr
Type: Girls Day 11–18
Fees: On application

England – London

W8

ABINGDON HOUSE SCHOOL[†]
4–6 Abingdon Road, London
W8 6AF
Tel: (0845) 230 0426
Fax: (020) 7361 0751
Email: ahs@
    abingdonhouseschool.co.uk
Head: Mr N Rees
Type: Co-educational Day 4–11
No of pupils: B38 G8
Fees: (September 08) Day £7325

W8

ASHBOURNE INDEPENDENT SIXTH FORM COLLEGE*
17 Old Court Place, Kensington,
London W8 4PL
Tel: (020) 7937 3858
Fax: (020) 7937 2207
Email: admin@
    ashbournecollege.co.uk
Head: Mr M J H Kirby
Type: Co-educational Day and
Boarding 14–19
No of pupils: B85 G90
Fees: (September 08) Day £17100

ASHBOURNE MIDDLE SCHOOL*
17 Old Court Place, Kensington,
London W8 4PL
Tel: (020) 7937 3858
Fax: (020) 7937 2207
Email: admin@
    ashbournecollege.co.uk
Head: Mr M J A Kirby
Type: Co-educational Day 12–16
No of pupils: B14 G11
Fees: (September 08) Day £17100

HAWKESDOWN HOUSE SCHOOL*
27 Edge Street, Kensington,
London W8 7PN
Tel: (020) 7727 9090
Fax: (020) 7727 9988
Email: admin@hawkesdown.co.uk
Head: Mrs C J Leslie
Type: Boys Day 3–8
No of pupils: 145
Fees: (September 08)
Day £10950–£12600

THOMAS'S PREPARATORY SCHOOL
17–19 Cottesmore Gardens,
London W8 5PR
Tel: (020) 7361 6500
Fax: (020) 7361 6501
Email: Dmaine@thomas-s.co.uk
Head: Mrs D Maine
Type: Co-educational Day 4–11
No of pupils: B158 G172
Fees: On application

W10

BALES COLLEGE
742 Harrow Road, London
W10 4AA
Tel: (020) 8960 5899
Fax: (020) 8960 8269
Email: info@balescollege.co.uk
Head: Mr W B Moore
Type: Co-educational Day and
Boarding 11–19
No of pupils: B50 G50
No of boarders: F18 W2
Fees: (September 08) F/WB £15300
Day £7950–£15300

BASSETT HOUSE SCHOOL*
60 Bassett Road, London W10 6JP
Tel: (020) 8969 0313
Fax: (020) 8960 9624
Email: info@bassetths.org.uk
Head: Mrs A Harris
Type: Co-educational Day 3–11
No of pupils: B66 G97
Fees: (September 08)
Day £5820–£12006

INSTITUTO ESPANOL VICENTE CANADA BLANCH
317 Portobello Road, London
W10 5SY
Tel: 020 89692664
Fax: 020 89689432
Email: canada.blanch.uk@mec.es
Head: Mr A Vitria
Type: Co-educational Day 4–19
No of pupils: B208 G227
Fees: On application

THE LLOYD WILLIAMSON SCHOOL
12 Telford Road, London W10 5SH
Tel: (020) 8962 0345
Fax: (020) 8962 0345
Email: office@
    lloydwilliamson.demon.co.uk
Head: Mrs L Meyer and
Mr A Williams
Type: Co-educational Day 0–14
No of pupils: B60 G60
Fees: (September 07)
Day £8220–£11250

W11

DAVID GAME COLLEGE*
69 Notting Hill Gate, London
W11 3JS
Tel: (020) 7221 6665
Fax: (020) 7243 1730
Email: nhg@
    davidgame-group.com
Head: Mr D Game
Type: Co-educational Day 15–25
No of pupils: B230 G190
Fees: On application

NORLAND PLACE SCHOOL
162–166 Holland Park Avenue,
London W11 4UH
Tel: (020) 7603 9103
Fax: (020) 7603 0648
Email: office@norlandplace.com
Head: Mr P Mattar
Type: Co-educational Day
Boys 4–8 Girls 4–11
No of pupils: B90 G150
Fees: (September 08)
Day £9327–£11775

NOTTING HILL PREPARATORY SCHOOL
95 Lancaster Road, London
W11 1QQ
Tel: (020) 7221 0727
Fax: (020) 7221 0332
Email: admin@
    nottinghillprep.com
Head: Mrs J Cameron
Type: Co-educational Day 5–13
No of pupils: B103 G113
Fees: (September 08) Day £12390

SOUTHBANK INTERNATIONAL SCHOOL, KENSINGTON

36–38 Kensington Park Road, London W11 3BU
Tel: (020) 7243 3803
Fax: (020) 7727 3290
Email: admissions@southbank.org
Head: Ms J Kingsbury
Type: Co-educational Day 3–11
No of pupils: B87 G101
Fees: (September 07)
Day £14100–£16500

TABERNACLE SCHOOL

32 St Ann's Villas, London W11 4RS
Tel: 08702 408207
Fax: 08702 408207
Email: tabernacleschool@ hotmail.co.uk
Head: Mrs P Wilson
Type: Co-educational Day 3–18
No of pupils: B16 G31
Fees: On application

THE WALMER ROAD SCHOOL

221 Walmer Road, London W11 4EY
Tel: 020 72292928
Fax: 020 73135258
Email: paul@rpt.org.uk
Head: Mr P Moody
Type: Co-educational Day 14–16
No of pupils: B6 G1
Fees: On application

WETHERBY PREPARATORY SCHOOL*

19 Pembridge Villas, London W11 3EP
Tel: (020) 7243 0243
Fax: (020) 7313 5244
Email: admin@ wetherbyprep.co.uk
Head: Mr N R Baker
Type: Boys Day 8–13
No of pupils: 103
Fees: (September 08) Day £12600

W13

AVENUE HOUSE SCHOOL

70 The Avenue, Ealing, London W13 8LS
Tel: (020) 8998 9981
Fax: (020) 8991 1533
Email: avenuehouseschool@ btinternet.com
Head: Mrs C Self
Type: Co-educational Day 3–11
No of pupils: B65 G75
Fees: (September 08)
Day £4920–£8250

EALING COLLEGE UPPER SCHOOL

83 The Avenue, Ealing, London W13 8JS
Tel: (020) 8248 2312
Fax: (020) 8248 3765
Email: head@ecus.org.uk
Head: Mr C P Morris
Type: Day
No of pupils: B136 G2
Fees: (September 08) Day £7800

NOTTING HILL AND EALING HIGH SCHOOL GDST

2 Cleveland Road, Ealing, London W13 8AX
Tel: (020) 8799 8400
Fax: (020) 8810 6891
Email: enquiries@nhehs.gdst.net
Head: Ms L Hunt
Type: Girls Day 4–18
No of pupils: 880
Fees: (September 08)
Day £8637–£11100

W14

FULHAM PREP SCHOOL (PREP DEPT)*

Prep Department, 200 Greyhound Road, London W14 9SD
Tel: (020) 7386 2444
Fax: (020) 7386 2449
Email: prepadmin@ fulhamprep.co.uk
Head: Mrs J Emmett
Type: Co-educational Day 7–13
No of pupils: B221 G114
Fees: (September 08)
Day £11385–£12645

HOLLAND PARK PRE-PREPARATORY SCHOOL

5 & 9 Holland Road, London W14 8HJ
Tel: (020) 7602 9066
Email: info@hpps.co.uk
Head: Miss K Mason and Ms Eleni Tsakanika
Type: Co-educational Day 0–8
No of pupils: B69 G58
Fees: (September 08)
Day £4504–£20800

ST JAMES INDEPENDENT SCHOOLS FOR BOYS AND GIRLS

Earsby Street, Nr. Kensington Olympia, London W14 8SH
Tel: (020) 7348 1777
Fax: (020) 7348 1790
Email: office@stjamesjunior.org
Head: Mr P Moss
Type: Co-educational Day 4–10
No of pupils: B93 G139
Fees: (September 08) Day £9750

ST JAMES SENIOR GIRLS' SCHOOL

Earsby Street, London W14 8SH
Tel: (020) 7348 1777
Fax: (020) 7348 1717
Email: admissions@sjsg.org.uk
Head: Mrs L A Hyde
Type: Girls Day 10–18
No of pupils: 266
Fees: (September 08) Day £11100

ST JAMES INDEPENDENT SCHOOLS FOR JUNIOR BOYS AND GIRLS

Earsby Street, near Kensington Olympia, London W14 8SH
Tel: (020) 7348 1777
Fax: (020) 7348 1790
Email: admissions@ stjamesjunior.org
Head: Mr P Moss
Type: Co-educational Day 4–10
No of pupils: B93 G139
Fees: (September 08) Day £9750

England – London

WC2

ROYAL BALLET SCHOOL
46 Floral Street, London
WC2E 9DA
Tel: (020) 7836 8899
Fax: (020) 7845 7080
Email: johnm@
 royalballetschool.co.uk
Head: Mr M Fosten
Type: Co-educational Boarding
and Day 11–18
No of pupils: B93 G109
No of boarders: F151
Fees: (September 08) FB £30011
Day £22221

GREATER MANCHESTER

BOLTON

AL JAMIAH AL ISLAMIYYAH
Hospital Road, Bromley Cross,
Bolton, Greater Manchester
BL7 9PY
Tel: (01204) 665779
Fax: (01204) 62622
Email: admin@
 al-jamiah-al-islamiyyah.org.uk
Head: Dr S J Haneef
Type: Boys Day 13–16
No of pupils: 150
Fees: On application

ECCLES

**BRANWOOD PREPARATORY
SCHOOL**
Stafford Road, Monton, Eccles,
Greater Manchester M30 9HN
Tel: (0161) 789 1054
Fax: (0161) 789 0561
Email: mail@
 branwoodschool.co.uk
Head: Mr W M Howard
Type: Co-educational Day 3–11
No of pupils: B95 G95
Fees: On application

**CLARENDON COTTAGE
SCHOOL**
Ivy Bank House, Half Edge Lane,
Eccles, Greater Manchester
M30 9BJ
Tel: (0161) 950 7868
Fax: (0161) 661 3822
Email: clarendon.cottage@
 dial.pipex.com
Head: Mrs E Bagnall
Type: Co-educational Day 1–11
No of pupils: B120 G100
Fees: On application

**MONTON PREP SCHOOL
WITH MONTESSORI
NURSERIES**
The School House, Francis Street,
Monton, Eccles,
Greater Manchester M30 9PR
Tel: (0161) 789 0472
Email: monton.village@
 dial.pipex.com
Head: Miss D S Bradburn
Type: Co-educational Day 2–13
No of pupils: B74 G80
Fees: On application

MANCHESTER

ABBEY COLLEGE
Cheapside, King Street,
Manchester, Greater Manchester
M2 4WG
Tel: (0161) 817 2700
Fax: (0161) 817 2705
Email: admin@
 abbeymanchester.co.uk
Head: Mrs J Thomas
Type: Co-educational Day 15–21
No of pupils: B90 G90
Fees: On application

**ABBOTSFORD
PREPARATORY SCHOOL**
211 Flixton Road, Urmston,
Manchester, Greater Manchester
M41 5PR
Tel: (0161) 748 3261
Fax: (0161) 748 7961
Email: secretary@
 abbotsford-prep.trafford.sch.uk
Head: Mr P Meehan
Type: Co-educational Day 3–11
No of pupils: B45 G47
Fees: (September 07)
Day £3927–£5217

BRIDGEWATER SCHOOL
Drywood Hall, Worsley Road,
Worsley, Manchester, Greater
Manchester M28 2WQ
Tel: (0161) 794 1463
Fax: (0161) 794 3519
Email: admin@
  bridgewater-school.org.uk
Head: Ms G A Shannon-Little
Type: Co-educational Day 3–18
No of pupils: B268 G248
Fees: On application

CHETHAM'S SCHOOL OF MUSIC
Long Millgate, Manchester,
Greater Manchester M3 1SB
Tel: (0161) 834 9644
Fax: (0161) 839 3609
Email: chets@chethams.com
Head: Mrs C J Hickman
Type: Co-educational Boarding
and Day 8–18
No of pupils: B140 G150
No of boarders: F229
Fees: On application

KASSIM DARWISH GRAMMAR SCHOOL FOR BOYS
Hartley Hall, Alexandra Road
South, Chorlton-cum-Hardy,
Manchester, Greater Manchester
M16 8NH
Tel: (0161) 860–7676
Fax: (0161) 860–0011
Email: kdgb_ad@hotmail.com
Head: Mrs M Mohamed
Type: Boys Day 11–16
No of pupils: 166
Fees: (September 08) Day £5664

KING OF KINGS SCHOOL
142 Dantzic Street, Manchester,
Greater Manchester M4 4DN
Tel: (0161) 834 4214
Email: staff@kingofkings.org.uk
Head: Mrs B Lewis
Type: Co-educational Day 3–16
No of pupils: B14 G10
Fees: On application

LIGHTHOUSE CHRISTIAN SCHOOL
193 Ashley Lane, Moston,
Manchester, Greater Manchester
M9 4NQ
Tel: 0161 2050957
Fax: 0161 2563973
Email: lighthousecsm9@aol.com
Head: Mr Akintayo Akinyele
Type: Co-educational Day 2–14
No of pupils: B12 G6
Fees: On application

THE MANCHESTER GRAMMAR SCHOOL
Old Hall Lane, Manchester,
Greater Manchester M13 0XT
Tel: (0161) 224 7201
Fax: (0161) 257 2446
Email: general@mgs.org
Head: Dr C Ray
Type: Boys Day 9–18
No of pupils: 1470
Fees: (September 08) Day £8976

MANCHESTER HIGH SCHOOL FOR GIRLS
Grangethorpe Road, Manchester,
Greater Manchester M14 6HS
Tel: (0161) 224 0447
Fax: (0161) 224 2255
Email: administration@
  mhsg.manchester.sch.uk
Head: Mrs C Hewitt
Type: Girls Day 4–18
No of pupils: 932
Fees: (September 08)
Day £6150–£8634

MANCHESTER ISLAMIC HIGH SCHOOL
55 High Lane, Chorlton,
Manchester, Greater Manchester
M21 9FA
Tel: (0161) 881 2127
Fax: (0161) 861 0534
Email: mihsg_ad@hotmail.com
Head: Mrs M Mohamed
Type: Girls Day 11–16
Fees: On application

MANCHESTER MUSLIM PREPARATORY SCHOOL
551 Wilmslow Road, Withington,
Manchester, Greater Manchester
M20 4BA
Tel: (0161) 445 5452
Fax: (0161) 445 2283
Email: admin@
  muslimprepschool.co.uk
Head: Mrs A Ali
Type: Co-educational Day 3–11
No of pupils: B79 G104
Fees: (September 08)
Day £3810–£4065

MOOR ALLERTON SCHOOL
131 Barlow Moor Road,
Manchester, Greater Manchester
M20 2PW
Tel: (0161) 445 4521
Fax: (0161) 434 5294
Email: office@moorallertonschool.
  manchester.sch.uk
Head: Mr P S Millard
Type: Co-educational Day 3–11
No of pupils: B117 G110
Fees: (September 08)
Day £5730–£6600

ST BEDE'S COLLEGE
Alexandra Park, Manchester,
Greater Manchester M16 8HX
Tel: (0161) 226 3323
Fax: (0161) 226 3813
Email: enquiries@
  stbedescollege.co.uk
Head: Mr J Byrne
Type: Co-educational Day 4–18
Fees: On application

WILLIAM HULME'S GRAMMAR SCHOOL
Spring Bridge Road, Manchester,
Greater Manchester M16 8PR
Tel: (0161) 226 2054
Fax: (0161) 232 5544
Email: enquiries@
  whgs-academy.org
Head: Mr Peter Mulholland
Type: Co-educational Day 3–18
No of pupils: B340 G168
Fees: (September 08)

England – Greater Manchester

WITHINGTON GIRLS' SCHOOL
100, Wellington Road,
Fallowfield, Manchester, Greater
Manchester M14 6BL
Tel: (0161) 224 1077
Fax: (0161) 248 5377
Email: office@
    withington.manchester.sch.uk
Head: Mrs J D Pickering
Type: Girls Day 7–18
No of pupils: 650
Fees: (September 08)
Day £6858–£9018

PRESTWICH

PRESTWICH PREPARATORY SCHOOL
400 Bury Old Road, Prestwich,
Greater Manchester M25 1PZ
Tel: (0161) 773 1223
Head: Miss Shiels and Mr D R
Sheldon
Type: Co-educational Day 2–11
No of pupils: B60 G60
Fees: On application

SALFORD

HUBERT JEWISH HIGH SCHOOL FOR GIRLS
10 Radford Street, Salford, Greater
Manchester M7 4NT
Tel: (0161) 792 2118
Head: Rabbi Y Goldblatt
Type: Girls Day 11–18
No of pupils: 165
Fees: On application

MERSEYSIDE

BIRKENHEAD

HIGHFIELD SCHOOL
96 Bidston Road, Oxton,
Birkenhead, Merseyside
CH43 6TW
Tel: (0151) 652 3708
Fax: (0151) 652 3708
Email: highfield.school@
    btinternet.com
Head: Mrs S Morris
Type: Co-educational Day 2–16
No of pupils: B20 G100
Fees: On application

FORMBY

CLARENCE HIGH SCHOOL
West Lane, Freshfield, Formby,
Merseyside L37 7AZ
Tel: (01704) 872151
Fax: (01704) 831001
Email: Clarence.High@
    nugentcare.org
Head: Mr D McKillop
Type: Co-educational Boarding
and Day 9–17
No of pupils: B45 G15
No of boarders: F30
Fees: On application

LIVERPOOL

ATHERTON HOUSE SCHOOL
6 Alexandra Road, Crosby,
Liverpool, Merseyside L23 7TF
Tel: (0151) 924 5578
Fax: (0151) 924 0421
Email: head@
    athertonhouse.ndo.co.uk
Head: Mrs A Apel
Type: Co-educational Day 2–11
No of pupils: B35 G40
Fees: On application

AUCKLAND COLLEGE
65–67 Parkfield Road, Liverpool,
Merseyside L17 4LE
Tel: 0151 7270083
Head: Ms G Akaraonye
Type: Co-educational Day 7–18
No of pupils: B98 G74
Fees: On application

BEECHENHURST PREPARATORY SCHOOL
145 Menlove Avenue, Liverpool,
Merseyside L18 3EE
Tel: (0151) 722 3279
Fax: (0151) 722 0697
Email: admin@
    beechenhurst-school.co.uk
Head: Mrs C Wright
Type: Co-educational Day 3–11
No of pupils: B55 G55
Fees: On application

CARLETON HOUSE PREPARATORY SCHOOL
Lyndhurst Road, Mossley Hill,
Liverpool, Merseyside L18 8AQ
Tel: (0151) 724 4880
Fax: (0151) 724 6086
Email: carleton@
    carletonhouse.fsbusiness.co.uk
Head: Mr P Andrew
Type: Co-educational Day 4–11
No of pupils: B88 G62
Fees: On application

LIVERPOOL COLLEGE
Queens's Drive, Mossley Hill,
Liverpool, Merseyside L18 8BG
Tel: (0151) 724 4000
Fax: (0151) 729 0105
Email: admin@
    liverpoolcollege.org.uk
Head: Mr H van Mourik Broekman
Type: Co-educational Day 3–18
No of pupils: B466 G328
Fees: (September 08)
Day £5415–£8595

MERCHANT TAYLORS' BOYS' SCHOOLS
Liverpool Road, Crosby, Liverpool,
Merseyside L23 0QP
Tel: (0151) 949 9333
Fax: (0151) 949 9300
Email: info@merchanttaylors.com
Head: Mr David Cook
Type: Boys Day 4–18
No of pupils: 794
Fees: (September 08)
Day £6012–£8181

MERCHANT TAYLORS' GIRLS' SCHOOL
Liverpool Road, Crosby, Liverpool, Merseyside L23 5SP
Tel: (0151) 924 3140
Fax: (0151) 932 1461
Email: officemtgs@
   merchanttaylors.co.uk
Head: Mrs L A Robinson
Type: Girls Day 4–18 (Boys 4–7)
No of pupils: 817
Fees: (September 08)
Day £6012–£8181

RUNNYMEDE ST EDWARD'S SCHOOL
North Drive, Sandfield Park, Liverpool, Merseyside L12 1LE
Tel: (0151) 281 2300
Fax: (0151) 281 4900
Email: podonnell@
   runnymede-school.org.uk
Head: Miss S Carter
Type: Co-educational Day 3–11
No of pupils: B190 G140
Fees: (September 08)
Day £5637–£5942

ST MARY'S COLLEGE
Crosby, Liverpool, Merseyside L23 5TW
Tel: (0151) 924 3926
Fax: (0151) 932 0363
Email: office@
   stmarys.lpool.sch.uk
Head: Mr M Kennedy
Type: Co-educational Day 0–18
No of pupils: B422 G390
Fees: (September 08)
Day £5178–£8061

STREATHAM HOUSE SCHOOL
Victoria Road West, Blundellsands, Liverpool, Merseyside L23 8UQ
Tel: (0151) 924 1514
Fax: (0151) 931 2780
Email: enquiries@
   streathamhouse.co.uk
Head: Mrs C Baxter
Type: Girls Day 2–16 (Boys 2–11)
No of pupils: B22 G139
Fees: (September 07)
Day £3390–£5685

NEWTON-LE-WILLOWS

NEWTON BANK SCHOOL
34 High Street, Newton-Le-Willows, Merseyside WA12 9SN
Tel: (01925) 225979
Head: Mrs J Butler
Type: Co-educational Day 2–10
No of pupils: B25 G38
Fees: On application

PRENTON

REDCOURT- ST ANSELMS
7 Devonshire Place, Prenton, Merseyside CH43 1TX
Tel: (0151) 652 5228
Fax: (0151) 653 5883
Email: admin@
   redcourt.wirral.sch.uk
Head: Mr K S Davey
Type: Co-educational Day 3–11
No of pupils: B141 G143
Fees: (September 07) Day £4101

PRESCOT

TOWER COLLEGE
Mill Lane, Rainhill, Prescot, Merseyside L35 6NE
Tel: (0151) 426 4333
Fax: (0151) 426 3338
Email: towercollege@lineone.net
Head: Miss R J Oxley
Type: Co-educational Day 3–16
No of pupils: B263 G276
Fees: (September 08)
Day £4644–£5445

SOUTHPORT

ARDEN COLLEGE
40 Derby Road, Southport, Merseyside PR9 0TZ
Tel: (01704) 534433
Fax: (01704) 549 711
Email: info@ardencollege.ac.uk
Head: Mr C A Mayho
Type: Co-educational Boarding and Day 16–25
No of pupils:
No of boarders: F60
Fees: (September 08)

SUNNYMEDE SCHOOL
4 Westcliffe Road, Birkdale, Southport, Merseyside PR8 2BN
Tel: (01704) 568593
Fax: (01704) 551745
Email: sunnymedeschool@
   btinternet.com
Head: Mr S J Pattinson
Type: Co-educational Day 3–11
No of pupils: B57 G59
Fees: (September 08)
Day £5100–£6300

WIRRAL

AVALON PREPARATORY SCHOOL
Caldy Road, West Kirby, Wirral, Merseyside CH48 2HE
Tel: (0151) 625 6993
Fax: (0151) 625 0332
Email: schooloffice@
   avalon-school.co.uk
Head: Dr B Scott
Type: Co-educational Day 2–11
No of pupils: B88 G89
Fees: (September 08)
Day £4785–£5205

BIRKENHEAD HIGH SCHOOL GDST
86 Devonshire Place, Prenton, Wirral, Merseyside CH43 1TY
Tel: (0151) 652 5777
Fax: (0151) 670 0639
Email: admissionssec@
   birkhs.gdst.net
Head: Mrs C H Evans
Type: Girls Day 3–19
No of pupils: 800
Fees: (September 08)
Day £5328–£8898

BIRKENHEAD SCHOOL
58 Beresford Road, Oxton, Wirral, Merseyside CH43 2JD
Tel: (0151) 652 4014
Fax: (0151) 651 3091
Email: enquire@
   birkenheadschool.co.uk
Head: Mr D J Clark
Type: Co-educational Day 3–18
No of pupils: B594 G117
Fees: (September 08)
Day £6147–£8727

England – Merseyside

HESWALL PREPARATORY SCHOOL
Carberry, 28 Quarry Road East, Heswall, Wirral, Merseyside CH60 6RB
Tel: (0151) 342 7851
Fax: (0151) 342 7851
Email: hesprep@aol.com
Head: Mrs M Hannaford
Type: Co-educational Day 3–11
No of pupils: B25 G25
Fees: (September 07)
Day £1150–£4200

KINGSMEAD SCHOOL
Bertram Drive, Hoylake, Wirral, Merseyside CH47 0LL
Tel: (0151) 632 3156
Fax: (0151) 632 0302
Email: enquiries@
   kingsmeadschool.com
Head: Mr J F Perry
Type: Co-educational Boarding and Day 3–16
No of pupils: B133 G79
No of boarders: F16 W3
Fees: (September 08)
FB £12930–£15075
WB £12390–£14535
Day £5025–£8625

PRENTON PREPARATORY SCHOOL
Mount Pleasant, Oxton, Wirral, Merseyside
Tel: (0151) 652 3182
Fax: (0151) 653 7428
Email: enquiry@
   prentonprep.co.uk
Head: Mrs N M Aloe
Type: Co-educational Day 2–11
No of pupils: B65 G87
Fees: On application

MIDDLESEX

ASHFORD

ST DAVID'S SCHOOL
Church Road, Ashford, Middlesex TW15 3DZ
Tel: (01784) 252494
Fax: (01784) 248652
Email: office@stdavidsschool.com
Head: Mrs T Smith
Type: Girls Day and Boarding 3–18
No of pupils: B10 G290
No of boarders: F25 W3
Fees: On application

BRENTFORD

LITTLE EDEN & EDEN HIGH SDA
St George's Hall, Green Dragaon Lane, Brentford, Middlesex TW8 0EN
Tel: (020) 8568 7756
Fax: (020) 8568 7756
Email: info@theedenschool.com
Head: Mrs L A Osei
Type: Co-educational Day 3–16
No of pupils: B37 G27
Fees: On application

EDGWARE

HOLLAND HOUSE
1 Broadhurst Avenue, Edgware, Middlesex HA8 8TP
Tel: (020) 8958 6979
Fax: (020) 8958 3591
Email: schooloffice@
   hollandhouse.org.uk
Head: Mrs I Tyk
Type: Co-educational Day 4–11
No of pupils: B70 G70
Fees: On application

NORTH LONDON COLLEGIATE
Canons Drive, Edgware, Middlesex HA8 7RJ
Tel: (020) 8952 0912
Fax: (020) 8951 1391
Email: office@nlcs.org.uk
Head: Mrs B McCabe
Type: Girls Day 4–18
No of pupils: 1057
Fees: On application

ENFIELD

ST JOHN'S SENIOR SCHOOL
North Lodge, The Ridgeway, Enfield, Middlesex EN2 8BE
Tel: (020) 8366 0035
Fax: (020) 8363 4439
Email: StJohnsSc@aol.com
Head: Mr A Tardios
Type: Co-educational Day Boys 11–18 Girls 10–18
No of pupils: B134 G106
Fees: On application

HAMPTON

ATHELSTAN HOUSE SCHOOL
36 Percy Road, Hampton, Middlesex TW12 2LA
Tel: (020) 8979 1045
Email: admin@
   athelstanhouseschool.co.uk
Head: Mrs E M Woolf
Type: Co-educational Day 3–7
No of pupils: B25 G32
Fees: (September 08)
Day £4200–£7128

DENMEAD SCHOOL
41–43 Wensleydale Road, Hampton, Middlesex TW12 2LP
Tel: (020) 8979 1844
Fax: (020) 8941 8773
Email: admissions@
   denmead.richmond.sch.uk
Head: Mr M T McKaughan
Type: Boys Day 2–11 (Girls 2–7)
No of pupils: B158 G18
Fees: (September 08)
Day £3885–£8970

HAMPTON SCHOOL
Hanworth Road, Hampton, Middlesex TW12 3HD
Tel: (020) 8979 5526
Fax: (020) 8783 4035
Email: headmaster@
   hamptonschool.org.uk
Head: Mr B R Martin
Type: Boys Day 11–18
No of pupils: 1130
Fees: (September 08) Day £12870

England – Middlesex

JACK AND JILL SCHOOL
30 Nightingale Road, Hampton,
Middlesex TW12 3HX
Tel: (020) 8979 3195
Fax: (020) 8979 3195
Email: jackandjillschool@
btconnect.com
Head: Miss K S Papirnik
Type: Girls Day 2–7 (Boys 3–5)
No of pupils: B22 G138
Fees: (September 08)
Day £3975–£8250

THE LADY ELEANOR HOLLES SCHOOL
102 Hanworth Road, Hampton,
Middlesex TW12 3HF
Tel: (020) 8979 1601
Fax: (020) 8979 8291
Email: office@lehs.org.uk
Head: Mrs G Low
Type: Girls Day 7–18
No of pupils: 860
Fees: (September 08)
Day £9450–£12540

TWICKENHAM PREPARATORY SCHOOL
Beveree, 43 High Street,
Hampton, Middlesex TW12 2SA
Tel: (020) 8979 6216
Fax: (020) 8979 1596
Email: office@
twickenhamprep.co.uk
Head: Mr D Malam
Type: Co-educational Day
Boys 4–13 Girls 4–11
No of pupils: B136 G130
Fees: (September 07)
Day £7584–£8196

HARROW

ALPHA PREPARATORY SCHOOL
21 Hindes Road, Harrow,
Middlesex HA1 1SH
Tel: (020) 8427 1471
Fax: (020) 8424 9324
Email: sec@alpha.harrow.sch.uk
Head: Mr P J Wylie
Type: Co-educational Day 4–11
No of pupils: B90 G70
Fees: (September 08)
Day £7230–£7920

BUCKINGHAM COLLEGE SCHOOL
15 Hindes Road, Harrow,
Middlesex HA1 1SH
Tel: (020) 8427 1220
Fax: (020) 8863 0816
Email: enquiries@buckcoll.org
Head: Mr D F T Bell
Type: Boys Day 11–18 (Co-ed VIth Form)
No of pupils: 150
Fees: On application

THE JOHN LYON SCHOOL
Middle Road, Harrow, Middlesex
HA2 0HN
Tel: (020) 8872 8400
Fax: (020) 8872 8455
Email: admissions@johnlyon.org
Head: Mr K J Riley
Type: Boys Day 11–18
No of pupils: 580
Fees: (September 07)

ORLEY FARM SCHOOL
South Hill Avenue, Harrow,
Middlesex HA1 3NU
Tel: (020) 8869 7600
Fax: (020) 8869 7601
Email: office@
orleyfarm.harrow.sch.uk
Head: Mr Mark Dunning
Type: Co-educational Day 4–13
No of pupils: B380 G90
Fees: (September 08)
Day £9600–£11550

QUAINTON HALL SCHOOL
91 Hindes Road, Harrow,
Middlesex HA1 1RX
Tel: (020) 8427 1304
Fax: (020) 8861 8861
Email: admin@quaintonhall.org.uk
Head: Mr D P Banister
Type: Co-educational Day
Boys 4–13 Girls 4–7
Fees: (September 08)
Day £7485–£8730

HARROW ON THE HILL

HARROW SCHOOL
1 High Street, Harrow on the Hill,
Middlesex HA1 3HT
Tel: (020) 8872 8003
Fax: (020) 8872 8012
Email: hm@harrowschool.org.uk
Head: Mr B J Lenon
Type: Boys Boarding 13–18
No of pupils: 800
No of boarders: F800
Fees: (September 07) FB £26445

ROXETH MEAD SCHOOL
Buckholt House, 25 Middle Road,
Harrow on the Hill, Middlesex
HA2 0HW
Tel: (020) 8422 2092
Fax: (020) 8426 4974
Email: info@roxethmead.com
Head: Mrs A J Isaacs
Type: Co-educational Day 3–7
No of pupils: B26 G35
Fees: On application

HILLINGDON

ACS HILLINGDON INTERNATIONAL SCHOOL*
Hillingdon Court, 108 Vine Lane,
Hillingdon, Middlesex UB10 0BE
Tel: (01895) 818402
Fax: (01895) 818404
Email: hillingdonadmissions@
acs-england.co.uk
Head: Mrs G Apple
Type: Co-educational Day 4–18
No of pupils: B294 G283
Fees: (September 08)
Day £8310–£17410

ST HELEN'S COLLEGE
Parkway, Hillingdon, Middlesex
UB10 9JX
Tel: (01895) 234371
Fax: (01895) 619818
Email: sthelenscoll@
easymail.rmplc.co.uk
Head: Mr D A Crehan and
Mrs G R Crehan
Type: Co-educational Day 3–11
No of pupils: B165 G175
Fees: (September 07)
Day £3750–£6300

ISLEWORTH

ASHTON HOUSE SCHOOL
50/52 Eversley Crescent,
Isleworth, Middlesex TW7 4LW
Tel: (020) 8560 3902
Fax: (020) 8568 1097
Email: principal@
ashtonhouse.com
Head: Mrs M Grundberg
Type: Co-educational Day 3–11
No of pupils: B70 G80
Fees: (September 08)
Day £5865–£8124

NORTHWOOD

MERCHANT TAYLORS' SCHOOL
Sandy Lodge, Northwood,
Middlesex HA6 2HT
Tel: (01923) 820644
Fax: (01923) 835110
Email: info@mtsn.org.uk
Head: Mr S N Wright
Type: Boys Day 11–18
No of pupils: 840
Fees: (September 08) Day £14280

NORTHWOOD COLLEGE*
Maxwell Road, Northwood,
Middlesex HA6 2YE
Tel: (01923) 825446
Fax: (01923) 836526
Email: admissions@
   northwoodcollege.co.uk
Head: Miss J Pain
Type: Girls Day 3–18
No of pupils: 817
Fees: (September 08)
Day £3334–£10975

ST HELEN'S SCHOOL*
Eastbury Road, Northwood,
Middlesex HA6 3AS
Tel: (01923) 843210
Fax: (01923) 843211
Email: enquiries@sthn.co.uk
Head: Mrs M Morris
Type: Girls Day 3–18
No of pupils: 1137
No of boarders: F5 W4
Fees: (September 08)
Day £8196–£11955

ST JOHN'S NORTHWOOD
Potter Street Hill, Northwood,
Middlesex HA6 3QY
Tel: (020) 8866 0067
Fax: (020) 8868 8770
Email: office@st-johns.org.uk
Head: Mr C R Kelly
Type: Boys Day 3–13
No of pupils: 390
Fees: (September 08)
Day £7100–£10580

ST MARTIN'S SCHOOL
40 Moor Park Road, Northwood,
Middlesex HA6 2DJ
Tel: (01923) 825740
Fax: (01923) 835452
Email: office@stmartins.org.uk
Head: Mr D T Tidmarsh
Type: Boys Day 3–13
No of pupils: 400
Fees: (September 07)
Day £3300–£10200

PINNER

BUCKINGHAM COLLEGE PREPARATORY SCHOOL
458 Rayners Lane, Pinner,
Middlesex HA5 5DT
Tel: (020) 8866 2737
Fax: (020) 8868 3228
Email: enquiries@buckprep.org
Head: Mr L Smith
Type: Boys Day 4–11
No of pupils: 117
Fees: (September 08)
Day £6660–£8712

HEATHFIELD SCHOOL*
Beaulieu Drive, Pinner, Middlesex
HA5 1NB
Tel: (020) 8868 2346
Fax: (020) 8868 4405
Email: j.moseley@hea.gdst.net
Head: Miss C Juett
Type: Girls Day 3–18
No of pupils: 550
Fees: (September 08)
Day £6663–£11100

INNELLAN HOUSE SCHOOL
44 Love Lane, Pinner, Middlesex
HA5 3EX
Tel: (020) 8866 1855
Fax: (020) 8866 1855
Email: innellan.house@virgin.net
Head: Ms J Watkins
Type: Co-educational Day 3–7
No of pupils: B27 G41
Fees: (September 08)
Day £4795–£5360

REDDIFORD
36–38 Cecil Park, Pinner,
Middlesex HA5 5HH
Tel: (020) 8866 0660
Fax: (020) 8866 4847
Email: office@reddiford.org.uk
Head: Mrs J Batt
Type: Co-educational Day 2–11
No of pupils: B180 G122
Fees: On application

SHEPPERTON

HALLIFORD SCHOOL
Russell Road, Shepperton,
Middlesex TW17 9HX
Tel: (01932) 223593
Fax: (01932) 229781
Email: registrar@
   hallifordschool.co.uk
Head: Mr P V Cottam
Type: Boys Day 11–19 (Co-ed VIth
Form)
No of pupils: B365 G7
Fees: (September 08) Day £9600

SOUTHALL

ACORN INDEPENDENT COLLEGE
39–47 High Street, Southall,
Middlesex UB1 3HF
Tel: (020) 85719900
Fax: (020) 85719901
Email: acorncollege@
   hotmail.co.uk
Head: Mrs Gladys Watt
Type: Co-educational Day 13–20
No of pupils: B65 G48
Fees: (September 07)
Day £1528–£12860

STAINES

STAINES PREPARATORY SCHOOL
3 Gresham Road, Staines,
Middlesex TW18 2BT
Tel: (01784) 450909
Fax: (01784) 464424
Email: registrar@stainesprep.co.uk
Head: Mr P Roberts
Type: Co-educational Day 3–11
No of pupils: B203 G122
Fees: (September 08)
Day £2205–£7650

STANMORE

PETERBOROUGH & ST MARGARET'S SCHOOL
Common Road, Stanmore,
Middlesex HA7 3JB
Tel: (020) 8950 3600
Fax: (020) 8421 8946
Email: psm@psmschool.org
Head: Mrs S R Watts
Type: Girls Day 4–16
No of pupils: 235
Fees: (September 07)
Day £6228–£9255

TWICKENHAM

THE MALL SCHOOL
185 Hampton Road, Twickenham,
Middlesex TW2 5NQ
Tel: (020) 8977 2523
Fax: (020) 8977 8771
Email: admissions@
mall.richmond.sch.uk
Head: Dr J G Jeanes
Type: Boys Day 4–13
No of pupils: 300
Fees: (September 08)
Day £8295–£9600

NEWLAND HOUSE SCHOOL
Waldegrave Park, Twickenham,
Middlesex TW1 4TQ
Tel: (020) 8892 7479
Fax: (020) 8744 0399
Email: school@
newlandhouse.co.uk
Head: Mr D J Ott
Type: Co-educational Day
Boys 4–13 Girls 4–11
No of pupils: B271 G152
Fees: On application

ST CATHERINE'S SCHOOL*
Cross Deep, Twickenham,
Middlesex TW1 4QJ
Tel: (020) 8891 2898
Fax: (020) 8744 9629
Email: info@
stcatherineschool.co.uk
Head: Sister P Thomas
Type: Day Girls 3–16 Boys 3–7
(Sixth form in 2010)
No of pupils: B4 G350
Fees: (September 07)
Day £7275–£10065

ST JAMES INDEPENDENT SCHOOL FOR BOYS (SENIOR)
Pope's Villa, 19 Cross Deep,
Twickenham, Middlesex
TW1 4QG
Tel: (020) 8892 2002
Fax: (020) 8892 4442
Email: admissions@
stjamesboys.co.uk
Head: Mr David Boddy
Type: Boys Day and Boarding
10–18
No of pupils: 300
No of boarders: W17
Fees: (September 08) WB £15450
Day £11100

SUNFLOWER MONTESSORI SCHOOL
8 Victoria Road, Twickenham,
Middlesex TW1 3HW
Tel: (020) 8891 2675
Fax: (020) 8891 1204
Email: deb@sunmont.fsnet.co.uk
Head: Mrs J Yandell and Mrs
Eileen Tiahlo
Type: Co-educational Day 2–6
No of pupils: B36 G22
Fees: (September 07)
Day £1050–£1650

WEMBLEY

BUXLOW PREPARATORY SCHOOL
5/6 Castleton Gardens, Wembley,
Middlesex HA9 7QJ
Tel: (020) 8904 3615
Fax: (020) 8904 3606
Email: buxlow@happychild.co.uk
Head: Mrs A Baines
Type: Co-educational Day 4–11
No of pupils: B50 G50
Fees: On application

ST CHRISTOPHER'S SCHOOL
71 Wembley Park Drive,
Wembley, Middlesex HA9 8HE
Tel: (020) 8902 5069
Fax: (020) 8903 5939
Email: stchris.head@
happychild.co.uk
Head: Mr J M B Edwards
Type: Co-educational Day 4–11
No of pupils: B49 G50
Fees: (September 08)
Day £6330–£6660

NORFOLK

CROMER

BEESTON HALL SCHOOL
West Runton, Cromer, Norfolk
NR27 9NQ
Tel: (01263) 837324
Fax: (01263) 838177
Email: office@beestonhall.co.uk
Head: Mr I K MacAskill
Type: Co-educational Boarding
and Day 7–13
No of pupils: B103 G70
No of boarders: F91
Fees: (September 07) FB £16575
Day £12375

DISS

RIDDLESWORTH HALL†
Diss, Norfolk IP22 2TA
Tel: (01953) 681246
Fax: (01953) 688124
Email: rhps@riddlesworthhall.com
Head: Mr P.I. Cochrane
Type: Co-educational Day and
Boarding Boys 2–11 Girls 2–13
(Girls' only boarding)
No of pupils: B24 G101
No of boarders: F16 W6
Fees: (September 07) FB £5300
WB £4990 Day £3045

HOLT

GRESHAM'S PREPARATORY SCHOOL
Cromer Road, Holt, Norfolk
NR25 6EY
Tel: (01263) 714600
Fax: (01263) 714060
Email: prep@greshams.com
Head: Mr J H W Quick
Type: Co-educational Day and
Boarding 8–13
No of pupils: B126 G126
No of boarders: F45
Fees: On application

England – Middlesex/Norfolk

GRESHAM'S SCHOOL
Cromer Road, Holt, Norfolk
NR25 6EA
Tel: (01263) 714500
Fax: (01263) 712028
Email: headmaster@greshams.com
Head: Mr P John
Type: Co-educational Boarding
and Day 13–18
No of pupils: B260 G216
No of boarders: F270
Fees: (September 08) FB £24150
Day £18450

HUNSTANTON

GLEBE HOUSE SCHOOL
2 Cromer Road, Hunstanton,
Norfolk PE36 6HW
Tel: (01485) 532809
Fax: (01485) 533900
Email: jpc@
glebehouseschool.co.uk
Head: Mr J Crofts
Type: Co-educational Boarding
and Day 4–13
No of pupils: B61 G54
No of boarders: W33
Fees: (September 07)
WB £11010–£12780
Day £7200–£10800

KINGS LYNN

DOWNHAM PREP SCHOOL AND MONTESSORI NURSERY
The Old Rectory, Stow Bardolph,
Kings Lynn, Norfolk PE34 3HT
Tel: (01366) 388066
Fax: (01366) 388066
Email: down.mont@talk21.com
Head: Mrs E J Laffeaty-Sharpe
Type: Co-educational Day 2–11
No of pupils: B72 G68
Fees: On application

NORTH WALSHAM

ST NICHOLAS HOUSE KINDERGARTEN & PREP SCHOOL
Yarmouth Road, North Walsham,
Norfolk NR28 9AT
Tel: (01692) 403143
Fax: (01692) 403143
Email: stnicholas@
yarmouth47.fsnet.co.uk
Head: Mr C Wardle
Type: Co-educational Day 3–11
No of pupils: B50 G60
Fees: (September 08) Day £3600

NORWICH

ALL SAINTS SCHOOL
School Road, Lessingham,
Norwich, Norfolk NR12 0DJ
Tel: (01692) 582083
Fax: (01692) 584999
Email: headmistress@
allsaintslessingham.co.uk
Head: Mrs J Gardiner
Type: Co-educational Day 2–16
No of pupils: B40 G40
Fees: (September 08) Day £4320

HETHERSETT OLD HALL SCHOOL
Hethersett, Norwich, Norfolk
NR9 3DW
Tel: (01603) 810390
Fax: (01603) 812094
Email: enquiries@hohs.co.uk
Head: Mr S Crump
Type: Co-educational Boarding
and Day Boys 4–11
Girls 4–18(Boys 4–7)
No of pupils: B10 G211
No of boarders: F13 W2
Fees: (September 07) FB £18585
WB £15000 Day £6300–£9900

LANGLEY PREPARATORY SCHOOL & NURSERY
Beech Hill, 11 Yarmouth Road,
Thorpe St Andrew, Norwich,
Norfolk NR7 0EA
Tel: (01603) 433861
Fax: (01603) 702639
Email: headmaster@
langleyprep.norfolk.sch.uk
Head: Mr S B Marfleet
Type: Co-educational Day 2–11
No of pupils: B70 G10
Fees: On application

LANGLEY SCHOOL
Langley Park, Loddon, Norwich,
Norfolk NR14 6BJ
Tel: (01508) 520210
Fax: (01508) 528058
Email: office@langleyschool.co.uk
Head: Dominic Findlay
Type: Co-educational Boarding
and Day 10–18
No of pupils: B302 G138
No of boarders: F54 W36
Fees: (September 07)
FB £15510–£18675
WB £13425–£15510
Day £7080–£9180

THE NEW ECCLES HALL SCHOOL
Quidenham, Norwich, Norfolk
NR16 2NZ
Tel: (01953) 887217
Fax: (01953) 887397
Email: admin@neweccleshall.com
Head: Mr R W Allard
Type: Co-educational Day and
Boarding 4–16
No of pupils: B170 G50
No of boarders: F70 W55
Fees: (September 07)
F/WB £12735–£15105
Day £4875–£8100

NORWICH HIGH SCHOOL FOR GIRLS GDST
Eaton Grove, 95 Newmarket
Road, Norwich, Norfolk NR2 2HU
Tel: (01603) 453265
Fax: (01603) 259891
Email: admissions@nor.gdst.net
Head: Mrs V C Bidwell
Type: Girls Day 3–18
No of pupils: 886
Fees: (September 08)
Day £6450–£8898

NORWICH SCHOOL
70 The Close, Norwich, Norfolk
NR1 4DD
Tel: (01603) 728430
Fax: (01603) 728491
Email: admissions@
norwich-school.org.uk
Head: Mr J B Hawkins
Type: Co-educational Day 7–18
(Co-ed VIth Form)
No of pupils: B839 G93
Fees: (September 07)
Day £9480–£9852

NOTRE DAME PREPARATORY SCHOOL
147 Dereham Road, Norwich, Norfolk NR2 3TA
Tel: (01603) 625593
Fax: (01603) 444139
Email: info@
notredameprepschool.co.u
Head: Mr KJ O'Herlihy
Type: Co-educational Day 3–11
No of pupils: B58 G55
Fees: On application

ST CHRISTOPHER'S SCHOOL
George Hill, Old Catton, Norwich, Norfolk NR6 7DE
Tel: (01603) 425179
Email: admin@
stchristophers.connectadsl.co.uk
Head: Mrs J Higgins
Type: Co-educational Day 2–8
No of pupils: B80 G60
Fees: On application

STRETTON SCHOOL
1 Albemarle Road, Norwich, Norfolk NR2 2DF
Tel: (01603) 451285
Fax: (01603) 458842
Email: enquiries@
stretton-school.co.uk
Head: Mrs Y D Barnett
Type: Co-educational Day 1–8
No of pupils: B50 G50
Fees: On application

TAVERHAM HALL PREPARATORY SCHOOL
Taverham Park, Taverham, Norwich, Norfolk NR8 6HU
Tel: (01603) 868206
Fax: (01603) 861061
Email: enquire@
taverhamhall.co.uk
Head: Mr M A Crossley
Type: Co-educational Boarding and Day 1–13
No of pupils: B130 G94
No of boarders: W25
Fees: (September 08) WB £13950 Day £7200–£12474

THORPE HOUSE SCHOOL
7 Yarmouth Road, Norwich, Norfolk NR7 0EA
Tel: (01603) 433055
Fax: (01603) 436323
Email: office@
thorpehouseschool.com
Head: Ms Anne Marie Sutcliffe
Type: Girls Day 3–16
No of pupils: 280
Fees: On application

TOWN CLOSE HOUSE PREPARATORY SCHOOL
14 Ipswich Road, Norwich, Norfolk NR2 2LR
Tel: (01603) 620180
Fax: (01603) 618256
Email: admissions@
townclose.com
Head: Mr Graeme Lowe
Type: Co-educational Day 3–13
No of pupils: B290 G207
Fees: (September 08) Day £5985–£9375

WOOD DENE SCHOOL
Aylmerton Hall, Holt Road, Aylmerton, Norwich, Norfolk NR11 8QA
Tel: (01263) 837224
Fax: (01263) 835837
Email: mail@wood-dene.co.uk
Head: Mrs D M Taylor
Type: Co-educational Day 2–16
No of pupils: B90 G110
Fees: On application

SWAFFHAM

SACRED HEART SCHOOL
17 Mangate Street, Swaffham, Norfolk PE37 7QW
Tel: (01760) 721330
Fax: (01760) 725557
Email: info@
sacredheartschool.co.uk
Head: Miss D Wynter
Type: Co-educational Day and Boarding 3–16
No of pupils: B13 G174
No of boarders: W12
Fees: (September 07)

THETFORD

THETFORD GRAMMAR SCHOOL
Bridge Street, Thetford, Norfolk IP24 3AF
Tel: (01842) 752840
Fax: (01842) 750220
Email: enquiries@
thetfordgrammarschool.
fsnet.co.uk
Head: Mr G J Price
Type: Co-educational Day 3–18
No of pupils: B200 G130
Fees: (September 08) Day £7872–£9519

England – Norfolk

NORTHAMPTONSHIRE

BLACKTHORN

ST PETER'S INDEPENDENT SCHOOL
Lingswood Park, Blackthorn,
Northamptonshire NN3 8TA
Tel: (01604) 411745
Head: Mr G J Smith
Type: Co-educational Day 4–18
No of pupils: 170
Fees: On application

BRACKLEY

BEACHBOROUGH SCHOOL
Westbury, Brackley,
Northamptonshire NN13 5LB
Tel: (01280) 700071
Fax: (01280) 704839
Email: office@beachborough.com
Head: Mr J Whybrow
Type: Co-educational Day and
Boarding 2–13
No of pupils: B132 G95
No of boarders: W49
Fees: On application

WINCHESTER HOUSE SCHOOL
Brackley, Northamptonshire
NN13 7AZ
Tel: (01280) 702483
Fax: (01280) 706400
Email: office@
winchester-house.org
Head: Mr M S Seymour
Type: Co-educational Boarding
and Day 3–13
No of pupils: B232 G144
No of boarders: F15 W54
Fees: (September 07) FB £16065
WB £12750–£16065
Day £5325–£12150

KETTERING

ST PETER'S SCHOOL
52 Headlands, Kettering,
Northamptonshire NN15 6DJ
Tel: (01536) 512066
Fax: (01536) 416469
Email: info@st-peters.org.uk
Head: Mrs M Chapman
Type: Co-educational Day 2–11
No of pupils: B57 G78
Fees: On application

NORTHAMPTON

BOSWORTH INDEPENDENT COLLEGE*
Nazareth House, Barrack Road,
Northampton, Northamptonshire
NN2 6AF
Tel: (01604) 235090
Fax: (01604) 239996
Email: info@bosworthcollege.com
Head: Mr M McQuin
Type: Co-educational Boarding
and Day 14–21
No of pupils: B170 G150
No of boarders: F240 W3
Fees: (September 08) FB £19500
WB £18600 Day £10600–£13600

GREAT HOUGHTON PREPARATORY SCHOOL
Great Houghton Hall,
Northampton, Northamptonshire
NN4 7AG
Tel: (01604) 761907
Fax: (01604) 761251
Email: office@ghps.co.uk
Head: Mr R O Barnes
Type: Co-educational Day 1–13
No of pupils: B216 G91
Fees: (September 08)
Day £6183–£10398

MAIDWELL HALL SCHOOL
Maidwell, Northampton,
Northamptonshire NN6 9JG
Tel: (01604) 686234
Fax: (01604) 686659
Email: headmaster@
maidwellhall.co.uk
Head: Mr R A Lankester
Type: Boys Boarding and Day
7–13
No of pupils: 102
No of boarders: F98 W4
Fees: (September 07) F/WB £18900
Day £14400

NORTHAMPTON HIGH SCHOOL
Newport Pagnell Road,
Hardingstone, Northampton,
Northamptonshire NN4 6UU
Tel: (01604) 765765
Fax: (01604) 709418
Email: admin@
northamptonhigh.co.uk
Head: Mrs S Dixon
Type: Girls Day 3–18
No of pupils: 770
Fees: (September 07)
Day £6870–£8970

QUINTON HOUSE SCHOOL
Upton Hall, Upton, Northampton,
Northamptonshire NN5 4UX
Tel: (01604) 752050
Fax: (01604) 581707
Email: info@
quintonhouseschool.co.uk
Head: Mr J R O'Leary
Type: Co-educational Day 3–18
No of pupils: B163 G162
Fees: On application

ST MATTHEWS SCHOOL
100 Park Avenue North,
Northampton, Northamptonshire
NN3 2JB
Tel: (01604) 712647
Email: principal@
st-matthewsschool.co.uk
Head: Mrs L Burgess
Type: Co-educational Day 2–9
No of pupils: B30 G30
Fees: On application

SPRATTON HALL
Spratton, Northampton,
Northamptonshire NN6 8HP
Tel: (01604) 847292
Fax: (01604) 820844
Email: office@sprattonhall.com
Head: Mr S Player
Type: Co-educational Day 4–13
No of pupils: B202 G200
Fees: (September 08)
Day £6975–£10275

NR PETERBOROUGH

LAXTON JUNIOR SCHOOL*
East Road, Oundle,
Nr Peterborough,
Northamptonshire PE8 4BX
Tel: (01832) 277275
Fax: (01832) 277271
Email: admissions@
  laxtonjunior.org.uk
Head: Mr M J Potter
Type: Co-educational Day 4–11
No of pupils: B124 G131
Fees: (September 08)
Day £8160–£8955

OUNDLE SCHOOL
The Great Hall, New Street,
Oundle, Nr Peterborough,
Northamptonshire PE8 4GH
Tel: (01832) 277125
Fax: (01832) 277128
Email: admissions@
  oundleschool.org.uk
Head: Mr C M P Bush
Type: Co-educational Boarding
and Day 11–19
No of pupils: B638 G433
No of boarders: F842
Fees: (September 08)
FB £19245–£25350
Day £12630–£16515

PITSFORD

**NORTHAMPTONSHIRE
GRAMMAR SCHOOL**
Pitsford Hall, Moulton Lane,
Pitsford, Northamptonshire
NN6 9AX
Tel: (01604) 880306
Fax: (01604) 882212
Email: office@ngs-school.com
Head: Mr N R Toone
Type: Co-educational Day 4–18
No of pupils: B161 G139
Fees: (September 08)
Day £6105–£10596

TOWCESTER

**SLAPTON
PRE-PREPARATORY SCHOOL**
Chapel Lane, Slapton, Towcester,
Northamptonshire NN12 8PE
Tel: (01327) 860158
Fax: (01327) 860158
Email: admin@slaptonpreprep.org
Head: Mrs P M Young
Type: Co-educational Day 4–8
(Pre-Prep)
No of pupils: B18 G18
Fees: On application

WELLINGBOROUGH

**WELLINGBOROUGH
SCHOOL**
Wellingborough,
Northamptonshire NN8 2BX
Tel: (01933) 222427
Fax: (01933) 271986
Email: headmaster@
  wellingboroughschool.org
Head: Mr G R Bowe
Type: Co-educational Day 3–18
No of pupils: B496 G337
Fees: On application

NORTHUMBERLAND

ALNWICK

ROCK HALL SCHOOL
Rock, Alnwick, Northumberland
NE66 3SB
Tel: (01665) 579224
Fax: (01665) 579467
Email: rockhallschool@
  btinternet.com
Head: Mrs L A Bosanquet
Type: Co-educational Day 3–13
No of pupils: B31 G29
Fees: On application

ST OSWALD'S SCHOOL
Spring Gardens, South Road,
Alnwick, Northumberland
NE66 2NU
Tel: (01665) 602739
Fax: (01665) 602817
Email: st-oswalds@
  alnwick.fsnet.co.uk
Head: Mr R Croft
Type: Co-educational Day 3–16
No of pupils: B52 G58
Fees: On application

BERWICK-UPON-TWEED

**LONGRIDGE TOWERS
SCHOOL**
Berwick-upon-Tweed,
Northumberland TD15 2XQ
Tel: (01289) 307584
Fax: (01289) 302581
Email: admissions@lts.org.uk
Head: Mr AE Clemit
Type: Co-educational Day and
Boarding 4–18
No of pupils: B165 G160
No of boarders: F21 W12
Fees: (September 07)
FB £17625–£18840
WB £15795–£17010
Day £5685–£8985

STOCKSFIELD

MOWDEN HALL SCHOOL
Newton, Stocksfield,
Northumberland NE43 7TP
Tel: (01661) 842147
Fax: (01661) 842529
Email: lb@mowdenhall.co.uk
Head: Mr B Beardmore Gray
Type: Co-educational Boarding
and Day 3–13
No of pupils: B136 G102
No of boarders: F110 W8
Fees: (September 08)
Day £7710–£17310

NOTTINGHAMSHIRE

MANSFIELD

MANSFIELD PREPARATORY SCHOOL
Welbeck Road, Mansfield,
Nottinghamshire NG19 9LA
Tel: (01623) 420940
Head: Miss J Sparrow
Type: Co-educational Day 3–11
No of pupils: B50 G39
Fees: On application

SAVILLE HOUSE SCHOOL
11 Church Street, Mansfield
Woodhouse, Mansfield,
Nottinghamshire NG19 8AH
Tel: (01623) 625068
Fax: (01623) 659983
Email: cherubsnurseries@aol.com
Head: Mrs J Nutter
Type: Co-educational Day 3–11
No of pupils: B39 G46
Fees: (September 08) Day £3600

NEWARK

HIGHFIELDS SCHOOL
London Road, Newark,
Nottinghamshire NG24 3AL
Tel: (01636) 704103
Fax: (01636) 680919
Email: office@
   highfieldsschool.co.uk
Head: Mr D R Wood
Type: Co-educational Day 3–11
No of pupils: B92 G90
Fees: (September 08) Day £6000

WELLOW HOUSE SCHOOL
Wellow, Newark,
Nottinghamshire NG22 0EA
Tel: (01623) 861054
Fax: (01623) 836665
Email: wellowhouse@
   btinternet.com
Head: Mr P W Cook
Type: Co-educational Day and
Boarding 3–13
No of pupils: B80 G64
Fees: (September 08) WB £12150
Day £5610–£9690

NOTTINGHAM

ATTENBOROUGH PREPARATORY SCHOOL
The Strand, Attenborough,
Beeston, Nottingham,
Nottinghamshire NG9 6AU
Tel: (0115) 943 6725
Email: attprepschl@hotmail.com
Head: Mr R Everist
Type: Co-educational Day 4–11
No of pupils: B40 G40
Fees: On application

COTESWOOD HOUSE SCHOOL
19 Thackeray's Lane,
Woodthorpe, Nottingham,
Nottinghamshire NG5 4HT
Tel: (0115) 967 6551
Type: Co-educational Day 3–11
No of pupils: B20 G20
Fees: On application

DAGFA HOUSE SCHOOL
57 Broadgate, Beeston,
Nottingham, Nottinghamshire
NG9 2FU
Tel: (0115) 913 8330
Fax: (0115) 913 8331
Email: enquiries@
   dagfahouse.notts.sch.uk
Head: Mr A Hampton
Type: Co-educational Day 2–16
No of pupils: B145 G105
Fees: On application

GREENHOLME SCHOOL
392 Derby Road, Nottingham,
Nottinghamshire NG7 2DX
Tel: (0115) 978 7329
Fax: (0115) 978 1160
Email: enquiries@
   greenholmeschool.co.uk
Head: Mrs A Fisher
Type: Co-educational Day 3–11
No of pupils: B102 G59
Fees: (September 08)
Day £7350–£7740

GROSVENOR SCHOOL
Edwalton, Nottingham,
Nottinghamshire NG12 4BS
Tel: (0115) 923 1184
Fax: (0115) 923 5184
Email: office@
   grosvenorschool.co.uk
Head: Mr C G J Oldershaw
Type: Co-educational Day 4–13
No of pupils: B109 G62
Fees: (September 08)
Day £7050–£7800

HAZEL HURST SCHOOL
400 Westdale Lane, Mapperley,
Nottingham, Nottinghamshire
NG3 6DG
Tel: (0115) 960 6759
Fax: (0115) 960 6759
Email: hazelhurst@onetel.com
Type: Co-educational Day 2–8
No of pupils: B25 G25
Fees: On application

HOLLYGIRT SCHOOL
Elm Avenue, Nottingham,
Nottinghamshire NG3 4GF
Tel: (0115) 9580596
Fax: (0115) 9897929
Email: info@hollygirt.co.uk
Head: Mrs M Connolly
Type: Girls Day 3–16
No of pupils: 300
Fees: (September 08)
Day £5850–£8280

THE KING'S SCHOOL
Green Street, The Meadows,
Nottingham, Nottinghamshire
NG2 2LA
Tel: (0115) 953 9194
Fax: (0115) 955 1148
Email: office@thekingsschool.info
Head: Mr R Southey
Type: Co-educational Day 4–16
No of pupils: B72 G55
Fees: (September 08) Day £3684

MOUNTFORD HOUSE SCHOOL
373 Mansfield Road, Nottingham,
Nottinghamshire NG5 2DA
Tel: (0115) 960 5676
Email: enquiries@
   mountfordhouse.nottingham.
   sch.uk
Head: Mrs D Williams
Type: Co-educational Day 3–11
No of pupils: B54 G30
Fees: On application

NOTTINGHAM HIGH SCHOOL FOR GIRLS GDST
9 Arboretum Street, Nottingham,
Nottinghamshire NG1 4JB
Tel: (0115) 941 7663
Fax: (0115) 924 0757
Email: enquiries@not.gdst.net
Head: Mrs S M Gorham
Type: Girls Day 4–18
No of pupils: 1078
Fees: On application

NOTTINGHAM HIGH JUNIOR SCHOOL
Waverley Mount, Nottingham,
Nottinghamshire NG7 4ED
Tel: (0115) 845 2214
Fax: (0115) 845 2298
Email: juniorinfo@
   nottinghamhigh.co.uk
Head: Mr A Earnshaw
Type: Boys Day 7–11
No of pupils: 145
Fees: (September 08) Day £8022

PLUMTREE SCHOOL
Church Hill, Plumtree,
Nottingham, Nottinghamshire
NG12 5ND
Tel: (0115) 937 5859
Fax: (0115) 937 5859
Email: plumtreeschool@
   tiscali.co.uk
Head: Mr N White
Type: Co-educational Day 3–11
No of pupils: B65 G50
Fees: (September 07)
Day £2925–£5025

ST JOSEPH'S SCHOOL
33 Derby Road, Nottingham,
Nottinghamshire NG1 5AW
Tel: (0115) 941 8356
Fax: (0115) 941 8356
Email: office@
   st-josephs.nottingham.sch.uk
Head: Mr J Crawley
Type: Co-educational Day 1–11
No of pupils: B115 G72
Fees: (September 08)
Day £6300–£18900

SALTERFORD HOUSE SCHOOL
Salterford Lane, Calverton,
Nottingham, Nottinghamshire
NG14 6NZ
Tel: (0115) 965 2127
Fax: (0115) 9652205
Email: office@
   salterfordhouseschool.co.uk
Head: Mrs M Venables
Type: Co-educational Day 2–11
No of pupils: B87 G73
Fees: (September 07)
Day £4875–£4950

TRENT COLLEGE
Long Eaton, Nottingham,
Nottinghamshire NG10 4AD
Tel: (0115) 849 4949
Fax: (0115) 849 4997
Email: enquiry@trentcollege.net
Head: Mr J S Lee
Type: Co-educational Boarding
and Day 3–18
No of pupils: B631 G452
No of boarders: F4 W124
Fees: On application

RETFORD

AL KARAM SECONDARY SCHOOL
Eaton Hall, Retford,
Nottinghamshire DN22 0PR
Tel: (01777) 706441
Fax: (01777) 711538
Email: info@alkaram.org
Head: Mr M I H Pirzada
Type: Boys Boarding 11–16
No of pupils: 140
No of boarders: F140
Fees: On application

RANBY HOUSE SCHOOL
Retford, Nottinghamshire
DN22 8HX
Tel: (01777) 703138
Fax: (01777) 702813
Email: office@
   ranbyhouseschool.co.uk
Head: Mr DWT Sibson
Type: Co-educational Day and
Boarding 3–13
No of pupils: B162 G137
No of boarders: F29 W20
Fees: (September 08) F/WB £4830
Day £2050–£3570

SUTTON IN ASHFIELD

LAMMAS SCHOOL
Lammas Road, Sutton in Ashfield,
Nottinghamshire NG17 2AD
Tel: (01623) 516879
Fax: (01623) 516879
Email: information@lammas.co.uk
Head: Mr C M Peck
Type: Co-educational Day 4–16
No of pupils: B90 G70
Fees: On application

England – Nottinghamshire

WORKSOP

WORKSOP COLLEGE
Worksop, Nottinghamshire
S80 3AP
Tel: (01909) 537100
Fax: (01909) 537102
Email: headmaster@
  worksopcollege.notts.sch.uk
Head: Mr R A Collard
Type: Co-educational Boarding
and Day 13–18
No of pupils: B254 G158
No of boarders: F92 W72
Fees: (September 08) F/WB £21555
Day £14610

OXFORDSHIRE

ABINGDON

ABINGDON SCHOOL
Park Road, Abingdon, Oxfordshire
OX14 IDE
Tel: (01235) 849041
Fax: (01235) 849085
Email: admissions@
  abingdon.org.uk
Head: Mr M Turner
Type: Boys Day and Boarding
11–18
No of pupils: 810
No of boarders: F70 W60
Fees: (September 07) FB £22770
WB £21120 Day £11940

**COTHILL HOUSE
PREPARATORY SCHOOL**
Cothill, Abingdon, Oxfordshire
OX13 6JL
Tel: (01865) 390800
Fax: (01865) 390205
Email: office@cothill.oxon.sch.uk
Head: Mr N R Brooks
Type: Boys Boarding 8–13
No of pupils:
No of boarders: F250
Fees: On application

**ABINGDON PREPARATORY
SCHOOL**
Josca's House, Kingston Road,
Frilford, Abingdon, Oxfordshire
OX13 5NX
Tel: (01865) 391570
Fax: (01865) 391042
Email: enquiries@
  abingdonprep.org.uk
Head: Mr C J Davies
Type: Boys Day 4–13 (Girls 4–7)
No of pupils: B250 G1
Fees: (September 08)
Day £9270–£9825

**THE MANOR PREPARATORY
SCHOOL***
Faringdon Road, Abingdon,
Oxfordshire OX13 6LN
Tel: (01235) 858462
Fax: (01235) 858458
Email: registrar@manorprep.org
Head: Mr P Heyworth
Type: Co-educational Day
Boys 2–7 Girls 2–11
No of pupils: B21 G309
Fees: (September 08)
Day £1650–£10050

**OUR LADY'S JUNIOR
SCHOOL**
St John's Road, Abingdon,
Oxfordshire OX14 2HB
Tel: (01235) 523147
Fax: (01235) 530387
Email: officejs@olab.org.uk
Head: Mr B O'Neill
Type: Co-educational Day 3–11
No of pupils: B60 G90
Fees: £5250

**OUR LADY'S ABINGDON
SCHOOL**
Radley Road, Abingdon,
Oxfordshire OX14 3PS
Tel: (01235) 524658
Fax: (01235) 535829
Email: office@olab.org.uk
Head: Mrs L Renwick
Type: Co-educational Day
Girls 11–18
No of pupils: 397
Fees: (September 08) Day £9545

RADLEY COLLEGE
Abingdon, Oxfordshire OX14 2HR
Tel: (01235) 543000
Fax: (01235) 543106
Email: admissions@radley.org.uk
Head: Mr A W McPhail
Type: Boys Boarding 13–18
No of pupils:
No of boarders: F644
Fees: (September 07) FB £24990

**THE SCHOOL OF ST HELEN
& ST KATHARINE**
Faringdon Road, Abingdon,
Oxfordshire OX14 1BE
Tel: (01235) 520173
Fax: (01235) 532934
Email: info@shsk.org.uk
Head: Miss R Edbrooke
Type: Girls Day 9–18
No of pupils: 622
Fees: (September 08) Day £10185

BANBURY

ASH-SHIFA SCHOOL
Merton Street, Banbury,
Oxfordshire OX16 8RU
Tel: (01295) 279954
Fax: (01295) 279954
Email: info@ash-shifa.org.uk
Head: Ms F Aslam
Type: Girls Day 11–16
No of pupils: 26
Fees: On application

BLOXHAM SCHOOL[†]
Bloxham, Banbury, Oxfordshire
OX15 4PE
Tel: (01295) 720222
Fax: (01295) 721897
Email: registrar@
   bloxhamschool.com
Head: Mr M E Allbrook
Type: Co-educational Boarding
and Day 11–18
No of pupils: B262 G147
No of boarders: F211 W18
Fees: On application

THE CARRDUS SCHOOL
Overthorpe Hall, Banbury,
Oxfordshire OX17 2BS
Tel: (01295) 263733
Fax: (01295) 263733
Email: office@carrdusschool.co.uk
Head: Miss S Carrdus
Type: Girls Day 3–11 (Boys 3–8)
No of pupils: B29 G122
Fees: (September 07)
Day £1485–£7686

ST JOHN'S PRIORY SCHOOL
St John's Road, Banbury,
Oxfordshire OX16 5HX
Tel: (01295) 259607
Fax: (01295) 273326
Email: enquiries@
   stjohnspriory.com
Head: Mrs S Holding
Type: Co-educational Day 2–11
No of pupils: B72 G52
Fees: (September 08)
Day £3240–£6990

SIBFORD SCHOOL[†]
Sibford Ferris, Banbury,
Oxfordshire OX15 5QL
Tel: (01295) 781200
Fax: (01295) 781204
Email: admissions@
   sibfordschool.co.uk
Head: Michael Goodwin
Type: Co-educational Boarding
and Day 4–18
No of pupils: B277 G148
No of boarders: F30 W30
Fees: (September 08)
FB £20322–£20727
WB £18927–£19302
Day £6648–£10668

TUDOR HALL SCHOOL
Wykham Park, Banbury,
Oxfordshire OX16 9UR
Tel: (01295) 756276
Fax: (01295) 253264
Email: admissions@
   tudorhallschool.com
Head: Miss W Griffiths
Type: Girls Boarding and Day
11–18
No of pupils: 290
No of boarders: F225
Fees: (September 08) FB £23595
Day £15336

CHIPPING NORTON

KINGHAM HILL SCHOOL*[†]
Kingham, Chipping Norton,
Oxfordshire OX7 6TH
Tel: (01608) 658999
Fax: (01608) 658658
Email: admissions@
   kingham-hill.oxon.sch.uk
Head: Mr N Seward
Type: Co-educational Boarding
and Day 11–18
No of pupils: B161 G74
No of boarders: F168
Fees: (September 08)
FB £18595–£22000
Day £12135–£14783

**WINDRUSH VALLEY
SCHOOL**
The Green, London Lane, Ascott-
U-Wychwood, Chipping Norton,
Oxfordshire OX7 6AN
Tel: (01993) 831793
Fax: (01993) 831793
Email: windrushvalley@aol.com
Head: Mr G A Wood
Type: Co-educational Day 3–11
No of pupils: B60 G60
Fees: (September 08)
Day £4983–£5130

FARINGDON

**FERNDALE PREPARATORY
SCHOOL**
5–7 Bromsgrove, Faringdon,
Oxfordshire SN7 7JF
Tel: (01367) 240618
Fax: (01367) 241429
Email: ferndaleprep.school@
   talk21.com
Head: Mr Andrew Mersh
Type: Co-educational Day 3–11
No of pupils: B55 G55
Fees: On application

ST HUGH'S SCHOOL
Carswell Manor, Faringdon,
Oxfordshire SN7 8PT
Tel: (01367) 870700
Fax: (01367) 870707
Email: registrar@st-hughs.co.uk
Head: Mr A J P Nott
Type: Co-educational Boarding
and Day 4–13
No of pupils: B161 G112
No of boarders: W35
Fees: (September 08)
WB £15165–£16185
Day £7965–£13515

HENLEY-ON-THAMES

RUPERT HOUSE
90 Bell Street, Henley-on-Thames,
Oxfordshire RG9 2BN
Tel: (01491) 574263
Fax: (01491) 573988
Email: office@
   ruperthouse.oxon.sch.uk
Head: Mrs N J Gan
Type: Co-educational Day
Boys 4–7 Girls 4–11
No of pupils: B41 G165
Fees: On application

England – Oxfordshire

ST MARY'S SCHOOL
13 St Andrew's Road, Henley-on-Thames, Oxfordshire RG9 1HS
Tel: (01491) 573118
Email: stmarys.henley@
    btinternet.com
Head: Mr T Ackroyd
Type: Co-educational Day 3–11
No of pupils: B72 G67
Fees: (September 08) Day £7470

SHIPLAKE COLLEGE*
Henley-on-Thames, Oxfordshire
RG9 4BW
Tel: (0118) 940 2455
Fax: (0118) 940 5204
Email: info@shiplake.org.uk
Head: Mr A G S Davies
Type: Co-educational Day and
Boarding Boys 13–18 Girls 16–18
(Day girls 16–18)
No of pupils: B294 G30
No of boarders: F171 W45
Fees: (September 08) F/WB £22998
Day £15513

OXFORD

ABACUS COLLEGE
Threeways House, George Street,
Oxford, Oxfordshire OX1 2BJ
Tel: (01865) 240111
Fax: (01865) 247259
Email: principal@
    abacuscollege.co.uk
Head: Dr R Carrington and Mrs J
Wasilewski
Type: Co-educational Boarding
and Day 16–19
No of pupils: B68 G52
No of boarders: F119
Fees: (September 07)
FB £11320–£13020
Day £7750–£8650

CHANDLINGS MANOR
SCHOOL
Bagley Wood, Kennington,
Oxford, Oxfordshire OX1 5ND
Tel: (01865) 730771
Fax: (01865) 735194
Email: office@chandlings.com
Head: Mrs Sophia Ashworth Jones
Type: Co-educational Day 4–11
No of pupils: B242 G138
Fees: (September 08)
Day £8610–£11250

CHERWELL COLLEGE
Greyfriars, Paradise Street, Oxford,
Oxfordshire OX1 1LD
Tel: (01865) 242670
Fax: (01865) 791761
Email: secretary@
    cherwell-college.co.uk
Head: Mr A R Thompson
Type: Co-educational Boarding
and Day 16+
No of pupils: B75 G75
No of boarders: F90 W10
Fees: (September 07)
FB £20500–£23500
Day £13500–£15500

CHRIST CHURCH
CATHEDRAL SCHOOL
3 Brewer Street, Oxford,
Oxfordshire OX1 1QW
Tel: (01865) 242561
Fax: (01865) 202945
Email: schooloffice@cccs.org.uk
Head: Mr M Bruce
Type: Boys Day 3–13 (Girls 2–4)
No of pupils: B139 G4
No of boarders: F22
Fees: (September 08)
FB £6585–£7275
Day £3330–£10665

D'OVERBROECK'S
COLLEGE*
The Swan Building, 111 Banbury
Road, Oxford, Oxfordshire
OX2 6JX
Tel: (01865) 310000
Fax: (01865) 552296
Email: mail@doverbroecks.com
Head: Mr S Cohen
Type: Co-educational Day and
Boarding 11–19 (Day only 11–16)
No of pupils: B182 G180
No of boarders: F120
Fees: (September 08)
FB £22095–£24270 Day £16845

DRAGON SCHOOL
Bardwell Road, Oxford,
Oxfordshire OX2 6SS
Tel: (01865) 315405
Fax: (01865) 311664
Email: admissions@
    dragonschool.org
Head: Mr J R Baugh
Type: Co-educational Boarding
and Day 4–13
No of pupils: B560 G270
No of boarders: F269
Fees: (September 08) FB £21810
Day £8280–£15240

EMMANUEL CHRISTIAN
SCHOOL
Sandford Road, Littlemore,
Oxford, Oxfordshire OX4 4PU
Tel: (01865) 395236
Email: admin@ecschool.org.uk
Head: Miss J P Dandy
Type: Co-educational Day 3–11
No of pupils: B23 G32
Fees: (September 08) Day £4092

GREENE'S TUTORIAL
COLLEGE
45 Pembroke Street, Oxford,
Oxfordshire OX1 1BP
Tel: (01865) 248308
Fax: (01865) 240700
Email: enquiries@greenes.org.uk
Head: Mr M Uffindell
Type: Co-educational Day and
Boarding 6–75 (Boarding (host
families))
No of pupils: B100 G100
No of boarders: F35 W35
Fees: On application

HEADINGTON SCHOOL
Oxford, Oxfordshire OX3 7TD
Tel: (01865) 759113
Fax: (01865) 760268
Email: admissions@
    headington.org
Head: Mrs A Coutts
Type: Girls Day and Boarding
3–18 (Co-ed 3–4)
No of pupils: 1017
No of boarders: F129 W48
Fees: (September 08)
FB £20745–£23325
WB £19110–£21390
Day £6570–£12150

IQRA SCHOOL
Lawn Upton House, David
Nicholls Close, Littlemore,
Oxford, Oxfordshire OX4 4PU
Tel: (01865) 777254
Email: iqraschooloxford@
    yahoo.co.uk
Head: Mr H Ramzy and
Mrs F Tenvir
Type: Girls Day 10–16
No of pupils: 80
Fees: On application

LECKFORD PLACE SCHOOL
Leckford Road, Oxford,
Oxfordshire OX2 6HX
Tel: (01865) 302 620
Fax: (01865) 302622
Email: corinna.hilton@
  leckfordplace.com
Head: Mr Mark Olejnik
Type: Co-educational Day 11–16
No of pupils: B70 G25
Fees: On application

MAGDALEN COLLEGE SCHOOL
Cowley Place, Oxford,
Oxfordshire OX4 1DZ
Tel: (01865) 242191
Fax: (01865) 240379
Email: admissions@mcsoxford.org
Head: Mr A D Halls
Type: Boys Day 7–18
No of pupils: 680
Fees: On application

NEW COLLEGE SCHOOL
2 Savile Road, Oxford,
Oxfordshire OX1 3UA
Tel: (01865) 243657
Fax: (01865) 201277
Email: office@
  newcollege.oxon.sch.uk
Head: Mr N.R. Gullifer
Type: Boys Day 4–13
No of pupils: 130
Fees: (September 08)
Day £6867–£11100

OXFORD HIGH SCHOOL GDST
Belbroughton Road, Oxford,
Oxfordshire OX2 6XA
Tel: (01865) 559888
Fax: (01865) 552343
Email: oxfordhigh@oxf.gdst.net
Head: Miss O F S Lusk
Type: Girls Day 3–18 (Boys 4 -6)
No of pupils: B39 G893
Fees: (September 08)
Day £2664–£8898

OXFORD MONTESSORI SCHOOLS
Forest Farm, Elsfield, Oxford,
Oxfordshire OX3 9UW
Tel: (01865) 358210
Fax: (01865) 358390
Email: oms.schools@
  btconnect.com
Type: Co-educational Day 2–12
No of pupils: B60 G50
Fees: (September 08)
Day £4563–£7605

OXFORD TUTORIAL COLLEGE
12 King Edward Street, Oxford,
Oxfordshire OX1 4HT
Tel: (01865) 793333
Fax: (01865) 793233
Email: info@otc.ac.uk
Head: Mrs F Pocock
Type: Co-educational Day and
Boarding 16+
No of pupils: B75 G70
No of boarders: F45
Fees: (September 08)
Day £16000–£19000

RYE ST ANTONY SCHOOL
Pullen's Lane, Oxford, Oxfordshire
OX3 0BY
Tel: (01865) 762802
Fax: (01865) 763611
Email: headmistress@
  ryestantony.co.uk
Head: Miss A M Jones
Type: Girls Boarding and Day
3–18 (Boys 3–8)
No of pupils: B20 G380
No of boarders: F60 W20
Fees: (September 08)
FB £15150–£17850
WB £14250–£16950
Day £6270–£10650

ST CLARE'S, OXFORD*
139 Banbury Road, Oxford,
Oxfordshire OX2 7AL
Tel: (01865) 552031
Fax: (01865) 513359
Email: admissions@stclares.ac.uk
Head: Mrs P Holloway
Type: Co-educational Boarding
and Day 15–19
No of pupils: 258
No of boarders: F238 W10
Fees: (September 08) FB £26449
WB £26134 Day £16355

ST EDWARD'S SCHOOL*
Woodstock Road, Oxford,
Oxfordshire OX2 7NN
Tel: (01865) 319200
Fax: (01865) 319202
Email: registrar@
  stedwards.oxon.sch.uk
Head: Mr A Trotman
Type: Co-educational Boarding
and Day 13–18
No of pupils: B423 G235
No of boarders: F506
Fees: (September 08) FB £27015
Day £21609

SUMMER FIELDS
Mayfield Road, Oxford,
Oxfordshire OX2 7EN
Tel: (01865) 454433
Fax: (01865) 459200
Email: schoolsec@
  summerfields.org.uk
Head: Mr R F Badham-Thornhill
Type: Boys Boarding and Day
7–13
No of pupils: 241
No of boarders: F211
Fees: (September 07) FB £19350
Day £14985

WYCHWOOD SCHOOL
74 Banbury Road, Oxford,
Oxfordshire OX2 6JR
Tel: (01865) 557976
Fax: (01865) 556806
Email: admin@
  wychwood-school.org.uk
Head: Mrs S M P Wingfield Digby
Type: Girls Boarding and Day
11–18
No of pupils: 150
No of boarders: F27 W31
Fees: (September 08) FB £5650
WB £5375 Day £3475

READING

THE ORATORY PREPARATORY SCHOOL*
Goring Heath, Reading RG8 7SF
Tel: (0118) 984 4511
Fax: (0118) 984 4806
Email: office@oratoryprep.co.uk
Head: Dr R J Hillier
Type: Co-educational Day and
Boarding 3–13
No of pupils: B250 G150
No of boarders: F20 W10
Fees: (September 08) FB £15135
WB £13935 Day £3285–£10980

WALLINGFORD

CRANFORD HOUSE SCHOOL
Moulsford, Wallingford,
Oxfordshire OX10 9HT
Tel: (01491) 651218
Fax: (01491) 652557
Email: admissions@
  cranfordhouse.oxon.sch.uk
Head: Mrs C Hamilton
Type: Girls Day 3–16 (Boys 3–7)
No of pupils: B33 G280
Fees: (September 08)
Day £2583–£11850

England – Oxfordshire

MOULSFORD PREPARATORY SCHOOL
Moulsford, Wallingford,
Oxfordshire OX10 9HR
Tel: (01491) 651438
Fax: (01491) 651868
Email: secretary@moulsford.com
Head: Mr M J Higham
Type: Boys Boarding and Day
4–13
No of boarders: W44
Fees: (September 08) WB £14985
Day £7575–£11955

WANTAGE

ST ANDREW'S
Wallingford Street, Wantage,
Oxfordshire OX12 8AZ
Tel: (01235) 762345
Fax: (01235) 768274
Email: admin@st-
    andrews-wantage.oxon.sch.uk
Head: Rabbi S Lawrence
Type: Co-educational Day 3–11
No of pupils: B57 G43
Fees: (September 08)
Day £5019–£5742

WITNEY

COKETHORPE SCHOOL*
Witney, Oxfordshire OX29 7PU
Tel: (01993) 703921
Fax: (01993) 773499
Email: admissions@
    cokethorpe.org
Head: Mr D J Ettinger
Type: Co-educational Day 4–18
No of pupils: B410 G250
Fees: (September 08)
Day £9285–£13485

THE KING'S SCHOOL, PRIMARY
New Yatt Road, Witney,
Oxfordshire OX29 6TA
Tel: (01993) 778463
Fax: (01993) 778463
Email: primary@occ.org.uk
Head: Mrs A Gibbon
Type: Co-educational Day 5–11
No of pupils: B60 G60
Fees: On application

RUTLAND

OAKHAM

BROOKE PRIORY SCHOOL
Station Approach, Oakham,
Rutland LE15 6QW
Tel: (01572) 724778
Fax: (01572) 724969
Email: info@brooke.rutland.sch.uk
Head: Mrs E Bell
Type: Co-educational Day 3–11
No of pupils: B120 G111
Fees: (September 08)
Day £5085–£6870

OAKHAM SCHOOL
Chapel Close, Oakham, Rutland
LE15 6DT
Tel: (01572) 758758
Fax: (01572) 758595
Email: admissions@
    oakham.rutland.sch.uk
Head:
Type: Co-educational Boarding
and Day 10–18
No of pupils: B553 G527
No of boarders: F616
Fees: (September 08)
FB £21360–£25050
WB £18150–£21300
Day £13560–£14970

UPPINGHAM

UPPINGHAM SCHOOL
Uppingham, Rutland LE15 9QE
Tel: (01572) 822216
Fax: (01572) 822332
Email: admissions@
    uppingham.co.uk
Head: Mr R S Harman
Type: Co-educational Boarding
and Day 13–18
No of pupils: B470 G293
No of boarders: F745
Fees: (September 07) FB £24900
Day £17430

WINDMILL HOUSE SCHOOL
22 Stockerston Road, Uppingham,
Rutland LE15 9UD
Tel: (01572) 823593
Email: head@
    windmillhouseschool.co.uk
Head: Mr T Collins
Type: Co-educational Day 3–11
No of pupils: B40 G40
Fees: On application

SHROPSHIRE

BRIDGNORTH

DOWER HOUSE SCHOOL
Quatt, Bridgnorth, Shropshire
WV15 6QW
Tel: (01746) 780309
Fax: (01746) 780309
Email: dowerhouseschool@
btconnect.com
Head: Miss D G Tunstall
Type: Co-educational Day 2–11
No of pupils: B31 G28
Fees: (September 07)
Day £5222–£5685

BUCKNELL

BEDSTONE COLLEGE
Bedstone, Bucknell, Shropshire
SY7 0BG
Tel: (01547) 530303
Fax: (01547) 530740
Email: admissions@bedstone.org
Head: Mr M S Symonds
Type: Co-educational Boarding
and Day 3–18
No of pupils: B139 G99
No of boarders: F118
Fees: (September 08)
FB £13680–£29250
Day £8070–£11190

ELLESMERE

ELLESMERE COLLEGE*†
Ellesmere, Shropshire SY12 9AB
Tel: (01691) 622321
Fax: (01691) 623286
Email: admissions.secretary@
ellesmere.com
Head: Mr B J Wignall
Type: Co-educational Boarding
and Day 7–18
No of pupils: B401 G211
No of boarders: F147 W87
Fees: (September 08) FB £22152
WB £17970 Day £13908

LUDLOW

MOOR PARK SCHOOL
Moor Park, Ludlow, Shropshire
SY8 4DZ
Tel: (01584) 876061
Fax: (01584) 877311
Email: head@moorpark.org.uk
Head: Mr J R Bartlett
Type: Co-educational Boarding
and Day 3–13
No of pupils: B135 G111
No of boarders: F5 W85
Fees: (September 08)
FB £4370–£5310
Day £1800–£3890

NEWPORT

CASTLE HOUSE SCHOOL
Chetwynd End, Newport,
Shropshire TF10 7JE
Tel: (01952) 811035
Fax: (01952) 810022
Email: admin@
castlehouseschool.co.uk
Head: Mr R M Walden
Type: Co-educational Day 2–11
No of pupils: B31 G37
Fees: (September 08)
Day £5751–£6096

OSWESTRY

MORETON HALL SCHOOL*
Weston Rhyn, Oswestry,
Shropshire SY11 3EW
Tel: (01691) 773671
Fax: (01691) 778552
Email: admin@moretonhall.com
Head: Mr J Forster
Type: Girls Boarding and Day
3–18 (Boys 3–11)
No of pupils: B10 G343
No of boarders: F238
Fees: (September 08)
FB £16050–£24900
Day £6900–£20100

OSWESTRY SCHOOL
Upper Brook Street, Oswestry,
Shropshire SY11 2TL
Tel: (01691) 655711
Fax: (01691) 662726
Email: admissions@
oswestryschool.org.uk
Head: Mr P D Stockdale
Type: Co-educational Day and
Boarding 0–18
No of pupils: B237 G222
No of boarders: F89 W12
Fees: (September 08) FB £20235
WB £17835 Day £6795–£11085

OSWESTRY SCHOOL BELLAN HOUSE
Bellan House, Church Street,
Oswestry, Shropshire SY11 2ST
Tel: (01691) 653453
Fax: (01691) 680552
Email: enquiries@
oswestryschool.org.uk
Head: Mrs J Greatores
Type: Co-educational Day 2–9
No of pupils: B60 G60
Fees: (September 07) Day £6867

SHREWSBURY

ADCOTE SCHOOL FOR GIRLS
Little Ness, Shrewsbury,
Shropshire SY4 2JY
Tel: (01939) 260202
Fax: (01939) 261300
Email: secretary@
adcoteschool.co.uk
Head: Mr Ryah Jervis
Type: Boarding and Day
No of pupils: 105
No of boarders: F35 W8
Fees: (September 08) FB £14640
WB £12885 Day £3960–£7020

CONCORD COLLEGE
Acton Burnell Hall, Shrewsbury,
Shropshire SY5 7PF
Tel: (01694) 731631
Fax: (01694) 731389
Email: theprincipal@
    concordcollegeuk.com
Head: Mr N G Hawkins
Type: Co-educational Boarding
and Day 13–19
No of pupils: B185 G185
No of boarders: F320
Fees: (September 08) FB £23400
Day £11120

KINGSLAND GRANGE
Old Roman Road, Shrewsbury,
Shropshire SY3 9AH
Tel: (01743) 232132
Fax: (01743) 352665
Email: mcjames@talk21.com
Head: Mr M C James
Type: Boys Day 4–13
No of pupils: 110
Fees: On application

**PACKWOOD HAUGH
SCHOOL**
Ruyton XI Towns, Shrewsbury,
Shropshire SY4 1HX
Tel: (01939) 260217
Fax: (01939) 262077
Email: head@
    packwood-haugh.co.uk
Head: Mr N T Westlake
Type: Co-educational Boarding
and Day 4–13
No of pupils: B176 G112
No of boarders: F140
Fees: (September 07) FB £15735
Day £5415–£12591

**PRESTFELDE PREPARATORY
SCHOOL**
London Road, Shrewsbury,
Shropshire SY2 6NZ
Tel: (01743) 245400
Fax: (01743) 241434
Email: office@prestfelde.co.uk
Head: Mr Mark Groome
Type: Co-educational Day and
Boarding 3–13
No of pupils: B200 G94
No of boarders: W23
Fees: (September 08) WB £14040
Day £3510–£10890

**ST WINEFRIDE'S CONVENT
SCHOOL**
Belmont, Shrewsbury, Shropshire
SY1 1TE
Tel: (01743) 369883
Fax: (01743) 341650
Email: stwinefridesschool@
    postmaster.co.uk
Head: Sister M Felicity
Type: Co-educational Day 3–11
No of pupils: B65 G86
Fees: On application

**SHREWSBURY HIGH
SCHOOL GDST**
32 Town Walls, Shrewsbury,
Shropshire SY1 1TN
Tel: (01743) 362872
Fax: (01743) 364942
Email: enquiries@shr.gdst.net
Head: Mrs M L R Cass
Type: Girls Day 2–18
No of pupils: B100 G660
Fees: (September 07)
Day £5028–£8400

SHREWSBURY SCHOOL
The Schools, Shrewsbury,
Shropshire SY3 7BA
Tel: (01743) 280552
Fax: (01743) 243107
Email: registrar@
    shrewsbury.org.uk
Head: Mr J Goulding
Type: Boys Boarding and Day
13–18
No of pupils: B670 G30
No of boarders: F558
Fees: (September 07) FB £25110
Day £17640

TELFORD

THE OLD HALL SCHOOL
Stanley Road, Wellington, Telford,
Shropshire TF1 3LB
Tel: (01952) 223117
Fax: (01952) 250035
Email: enq@oldhall.co.uk
Head: Mr M C Stott
Type: Co-educational Day 4–11
No of pupils: B136 G118
Fees: (September 08)
Day £6060–£9402

WREKIN COLLEGE
Wellington, Telford, Shropshire
TF1 3BH
Tel: (01952) 240131/242305
Fax: (01952) 240338
Email: info@wrekincollege.ac.uk
Head: Mr S G Drew
Type: Co-educational Boarding
and Day 11–19
No of pupils: B269 G184
No of boarders: F114
Fees: On application

WHITCHURCH

WHITE HOUSE SCHOOL
Heath Road, Whitchurch,
Shropshire SY13 2AA
Tel: (01948) 662730
Email: whitehouseschool@
    btconnect.com
Head: Mrs H Clarke
Type: Co-educational Day 3–11
No of pupils: B75 G75
Fees: On application

SOMERSET

BATH

DOWNSIDE SCHOOL
Stratton-on-the-Fosse, Radstock,
Bath, Somerset BA3 4RJ
Tel: (01761) 235100
Fax: (01761) 235105
Email: registrar@downside.co.uk
Head: Dom Leo Maidlow Davis
Type: Co-educational Boarding
and Day 9–18
No of pupils: B367 G60
No of boarders: F229
Fees: (September 08)
FB £18705–£23550
Day £11469–£12759

BRUTON

BRUTON SCHOOL FOR GIRLS
Sunny Hill, Bruton, Somerset
BA10 0NT
Tel: (01749) 814400
Fax: (01749) 812537
Email: info@brutonschool.co.uk
Head: Mr John Burrough
Type: Girls Day and Boarding
3–18
No of pupils: B5 G359
No of boarders: F86 W20
Fees: (September 08)
FB £16641–£20889
WB £15402–£17769
Day £6312–£11571

KING'S BRUTON*†
Bruton, Somerset BA10 0ED
Tel: (01749) 814200
Fax: (01749) 813426
Email: registrar@kingsbruton.com
Head: Mr N M Lashbrook
Type: Co-educational Boarding
and Day 13–18
No of pupils: B229 G105
No of boarders: F226
Fees: (September 08) FB £23910
Day £17424

BURNHAM-ON-SEA

SOUTHLEIGH KINDERGARTEN
11 Rectory Road, Burnham-on-
Sea, Somerset TA8 2BY
Tel: (01278) 783999
Email: magna9uk@yahoo.co.uk
Head: Mrs L Easton
Type: Co-educational Day 2–7
No of pupils: B40 G40
Fees: On application

CHARD

CHARD SCHOOL
Fore Street, Chard, Somerset
TA20 1QA
Tel: (01460) 63234
Fax: (01460) 68988
Email: headmaster@
   chardschool.co.uk
Head: Mr J G Stotesbury
Type: Co-educational Day 2–11
No of pupils: B52 G52
Fees: (September 08)
Day £4020–£4815

CREWKERNE

PERROTT HILL SCHOOL
North Perrott, Crewkerne,
Somerset TA18 7SL
Tel: (01460) 72051
Fax: (01460) 78246
Email: headmaster@
   perrotthill.com
Head: Mr M J Davies
Type: Co-educational Boarding
and Day 3–13
No of pupils: B100 G80
No of boarders: F10 W25
Fees: On application

GLASTONBURY

MILLFIELD PREPARATORY SCHOOL
Edgarley Hall, Glastonbury,
Somerset BA6 8LD
Tel: (01458) 832446
Fax: (01458) 833679
Email: admissions@
   millfieldprep.com
Head: Mr K Cheney
Type: Co-educational Boarding
and Day 2–13
No of pupils: B262 G209
No of boarders: F149
Fees: On application

SHEPTON MALLET

ALL HALLOWS
Cranmore Hall, East Cranmore,
Shepton Mallet, Somerset BA4 4SF
Tel: (01749) 881600
Fax: (01749) 880709
Email: info@allhallwsschool.co.uk
Head: Mr Ian Murphy
Type: Co-educational Boarding
and Day 4–13
No of pupils: B168 G125
No of boarders: F65
Fees: (September 08) FB £17100
Day £5850–£11400

STREET

MILLFIELD SCHOOL
Butleigh Road, Street, Somerset
BA16 0YD
Tel: (01458) 442291
Fax: (01458) 447276
Email: admissions@
   millfieldschool.com
Head: Mr C A Considine
Type: Co-educational Boarding
and Day 13–18
No of pupils: B766 G465
No of boarders: F945
Fees: On application

TAUNTON

KING'S COLLEGE
South Road, Taunton, Somerset
TA1 3LA
Tel: (01823) 328200
Fax: (01823) 328202
Email: admissions@
kings-taunton.co.uk
Head: Mr R R Biggs
Type: Co-educational Boarding
and Day 13–18
No of pupils: B278 G145
No of boarders: F264
Fees: (September 08) FB £23385
Day £15825

KING'S HALL
Kingston Road, Taunton, Somerset
TA2 8AA
Tel: (01823) 285920
Fax: (01823) 285922
Email: schooloffice@
kingshall.rmplc.co.uk
Head: Mr J K Macpherson
Type: Co-educational Boarding
and Day 3–13
No of pupils: B211 G161
No of boarders: F265 W145
Fees: (September 08)
F/WB £13110–£17040
Day £4350–£11520

QUEEN'S COLLEGE JUNIOR, PRE-PREP & NURSERY SCHOOLS
Trull Road, Taunton, Somerset
TA1 4QP
Tel: (01823) 272990
Fax: (01823) 323811
Email: admissions@
queenscollege.org.uk
Head: Mr J M Backhouse and
Mrs J Williams
Type: Co-educational Day and
Boarding 3–11
No of pupils: B118 G98
No of boarders: F11
Fees: (September 08)
FB £9555–£14535
Day £4635–£9315

QUEEN'S COLLEGE
Trull Road, Taunton, Somerset
TA1 4QS
Tel: (01823) 340830
Fax: (01823) 338430
Email: admissions@
queenscollege.org.uk
Head: Mr C J Alcock
Type: Co-educational Day and
Boarding 3–18
No of pupils: B405 G365
No of boarders: F175
Fees: On application

TAUNTON INTERNATIONAL STUDY CENTRE (TISC)
Taunton School, Taunton,
Somerset TA2 6AD
Tel: (01823) 348100
Fax: (01823) 349206
Email: tisc@tauntonschool.co.uk
Head: Mrs C G Nixon
Type: Co-educational Boarding
13–17
No of pupils: B51 G24
No of boarders: F75
Fees: (September 07)
FB £24000–£25500

TAUNTON PREPARATORY SCHOOL
Staplegrove Road, Taunton,
Somerset TA2 6AE
Tel: (01823) 349250
Fax: (01823) 349202
Email: tps.enquiries@
tauntonschool.co.uk
Head: Mr M Anderson
Type: Co-educational Day and
Boarding 2–13
No of pupils: B254 G211
No of boarders: F46
Fees: (September 08)
FB £3275–£5930
Day £2030–£3820

TAUNTON SCHOOL
Staplegrove Road, Taunton,
Somerset TA2 6AD
Tel: (01823) 349200/349223
Fax: (01823) 349201
Email: enquiries@
tauntonschool.co.uk
Head: Dr J Newton
Type: Co-educational Boarding
and Day 13–18
No of pupils: B293 G205
No of boarders: F200
Fees: (September 08) FB £22590
Day £14100

WELLINGTON

WELLINGTON SCHOOL
South Street, Wellington, Somerset
TA21 8NT
Tel: (01823) 668800
Fax: (01823) 668844
Email: admin@
wellington-school.org.uk
Head: Mr Martin Reader
Type: Co-educational Boarding
and Day 10–18
No of pupils: B413 G340
No of boarders: F140 W15
Fees: (September 07)
FB £14046–£17658
WB £11097–£13950
Day £7158–£9480

WELLS

WELLS CATHEDRAL JUNIOR SCHOOL
8 New Street, Wells, Somerset
BA5 2LQ
Tel: (01749) 834400
Fax: (01749) 834401
Email: juniorschool@
wells-cathedral-school.com
Head: Mr E Cairncross
Type: Co-educational Boarding
and Day 3–11
No of pupils: B94 G93
No of boarders: F4 W4
Fees: On application

WELLS CATHEDRAL SCHOOL
Wells, Somerset BA5 2ST
Tel: (01749) 834200
Fax: (01749) 834201
Email: admissions@
wells-cathedral-school.com
Head: Mrs E C Cairncross
Type: Co-educational Boarding
and Day 3–18
No of pupils: B342 G310
No of boarders: F205
Fees: On application

YEOVIL

CHILTON CANTELO SCHOOL

Chilton Cantelo, Yeovil, Somerset
BA22 8BG
Tel: (01935) 850555
Fax: (01935) 850482
Email: ccs@pavilion.co.uk
Head: Mr D S von Zeffman
Type: Co-educational Boarding
and Day 7–16
No of pupils: B230 G180
No of boarders: F210
Fees: On application

HAZLEGROVE (KING'S BRUTON PREPARATORY SCHOOL)†

Hazlegrove House, Sparkford,
Yeovil, Somerset BA22 7JA
Tel: (01963) 440314
Fax: (01963) 440569
Email: office@hazlegrove.co.uk
Head: Mr R Fenwick
Type: Co-educational Day and
Boarding 2–13
No of pupils: B191 G171
No of boarders: F88
Fees: (September 08)
F/WB £14505–£18507
Day £6441–£13056

THE PARK SCHOOL

The Park, Yeovil, Somerset
BA20 1DH
Tel: (01935) 423514
Fax: (01935) 411257
Email: admin@parkschool.com
Head: Mr P W Bate
Type: Co-educational Day and
Boarding 3–18
No of pupils: B128 G130
No of boarders: F28 W4
Fees: (September 08)
FB £15045–£16095
WB £14385–£15405
Day £4245–£7680

BATH & NORTH EAST SOMERSET

BATH

BATH ACADEMY

27 Queen Square, Bath, Bath &
North East Somerset BA1 2HX
Tel: (01225) 334577
Fax: (01225) 482414
Email: principal@
 bathacademy.co.uk
Head: Mrs L Brown
Type: Co-educational Boarding
and Day 16–20
No of pupils: B70 G70
No of boarders: F140
Fees: (September 08)
FB £12850–£15530
Day £3200–£8700

KING EDWARD'S JUNIOR SCHOOL

North Road, Bath, Bath & North
East Somerset BA2 6JA
Tel: (01225) 463218
Fax: (01225) 442178
Email: juniorschhead@
 kesbath.biblio.net
Head: Mr G Taylor
Type: Co-educational Day 7–11
Fees: (September 08) Day £8010

KING EDWARD'S PRE-PREP SCHOOL

Weston Lane, Bath, Bath & North
East Somerset BA1 4AQ
Tel: (01225) 421681
Fax: (01225) 428006
Email: kespp@btopenworld.com
Head: Mrs J A Siderfin
Type: Co-educational Day 3–7
No of pupils: B63 G24
Fees: On application

KING EDWARD'S SCHOOL, BATH

North Road, Bath, Bath & North
East Somerset BA2 6HU
Tel: (01225) 464313
Fax: (01225) 481363
Email: headmaster@kesbath.com
Head: Mr Martin Boden
Type: Co-educational Day 3–18
No of pupils: B473 G211
Fees: (September 08)
Day £6150–£10260

KINGSWOOD PREPARATORY SCHOOL

College Road, Lansdown, Bath,
Bath & North East Somerset
BA1 5SD
Tel: (01225) 734460
Fax: (01225) 464434
Email: enquiries@
 kingswood.bath.sch.uk
Head: Mr Marcus Cornah
Type: Co-educational Day and
Boarding 3–11
No of pupils: B178 G133
No of boarders: F7 W10
Fees: (September 08)
FB £16806–£17808 WB £14118
Day £7125–£8250

KINGSWOOD SCHOOL*

Lansdown, Bath, Bath & North
East Somerset BA1 5RG
Tel: (01225) 734210
Fax: (01225) 734305
Email: enquiries@
 kingswood.bath.sch.uk
Head: Mr S Morris
Type: Co-educational Boarding
and Day 3–18
No of pupils: B550 G421
No of boarders: F128 W40
Fees: (September 08)
FB £19407–£23247
WB £16953–£21003
Day £10425–£10425

England – Somerset/Bath & North East Somerset

MONKTON PREP
Combe Down, Bath, Bath & North
East Somerset BA2 7ET
Tel: (01225) 837912
Fax: (01225) 840312
Email: admin@
  monktonprep.org.uk
Head: Mr C J Stafford
Type: Co-educational Day and
Boarding 2–13
No of pupils: B221 G151
No of boarders: F19 W41
Fees: (September 08)
FB £17154–£17997
WB £14998–£16425
Day £9948–£12753

**MONKTON SENIOR
SCHOOL**[†]
Church Lane, Bath, Bath & North
East Somerset BA2 7HG
Tel: (01225) 721133
Fax: (01225) 721181
Email: admissions@
  monkton.org.uk
Head: Mr R P Backhouse
Type: Co-educational Boarding
and Day 11–19
No of pupils:
No of boarders: F212
Fees: (September 08)
FB £17997–£24534
WB £19716–£21885
Day £12753–£16572

**PARAGON SCHOOL, PRIOR
PARK COLLEGE JUNIOR**
Lyncombe House, Lyncombe
Vale, Bath, Bath & North East
Somerset BA2 4LT
Tel: (01225) 310837
Fax: (01225) 427980
Email: office@
  paragonschool.co.uk
Head: Mr T Mills
Type: Co-educational Day 3–11
No of pupils: B116 G86
Fees: (September 08)
Day £6390–£7122

PRIOR PARK COLLEGE*
Ralph Allen Drive, Bath, Bath &
North East Somerset BA2 5AH
Tel: (01225) 831000
Fax: (01225) 835753
Email: admissions@
  priorpark.co.uk
Head: Dr G Mercer
Type: Co-educational Boarding
and Day 11–18 (Boarding from 13)
No of pupils: B301 G268
No of boarders: F114
Fees: (September 08) FB £22338
Day £11118–£12387

THE ROYAL HIGH SCHOOL*
Lansdown Road, Bath, Bath &
North East Somerset BA1 5SZ
Tel: (01225) 313877
Fax: (01225) 465446
Email: royalhigh@bat.gdst.net
Head: Mr J Graham-Brown
Type: Girls Boarding and Day
3–18 (Boys admitted (day only)
into Sixth Form)
No of pupils: 835
No of boarders: F75 W10
Fees: (September 08) FB £17445
WB £15486 Day £8898

NORTH SOMERSET

WESTON-SUPER-MARE

ASHBROOKE HOUSE
9 Ellenborough Park North,
Weston-Super-Mare, North
Somerset BS23 1XH
Tel: (01934) 629515
Fax: (01934) 629685
Email: headteacher@
  ashbrookehouse.n-somerset.
  sch.uk
Head: Mrs R Thomas
Type: Co-educational Day 3–11
No of pupils: B60 G50
Fees: On application

**LANCASTER HOUSE
SCHOOL**
38 Hill Road, Weston-Super-Mare,
North Somerset BS23 2RY
Tel: (01934) 624116
Email: susanlewisbrent@
  supanet.com
Head: Mrs S Lewis
Type: Co-educational Day 4–11
No of pupils: B23 G23
Fees: (September 07) Day £2700

WINSCOMBE

SIDCOT SCHOOL*
Oakridge Lane, Winscombe,
North Somerset BS25 1PD
Tel: (01934) 843102
Fax: (01934) 844181
Email: admissions@sidcot.org.uk
Head: Mr J Walmsley
Type: Co-educational Boarding
and Day 3–18
No of pupils: B290 G221
No of boarders: F139 W16
Fees: (September 08) F/WB £19800
Day £4875–£11850

STAFFORDSHIRE

ABBOTS BROMLEY

ABBOTS BROMLEY SCHOOL FOR GIRLS
Abbots Bromley, Staffordshire WS15 3BW
Tel: (01283) 840232
Fax: (01283) 840988
Email: registar@abbotsbromley.net
Head: Mrs P Woodhouse
Type: Girls Boarding and Day 3–18
No of pupils: 297
No of boarders: F40 W30
Fees: (September 07)
FB £14490–£20010
WB £11490–£16560
Day £6090–£11955

BREWOOD

VERNON LODGE PREPARATORY SCHOOL
School Lane, Stretton, Brewood, Staffordshire ST19 9LJ
Tel: (01902) 850568
Fax: (01902) 850568
Email: info@vernonlodge.co.uk
Head: Mrs P Sills
Type: Co-educational Day 2–11
No of pupils: B46 G41
Fees: (September 08)
Day £5685–£6435

CANNOCK

CHASE ACADEMY
Lyncroft House, St John's Road, Cannock, Staffordshire WS11 0UR
Tel: (01543) 501800
Fax: (01543) 501801
Email: info@chaseacademy.com
Head: Mr D R Holland
Type: Co-educational Day and Boarding 3–18
No of pupils: B109 G82
No of boarders: F6
Fees: On application

LICHFIELD

LICHFIELD CATHEDRAL SCHOOL
The Close, Lichfield, Staffordshire WS13 7LH
Tel: (01543) 306170
Fax: (01543) 306176
Email: reception@
lichfieldcathedralschool.com
Head: Mr P Allwood
Type: Co-educational Day and Boarding 3–16
No of pupils: 273
No of boarders: F18 W6
Fees: On application

NEWCASTLE-UNDER-LYME

EDENHURST SCHOOL
Westlands Avenue, Newcastle-under-Lyme, Staffordshire ST5 2PU
Tel: (01782) 619348
Fax: (01782) 662402
Email: headmaster@
edenhurst.co.uk
Head: Mr N H F Copestick
Type: Co-educational Day 3–14
No of pupils: B118 G122
Fees: On application

NEWCASTLE-UNDER-LYME SCHOOL
Mount Pleasant, Newcastle-under-Lyme, Staffordshire ST5 1DB
Tel: (01782) 631197
Fax: (01782) 632582
Email: info@nuls.org.uk
Head: Mr N A Rugg
Type: Co-educational Day 3–18
No of pupils: B550 G550
Fees: (September 08)
Day £6420–£8241

STAFFORD

BROOKLANDS SCHOOL & LITTLE BROOKLANDS NURSERY
167 Eccleshall Road, Stafford, Staffordshire ST16 1PD
Tel: (01785) 251399
Fax: (01785) 244379
Email: enquiries@
brooklandsschool.com
Head: Mr D R Williams
Type: Co-educational Day 0–11
No of pupils: B57 G55
Fees: On application

ST BEDE'S SCHOOL
Bishton Hall, Wolseley Bridge, Stafford, Staffordshire ST17 0XN
Tel: (01889) 881277
Fax: (01889) 882749
Email: admin@saintbedes.com
Head: Mr H Stafford Northcote
Type: Co-educational Boarding and Day 2–13
No of pupils: B68 G50
No of boarders: F10 W15
Fees: On application

ST DOMINIC'S SCHOOL
32 Bargate Street, Brewood, Stafford, Staffordshire ST19 9BA
Tel: (01902) 850248
Fax: (01902) 851154
Email: enquiries@
stdominicsschool.co.uk
Head: Mrs S White
Type: Girls Day 2–18 (Co-ed 2–7)
No of pupils: B3 G295
Fees: (September 08)
Day £3030–£9750

STAFFORD GRAMMAR SCHOOL
Burton Manor, Stafford, Staffordshire ST18 9AT
Tel: (01785) 249752
Fax: (01785) 255005
Email: headsec@
staffordgs.plus.com
Head: Mr M R Darley
Type: Co-educational Day 11–18
No of pupils: B197 G160
Fees: On application

YARLET SCHOOL
Yarlet, Near Stafford, Stafford,
Staffordshire ST18 9SU
Tel: (01785) 286568
Fax: (01785) 286569
Email: headmaster@
 yarletschool.co.uk
Head: Mr R S Plant
Type: Co-educational Day and
Boarding 2–13
No of pupils: B92 G75
Fees: On application

STOKE-ON-TRENT

ST DOMINIC'S INDEPENDENT JUNIOR SCHOOL
Hartshill Road, Stoke-on-Trent,
Staffordshire ST4 7LY
Tel: (01782) 848588
Fax: (01782) 413778
Email: saintdominics@
 btconnect.com
Head: Mr J F Butler
Type: Co-educational Day 3–11
No of pupils: B45 G35
Fees: (September 08)
Day £3618–£4740

ST JOSEPH'S PREPARATORY SCHOOL
London Road, Trent Vale,
Stoke-on-Trent, Staffordshire
ST4 5RF
Tel: (01782) 417533
Fax: (01782) 849327
Email: enquiries@
 stjosephprepschool.co.uk
Head: Mrs S D Hutchinson
Type: Co-educational Day 3–11
No of pupils: 120
Fees: On application

STONE

ST DOMINIC'S PRIORY SCHOOL
21 Station Road, Stone,
Staffordshire ST15 8EN
Tel: (01785) 814181
Fax: (01785) 819361
Email: head@
 st-dominicspriory.staffs.sch.uk
Head: Mrs P Adamson
Type: Co-educational Day
Boys 2–7 Girls 2–18 (Boys 3–11)
No of pupils: B12 G250
Fees: (September 08)
Day £5148–£8208

UTTOXETER

ABBOTSHOLME SCHOOL*
Rocester, Uttoxeter, Staffordshire
ST14 5BS
Tel: (01889) 590217
Fax: (01889) 591001
Email: admissions@
 abbotsholme.co.uk
Head: Mr S Fairclough
Type: Co-educational Boarding
and Day 5–18
No of pupils: B196 G122
No of boarders: F55 W76
Fees: (September 08)
FB £20700–£24000
WB £15900–£20100
Day £8850–£16350

DENSTONE COLLEGE
Uttoxeter, Staffordshire ST14 5HN
Tel: (01889) 591415
Fax: (01889) 591295
Email: admissions@
 denstonecollege.org
Head: Mr D M Derbyshire
Type: Co-educational Boarding
and Day 11–18
No of pupils: B345 G199
No of boarders: F125
Fees: (September 08)
FB £17205–£18861
Day £8964–£10830

SMALLWOOD MANOR PREPARATORY SCHOOL
Uttoxeter, Staffordshire ST14 8NS
Tel: (01889) 562083
Fax: (01889) 568682
Email: headmaster@
 smallwoodmanor.co.uk
Head: Mr C J Cann
Type: Co-educational Day 2–11
No of pupils: B110 G73
Fees: (September 08)
Day £6525–£8355

STOCKTON-ON-TEES

EAGLESCLIFFE

TEESSIDE HIGH SCHOOL
The Avenue, Eaglescliffe,
Stockton-on-Tees TS16 9AT
Tel: (01642) 782095
Fax: (01642) 791207
Email: info@teessidehigh.co.uk
Head: Mr T A Packer
Type: Co-educational Day 3–18
No of pupils: B52 G313
Fees: (September 08)
Day £4197–£9504

NORTON

RED HOUSE SCHOOL
36 The Green, Norton, Stockton-
on-Tees TS20 1DX
Tel: (01642) 553370
Fax: (01642) 361031
Email: headmaster@
    redhouseschool.co.uk
Head: Mr A R W Taylor
Type: Co-educational Day 3–16
No of pupils: B239 G193
Fees: On application

YARM

YARM SCHOOL
The Friarage, Yarm, Stockton-on-
Tees TS15 9EJ
Tel: (01642) 786023/781447
Fax: (01642) 789216
Email: dmd@yarmschool.org
Head: Mr D M Dunn
Type: Co-educational Day 3–18
No of pupils: B590 G400
Fees: (September 08)
Day £4167–£9501

SUFFOLK

BECCLES

THE OLD SCHOOL
Henstead, Beccles, Suffolk
NR34 7LG
Tel: (01502) 741150
Fax: (01502) 741150
Email: oldschool@btclick.com
Head: Mr M J Hewett
Type: Co-educational Day 4–11
No of pupils: B60 G45
Fees: On application

BRANDESTON

BRANDESTON HALL, THE PREPARATORY SCHOOL FOR FRAMLINGHAM COLLEGE
Brandeston Hall, Brandeston,
Suffolk IP13 7AH
Tel: (01728) 685331
Fax: (01728) 685437
Email: office@
    brandestonhall.co.uk
Head: Mr MK Myers-Allen
Type: Co-educational Boarding
and Day 3–13
No of pupils: B149 G96
No of boarders: F32
Fees: (September 07) F/WB £16311
Day £5832–£10143

BURY ST EDMUNDS

CHERRY TREES SCHOOL
Flempton Road, Risby, Bury St
Edmunds, Suffolk IP28 6QJ
Tel: (01284) 760531
Fax: (01284) 750177
Email: admin@
    cherrytrees-school.co.uk
Head: Ms W Compson
Type: Co-educational Day 0–11
No of pupils: B130 G126
Fees: (September 08)
Day £6495–£11271

CULFORD SCHOOL*
Bury St Edmunds, Suffolk IP28 6TX
Tel: (01284) 728615
Fax: (01284) 729146
Email: admissions@culford.co.uk
Head: Mr J F Johnson-Munday
Type: Co-educational Boarding
and Day 3–18
No of pupils: B357 G295
No of boarders: F192
Fees: (September 08)
F/WB £16380–£22800
Day £6900–£14520

MORETON HALL PREPARATORY SCHOOL
Mount Road, Bury St Edmunds,
Suffolk IP32 7BJ
Tel: (01284) 753532
Fax: (01284) 769197
Email: office@moretonhall.net
Head: Mr B H Dunhill
Type: Co-educational Boarding
and Day 2–13
No of pupils: B65 G51
No of boarders: F8 W4
Fees: (September 07) FB £5375
WB £4800 Day £2115–£3575

SOUTH LEE PREPARATORY SCHOOL
Nowton Road, Bury St Edmunds,
Suffolk IP33 2BT
Tel: (01284) 754654
Fax: (01284) 706178
Email: office@southlee.co.uk
Head: Mr D Whipp
Type: Co-educational Day 2–13
No of pupils: B162 G158
Fees: (September 08)
Day £6870–£8550

FELIXSTOWE

FELIXSTOWE INTERNATIONAL COLLEGE
Maybush House, Maybush Lane, Felixstowe, Suffolk IP11 7NA
Tel: (01394) 282388
Fax: (01394) 276926
Email: felixc@fmplc.co.uk
Head: Mrs J S Lee
Type: Co-educational Boarding 9–17
No of pupils: B15 G10
No of boarders: F15
Fees: (September 08) FB £19500

HAVERHILL

BARNARDISTON HALL PREPARATORY SCHOOL[†]
Barnardiston, Haverhill, Suffolk CB9 7TG
Tel: (01440) 786316
Fax: (01440) 786355
Email: info@barnardiston.com
Head: Lt Col K A Boulter
Type: Co-educational Day and Boarding 2–13
No of pupils: B121 G128
No of boarders: F30 W16
Fees: (September 08)
Day £3645–£9765

IPSWICH

AMBERFIELD SCHOOL
Nacton, Ipswich, Suffolk IP10 0HL
Tel: (01473) 659265
Fax: (01473) 659843
Email: registrar@amberfield.suffolk.sch.uk
Head: Mrs H Kay
Type: Girls Day 3–16 (Boys 3–7)
No of pupils: B10 G262
Fees: (September 07)
Day £6165–£8715

IPSWICH HIGH SCHOOL GDST
Woolverstone, Ipswich, Suffolk IP9 1AZ
Tel: (01473) 780201
Fax: (01473) 780985
Email: admissions@ihs.gdst.net
Head: Ms Elaine Purves
Type: Girls Day 3–18
No of pupils: 680
Fees: On application

IPSWICH PREPARATORY SCHOOL
3 Ivry Street, Ipswich, Suffolk IP1 3QW
Tel: (01473) 281302
Fax: (01473) 400068
Email: prepregistrar@ipswich.suffolk.sch.uk
Head: Mrs J M Jones
Type: Co-educational Day 3–11
No of pupils: B187 G117
Fees: (September 08)
Day £7101–£7905

IPSWICH SCHOOL
Henley Road, Ipswich, Suffolk IP1 3SG
Tel: (01473) 408300
Fax: (01473) 400058
Email: registrar@ipswich.suffolk.sch.uk
Head: Mr I G Galbraith
Type: Co-educational Day and Boarding 11–18
No of pupils: B528 G274
No of boarders: F34 W11
Fees: (September 08)
FB £15888–£18159
WB £15168–£17046
Day £9444–£10353

OLD BUCKENHAM HALL SCHOOL
Brettenham Park, Brettenham, Ipswich, Suffolk IP7 7PH
Tel: (01449) 740252
Fax: (01449) 740955
Email: registrar@obh.co.uk
Head: Mr M A Ives
Type: Co-educational Day and Boarding 2–13
No of pupils: B164 G96
No of boarders: F81 W32
Fees: (September 07) F/WB £17790
Day £6750–£14310

ORWELL PARK
Nacton, Ipswich, Suffolk IP10 0ER
Tel: (01473) 659225
Fax: (01473) 659822
Email: headmaster@orwellpark.co.uk
Head: Mr R Constantine
Type: Co-educational Boarding and Day 3–13
No of pupils: B210 G89
No of boarders: F78 W77
Fees: On application

THE ROYAL HOSPITAL SCHOOL*
Holbrook, Ipswich, Suffolk IP9 2RX
Tel: (01473) 326200
Fax: (01473) 326213
Email: admissions@royalhospitalschool.org
Head: Mr H W Blackett
Type: Co-educational Boarding and Day 11–18
No of pupils: B380 G288
No of boarders: F604
Fees: (September 08) F/WB £19668
Day £10521

ST JOSEPH'S COLLEGE
Belstead Road, Birkfield, Ipswich, Suffolk IP2 9DR
Tel: (01473) 690281
Fax: (01473) 602409
Email: registrar@stjos.co.uk
Head: Mrs S Grant and Mrs D Clarke
Type: Co-educational Day and Boarding 2–18
No of pupils: B428 G188
No of boarders: F97 W10
Fees: (September 08)
FB £16875–£18345
WB £13080–£17625
Day £6285–£10605

LEISTON

SUMMERHILL SCHOOL
Westward Ho, Leiston, Suffolk IP16 4HY
Tel: (01728) 830540
Fax: (01728) 830540
Email: office@summerhillschool.co.uk
Head: Mrs Z S Readhead
Type: Co-educational Boarding and Day 5–17
No of pupils:
No of boarders: F68
Fees: (September 08)
FB £7581–£13176
Day £3303–£7902

NEWMARKET

FAIRSTEAD HOUSE SCHOOL
Fordham Road, Newmarket,
Suffolk CB8 7AA
Tel: (01638) 662318
Fax: (01638) 561685
Email: secretary@
fairsteadhouse.co.uk
Head: Mrs D J Buckenham
Type: Co-educational Day 3–11
No of pupils: B57 G69
Fees: (September 08)
Day £6864–£7356

SOUTHWOLD

SAINT FELIX SCHOOL
Southwold, Suffolk IP18 6SD
Tel: (01502) 722175
Fax: (01502) 722641
Email: schooladmin@
stfelix.suffolk.sch.uk
Head: Mr David Ward
Type: Co-educational Boarding
and Day 1–18 (Boarding (girls
only) 11[†])
No of pupils: B204 G277
No of boarders: F57 W23
Fees: (September 08)
FB £16485–£20985
WB £12435–£16935
Day £5085–£11985

STOWMARKET

FINBOROUGH SCHOOL[†]
The Hall, Great Finborough,
Stowmarket, Suffolk IP14 3EF
Tel: (01449) 773600
Fax: (01449) 773601
Email: admin@
finborough.suffolk.sch.uk
Head: Mr J Sinclair
Type: Co-educational Boarding
and Day 2–18
No of pupils: 240
No of boarders: F108 W9
Fees: On application

SUDBURY

STOKE COLLEGE
Stoke by Clare, Sudbury, Suffolk
CO10 8JE
Tel: (01787) 278141
Fax: (01787) 277904
Email: office@stokecollege.co.uk
Head: Mr J Gibson
Type: Co-educational Day and
Boarding 3–16
No of pupils: B155 G90
No of boarders: W16
Fees: On application

WOODBRIDGE

THE ABBEY
The Prep School for Woodbridge
School, Church Street,
WOODBRIDGE, Suffolk IP12 1DS
Tel: (01394) 382673
Fax: (01394) 383880
Email: office@
theabbeyschool-suffolk.org.uk
Head: Mr N J Garrett
Type: Co-educational Day 4–11
No of pupils: B175 G175
Fees: (September 08)
Day £6600–£9900

ALEXANDERS INTERNATIONAL SCHOOL*
Bawdsey Manor, Bawdsey,
Woodbridge, Suffolk IP12 3AZ
Tel: (01394) 411633
Fax: (01394) 411357
Email: office@
alexandersschool.com
Head: Mr A Laidlaw
Type: Co-educational Boarding
11–17
No of pupils: B20 G20
No of boarders: F40
Fees: On application

FRAMLINGHAM COLLEGE*
Framlingham, Woodbridge,
Suffolk IP13 9EY
Tel: (01728) 723789
Fax: (01728) 724546
Email: admissions@
framcollege.co.uk
Head: Mrs G M Randall
Type: Co-educational Boarding
and Day 13–18
No of pupils: B255 G177
No of boarders: F265
Fees: (September 07) F/WB £20691
Day £13299

WOODBRIDGE SCHOOL
Burkitt Road, Woodbridge, Suffolk
IP12 4JH
Tel: (01394) 615041
Fax: (01394) 380944
Email: admissions@
woodbridge.suffolk.sch.uk
Head: Mr S H Cole
Type: Co-educational Day and
Boarding 11–18
No of pupils: B325 G325
No of boarders: F40
Fees: (September 08) F/WB £21192
Day £11382–£11994

England – Suffolk

SURREY

ASHTEAD

CITY OF LONDON FREEMEN'S SCHOOL
Ashtead Park, Ashtead, Surrey
KT21 1ET
Tel: (01372) 277933
Fax: (01372) 276165
Email: admissions.clfs@
  cityoflondon.gov.uk
Head: Mr Philip MacDonald
Type: Co-educational Day and
Boarding 7–18
No of pupils: B440 G420
No of boarders: F46
Fees: (September 08) FB £21771
Day £10185–£13680

DOWNSEND SCHOOL–ASHTEAD LODGE
22 Oakfield Road, Ashtead, Surrey
KT21 2RE
Tel: (01372) 385439
Fax: (01372) 273816
Email: ashteadlodge@
  downsend.co.uk
Head: Mrs K Barrett
Type: Co-educational Day 2–6
No of pupils: B35 G31
Fees: (September 08)
Day £2085–£7875

BAGSHOT

HALL GROVE SCHOOL
London Road, Bagshot, Surrey
GU19 5HZ
Tel: (01276) 473059
Fax: (01276) 452003
Email: office@
  hallgrove.surrey.sch.uk
Head: Mr A R Graham
Type: Co-educational Day and
Boarding 4–13
No of pupils: B238 G79
No of boarders: W10
Fees: (September 08)
WB £12375–£13350
Day £7635–£10575

BANSTEAD

GREENACRE SCHOOL FOR GIRLS*
Sutton Lane, Banstead, Surrey
SM7 3RA
Tel: (01737) 352114
Fax: (01737) 373485
Email: admin@
  greenacre.surrey.sch.uk
Head: Mrs P M Wood
Type: Girls Day 3–18
No of pupils: 410
Fees: (September 07)
Day £6300–£10800

PRIORY PREPARATORY SCHOOL*
Bolters Lane, Banstead, Surrey
SM7 2AJ
Tel: (01737) 366920
Fax: (01737) 366921
Email: office@prioryprep.co.uk
Head: Mr G D Malcolm
Type: Boys Day 2–13
No of pupils: 160
Fees: (September 08)
Day £3750–£9105

CAMBERLEY

HAWLEY PLACE SCHOOL
Fernhill Road, Blackwater,
Camberley, Surrey GU17 9HU
Tel: (01276) 32028
Fax: (01276) 609695
Email: office@hawleyplace.com
Head: Mr T G Pipe and
Mrs M L PIPE
Type: Co-educational Day
Boys 2–11 Girls 2–16
No of pupils: B115 G265
Fees: On application

LYNDHURST SCHOOL
36 The Avenue, Camberley, Surrey
GU15 3NE
Tel: (01276) 22895
Fax: (01276) 709186
Email: office@
  lyndhurstschool.com
Head: Mr S G Yeo
Type: Co-educational Day 2–12
No of pupils: B92 G80
Fees: On application

CATERHAM

CATERHAM PREPARATORY SCHOOL
Harestone Valley Road, Caterham,
Surrey CR3 6YB
Tel: (01883) 342097
Fax: (01883) 341230
Email: howard.tuckett@
  caterhamschool.co.uk
Head: Mr H W G Tuckett
Type: Co-educational Day 3–11
No of pupils: B153 G121
Fees: (September 07)
Day £3831–£9861

CATERHAM SCHOOL
Harestone Valley Road, Caterham,
Surrey CR3 6YA
Tel: (01883) 343028
Fax: (01883) 347795
Email: admissions@
  caterhamschool.co.uk
Head: Mr J P Thomas
Type: Co-educational Day and
Boarding 11–18
No of pupils: B464 G339
No of boarders: F160 W4
Fees: (September 08)
F/WB £22818–£24054
Day £12318–£12894

ESSENDENE LODGE SCHOOL
Essendene Road, Caterham, Surrey
CR3 5PB
Tel: (01883) 348349
Fax: (01883) 348349
Email: office@
  essendenelodge.surrey.sch.uk
Head: Mr S J Haydock
Type: Co-educational Day 2–11
No of pupils: B71 G86
Fees: (September 08)
Day £2535–£5040

OAKHYRST GRANGE SCHOOL
160 Stanstead Road, Caterham,
Surrey CR3 6AF
Tel: (01883) 343344
Fax: (01883) 342021
Email: office@
  oakhyrstgrangeschool.co.uk
Head: Mrs E A Stanford
Type: Co-educational Day 4–11
No of pupils: B65 G63
Fees: On application

CHERTSEY

SIR WILLIAM PERKINS'S SCHOOL
Guildford Road, Chertsey, Surrey
KT16 9BN
Tel: (01932) 574900
Fax: (01932) 574901
Email: reg@swps.org.uk
Head: Mrs S D Cooke
Type: Girls Day 11–18
No of pupils: 570
Fees: (September 08) Day £10956

COBHAM

ACS COBHAM INTERNATIONAL SCHOOL*
Heywood, Portsmouth Road,
Cobham, Surrey KT11 1BL
Tel: (01932) 867251
Fax: (01932) 869789
Email: cobhamadmissions@
    acs-england.co.uk
Head: Mr T J Lehman
Type: Co-educational Boarding
and Day 2–18
No of pupils: B763 G606
No of boarders: F60 W30
Fees: (September 08)
FB £30600–£32040
WB £26890–£28330
Day £8310–£18280

FELTONFLEET SCHOOL
Cobham, Surrey KT11 1DR
Tel: (01932) 862264
Fax: (01932) 860280
Email: p.ward@feltonfleet.co.uk
Head: Mr Phil Ward
Type: Co-educational Boarding
and Day 3–13
No of pupils: B228 G137
No of boarders: W45
Fees: On application

NOTRE DAME PREPARATORY SCHOOL
Burwood House, Cobham, Surrey
KT11 1HA
Tel: (01932) 869991
Fax: (01932) 589480
Email: headmaster@
    notredame.co.uk
Head: Mr D Plummer
Type: Girls Day 2–11 (Boys 2–5)
No of pupils: B10 G340
Fees: (September 08)
Day £3270–£9480

NOTRE DAME SENIOR SCHOOL
Burwood House, Cobham, Surrey
KT11 1HA
Tel: (01932) 869990
Fax: (01932) 589481
Email: headmistress@
    notredame.co.uk
Head: Mrs B Williams
Type: Girls Day 11–18
No of pupils: 375
Fees: (September 08) Day £11130

PARKSIDE SCHOOL*
The Manor, Stoke D'Abernon,
Cobham, Surrey KT11 3PX
Tel: (01932) 862749
Fax: (01932) 860251
Email: enquiries@
    parkside-school.co.uk
Head: Mr D Aylward
Type: Boys Day 4–13 (Co-ed 2–4)
No of pupils: B390 G20
Fees: (September 08)
Day £786–£10950

REED'S SCHOOL
Sandy Lane, Cobham, Surrey
KT11 2ES
Tel: (01932) 869001
Fax: (01932) 869046
Email: admissions@
    reeds.surrey.sch.uk
Head: Mr D W Jarrett
Type: Boys Boarding and Day
11–18 (Co-ed VIth Form)
No of pupils: B500 G50
No of boarders: F86
Fees: On application

YEHUDI MENUHIN SCHOOL
Stoke D'Abernon, Cobham, Surrey
KT11 3QQ
Tel: (01932) 864739
Fax: (01932) 864633
Email: admin@
    yehudimenuhinschool.co.uk
Head: Mr N Chisholm
Type: Co-educational Boarding
8–18
No of pupils: B26 G34
No of boarders: F60
Fees: (September 07) F/WB £36636
Day £35685

CRANLEIGH

CRANLEIGH PREPARATORY SCHOOL
Horseshoe Lane, Cranleigh, Surrey
GU68 8QH
Tel: (01483) 274199
Fax: (01483) 277136
Email: enquiry@cranleigh.org
Head: Mr M W Roulston
Type: Co-educational Boarding
and Day 7–13
No of pupils: 231
No of boarders: F40
Fees: On application

CRANLEIGH SCHOOL
Horseshoe Lane, Cranleigh, Surrey
GU6 8QQ
Tel: (01483) 273666
Fax: (01483) 267398
Email: enquiry@cranleigh.org
Head: Mr G de W Waller
Type: Co-educational Boarding
and Day 13–18
No of pupils: B410 G207
No of boarders: F455
Fees: (September 08) FB £26040
Day £21225

CROYDON

CAMBRIDGE TUTORS COLLEGE
Water Tower Hill, Croydon,
Surrey CR0 5SX
Tel: (020) 8688 5284
Fax: (020) 8686 9220
Email: admin@ctc.ac.uk
Head: Mr M Di Clemente
Type: Co-educational Boarding
and Day Boys 15–21 Girls 15–22
No of pupils: B160 G140
No of boarders: F240
Fees: (September 07) FB £18600
Day £14600

NEW LIFE CHRISTIAN SCHOOL
Cairo New Road, Croydon, Surrey
CR0 1XP
Tel: (020) 8680 7671
Fax: (020) 8686 7692
Email: nlcs@btconnect.com
Head: Mrs S Kehinde
Type: Co-educational Day 4–11
Fees: (September 08) Day £4032

England – Surrey

OLD PALACE OF JOHN WHITGIFT SCHOOL
Old Palace Road, Croydon, Surrey
CR0 1AX
Tel: (020) 8688 2027
Fax: (020) 8680 5877
Email: info@
oldpalace.croydon.sch.uk
Head: Ms J Harris
Type: Girls Day 4–18
Fees: (September 08)
Day £7371–£9858

ROYAL RUSSELL SCHOOL
Coombe Lane, Croydon, Surrey
CR9 5BX
Fax: (020) 8657 9555
Email: headmaster@
royalrussell.croydon.sch.uk
Head: Dr J R Jennings
Type: Co-educational Boarding
and Day 3–18
No of pupils: B483 G355
No of boarders: F115 W10
Fees: (September 08)
F/WB £18570–£25110
Day £7680–£12690

TRINITY SCHOOL*
Shirley Park, Croydon, Surrey
CR9 7AT
Tel: (020) 8656 9541
Fax: (020) 8655 0522
Email: admissions@
trinity.croydon.sch.uk
Head: Mr M J Bishop
Type: Boys Day 10–18
No of pupils: 890
Fees: (September 08) Day £11274

WARLINGHAM PARK SCHOOL
Chelsham Common, Warlingham,
Croydon, Surrey CR6 9PB
Tel: (01883) 626844
Fax: (01883) 625501
Email: info@
warlinghamparkschool.com
Head: Mr M R Donald
Type: Co-educational Day 2–11
No of pupils: B64 G66   .
Fees: (September 08)
Day £5445–£6585

DORKING

ABINGER HAMMER VILLAGE SCHOOL
Hackhurst Lane, Abinger Hammer,
Dorking, Surrey RH5 6SE
Tel: (01306) 730343
Email: enquiries@ahvst.org
Head: Mrs C Townsend
Type: Co-educational Day 4–8
No of pupils: B4 G8
Fees: On application

BELMONT SCHOOL
Feldemore, Holmbury St Mary,
Dorking, Surrey RH5 6LQ
Tel: (01306) 730852/730829
Fax: (01306) 731220
Email: schooloffice@
belmont-school.org
Head: Mrs H C Skrine
Type: Co-educational Boarding
and Day Boys 2–13 Girls 4–13
No of pupils: B180 G60
No of boarders: W42
Fees: (September 08) WB £5040
Day £2010–£3425

BOX HILL SCHOOL*
Mickleham, Dorking, Surrey
RH5 6EA
Tel: (01372) 373382
Fax: (01372) 363942
Email: enquiries@
boxhillschool.org.uk
Head: Mr M Eagers
Type: Co-educational Boarding
and Day 11–18
No of pupils: B264 G135
No of boarders: F95 W59
Fees: (September 08) FB £21000
WB £19050 Day £12000–£13500

HURTWOOD HOUSE*
Holmbury St Mary, Dorking,
Surrey RH5 6NU
Tel: (01483) 279000
Fax: (01483) 267586
Email: info@hurtwood.net
Head: Mr CM Jackson
Type: Co-educational Boarding
and Day 16–18
No of pupils: B145 G155
No of boarders: F283 W283
Fees: (September 07)
F/WB £29250–£33600
Day £19500

NEW LODGE SCHOOL
Chichester Road, Dorking, Surrey
RH4 1LR
Tel: (01306) 882151
Fax: (01306) 882656
Email: office@
newlodgeschool.com
Head: Mrs S Watt
Type: Co-educational Day 2–11
No of pupils: B95 G75
Fees: On application

ST TERESA'S SCHOOL*
Effingham Hill, Dorking, Surrey
RH5 6ST
Tel: (01372) 452037
Fax: (01372) 450311
Email: info@stteresas.surrey.sch.uk
Head: Mrs L Falconer and
Mrs A M Stewart
Type: Girls Boarding and Day
11–18
No of pupils: 518
No of boarders: F77 W13
Fees: (September 08)
FB £17865–£21900
WB £16230–£20265
Day £6450–£12870

EAST MOLESEY

HAMPTON COURT HOUSE
Hampton Court Road, East
Molesey, Surrey KT8 9BS
Tel: (020) 8943 0889
Fax: (020) 8977 5357
Email: office@
hamptoncourthouse.co.uk
Head: Lady E Houston-Boswall
Type: Co-educational Day 3–17
No of pupils: B120 G71
Fees: (September 08)
Day £7860–£12405

EFFINGHAM

ST TERESA'S PREPARATORY SCHOOL
Grove House, Guildford Road,
Effingham, Surrey KT24 5QA
Tel: (01372) 453456
Fax: (01372) 451562
Email: info@stteresasprep.co.uk
Head: Mrs A Stewart
Type: Girls Day and Boarding
2–11
No of pupils: 120
No of boarders: F2
Fees: (September 07)
FB £17040–£17790
WB £15480–£16230
Day £3150–£9180

EGHAM

ACS EGHAM INTERNATIONAL SCHOOL*
Woodlee, London Road (A30), Egham, Surrey TW20 0HS
Tel: (01784) 430800
Fax: (01784) 430626
Email: eghamadmissions@
    acs-england.co.uk
Head: Ms M Hadley
Type: Co-educational Day 2–18
No of pupils: B302 G284
Fees: (September 07)
Day £8310–£18050

BISHOPSGATE SCHOOL
Englefield Green, Egham, Surrey
TW20 0YJ
Tel: (01784) 432109
Fax: (01784) 430460
Email: admissions@
    bishopsgate.surrey.sch.uk
Head: Mr A Cowell
Type: Co-educational Day and
Boarding 2–13
No of pupils: B190 G103
No of boarders: W14
Fees: (September 07)
WB £12225–£13470

EPSOM

DOWNSEND SCHOOL–EPSOM LODGE
6 Norman Avenue, Epsom, Surrey
KT17 3AB
Tel: (01372) 385438
Fax: (01372) 721824
Email: epsomlodge@
    downsend.co.uk
Head: Miss J Birchall
Type: Co-educational Day 2–6
No of pupils: B65 G47
Fees: (September 08)
FB £2085–£7875

EPSOM COLLEGE
College Road, Epsom, Surrey
KT17 4JQ
Tel: (01372) 821004
Fax: (01372) 821237
Email: admissions@
    epsomcollege.org.uk
Head: Mr S R Borthwick
Type: Co-educational Boarding
and Day 13–18
No of pupils: B498 G222
No of boarders: F99 W232
Fees: (September 08) FB £26895
WB £24540 Day £18372

EWELL CASTLE SCHOOL
Church Street, Ewell, Epsom,
Surrey KT17 2AW
Tel: (020) 8393 1413
Fax: (020) 8786 8218
Email: admissions@
    ewellcastle.co.uk
Head: Mr A J Tibble
Type: Boys Day 3–18 (Co-ed 3–11)
No of pupils: B480 G65
Fees: (September 08)
Day £5700–£10650

KINGSWOOD HOUSE SCHOOL†
56 West Hill, Epsom, Surrey
KT19 8LG
Tel: (01372) 723590
Fax: (01372) 749081
Email: office@
    kingswoodhouse.org
Head: Mr P Brooks
Type: Boys Day 3–13
No of pupils: 210
Fees: (September 08)
Day £7245–£9570

ST CHRISTOPHER'S SCHOOL
6 Downs Road, Epsom, Surrey
KT18 5HE
Tel: (01372) 721807
Fax: (01372) 726717
Email: office@
    st-christophers.surrey.sch.uk
Head: Mrs M V Evans
Type: Co-educational Day 3–7
No of pupils: B76 G75
Fees: (September 08)
Day £6375–£6960

ESHER

CLAREMONT FAN COURT SCHOOL*
Claremont Drive, Esher, Surrey
KT10 9LY
Tel: (01372) 467841
Fax: (01372) 471109
Email: jtilson@
    claremont.surrey.sch.uk
Head: Mrs A Stanley
Type: Co-educational Day 3–18
No of pupils: B325 G325
Fees: (September 07)
Day £3651–£12216

EMBERHURST
94 Ember Lane, Esher, Surrey
KT10 8EN
Tel: (020) 8398 2933
Email: emberhurst.school@
    ntlworld.com
Head: Mrs P Chadwick
Type: Co-educational Day 2–8
No of pupils: B40 G35
Fees: On application

GRANTCHESTER HOUSE
5 Hinchley Way, Hinchley Wood,
Esher, Surrey KT10 0BD
Tel: (020) 8398 1157
Fax: (020) 8398 1157
Email: enquiries@
    grantchesterhouseschool.com
Head: Mrs A E Fry
Type: Co-educational Day 3–7
No of pupils: B49 G37
Fees: On application

MILBOURNE LODGE SCHOOL
43 Arbrook Lane, Esher, Surrey
KT10 9EG
Tel: (01372) 462737
Fax: (01372) 471164
Email: headmaster@
    milbournelodge.co.uk
Head: Mr P Fawkes and
Mr P Angus
Type: Co-educational Day 8–13
No of pupils: B141 G18
Fees: (September 08)
Day £9870–£10350

ROWAN PREPARATORY SCHOOL
6 Fitzalan Road, Claygate, Esher,
Surrey KT10 0LX
Tel: (01372) 462627
Fax: (01372) 470782
Email: office@rowan.surrey.sch.uk
Head: Mrs K Kershaw
Type: Girls Day 2–11
No of pupils: 280
Fees: On application

FARNHAM

BARFIELD SCHOOL
Guildford Road, Runfold,
Farnham, Surrey GU10 1PB
Tel: (01252) 782271
Fax: (01252) 781480
Email: admin@barfieldschool.com
Head: Mr Robin L Davies
Type: Co-educational Day 3–13
No of pupils: B170 G80
Fees: On application

England – Surrey

EDGEBOROUGH
Frensham, Farnham, Surrey
GU10 3AH
Tel: (01252) 792495
Fax: (01252) 795156
Email: office@edgeborough.co.uk
Head: Mrs M A Jackson and Mr R
A Jackson
Type: Co-educational Day and
Boarding 2–13
No of pupils: B198 G142
No of boarders: W48
Fees: (September 08)
WB £15405–£16740
Day £7980–£13020

**FRENSHAM HEIGHTS
SCHOOL**
Rowledge, Farnham, Surrey
GU10 4EA
Tel: (01252) 792561
Fax: (01252) 794335
Email: admissions@
  frensham-heights.org.uk
Head: Mr A Fisher
Type: Co-educational Boarding
and Day 3–18
No of pupils: B286 G240
No of boarders: F100
Fees: (September 07)
FB £20505–£21915
Day £5013–£14715

MORE HOUSE SCHOOL†
Moons Hill, Frensham, Farnham,
Surrey GU10 3AP
Tel: (01252) 792303
Fax: (01252) 797601
Email: schooloffice@
  morehouseschool.co.uk
Head: Mr B G Huggett
Type: Boys Boarding and Day
9–18
No of pupils: 260
No of boarders: F16 W85
Fees: On application

GODALMING

ALDRO SCHOOL
Lombard Street, Shackleford,
Godalming, Surrey GU8 6AS
Tel: (01483) 409020
Fax: (01483) 409010
Email: hmsec@aldro.org
Head: Mr D W N Aston
Type: Boys Boarding and Day
7–13
No of pupils: 220
No of boarders: F50
Fees: (September 08) FB £18795
Day £14610

BARROW HILLS SCHOOL
Roke Lane, Witley, Godalming,
Surrey GU8 5NY
Tel: (01428) 683639
Fax: (01428) 681906
Email: info@barrowhills.org.uk
Head: Mr M Unsworth
Type: Co-educational Day 3–13
No of pupils: B173 G101
Fees: (September 08)
Day £4875–£10815

CHARTERHOUSE
Godalming, Surrey GU7 2DX
Tel: (01483) 291501
Fax: (01483) 291507
Email: admissions@
  charterhouse.org.uk
Head: Rev J S Witheridge
Type: Boys Boarding 13–18 (Co-ed
VIth Form)
No of pupils: B635 G104
No of boarders: F720
Fees: (September 08) FB £27480
Day £22716

**KING EDWARD'S SCHOOL
WITLEY**
Petworth Road, Wormley,
Godalming, Surrey GU8 5SG
Tel: (01428) 686735
Fax: (01428) 685260
Email: admissions@
  kesw.surrey.sch.uk
Head: Mr P Kerr Fulton-Peebles
Type: Co-educational Boarding
and Day 11–18
No of pupils: B250 G190
No of boarders: F265
Fees: On application

PRIOR'S FIELD SCHOOL*
Priorsfield Road, Godalming,
Surrey GU7 2RH
Tel: (01483) 810551
Fax: (01483) 810180
Email: registrar@
  priorsfieldschool.com
Head: Mrs J Roseblade
Type: Girls Boarding and Day
11–18
No of pupils: 379
No of boarders: F43 W84
Fees: (September 08) F/WB £21450
Day £13260

ST HILARY'S SCHOOL*
Holloway Hill, Godalming, Surrey
GU7 1RZ
Tel: (01483) 416551
Fax: (01483) 418325
Email: registrar@
  sthilarysschool.com
Head: Mrs S Bailes
Type: Co-educational Day
Boys 2½–7 Girls 2½–11
No of pupils: B91 G197
Fees: (September 08)
Day £7335–£10575

GUILDFORD

DRAYTON HOUSE SCHOOL
35 Austen Road, Guildford, Surrey
GU1 3NP
Tel: (01483) 504707
Email: ask@draytonhouse.co.uk
Head: Mrs J Tyson-Jones
Type: Co-educational Day 3–8
(Nursery 1–3)
No of pupils: 90
Fees: On application

DUKE OF KENT SCHOOL
Peaslake Road, Ewhurst,
Guildford, Surrey GU6 7NS
Tel: (01483) 277313
Fax: (01483) 273862
Email: dok.school@virgin.net
Head: Dr A Cameron
Type: Co-educational Boarding
and Day 3–16
No of pupils: B114 G59
No of boarders: F10 W7
Fees: (September 08)
FB £14205–£16995
WB £10965–£13965
Day £4155–£12510

GUILDFORD HIGH SCHOOL
London Road, Guildford, Surrey
GU1 1SJ
Tel: (01483) 561440
Fax: (01483) 306516
Email: alex.kearney@
  church-schools.com
Head: Mrs F J Boulton
Type: Girls Day 4–18
No of pupils: 930
Fees: (September 08)
Day £6891–£11616

LANESBOROUGH
Maori Road, Guildford, Surrey
GU1 2EL
Tel: (01483) 880650
Fax: (01483) 880651
Email: secretary@
  lanesborough.surrey.sch.uk
Head: Mrs C Turnbull
Type: Boys Day 3–13
No of pupils: 358
Fees: (September 08)
Day £6975–£9405

LONGACRE SCHOOL
Hullbrook Lane, Shamley Green,
Guildford, Surrey GU5 0NQ
Tel: (01483) 893225
Fax: (01483) 893501
Email: office@
  longacre.surrey.sch.uk
Head: Mr M Beach
Type: Co-educational Day 2–11
No of pupils: B113 G106
Fees: On application

PEASLAKE SCHOOL
Colmans Hill, Peaslake, Guildford,
Surrey GU5 9ST
Tel: (01306) 730411
Email: info@
  peaslake.surrey.sch.uk
Head: Mrs J George
Type: Co-educational Day 3–7
No of pupils: B18 G24
Fees: On application

ROYAL GRAMMAR SCHOOL
High Street, Guildford, Surrey
GU1 3BB
Tel: (01483) 880600
Fax: (01483) 306127
Email: tmsyoung@
  rgs.guildford.co.uk
Head: Dr J M Cox
Type: Boys Day 11–18
No of pupils: 890
Fees: On application

RYDES HILL PREPARATORY SCHOOL
Aldershot Road, Guildford, Surrey
GU2 8BP
Tel: (01483) 563160
Fax: (01483) 306714
Email: enquiries@rydeshill.com
Head: Mrs Stephanie Bell
Type: Co-educational Day
Boys 3–7 Girls 3–11
No of pupils: B10 G150
Fees: (September 08)
Day £7200–£8880

ST CATHERINE'S SCHOOL
Station Road, Bramley, Guildford,
Surrey GU5 0DF
Tel: (01483) 899609
Fax: (01483) 899608
Email: admissions@
  stcatherines.info
Head: Mrs A M Phillips and
Mrs K Jefferies
Type: Girls Day and Boarding
4–18
No of pupils: 780
No of boarders: F24 W96
Fees: (September 08) F/WB £20520
Day £6025–£12465

TORMEAD SCHOOL
27 Cranley Road, Guildford,
Surrey GUI 2JD
Tel: (01483) 575101
Fax: (01483) 450592
Email: registrar@
  tormeadschool.org.uk
Head: Mrs S Marks
Type: Girls Day 4–18
No of pupils: 760
Fees: On application

HASLEMERE

HASLEMERE PREPARATORY SCHOOL
The Heights, Hill Road,
Haslemere, Surrey GU27 2JP
Tel: (01428) 642350
Fax: (01428) 645314
Email: office@
  haslemere-prep.surrey.sch.uk
Head: Mr K J Merrick
Type: Boys Day 2–14
No of pupils: B235 G13
Fees: On application

THE ROYAL SCHOOL
Farnham Lane, Haslemere, Surrey
GU27 1HQ
Tel: (01428) 605805
Fax: (01428) 603028
Email: admissions@
  royal.surrey.sch.uk
Head: Mrs L Taylor-Gooby
Type: Girls Day and Boarding
3–18 (Boys 2–4)
No of pupils: 334
No of boarders: F66
Fees: On application

ST IVES SCHOOL
Three Gates Lane, Haslemere,
Surrey GU27 2ES
Tel: (01428) 643734
Fax: (01428) 644788
Email: admin@
  stiveshaslemere.com
Head: Mrs S E Cattaneo
Type: Girls Day 3–11 (Boys 3–5)
No of pupils: B5 G140
Fees: (September 08)
Day £7320–£10245

HINDHEAD

AMESBURY
Hazel Grove, Hindhead, Surrey
GU26 6BL
Tel: (01428) 604322
Fax: (01428) 607715
Email: enquiries@
  amesburyschool.co.uk
Head: Mr N Taylor
Type: Co-educational Day 3–13
No of pupils: B210 G115
No of boarders: W10
Fees: On application

ST EDMUND'S SCHOOL
Portsmouth Road, Hindhead,
Surrey GU26 6BH
Tel: (01428) 609875
Fax: (01428) 607898
Email: registrar@
  saintedmunds.co.uk
Head: Mr A J Walliker
Type: Boys Boarding and Day
2–13 (Co-ed day 2–7)
No of pupils: B220 G47
No of boarders: W25
Fees: On application

HORLEY

REDEHALL PREPARATORY SCHOOL
Redehall Road, Smallfield, Horley,
Surrey RH6 9QA
Tel: (01342) 842987
Fax: (01342) 842987
Email: enquiries@
  redehall.surrey.sch.uk
Head: Mrs E Boak
Type: Co-educational Day 4–11
No of pupils: B60 G60
Fees: (September 07) Day £3150

England – Surrey

KINGSTON-UPON-THAMES

CANBURY SCHOOL
Kingston Hill, Kingston-upon-Thames, Surrey KT2 7LN
Tel: (020) 8549 8622
Fax: (020) 8974 6018
Email: head@canburyschool.co.uk
Head: Mr R Metters
Type: Co-educational Day
Boys 10–16 Girls 11–16
No of pupils: B45 G25
Fees: On application

HOLY CROSS PREPARATORY SCHOOL
George Road, Kingston-upon-Thames, Surrey KT2 7NU
Tel: (020) 8942 0729
Fax: (020) 8336 0764
Email: admissions@
   holycrossprep.co.uk
Head: Mrs K Hayes
Type: Girls Day 4–11
No of pupils: 250
Fees: On application

KINGSTON GRAMMAR SCHOOL*
London Road, Kingston-upon-Thames, Surrey KT2 6PY
Tel: (020) 8546 5875
Fax: (020) 8547 1499
Email: registar@kgs.org.uk
Head: Mr C D Baxter
Type: Co-educational Day 10–18
No of pupils: B462 G340
Fees: (September 08)
Day £12687–£13029

MARYMOUNT INTERNATIONAL SCHOOL*
George Road, Kingston-upon-Thames, Surrey KT2 7PE
Tel: (020) 8949 0571
Fax: (020) 8336 2485
Email: admissions@
   marymountlondon.com
Head: Sister K Fagan
Type: Girls Day and Boarding 11–18
No of pupils: 245
No of boarders: F90 W10
Fees: (September 08)
FB £26340–£28390
WB £25135–£27185
Day £14895–£16945

PARK HILL SCHOOL
8 Queens Road, Kingston-upon-Thames, Surrey KT2 7SH
Tel: (020) 8546 5496
Fax: (020) 8546 4558
Email: secretary@
   parkhillschool.com
Head: Mrs M D Christie
Type: Co-educational Day
Boys 3–8 Girls 3–11
No of pupils: B45 G75
Fees: (September 08)
Day £3885–£7560

ROKEBY SCHOOL
George Road, Kingston-upon-Thames, Surrey KT2 7PB
Tel: (020) 8942 2247
Fax: (020) 8942 5707
Email: hmsec@rokeby.org.uk
Head: Mr J R Peck
Type: Boys Day 4–13
No of pupils: 370
Fees: (September 08)
Day £7770–£11295

SURBITON HIGH SCHOOL*
Surbiton Crescent, Kingston-upon-Thames, Surrey KT1 2JT
Tel: (020) 8546 5245
Fax: (020) 8547 0026
Email: surbiton.high@
   church-schools.com
Head: Miss A Haydon
Type: Girls Day 4–18 (Boys 4–11)
No of pupils: B133 G1101
Fees: (September 08)
Day £6555–£11163

LEATHERHEAD

CRANMORE SCHOOL
West Horsley, Leatherhead, Surrey KT24 6AT
Tel: (01483) 280340
Fax: (01483) 280341
Email: office@cranmoreprep.co.uk
Head: Mr A J Martin
Type: Boys Day 3–13
No of pupils: 520
Fees: On application

DANES HILL SCHOOL†
Leatherhead Road, Oxshott, Leatherhead, Surrey KT22 0JG
Tel: (01372) 842509
Fax: (01372) 844452
Email: registrar@
   daneshillschool.co.uk
Head: Mr William Murdock
Type: Co-educational Day 3–13
No of pupils: B477 G395
Fees: On application

DOWNSEND SCHOOL
1 Leatherhead Road, Leatherhead, Surrey KT22 8TJ
Tel: (01372) 372197
Fax: (01372) 363367
Email: admissions@
   downsend.co.uk
Head: Mr F Steadman
Type: Co-educational Day 6–13
No of pupils: B313 G257
Fees: (September 08)
Day £8640–£10485

DOWNSEND SCHOOL–LEATHERHEAD LODGE
13 Epsom Road, Leatherhead, Surrey KT22 8ST
Tel: (01372) 385437
Fax: (01372) 376574
Email: leatherheadlodge@
   downsend.co.uk
Head: Mrs G Brooks
Type: Co-educational Day 2–6
No of pupils: B68 G55
Fees: (September 08)
Day £2085–£7875

GLENESK SCHOOL
Ockham Road North, East Horsley, Leatherhead, Surrey KT24 6NS
Tel: (01483) 282329
Fax: (01483) 281489
Email: info@glenesk.co.uk
Head: Mrs S J Christie-Hall
Type: Co-educational Day 2–7
No of pupils: B74 G57
Fees: (September 08)
Day £950–£8610

MANOR HOUSE SCHOOL
Manor House Lane, Little Bookham, Leatherhead, Surrey KT23 4EN
Tel: (01372) 458538
Fax: (01372) 450414
Email: admin@
   manorhouseschool.org
Head: Miss Z Axton
Type: Girls Day 2–16
No of pupils: 396
Fees: (September 07)
Day £2160–£11385

ST JOHN'S SCHOOL
Epsom Road, Leatherhead, Surrey
KT22 8SP
Tel: (01372) 373000
Fax: (01372) 386606
Email: secretary@
   stjohns.surrey.sch.uk
Head: Mr N J R Haddock
Type: Co-educational Boarding
and Day Boys 13–18 Girls 16–18
(Co-ed VIth Form)
No of pupils: B410 G62
Fees: (September 08) FB £7960
Day £5790

LINGFIELD

LINGFIELD NOTRE DAME SCHOOL
St Piers Lane, Lingfield, Surrey
RH7 6PH
Tel: (01342) 833176
Fax: (01342) 836048
Email: office@
   lingfieldnotredame.co.uk
Head: Mrs N E Shepley
Type: Co-educational Day 2–18
No of pupils: B360 G390
Fees: (September 08)
Day £810–£9090

MITCHAM

DATE VALLEY SCHOOL
9–11 Commonside East, Mitcham,
Surrey CR4 2QA
Tel: (020) 86484647
Head: Mrs Razina Karim
Type: Co-educational Day 2–11
No of pupils: B40 G40
Fees: On application

NEW MALDEN

THE STUDY SCHOOL
57 Thetford Road, New Malden,
Surrey KT3 5DP
Tel: (020) 8942 0754
Fax: (020) 8942 0754
Email: info@study.kingston.sch.uk
Head: Mrs A. Farnish
Type: Co-educational Day 3–11
No of pupils: B77 G58
Fees: (September 08)
Day £1164–£2716

WESTBURY HOUSE SCHOOL
80 Westbury Road, New Malden,
Surrey KT3 5AS
Tel: (020) 8942 5885
Fax: (020) 8942 5885
Email: info@
   westburyhouse.surrey.sch.uk
Head: Mrs M T Morton
Type: Co-educational Day 3–11
No of pupils: B65 G55
Fees: (September 08)
Day £1045–£2443

OXTED

HAZELWOOD SCHOOL*
Wolf's Hill, Limpsfield, Oxted,
Surrey RH8 0QU
Tel: (01883) 712194
Fax: (01883) 716135
Email: registrar@
   hazelwoodschool.com
Head: Mr Roger McDuff
Type: Co-educational Day 2–13
No of pupils: B229 G157
Fees: (September 08)
Day £3825–£11865

LAVEROCK SCHOOL
19 Bluehouse Lane, Oxted, Surrey
RH8 0AA
Tel: (01883) 714171
Fax: (01883) 722206
Email: office@
   laverock.surrey.sch.uk
Head: Mrs A C Paterson
Type: Girls Day 3–11
No of pupils: 125
Fees: (September 07) Day £8985

PURLEY

LALEHAM LEA SCHOOL
29 Peaks Hill, Purley, Surrey
CR8 3JJ
Tel: (020) 8660 3351
Fax: (020) 8763 0901
Email: enquiries@
   lalehamlea.co.uk
Head: Mr John Power
Type: Co-educational Day 3–11
No of pupils: B100 G50
Fees: (September 08) Day £5820

LODGE SCHOOL
11 Woodcote Lane, Purley, Surrey
CR8 3HB
Tel: (020) 8660 3179
Fax: (020) 8660 1385
Email: principal@
   lodgeschool.co.uk
Head: Miss P Maynard
Type: Girls Day 2–19 (Boys 3–11)
No of pupils: B102 G201
Fees: (September 08)
Day £1560–£11175

OAKWOOD SCHOOL & NURSERY
Godstone Road, Purley, Surrey
CR8 2AN
Tel: (020) 8668 8080
Fax: (020) 8668 2895
Email: enquiries@
   oakwoodschool.org.uk
Head: Mr C Candia
Type: Co-educational Day 2–11
No of pupils: B75 G68
Fees: On application

ST DAVID'S SCHOOL
23 Woodcote Valley Road, Purley,
Surrey CR8 3AL
Tel: (020) 8660 0723
Fax: (020) 8645 0426
Email: office@
   stdavidsschool.co.uk
Head: Mrs L Nash
Type: Co-educational Day 3–11
No of pupils: B80 G82
Fees: On application

WEST DENE SCHOOL
167 Brighton Road, Purley, Surrey
CR8 4HE
Tel: (020) 8660 2404
Fax: (020) 8660 1189
Email: head@
   westdeneschool.fsnet.co.uk
Head: Mr P Kelly
Type: Co-educational Day 2–11
No of pupils: B52 G62
Fees: (September 08)
Day £2120–£2290

England – Surrey

REDHILL

THE HAWTHORNS SCHOOL
Pendell Court, Bletchingley,
Redhill, Surrey RH1 4QJ
Tel: (01883) 743048
Fax: (01883) 744256
Email: admissions@
  hawthorns.com
Head: Mr T R Johns
Type: Co-educational Day 2–13
No of pupils: B322 G218
Fees: (September 07)
Day £1374–£9300

REIGATE

BURYS COURT SCHOOL AND MOON HALL COLLEGE
Flanchford Road, Leigh, Reigate,
Surrey RH2 8RE
Tel: (01306) 611372
Fax: (01306) 611037
Email: enquiries@
  buryscourtschool.co.uk
Head: Mr David Rowlands and
Mrs B E Baker
Type: Co-educational Day 3–16
No of pupils: B64 G27
Fees: (September 07)
Day £4980–£14970

DUNOTTAR SCHOOL
High Trees Road, Reigate, Surrey
RH2 7EL
Tel: (01737) 761945
Fax: (01737) 779450
Email: info@
  dunottar.surrey.sch.uk
Head: Mrs J Hellier
Type: Girls Day 3–18
No of pupils: 380
Fees: On application

MICKLEFIELD SCHOOL
10 Somers Road, Reigate, Surrey
RH2 9DU
Tel: (01737) 242615
Fax: (01737) 248889
Email: office@
  micklefieldschool.co.uk
Head: Mrs L Rose
Type: Co-educational Day 3–11
No of pupils: B129 G141
Fees: (September 08)
Day £2490–£8220

REIGATE GRAMMAR SCHOOL
Reigate Road, Reigate, Surrey
RH2 0QS
Tel: (01737) 222231
Fax: (01737) 224201
Email: info@reigategrammar.org
Head: Mr D S Thomas
Type: Co-educational Day 11–18
No of pupils: B529 G335
Fees: (September 07) Day £12072

REIGATE ST MARY'S PREPARATORY AND CHOIR SCHOOL
Chart Lane, Reigate, Surrey
RH2 7RN
Tel: (01737) 244880
Fax: (01737) 221540
Email: office@reigatestmarys.org
Head: Mr M Culverwell
Type: Co-educational Day 3–11
No of pupils: B195 G94
Fees: (September 08)
Day £2861–£3368

ROYAL ALEXANDRA AND ALBERT SCHOOL*
Gatton Park, Reigate, Surrey
RH2 0TD
Tel: (01737) 649000
Fax: (01737) 649002
Email: admissions@
  gatton-park.org.uk
Head: Mr Paul D Spencer Ellis
Type: Co-educational Boarding
and Day 7–18
No of pupils: B400 G380
No of boarders: F400
Fees: (September 08)
FB £11625–£11985
Day £2670–£3810

RICHMOND

BROOMFIELD HOUSE SCHOOL
10 Broomfield Road, Kew
Gardens, Richmond, Surrey
TW9 3HS
Tel: (020) 8940 3884
Fax: (020) 8332 6485
Email: office@
  broomfieldhouse.com
Head: Mr N O York
Type: Co-educational Day 3–11
No of pupils: B73 G87
Fees: (September 08)
Day £4404–£9321

THE GERMAN SCHOOL
Douglas House, Petersham Road,
Richmond, Surrey TW10 7AH
Tel: (020) 8940 2510
Fax: (020) 8332 7446
Email: gerd.koehncke@
  dsLondon.org.uk
Head: Mr G Koehncke
Type: Co-educational Day 5–19
No of pupils: B320 G310
Fees: On application

KEW COLLEGE
24/26 Cumberland Road, Kew,
Richmond, Surrey TW9 3HQ
Tel: (020) 8940 2039
Fax: (020) 8332 9945
Email: enquiries@kewcollege.com
Head: Mrs D E Lyness
Type: Co-educational Day 3–11
No of pupils: B126 G141
Fees: (September 08)
Day £3975–£7485

KEW GREEN PREPARATORY SCHOOL*
Layton House, Ferry Lane,
Richmond, Surrey TW9 3AF
Tel: (020) 8948 5999
Fax: (020) 8948 4774
Email: secretary@kgps.co.uk
Head: Mrs M Gardener
Type: Co-educational Day 4–11
No of pupils: B140 G140
Fees: (September 08) Day £11907

KING'S HOUSE SCHOOL
68 Kings Road, Richmond, Surrey
TW10 6ES
Tel: (020) 8940 1878
Fax: (020) 8939 2501
Email: secretary1@
  kingshouse.richmond.sch.uk
Head: Mrs S Piper
Type: Boys Day 4–13
No of pupils: 380
Fees: On application

OLD VICARAGE SCHOOL
48 Richmond Hill, Richmond,
Surrey TW10 6QX
Tel: (020) 8940 0922
Fax: (020) 8948 6834
Email: office@
  oldvicarage-richmond.co.uk
Head: Mrs J Harrison
Type: Girls Day 4–11
No of pupils: 170
Fees: (September 07)
Day £7290–£8085

ROYAL BALLET SCHOOL
White Lodge, Richmond Park,
Richmond, Surrey TW10 5HR
Tel: (020) 8392 8000
Fax: (020) 8392 8037
Email: enquiries@
   royalballetschool.co.uk
Head: Mrs P Hogg
Type: Co-educational Day and
Boarding 11–16
No of pupils: B101 G106
No of boarders: F115
Fees: On application

UNICORN SCHOOL
238 Kew Road, Kew, Richmond,
Surrey TW9 3JX
Tel: (020) 8948 3926
Fax: (020) 8332 6814
Email: registrar@
   unicornschool.org.uk
Head: Mrs R Linehan and
Miss R Box
Type: Co-educational Day 3–11
No of pupils: B80 G89
Fees: (September 08)
Day £5130–£9405

SOUTH CROYDON

**CROYDON HIGH SCHOOL
GDST**
Old Farleigh Road, Selsdon, South
Croydon, Surrey CR2 8YB
Tel: (020) 8651 5020
Fax: (020) 8657 5413
Email: info2@cry.gdst.net
Head: Mrs Z Braganza
Type: Girls Day 3–18
No of pupils: 701
Fees: On application

CUMNOR HOUSE SCHOOL
168 Pampisford Road, South
Croydon, Surrey CR2 6DA
Tel: (020) 8660 3445
Fax: (020) 8660 3445
Email: admin@cumnorhouse.com
Head: Mr P Clare-Hunt
Type: Boys Day 4–13
No of pupils: 360
Fees: (September 07)
Day £6990–£8400

ELMHURST SCHOOL
44–48 South Park Hill Road, South
Croydon, Surrey CR2 7DW
Tel: (020) 8688 0661
Fax: (020) 8686 7675
Email: office@elmhurstschool.net
Head: Mr Matthew Apsley
Type: Boys Day 4–11
No of pupils: 254
Fees: On application

WHITGIFT SCHOOL
Haling Park, South Croydon,
Surrey CR2 6YT
Tel: (020) 8688 9222
Fax: (020) 8760 0682
Email: office@whitgift.co.uk
Head: Dr C A Barnett and
Mr J D Pitt
Type: Boys Day 10–18
No of pupils: 1200
Fees: (September 08) Day £12816

SURBITON

LINLEY HOUSE
6 Berrylands Road, Surbiton,
Surrey KT5 8RA
Tel: (020) 8399 4979
Fax: (020) 8399 4979
Email: office@
   linleyhouseschool.com
Head: Mrs S Mallin
Type: Co-educational Day 3–7
No of pupils: B18 G17
Fees: (September 08)
Day £3429–£6951

**SHREWSBURY HOUSE
SCHOOL**
107 Ditton Road, Surbiton, Surrey
KT6 6RL
Tel: (020) 8399 3066
Fax: (020) 8339 9529
Email: office@shspost.co.uk
Head: Mr C M Ross
Type: Boys Day 7–13
No of pupils: 290
Fees: On application

**SURBITON PREPARATORY
SCHOOL**
3 Avenue Elmers, Surbiton, Surrey
KT6 4SP
Tel: (020) 8390 6640
Fax: (020) 8255 3049
Email: surbiton.prep@
   church-schools.com
Head: Mr S J Pryce
Type: Boys Day 4–11
No of pupils: 125
Fees: (September 07)
Day £6390–£8706

SUTTON

HOMEFIELD SCHOOL*
Western Road, Sutton, Surrey
SM1 2TE
Tel: (020) 8642 0965
Fax: (020) 87701668
Email: administration@
   homefield.sutton.sch.uk
Head: Mr P R Mowbray
and Mr M Till
Type: Boys Day 2½–13
No of pupils: 430
Fees: (September 08)
Day £3825–£8925

SEATON HOUSE SCHOOL
67 Banstead Road South, Sutton,
Surrey SM2 5LH
Tel: (020) 8642 2332
Fax: (020) 8642 2332
Email: office@
   seatonhouse.sutton.sch.uk
Head: Mrs V Rickus
Type: Girls Day 3–11 (Boys 3–5)
No of pupils: B2 G138
Fees: (September 08)
Day £2457–£6960

STOWFORD COLLEGE[†]
95 Brighton Road, Sutton, Surrey
SM2 5SJ
Tel: (020) 8661 9444
Fax: (020) 8661 6136
Email: stowfordsch@
   btinternet.com
Head: Mr R J Shakespeare
Type: Co-educational Day 6–16
No of pupils: B55 G28
Fees: On application

**SUTTON HIGH SCHOOL
GDST**
55 Cheam Road, Sutton, Surrey
SM1 2AX
Tel: (020) 8642 0594
Fax: (020) 8642 2014
Email: office@sut.gdst.net
Head: Mr S Callaghan
Type: Girls Day 3–18
No of pupils: 769
Fees: (September 07)
Day £6285–£10470

England – Surrey

TADWORTH

ABERDOUR
Brighton Road, Burgh Heath,
Tadworth, Surrey KT20 6AJ
Tel: (01737) 354119
Fax: (01737) 363044
Email: enquiries@
aberdourschool.co.uk
Head: Mr S Collins
Type: Co-educational Day 2–13
No of pupils: B160 G105
Fees: (September 07)
Day £2625–£9765

BRAMLEY SCHOOL
Chequers Lane, Walton-on-the-
Hill, Tadworth, Surrey KT20 7ST
Tel: (01737) 812004
Fax: (01737) 819945
Email: office@
bramleyschool.surrey.sch.uk
Head: Mrs P Burgess
Type: Girls Day 3–11
No of pupils: 110
Fees: (September 08)
Day £3858–£8418

CHINTHURST SCHOOL
Tadworth Street, Tadworth, Surrey
KT20 5QZ
Tel: (01737) 812011
Fax: (01737) 814835
Email: enquiries@
chinthurst.surrey.sch.uk
Head: Mr T J Egan
Type: Boys Day 3–13
No of pupils: 275
Fees: (September 08)
Day £1935–£9195

THAMES DITTON

WESTON GREEN SCHOOL
Weston Green Road, Thames
Ditton, Surrey KT7 0JN
Tel: (020) 8398 2778
Fax: (020) 8398 2778
Email: info@
westongreenschool.org.uk
Head: Mrs L Harvey
Type: Co-educational Day 2–8
No of pupils: 180
Fees: (September 08)
Day £6315–£6660

THORPE

TASIS THE AMERICAN SCHOOL IN ENGLAND*
Coldharbour Lane, Thorpe, Surrey
TW20 8TE
Tel: (01932) 565252
Fax: (01932) 564644
Email: ukadmissions@
tasisengland.org
Head: Dr J A Doran
Type: Co-educational Boarding
and Day 3–18
No of pupils: B345 G405
No of boarders: F160
Fees: (September 08) FB £26750
Day £5500–£17500

WALLINGTON

COLLINGWOOD SCHOOL
3 Springfield Road, Wallington,
Surrey SM6 0BD
Tel: (020) 8647 4607
Fax: (020) 8669 2884
Email: headmaster@
collingwood.sutton.sch.uk
Head: Mr G M Barham
Type: Co-educational Day 2–11
No of pupils: B112 G64
Fees: (September 08)
Day £1725–£6120

WALTON-ON-THAMES

DANESFIELD MANOR SCHOOL
Rydens Avenue, Walton-on-
Thames, Surrey KT12 3JB
Tel: (01932) 220930
Fax: (01932) 225640
Email: danesfieldmanoradmin@
cfbt.com
Head: Mrs L Fidler
Type: Co-educational Day 1–11
No of pupils: B84 G85
Fees: (September 08)
Day £6012–£6525

WESTWARD PREPARATORY SCHOOL
47 Hersham Road, Walton-on-
Thames, Surrey KT12 1LE
Tel: (01932) 220911
Fax: (01932) 220911
Email: westwardschool@
btconnect.com
Head: Mrs P Robertson
Type: Co-educational Day 3–11
No of pupils: B70 G70
Fees: (September 07)
Day £4230–£5235

WEYBRIDGE

ST GEORGE'S COLLEGE
Weybridge Road, Addlestone,
Weybridge, Surrey KT15 2QS
Tel: (01932) 839300
Fax: (01932) 839301
Email: contact@
st-georges-college.co.uk
Head: Mr J A Peake
Type: Co-educational Day 11–18
No of pupils: B525 G325
Fees: (September 08)
Day £11610–£13365

ST GEORGE'S COLLEGE JUNIOR SCHOOL
Thames Street, Weybridge, Surrey
KT13 8NL
Tel: (01932) 839400
Fax: (01932) 839401
Email: jshead@
st-georges-college.co.uk
Head: Mr A J W Hudson
Type: Co-educational Day 3–11
No of pupils: B333 G290
Fees: (September 07)
Day £1755–£9495

WINDLESHAM

WOODCOTE HOUSE SCHOOL
Snows Ride, Windlesham, Surrey
GU20 6PF
Tel: (01276) 472115
Fax: (01276) 472890
Email: info@
woodcotehouseschool.co.uk
Head: Mr N H K Paterson
Type: Boys Boarding and Day
7–14
No of pupils: 100
No of boarders: F75
Fees: On application

WOKING

COWORTH-FLEXLANDS SCHOOL
Valley End, Chobham, Woking, Surrey GU24 8TE
Tel: (01276) 855707
Fax: (01276) 856043
Email: admissions@ coworthflexlands.co.uk
Head: Mrs S O E Stephen
Type: Co-educational Day
Boys 3–7 Girls 3–11
No of pupils: B15 G166
Fees: (September 08)
Day £3765–£9135

GREENFIELD SCHOOL
Brooklyn Road, Woking, Surrey GU22 7TP
Tel: (01483) 772525
Fax: (01483) 728907
Email: principal@ greenfield.surrey.sch.uk
Head: Ms Janis Radcliffe
Type: Co-educational Day 3–11
No of pupils: B105 G115
Fees: On application

HALSTEAD PREPARATORY SCHOOL
Woodham Rise, Woking, Surrey GU21 4EE
Tel: (01483) 772682
Fax: (01483) 757611
Email: registrar@ halstead-school.org.uk
Head: Mrs Sabine Fellows
Type: Girls Day 3–11
No of pupils: 208
Fees: (September 08)
Day £2160–£9924

HOE BRIDGE SCHOOL*
Hoe Place, Old Woking Road, Woking, Surrey GU22 8JE
Tel: (01483) 760018
Fax: (01483) 757560
Email: enquiriesprep@ hoebridgeschool.co.uk
Head: Mr R W K Barr
Type: Co-educational Day 2–13
No of pupils: B337 G145
Fees: (September 08)
Day £1620–£11640

OAKFIELD SCHOOL
Coldharbour Road, Pyrford, Woking, Surrey GU22 8SJ
Tel: (01932) 342465
Fax: (01932) 342745
Email: education@ oakfieldschool.co.uk
Head: Mrs S H Goddard
Type: Co-educational Day
Boys 3–7 Girls 3–16
No of pupils: B20 G168
Fees: On application

PRINS WILLEM-ALEXANDER SCHOOL
Old Woking Road, Woking, Surrey GU22 8HY
Tel: (01483) 750409
Fax: (01483) 730962
Email: info@ prinswillemalexander.com
Head: Mr M Damhuis and Mr D Hooijberg
Type: Co-educational Day 4–12
No of pupils: B68 G71
Fees: (September 08)
Day £8205–£12885

RIPLEY COURT SCHOOL
Rose Lane, Ripley, Woking, Surrey GU23 6NE
Tel: (01483) 225217
Fax: (01483) 223854
Email: head@ripleycourt.co.uk
Head: Mr A J Gough
Type: Co-educational Day 3–13
No of pupils: B170 G86
Fees: (September 08)
Day £6900–£9840

ST ANDREW'S (WOKING) SCHOOL TRUST*
Church Hill House, Wilson Way, Horsell, Woking, Surrey GU21 4QW
Tel: (01483) 760943
Fax: (01483) 740314
Email: admin@ st-andrews.woking.sch.uk
Head: Mr A K Perks
Type: Co-educational Day 3–13
No of pupils: B220 G76
Fees: (September 08)
Day £2790–£11550

WOLDINGHAM

WOLDINGHAM SCHOOL*
Marden Park, Woldingham, Surrey CR3 7YA
Tel: (01883) 349431
Fax: (01883) 348653
Email: registrar@ woldingham.surrey.sch.uk
Head: Mrs Jayne Triffitt
Type: Girls Boarding and Day 11–18
No of pupils: 516
No of boarders: F324
Fees: (September 08) FB £24870
Day £14985

England – Surrey

EAST SUSSEX

BATTLE

BATTLE ABBEY SCHOOL*
High Street, Battle, East Sussex
TN33 0AD
Tel: (01424) 772385
Fax: (01424) 773573
Email: office@
 battleabbeyschool.com
Head: Mr R Clark
Type: Co-educational Boarding
and Day 2–18
No of pupils: B181 G189
No of boarders: F40
Fees: (September 08) FB £20790
Day £6225–£12600

BRIGHTON

BRIGHTON AND HOVE HIGH SCHOOL GDST
Montpelier Road, Brighton,
East Sussex BN1 3AT
Tel: (01273) 734112
Fax: (01273) 737120
Email: enquiries@bhhs.gdst.net
Head: Mrs A Greatorex
Type: Girls Day 3–18
No of pupils: 780
Fees: On application

BRIGHTON COLLEGE
Eastern Road, Brighton,
East Sussex BN2 0AL
Tel: (01273) 704200
Fax: (01273) 704204
Email: registrar@
 brightoncollege.net
Head: Mr R Cairns
Type: Co-educational Day and
Boarding 11–18
No of pupils: B430 G254
No of boarders: F74 W90
Fees: (September 07) FB £24078
WB £21150 Day £15387–£15534

BRIGHTON COLLEGE PRE-PREPARATORY SCHOOL
Sutherland Road, Brighton,
East Sussex BN2 0EQ
Tel: (01273) 704201
Fax: (01273) 704204
Email: registrar@
 brightoncollege.net
Head: Mrs S P Wicks
Type: Co-educational Day 3–8
No of pupils: B110 G85
Fees: (September 07)
Day £3000–£8200

BRIGHTON COLLEGE PREP SCHOOL
Walpole Lodge, Walpole Road,
Brighton, East Sussex BN2 0EU
Tel: (01273) 704201
Fax: (01273) 704286
Email: paprep@
 brightoncollege.net
Head: Mr B Melia
Type: Co-educational Day 8–13
No of pupils: B166 G131
Fees: (September 07)
Day £9909–£12582

BRIGHTON STEINER SCHOOL LIMITED
Roedean Road, Brighton,
East Sussex BN2 5RA
Tel: (01273) 386300
Fax: (01273) 386313
Email: enquiries@
 brightonsteinerschool.org.uk
Head: Ms R Harrison
Type: Co-educational Day 2–16
Fees: (September 08) Day £5850

DHARMA SCHOOL
White House, Ladies Mile Road,
Patcham, Brighton, East Sussex
BN1 8TB
Tel: (01273) 502055
Fax: (01273) 556580
Email: office@
 dharmaschool.f9.co.uk
Head: Mr P Murdock
Type: Co-educational Day 3–11
No of pupils: B34 G36
Fees: (September 07)
Day £3973–£4675

ROEDEAN SCHOOL
Roedean Way, Brighton,
East Sussex BN2 5RQ
Tel: (01273) 603181
Fax: (01273) 680791
Email: admissions@roedean.co.uk
Head: Mrs Frances King
Type: Girls Boarding and Day
11–18
No of pupils: 377
No of boarders: F316
Fees: On application

ST AUBYNS SCHOOL
76 High Street, Rottingdean,
Brighton, East Sussex BN2 7JN
Tel: (01273) 302170
Fax: (01273) 304004
Email: office@
 staubyns-school.org.uk
Head: Mr S L Hitchings
Type: Co-educational Day and
Boarding 3–13
No of pupils: B119 G60
No of boarders: W4
Fees: (September 08) WB £16950
Day £4800–£13650

ST MARY'S HALL*
Eastern Road, Brighton,
East Sussex BN2 5JF
Tel: (01273) 606061
Fax: (01273) 620782
Email: registrar@stmaryshall.co.uk
Head: Mrs S M Meek
Type: Co-educational Day and
Boarding Boys 3–8 Girls 3–18
(Co-ed Junior School 3–11)
No of pupils: B15 G290
No of boarders: F79 W9
Fees: (September 08)
FB £15741–£20817
WB £14985–£19956
Day £5478–£12609

EASTBOURNE

EASTBOURNE COLLEGE
Old Wish Road, Eastbourne,
East Sussex BN21 4JX
Tel: (01323) 452323
Fax: (01323) 452354
Email: EDeacon@
   eastbourne-college.co.uk
Head: Mr S P Davies
Type: Co-educational Boarding
and Day 13–18
No of pupils: B382 G228
No of boarders: F290
Fees: On application

MOIRA HOUSE GIRLS SCHOOL
Upper Carlisle Road, Eastbourne,
East Sussex BN20 7TE
Tel: (01323) 644144
Fax: (01323) 649720
Email: info@moirahouse.co.uk
Head: Mrs L A Watson
Type: Girls Boarding and Day
3–19
No of pupils: 420
No of boarders: F110 W12
Fees: On application

MOIRA HOUSE SCHOOL*
Upper Carlisle Road, Eastbourne,
East Sussex BN20 7TE
Tel: (01323) 636800
Fax: (01323) 649720
Email: lyoung@
   moirahouse.e-sussex.sch.uk
Head: Mrs L Young
Type: Girls Day and Boarding
2–11
No of pupils: 85
No of boarders: F4
Fees: (September 08)
FB £15540–£20670
WB £16380–£17625
Day £5460–£10290

ST ANDREW'S SCHOOL
Meads, Eastbourne, East Sussex
BN20 7RP
Tel: (01323) 733203
Fax: (01323) 646860
Email: info@androvian.com
Head: Mr J Griffith
Type: Co-educational Boarding
and Day 2–13
No of pupils: B267 G151
No of boarders: F16 W4
Fees: (September 08) FB £6000
WB £5330 Day £2427–£4225

ST BEDE'S PREP SCHOOL
Duke's Drive, Eastbourne,
East Sussex BN20 7XL
Tel: (01323) 734222
Fax: (01323) 746438
Email: prep.school@
   stbedesschool.org
Head: Mr N Bevington
Type: Co-educational Boarding
and Day 2–13
No of pupils: B263 G185
No of boarders: F32 W5
Fees: (September 08) F/WB £18045
Day £7665–£12420

FOREST ROW

ASHDOWN HOUSE SCHOOL
Forest Row, East Sussex RH18 5JY
Tel: (01342) 822574
Fax: (01342) 824380
Email: secretary@
   ashdownhouse.com
Head: Mr A R Taylor
Type: Co-educational Boarding
8–13
No of pupils: B90 G52
No of boarders: F142
Fees: (September 08) FB £20085
Day £16917

GREENFIELDS SCHOOL
Priory Road, Forest Row,
East Sussex RH18 5JD
Tel: (01342) 822189
Fax: (01342) 825289
Email: info@
   greenfieldsschool.com
Head: Mrs V Tupholme
Type: Co-educational Day and
Boarding 2–19
No of pupils: B80 G65
No of boarders: F32
Fees: (September 07)
F/WB £14100–£17100
Day £3000–£10000

MICHAEL HALL (STEINER WALDORF SCHOOL)
Kidbrooke Park, Forest Row,
East Sussex RH18 5JA
Tel: (01342) 822275
Fax: (01342) 826593
Email: info@michaelhall.co.uk
Type: Co-educational Day and
Boarding 3–19
No of pupils: B239 G265
No of boarders: F18
Fees: (September 07)
FB £12702–£14337
WB £11777–£13412
Day £3990–£8985

HAILSHAM

ST BEDE'S SCHOOL
Upper Dicker, Hailsham,
East Sussex BN27 3QH
Tel: (01323) 843252
Fax: (01323) 442628
Email: school.office@
   stbedesschool.org
Head: Mr S W Cole
Type: Co-educational Boarding
and Day 13–19
No of pupils: B542 G317
No of boarders: F343
Fees: (September 08) FB £23340
Day £14355

HASTINGS

BUCKSWOOD SCHOOL*
Broomham Hall, Rye Road,
Guestling, Hastings, East Sussex
TN35 4LT
Tel: (01424) 813813
Fax: (01424) 812100
Email: achieve@buckswood.co.uk
Head: Mr T Fish
Type: Co-educational Day and
Boarding 10–19
No of pupils: B180 G170
No of boarders: F197
Fees: (September 08)
FB £16440–£20790 WB £15720
Day £9735

HOVE

BELLERBYS COLLEGE
Manor Campus, 44 Cromwell Road, Hove, East Sussex BN3 3ER
Tel: (01273) 323374
Fax: (01273) 749322
Email: hove@bellerbys.com
Head: Mr N Addison
Type: Co-educational Boarding and Day 14+
No of pupils: B270 G210
No of boarders: F390
Fees: (September 07)
FB £18480–£22410
Day £8075–£14280

DEEPDENE SCHOOL
Hove, East Sussex BN3 4ED
Tel: (01273) 418984
Fax: (01273) 415543
Email: info@deepdeneschool.com
Head: Mrs L V Clark-Darby and Mrs N K Gane
Type: Co-educational Day 1–8
No of pupils: B108 G122
Fees: (September 08)
Day £5175–£7500

THE DRIVE PREP SCHOOL
101 The Drive, Hove, East Sussex BN3 6GE
Tel: (01273) 738444
Fax: (01273) 738444
Email: enquiries@driveprep.co.uk
Head: Mrs S Parkinson
Type: Co-educational Day 3–16
No of pupils: 109
Fees: (September 08)
Day £3000–£6000

THE FOLD SCHOOL
201 New Church Road, Hove, East Sussex BN3 4ED
Tel: (01273) 410901
Email: thefoldschool@
  ntlworld.com
Head: Dr C J Drake
Type: Co-educational Day 3–11
No of pupils: B37 G38
Fees: On application

LANCING COLLEGE PREPARATORY SCHOOL AT MOWDEN
The Droveway, Hove, East Sussex BN3 6LU
Tel: (01273) 503452
Fax: (01273) 503457
Email: info@lancingprep.co.uk
Head: Mr A P Laurent
Type: Co-educational Day 3–13
No of pupils: B133 G43
Fees: (September 07)
Day £5070–£11175

ST CHRISTOPHER'S SCHOOL
33 New Church Road, Hove, East Sussex BN3 4AD
Tel: (01273) 735404
Fax: (01273) 747956
Email: office@
  stchristophershove.org.uk
Head: Mr I McIntyre
Type: Co-educational Day 4–13
No of pupils: B177 G65
Fees: On application

STONELANDS SCHOOL OF BALLET & THEATRE ARTS
170A Church Road, Hove, East Sussex BN3 2DJ
Tel: (01273) 770445
Fax: (01273) 770444
Email: dianacarteur@
  stonelandsschool.co.uk
Head: Mrs D Carteur
Type: Co-educational Boarding and Day 5–16
No of pupils: B6 G44
No of boarders: F10 W10
Fees: (September 08) FB £16530
Day £4000–£6500

LEWES

LEWES OLD GRAMMAR SCHOOL
140 High Street, Lewes, East Sussex BN7 1XS
Tel: (01273) 472634
Fax: (01273) 476948
Email: office@logs.uk.com
Head: Mr R Blewitt
Type: Co-educational Day 3–18
No of pupils: B210 G120
Fees: On application

MAYFIELD

ST LEONARDS-MAYFIELD SCHOOL
The Old Palace, Mayfield, East Sussex TN20 6PH
Tel: (01435) 874600
Fax: (01435) 872627
Email: admissions@
  mayfieldgirls.org
Head: Miss A Beary
Type: Girls Boarding and Day 11–18
No of pupils: 407
No of boarders: F75 W28
Fees: (September 08) FB £22560
WB £22335 Day £14985

SKIPPERS HILL MANOR PREPARATORY SCHOOL
Five Ashes, Mayfield, East Sussex TN20 6HR
Tel: (01825) 830234
Fax: (01825) 831040
Email: info@skippershill.com
Head: Mr T W Lewis
Type: Co-educational Day 3–13
No of pupils: B63 G56
Fees: On application

ROBERTSBRIDGE

BODIAM MANOR SCHOOL
Bodiam, Robertsbridge, East Sussex TN32 5UJ
Tel: (01580) 830225
Fax: (01580) 830227
Email: headmaster@
  bodiammanorschool.fsnet.co.uk
Head: Mr S Flutter
Type: Co-educational Day 2–13
No of pupils: B73 G72
Fees: (September 08)
Day £5970–£10797

DARVELL SCHOOL
Darvell Bruderhof, Robertsbridge, East Sussex TN32 5DR
Tel: (01580) 883300
Fax: (01580) 883317
Head: Mr R A Meier
Type: Co-educational Day 4–16
No of pupils: B55 G55
Fees: On application

VINEHALL SCHOOL
Robertsbridge, East Sussex
TN32 5JL
Tel: (01580) 880413
Fax: (01580) 882119
Email: office@vinehallschool.com
Head: Mrs J L Robinson
Type: Co-educational Boarding
and Day 2–13
No of pupils: B184 G154
No of boarders: F40
Fees: (September 08) F/WB £17226
Day £13185

SEAFORD

NEWLANDS SCHOOL[†]
Eastbourne Road, Sutton Avenue,
Seaford, East Sussex BN25 4NP
Tel: (01323) 892334 / 490000
Fax: (01323) 898420
Email: newlands1@msn.com
Head: Mr C M Bridgman
Type: Co-educational Boarding
and Day 0–18 (nursery & pre-prep)
No of pupils: B70 G80
No of boarders: F10
Fees: On application

ST LEONARDS-ON-SEA

CLAREMONT SCHOOL
Baldslow, St Leonards-on-Sea,
East Sussex TN37 7PW
Tel: (01424) 751555
Fax: (01424) 754310
Email: enquiries@
   claremontschool.co.uk
Head: Mr M Beaumont and
Mr I Culley
Type: Co-educational Day 1–14
No of pupils: B200 G200
Fees: On application

WADHURST

BRICKLEHURST MANOR PREPARATORY
Bardown Road, Stonegate,
Wadhurst, East Sussex TN5 7EL
Tel: (01580) 200448
Fax: (01580) 200998
Email: office@bricklehurst.co.uk
Head: Mrs C Flowers
Type: Co-educational Day 3–11
No of pupils: B48 G77
Fees: On application

SACRED HEART R C PRIMARY SCHOOL
Mayfield Lane, Durgates,
Wadhurst, East Sussex TN5 6DQ
Tel: (01892) 783414
Fax: (01892) 783510
Email: admin@
   wadhurstsacredheart.
   freeserve.co.uk
Head: Mrs H Blake
Type: Co-educational Day 3–11
No of pupils: B60 G60
Fees: (September 08)
Day £5085–£5385

WEST SUSSEX

ARUNDEL

SLINDON COLLEGE[†]
Slindon, Arundel, West Sussex
BN18 0RH
Tel: (01243) 814320
Fax: (01243) 814702
Email: registrar@
   slindoncollege.co.uk
Head: Mr I P Graham
Type: Boys Boarding and Day
9–16
No of pupils: 110
No of boarders: F20 W20
Fees: (September 07) F/WB £22035
Day £12945

BURGESS HILL

BURGESS HILL SCHOOL FOR GIRLS*
Keymer Road, Burgess Hill,
West Sussex RH15 0EG
Tel: (01444) 241050
Fax: (01444) 870314
Email: registrar@
   burgesshill-school.com
Head: Mrs A Aughwane
Type: Girls Boarding and Day
2–18
No of pupils: B50 G624
No of boarders: F54
Fees: (September 07) FB £20850
Day £5730–£12000

CHICHESTER

GREAT BALLARD SCHOOL
Eartham, Chichester, West Sussex
PO18 0LR
Tel: (01243) 814236
Fax: (01243) 814586
Email: office@greatballard.co.uk
Head: Mr R E Jennings
Type: Co-educational Boarding
and Day 2–13
No of pupils: B88 G102
Fees: (September 08) WB £4325
Day £1000–£3600

LAVANT HOUSE

West Lavant, Chichester,
West Sussex PO18 9AB
Tel: (01243) 527211
Fax: (01243) 530490
Email: office@lavanthouse.org.uk
Head: Mrs M Scott
Type: Girls Day and Boarding
3–18
No of pupils: 165
No of boarders: F15 W10
Fees: (September 08)
F/WB £15720–£18855
Day £5910–£11985

OAKWOOD SCHOOL

Oakwood, Chichester, West Sussex
PO18 9AN
Tel: (01243) 575209
Fax: (01243) 575433
Email: office@
   oakwoodschool.co.uk
Head: Mr J Kittermaster
Type: Co-educational Day 2–11
No of pupils: B140 G140
Fees: (September 08)
Day £6480–£10260

THE PREBENDAL SCHOOL

54 West Street, Chichester,
West Sussex PO19 1RT
Tel: (01243) 782026/784828
Fax: (01243) 771821
Email: secretary.prebendal@
   btconnect.com
Head: Mr T R Cannell
Type: Co-educational Day and
Boarding 3–14
No of pupils: B167 G121
No of boarders: F18 W12
Fees: On application

PREBENDAL SCHOOL
(NORTHGATE HOUSE)

38 North Street, Chichester,
West Sussex PO19 1LX
Tel: (01243) 784828
Email: secretary.prebendal@
   btconnect.com
Head: Mrs L M Greenall
Type: Co-educational Day 3–7
No of pupils: B53 G42
Fees: (September 08)
Day £5484–£6594

WESTBOURNE HOUSE
SCHOOL

Coach Road, Shopwyke,
Chichester, West Sussex
PO20 2BH
Tel: (01243) 782739
Fax: (01243) 770759
Email: office@westbournehouse.
   w-sussex.sch.uk
Head: Mr B G Law
Type: Co-educational Boarding
and Day 2–13
No of pupils: B238 G187
No of boarders: F48 W32
Fees: (September 08) FB £15450
Day £2250–£12600

COPTHORNE

COPTHORNE PREP SCHOOL

Effingham Lane, Copthorne,
West Sussex RH10 3HR
Tel: (01342) 712311
Fax: (01342) 714014
Email: office@
   copthorneprep.co.uk
Head: Mr C Jones
Type: Co-educational Day and
Boarding 2–13
No of pupils: B150 G150
No of boarders: W10
Fees: On application

CRAWLEY

WILLOW TREE MONTESSORI
SCHOOL

Charlwood House, Charlwood
Road, Lowfield Heath, Crawley,
West Sussex RH11 0QA
Tel: (01293) 565544
Fax: (01293) 611705
Email: gkerfante@hotmail.com
Head: Mrs G Kerfante
Type: Co-educational Day 1–8
No of pupils: B84 G66
Fees: (September 08)
Day £2970–£4185

EAST GRINSTEAD

BRAMBLETYE

Lewes Road, Brambletye, East
Grinstead, West Sussex RH19 3PD
Tel: (01342) 321004
Fax: (01342) 317562
Email: registrar@brambletye.com
Head: Mr H D Cocke
Type: Co-educational Boarding
and Day 3–13
No of pupils: B150 G105
No of boarders: F80
Fees: (September 07) FB £17475
Day £13275–£16725

FONTHILL LODGE

Coombe Hill Road, East Grinstead,
West Sussex RH9 4LY
Tel: (01342) 321635
Fax: (01342) 326844
Email: enquiries@
   fonthill-lodge.co.uk
Head: Mrs Margaret Neal
Type: Co-educational Day 2–11
(Single-sex ed 8–11)
No of pupils: B91 G99
Fees: (September 08)
Day £6855–£11271

STOKE BRUNSWICK

Ashurstwood, East Grinstead,
West Sussex RH19 3PF
Tel: (01342) 828200
Fax: (01342) 828201
Email: headmaster@
   stokebrunswick.co.uk
Head: Mr R Taylor
Type: Co-educational Boarding
and Day 3–13
No of pupils: B100 G55
No of boarders: W10
Fees: On application

HAYWARDS HEATH

ARDINGLY COLLEGE

Haywards Heath, West Sussex
RH17 6SQ
Tel: (01444) 893000
Fax: (01444) 893001
Email: registrar@ardingly.com
Head: Mr P R A Green
Type: Co-educational Boarding
and Day 3–18
No of pupils: B485 G303
No of boarders: F228 W11
Fees: (September 07)
FB £22800–£23700
WB £14625–£14775
Day £5655–£17700

ARDINGLY COLLEGE JUNIOR SCHOOL
Haywards Heath, West Sussex
RH17 6SQ
Tel: (01444) 893200
Fax: (01444) 892001
Email: mark.groome@
  ardingly.com
Head: Mr M Groome
Type: Co-educational Boarding
and Day 7–13 (and pre-prep)
No of pupils: B146 G90
No of boarders: W14
Fees: On application

CUMNOR HOUSE SCHOOL
Danehill, Haywards Heath,
West Sussex RH17 7HT
Tel: (01825) 790347
Fax: (01825) 790910
Email: office@cumnor.co.uk
Head: Mr C St J Heinrich
Type: Co-educational Boarding
and Day 4–13
No of pupils: B185 G174
No of boarders: F26
Fees: (September 08) FB £17205
Day £7665–£14490

GREAT WALSTEAD
East Mascalls Lane, Lindfield,
Haywards Heath, West Sussex
RH16 2QL
Tel: (01444) 483528
Fax: (01444) 482122
Email: admin@
  greatwalstead.co.uk
Head: Mr J Sykes
Type: Co-educational Day and
Boarding 2–13
No of pupils: B245 G166
No of boarders: W30
Fees: On application

HANDCROSS PARK SCHOOL
Handcross, Haywards Heath,
West Sussex RH17 6HF
Tel: (01444) 400526
Fax: (01444) 400527
Email: info@handxpark.com
Head: Mr W J Hilton
Type: Co-educational Day and
Boarding 2–13
No of pupils: B151 G113
No of boarders: W10
Fees: (September 08) WB £15879
Day £1590–£13551

TAVISTOCK & SUMMERHILL SCHOOL
Summerhill Lane, Haywards
Heath, West Sussex RH16 1RP
Tel: (01444) 450256
Fax: (01444) 458251
Email: info@
  tavistockandsummerhill.co.uk
Head: Mr M Barber
Type: Co-educational Day 3–13
No of pupils: B99 G53
Fees: On application

HORSHAM

CHRIST'S HOSPITAL
Horsham, West Sussex RH13 0YP
Tel: (01403) 211293
Fax: (01403) 211580
Email: enquiries@
  christs-hospital.org.uk
Head: Mr J R Franklin
Type: Co-educational Boarding
11–18
No of pupils: B442 G395
No of boarders: F837
Fees: (September 07) FB £19752

FARLINGTON SCHOOL*
Strood Park, Horsham, West Sussex
RH12 3PN
Tel: (01403) 254967
Fax: (01403) 272258
Email: office@farlingtonschool.net
Head: Mrs J Goyer
Type: Girls Boarding and Day
3–18
No of pupils: 480
No of boarders: F29 W9
Fees: (September 07)
FB £15501–£18888
WB £15120–£18507
Day £5580–£11877

PENNTHORPE SCHOOL
Church Street, Rudgwick,
Horsham, West Sussex RH12 3HJ
Tel: (01403) 822391
Fax: (01403) 822438
Email: enquiries@pennthorpe.com
Head: Mr S Moll
Type: Co-educational Day 2–14
No of pupils: B197 G109
Fees: On application

HURSTPIERPOINT

HURSTPIERPOINT COLLEGE
College Lane, Hurstpierpoint,
West Sussex BN6 9JS
Tel: (01273) 833636
Fax: (01273) 835257
Email: info@hppc.co.uk
Head: Mr T J Manly
Type: Co-educational Boarding
and Day 7–18
No of pupils: B479 G307
No of boarders: F18 W311
Fees: (September 08) FB £23175
WB £13710–£21930
Day £10350–£17235

LANCING

ARDMORE MONTESSORI SCHOOL
Wembley Gardens, Lancing,
West Sussex BN15 9LA
Tel: (01903) 755583
Head: Mr N Peck
Type: Co-educational Day 2–12
No of pupils: 60
Fees: On application

LANCING COLLEGE
Lancing, West Sussex BN15 0RW
Tel: (01273) 452213
Fax: (01273) 464720
Email: admissions@
  lancingcollege.org.uk
Head: Mr J Gillespie
Type: Co-educational Boarding
and Day 13–18
No of pupils: B355 G150
No of boarders: F300
Fees: (September 07) FB £24600
Day £17085

MIDHURST

CONIFERS SCHOOL
Egmont Road, Midhurst,
West Sussex GU29 9BG
Tel: (01730) 813243
Fax: (01730) 813382
Email: admin@conifersschool.com
Head: Mrs L R Fox
Type: Co-educational Day
Boys 3–8 Girls 3–11
No of pupils: B30 G70
Fees: On application

ST MARGARET'S SCHOOL
Petersfield Road, Midhurst,
West Sussex GU29 9JN
Tel: (01730) 813956
Fax: (01730) 810829
Email: smsadmin@
  conventofmercy.org
Head: Sister M Joseph Clare
Type: Co-educational Day 2–11
No of pupils: B81 G112
Fees: (September 07)
Day £1410–£6255

PEASE POTTAGE

COTTESMORE SCHOOL*
Buchan Hill, Pease Pottage,
West Sussex RH11 9AU
Tel: (01293) 520648
Fax: (01293) 614784
Email: office@
  cottesmoreschool.com
Head: Mr T F Rogerson
Type: Co-educational Day and
Boarding 7–13
No of pupils: B100 G50
No of boarders: F150 W10
Fees: (September 08) F/WB £17910
Day £13440–£16119

PETWORTH

SEAFORD COLLEGE*
Lavington Park, Petworth,
West Sussex GU28 0NB
Tel: (01798) 867392
Fax: (01798) 867606
Email: seaford@clara.co.uk
Head: Mr T J Mullins
Type: Co-educational Boarding
and Day 10–18
No of pupils: B366 G185
No of boarders: F30 W103
Fees: (September 08)
FB £17010–£22680
WB £14925–£19200
Day £12000–£14850

PULBOROUGH

**ARUNDALE PREPARATORY
SCHOOL**
Lower Street, Pulborough,
West Sussex RH20 2BX
Tel: (01798) 872520
Fax: (01798) 875202
Email: arundale@easynet.co.uk
Head: Miss K Lovejoy
Type: Co-educational Day 2–11
No of pupils: B36 G63
Fees: (September 07)
Day £905–£8610

DORSET HOUSE SCHOOL
The Manor, Church Lane, Bury,
Pulborough, West Sussex
RH20 1PB
Tel: (01798) 831456
Fax: (01798) 831141
Email: headmaster@
  dorsethouse.w-sussex.sch.uk
Head: Mr E J D Clarke
Type: Co-educational Boarding
and Day 3–13
No of pupils: B130 G9
No of boarders: W32
Fees: (September 07)
WB £13935–£15660
Day £6426–£12960

WINDLESHAM HOUSE*
London Road, Washington,
Pulborough, West Sussex
RH20 4AY
Tel: (01903) 874700
Fax: (01903) 874702
Email: office@windlesham.com
Head: Mr R Foster
Type: Co-educational Boarding
and Day 4–13 (Day pre-prep 4–7)
No of pupils: B187 G114
No of boarders: F191
Fees: (September 08)
FB £10890–£18750
Day £6810–£15750

SHOREHAM-BY-SEA

SHOREHAM COLLEGE
St Julian's Lane, Shoreham-by-Sea,
West Sussex BN43 6YW
Tel: (01273) 592681
Fax: (01273) 591673
Email: info@
  shorehamcollege.co.uk
Head: Mr R K Iremonger
Type: Co-educational Day 3–16
No of pupils: B280 G144
Fees: On application

SOMPTING

**SOMPTING ABBOTTS
SCHOOL***
Church Lane, Sompting,
West Sussex BN15 0AZ
Tel: (01903) 235960
Fax: (01903) 210045
Email: office@
  somptingabbotts.com
Head: Mrs P M Sinclair and
Mr T R Sinclair
Type: Co-educational Day and
Boarding 3–13
No of pupils: B125 G60
No of boarders: W12
Fees: (September 08) WB £10650
Day £6840–£8760

STEYNING

**THE TOWERS CONVENT
SCHOOL**
Henfield Road, Upper Beeding,
Steyning, West Sussex BN44 3TF
Tel: (01903) 812185
Fax: (01903) 813858
Email: admin@
  towers.w-sussex.sch.uk
Head: Mrs C Baker
Type: Girls Day and Boarding
3–16 (Boys 3–11)
No of pupils: B4 G271
No of boarders: F44 W1
Fees: On application

TURNERS HILL

WORTH SCHOOL
Paddockhurst Road, Turners Hill,
West Sussex RH10 4SD
Tel: (01342) 710200
Fax: (01342) 710230
Email: registry@worth.org.uk
Head: Mr G Carminati
Type: Co-educational Boarding
and Day Boys 11–18 Girls 16–18
No of pupils: B443 G32
No of boarders: F320
Fees: (September 08)
FB £20997–£24036
Day £15558–£17805

WORTHING

BROADWATER MANOR SCHOOL

Broadwater Road, Worthing,
West Sussex BN14 8HU
Tel: (01903) 201123
Fax: (01903) 821777
Email: info@
broadwatermanor.com
Head: Mrs E K Woodley
Type: Co-educational Day 2–13
No of pupils: B137 G117
Fees: On application

OUR LADY OF SION SCHOOL

Gratwicke Road, Worthing,
West Sussex BN11 4BL
Tel: (01903) 204063
Fax: (01903) 214434
Email: enquiries@
sionschool.org.uk
Head: Mr M Scullion and
Mr J Summers
Type: Co-educational Day 2–18
No of pupils: B253 G266
Fees: (September 07)
Day £5715–£9150

TYNE AND WEAR

NEWCASTLE UPON TYNE

CENTRAL NEWCASTLE HIGH SCHOOL GDST

Eskdale Terrace, Newcastle upon
Tyne, Tyne and Wear NE2 4DS
Tel: (0191) 281 1768
Fax: (0191) 281 6192
Email: cnhs@cnw.gdst.net
Head: Mrs H French
Type: Girls Day 3–18
No of pupils: 967
Fees: (September 08)
Day £5328–£8898

DAME ALLAN'S BOYS SCHOOL

Fowberry Crescent, Fenham,
Newcastle upon Tyne,
Tyne and Wear NE4 9YJ
Tel: (0191) 275 0608
Fax: (0191) 275 1502
Email: enquiries@
dameallans.co.uk
Head: Dr J R Hind
Type: Boys Day 8–18 (Co-ed VIth
Form)
No of pupils: 510
Fees: On application

DAME ALLAN'S GIRLS SCHOOL

Fowberry Crescent, Fenham,
Newcastle upon Tyne,
Tyne and Wear NE4 9YJ
Tel: (0191) 275 0708
Fax: (0191) 275 1502
Email: enquiries@
dameallans.co.uk
Head: Dr J R Hind
Type: Girls Day 8–18 (Co-ed VIth
Form)
No of pupils: 422
Fees: On application

LINDEN SCHOOL

72 Station Road, Forest Hall,
Newcastle upon Tyne,
Tyne and Wear NE12 9BQ
Tel: (0191) 266 2943
Fax: (0191) 266 2943
Head: Mr A J Edge
Type: Co-educational Day 3–11
No of pupils: B60 G58
Fees: On application

NEWCASTLE PREPARATORY SCHOOL

6 Eslington Road, Jesmond,
Newcastle upon Tyne,
Tyne and Wear NE2 4RH
Tel: (0191) 281 1769
Fax: (0191) 281 5668
Email: enquiries@
newcastleprepschool.org.uk
Head: Mrs M Coates
Type: Co-educational Day 3–11
No of pupils: B160 G60
Fees: On application

NEWCASTLE SCHOOL FOR BOYS

30 West Avenue, Gosforth,
Newcastle upon Tyne,
Tyne and Wear NE3 4ES
Tel: (0191) 285 1619
Fax: (0191) 213 1105
Email: office@
newcastleschool.co.uk
Head: Mr C J Hutchinson
Type: Boys Day 3–13
No of pupils: 392
Fees: (September 08)
Day £6900–£8670

NEWCASTLE UPON TYNE CHURCH HIGH SCHOOL

Tankerville Terrace, Jesmond,
Newcastle upon Tyne,
Tyne and Wear NE2 3BA
Tel: (0191) 281 4306
Fax: (0191) 281 0806
Email: info@churchhigh.com
Head: Mrs J Gatenby
Type: Girls Day 2–18
No of pupils: 609
Fees: (September 08)
Day £5448–£9219

ROYAL GRAMMAR SCHOOL

Eskdale Terrace, Newcastle upon
Tyne, Tyne and Wear NE2 4DX
Tel: (0191) 281 5711
Fax: (0191) 212 0392
Email: hm@rgs.newcastle.sch.uk
Head: Dr B Trafford
Type: Boys Day 8–18 (Co-ed VIth
form)
No of pupils: B1067 G74
Fees: (September 08)
Day £7416–£8799

WESTFIELD SCHOOL
Oakfield Road, Gosforth,
Newcastle upon Tyne,
Tyne and Wear NE3 4HS
Tel: (0191) 255 3980
Fax: (0191) 255 3983
Email: westfield@
    westfield.newcastle.sch.uk
Head: Mrs M Farndale
Type: Girls Day 3–18
No of pupils: 370
Fees: On application

SUNDERLAND

ARGYLE HOUSE SCHOOL
19/20 Thornhill Park, Sunderland,
Tyne and Wear SR2 7LA
Tel: (0191) 510 0726
Fax: (0191) 567 2209
Email: info@
    argylehouseschool.co.uk
Head: Mr C Johnson
Type: Co-educational Day 3–16
No of pupils: B156 G81
Fees: On application

GRINDON HALL CHRISTIAN SCHOOL
Nookside, Sunderland,
Tyne and Wear SR4 8PG
Tel: (0191) 534 4444
Fax: (0191) 534 4111
Email: info@grindonhall.com
Head: Mr C J Gray
Type: Co-educational Day 3–18
(VIth Form from Sept 2005)
Fees: (September 08)
Day £4500–£5994

SUNDERLAND HIGH SCHOOL
Mowbray Road, Sunderland,
Tyne and Wear SR2 8HY
Tel: (0191) 567 4984
Fax: (0191) 510 3953
Email: info@sunderlandhigh.co.uk
Head: Dr A Slater
Type: Co-educational Day 2–18
No of pupils: B318 G257
Fees: (September 08)
Day £6678–£7818

TYNEMOUTH

THE KING'S SCHOOL
Huntington Place, Tynemouth,
Tyne and Wear NE30 4RF
Tel: (0191) 258 5995
Fax: (0191) 296 3826
Email: hm@
    kings-tynemouth.co.uk
Head: Mr P J S Cantwell
Type: Co-educational Day 4–18
No of pupils: B540 G280
Fees: (September 08)
Day £7026–£8853

WARWICKSHIRE

ATHERSTONE

TWYCROSS HOUSE SCHOOL
Twycross, Atherstone,
Warwickshire CV9 3PL
Tel: (01827) 880651
Fax: (01827) 880651
Email: enquiries@
    twycrosshouseschool.org.uk
Head: Mr S D Assinder and
Mrs N J Lilley
Type: Co-educational Day 8–19
No of pupils: B163 G163
Fees: (September 07)
Day £6375–£7200

KENILWORTH

ABBOTSFORD SCHOOL
Bridge Street, Kenilworth,
Warwickshire CV8 1BP
Tel: (01926) 852826
Fax: (01926) 852753
Email: office@
    abbotsfordschool.co.uk
Head: Mr J P Skuse
Type: Co-educational Day 3–11
No of pupils: B50 G46
Fees: (September 07)
Day £4485–£5610

CRACKLEY HALL SCHOOL
St Joseph's Park, Kenilworth,
Warwickshire CV8 2FT
Tel: (01926) 514444
Fax: (01926) 514455
Email: post@crackleyhall.co.uk
Head: Mrs J Le Poidevin
Type: Co-educational Day 2–11
No of pupils: B79 G88
Fees: (September 07)
Day £5865–£6390

LEAMINGTON SPA

ARNOLD LODGE SCHOOL
Kenilworth Road, Leamington Spa,
Warwickshire CV32 5TW
Tel: (01926) 778050
Fax: (01926) 743311
Email: info@arnoldlodge.com
Head: Mrs E M Hickling
Type: Co-educational Day 3–13
No of pupils: B187 G80
Fees: On application

EMSCOTE HOUSE SCHOOL AND NURSERY
46 Warwick Place, Leamington
Spa, Warwickshire CV32 5DE
Tel: (01926) 425067
Email: headteacher@
    emscotehouse.demon.co.uk
Head: Mrs G J Andrews
Type: Co-educational Day 2–8
No of pupils: B26 G15
Fees: On application

THE KINGSLEY SCHOOL
Beauchamp Avenue, Leamington Spa, Warwickshire CV32 5RD
Tel: (01926) 425127
Fax: (01926) 831691
Email: admin@
kingsley.warwickshire.sch.uk
Head: Mrs C Mannion Watson
Type: Girls Day 3–18 (Boys 2–7)
No of pupils: B2 G500
Fees: On application

THE TERRACE SCHOOL
54 High Street, Leamington Spa, Warwickshire CV31 1LW
Tel: (01926) 421222
Fax: (01926) 421222
Head: Mrs Celia Lowe
Type: Co-educational Day 2–13
No of pupils: B20 G20
Fees: On application

NUNEATON

THE DIXIE GRAMMAR JUNIOR SCHOOL
Temple Hall, Wellsborough, Nuneaton, Warwickshire CV13 6PA
Tel: (01455) 293024
Fax: (01455) 293040
Email: info@dixiejs.org.uk
Head: Mr S Barnett
Type: Co-educational Day 3–10
No of pupils: B85 G67
Fees: On application

MILVERTON HOUSE SCHOOL
Holman Way, Park Street, Attleborough, Nuneaton, Warwickshire CV11 4NS
Tel: (024) 7664 1722
Email: reception@
milvertonschool.com
Head: Mrs S D Latham
Type: Co-educational Day 0–11
No of pupils: B150 G150
Fees: On application

RUGBY

BILTON GRANGE
Rugby Road, Dunchurch, Rugby, Warwickshire CV22 6QU
Tel: (01788) 810217
Fax: (01788) 816922
Email: headmaster@
biltongrange.co.uk
Head: Mr J P Kirk
Type: Co-educational Boarding and Day 4–13
No of pupils: B207 G129
No of boarders: F25 W16
Fees: (September 07) F/WB £17700 Day £7800–£14800

THE CRESCENT SCHOOL
Bawnmore Road, Bilton, Rugby, Warwickshire CV22 7QH
Tel: (01788) 521595
Fax: (01788) 816185
Email: admin@
crescentschool.co.uk
Head: Mr R H Marshall
Type: Co-educational Day 3–11
No of pupils: B70 G87
Fees: On application

PRINCETHORPE COLLEGE
Leamington Road, Princethorpe, Rugby, Warwickshire CV23 9PX
Tel: (01926) 634200
Fax: (01926) 633365
Email: post@princethorpe.co.uk
Head: Mr J M Shinkwin
Type: Co-educational Day 11–18
No of pupils: B401 G346
Fees: (September 08) Day £2815

RUGBY SCHOOL
Rugby, Warwickshire CV22 5EH
Tel: (01788) 556276
Fax: (01788) 556277
Email: registry@rugbyschool.net
Head: Mr P S J Derham
Type: Co-educational Boarding and Day 11–18
No of pupils: B441 G341
No of boarders: F643
Fees: (September 07) FB £24915 Day £15750

STRATFORD-UPON-AVON

THE CROFT PREPARATORY SCHOOL
Alveston Hill, Loxley Road, Stratford-upon-Avon, Warwickshire CV37 7RL
Tel: (01789) 293795
Fax: (01789) 414960
Email: office@croftschool.co.uk
Head: Dr P Thompson
Type: Co-educational Day 2–11
No of pupils: B250 G210
Fees: (September 07) Day £1185–£8130

STRATFORD PREPARATORY SCHOOL
Church House, Old Town, Stratford-upon-Avon, Warwickshire CV37 6BG
Tel: (01789) 297993
Fax: (01789) 263993
Email: enquiries@
stratfordprep.co.uk
Head: Mrs C Quinn
Type: Co-educational Day 2–11
No of pupils: B58 G56
Fees: (September 08) Day £6285–£6915

WARWICK

KING'S HIGH SCHOOL, WARWICK
Smith Street, Warwick, Warwickshire CV34 4HJ
Tel: (01926) 494485
Fax: (01926) 403089
Email: enquiries@
kingshighwarwick.co.uk
Head: Mrs E Surber
Type: Girls Day 10–18
No of pupils: 596
Fees: (September 08) Day £9126

WARWICK PREPARATORY SCHOOL
Bridge Field, Banbury Road, Warwick, Warwickshire CV34 6PL
Tel: (01926) 491545
Fax: (01926) 403456
Email: info@warwickprep.com
Head: Mrs D M Robinson
Type: Co-educational Day Boys 3–7 Girls 3–11
No of pupils: B106 G336
Fees: On application

England – Warwickshire

WARWICK SCHOOL
Myton Road, Warwick,
Warwickshire CV34 6PP
Tel: (01926) 776400
Fax: (01926) 401259
Email: enquiries@
   warwickschool.org
Head: Mr E B Halse
Type: Boys Day and Boarding
7–18
No of pupils: 1090
No of boarders: F35 W11
Fees: (September 08)
FB £18522–£20676
WB £17172–£19326
Day £7536–£9690

WEST MIDLANDS

BIRMINGHAM

ABBEY COLLEGE
10 St Pauls Square, Birmingham,
West Midlands B3 1QU
Tel: (0121) 236 7474
Fax: (0121) 236 3937
Email: adminbir@
   abbeycollege.co.uk
Head: Mr Andrew Jedras
Type: Co-educational Day 13+
No of pupils: B95 G61
No of boarders: F1
Fees: On application

AL HIJRAH SCHOOL
Cherrywood Centre, Burbidge
Road, Bordesley Green,
Birmingham, West Midlands
B9 4US
Tel: (0121) 773 7979
Fax: (0121) 773 7111
Email: enquiry@
   al-hijrah.ghan.sch.uk
Head: Mr M A K Saqib
Type: Co-educational Day 4–11
No of pupils: B128 G128
Fees: On application

**AL-BURHAN GRAMMAR
SCHOOL**
28A George Street, Balsall Heath,
Birmingham, West Midlands
B12 9RG
Tel: 0121 4405454
Fax: 0121 4405454
Email: info@alburhan.org.uk
Head: Dr Mohammad Nasrullah
Type: Girls Day 11–16
No of pupils: 85
Fees: On application

**BIRCHFIELD INDEPENDENT
GIRLS SCHOOL**
Beacon House, 30 Beacon Hill,
Aston, Birmingham,
West Midlands B6 6JU
Tel: (0121) 327 7707
Fax: (0121) 327 6888
Email: anwar.telodia@bigs.org.uk
Head: Mrs K Chawdhry
Type: Girls Day 11–16
No of pupils: 170
Fees: On application

THE BLUE COAT SCHOOL
Somerset Road, Edgbaston,
Birmingham, West Midlands
B17 0HR
Tel: (0121) 410 6800
Fax: (0121) 454 7757
Email: admissions@
   bluecoat.bham.sch.uk
Head: Mr A D J Browning
Type: Co-educational Day 2–11
No of pupils: B331 G218
Fees: (September 07)
Day £5575–£8895

**DARUL ULOOM ISLAMIC
HIGH SCHOOL & COLLEGE**
521–527 Coventry Road,
Smallheath, Birmingham,
West Midlands B10 0LL
Tel: (0121) 772 6408
Fax: (0121) 773 4340
Email: contact@darululoom.org.uk
Head: Dr A A Rahim
Type: Co-educational Day and
Boarding
No of pupils: B77 G13
No of boarders: F14
Fees: On application

**EDGBASTON HIGH
SCHOOL FOR GIRLS**
Westbourne Road, Edgbaston,
Birmingham, West Midlands
B15 3TS
Tel: (0121) 454 5831
Fax: (0121) 454 2363
Email: genoffice@
   edgbastonhigh.bham.sch.uk
Head: Dr R Weeks
Type: Girls Day 2–18
No of pupils: 922
Fees: On application

ELMHURST SCHOOL FOR DANCE
247–249 Bristol Road, Edgbaston, Birmingham, West Midlands B5 7UH
Tel: (0121) 472 6655
Fax: (0121) 472 6654
Email: enquiries@ elmhurstdance.co.uk
Head: Elaine Brook
Type: Co-educational Boarding and Day 11–19
No of pupils: B26 G159
No of boarders: F158
Fees: (September 08)
FB £21150–£22800
Day £16500–£17100

HALLFIELD SCHOOL
48 Church Road, Edgbaston, Birmingham, West Midlands B15 3SJ
Tel: (0121) 454 1496
Fax: (0121) 454 9182
Email: admissions@ hallfield.bham.sch.uk
Head: Mr J A Shackleton
Type: Co-educational Day 2–11
No of pupils: B327 G130
Fees: (September 08)
Day £6060–£9180

HARPER BELL SCHOOL
29 Ravenhurst Street, Birmingham, West Midlands B2 0EP
Tel: 0121 6937742
Fax: 0121 6930752
Email: harperbellsdaschool@ hotmail.co.uk
Head: Mr O F Stewart
Type: Co-educational Day 2–11
Fees: On application

HIGHCLARE SCHOOL
10 Sutton Road, Erdington, Birmingham, West Midlands B23 6QL
Tel: (0121) 373 7400
Fax: (0121) 373 7445
Email: abbey@ highclareschool.co.uk
Head: Mrs M Viles
Type: Co-educational Day Boys 1–11 Girls 1–18(Boys 1–11 & 16–18)
No of pupils: B225 G520
Fees: (September 08)
Day £4005–£9150

KING EDWARD VI HIGH SCHOOL FOR GIRLS
Edgbaston Park Road, Birmingham, West Midlands B15 2UB
Tel: (0121) 472 1834
Fax: (0121) 471 3808
Email: admissions@kehs.co.uk
Head: Miss S H Evans
Type: Girls Day 11–18
No of pupils: 540
Fees: (September 08) Day £8850

KING EDWARD'S SCHOOL
Edgbaston Park Road, Birmingham, West Midlands B15 2UA
Tel: (0121) 472 1672
Fax: (0121) 415 4327
Email: admissions@kes.org.uk
Head: Mr J A Claughton
Type: Boys Day 11–18
No of pupils: 840
Fees: (September 08) Day £8970

LAMBS CHRISTIAN SCHOOL
86–95 Bacchus Road, Winson Green, Birmingham, West Midlands B18 4QY
Tel: 0121 5544 744
Email: jevekhuemelo@aol.com
Head: Mrs Patricia Ekhuenelo
Type: Co-educational Day 4–11
No of pupils: B6 G6
Fees: On application

MANDER PORTMAN WOODWARD
17–18 Greenfield Crescent, Edgbaston, Birmingham, West Midlands B15 3AU
Tel: (0121) 454 9637
Fax: (0121) 454 6433
Email: enq@ birmingham.mpw.co.uk
Head: Mrs D Jewell
Type: Co-educational Day 14+
No of pupils: B50 G50
Fees: On application

NORFOLK HOUSE SCHOOL
4 Norfolk Road, Edgbaston, Birmingham, West Midlands B15 3PS
Tel: (0121) 454 7021
Fax: (0121) 454 7021
Email: norfolkhs@aol.com
Head: Mrs Helen Maresca
Type: Co-educational Day 3–11
No of pupils: B80 G78
Fees: (September 08)
Day £3132–£5430

PRIORY SCHOOL
39 Sir Harry's Road, Edgbaston, Birmingham, West Midlands B15 2UR
Tel: (0121) 440 4103
Fax: (0121) 440 3639
Email: enquiries@prioryschool.net
Head: Mrs E Brook
Type: Co-educational Day Boys 0–13 Girls 0–18(Co-ed 1–11)
No of pupils: B131 G205
Fees: (September 07)
Day £5898–£8934

RATHVILLY SCHOOL
119 Bunbury Road, Birmingham, West Midlands B31 2NB
Tel: (0121) 475 1509
Email: enquiries@ rathvillyschool.co.uk
Head: Mrs D P Edwards
Type: Co-educational Day 3–11
No of pupils: B55 G65
Fees: On application

ROSSLYN SCHOOL
1597 Stratford Road, Hall Green, Birmingham, West Midlands B28 9JB
Tel: (0121) 744 2743
Fax: (0121) 744 2743
Email: office@rosslynschool.co.uk
Head: Mrs P J Scott
Type: Co-educational Day 2–11
No of pupils: B49 G55
Fees: (September 08)
Day £2325–£4350

ST GEORGE'S SCHOOL, EDGBASTON
31 Calthorpe Road, Edgbaston, Birmingham, West Midlands B15 1RX
Tel: (0121) 625 0398
Fax: (0121) 625 3340
Email: admin@sgse.co.uk
Head: Miss H J Phillips
Type: Co-educational Day 3–18
No of pupils: B280 G140
Fees: On application

England – West Midlands

WEST HOUSE SCHOOL
24 St James's Road, Edgbaston,
Birmingham, West Midlands
B15 2NX
Tel: (0121) 440 4097
Fax: (0121) 440 5839
Email: secretary@
    westhouseschool.demon.co.uk
Head: Mr A Lyttle
Type: Boys Day 1–11 (Girls 1–4)
No of pupils: B190 G25
Fees: (September 08)
Day £3552–£8970

**WOODSTOCK GIRLS'
SCHOOL**
11–15 Woodstock Road, Moseley,
Birmingham, West Midlands
B13 9BB
Tel: (0121) 449 6690
Fax: (0121) 449 6690
Head: Mr Tahir Rehman
Type: Girls Day 11–15
No of pupils: 120
Fees: (September 08) Day £3600

COVENTRY

BABLAKE JUNIOR SCHOOL
Coundon Road, Coundon,
Coventry, West Midlands
CV1 4AU
Tel: (44 (024) 7627 1260
Fax: (44 (024) 7627 1294
Email: jhmsec@bablakejs.co.uk
Head: Mr N A Price
Type: Co-educational Day 7–11
No of pupils: B104 G85
Fees: (September 07) Day £6015

BABLAKE SCHOOL
Coundon Road, Coventry,
West Midlands CV1 4AU
Tel: (024) 7627 1200
Fax: (024) 7627 1290
Email: info@
    bablake.coventry.sch.uk
Head: Mr J W Watson
Type: Co-educational Day 11–19
No of pupils: B460 G410
Fees: (September 08) Day £8379

**CHESHUNT PRE-
PREPARATORY SCHOOL**
8 Park Road, Coventry,
West Midlands CV1 2LH
Tel: (024) 7622 1677
Fax: (024) 7623 1630
Head: Mrs F Ward
Type: Co-educational Day 3–8
No of pupils: 100
Fees: On application

**COVENTRY MUSLIM
SCHOOL**
643 Foleshill Road, Coventry,
West Midlands CV6 5JQ
Tel: (024) 7626 1803
Fax: (024) 7626 1803
Email: admin@
    coventrymuslimschool.
    freeserve.co.uk
Head: Mrs M Ashique
Type: Girls Day 4–16
No of pupils: B8 G52
Fees: On application

COVENTRY PREP SCHOOL
Kenilworth Road, Coventry,
West Midlands CV3 6PT
Tel: (024) 7627 1307
Fax: (024) 7627 1308
Email: headmaster@
    coventryprep.co.uk
Head: Mr N Lovell
Type: Co-educational Day 3–11
No of pupils: B147 G97
Fees: On application

**DAVENPORT LODGE
SCHOOL**
21 Davenport Road, Earlsdon,
Coventry, West Midlands
CV5 6QA
Tel: (024) 7667 5051
Fax: (024) 76679370
Email: office@
    davenportlodgeschool.co.uk
Head: Mrs M D Martin
Type: Co-educational Day 0–8
Fees: (September 07)
Day £1512–£5040

KING HENRY VIII SCHOOL
Warwick Road, Coventry,
West Midlands CV3 6AQ
Tel: (024) 7672 1111
Fax: (024) 7672 1188
Email: info@khviii.com
Head: Mr G D Fisher
Type: Co-educational Day 7–18
No of pupils: B457 G405
Fees: (September 08) Day £8379

PATTISON COLLEGE
90 Binley Road, Coventry,
West Midlands CV3 1FQ
Tel: (024) 7645 5031
Email: pattisonsinfo@
    btconnect.com
Head: Mrs E A P Connell and Mrs J
A Satchell
Type: Co-educational Day 3–16
No of pupils: B38 G108
Fees: On application

SOLIHULL

**EVERSFIELD PREPARATORY
SCHOOL**
Warwick Road, Solihull,
West Midlands B91 1AT
Tel: (0121) 705 0354
Fax: (0121) 709 0168
Email: enquiries@eversfield.co.uk
Head: Mr R A Yates
Type: Co-educational Day 2–11
No of pupils: B196 G65
Fees: (September 08)
Day £2478–£8199

KINGSWOOD SCHOOL
St James Place, Shirley, Solihull,
West Midlands B90 2BA
Tel: (0121) 744 7883
Fax: (0121) 744 1282
Email: kingswoodhm@aol.com
Head: Mr N Shaw
Type: Co-educational Day 2–11
No of pupils: B40 G40
Fees: (September 07)
Day £4680–£6000

RUCKLEIGH SCHOOL
17 Lode Lane, Solihull,
West Midlands B91 2AB
Tel: (0121) 705 2773
Fax: (0121) 704 4883
Email: admin@ruckleigh.co.uk
Head: Mrs B M Forster
Type: Co-educational Day 2–11
No of pupils: B144 G100
Fees: (September 07)
Day £2265–£6564

SAINT MARTIN'S SCHOOL
Malvern Hall, Brueton Avenue,
Solihull, West Midlands B91 3EN
Tel: (0121) 705 1265
Fax: (0121) 711 4529
Email: mail@
    saintmartins-school.com
Head: Mrs J Carwithen
Type: Girls Day 3–18
No of pupils: 520
Fees: On application

SOLIHULL SCHOOL
Warwick Road, Solihull,
West Midlands B91 3DJ
Tel: (0121) 705 4273
Fax: (0121) 711 4439
Email: enquiries@solsch.org.uk
Head: Mr P J Griffiths
Type: Co-educational Day 7–18
No of pupils: B710 G307
Fees: (September 08)
Day £7515–£9249

SUTTON COLDFIELD

THE SHRUBBERY SCHOOL
Walmley Ash Road, Walmley,
Sutton Coldfield, West Midlands
B76 1HY
Tel: (0121) 351 1582
Fax: (0121) 351 1124
Email: info@
  shrubbery.bham.sch.uk
Head: Mrs H Cook
Type: Co-educational Day 3–11
No of pupils: B152 G118
Fees: (September 08)
Day £2775–£5820

WALSALL

ABU BAKR INDEPENDENT SCHOOL
154–160 Wednesbury Road,
Palfrey, Walsall, West Midlands
WS1 4JJ
Tel: 01922 620618
Fax: 01922 646175
Email: info@abubakrtrust.org
Head: Mr M Ramzan
Type: Co-educational Day 11–16
No of pupils: B60 G198
Fees: On application

EMMANUEL SCHOOL
Bath Street Centre, Bath Street,
Walsall, West Midlands WS1 3DB
Tel: (01922) 635810
Email: office@
  emmanuel.walsall.sch.uk
Head: Mr J Swain
Type: Co-educational Day 3–16
No of pupils: B27 G32
Fees: On application

HYDESVILLE TOWER SCHOOL
25 Broadway North, Walsall,
West Midlands WS1 2QG
Tel: (01922) 624374
Fax: (01922) 746169
Email: info@hydesville.com
Head: Dr Leslie Fox
Type: Co-educational Day 3–16
No of pupils: B217 G163
Fees: (September 08)
Day £5250–£9135

MAYFIELD PREPARATORY SCHOOL
Sutton Road, Walsall,
West Midlands WS1 2PD
Tel: (01922) 624107
Fax: (01299) 746908
Email: info@mayfieldprep.co.uk
Head: Mr M Draper
Type: Co-educational Day 3–11
No of pupils: B105 G86
Fees: (September 07) Day £6150

WOLVERHAMPTON

BIRCHFIELD SCHOOL
Albrighton, Wolverhampton,
West Midlands WV7 3AF
Tel: (01902) 372534
Fax: (01902) 373516
Email: office@
  birchfieldschool.co.uk
Head: Mr R P Merriman
Type: Co-educational Day and
Boarding Boys 4–13 Girls 4–7
No of pupils: B145 G16
No of boarders: W19
Fees: (September 08) WB £14925
Day £6765–£10845

THE DRIVE PREPARATORY SCHOOL
Wood Road, Tettenhall,
Wolverhampton, West Midlands
WV6 8RX
Tel: (01902) 751125
Fax: (01902) 741940
Email: head@
  tettcoll.wolverhants.sch.uk
Head: Mr P Cochrane
Type: Co-educational Day 2–7
No of pupils: 142
Fees: On application

NEWBRIDGE PREPARATORY SCHOOL
51 Newbridge Crescent,
Tettenhall, Wolverhampton,
West Midlands WV6 0LH
Tel: (01902) 751088
Fax: (01902) 751333
Email: office@
  newbridge.wolverhampton.
  sch.uk
Head: Mrs B Pring
Type: Girls Day 3–11
No of pupils: 148
Fees: On application

THE ROYAL WOLVERHAMPTON JUNIOR SCHOOL
Penn Road, Wolverhampton,
West Midlands WV3 0EG
Tel: (01902) 341230
Fax: (01902) 344496
Email: mo@
  royal.wolverhampton.sch.uk
Head: Mrs M Saunders
Type: Co-educational Day and
Boarding 2–11
No of pupils: B86 G78
No of boarders: F1
Fees: On application

THE ROYAL WOLVERHAMPTON SCHOOL[†]
Penn Road, Wolverhampton,
West Midlands WV3 0EG
Tel: (01902) 349109
Fax: (01902) 349119
Email: mo@
  royal.wolverhampton.sch.uk
Head: Mr S.M Bailey
Type: Co-educational Boarding
and Day 2–18
No of pupils: B262 G211
No of boarders: F134 W16
Fees: (September 08)
FB £19380–£22260 WB £19845
Day £5700–£10650

TETTENHALL COLLEGE[†]
Wood Road, Tettenhall,
Wolverhampton, West Midlands
WV6 8QX
Tel: (01902) 751119
Fax: (01902) 741940
Email: head@tettcoll.co.uk
Head: Dr P C Bodkin
Type: Co-educational Boarding
and Day 2–18
No of pupils: B289 G198
No of boarders: F66 W11
Fees: (September 08)
FB £16044–£19539
WB £13020–£16260
Day £5394–£11136

**WOLVERHAMPTON
GRAMMAR SCHOOL**
Compton Road, Wolverhampton,
West Midlands WV3 9RB
Tel: (01902) 421326
Fax: (01902) 421819
Email: wgs@wgs.org.uk
Head: Mr J V Darby
Type: Co-educational Day 10–18
No of pupils: B395 G271
Fees: (September 08)
Day £7665–£10275

WILTSHIRE

CALNE

**ST MARGARET'S
PREPARATORY SCHOOL**
Curzon Street, Calne, Wiltshire
SN11 0DF
Tel: (01249) 857220
Fax: (01249) 857227
Email: office@
   stmargaretsprep.org.uk
Head: Mrs K E Cordon
Type: Co-educational Day 3–11
No of pupils: B77 G120
Fees: (September 08)
Day £4200–£8670

ST MARY'S CALNE*
Curzon Street, Calne, Wiltshire
SN11 0DF
Tel: (01249) 857200
Fax: (01249) 857207
Email: admissions@
   stmaryscalne.org
Head: Dr H M Wright
Type: Girls Boarding and Day
11–18
No of pupils: 300
No of boarders: F250
Fees: (September 08) FB £26400
Day £18900

CHIPPENHAM

**GRITTLETON HOUSE
SCHOOL***
Grittleton, Chippenham, Wiltshire
SN14 6AP
Tel: (01249) 782434
Fax: (01249) 782669
Email: secretary@
   grittletonhouseschool.org
Head: Mrs C Whitney
Type: Co-educational Day 2–16
No of pupils: B174 G141
Fees: (September 08)
Day £6150–£9270

CORSHAM

**HEYWOOD PREPARATORY
SCHOOL**
The Priory, Priory Street, Corsham,
Wiltshire SN13 0AP
Tel: (01249) 713379
Fax: (01249) 701757
Email: principals@
   heywoodprep.com
Head: Mrs P Hall and Mr M Hall
Type: Co-educational Day 2–11
No of pupils: B94 G64
Fees: On application

CRICKLADE

**MEADOWPARK NURSERY &
PRE-PREP SCHOOL**
Calcutt Street, Cricklade, Wiltshire
SN6 6BA
Tel: (01793) 752600
Fax: (01793) 752600
Email: mpschoffice@aol.com
Head: Mrs R Kular
Type: Co-educational Day 0–7
No of pupils: B122 G105
Fees: On application

**PRIOR PARK PREPARATORY
SCHOOL***†
Calcutt Street, Cricklade, Wiltshire
SN6 6BB
Tel: (01793) 750275
Fax: (01793) 750910
Email: officepriorparkprep@
   priorpark.co.uk
Head: Mr G B Hobern
Type: Co-educational Boarding
and Day 7–13
No of pupils: B100 G87
No of boarders: F37 W4
Fees: (September 08)
F/WB £13803–£16224
Day £9438–£11607

DEVIZES

DAUNTSEY'S SCHOOL*
High Street, West Lavington,
Devizes, Wiltshire SN10 4HE
Tel: (01380) 814500
Fax: (01380) 814501
Email: information@
   dauntseys.wilts.sch.uk
Head: Mr S B Roberts
Type: Co-educational Boarding
and Day 11–18
No of pupils: B430 G360
No of boarders: F300
Fees: (September 08) FB £23850
Day £14145

THE MILL SCHOOL
Whistley Road, Potterne, Devizes,
Wiltshire SN10 5TE
Tel: (01380) 723011
Fax: (01380) 736530
Email: office@mill.wilts.sch.uk
Head: Mrs L Gill
Type: Co-educational Day 3–11
No of pupils: B41 G46
Fees: (September 08)
Day £5550–£6750

MARLBOROUGH

MARLBOROUGH COLLEGE
Marlborough, Wiltshire SN8 1PA
Tel: (01672) 892300
Fax: (01672) 892307
Email: admissions@
   marlboroughcollege.org
Head: Mr N A Sampson
Type: Co-educational Boarding
and Day 13–18
No of pupils: B549 G331
No of boarders: F880
Fees: (September 08)
FB £27690–£9230
Day £20790–£6930

STEPPING STONES NURSERY AND PRE-PREPARATORY SCHOOL
Oakhill Farm, Froxfield,
Marlborough, Wiltshire SN8 3JT
Tel: (01488) 681067
Fax: (01488) 681067
Email: info@
   steppingstonesschool.org.uk
Head: Miss S Corfield and
Miss A Harron
Type: Co-educational Day 2–8
No of pupils: B89 G80
Fees: On application

MELKSHAM

STONAR SCHOOL*
Cottles Park, Atworth, Melksham,
Wiltshire SN12 8NT
Tel: (01225) 701740
Fax: (01225) 790830
Email: admissions@
   stonarschool.com
Head: Mrs S Shayler
Type: Girls Boarding and Day
2–18
No of pupils: 355
No of boarders: W156
Fees: (September 07)
F/WB £16350–£19050
Day £5550–£10800

PEWSEY

ST FRANCIS SCHOOL
Marlborough Road, Pewsey,
Wiltshire SN9 5NT
Tel: (01672) 563228
Fax: (01672) 564323
Email: admissions@
   st-francis.wilts.sch.uk
Head: Mr B Brown
Type: Co-educational Day 2–13
No of pupils: B150 G130
Fees: (September 08)
Day £624–£9285

SALISBURY

APPLEFORD SCHOOL[†]
Elston Lane, Shrewton, Salisbury,
Wiltshire SP3 4HL
Tel: (01980) 621020
Fax: (01980) 621366
Email: secretary@
   appleford.wilts.sch.uk
Head: Ms S M Wilson
Type: Co-educational Boarding
and Day 7–13
No of pupils: B87 G15
No of boarders: F22 W33
Fees: (September 07) F/WB £6927
Day £4727

AVONDALE SCHOOL
High Street, Bulford, Salisbury,
Wiltshire SP4 9DR
Tel: (01980) 632387
Email: avondale.school@
   tiscali.co.uk
Head: Mr R McNeall and
Mrs S McNeall
Type: Co-educational Day 3–11
No of pupils: B50 G50
Fees: On application

CHAFYN GROVE SCHOOL
Bourne Avenue, Salisbury,
Wiltshire SP1 1LR
Tel: (01722) 333423
Fax: (01722) 323114
Email: office@chafyngrove.co.uk
Head: Mr E J Newton
Type: Co-educational Boarding
and Day 3–13
No of pupils: B224 G85
No of boarders: F46
Fees: (September 07)
FB £13875–£16965
Day £505–£12525

GODOLPHIN PREPARATORY SCHOOL
Laverstock Road, Salisbury,
Wiltshire SP1 2RB
Tel: (01722) 430652
Fax: (01722) 430651
Email: prep@
   godolphin.wilts.sch.uk
Head: Mrs P White
Type: Girls Day 3–11
Fees: (September 07)
Day £1582–£3090

THE GODOLPHIN SCHOOL
Milford Hill, Salisbury, Wiltshire
SP1 2RA
Tel: (01722) 430511
Fax: (01722) 430501
Email: admissions@
   godolphin.wilts.sch.uk
Head: Miss M J Horsburgh
Type: Girls Boarding and Day
11–18
No of pupils: 440
No of boarders: F177
Fees: (September 08) FB £7397
Day £5093

LEEHURST SWAN
Campbell Road, Salisbury,
Wiltshire SP1 3BQ
Tel: (01722) 333094
Fax: (01722) 330868
Email: registrar@
   leehurstswan.org.uk
Head: Mr R N S Leake
Type: Co-educational Day 2–16
No of pupils: B178 G165
Fees: (September 08)
Day £5910–£10314

England – Wiltshire

LEADEN HALL SCHOOL
70 The Close, Salisbury, Wiltshire
SP1 2EP
Tel: (01722) 439269
Fax: (01722) 410575
Email: admin@leaden-hall.com
Head: Mrs D Watkins
Type: Girls Day and Boarding
3–11 (Boys 3–4)
No of pupils: B2 G237
No of boarders: F29
Fees: On application

NORMAN COURT PREPARATORY SCHOOL
West Tytherley, Salisbury,
Wiltshire SP5 1NH
Tel: (01980) 862345
Fax: (01980) 862082
Email: office@normancourt.co.uk
Head: Mr P G Savage
Type: Co-educational Boarding
and Day 3–13
No of pupils: B146 G71
No of boarders: F24 W40
Fees: (September 08) F/WB £18480
Day £6375–£13710

SALISBURY CATHEDRAL SCHOOL
1 The Close, Salisbury, Wiltshire
SP1 2EQ
Tel: (01722) 555300
Fax: (01722) 410910
Email: admissions@
   salisburycathedralschool.com
Head: Mr P M Greenfield
Type: Co-educational Day and
Boarding 3–13
No of pupils: B132 G67
No of boarders: F35
Fees: (September 07) FB £16770
Day £3780–£11475

SANDROYD SCHOOL
Rushmore, Tollard Royal,
Salisbury, Wiltshire SP5 5QD
Tel: (01725) 516264
Fax: (01725) 516441
Email: office@sandroyd.com
Head: Mr Martin Harris
Type: Co-educational Boarding
and Day 7–13
No of pupils: B197 G24
No of boarders: F110
Fees: On application

SOUTH HILLS SCHOOL
Home Farm Road, Wilton,
Salisbury, Wiltshire SP2 8PJ
Tel: (01722) 744971
Fax: (01722) 744971
Email: southhillsschool@
   btinternet.com
Head: Mrs A Proctor
Type: Co-educational Day 0–7
No of pupils: B80 G80
Fees: On application

SHRIVENHAM

PINEWOOD SCHOOL
Bourton, Shrivenham, Wiltshire
SN6 8HZ
Tel: (01793) 782205
Fax: (01793) 783476
Email: office@
   pinewoodschool.co.uk
Head: Mr P J Hoyland
Type: Co-educational Boarding
and Day 3–13
No of pupils: B147 G149
No of boarders: W30
Fees: On application

SWINDON

MARANATHA CHRISTIAN SCHOOL
Queenlaines Farm,
Sevenhampton, Swindon,
Wiltshire SN6 7SQ
Tel: (01793) 762075
Fax: (01793) 783783
Head: Mr P Medlock
Type: Co-educational Day 3–18
No of pupils: B20 G20
Fees: On application

TROWBRIDGE

EMMAUS SCHOOL
School Lane, Staverton,
Trowbridge, Wiltshire BA14 6NZ
Tel: (01225) 782684
Email: info@
   emmaus-school.org.uk
Head: Mrs M Wiltshire
Type: Co-educational Day 5–16
No of pupils: B22 G23
Fees: On application

ROUNDSTONE PREPARATORY SCHOOL
Courtfield House, Polebarn Road,
Trowbridge, Wiltshire BA14 7EG
Tel: (01225) 752847
Email: admin@
   roundstone.wilts.sch.uk
Head: Mrs M E Pearce
Type: Co-educational Day 4–11
No of pupils: B30 G30
Fees: (September 07)
Day £3300–£3600

WARMINSTER

STOURBRIDGE HOUSE SCHOOL
Castle Street, Mere, Warminster,
Wiltshire BA12 6JQ
Tel: (01747) 860165
Fax: (01747) 861945
Email: office@
   stourbridgehouse.wilts.sch.uk
Head: Mrs E Coward
Type: Co-educational Day 3–9
No of pupils: B25 G19
Fees: On application

WARMINSTER SCHOOL*
Church Street, Warminster,
Wiltshire BA12 8PJ
Tel: (01985) 210160
Fax: (01985) 210154
Email: admissions@
   warminsterschool.org.uk
Head: Mr M Priestley
Type: Co-educational Boarding
and Day 3–19
No of pupils: B360 G240
No of boarders: F200
Fees: (September 08) F/WB £20640
Day £12084

WORCESTERSHIRE

BEWDLEY

MOFFATS SCHOOL*
Kinlet Hall, Kinlet, Bewdley,
Worcestershire DY12 3AY
Tel: (01299) 841230
Fax: (01299) 841444
Email: office@moffats.co.uk
Head: Mr M H Daborn
Type: Co-educational Boarding
and Day 4–13
No of pupils: B46 G25
No of boarders: F25 W2
Fees: (September 08) F/WB £13425
Day £1000–£8415

BROMSGROVE

BROMSGROVE PRE-PREPARATORY AND NURSERY SCHOOL
Avoncroft House, Hanbury Road,
Bromsgrove, Worcestershire
B60 4JS
Tel: (01527) 873007
Fax: (01527) 873007
Email: preprep@
   bromsgrove-school.co.uk
Head: Mrs S Pickering
Type: Co-educational Day 2–7
No of pupils: B100 G79
Fees: On application

BROMSGROVE PREPARATORY SCHOOL
Old Station Road, Bromsgrove,
Worcestershire B60 2BU
Tel: (01527) 579600
Fax: (01527) 579571
Email: admissions@
   bromsgrove-school.co.uk
Head: Mr Richard Evans
Type: Co-educational Boarding
and Day 7–13
No of pupils: B227 G178
No of boarders: F50
Fees: (September 08)
FB £5600–£6935
Day £2815–£3675

BROMSGROVE SCHOOL*
Worcester Road, Bromsgrove,
Worcestershire B61 7DU
Tel: (01527) 579679
Fax: (01527) 576177
Email: admissions@
   bromsgrove-school.co.uk
Head: Mr C Edwards
Type: Co-educational Boarding
and Day 13–18
No of pupils: B451 G290
No of boarders: F367
Fees: (September 08) FB £23220
Day £11850

DROITWICH SPA

DODDERHILL SCHOOL
Droitwich Spa, Worcestershire
WR9 0BE
Tel: (01905) 778290
Fax: (01905) 790623
Email: enquiries@dodderhill.co.uk
Head: Mrs J Mumby
Type: Girls Day 3–16 (Boys 3–9)
No of pupils: B20 G220
Fees: On application

EVESHAM

GREEN HILL SCHOOL
Evesham, Worcestershire
WR11 4NG
Tel: (01386) 442364
Fax: (01386) 442364
Email: kay.barrett.ghs@
   btconnect.com
Head: Mr O Lister
Type: Co-educational Day 3–13
No of pupils: B48 G53
Fees: (September 07)
Day £4635–£6165

KIDDERMINSTER

HEATHFIELD SCHOOL
Wolverley, Kidderminster,
Worcestershire DY10 3QE
Tel: (01562) 850204
Fax: (01562) 852609
Email: info@
   heathfieldschool.co.uk
Head: Mr Roger Brierly
Type: Co-educational Day 3–16
No of pupils: B126 G116
Fees: On application

HOLY TRINITY SCHOOL
Birmingham Road, Kidderminster,
Worcestershire DY10 2BY
Tel: (01562) 822929
Fax: (01562) 865137
Email: office@holytrinity.co.uk
Head: Mrs Y L Wilkinson
Type: Co-educational Day
Boys 0–11 Girls 0–18
No of pupils: B44 G316
Fees: (September 08)
Day £5175–£8595

THE KNOLL SCHOOL
33 Manor Avenue, Kidderminster,
Worcestershire DY11 6EA
Tel: (01562) 822622
Fax: (01562) 865686
Email: info@knollschool.co.uk
Head: Mr N J Humphreys
Type: Co-educational Day 2–11
No of pupils: B77 G42
Fees: (September 08)
Day £2580–£3396

WINTERFOLD HOUSE
Chaddesley Corbett,
Kidderminster, Worcestershire
DY10 4PW
Tel: (01562) 777234
Fax: (01562) 777078
Email: head@
   winterfoldhouse.co.uk
Head: Mr W C R Ibbetson-Price
Type: Co-educational Day
Boys 2–13 Girls 3–13
No of pupils: B200 G120
Fees: On application

MALVERN

THE DOWNS, MALVERN COLLEGE PREPARATORY SCHOOL
Brockhill Road, Colwall, Malvern,
Worcestershire WR13 6EY
Tel: (01684) 540277
Fax: (01684) 540094
Email: enquiries@
   thedowns.malcol.org
Head: Mr A P Ramsay
Type: Co-educational Boarding
and Day 2–13
No of pupils: B170 G150
No of boarders: F30 W30
Fees: (September 08)
FB £3500–£5403
Day £1700–£4082

THE ELMS

Colwall, Malvern, Worcestershire
WR13 6EF
Tel: (01684) 540344
Fax: (01684) 571174
Email: office@elmsschool.co.uk
Head: Mr L A C Ashby
Type: Co-educational Boarding
and Day 3–13
No of pupils: B111 G81
No of boarders: F86
Fees: (September 08) FB £18870
Day £6720–£17520

MADRESFIELD EARLY YEARS CENTRE

Hayswood Farm, Madresfield,
Malvern, Worcestershire
WR13 5AA
Tel: (01684) 574378
Fax: (01684) 567772
Email: info@meyc.co.uk
Head: Mrs B J Bennett
Type: Co-educational Day 1–8
No of pupils: B117 G102
Fees: On application

MALVERN COLLEGE*

College Road, Malvern,
Worcestershire WR14 3DF
Tel: (01684) 581500
Fax: (01684) 581617
Email: registrar@malcol.org
Head: Mr Antony Clark
Type: Co-educational Boarding
and Day 3–18
No of pupils: B364 G276
No of boarders: F516
Fees: (September 08)
FB £25889–£26700
Day £17163–£17697

MALVERN ST JAMES*†

15 Avenue Road, Great Malvern,
Worcestershire WR14 3BA
Tel: (01684) 584624
Fax: (01684) 566204
Email: registrar@
   malvernstjames.co.uk
Head: Mrs R Hayes
Type: Girls Boarding and Day
5–18
No of pupils: 360
No of boarders: F168 W13
Fees: (September 08)
FB £17400–£24420
WB from £23520 Day £6000

MALVERN WELLS

THE ABBEY COLLEGE

253 Wells Road, Malvern Wells,
Worcestershire WR14 4JF
Tel: (01684) 892300
Fax: (01684) 892757
Email: enquiries@
   abbeycollege.co.uk
Head: Mr P Moere
Type: Co-educational Boarding
and Day 13+
No of pupils: B75 G23
No of boarders: 98
Fees: (September 08)
FB £17950–£18950

PERSHORE

BOWBROOK HOUSE SCHOOL

Peopleton, Pershore,
Worcestershire WR10 2EE
Tel: (01905) 841242
Fax: (01905) 840716
Email: enquiries@
   bowbrookhouseschool.co.uk
Head: Mr C D Allen
Type: Co-educational Day 3–16
No of pupils: B117 G55
Fees: (September 07)
Day £4400–£7140

TENBURY WELLS

SAINT MICHAEL'S COLLEGE

Oldwood Road, St Michaels,
Tenbury Wells, Worcestershire
WR15 8PH
Tel: (01584) 811300
Fax: (01584) 811221
Email: info@st-michaels.uk.com
Head: Mr S Higgins
Type: Co-educational Day and
Boarding 14–19
No of pupils: B110 G75
No of boarders: F110
Fees: (September 08)
FB £17935–£19423

WORCESTER

ABBERLEY HALL

Abberley Hall, Worcester,
Worcestershire WR6 6DD
Tel: (01299) 896275
Fax: (01299) 896875
Email: john.walker@
   abberleyhall.co.uk
Head: Mr J G W Walker
Type: Co-educational Boarding
and Day 2–13
No of pupils: B185 G107
No of boarders: F101
Fees: (September 08) FB £17220
Day £5160–£13710

SPRINGFIELD SCHOOL

Britannia Square, Worcester,
Worcestershire WR1 3DL
Tel: (01905) 24999
Fax: (01905) 27957
Email: springfield@rgsao.org
Head: Mrs M Lloyd
Type: Co-educational Day 2–11
No of pupils: B11 G82
Fees: (September 08)
Day £1648–£2928

KING'S HAWFORD

Lock Lane, Worcester,
Worcestershire WR3 7SE
Tel: (01905) 451292
Fax: (01905) 756502
Email: hawford@ksw.org.uk
Head: Mr J Turner
Type: Co-educational Day 2–11
No of pupils: B200 G142
Fees: On application

THE KING'S SCHOOL

5 College Green, Worcester,
Worcestershire WR1 2LL
Tel: (01905) 721700
Fax: (01905) 721710
Email: info@ksw.org.uk
Head: Mr T H Keyes
Type: Co-educational Day 3–18
No of pupils: B798 G618
Fees: (September 07)
Day £5400–£9783

RGS THE GRANGE

Grange Lane, Claines, Worcester,
Worcestershire WR3 7RR
Tel: (01905) 451205
Fax: (01905) 757917
Email: grange@rgsao.org
Head: Mr T Lowe
Type: Co-educational Day 2–11
No of pupils: B253 G126
Fees: (September 08)
Day £1812–£2844

RIVER SCHOOL
Oakfield House, Droitwich Road,
Worcester, Worcestershire
WR3 7ST
Tel: (01905) 457047
Fax: (01905) 754492
Email: info@riverschool.co.uk
Head: Mr G Coyle
Type: Co-educational Day 5–16
No of pupils: B67 G82
Fees: On application

RGS WORCESTER & THE ALICE OTTLEY SCHOOL
Upper Tything, Worcester,
Worcestershire WR1 1HP
Tel: (01905) 613391
Fax: (01905) 726892
Email: office@rgsao.org
Head: Mr A R Rattue
Type: Co-educational Day 11–18
No of pupils: B574 G141
Fees: (September 08) Day £3012

ST MARY'S CONVENT SCHOOL
Mount Battenhall, Worcester,
Worcestershire WR5 2HP
Tel: (01905) 357786
Fax: (01905) 351718
Email: head@stmarys.org.uk
Head: Mrs S K Cookson
Type: Girls Day 0–18 (Boys 2–8)
No of pupils: B57 G361
Fees: (September 08)
Day £885–£9315

EAST RIDING OF YORKSHIRE

ANLABY

HULL COLLEGIATE SCHOOL
Tranby Croft, Anlaby, East Riding
of Yorkshire HU10 7EH
Tel: (01482) 657016
Fax: (01482) 655389
Email: enquiries.hull@
church-schools.com
Head: Mr R Haworth
Type: Co-educational Day 3–18
No of pupils: B367 G435
Fees: (September 07)
Day £5106–£8475

HESSLE

HESSLE MOUNT SCHOOL
Jenny Brough Lane, Hessle, East
Riding of Yorkshire HU13 0JX
Tel: (01482) 643371/641948
Fax: (01482) 643371
Email: info@
hesslemountschool.org.uk
Head: Mrs Cutting
Type: Co-educational Day 3–8
No of pupils: 160
Fees: On application

HULL

FROEBEL HOUSE SCHOOL
5 Marlborough Avenue, Princes
Avenue, Hull, East Riding of
Yorkshire HU5 3JP
Tel: (01482) 342272
Fax: (01482) 342272
Email: froebel@
froebel.karoo.co.uk
Head: Mrs L A Roberts
Type: Co-educational Day 4–11
No of pupils: B56 G51
Fees: On application

HYMERS COLLEGE
Hymers Avenue, Hull, East Riding
of Yorkshire HU3 1LW
Tel: (01482) 343555
Fax: (01482) 472854
Email: enquiries@
hymers.hull.sch.uk
Head: Mr D C Elstone
Type: Co-educational Day 8–18
No of pupils: B549 G429
Fees: (September 07)
Day £6165–£7407

POCKLINGTON

POCKLINGTON MONTESSORI SCHOOL
Carr Lane, Pocklington, East
Riding of Yorkshire YO42 1NT
Tel: (01759) 305436
Fax: (01759) 321421
Email: info@
pocklingtonmontessori.com
Head: Ms R Pressland
Type: Co-educational Day 0–7
No of pupils: B106 G108
Fees: (September 08) Day £5683

POCKLINGTON SCHOOL
West Green, Pocklington, East
Riding of Yorkshire YO42 2NJ
Tel: (01759) 321200
Fax: (01759) 306366
Email: enquiry@
pocklingtonschool.com
Head: Mr N Clements
Type: Co-educational Boarding
and Day 7–18
No of pupils: B433 G377
No of boarders: F115 W20
Fees: On application

England – Worcestershire/East Riding of Yorkshire

NORTH YORKSHIRE

BEDALE

AYSGARTH PREPARATORY SCHOOL*
Newton-Le-Willows, Bedale,
North Yorkshire DL8 1TF
Tel: (01677) 450240
Fax: (01677) 450736
Email: lfoster@
    aysgarthschool.co.uk
Head: Mr C A A Goddard
Type: Boys Boarding 3–13 (Co-ed
day 3–8)
No of pupils: B159 G19
No of boarders: F89 W/D 35
Fees: (September 08) F/WB £17670
Day £14850

HARROGATE

ASHVILLE COLLEGE
Green Lane, Harrogate,
North Yorkshire HG2 9JP
Tel: (01423) 566358
Fax: (01423) 505142
Email: ashville@ashville.co.uk
Head: Mr A Fleck
Type: Co-educational Day and
Boarding 4–18
No of pupils: B480 G320
No of boarders: F96 W18
Fees: (September 08)
FB £13155–£20280
WB £12570–£18480
Day £6045–£10335

BELMONT GROSVENOR SCHOOL
Swarcliffe Hall, Birstwith,
Harrogate, North Yorkshire
HG3 2JG
Tel: (01423) 771029
Fax: (01423) 772600
Email: admin@
    belmontgrosvenor.co.uk
Head: Miss J Merriman
Type: Co-educational Day 2–11
No of pupils: B122 G111
Fees: On application

BRACKENFIELD SCHOOL
128 Duchy Road, Harrogate,
North Yorkshire HG1 2HE
Tel: (01423) 508558
Fax: (01423) 524841
Email: admin@
    brackenfieldschool.co.uk
Head: Mrs J Skillington
Type: Co-educational Day 2–11
No of pupils: B86 G74
Fees: (September 08)
Day £1500–£6255

HARROGATE LADIES' COLLEGE
Clarence Drive, Harrogate,
North Yorkshire HG1 2QG
Tel: (01423) 504543
Fax: (01423) 568893
Email: enquire@hlc.org.uk
Head: Mr Geoffrey Hazell
Type: Girls Boarding and Day
10–18
No of pupils: 329
No of boarders: F157 W11
Fees: (September 08)
F/WB £21180–£23085
Day £12450

HARROGATE TUTORIAL COLLEGE
2 The Oval, Harrogate,
North Yorkshire HG2 9BA
Tel: (01423) 501041
Fax: (01423) 531110
Email: enquiries@htcuk.org
Head: Mr K W Pollard
Type: Co-educational Day and
Boarding 15–20
No of pupils: B36 G34
No of boarders: F20 W20
Fees: On application

HIGHFIELD PREPARATORY SCHOOL
Clarence Drive, Harrogate,
North Yorkshire HG1 2QG
Tel: (01423) 537060
Fax: (01423) 568893
Email: enquire@hlc.org.uk
Head: Mrs C Cameron
Type: Co-educational Day and
Boarding 4–11
No of pupils: B70 G151
Fees: On application

MALTON

WOODLEIGH SCHOOL[†]
Langton, Malton, North Yorkshire
YO17 9QN
Tel: (01653) 658215
Fax: (01653) 658423
Email: dme@
    woodleighschool.com
Head: Mr D M England
Type: Co-educational Boarding
and Day 3–13
No of pupils: B70 G40
No of boarders: F10 W25
Fees: (September 08)
F/WB £10650–£12750
Day £4575–£9675

NEAR SKIPTON

MALSIS SCHOOL
Cross Hills, Near Skipton,
North Yorkshire BD20 8DT
Tel: (01535) 633027
Fax: (01535) 630571
Email: admin@malsis.com
Head: Mr M R Peel
Type: Co-educational Boarding
and Day 3–13
No of pupils: B92 G44
No of boarders: F35
Fees: (September 08) FB £16695
Day £7185–£12795

RIPON

RIPON CATHEDRAL CHOIR SCHOOL
Whitcliffe Lane, Ripon,
North Yorkshire HG4 2LA
Tel: (01765) 602134
Fax: (01765) 608760
Email: admin@
    cathedralchoirschool.co.uk
Head: Mrs P Burton
Type: Co-educational Boarding
and Day 3–13
No of pupils: B50 G40
No of boarders: F19 W5
Fees: (September 08) FB £18420
Day £6000

SCARBOROUGH

BRAMCOTE SCHOOL
Filey Road, Scarborough,
North Yorkshire YO11 2TT
Tel: (01723) 373086
Fax: (01723) 364186
Email: office@
  bramcoteschool.com
Head: Mr A G W Lewin
Type: Co-educational Boarding
and Day 4–13
No of pupils: B61 G55
No of boarders: F59 W25
Fees: On application

LISVANE, SCARBOROUGH COLLEGE JUNIOR SCHOOL
Filey Road, Scarborough,
North Yorkshire YO11 3BA
Tel: (01723) 380606
Fax: (01723) 380607
Email: lisvane@
  scarboroughcoll.co.uk
Head: Mr G S Twist
Type: Co-educational Day and
Boarding 3–11
No of pupils: B69 G69
No of boarders: W2
Fees: On application

SCARBOROUGH COLLEGE & LISVANE SCHOOL
Filey Road, Scarborough,
North Yorkshire YO11 3BA
Tel: (01723) 360620
Fax: (01723) 377265
Email: admin@
  scarboroughcollege.co.uk
Head: Mr T L Kirkup
Type: Co-educational Boarding
and Day 3–18
No of pupils: B289 G228
No of boarders: F41 W20
Fees: On application

SELBY

READ SCHOOL
Drax, Selby, North Yorkshire
YO8 8NL
Tel: (01757) 618248
Fax: (01757) 617432
Email: richard.hadfield@virgin.net
Head: Mr R A Hadfield
Type: Co-educational Day and
Boarding 4–18
No of pupils: B209 G147
No of boarders: F68 W2
Fees: (September 07)
FB £14358–£16512
WB £13464–£15486
Day £5370–£7629

SETTLE

GIGGLESWICK JUNIOR SCHOOL
Giggleswick, Settle,
North Yorkshire BD24 0DG
Tel: (01729) 893100
Fax: (01729) 893158
Email: catteralhall@
  giggleswick.org.uk
Head: Mr G P Boult
Type: Co-educational Boarding
and Day 7–13
No of pupils: B69 G43
No of boarders: F54
Fees: On application

GIGGLESWICK SCHOOL
Giggleswick, Settle,
North Yorkshire BD24 0DE
Tel: (01729) 893000
Fax: (01729) 893150
Email: enquiries@
  giggleswick.org.uk
Head: Mr G P Boult
Type: Co-educational Boarding
and Day 4–18
No of pupils: B199 G119
No of boarders: F203
Fees: On application

THIRSK

QUEEN MARY'S SCHOOL
Baldersby Park, Topcliffe, Thirsk,
North Yorkshire YO7 3BZ
Tel: 01845 575000
Fax: (01845) 575001
Email: admin@queenmarys.org
Head: Mr R A McKenzie Johnson
Type: Girls Boarding and Day
3–16 (Boys 3–7)
No of pupils: B66 G161
No of boarders: F20 W46
Fees: (September 07)
FB £13860–£16350
Day £5235–£12555

WHITBY

BOTTON VILLAGE SCHOOL
Danby, Whitby, North Yorkshire
YO21 2NJ
Tel: (01287) 661206
Email: school.botton@
  camphill.org.uk
Type: Co-educational Day 4–14
No of pupils: B53 G41
Fees: On application

FYLING HALL SCHOOL
Robin Hood's Bay, Whitby,
North Yorkshire YO22 4QD
Tel: (01947) 880353
Fax: (01947) 881097
Email: office@fylinghall.org
Head: Mr K D James
Type: Co-educational Boarding
and Day 4–19
No of pupils: B98 G88
No of boarders: F90 W6
Fees: (September 08)
FB £12750–£15585
WB £11970–£13020
Day £5025–£6825

YORK

AMPLEFORTH COLLEGE
York, North Yorkshire YO62 4ER
Tel: (01439) 766000
Fax: (01439) 788330
Email: admissions@
  ampleforth.org.uk
Head: Rev C G E Everitt
Type: Co-educational Boarding
and Day 13–18
No of pupils: B457 G171
No of boarders: F529
Fees: (September 08) FB £25725
Day £15735

England – North Yorkshire

BOOTHAM SCHOOL
Bootham, York, North Yorkshire
YO30 7BU
Tel: (01904) 623261
Fax: (01904) 652106
Email: enquiries@
   boothamschool.com
Head: Mr J Taylor
Type: Co-educational Boarding
and Day 11–18
No of pupils: B294 G199
No of boarders: F86 W29
Fees: (September 08)
FB £13800–£21750
WB £13800–£19920
Day £12630–£13590

CUNDALL MANOR SCHOOL
Helperby, York, North Yorkshire
YO6 2RW
Tel: (01423) 360200
Fax: (01423) 360754
Email: headmaster@
   cundallmanor.co.uk
Head: Mr P Phillips
Type: Co-educational Boarding
and Day 2–13
No of pupils:
No of boarders: F30 W35
Fees: (September 08)
Day £6909–£9528

EBOR PREPARATORY
SCHOOL
Rawcliffe Lane, York,
North Yorkshire YO30 6NP
Tel: (01904) 655021
Fax: (01904) 651666
Email: office@
   eborschool.york.sch.uk
Head: Ms S Ratcliffe
Type: Co-educational Day 3–11
No of pupils: B70 G60
Fees: On application

THE MINSTER SCHOOL
Deangate, York, North Yorkshire
YO1 7JA
Tel: (01904) 557230
Fax: (01904) 557232
Email: school@yorkminster.org
Head: Mr R Moore
Type: Co-educational Day 3–13
No of pupils: B100 G80
Fees: On application

TREGELLES
The Mount Junior School, Dalton
Terrace, York, North Yorkshire
YO24 4DD
Tel: (01904) 667513
Fax: (01904) 667524
Email: registrar@
   mount.n-yorks.sch.uk
Head: Mrs J Lodrick
Type: Co-educational Day 3–11
No of pupils: B59 G135
Fees: (September 08)
Day £7950–£20520

THE MOUNT SCHOOL
Dalton Terrace, York,
North Yorkshire YO24 4DD
Tel: (01904) 667500
Fax: (01904) 667524
Email: enquiries@
   mount.n-yorks.sch.uk
Head: Mrs Diana Gant
Type: Co-educational Day and
Boarding Boys 3–11 Girls 3–18
No of pupils: B23 G360
No of boarders: F46 W13
Fees: (September 08) FB £20520
WB £19350 Day £5985–£13200

QUEEN ETHELBURGA'S
COLLEGE*
Thorpe Underwood Hall,
Ouseburn, York, North Yorkshire
YO26 9SS
Tel: (01423) 333330
Fax: (01423) 331444
Email: remember@
   compuserve.com
Head: Mr S Jandrell
Type: Co-educational Boarding
and Day 2–20
No of pupils: B362 G404
No of boarders: 498
Fees: (September 08)
F/WB £18735–£31005
Day £4185–£9225

QUEEN MARGARET'S
SCHOOL
Escrick Park, York, North Yorkshire
YO19 6EU
Tel: (01904) 728261
Fax: (01904) 728150
Email: enquiries@
   queenmargaretsschool.co.uk
Head: Dr G A H Chapman
Type: Girls Boarding and Day
11–18
No of pupils: 365
No of boarders: F251 W85
Fees: On application

ST MARTIN'S AMPLEFORTH
Gilling Castle, Gilling East, York,
North Yorkshire YO62 4HP
Tel: (01439) 766600
Fax: (01439) 788538
Email: headmaster@
   stmartins.ampleforth.org.uk
Head: Mr N J Higham
Type: Co-educational Boarding
and Day 3–13
No of pupils: B135 G71
No of boarders: F75
Fees: (September 08) FB £17577
Day £10863

ST PETER'S SCHOOL
York, North Yorkshire YO30 6AB
Tel: (01904) 527 300
Fax: (01904) 527 302
Email: enquiries@
   st-peters.york.sch.uk
Head: Mr R I Smyth
Type: Co-educational Boarding
and Day 13–18
No of pupils: B320 G222
No of boarders: F169
Fees: On application

TERRINGTON HALL
Terrington, York, North Yorkshire
YO60 6PR
Tel: (01653) 648227
Fax: (01653) 648458
Email: enquiries@
   terringtonhall.com
Head: Mr J Glen
Type: Co-educational Boarding
and Day 3–13
No of pupils: B120 G88
No of boarders: F35 W5
Fees: (September 08) FB £14790
Day £5730–£10410

SOUTH YORKSHIRE

BARNSLEY

BARNSLEY CHRISTIAN SCHOOL
Hope House, 2 Blucher Street, Barnsley, South Yorkshire S70 1AP
Tel: (01226) 211011
Fax: (01226) 211011
Email: hopehouseadmin@ tiscali.co.uk
Head: Mr G-J Barnes
Type: Co-educational Day 5–16
No of pupils: B49 G45
Fees: (September 08)
Day £3360–£3960

DONCASTER

HILL HOUSE SCHOOL
Sixth Avenue, Auckley, Doncaster, South Yorkshire DN9 3GG
Tel: 0845 302 1929
Fax: 0845 302 1928
Email: info@ hillhouse.doncaster.sch.uk
Head: Mr D.R. Holland
Type: Co-educational Day 2–16
No of pupils: B226 G206
Fees: (September 07)
Day £6150–£8790

SYCAMORE HALL PREPARATORY SCHOOL
1 Hall Flat Lane, Balby, Doncaster, South Yorkshire DN4 8PT
Tel: (01302) 856800
Email: sycamorehall@tiscali.co.uk
Head: Miss J Spencer
Type: Co-educational Day 3–11
No of pupils: B41 G43
Fees: On application

ROTHERHAM

RUDSTON PREPARATORY SCHOOL
59–63 Broom Road, Rotherham, South Yorkshire S60 2SW
Tel: (01709) 837774
Fax: (01709) 837975
Email: office@rudstonschool.com
Head: Mrs L J Sharpe
Type: Co-educational Day 2–11
No of pupils: B114 G101
Fees: (September 08) Day £5355

SHEFFIELD

ASHDELL PREPARATORY SCHOOL
266 Fulwood Road, Sheffield, South Yorkshire S10 3BL
Tel: (0114) 266 3835
Fax: (0114) 267 1762
Email: headteacher@ ashdell-prep.sheffield.sch.uk
Type: Girls Day 4–11
No of pupils: 123
Fees: (September 08)
Day £6720–£7740

BIRKDALE SCHOOL
Oakholme Road, Sheffield, South Yorkshire S10 3DH
Tel: (0114) 266 8409
Fax: (0114) 267 1947
Email: enquiries@ birkdaleschool.org.uk
Head: Mr R J Court
Type: Boys Day 4–18 (Co-ed VIth Form)
No of pupils: B750 G50
Fees: (September 08)
Day £6801–£9744

BRANTWOOD SCHOOL
1 Kenwood Bank, Sheffield, South Yorkshire S7 1NU
Tel: (0114) 258 1747
Fax: (0114) 258 1847
Email: enquiries@ brantwoodschool.co.uk
Head: Mrs L Marriott
Type: Girls Day 3–16
No of pupils: 200
Fees: (September 08)
Day £4475–£8574

HANDSWORTH CHRISTIAN SCHOOL
231 Handsworth Road, Handsworth, Sheffield, South Yorkshire S13 9BJ
Tel: (0114) 243 0276
Email: rmarks@ handsworthchristianschool. co.uk
Head: Mrs P Arnott
Type: Co-educational Day 4–16
Fees: (September 07) Day £2628

MYLNHURST PREPARATORY SCHOOL & NURSERY
Button Hill, Ecclesall, Sheffield, South Yorkshire S11 9HJ
Tel: (0114) 236 1411
Fax: (0114) 236 1411
Email: enquiries@mylnhurst.co.uk
Head: Mr C Emmott
Type: Co-educational Day 3–11
No of pupils: B97 G85
Fees: (September 08)
Day £2191–£6573

SHEFFIELD HIGH SCHOOL GDST
10 Rutland Park, Broomhill, Sheffield, South Yorkshire S10 2PE
Tel: (0114) 266 0324
Email: enquiries@she.gdst.net
Head: Mrs V A Dunsford
Type: Girls Day 4–18
No of pupils: 974
Fees: (September 08)
Day £6450–£26694

WESTBOURNE SCHOOL
60 Westbourne Road, Sheffield, South Yorkshire S10 2QT
Tel: (0114) 266 0374
Fax: (0114) 263 8176
Email: admin@ westbourneschool.co.uk
Head: Mr J Hicks
Type: Co-educational Day 4–16
No of pupils: B224 G106
Fees: On application

WEST YORKSHIRE

APPERLEY BRIDGE

WOODHOUSE GROVE SCHOOL
Apperley Bridge, West Yorkshire
BD10 0NR
Tel: (0113) 250 2477
Fax: (0113) 250 5290
Email: enquiries@
woodhousegrove.co.uk
Head: Mr D C Humphreys
Type: Co-educational Boarding
and Day 11–18
No of pupils: B468 G280
No of boarders: F84 W19
Fees: (September 08)
FB £18540–£18765
WB £17010–£17265
Day £9420–£9660

BATLEY

BATLEY GRAMMAR SCHOOL
Carlinghow Hill, Batley,
West Yorkshire WF17 0AD
Tel: (01924) 474980
Fax: (01924) 471960
Email: hmsec@
batleygrammar.co.uk
Head: Mrs B Tullie
Type: Co-educational Day 2–18
No of pupils: B210 G144
Fees: (September 08)
Day £5805–£8307

DALE HOUSE SCHOOL
Ruby Street, Carlinghow, Batley,
West Yorkshire WF17 8HL
Tel: (01924) 422215
Fax: (01924) 422215
Email: admin@
dhschool.freeserve.co.uk
Head: Mrs S M G Fletcher
Type: Co-educational Day 2–11
No of pupils: B45 G45
Fees: (September 08)
Day £4770–£5148

BINGLEY

LADY LANE PARK SCHOOL
Lady Lane, Bingley, West Yorkshire
BD16 4AP
Tel: (01274) 551168
Fax: (01274) 569732
Email: secretary@
ladylanepark.co.uk
Head: Mrs G Wilson and Mr D
Robinson
Type: Co-educational Day 2–11
No of pupils: B84 G92
Fees: (September 07)
Day £1688–£1792

BRADFORD

BRADFORD CHRISTIAN SCHOOL
Livingstone Road, Bolton Woods,
Bradford, West Yorkshire BD2 1BT
Tel: (01274) 595819
Fax: (01274) 620738
Email: bchristians@btconnect.com
Head: Mr P J Moon
Type: Co-educational Day 4–16
No of pupils: 197
Fees: On application

BRADFORD GIRLS' GRAMMAR SCHOOL
Squire Lane, Bradford,
West Yorkshire BD9 6RB
Tel: (01274) 545395
Fax: (01274) 482595
Email: headsec@bggs.com
Head: Mrs L J Warrington
Type: Girls Day 2–18
No of pupils: B27 G473
Fees: (September 08)
Day £6441–£10533

BRADFORD GRAMMAR SCHOOL
Keighley Road, Bradford,
West Yorkshire BD9 4JP
Tel: (01274) 553702
Fax: (01274) 548129
Email: hmsec@
bradfordgrammar.com
Head: Mr S R Davidson
Type: Co-educational Day 6–18
No of pupils: B756 G362
Fees: (September 08)
Day £7424–£9890

BRONTE HOUSE SCHOOL
Apperley Bridge, Bradford,
West Yorkshire BD10 0PQ
Tel: (0113) 250 2811
Fax: (0113) 250 0666
Email: enquiries@
brontehouse.co.uk
Head: Mr S Dunn
Type: Co-educational Boarding
and Day 3–11
No of pupils: B170 G110
No of boarders: F5
Fees: (September 08) FB £16500
WB £14820 Day £7470–£8490

NETHERLEIGH AND ROSSEFIELD SCHOOL
Parsons Road, Heaton, Bradford,
West Yorkshire BD9 4AY
Tel: (01274) 543162
Fax: (01274) 93011
Email: headteacher@
netherleighandrossefieldschoo-
l.co.uk
Head: Mrs M Midgley
Type: Co-educational Day 3–11
No of pupils: B110 G65
Fees: (September 07)
Day £2610–£4680

OLIVE SECONDARY
8 Cunliffe Villas, Bradford,
West Yorkshire BD8 7AN
Tel: 07909 541855
Fax: 01274 549900
Email: info@olivesecondary.org.uk
Head: Mr Amjad Mohammed
Type: Boys Day 11–18
No of pupils: 40
Fees: On application

BRIGHOUSE

THE RASTRICK INDEPENDENT SCHOOL
Ogden Lane, Rastrick, Brighouse,
West Yorkshire HD6 3HF
Tel: (01484) 400344
Fax: (01484) 718318
Email: info@
rastrick-independent.co.uk
Head: Mrs S A Vaughey
Type: Co-educational Day 0–16
No of pupils: B90 G100
Fees: (September 08)
Day £5550–£8500

HALIFAX

THE GLEDDINGS SCHOOL
Birdcage Lane, Halifax,
West Yorkshire HX3 0JB
Tel: (01422) 354605
Email: TheGleddings@aol.com
Head: Mrs Wilson
Type: Co-educational Day 3–11
No of pupils: B80 G80
Fees: On application

HIPPERHOLME GRAMMAR SCHOOL
Bramley Lane, Hipperholme,
Halifax, West Yorkshire HX3 8JE
Tel: (01422) 202256
Fax: (01422) 204592
Email: headmaster@
   hipperholmegrammar.org.uk
Head: Dr J Scarth
Type: Co-educational Day 11–18
No of pupils: B160 G145
Fees: On application

LIGHTCLIFFE PREPARATORY
Wakefield Road, Halifax,
West Yorkshire HX3 8AQ
Tel: (01422) 201330
Fax: (01422) 204845
Email: thesecretary@
   lightcliffepreparatoryschool.
   co.uk
Head: Mrs J A Pickersgill
Type: Co-educational Day 2–11
No of pupils: B85 G85
Fees: On application

HEBDEN BRIDGE

GLEN HOUSE MONTESSORI SCHOOL
Cragg Vale, Hebden Bridge,
West Yorkshire HX7 5SQ
Tel: (01422) 884682
Email: glenhouseschool@3-c.coop
Head: Mrs M Scaife
Type: Co-educational Day 3–15
No of pupils: B16 G10
Fees: On application

HECKMONDWIKE

THE BRANCH CHRISTIAN SCHOOL
8–10 Thomas Street,
Heckmondwike, West Yorkshire
WF16 0NW
Tel: (01924) 235637
Fax: (01924) 411021
Email: branchschool@tiscali.co.uk
Head: Mr R Ward
Type: Co-educational Day 3–17
No of pupils: B8 G12
Fees: On application

HUDDERSFIELD

HUDDERSFIELD GRAMMAR SCHOOL
Royds Mount, Luck Lane, Marsh,
Huddersfield, West Yorkshire
HD1 4QX
Tel: (01484) 424549
Fax: (01484) 531835
Email: admin@huddersfield-
   grammarschool.co.uk
Head: Mrs J L Straughan
Type: Co-educational Day 3–16
No of pupils: B194 G156
Fees: (September 07)
Day £5025–£6225

ISLAMIA GIRLS HIGH SCHOOL
Thornton Lodge Road, Thornton
Lodge, Huddersfield,
West Yorkshire HD1 3JQ
Tel: (01484) 432928
Head: Mr I Meer
Type: Girls Day 11–16
No of pupils: 77
Fees: On application

MOUNT SCHOOL
3 Binham Road, Edgerton,
Huddersfield, West Yorkshire
HD2 2AP
Tel: (01484) 426432
Fax: (01484) 426432
Email: info@themount.org.uk
Head: Mr N M Smith
Type: Co-educational Day 3–11
No of pupils: B75 G75
Fees: (September 08) Day £5235

MOUNTJOY HOUSE SCHOOL
63 New North Road,
Huddersfield, West Yorkshire
HD1 5ND
Tel: (01484) 429967
Fax: (01484) 362653
Email: mjhhuddersfield@aol.com
Head: Mrs C Rogers
Type: Co-educational Day 3–11
No of pupils: B43 G43
Fees: On application

ILKLEY

GHYLL ROYD SCHOOL
Greystone Manor, Ilkley Road,
Burley in Wharfedale, Ilkley,
West Yorkshire LS29 7HW
Tel: (01943) 865575
Fax: (01943) 865574
Email: information@
   ghyllroydschool.co.uk
Head: Mrs I Connor
Type: Boys Day 2–11
No of pupils: 90
Fees: (September 08)
Day £6246–£6867

MOORFIELD SCHOOL
Wharfedale Lodge, Ben Rhydding
Road, Ilkley, West Yorkshire
LS29 8RL
Tel: (01943) 607285
Fax: (01943) 603186
Email: enquiries@
   moorfieldschool.co.uk
Head: Mrs T Holden
Type: Girls Day 2–11
No of pupils: 134
Fees: (September 07)
Day £972–£4860

WESTVILLE HOUSE PREPARATORY SCHOOL
Carter's Lane, Middleton, Ilkley,
West Yorkshire LS29 0DQ
Tel: (01943) 608053
Fax: (01943) 817410
Email: westville@epals.com
Head: Mr C A Holloway
Type: Co-educational Day 3–11
No of pupils: B74 G63
Fees: (September 08)
Day £4110–£7140

England – West Yorkshire

LEEDS

ALCUIN SCHOOL
64 Woodland Lane, Leeds,
West Yorkshire LS7 4PD
Tel: (0113) 269 1173
Email: office@alcuinschool.co.uk
Head: Mr J Hipshon
Type: Co-educational Day 4–11
No of pupils: B20 G16
Fees: (September 08)
Day £1525–£1525

BROWNBERRIE SCHOOL
173–179 New Road Side,
Horsforth, Leeds, West Yorkshire
LS18 4DR
Tel: 0113 3053350
Head: Mr B Hargreaves
Type: Co-educational Day 11–17
No of pupils: B29 G15
Fees: On application

THE FROEBELIAN SCHOOL
Clarence Road, Horsforth, Leeds,
West Yorkshire LS18 4LB
Tel: (0113) 258 3047
Fax: (0113) 258 0173
Email: office@froebelian.co.uk
Head: Mr J Tranmer
Type: Co-educational Day 3–11
No of pupils: B94 G91
Fees: (September 07)
Day £3678–£5535

FULNECK SCHOOL[†]
Fulneck, Leeds, West Yorkshire
LS28 8DS
Tel: (0113) 257 0235
Fax: (0113) 255 7316
Email: enquiries@
  fulneckschool.co.uk
Head: Mr T Kernohan
Type: Co-educational Day and
Boarding 3–18
No of pupils: B228 G179
No of boarders: F55 W8
Fees: (September 08)
FB £14280–£17370
WB £13200–£15810
Day £5340–£9495

GATEWAYS SCHOOL
Harewood, Leeds, West Yorkshire
LS17 9LE
Tel: (0113) 288 6345
Fax: (0113) 288 6148
Email: gateways@
  gatewayschool.co.uk
Head: Mrs D Davidson
Type: Girls Day 3–18 (Boys 3–7)
No of pupils: B15 G490
Fees: On application

MOORLANDS SCHOOL
Foxhill Drive, Weetwood Lane,
Leeds, West Yorkshire LS16 5PF
Tel: (0113) 278 5286
Fax: (0113) 230 3193
Email: info@
  moorlands-school.co.uk
Head: Mr J G Davies
Type: Co-educational Day 2–13
No of pupils: B140 G59
Fees: (September 08)
Day £3762–£7935

NEW HORIZON COMMUNITY SCHOOL
Newton Hill House, Newton Hill
Road, Leeds, West Yorkshire
LS7 4JE
Tel: (0113) 262 4001
Fax: (0113) 262 4912
Email: nhcsleeds@
  newtonhillhouse.wanadoo.
  co.uk
Head: Mrs Sakinah Dambatta
Type: Girls Day 11–16
No of pupils: 100
Fees: On application

RICHMOND HOUSE SCHOOL
170 Otley Road, Leeds,
West Yorkshire LS16 5LG
Tel: (0113) 275 2670
Fax: (0113) 230 4868
Email: enquiries@rhschool.org
Type: Co-educational Day 3–11
No of pupils: B146 G111
Fees: (September 07)
Day £1300–£2030

ST AGNES PNEU SCHOOL
25 Burton Crescent, Leeds,
West Yorkshire LS6 4DN
Tel: (0113) 278 6722
Email: info@st-agnes.demon.co.uk
Head: Mrs S McMeeking
Type: Co-educational Day 2–7
No of pupils: B22 G24
Fees: On application

THE GRAMMAR SCHOOL AT LEEDS
Alwoodley Gates, Harrogate
Road, Leeds, West Yorkshire
LS17 8GS
Tel: (0113) 229 1552
Fax: (0113) 228 5111
Email: enquiries@gsal.org.uk
Head: Dr M Bailey
Type: Co-educational Day
Boys 3–18 Girls 3–19
No of pupils: B1346 G978
Fees: (September 08)
Day £6570–£9594

WAKEFIELD TUTORIAL PREPARATORY SCHOOL
Commercial Street, Morley, Leeds,
West Yorkshire LS27 8HY
Tel: (0113) 253 4033
Fax: (0113) 253 3581
Email: Headteacher@
  wtschool.co.uk
Head: Mrs J A Tanner
Type: Co-educational Day 4–11
No of pupils: B25 G25
Fees: (September 07)
Day £4170–£4575

PONTEFRACT

ACKWORTH SCHOOL
Ackworth, Pontefract,
West Yorkshire WF7 7LT
Tel: (01977) 611401
Fax: (01977) 616225
Email: admissions@
  ackworthschool.com
Head: Mr P Simpson
Type: Co-educational Boarding
and Day 4–18
No of pupils: B259 G266
No of boarders: F100
Fees: (September 08) FB £17817
Day £10884

ACKWORTH SCHOOL
Ackworth, Pontefract,
West Yorkshire WF7 7LT
Tel: (01977) 611401
Fax: (01977) 616225
Email: admissions@
  ackworthschool.com
Head: Mr P J Simpson
Type: Co-educational Day and
Boarding 2–18
No of pupils: B266 G273
No of boarders: F99
Fees: (September 08)
FB £17817–£7817
Day £6759–£10884

INGLEBROOK SCHOOL
Northgate Close, Pontefract,
West Yorkshire WF8 1HJ
Tel: (01977) 700120
Head: Mrs J Bellamy
Type: Co-educational Day 2–11
No of pupils: B90 G90
Fees: On application

RISHWORTH

RISHWORTH SCHOOL
Rishworth, West Yorkshire
HX6 4QA
Tel: (01422) 822217
Fax: (01422) 820911
Email: admin@
    rishworth-school.co.uk
Head: Mr R A Baker
Type: Co-educational Day and
Boarding 3–18
No of pupils: B290 G280
No of boarders: F78 W14
Fees: On application

WAKEFIELD

CLIFF SCHOOL
St John's Lodge, 2 Leeds Road,
Wakefield, West Yorkshire
WF1 3JT
Tel: (01924) 373597
Fax: (01924) 211137
Email: info@cliffschool.com
Head: Mr G Milne
Type: Co-educational Day 2–11
No of pupils: B70 G80
Fees: (September 08)
Day £3234–£8526

QUEEN ELIZABETH GRAMMAR SCHOOL
154 Northgate, Wakefield,
West Yorkshire WF1 3QX
Tel: (01924) 373943
Fax: (01924) 231603
Email: admissions@qegsss.org.uk
Head: Mr M R Gibbons
Type: Boys Day 7–18
Fees: On application

ST HILDA'S SCHOOL
Dovecote Lane, Horbury,
Wakefield, West Yorkshire
WF4 6BB
Tel: (01924) 260706
Fax: (01924) 272516
Email: head@sthildasschool.org.uk
Head: Mrs J Sharpe
Type: Co-educational Day
Boys 3–7 Girls 3–11
No of pupils: B44 G89
Fees: (September 08)
Day £4498–£4798

SILCOATES SCHOOL
Wrenthorpe, Wakefield,
West Yorkshire WF2 0PD
Tel: (01924) 291614
Fax: (01924) 368693
Email: head@silcoates.org.uk
Head: Mr D S Wideman
Type: Co-educational Day 7–18
No of pupils: B392 G345
Fees: (September 08)
Day £6492–£10968

SUNNY HILL HOUSE SCHOOL
Wrenthorpe Lane, Wrenthorpe,
Wakefield, West Yorkshire
WF2 0QB
Tel: (01924) 291717
Fax: (01924) 291717
Email: shhschool@aol.com
Head: Mrs H K Cushing
Type: Co-educational Day 2–7
No of pupils: B62 G47
Fees: (September 07) Day £5256

WAKEFIELD GIRLS' HIGH SCHOOL
Wentworth Street, Wakefield,
West Yorkshire WF1 2QS
Tel: (01924) 372490
Fax: (01924) 231601
Email: admissions@wghsss.org.uk
Head: Mrs P A Langham
Type: Girls Day 11–18
No of pupils: 734
Fees: On application

WAKEFIELD INDEPENDENT SCHOOL
The Nostell Centre, Doncaster
Road, Nostell, Wakefield,
West Yorkshire WF4 1QG
Tel: (01924) 865757
Fax: (01924) 865757
Email: headatwis@fsmail.net
Head: Mrs K E Caryl
Type: Co-educational Day 3–16
No of pupils: B95 G92
Fees: (September 08)
Day £4452–£6183

England – West Yorkshire

2.3

Northern Ireland

COUNTY ANTRIM

BELFAST

BELFAST ROYAL ACADEMY
Belfast, County Antrim BT14 6JL
Tel: (028) 9074 0423
Fax: (028) 9075 0607
Email: enquiries@
  bfsra.belfast.ni.sch.uk
Head: Mr J M G Dickson
Type: Co-educational Day 4–19
No of pupils: B764 G816
Fees: (September 08) Day £240

CABIN HILL SCHOOL
562–594 Upper Newtownards
Road, Knock, Belfast,
County Antrim BT4 3HJ
Tel: (028) 9065 3368
Fax: (028) 9065 1966
Email: info@
  cabinhill.belfast.ni.sch.uk
Head: Mrs H M Rowan
Type: Boys Day and Boarding
3–13 (Co-ed kindergarten)
No of pupils: B284 G8
No of boarders: F6 W21
Fees: On application

CAMPBELL COLLEGE
Belmont Road, Belfast,
County Antrim BT4 2ND
Tel: (028) 9076 3076
Fax: (028) 9076 1894
Email: hmoffice@
  campbellcollege.co.uk
Head: Mr J A Piggot
Type: Boys Boarding and Day
11–18
No of pupils: 876
Fees: (September 07)
FB £9300–£12900
Day £1900–£5500

METHODIST COLLEGE
1 Malone Road, Belfast,
County Antrim BT9 6BY
Tel: (028) 9020 5205
Fax: (028) 9020 5230
Email: school@methody.org
Head: Dr T W Mulryne
Type: Co-educational Day and
Boarding 4–19
No of pupils: B1300 G1100
No of boarders: F170
Fees: On application

**ROYAL BELFAST
ACADEMICAL INSTITUTION**
College Square East, Belfast,
County Antrim BT1 6DL
Tel: (028) 9024 0461
Fax: (028) 9023 7464
Email: prinsec@
  rbai.belfast.ni.sch.uk
Head: Miss J Williamson
Type: Boys Day 4–18
No of pupils: 1300
Fees: On application

**VICTORIA COLLEGE
BELFAST**
Cranmore Park, Belfast,
County Antrim BT9 6JA
Tel: (028) 9066 1506
Fax: (028) 9066 6898
Email: vcbinfo@aol.com
Head: Ms P Slevin
Type: Girls Day and Boarding
4–18
No of pupils: 1010
No of boarders: F49
Fees: (September 08)
F/WB £7875–£13125

COUNTY ARMAGH

ARMAGH

THE ROYAL SCHOOL ARMAGH
College Hill, Armagh,
County Armagh BT61 9DH
Tel: (028) 3752 2807
Fax: (028) 3752 5014
Email: info@
  royalschoolarmagh.com
Head: Mr P Crute
Type: Co-educational Boarding
and Day 4–19
No of pupils: B333 G336
No of boarders: F16 W65
Fees: On application

COUNTY DOWN

BANGOR

BANGOR GRAMMAR SCHOOL
13 College Avenue, Bangor,
County Down BT20 5HJ
Tel: (028) 9147 3734
Fax: (028) 9127 3245
Email: info@bgs.bangor.ni.sch.uk
Head: Mr S D Connolly
Type: Boys Day 11–18
No of pupils: 888
Fees: On application

BANGOR INDEPENDENT CHRISTIAN SCHOOL
277A Clandeboye Road, Bangor,
County Down BT19 1AA
Tel: (028) 9145 0240
Fax: (028) 9145 0240
Email: ics.bangor@gmail.com
Head: Mrs Ruth Daly
Type: Co-educational Day 4–16
No of pupils: B10 G12
Fees: On application

HOLYWOOD

THE HOLYWOOD RUDOLF STEINER SCHOOL
The Highlands, 34 Croft Road,
Holywood, County Down
BT18 0PR
Tel: (028) 9042 8029
Fax: (028) 9042 8029
Email: info@
  holywood-steiner.co.uk
Type: Co-educational Day 4–17
No of pupils: B71 G62
Fees: (September 07)
Day £225–£255

ROCKPORT SCHOOL
15 Rockport Road, Craigavad,
Holywood, County Down
BT18 0DD
Tel: (028) 9042 8372
Fax: (028) 9042 2608
Email: info@rockportschool.com
Head: Ms C A Osborne
Type: Co-educational Boarding
and Day 3–16 (Boarding 7–13)
No of pupils: B84 G113
No of boarders: W20
Fees: (September 08)
WB £9225–£13350
Day £3900–£10050

COUNTY LONDONDERRY

COLERAINE

COLERAINE ACADEMICAL INSTITUTION
Castlerock Road, Coleraine,
County Londonderry BT51 3LA
Tel: (028) 7034 4331
Fax: (028) 7035 2632
Email: enquiries@
   coleraineai.coleraine.ni.sch.uk
Head: Dr D Carruthers
Type: Boys Day 11–19
No of pupils: 720
Fees: On application

COUNTY TYRONE

DUNGANNON

THE ROYAL SCHOOL DUNGANNON
1 Ranfurly Road, Dungannon,
County Tyrone BT71 6EG
Tel: (028) 8772 2710
Fax: (028) 8775 2845
Email: acullen584@
   rsd.dungannon.ni.sch.uk
Head: Mr P D Hewitt
Type: Co-educational Day and
Boarding 11–19
No of pupils: B325 G325
No of boarders: F40 W5
Fees: (September 08)
F/WB £5000–£10000 Day £5000

SIXMILECROSS

COOLEY PRIMARY SCHOOL
90 Cooley Road, Omagh,
Sixmilecross, County Tyrone
BT79 9DH
Tel: (028) 8075 8742
Fax: (028) 8075 8744
Email: info@
   cooley.omagh.ni.sch.uk
Head: Mrs Anne Anderson and
Mrs Karen Atchison
Type: Co-educational Day 4–11
No of pupils: B62 G69
Fees: On application

2.4

Scotland

ABERDEENSHIRE

ABERDEEN

ABERDEEN WALDORF SCHOOL
Craigton Road, Cults, Aberdeen,
Aberdeenshire AB15 9QD
Tel: (01224) 869932
Fax: (01224) 868366
Email: aws@talk21.com
Head: Mr P Hansmann
Type: Day
No of pupils: B70 G55
Fees: On application

ALBYN SCHOOL
17–23 Queen's Road, Aberdeen,
Aberdeenshire AB15 4PB
Tel: (01224) 322408
Fax: (01224) 209173
Email: information@
  albynschool.co.uk
Head: Dr I E Long
Type: Co-educational Day
Boys 1–13 Girls 1–18
No of pupils: B205 G497
Fees: (September 08)
Day £5460–£8960

THE HAMILTON SCHOOL
55–57 Queens Road, Aberdeen,
Aberdeenshire AB15 4YP
Tel: (01224) 317295
Fax: (01224) 312656
Email: admin@
  thehamilton.aberdeen.sch.uk
Head: Mrs K Taylor
Type: Co-educational Day 0–12
No of pupils: B140 G150
Fees: On application

INTERNATIONAL SCHOOL OF ABERDEEN
'Fairgirth', 296 North Deeside
Road, Milltimber, Aberdeen,
Aberdeenshire AB13 OAB
Tel: (01224) 732267
Fax: (01224) 735648
Email: admin@
  isa.aberdeen.sch.uk
Head: Dr D A Hovde
Type: Co-educational Day 3–18
No of pupils: B264 G216
Fees: (September 07)
Day £14335–£16050

ROBERT GORDONS COLLEGE
Schoolhill, Aberdeen,
Aberdeenshire AB10 1FE
Tel: (01224) 646346
Fax: (01224) 630301
Email: enquiries@
  rgc.aberdeen.sch.uk
Head: Mr Hugh Ouston
Type: Co-educational Day 4–18
No of pupils: B910 G558
Fees: (September 08)
Day £10395–£24840

ST MARGARET'S SCHOOL FOR GIRLS
17 Albyn Place, Aberdeen,
Aberdeenshire AB10 1RU
Tel: (01224) 584466
Fax: (01224) 585600
Email: info@
  st-margaret.aberdeen.sch.uk
Head: Mrs Anne McKay
Type: Girls Day 3–18 (Boys 3–5)
No of pupils: B2 G380
Fees: (September 08)
Day £5199–£9069

ANGUS

DUNDEE

THE HIGH SCHOOL OF DUNDEE
Euclid Crescent, Dundee, Angus
DD1 1HU
Tel: (01382) 202921
Fax: (01382) 229822
Email: admissions@
  highschoolofdundee.co.uk
Head: Mr A M Duncan
Type: Co-educational Day 5–18
No of pupils: B549 G503
Fees: (September 07)
Day £6126–£8712

MONTROSE

LATHALLAN SCHOOL
Brotherton Castle, Johnshaven,
Montrose, Angus DD10 0HN
Tel: (01561) 362220
Fax: (01561) 361695
Email: office@lathallan.com
Head: Mr Andrew Giles
Type: Co-educational Boarding
and Day 5–15
No of pupils: B90 G64
No of boarders: W21
Fees: (September 08) WB £1113
Day £2717–£4651

ARGYLL AND BUTE

HELENSBURGH

LOMOND SCHOOL
10 Stafford Street, Helensburgh,
Argyll and Bute G84 9JX
Tel: (01436) 672476
Fax: (01436) 678320
Email: admin@
  lomond-school.demon.co.uk
Head: Mr A D Macdonald
Type: Co-educational Day and
Boarding 3–19
No of pupils: B280 G282
No of boarders: F64
Fees: On application

SOUTH AYRSHIRE

AYR

WELLINGTON SCHOOL
Carleton Turrets, Craigweil Road,
Ayr, South Ayrshire KA7 2XH
Tel: (01292) 269321
Fax: (01292) 272161
Email: info@wellingtonschool.org
Head: Mr M Parlour
Type: Co-educational Day 3–18
No of pupils: B286 G311
Fees: (September 07)
Day £4470–£8775

CLACKMANNANSHIRE

DOLLAR

DOLLAR ACADEMY
Dollar, Clackmannanshire
FK14 7DU
Tel: (01259) 742511
Fax: (01259) 742867
Email: rector@
   dollaracademy.org.uk
Head: Mr J S Robertson
Type: Co-educational Day and
Boarding 5–18
No of pupils: B621 G579
No of boarders: F85 W9
Fees: (September 07)
FB £16524–£18585
WB £15525–£17586
Day £6084–£8145

DUMFRIES & GALLOWAY

THORNHILL

**CADEMUIR
INTERNATIONAL SCHOOL**
Crawfordton House, Moniaive,
Thornhill, Dumfries & Galloway
DG3 4HG
Tel: (01848) 200212
Fax: (01848) 200212
Email: cademuir1@aol.com
Head: Mr Ian Hornby
Type: Co-educational Day and
Boarding
No of pupils: 34 *No of boarders:* F33
Fees: On application

FIFE

KIRKCALDY

SEA VIEW PRIVATE SCHOOL
102 Loughborough Road,
Kirkcaldy, Fife KY1 3DD
Tel: (01592) 652244
Fax: (01592) 655929
Email: seaviewkdy@sol.co.uk
Head: Mr Andrew Moss and Mrs
Louise Moss
Type: Co-educational Day 3–12
No of pupils: B32 G25
Fees: On application

ST ANDREWS

ST LEONARDS SCHOOL
St Andrews, Fife KY16 9QJ
Tel: (01334) 472126
Fax: (01334) 476152
Email: info@stleonards-fife.org
Head: Dr M Carslaw
Type: Co-educational Boarding
and Day 5–18
No of pupils: B222 G231
No of boarders: F120 W2
Fees: (September 08) FB £23346
Day £7110–£9807

GLASGOW

GLASGOW

CRAIGHOLME SCHOOL
72 St. Andrew's Drive,
Pollokshields, Glasgow G41 4HS
Tel: (0141) 427 0375
Fax: (0141) 427 6396
Email: principal@
craigholme.co.uk
Head: Mrs G Stobo
Type: Girls Day 3–18 (Boys 3–5)
No of pupils: B10 G500
Fees: (September 08)
Day £6774–£8634

THE GLASGOW ACADEMY
Colebrooke Street, Glasgow
G12 8HE
Tel: (0141) 334 8558
Fax: (0141) 337 3473
Email: enquiries@tga.org.uk
Head: Mr P J Brodie
Type: Co-educational Day 3–18
No of pupils: B643 G550
Fees: On application

**THE GLASGOW ACADEMY
DAIRSIE**
54 Newlands Road, Glasgow
G43 2JG
Tel: (0141) 632 0736
Fax: (0141) 632 1303
Email: dairsie@tga.org.uk
Head: Mrs S S McKnight
Type: Co-educational Day 3–9
No of pupils: B44 G27
Fees: On application

**GLASGOW STEINER
SCHOOL**
52 Lumsden Street, Glasgow
G3 8RH
Tel: (0141) 334 8855
Fax: (0141) 334 8855
Email: admin@
glasgowsteinerschool.org.uk
Head: Ms S Noakes
Type: Co-educational Day 3–14
No of pupils: B53 G38
Fees: On application

**THE HIGH SCHOOL OF
GLASGOW**
637 Crow Road, Glasgow G13 1PL
Tel: (0141) 954 9628
Fax: (0141) 435 5708
Email: rector@hsog.co.uk
Head: Mr C D R Mair
Type: Co-educational Day 3–18
No of pupils: B535 G524
Fees: On application

**HUTCHESONS' GRAMMAR
SCHOOL**
21 Beaton Road, Glasgow
G41 4NW
Tel: (0141) 423 2933
Fax: (0141) 424 0251
Email: admissions@
hutchesons.org
Head: Dr K M Greig
Type: Co-educational Day 5–18
No of pupils: B907 G820
Fees: (September 08)
Day £6722–£8634

KELVINSIDE ACADEMY
33 Kirklee Road, Glasgow
G12 0SW
Tel: (0141) 357 3376
Fax: (0141) 357 5401
Email: rector@
kelvinsideacademy.org.uk
Head: Mr J L Broadfoot
Type: Co-educational Day 3–18
No of pupils: B408 G220
Fees: (September 08)
Day £5667–£9294

ST ALOYSIUS' COLLEGE
45 Hill Street, Glasgow G3 6RJ
Tel: (0141) 331 9259
Fax: (0141) 353 0426
Email: mail@staloysius.org
Head: Mr J E Stoer
Type: Co-educational Day 3–18
No of pupils: B672 G610
Fees: (September 08)
Day £6120–£8010

**ST ALOYSIUS JUNIOR
SCHOOL**
56–58 Hill Street, Glasgow
G3 6RH
Tel: (0141) 331 9200
Email: mail@staloysiuscollege.org
Head: Mrs F Davidson
Type: Co-educational Day 5–12
No of pupils: 431
Fees: On application

INVERCLYDE

GREENOCK

CEDARS SCHOOL OF EXCELLENCE
31 Ardgowan Square, Greenock,
Inverclyde PA16 8NJ
Tel: (01475) 723905
Fax: (01475) 723905
Email: alison@speirs.org
Type: Co-educational Day 5–14
No of pupils: 50
Fees: On application

KILMACOLM

ST COLUMBA'S SCHOOL
Duchal Road, Kilmacolm,
Inverclyde PA13 4AU
Tel: (01505) 872238
Fax: (01505) 873995
Email: secretary@st-columbas.org
Head: Mr D G Girdwood
Type: Co-educational Day 3–18
No of pupils: B364 G365
Fees: (September 08)
Day £2200–£8580

LANARKSHIRE

HAMILTON

HAMILTON COLLEGE
Bothwell Road, Hamilton,
Lanarkshire ML3 0AY
Tel: (01698) 282700
Fax: (01698) 281589
Email: principal@
    hamiltoncollege.co.uk
Head: Mr A J Leach
Type: Co-educational Day 3–18
No of pupils: B400 G400
Fees: On application

SOUTH LANARKSHIRE

GLASGOW

FERNHILL SCHOOL
Fernbrae Avenue, Rutherglen,
Glasgow, South Lanarkshire
G73 4SG
Tel: (0141) 634 2674
Fax: (0141) 631 4343
Email: info@fernhillschool.co.uk
Head: Mrs J Sexton
Type: Co-educational Day
Boys 4–11 Girls 4–18(Boys 4–11)
No of pupils: B61 G270
Fees: (September 07)
Day £6330–£7590

LOTHIAN

DUNBAR

BELHAVEN HILL
Dunbar, Lothian EH42 1NN
Tel: (01368) 862785
Fax: (01368) 865225
Email: headmaster@
  belhavenhill.com
Head: Mr I K MacAskill
Type: Co-educational Boarding
and Day 7–13
No of pupils: B71 G57
No of boarders: F107
Fees: (September 08) FB £17280
Day £11985

EDINBURGH

BASIL PATERSON TUTORIAL COLLEGE
66 Queen Street, Edinburgh,
Lothian EH2 4NA
Tel: (0131) 225 3802
Fax: (0131) 226 6701
Email: info@basilpaterson.co.uk
Head: Mr C Smith
Type: Co-educational Boarding
and Day 15+
No of pupils: B15 G15
No of boarders: F7
Fees: On application

CARGILFIELD
Barnton Avenue West, Edinburgh,
Lothian EH4 6HU
Tel: (0131) 336 2207
Fax: (0131) 336 3179
Email: admin@cargilfield.com
Head: Mr J Elder
Type: Co-educational Boarding
and Day 3–13
No of pupils: B127 G53
No of boarders: F21
Fees: On application

CLIFTON HALL SCHOOL
Newbridge, Edinburgh, Lothian
EH28 8LQ
Tel: (0131) 333 1359
Fax: (0131) 333 4609
Email: office@cliftonhall.org.uk
Head: Mr R Grant
Type: Co-educational Day 3–18
No of pupils: B128 G102
Fees: (September 07) Day £7875

DUNEDIN SCHOOL
Liberton Bank House, 5 Nether
Liberton Lane, Edinburgh, Lothian
EH16 5TY
Tel: (0132) 672 2638
Email: staff@dunedin.edin.sch.uk
Head: Mrs S Peck and Mrs S Ford
Type: Co-educational Day 10–17
No of pupils: B10 G10
Fees: On application

THE EDINBURGH ACADEMY
42 Henderson Row, Edinburgh,
Lothian EH3 5BL
Tel: (0131) 556 4603
Fax: (0131) 624 4994
Email: rector@
  edinburghacademy.org.uk
Head: Mr J V Light
Type: Boys Day and Boarding
5–18 (Co-ed VIth Form)
No of pupils: B451 G25
No of boarders: F17 W2
Fees: On application

THE EDINBURGH RUDOLF STEINER SCHOOL
60 Spylaw Road, Edinburgh,
Lothian EH10 5BR
Tel: (0131) 337 3410
Fax: (0131) 538 6066
Email: steinersch@aol.com
Head: Mr A Farquharson
Type: Co-educational Day 3–18
No of pupils: B150 G150
No of boarders: F8 W1
Fees: On application

FETTES COLLEGE
Carrington Road, Edinburgh,
Lothian EH4 1QX
Tel: (0131) 311 6744
Fax: (0131) 311 6714
Email: enquiries@fettes.com
Head: Mr M C B Spens
Type: Co-educational Boarding
and Day 7–18
No of pupils: B363 G288
No of boarders: F429
Fees: (September 08)
FB £17739–£24498
Day £11331–£17838

GEORGE HERIOT'S SCHOOL
Lauriston Place, Edinburgh,
Lothian EH3 9EQ
Tel: (0131) 229 7263
Fax: (0131) 229 6363
Email: admissions@
  george-heriots.com
Head: Mr A G Hector and
Mr C D Wyllie
Type: Co-educational Day 4–18
No of pupils: B853 G743
Fees: (September 08)
Day £5850–£8811

GEORGE WATSON'S COLLEGE
67–71 Colinton Road, Edinburgh,
Lothian EH10 5EG
Tel: (0131) 446 6000
Fax: (0131) 446 6090
Email: admissions@gwc.org.uk
Head: Mr Gareth Edwards
Type: Co-educational Day 3–18
No of pupils: B1236 G1071
Fees: (September 08)
Day £5712–£8856

MANNAFIELDS CHRISTIAN SCHOOL
170 Easter Road, Edinburgh,
Lothian EH7 5QE
Tel: (0131) 659 5602
Email: ht@mannafields.org.uk
Head: Mr G S Ackerman
Type: Co-educational Day 5–14
No of pupils: B16 G15
Fees: (September 08)
Day £200–£3600

THE MARY ERSKINE SCHOOL
Ravelston, Edinburgh, Lothian
EH4 3NT
Tel: (0131) 347 5700
Fax: (0131) 347 5799
Email: schoolsecretary@
  esmgc.com
Head: Mr J N D Gray
Type: Girls Day and Boarding
12–18 (Co-ed VIth Form)
No of pupils: 746
No of boarders: F25
Fees: (September 08) FB £16938
WB £16515 Day £8919

MERCHISTON CASTLE SCHOOL*

Colinton, Edinburgh, Lothian
EH13 0PU
Tel: (0131) 312 2200
Fax: (0131) 441 6060
Email: admissions@
  merchiston.co.uk
Head: Mr A R Hunter
Type: Boys Boarding and Day
8–18
No of pupils: 453
No of boarders: F289
Fees: (September 08)
FB £15585–£23760
Day £10995–£17205

REGIUS CHRISTIAN SCHOOL

41a South Clerk·Street, Edinburgh,
Lothian EH8 8NZ
Tel: 0131 466 8662
Email: jenny@regius.edin.sch.uk
Head: Mrs Jenny Taylor
Type: Co-educational Day
No of pupils: 16
Fees: On application

ST GEORGE'S SCHOOL FOR GIRLS*

Garscube Terrace, Edinburgh,
Lothian EH12 6BG
Tel: (0131) 311 8000
Fax: (0131) 311 8120
Email: admissions@
  st-georges.edin.sch.uk
Head: Dr J McClure
Type: Girls Day and Boarding
2–18 (Boys 2–4)
No of pupils: B8 G837
No of boarders: F54 W6
Fees: (September 08)
FB £16215–£20130
Day £3195–£10110

ST MARGARET'S SCHOOL

East Suffolk Road, Edinburgh,
Lothian EH16 5PJ
Tel: (0131) 668 1986
Fax: (0131) 667 9814
Email: admissions@
  st-margarets.sch.edin.uk
Head: Mrs E M Davis
Type: Girls Day 1–18 (Boys 1–8)
No of pupils: B68 G472
Fees: (September 08)
Day £5850–£9537

ST MARY'S MUSIC SCHOOL

Coates Hall, 25 Grosvenor
Crescent, Edinburgh, Lothian
EH12 5EL
Tel: (0131) 538 7766
Fax: (0131) 467 7289
Email: info@
  st-marys-music-school.co.uk
Head: Mrs J J Rimer
Type: Co-educational Boarding
and Day 9–19
No of pupils: B31 G40
No of boarders: F32
Fees: On application

ST SERF'S SCHOOL

5 Wester Coates Gardens,
Edinburgh, Lothian EH12 5LT
Tel: (0131) 337 1015
Fax: (0131) 346 7829
Email: office@
  stserfsschool.freeserve.co.uk
Head: Mrs K D Hume
Type: Co-educational Day 5–18
No of pupils: B65 G50
Fees: On application

STEWART'S MELVILLE COLLEGE

Queensferry Road, Edinburgh,
Lothian EH4 3EZ
Tel: (0131) 311 1000
Fax: (0131) 311 1099
Email: secretary@esmgc.com
Head: Mr J N D Gray
Type: Boys Day and Boarding
12–18 (Co-ed VIth Form)
No of pupils: 716
No of boarders: F21
Fees: (September 08) FB £16938
WB £16515 Day £8919

HADDINGTON

THE COMPASS SCHOOL

West Road, Haddington, Lothian
EH41 3RD
Tel: (01620) 822642
Fax: (01620) 822144
Email: office@
  thecompassschool.co.uk
Head: Mr M Becher
Type: Co-educational Day 4–12
No of pupils: B54 G60
Fees: (September 07)
Day £1460–£2243

MUSSELBURGH

LORETTO JUNIOR SCHOOL

North Esk Lodge, 1 North High
Street, Musselburgh, Lothian
EH21 6JA
Tel: (0131) 653 4570
Fax: (0131) 653 4571
Email: juniorschool@loretto.com
Head: Mr R G Selley
Type: Co-educational Day and
Boarding 3–12
No of pupils: B100 G92
No of boarders: F7
Fees: (September 07) F/WB £13500
Day £6210–£11550

LORETTO SCHOOL*

Linkfield Road, Musselburgh,
Lothian EH21 7RE
Tel: (0131) 653 4455
Fax: (0131) 653 4401
Email: admissions@loretto.com
Head: Mr P A Hogan
Type: Co-educational Boarding
and Day 3–18
No of pupils: B303 G227
No of boarders: F245
Fees: (September 08)
FB £15975–£24450
Day £3000–£16620

Scotland – Lothian

MORAYSHIRE

ELGIN

GORDONSTOUN SCHOOL*
Elgin, Morayshire IV30 5RF
Tel: (01343) 837837
Fax: (01343) 837808
Email: admissions@
gordonstoun.org.uk
Head: Mr M C Pyper
Type: Co-educational Boarding
and Day 8–18
No of pupils: B359 G248
No of boarders: F456 W23
Fees: (September 08)
FB £16731–£27390 WB £15366
Day £10290–£20451

ROSEBRAE SCHOOL
Spynie, Elgin, Morayshire IV30 8XT
Tel: (01343) 544841
Fax: (01343) 544841
Email: enquiries@
rosebrae.moray.sch.uk
Head: Mrs B MacPherson
Type: Co-educational Day 2–8
No of pupils: B32 G32
Fees: On application

PERTH AND KINROSS

CRIEFF

ARDVRECK SCHOOL
Gwydyr Road, Crieff, Perth and
Kinross PH7 4EX
Tel: (01764) 653112
Fax: (01764) 654920
Email: headmaster@
ardvreck.org.uk
Head: Mr P Watson
Type: Co-educational Day and
Boarding 3–13
No of pupils: B80 G70
No of boarders: F105
Fees: On application

PERTH

STRATHALLAN SCHOOL*
Forgandenny, Perth, Perth and
Kinross PH2 9EG
Tel: (01738) 812546
Fax: (01738) 812549
Email: admissions@
strathallan.co.uk
Head: Mr B K Thompson
Type: Co-educational Boarding
and Day 9–18
No of pupils: B297 G205
No of boarders: F326
Fees: (September 08)
FB £16770–£23520
Day £10470–£15960

RENFREWSHIRE

NEWTON MEARNS

BELMONT HOUSE
Sandringham Avenue, Newton
Mearns, Renfrewshire G77 5DU
Tel: (0141) 639 2922
Fax: (0141) 639 9860
Email: admin@
  belmontschool.co.uk
Head: Mr M D Shanks
Type: Co-educational Day 3–18
No of pupils: B277 G66
Fees: (September 08)
Day £3771–£8556

ROXBURGHSHIRE

MELROSE

ST MARY'S PREPARATORY SCHOOL
Abbey Park, Melrose,
Roxburghshire TD6 9LN
Tel: (01896) 822517
Fax: (01896) 823550
Email: enquiries@
  stmarys.newnet.co.uk
Head: Mr J Brett
Type: Co-educational Day and
Boarding 2–13
No of pupils: B57 G80
No of boarders: W21
Fees: (September 08)
Day £8700–£14250

STIRLING

STIRLING

BEACONHURST SCHOOL*
52 Kenilworth Road, Bridge of
Allan, Stirling FK9 4RR
Tel: (01786) 832146
Fax: (01786) 833415
Email: secretary@
    beaconhurst.stirling.sch.uk
Head: Mr I W Kilpatrick
Type: Co-educational Day 3–18
No of pupils: B205 G196
Fees: (September 08)
Day £2862–£9210

2.5

Wales

ANGLESEY

MENAI BRIDGE

TREFFOS SCHOOL
Llansadwrn, Menai Bridge,
Anglesey LL59 5SL
Tel: (01248) 712322
Fax: (01248) 715276
Email: treffos@aol.com
Head: Mrs J E Humphreys and Dr S
Humphreys
Type: Co-educational Day 0–11
No of pupils: B45 G42
Fees: On application

BRIDGEND

PORTHCAWL

ST CLARE'S SCHOOL
Newton, Porthcawl, Bridgend
CF36 5NR
Tel: (01656) 782509
Fax: (01656) 789960
Email: info@stclares-school.co.uk
Head: Mrs C M Barnard
Type: Co-educational Day 3–18
No of pupils: B130 G176
Fees: (September 08)
Day £3930–£7380

ST JOHN'S SCHOOL
Church Street, Newton,
Porthcawl, Bridgend CF36 5NP
Tel: (01656) 783404
Fax: (01656) 783535
Email: office@
  stjohnsschool-porthcawl.com
Head: Mrs C A Clint
Type: Co-educational Day 3–16
Fees: (September 08)
Day £3885–£8985

CAERPHILLY

MACHEN

WYCLIF INDEPENDENT CHRISTIAN SCHOOL
Ebenezer Baptist Chapel,
Wyndham Street, Machen,
Caerphilly NP1 8PU
Tel: 01633 441582
Fax: 01633 441582
Email: info@
  wyclifchristianschool.org
Head: Mr Andrew Tamplin
Type: Co-educational Day 4–16
No of pupils: B48 G51
Fees: On application

CARDIFF

CARDIFF

THE CARDIFF ACADEMY
40–41 The Parade, Roath, Cardiff
CF24 3AB
Tel: (02920) 409630
Fax: (02920) 455273
Email: 40–41@
  theparade.fsbusiness.co.uk
Head: Dr S R Wilson
Type: Co-educational Day 14–18
No of pupils: B25 G25
Fees: On application

THE CATHEDRAL SCHOOL
Cardiff Road, Llandaff, Cardiff
CF5 2YH
Tel: (029) 2056 3179
Fax: (029) 2056 7752
Email: Registrar@
  cathedral-school.co.uk
Head: Mr P L Gray
Type: Co-educational Day 3–16
No of pupils: B437 G212
Fees: (September 08)
Day £6210–£9105

HOWELL'S SCHOOL, LLANDAFF GDST
Cardiff Road, Llandaff, Cardiff
CF5 2YD
Tel: (029) 2056 2019
Fax: (029) 2057 8879
Email: mail@how.gdst.net
Head: Mrs Sally Davis
Type: Co-educational Day
Boys 16–18 Girls 3–18
No of pupils: B82 G787
Fees: (September 08)
Day £1854–£8955

KINGS MONKTON SCHOOL
6 West Grove, Cardiff CF24 3XL
Tel: (029) 2048 2854
Fax: (029) 2049 0484
Email: lauriehill@
  kingsmonkton.org.uk
Head: Mr P Cox
Type: Co-educational Day 2–18
No of pupils: B220 G140
Fees: (September 08)
Day £5880–£7665

ST JOHN'S COLLEGE
College Green, Newport Road,
Old St Mellons, Cardiff CF3 5YX
Tel: (029) 2077 8936
Fax: (029) 20779099
Email: admin@
  stjohnscollegecardiff.co.uk
Head: Dr D Neville
Type: Co-educational Day 3–18
No of pupils: B240 G200
Fees: On application

WESTBOURNE SCHOOL
Hickman Road, Penarth, Cardiff
CF64 2AJ
Tel: (029) 2070 5705
Fax: (029) 2070 9988
Email: enquiries@
  westbourneschool.com
Head: Mr K W Underhilll
Type: Co-educational Day and
Boarding 3–16
No of pupils: B105 G56
Fees: On application

CARMARTHENSHIRE

LLANDOVERY

LLANDOVERY COLLEGE
Llandovery, Carmarthenshire
SA20 0EE
Tel: (01550) 723000
Fax: (01550) 723002
Email: mail@
 llandoverycollege.com
Head: Mr I M Hunt
Type: Co-educational Boarding
and Day 3–18
No of pupils: B173 G125
No of boarders: F145 W8
Fees: (September 08)
FB £4083–£6918 WB £3040
Day £1950–£4270

LLANELLI

ST MICHAEL'S SCHOOL
Bryn, Llanelli, Carmarthenshire
SA14 9TU
Tel: (01554) 820325
Fax: (01554) 821716
Email: office@stmikes.co.uk
Head: Mr D T Sheehan
Type: Co-educational Day 3–18
No of pupils: B227 G206
No of boarders: F19
Fees: (September 07) FB £18800

CONWY

COLWYN BAY

LYNDON PREPARATORY SCHOOL
Pwllycrochan Avenue, Colwyn
Bay, Conwy LL29 7BP
Tel: (01492) 530381
Fax: (01492) 539720
Email: lyndon@
 rydal-penrhos.co.uk
Head: Mr P J Bendall
Type: Co-educational Boarding
and Day 2–11
No of pupils: B146 G120
Fees: (September 08)
FB £13830–£16005
WB £12450–£14415
Day £4950–£7080

RYDAL PENRHOS SENIOR SCHOOL
Pwllycrochan Avenue, Colwyn
Bay, Conwy LL29 7BT
Tel: (01492) 530155
Fax: (01492) 534072
Email: info@rydal-penrhos.com
Head: Mr P Lee-Browne
Type: Co-educational Boarding
and Day 11–18 (Single-sex ed
11–16)
No of pupils: B266 G196
No of boarders: F153 W20
Fees: (September 07)
FB £17745–£21900
WB £15972–£19770
Day £9120–£13020

LLANDUDNO

ST DAVID'S COLLEGE[†]
Llandudno, Conwy LL30 1RD
Tel: (01492) 875974
Fax: (01492) 870383
Email: hmsec@
 stdavidscollege.co.uk
Head: Mr S Hay
Type: Co-educational Boarding
and Day 11–18
No of pupils: B185 G65
No of boarders: F132 W5
Fees: (September 08)
F/WB £17985–£22665
Day £10425–£15210

DENBIGHSHIRE

DENBIGH

HOWELL'S SCHOOL
Denbigh, Denbighshire LL16 3EN
Tel: (01745) 813631
Fax: (01745) 814443
Email: enquiries@howells.org
Head: Miss R Hodgson
Type: Girls Boarding and Day
2–18
No of pupils: B5 G240
No of boarders: F78 W20
Fees: (September 08)
F/WB £10500–£18150
Day £4950–£11100

RUTHIN

RUTHIN SCHOOL
Mold Road, Ruthin, Denbighshire
LL15 1EE
Tel: (01824) 702543
Fax: (01824) 707141
Email: secretary@
  ruthinschool.co.uk
Head: Mr J S Rowlands
Type: Co-educational Boarding
and Day 3–18
No of pupils: B120 G70
No of boarders: F54 W6
Fees: (September 08) FB £19500
WB £15000 Day £6000–£10500

ST ASAPH

FAIRHOLME PREPARATORY SCHOOL
Mount Road, St Asaph,
Denbighshire LL17 0DH
Tel: (01745) 583505
Fax: (01745) 584332
Email: success@
  fairholmeschool.com
Head: Mrs M Cashman
Type: Co-educational Day 3–11
No of pupils: B70 G60
Fees: (September 08) Day £4800

GWYNEDD

BANGOR

HILLGROVE SCHOOL
Ffriddoedd Road, Bangor,
Gwynedd LL57 2TW
Tel: (01248) 353568
Fax: (01248) 353971
Email: headmaster@
  hillgrove.gwynedd.sch.uk
Head: Mr J G Porter
Type: Co-educational Day 3–16
No of pupils: B72 G82
Fees: (September 07)
Day £760–£1290

ST GERARD'S SCHOOL
Ffriddoedd Road, Bangor,
Gwynedd LL57 2EL
Tel: (01248) 351656
Fax: (01248) 351204
Email: st_gerards@lineone.net
Head: Miss A Parkinson
Type: Co-educational Day 3–18
No of pupils: B169 G184
Fees: On application

MONMOUTHSHIRE

CHEPSTOW

ST JOHN'S-ON-THE-HILL
Tutshill, Chepstow,
Monmouthshire NP16 7LE
Tel: (01291) 622045
Fax: (01291) 623932
Email: registrar@
  stjohnsonthehill.co.uk
Head: Mr I K Etchells
Type: Co-educational Boarding
and Day 0–13 (Nursery from 3
months)
No of pupils: B192 G133
No of boarders: F30
Fees: (September 07) F/WB £13500
Day £5805–£9600

MONMOUTH

HABERDASHERS' MONMOUTH SCHOOL FOR GIRLS
Hereford Road, Monmouth,
Monmouthshire NP25 5XT
Tel: (01600) 711100
Fax: (01600) 711233
Email: admissions@hmsg.co.uk
Head: Dr B Despontin
Type: Girls Day and Boarding
7–18
No of pupils: 655
No of boarders: F90
Fees: On application

LLANGATTOCK SCHOOL
Llangattock-Vibon-Avel,
Monmouth, Monmouthshire
NP25 5NG
Tel: (01600) 772213
Fax: (01600) 772213
Email: admin@
  llangattockschool.co.uk
Head: Mrs Rosemary Whaley
Type: Co-educational Day 2–12
No of pupils: B53 G43
Fees: On application

MONMOUTH SCHOOL
Almshouse Street, Monmouth,
Monmouthshire NP25 3XP
Tel: (01600) 713143
Fax: (01600) 772701
Email: admissions@
  monmouthschool.org
Head: Dr S G Connors
Type: Boys Boarding and Day
7–18 (Boarding 11–18)
No of pupils: 692
No of boarders: F140
Fees: (September 07)
F/WB £14847–£17973
Day £7551–£10677

NEWPORT

NEWPORT

ROUGEMONT SCHOOL
Llantarnam Hall, Malpas Road,
Newport NP20 6QB
Tel: (01633) 820800
Fax: (01633) 855598
Email: registrar@rsch.co.uk
Head: Dr J Tribbick
Type: Co-educational Day 3–18
No of pupils: B356 G332
Fees: On application

PEMBROKESHIRE

SAUNDERSFOOT

NETHERWOOD SCHOOL
Saundersfoot, Pembrokeshire
SA69 9BE
Tel: (01834) 811057
Fax: (01834) 811023
Email: netherwood.school@
  virgin.net
Head: Mr D H Morris
Type: Co-educational Day and
Boarding 3–18
No of pupils: B76 G59
No of boarders: F24 W4
Fees: On application

POWYS

BRECON

CHRIST COLLEGE
Brecon, Powys LD3 8AG
Tel: (01874) 615440
Fax: (01874) 615475
Email: enquiries@
  christcollegebrecon.com
Head: Mrs Emma Taylor
Type: Co-educational Boarding
and Day 11–18
No of pupils: B180 G130
No of boarders: F207 W40
Fees: (September 07)
FB £15090–£19275
Day £10950–£12465

SWANSEA

BISHOPTSTON

CRAIG-Y-NOS SCHOOL
Clyne Common, Bishoptston,
Swansea SA3 3JB
Tel: (01792) 234288
Fax: (01792) 233813
Email: craigynos.school@
btinternet.com
Head: Mr G W Fursland
Type: Co-educational Day 2–11
No of pupils: B64 G52
Fees: (September 08)
Day £3720–£4875

SWANSEA

FFYNONE HOUSE SCHOOL
36 St James' Crescent, Swansea
SA1 6DR
Tel: (01792) 464967
Fax: (01792) 455202
Email: snrsec@
ffynonetrustschools.co.uk
Head: Mrs Edwina Jones
Type: Co-educational Day 9–18
No of pupils: B87 G126
Fees: On application

FFYNONE HOUSE SCHOOL
36 St James' Crescent, Uplands,
Swansea SA1 6DR
Tel: (01792) 464967
Fax: (01792) 455202
Email: snrsec@
ffynonetrustschools.co.uk
Head: Mrs E Jones
Type: Co-educational Day 9–18
No of pupils: B87 G128
Fees: (September 07)
Day £5025–£8100

OAKLEIGH HOUSE SCHOOL
38 Penlan Crescent, Uplands,
Swansea SA2 0RL
Tel: (01792) 298537
Fax: (01792) 280371
Email: info@
oakleighhouseschool.co.uk
Head: Mrs R Ferriman
Type: Co-educational Day 3–11
No of pupils: B60 G60
Fees: (September 08)
Day £4200–£5520

2.6
Overseas Schools

FRANCE

**CHAVAGNES
INTERNATIONAL COLLEGE***
96 rue du Calvaire, 85250,
CHAVAGNES-EN-PAILLERS,
France, France
Tel: (33 (0)) 51 42 39 82
Fax: (33(0)) 51 42 39 83
Email: info@chavagnes.org
Head: Mr F D McDermott
Type: Boys Boarding and Day
10–18
No of pupils: 30
No of boarders: F26 W3
Fees: FB from €14000 WB from
€11000 DAY from €6500 (various
bursaries are available)

MOUGINS SCHOOL*
615 Avenue Dr Maurice Donat,
Font de l'Orme, BP 401, 06251
Mougins Cedex, France, France
Tel: (33 (0) 4 93 90 15 47
Fax: (33 (0) 4 93 75 31 40
Email: information@
   mougins-school.com
Head: Mr B G Hickmore
Type: Co-educational Day 3–18
No of pupils: B273 G186

SPAIN

KING'S COLLEGE MADRID*
Paseo de los Andes, 35, 28761
Soto de Vinuelas, Madrid, Spain,
Spain
Tel: (†34) 918 034 800
Fax: (†34) 918 036 557
Email: info@kingscollege.es
Head: Mr D Johnson
Type: Co-educational Day and
Boarding 2–18
No of pupils: B924 G956
No of boarders: F20
Fees: FB €16,830–€18,357 Day
€5,454–€10,476

SWITZERLAND

AIGLON COLLEGE*
1885 Chesieres-Villars,
Switzerland, Switzerland
Tel: (41 (0) 24 496 6126
Fax: (41 (0) 24 469 6162
Email: info@aiglon.ch
Head: Mr P J Armstrong
Type: Co-educational Day and
Boarding 9–18
No of pupils: B206 G172
Fees: FB SFr58000–SFr73300
WB SFr49700
Day SFr38300–SFr51300

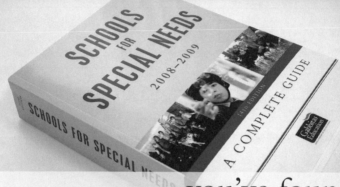

Part 3

School Profiles

COUNTIES OF ENGLAND, SCOTLAND AND WALES

SCOTLAND

Moray

Highland

Aberdeenshire

Aberdeen City

1. Inverclyde
2. North Ayrshire
3. Renfrewshire
4. West Dunbartonshire
5. East Dunbartonshire
6. North Lanarkshire

7. Falkirk
8. Clackmannanshire
9. West Lothian
10. City of Edinburgh
11. Midlothian
12. East Lothian

Perth
and
Kinross

Angus

Argyll
and
Bute

Stirling

Fife

South
Lanarkshire

East
Ayrshire

South
Ayrshire

Borders

Dumfries and
Galloway

Isle
of
Man

NORTHERN
ENGLAND

Northumberland

Newcastle upon Tyne

Hartlepool

Stockton-on-Tees

Middlesbrough

Durham

Cumbria

North
Yorkshire

York

East Riding
of Yorkshire

North Lincolnshire

North East Lincolnshire

Lancashire

West
Yorkshire

Merseyside

G. M.

South
Yorkshire

EASTERN
ENGLAND

Cheshire

Derbyshire

Nottingham-
shire

Lincoln-
shire

Rutland

WALES

Denbighshire

Flintshire

Conwy

Wrexham

Stafford-
shire

Norfolk

1. Monmouthshire
2. Torfean
3. Newport
4. Blaenau Gwent
5. Caerphilly
6. Cardiff
7. Merthyr Tydfil
8. Cynon Taff
9. Vale of Glamorgan
10. Bridgend
11. Neath Port Talbot
12. Swansea

Gwynedd

Shropshire

W.M.

Leicester-
shire

Cambridge-
shire

Suffolk

Northampton-
shire

Ceredigion

Powys

Worcester-
shire

Warwick-
shire

Hereford-
shire

Bedford-
shire

Carmarthenshire

Gloucester-
shire

Oxford-
shire

Buckingham-
shire

Hertford-
shire

Essex

HOME
COUNTIES
(North)

Pembrokeshire

CENTRAL
ENGLAND

Berkshire

Greater
London

LONDON

13. South Gloucestershire
14. Bath and North East Somerset
15. City of Bristol
16. North Somerset

Wiltshire

Somerset

Hampshire

Surrey

Kent

Devon

Dorset

West
Sussex

East
Sussex

Cornwall

Isle of
Wight

HOME COUNTIES
(South)

SOUTH WEST
ENGLAND

3.1 England

MAP OF NORTHERN ENGLAND

PROFILED SCHOOLS IN NORTHERN ENGLAND

(Incorporating the counties of Cheshire, Cumbria, Derbyshire, Durham, Hartlepool, Lancashire, North East Lincolnshire, North Lincolnshire, Greater Manchester, Merseyside, Middlesbrough, Northumberland, Nottinghamshire, Staffordshire, Stockton-on-Tees, East Riding of Yorkshire, North Yorkshire, South Yorkshire, West Yorkshire)

England

Chetwynde School

Croslands, Rating Lane, Barrow-in-Furness, Cumbria LA13 0NY   Tel: (01229) 824210
Fax: (01229) 871440   E-mail: info@chetwynde.cumbria.sch.uk
Website: www.chetwynde.cumbria.sch.uk   www.gabbitas.co.uk

Head of School Mrs I Nixon
Founded 1938
School status Independent. Co-educational
Day 3–18
Religious denomination Inter-Denominational
Member of SHMIS
Accredited by ISC
Learning difficulties CA WI/DYC DYP DYS
Physical and medical conditions EPI HEA HI
Fees per annum *(day)* £5994–£6996

Chetwynde School occupies an attractive site situated near the Lake District. It has grown into a substantial and successful school with an excellent academic and outstanding sporting reputation.

The school prides itself on high academic standards based on good teaching and individual attention. The GCSE pass rate has been at or above 97 per cent five Grades A–C for over three years and the A level pass rate stands at or above 99 per cent over the same period. All our Sixth Form pupils go on to higher education. The curriculum is broad and challenging, but there is also an emphasis on music, sport and outdoor pursuits including a vibrant Duke of Edinburgh Award Scheme.

Lime House School

Holm Hill, Dalston, Carlisle, Cumbria CA5 7BX   Tel: (01228) 710225   Fax: (01228) 710508
E-mail: lhsoffice@aol.com   Website: www.limehouseschool.co.uk

Headmaster Mr N A Rice MA BA CertEd
Bursar Mrs J Fisher   **Founded** 1809
School status Independent. Co-educational
Boarding and Day 3½–18. Boarders from 9
Member of CReSTeD, IAPS, ISA
Accredited by IAPS, ISA
Learning difficulties CA SC SNU WI/DYP DYS
MLD
No of pupils 201; *(full boarding)* 110; *(weekly boarding)* 4; *(day)* 116; *Girls* 86; *Boys* 115
Fees per annum *(full boarding)* £9000–£16500; *(weekly)* £9000–£16500; *(day)* £3000–£7350

Lime House School is a fully independent co-educational boarding and day school for pupils aged 3½ to 18. Our aim is to ensure that each pupil achieves their potential both academically and socially, with each child treated individually. Our pupils are cared for in a safe rural environment and every possible attempt is made to ensure that they develop confidence and self-esteem.

Boarding is available to all pupils, with the majority being full boarders. Each pupil's pastoral care is the shared responsibility of the residential care team and the pupil's form teacher. Foreign students whose first language is not English add to the cosmopolitan atmosphere of the school. They are prepared for Cambridge English examinations and follow the same curriculum as all other students. Games and sport form an important part of school life. All students participate and a wide range of team and individual sports is offered. Most pupils take games to GCSE level, with many continuing to A level.

We would welcome a visit to our school to see it in action. Simply contact the school and we will arrange a time convenient for you.

Sedbergh School

Sedbergh, Cumbria LA10 5HG   Tel: (015396) 20535   Fax: (015396) 21301
E-mail: hm@sedberghschool.org   Website: www.sedberghschool.org

Headmaster Mr C H Hirst MA (Cantab)
Founded 1525
School status Independent. Co-educational
Boarding and Day 13–18
Religious denomination Church of England
Member of AGBIS, HMC
Learning difficulties SNU WI/DYS
Behavioural and emotional disorders TS/ADD
Physical and medical conditions RA SM/HEA
HI VI
No of pupils 480; *(full boarding)* 465; *(day)* 15;
Sixth Form 200; *Girls* 135; *Boys* 345
Teacher:pupil ratio 1:6 **Ave class size** 12–15
Fees per annum *(full boarding)* £8250

Sedbergh School offers a blend of academic learning and all-round development of the individual through a strong and caring house system and a wide range of extra-curricular activities. It is known for its excellence in sport, art and music, magnificent location and happy atmosphere.

It has faced up to the demands of the 21st century without losing its traditional values and ethos. Almost all pupils are seven-day-a-week boarders in a house system providing pastoral care of the highest standard. There are no formal exeat weekends and over 90 per cent of the pupils will be present on Saturdays and Sundays.

Academic success is taken for granted with most pupils leaving to go on to university or gap year activities. Scholarships and awards are awarded in various disciplines, and bursaries are available for promising individuals who might not otherwise be able to consider the school.

Sedbergh has its own co-educational Junior School which has recently moved back to Sedbergh to sit alongside its parent school.

England

Barlborough Hall School

Barlborough, Chesterfield, Derbyshire S43 4TJ   Tel: (01246) 810511   Fax: (01246) 570605
E-mail: barlborough.hall@virgin.net
Website: www.barlboroughhallschool.co.uk   www.msmcollege.com

Headteacher Mrs W E Parkinson BEd
Founded 1939
School status Co-educational Day 3–11
Religious denomination Roman Catholic
Member of HMC **Accredited by** HMC, ISC
Learning difficulties CA WI/DYP DYS
Physical and medical conditions VI
No of pupils 259; *(day)* 259; *Nursery* 39;
Pre-prep 83; *Prep* 137; *Girls* 138; *Boys* 122
Teacher:pupil ratio 1:12 **Average class size** 15
Fees *Nursery and Pre-prep* £5250; *Prep* £7500
Private music lessons £26 per hour

Barlborough Hall School, preparatory school to Mount St Mary's College, is seen as one of the premier independent Catholic schools in the South Yorkshire/Derbyshire area, welcoming pupils of all denominations.

Set in 300 acres of beautiful surroundings, small classes, well-motivated teachers and exceptional specialist facilities, including a technology centre, science laboratory, art studio, IT suite, theatre and indoor heated pool ensure that our pupils receive the very best educational opportunities.

The school has an excellent nursery provision (from 3 years) in a secure and safe environment.

A regular minibus service and an 'out of school club', with a full range of activities and run by qualified staff until 6pm, ensure the flexibility and peace of mind required by many working parents.

Mount St Mary's College

Spinkhill, Derbyshire S21 3YL   Tel: (01246) 433388   Fax: (01246) 435511
E-mail: info@msmcollege.com   Website: www.msmcollege.com   www.gabbitas.co.uk
Admissions secretary: Mrs Sarah Birks   (01246) 432872

Headmaster Mr L McKell MA, MEd
College status Independent. Co-educational
Boarding and Day 11–18   **Founded** 1842
Religious denomination Roman Catholic
Member of BSA, CIS, HMC, ISCis
Accredited by HMC, ISC
Learning difficulties CA SC SNU WI/DYC DYP
DYS
Behavioural and emotional disorders CA
RA/ADD ADHD ASP AUT
Physical and medical conditions CA IT SM
WA3/EPI HEA HI VI
No of pupils 405; *(full boarding)* 51; *(weekly
boarding)* 18; *(day)* 336; *Sixth Form* 107;
Girls 153; *Boys* 252
Teacher:pupil ratio 1:10 **Average class size** 20
Fees per annum *(full boarding)* £14160–
£18690; *(weekly)* £12000–£16140; *(day)*
£8445–£9780. Private music lessons £26 per
hour EAL lessons £585pa £195 per term

Mount St Mary's College welcomes children of all denominations. In beautiful surroundings close to the M1 junction 30, with minibus services to local areas, the school is also popular with local, national and international boarders. Proudly non-academically selective, the school achieves success for pupils at all levels; value-added scores show that many pupils achieve higher than predicted results.

Emphasis is placed on developing the whole person, with a wide range of extra-curricular activities. Sport, drama and music are particularly strong. The new international standard athletics facility has attracted much interest. The jazz band, several choirs, ensembles and orchestra provide many opportunities for music-making.

Stonyhurst College

Stonyhurst, Clitheroe, Lancashire BB7 9PZ   Tel: (01254) 827073   Fax: (01254) 827135
E-mail: admissions@stonyhurst.ac.uk   Website: www.stonyhurst.ac.uk

Headmaster Mr A R Johnson BA
Founded 1593
College status Independent. Co-educational
Boarding and Day 13–18. Boarders from 13
Religious denomination Roman Catholic
Member of BSA, CASE, HMC, ISBA, SATIPS
Accredited by HMC, ISC
Learning difficulties SNU WI/DYC DYP DYS
MLD
Behavioural and emotional disorders CO
ST/ADD ADHD ASP
Physical and medical conditions SM WA3/EPI
HEA HI
No of pupils 185; *(full boarding)* 242; *(weekly boarding)* 50; *(day)* 171; *Senior* 248; *Sixth Form* 217; *Girls* 154; *Boys* 309
Teacher:pupil ratio 1:8
Fees per annum *(full boarding)* £24192; *(weekly)* £20700; *(day)* £14142

We attach particular importance to emotional and spiritual development as well as academic excellence. In addition to young Catholics, we have young people here who belong to other Christian traditions, and other faiths, and we encourage all of them to play a full part in the spiritual life of the school. At the heart of the Jesuit educational philosophy is knowing each individual pupil in our care so we can help them to achieve their full potential in all that they do.

St Mary's Hall

Stonyhurst, Lancashire BB7 9PU   Tel: (01254) 826242   Fax: (01254) 827316
E-mail: t.ashton@stonyhurst.ac.uk   Website: www.stonyhurst.ac.uk

Headmaster Mr L A Crouch BA, MA, PGCE
Founded 1946
School status Independent. Co-educational
Boarding and Day 3–13. Flexi-boarding
available. Boarders from 7
Religious denomination Roman Catholic
Member of IAPS, ISBA, SATIPS
Accredited by IAPS, ISC
Learning difficulties CA SNU WI/DYP DYS
Behavioural and emotional disorders CO/ADD
Physical and medical conditions RA
No of pupils 269; *(full boarding)* 43; *(weekly boarding)* 9; *(day)* 217; *Nursery* 16; *Pre-prep* 27; *Prep* 226; *Girls* 112; *Boys* 157
Teacher:pupil ratio 1:9
Average class size 17
Fees per annum *(full boarding)* £17049; *(weekly)* £14997; *(day)* £5934–£11832

Stonyhurst St Mary's Hall is a Roman Catholic school in the Jesuit Charism providing co-education for boarders and day pupils between the ages of 3–13 and offering a warm welcome to Christians of other denominations. As a result of its close ties with Stonyhurst College, which was founded in 1593 and is one of the oldest Jesuit colleges in the world, St Mary's Hall is part of a stimulating and well-proven educational tradition. Set in the beautiful Stonyhurst estate in rural Lancashire, the school has outstanding facilities for teaching, sports and cultural activities.

England

Abbotsholme School

Rocester, Uttoxeter, Staffordshire ST14 5BS   Tel: (01889) 590217   Fax: (01889) 591001
E-mail: admissions@abbotsholme.co.uk   Website: www.abbotsholme.com

The Headmaster Mr S Fairclough MSc
Deputy Head Mrs D H Wainwright BA
School status Independent. Co-educational
Boarding and Day 5–18   **Founded** 1889
Religious denomination Inter-Denominational
Member of BHS, BSA, ISCis, Round Square,
SHMIS **Learning difficulties** WI/DYS
No of pupils 318; *(full boarding)* 55; *(weekly boarding)* 76; *Pre-prep* 9; *Prep* 62; *Senior* 194;
Sixth Form 69; *Girls* 122; *Boys* 196
Teacher:pupil ratio 1:15 **Average class size** 15
Fees per annum *(full boarding)* £20700–
£24000; *(weekly)* £15900–£20100; *(day)*
£8850–£16350

Abbotsholme is a small school set in a 140-acre estate.

With just over 320 pupils, class sizes are deliberately kept small and the school caters for a broad ability range maintaining high academic standards.

Great emphasis is placed on providing an educational experience beyond the classroom, which is achieved in a number of areas:

- In the boarding environment, with flexible boarding options providing small houses with excellent pastoral care and a full programme of weekend activities.
- In the arts, through involvement in theatre work, music and the visual arts.
- In the outdoor world, through involvement in an extensive programme of outdoor education, which has taken pupils and staff on adventures all over the world.
- In the natural world through involvement with the working farm, BHS-Approved Equestrian Centre and conservation activities throughout the estate.
- In the world of technology, with activities in CDT, engineering, cookery and life skills.

Aysgarth Preparatory School

Newton-Le-Willows, Bedale, North Yorkshire DL8 1TF   Tel: (01677) 450240   Fax: (01677) 450736
E-mail: lfoster@aysgarthschool.co.uk   Website: www.aysgarthschool.com

Head Mr C A A Goddard
School status Independent. Boys Boarding 3–13 (Co-ed day 3–8). Flexi-boarding available. Boarders from 8
Religious denomination Church of England
Learning difficulties CA SNU WI/DYC DYP DYS
Behavioural and emotional disorders RA/ADD
Physical and medical conditions CA RA SM TW WA3/HEA HI
No of pupils 178; *(full boarding)* 89; *(weekly/day)* 35; *Girls* 19; *Boys* 159
Fees per annum *(full boarding)* £17670; *(weekly)* £17670; *(day)* £14850

Where boys can be boys!

Aysgarth School set in the foothills of the Yorkshire Dales is the only all-boys boarding and day prep school in the North of England. It is one of the leading preparatory schools in the country and in the North has an unmatched record of sending boys to Eton, Harrow, Radley, Shrewsbury, Stowe, Uppingham and Winchester as well as Ampleforth and Sedbergh closer by. Staff at Aysgarth are passionate about the benefits that boarding provides. Boys are introduced to a wide range of opportunities and become happy, confident, courteous and independent – well prepared to move on to their chosen public school.

Outstanding early years education for both boys and girls aged 3–8 is also provided in the Pre-prep and Nursery.

England

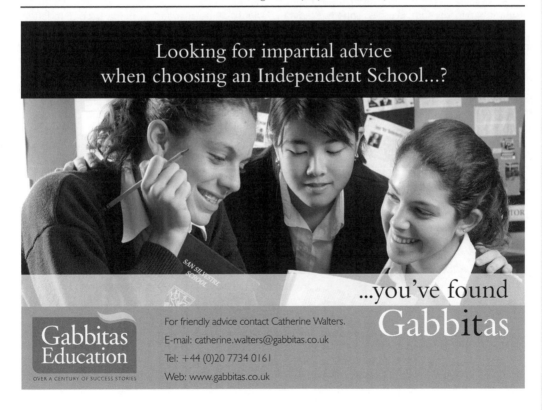

Queen Ethelburga's College

Thorpe Underwood Hall, Ouseburn, York, North Yorkshire YO26 9SS
Tel: (01423) 333330   Fax: (01423) 331444
E-mail: remember@compuserve.com
Website: www.queenethelburgas.edu   www.gabbitas.co.uk

Headmaster Mr S Jandrell BA
Provost Mr Brian Martin
Founded 1912
College status Co-educational Boarding and
Day 2–20. Boarders from 6
Religious denomination Church of England
Member of BHS, BSA
Accredited by British Council, ISA, ISC
Learning difficulties RA/DYS
No of pupils 766; *(full boarding)* 448; *(day)*
268; *Nursery* 14; *Pre-prep* 12; *Prep* 130; *Senior*
351; *Sixth Form* 261; *Girls* 404; *Boys* 362
Teacher:pupil ratio 1:10
Average class size 20
Fees per annum *(full boarding)* £18735–
£31005; *(weekly)* £22485–£31005; *(day)*
£4185–£9225

Broad-based curriculum following National Curriculum in key subject areas. Entry to Preparatory School by assessment and interview. Students move through to Senior School. External entry to Senior School is by test, reports and interview. Senior students are prepared for GCSE, A Levels, IB and advanced vocational courses including fashion and design, photography and business, as well as BTEC National Diploma in horse studies and BHSAI for riders. Recent heavy investment has been made in living accommodation, the equestrian centre, business and computing suite, cookery area, purpose-built laboratories and lecture theatre. There is a large programme of sport and extra activities. Scholarships for academic excellence and riding competence are available.

MAP OF EASTERN ENGLAND

PROFILED SCHOOLS IN EASTERN ENGLAND

(Incorporating the counties of Cambridgeshire, Leicestershire, Lincolnshire, Norfolk, Northamptonshire, Suffolk)

England

Cambridge Centre for Sixth-form Studies

1 Salisbury Villas, Station Road, Cambridge, Cambridgeshire CB1 2JF   Tel: (01223) 716890
Fax: (01223) 517530   E-mail: enquiries@ccss.co.uk   Website: www.ccss.co.uk   www.ccss.co.uk

The Principal Mr N Roskilly BA, PGCE, FRSA, FRGS   **Founded** 1981
School status Independent Sixth Form College
Religious denomination Non-Denominational
Member of CIFE, ISA, ISCis
Accredited by ISA, ISC Registered charity.
Member of the European Council of
International Schools (ECIS)
Learning difficulties CA WI/DYP DYS MLD SP&LD
Behavioural and emotional disorders CA CO TS/ADD ADHD ASP AUT
Physical and medical conditions RA SM/HEA
No of pupils 200; *(full boarding)* 116; *(weekly boarding)* 4; *(day)* 109; *Sixth Form* 200; *Girls* 87; *Boys* 113
Fees per annum *(full boarding)* £15762–£26091; *(day)* £6285–£16614

Cambridge Centre for Sixth-form Studies (CCSS) is a co-educational college offering GCSE and A level courses to 200 students, supported by 90 staff. The college provides close academic supervision, a friendly, informal atmosphere and high levels of pastoral care. One-to-one private tutorials are an important and unique part of all A level courses on top of group lessons. The small class sizes allow plenty of opportunity for individual involvement and for developing each student's level of understanding. A full and flexible GCSE curriculum is offered and at A level there are over 36 subjects to choose from.

CCSS is based in the exciting university town of Cambridge, close to the railway station and 50-minutes' train-ride from London, with easy connections to international airports.

CATS Cambridge

13–14 Round Church Street, Cambridge, Cambridgeshire CB5 8AD
Tel: (01223) 314431   Fax: (01223) 467773
E-mail: enquiries@catscambridge.com   Website: www.catscambridge.com   www.ceg-uk.com

Principal Dr G Hawkins BSc, PhD, MBS
Director of Studies Mr A Sweatman BSc Pure Mathematics
Registrar Mrs J Mullan   **Founded** 1985
School status Independent Sixth Form College. Co-educational Boarding and Day 14–19. Boarders from 14
Religious denomination Non-Denominational
Member of ISA
Accredited by BAC, ISA ISIS Member
No of pupils 312; *(full boarding)* 279; *(day)* 33; *Girls* 131; *Boys* 181
Teacher:pupil ratio 1:3 **Average class size** 6
Fees per annum *(full boarding)* £20850–£32625; *(day)* £15000–£23475

CATS Cambridge is a leading Sixth Form college, located in the centre of Cambridge, set up to help students' focus on success and seize opportunity. Ambition is encouraged, potential is recognized and students are given the opportunity to stretch their abilities in an atmosphere that is dynamic yet safe and supportive.

Established in 1982, the college houses around 300 students from around the world studying A levels, GCSE, university foundation and Academic English Language programmes. Our student success rate is high. In 2008 73 per cent of students achieved A–C grades at A level – 40 per cent above the national average – before departing for University destinations including London School of Economics, Manchester University, Queen Mary's and Edinburgh.

The Leys School

Trumpington Road, Cambridge, Cambridgeshire CB2 7AD Tel: (01223) 508900 Fax: (01223) 505303
E-mail: office@theleys.net   Website: www.theleys.net

Headmaster Mr Mark Slater MA
Founded 1875
School status Co-educational Boarding and
Day 11–18
Religious denomination Inter-Denominational,
Methodist   **Member of** HMC
Accredited by British Council, HMC
Learning difficulties DYS
Behavioural and emotional disorders RA/ADD
ADHD
Physical and medical conditions RA/HI
No of pupils 526; *(full boarding)* 280; *Girls* 202;
Boys 324
Teacher:pupil ratio 1:9 **Ave class size** 1–20
Fees per annum *(full boarding)* £17250–
£23940; *(day)* £11145–£15630

Made famous by the novel *Goodbye Mr Chips*
the author James Hilton was an old boy of the
school, which has kept true to its original ethos
and values with pastoral care a major selling
point. Current day Leys pupils enjoy a myriad of
extra curricular activities, the finest sports facilities and coaches, music in the state-of-the-art
music school and drama that is the envy of most
– life at the school is full. The Leys is primarily a
boarding school and Headmaster Mark Slater
places great importance on providing a caring,
friendly and secure environment for all its pupils.

The Leys is one of East Anglia's finest co-educational Boarding and Day Schools for 11–18-year-
olds, situated in the thriving hub that is Cambridge, in a 50 acre campus.

Peterborough High School

Thorpe Road, Peterborough, Cambridgeshire PE3 6JF   Tel: (01733) 343357   Fax: (01733) 355710
E-mail: phs@peterboroughhigh.co.uk   Website: www.peterboroughhigh.co.uk
Peterborough's only independent day and boarding school

Headmaster Mr A D Meadows BSc (Hons),
NPQH   **Founded** 1895
School status Independent. Girls Day and
Boarding 3–18 (Boys 3–11). Flexi-boarding
available. Boarders from 8
Religious denomination Church of England,
Inter-Denominational
Member of GSA, Woodard Schools
Accredited by GSA, ISC
Learning difficulties DYS
Behavioural and emotional disorders CO
No of pupils 355; *(full boarding)* 16; *(weekly
boarding)* 14; *Prep* 160; *Senior* 180; *Sixth
Form* 40; *Girls* 285; *Boys* 70
Teacher:pupil ratio 1:15 **Average class size** 15
Fees per annum *(full boarding)* £17909–
£19371; *(weekly)* £15756–£16719; *(day)*
£7428–£10491

Peterborough   High
School has an excellent
academic reputation,
combining traditional
high expectations with
modern methods, instil-
ling independent study
habits and bringing top
results.

The Preparatory department provides a broad
and balanced curriculum to meet the needs of
each boy and girl. The key characteristics which
are developed in our children are pride, courtesy,
self-esteem and the will to achieve and take on
further challenges.

The Senior School, for girls only, is distinguished by its small class sizes, which provide
excellent individual attention for academic and
social development.

England

St Mary's School

Bateman Street, Cambridge, Cambridgeshire CB2 1LY   Tel: (01223) 353253   Fax: (01223) 357451
E-mail: enquiries@stmaryscambridge.co.uk   Website: www.stmaryscambridge.co.uk
www.gabbitas.co.uk   St Mary's Junior School   Tel: 01223 311666   Fax: 01223 472168

Headmistress Miss C Avery MA (Oxon)
Headmistress (Junior School) Mrs Deirdre
O'Sullivan   **Founded** 1898
School status Independent. Girls Day and
Boarding 4–18. Boarders from 13
Religious denomination Roman Catholic
Member of GSA **Accredited by** GSA
Learning difficulties RA WI/DYP DYS MLD
Behavioural and emotional disorders RA/
ADHD ASP
Physical and medical conditions AT CA IT SM
TW WA2/EPI HEA HI IM VI
No of pupils *(full boarding)* 53; *(weekly
boarding)* 7; *(day)* 609   **Average class size** 20
in Senior School, fewer in Sixth Form
Fees per annum *(full boarding)* £23310;
(weekly) £20475; *(day)* £11625. The above are
fees for Senior School.

St Mary's is a purposeful and happy school.

Founded in 1898, we provide an all-round education in a welcoming Christian community that
encourages all girls to reach their full potential.
We are situated in the centre of the beautiful
university city of Cambridge, close to the railway
station, 50 miles from London and within easy
reach of four major airports. Both St Mary's Senior
and Junior Schools offer an excellent academic
education and a strong tradition of superlative
pastoral care. In the Senior School, there is a lively
programme of extra-curricular activities: rowing,
yoga and a thriving Duke of Edinburgh's Award
Scheme.

Brooke House College

Leicester Road, Market Harborough, Leicestershire LE16 7AU Tel: (01858) 462452 Fax: (01858) 462487
E-mail: enquiries@brookehouse.com   Website: www.brookehouse.com   www.gabbitas.co.uk

Director Mr G E I Williams MA (Oxon)
Director of Studies Mr J Fuller BA, PGCE
Founded 1967
College status Independent. Co-educational
Boarding and Day 14–19. Flexi-boarding
available. Boarders from 14 International
Religious denomination Non-Denominational
Member of CIFE **Accredited by** BAC
Learning difficulties CA SC WI/DYC DYS MLD
Physical and medical conditions RA
No of pupils 180; *(full boarding)* 175; *(day)* 5;
Senior 30; *Sixth Form* 150; *Girls* 80; *Boys* 100
Teacher:pupil ratio 1:5 **Average class size** 1:8
Fees per annum *(full boarding)* £19350;
(weekly) £10900; *(day)* £10900

Situated in the heart of rural England in the historic town of Market Harborough, Brooke House is a fully residential, international college, offering GCSE, A level and pre-university foundation courses in intensive, small classes. The college possesses excellent academic facilities including science laboratories, an art and design studio and two recently developed IT suites. The academic and social welfare of students is paramount and is safeguarded by a system of personal tutors and by a secure and friendly learning environment. The college's full-time Universities Admissions Adviser gives advice and guidance, and Brooke House has an enviable tradition of assisting international and UK students to gain places at the most prestigious of universities in the UK and the USA.

Ratcliffe College

Fosse Way, Ratcliffe on the Wreake, Leicester, Leicestershire LE7 4SG   Tel: (01509) 817000
Fax: (01509) 817004   E-mail: registrar@ratcliffe.leics.sch.uk   Website: www.ratcliffecollege.com

Headmaster Mr G Lloyd MA
College status Independent. Co-educational
Day and Boarding 3–18. Flexi-boarding
available. Boarders from age 10
Religious denomination Roman Catholic
Learning difficulties SNU/DYC DYP DYS
SP&LD
Behavioural & emotional disorders AT RA SM W
No of pupils 677; *(full boarding)* 94; *(weekly boarding)* 1; *(day)* 583; *Nursery* 32; *Prep* 136;
Senior 353; *Sixth Form* 156; *Girls* 289;
Boys 388 **Average class size** 17 (Junior Dept);
21 (Senior School); smaller in Sixth Form
Fees per annum *(full boarding)* £18846;
(weekly) £15198; *(day)* £6690–£12498

Ratcliffe College offers a balanced all-round day and boarding education to boys and girls aged 3–18 on a superb 100-acre campus; there are good class sizes, well-resourced classrooms, high academic standards, excellent pastoral care, full extra-curricular programme and extended school day. While it is a Catholic school, Ratcliffe welcomes children from other denominations.

In the Senior School (11–18-year-olds) a broad and balanced curriculum is offered, with most students taking 9 or 10 GCSEs, while also being encouraged to participate fully in extra-curricular activities. In the Sixth Form, students study three or four A level courses, from a list of 21 subjects available. A state-of-the-art Sixth Form Centre opened in January 2007 and is proving an outstanding resource, offering Sixth Formers the combination of an extensively resourced private study area, together with a social area that provides an informal, relaxed setting for breaks and lunchtime. In the Junior Department, (5–11-year-olds), as well as the core subjects, children also learn French and subjects like PE, music, history and geography are emphasized. The Nursery School (3–5-year-olds) is situated in a purpose-built secure building with excellent facilities.

England

Lincoln Minster School

Upper Lindunn Street, Lincoln, Lincolnshire LN2 5RW   Tel: (01552) 551300   Fax: (01522) 551310
E-mail: enquiries.lincoln@church-schools.com   Website: www.lincolnminster.co.uk

Headmaster Mr Clive Rickart BA (Hons), PGCE
School status Independent. Co-educations day and boarding 2–18
Religious denomination Church of England
Member of IAPS, SHMIS
Accredited by IAPS, ISC, UCST
Learning difficulties CA SNU/DYC DYP DYS
Behavioural and emotional disorders RA/ADD ADHD ASD ASP
Physical and medical conditions CA/CP RM SM TW WA2
No of pupils 802
Fees per annum *(full boarding)* £16266–£18867; *(weekly)* £15075–£17457; *(day)* £6834–£9969. Second sibling 5% discount

- Small class sizes with specialist teaching across the curriculum.
- New £10 million Music School, Recital Hall and Sports Hall under construction (opening 2010).
- Cutting edge interactive technology in all classrooms.
- Exceptionally well balanced / nutritional catering.
- Full and weekly boarding.
- Excellent transport links – daily buses across the county and beyond.

Bosworth Independent College

Nazareth House, Barrack Road, Northampton, Northamptonshire NN2 6AF   Tel: (01604) 235090
Fax: (01604) 239996   E-mail: info@bosworthcollege.com   Website: www.bosworthcollege.com

The Principal Mr M McQuin MEd
College status Independent. Co-educational
Boarding and Day 14–21   **Founded** 1977
Member of CIFE **Accredited by** BAC
Learning difficulties WI/DYS
Behavioural and emotional disorders RA
Physical and medical conditions RA SM TW
WA2/HEA
No of pupils 320; *(full boarding)* 240; *(weekly*
boarding) 3; *(day)* 77; *Girls* 150; *Boys* 170
Teacher:pupil ratio 1:7 **Average class size** 6–8
Fees per annum *(full boarding)* £19500;
(weekly) £18600; *(day)* £10600–£13600

'A tradition of hard work, integrity and youthful ambition.'

Bosworth Independent College was established in 1977 and is now considered to be one of the leading independent schools in the UK. With 320 students representing over 25 nationalities it is also one of the most diverse.

Over the past three years our A level programme has achieved a 100 per cent pass rate and students have entered well known universities: Cambridge, LSE, UCL, Warwick.

The combination of small classes, study hall sessions and a heightened sense of responsibility empowers each student to work hard to achieve the top grades.

Laxton Junior School

East Road, Oundle, Nr Peterborough, Northamptonshire PE8 4BX
Tel: (01832) 277275   Fax: (01832) 277271
E-mail: admissions@laxtonjunior.org.uk   Website: www.laxtonjunior.org.uk   www.gabbitas.co.uk

Head Mr M J Potter BEd (Hons) (Liverpool)
Deputy Head Miss J R Bass BA (Hons) (Wales)
Dir of Curriculum Mr D M Worthington BEd
(Hons) (York)   **Founded** 1973
School status Independent. Co-educational
Day 4–11
Religious denomination Church of England
Member of IAPS **Accredited by** IAPS
Learning difficulties SNU WI/DYP DYS MLD
Physical and medical conditions CA TW WA1
No of pupils 255; *(day)* 255; *Pre-prep* 102; *Prep*
153; *Girls* 131; *Boys* 124
Average class size Max 20
Fees per annum *(day)* £8160–£8955. Cooked
lunch and most extra curricular clubs included
in fees

located in the picturesque market town of Oundle, Northamptonshire. The school offers a broad and well-balanced curriculum where children are encouraged to fulfil their potential in a happy and secure environment, supported by a dedicated team of professionals.

Through the academic curriculum and caring pastoral system, the school aims to lay solid foundations in the development of well-motivated, confident and happy individuals who are always willing to give of their best on the road to high achievement.

Founded in 1973, Laxton Junior School is a co-educational day school for 4–11-year-olds. Since 2002 housed in new, purpose-built premises

Alexanders International School

Bawdsey Manor, Bawdsey, Woodbridge, Suffolk IP12 3AZ Tel: (01394) 411633 Fax: (01394) 411357
E-mail: office@alexandersschool.com   Website: www.skola.co.uk

Head Mr A Laidlaw
School status Independent. Co-educational
Boarding 11–17
Religious denomination Inter-Denominational
Learning difficulties WI
No of pupils 40; *(full boarding)* 40; *Girls* 20;
Boys 20

Alexanders International School (AIS) is a founder member of the SKOLA Group of Schools established over 30 years ago and comprising five British Council accredited centres. AIS is situated on a 120-acre campus on the Suffolk coast which has student residences, classrooms, sports and recreational facilities and our own watersports centre.

Boarding School Foundation Course: This one-year course prepares students who wish to enter a UK boarding school but students may join at any time of the year. As we are wholly independent we can advise and support students in their applications for their chosen school. AIS students have gone on to schools such as Lancing College, Roedean School, Merchiston Castle School and Wellington College.

English language classes at all levels, from beginners to advanced, run throughout the academic year. I/GCSEs in English language, maths, art, business studies and IT are available as well as GCSE combined science. Students can be entered for UCLES examinations (KET, PET, FCE and IELTS) or I/GCSE English Language.

Culford School

Bury St Edmunds, Suffolk IP28 6TX   Tel: (01284) 728615   Fax: (01284) 729146
E-mail: admissions@culford.co.uk   Website: www.culford.co.uk

Headmaster Mr J F Johnson-Munday MA, MBA
Registrar Mrs K Tompkinson   **Founded** 1881
School status Independent. Co-educational
Boarding and Day 3–18. Flexi-boarding
available. Boarders from 7
Religious denomination Methodist
Member of AGBIS, HMC, IAPS
Accredited by HMC, IAPS
Learning difficulties WI/DYC DYP DYS
Physical and medical conditions RA/EPI HEA HI
No of pupils 652; *(full boarding)* 192; *(day)*
460; *Nursery* 19; *Pre-prep* 56; *Prep* 234; *Senior*
343; *Sixth Form* 139; *Girls* 295; *Boys* 357
Teacher:pupil ratio 1:9 **Average class size** 18
Fees per annum *(boarding)* £16380–£22800;
(day) £6900–£14520

academic facilities and aims to educate the whole person. We offer a rich after-school and weekend activities programme including art, music and drama through to the Combined Cadet Force and the Duke of Edinburgh's Award Scheme.

Academic facilities include new ICT suites;

Culford is set in 480 acres of beautiful Suffolk parkland, located 40 minutes from Cambridge and 90 minutes from London. Culford is a friendly, caring school with superb sporting and a dedicated centre for art and design technology; and superb facilities in the William Miller Science Centre. Music and drama are well catered for in the new studio theatre and redevelopment of the Music School in Culford Hall. The sports centre boasts impressive facilities including an indoor climbing wall, 25 metre pool and a new championship standard indoor tennis centre.

Framlingham College

Framlingham College (13–18): Framlingham, Woodbridge, Suffolk IP13 9EY   Tel: (01728) 723789
Fax: (01728) 724546   E-mail: admissions@framcollege.co.uk
Brandeston Hall (2½–13): Brandeston, Woodbridge, Suffolk IP13 7AH   Tel: (01728) 685331
Fax: (01728) 685437 E-mail: office@brandestonhall.co.uk Website: www.framlingham.suffolk.sch.uk

The Headteacher Mrs G M Randall
College status Independent. Co-educational
Boarding and Day 2½–18. Flexi-boarding
available
Religious denomination Church of England
Member of HMC, IAPS, SHMIS
Accredited by HMC, IAPS
Learning difficulties DYC DYP DYS
Physical and medical conditions SM TW W
No of pupils 680; *(full boarding)* 292; *(day)*
388; *Girls* 278; *Boys* 402
Fees per annum *(full boarding)* £20691;
(weekly) £20691; *(day)* £13299

Framlingham College is a centre of all-round
excellence, providing co-educational boarding
and day schooling from 2½–18. It enjoys a

magnificent rural situation, looking across to the
12th-century Framlingham Castle, and is within
easy striking distance of Ipswich, Cambridge,
Colchester and Norwich. The college grounds
and facilities are extensive; the latest addition is
a state-of-the-art specialist theatre and music
facility, which was opened in November 2006.
The exceptional facilities create a lively academic, cultural and social environment in which
pupils are encouraged to be industrious and ambitious and where all can take full advantage of the
rich mix of extra-curricular activities on offer. At
Framlingham we believe that the academic
potential of the individual is unlocked in an
environment where opportunities abound and in
which a firm sense of community prevails.

The Royal Hospital School

Holbrook, Ipswich, Suffolk IP9 2RX   Tel: (01473) 326200   Fax: (01473) 326213
E-mail: admissions@royalhospitalschool.org   Website: www.royalhospitalschool.org
Admissions Officer Sue Toner 01473 326210

Headmaster Mr H W Blackett MA (Oxon)
Deputy Headmaster Mr I S Wilmshurst MA
Chaplain Rev Dr CE Stewart BSc, BD, MTh
Founded 1715
School status Independent. Co-educational
Boarding and Day 11–18
Religious denomination Christian
Member of SHMIS **Accredited by** HMC, ISC,
SHMIS. The School is owned by the Crown
Charity, Greenwich Hospital
Learning difficulties SNU WI/DYP DYS MLD
Behavioural and emotional disorders CO RA
Physical and medical conditions RA SM
WA2/EPI HEA
No of pupils 668; *(full boarding)* 604; *(day)* 64;
Senior 668; *Sixth Form* 205; *Girls* 288;
Boys 380
Teacher:pupil ratio 1:8 **Average class size** 16
Fees per annum *(full boarding)* £19668; *(day)*
£10521. Seafarer Bursaries, academic, sport,

music, sailing and art scholarships and Special
Forces rates are available

As well as being encouraged to nurture academic
excellence, every pupil at the school has the
opportunity to pursue a huge range of interests,
to discover new passions and develop values that
will last for life.

Supported by high-quality enthusiastic teaching, excellent resources and dedicated tutorial
support, pupils are encouraged to aim high, attain
their personal best and most importantly to enjoy
achieving it.

MAP OF CENTRAL ENGLAND

PROFILED SCHOOLS IN CENTRAL ENGLAND

(Incorporating the counties of Gloucestershire, Herefordshire, Oxfordshire, West Midlands, Shropshire, Warwickshire, Worcestershire)

Map
Number

Page
Number

England

Airthrie School

27–29 Christchurch Road, Cheltenham, Gloucestershire GL50 2NY
Tel: (01242) 512837   Fax: (01242) 579583
E-mail: mail@airthrie-school.co.uk   Website: www.airthrie-school.co.uk

Principal Mrs A E Sullivan Dip Ed
School status Co-educational Day 3–11
Religious denomination Church of England
Learning difficulties CA SNU DYP DYS
Physical and medical conditions HEA HI VI
No of pupils 166; *(day)* 162; *Nursery* 17;
Pre-prep 56; *Prep* 93; *Girls* 86; *Boys* 80
Teacher:pupil ratio Average 1:5
Average class size 15
Fees per annum *(day)* £4935–£6894

Airthrie is a long-established school with an out-standing reputation for high academic standards and successful entry to a wide spectrum of senior schools including grammar and independent. It has achieved excellent Ofsted reports – 'Everyone at the school works together to create a warm family atmosphere ... The teaching is effective and pupils make very good progress'.

Highly committed teachers work with small groups enabling pupils to enjoy much individual instruction. A full range of sports and swimming is pursued at The Cheltenham Ladies' College Sports Complex. Music, French and drama are taught throughout the whole age range enhancing a full academic curriculum.

Each child is valued for their unique talents, and is encouraged to work hard and join in all aspects of the 'family' community.

Dean Close Preparatory School

Lansdown Road, Cheltenham, Gloucestershire GL51 6QS Tel: (01242) 512217 Fax: (01242) 258005
E-mail: dcpsoffice@deanclose.org.uk   Website: www.deanclose.org.uk   www.gabbitas.co.uk

Headmaster Rev L Browne MA
Founded 1886
School status Independent. Co-educational
Boarding and Day 2–13. Flexi-boarding
available. Boarders from 7
Religious denomination Church of England
Member of IAPS **Accredited by** IAPS
Learning difficulties SNU/DYC DYP DYS MLD
Behavioural and emotional disorders CA/
ADHD
No of pupils 428; *(full boarding)* 60; *(day)* 225;
Nursery 24; *Pre-prep* 121; *Prep* 285; *Senior*
270; *Sixth Form* 226; *Girls* 208; *Boys* 220
Teacher:pupil ratio 1:8
Average class size 15
Fees per annum *(full boarding)* £14610–
£18495; *(day)* £8760–£12930

Chorister scholarships
to join the Tewkesbury
Abbey Schola Cantorum
of Dean Close Prep
School are available for
boys aged 7–11. Aca-
demic and music
scholarships and exhibi-
tions, and sports awards
are offered at 11+.

There are three board-
ing houses run by house-
parents. The number of day boarders in each
house is limited to ensure a large full-time boarding community. There are also three day houses
offering pastoral care of the highest order. The
school has outstanding facilities including a
swimming pool, climbing wall, shooting range

Dean Close Preparatory School is a Christian
family school committed to the development of
the individual child in all aspects of education.

and two theatres. A new sports complex with
extensive hall, dance studio and gym has also just
been opened.

Dean Close School

Shelburne Road, Cheltenham, Gloucestershire GL51 6HE Tel: (01242) 258044 Fax: (01242) 258003
E-mail: registrar@deanclose.org.uk   Website: www.deanclose.org.uk   www.gabbitas.co.uk

Acting Head Jonathan Lancashire MA, FCA
Founded 1886
School status Independent. Co-educational
Boarding and Day 13–18. Boarders from 8
Religious denomination Christian
Member of HMC
Accredited by HMC HMC
Learning difficulties WI/DYC DYP DYS
Behavioural and emotional disorders RA/ADD
ADHD ASP
Physical and medical conditions RA SM
No of pupils 492; *(full boarding)* 289; *(day)*
203; *Pre-prep* 112; *Prep* 300; *Senior* 273; *Sixth
Form* 219; *Girls* 207; *Boys* 285
Teacher:pupil ratio 1:9
Fees per annum *(full boarding)* £26160; *(day)*
£18480

Dean Close is truly co-educational, with almost
40 years experience and almost equal numbers of
girls and boys. The school aims to broaden the

opportunities of each and every pupil through an
exceptional array of facilities and coaching in
sport, music, theatre and art, and offers a huge
number of extra-curricular clubs and societies.
Facilities include a recent £3 million sports hall,
a 25-metre indoor pool, two astro-turf pitches, an
impressive 550-seat theatre, a purpose-built arts
centre and a music school. A level results in 2008
generated over 75 per cent of passes at grade A or
B, and at GCSE 52 per cent achieved A* or A.

England

Wycliffe

Bath Road, Stonehouse, Gloucestershire GL10 2JQ
Tel: (01453) 822432   Fax: (01453) 827634
E-mail: senior@wycliffe.co.uk
Website: www.wycliffe.co.uk www.gabbitas.co.uk, www.crested.org.uk

Head Mrs M E Burnet Ward MA (Hons)
Head of Preparatory School Mr A Palmer BEd
Founded 1882
School status Independent. Co-educational
Boarding and Day 2–18. Flexi-boarding
available.
Religious denomination Inter-Denominational
Member of CReSTeD, GSA, HMC, IAPS, ISBA,
NACE, SHA
Accredited by GSA, HMC, IAPS
Learning difficulties SNU WI/DYC DYP DYS
Behavioural and emotional disorders TOU
Physical and medical conditions RA
No of pupils 419; *(full boarding)* 233; *(day)*
186; *Girls* 141; *Boys* 278
No of pupils 773; *(full boarding)* 304; *(day)*
469; *Girls* 181; *Boys* 288; *Nursery* 75
Teacher:pupil ratio 1:7 **Average class size** 12
Fees per annum *(boarding)* £13230–£23520;
(day) £5160–£15465. Development year (pre-
A level year) £28335

Wycliffe is a thriving day, boarding and flexi-boarding school set conveniently within the heart of the Cotswolds. The school has excellent links to London both by road and rail, is close to the amenities offered in Cheltenham, Bristol and Bath, making Wycliffe an ideal destination for students who want all the advantages of a contemporary environment without the distractions of studying in a large city.

The school is committed to fostering individual learning in all areas of the curriculum and pupils benefit from small class sizes with a high teacher to pupil ratio. One of Wycliffe's aims is to cultivate each pupil's unique talents and bring out the best in its pupils by creating a supportive learning environment which promotes individual achievements in all fields. Specialist teachers ensure outstanding teaching delivery across the curriculum and a wide variety of co-curricular activities enables the school to offer a fully-rounded education designed to develop confidence and self-esteem.

Academic excellence is something pupils are encouraged to attain and the fact that some of our pupils have been registered with the National Programme for Gifted and Talented in Education, attests to the high-achieving nature of many of our students and the school's ability to nurture this. Wycliffe recently became the only school in the UK to win the NACE Challenge Award for Excellence in teaching the gifted and talented across every one of the six stages of education – from pre-prep to A level, and is the first independent school in the country to collect this award.

For the sixth year in succession, the pass rate at A level was 100 per cent, with over 60 per cent of our pupils achieving A to B grades over the same period. Wycliffe is not academically selective yet the GCSE pass rate is also high, with 90 per cent of pupils gaining A* to C grades. There are over 27 subjects available at AS level including theatre studies, media studies, travel and tourism, psychology and Japanese.

Wycliffe is very experienced in the education of pupils of UK parents living overseas. We offer a very high standard of pastoral care, excellent weekend activities with organized trips to the theatre, Drayton Manor Theme Park, ice skating and when warmer, barbeques on the campus or picnics at Stratford Park.

Cokethorpe School

Witney, Oxfordshire OX29 7PU   Tel: (01993) 703921   Fax: (01993) 773499
E-mail: admissions@cokethorpe.org   Website: www.cokethorpe.org.uk   www.gabbitas.co.uk

Headmaster Mr D J Ettinger BA, MA, PGCE
Registrar Mrs L M Berry BA
Admissions Secretary Ms C Bowerman
Founded 1957
School status Independent. Co-educational
Day 4–18
Religious denomination Inter-Denominational
Member of AGBIS, ISBA, SHMIS
Learning difficulties SNU/DYS MLD
Physical and medical conditions AT RA TW/EPI
HEA HI VI
No of pupils 660; *(day)* 660; *Pre-prep* 20; *Prep*
110; *Senior* 390; *Sixth Form* 140; *Girls* 250;
Boys 410
Teacher:pupil ratio 1:10 **Average class size** 17
Fees per annum *(day)* £9285–£13485

Set in 150 acres of stunningly beautiful Oxford-shire parkland just south of Witney, Cokethorpe offers a broad and exciting education to girls and boys aged from 4 to 18. A network of buses brings pupils from a wide area, classes are small and there is an unparalleled range of extra-curricular activities. Expectations and aspirations are high, with many academic, sporting and other achievements at local and national level, as well as Oxbridge success and value added scores among the very best in the country, which have established Cokethorpe among the best independent schools in the area. Its growing reputation reflects the inspirational teaching, safe and tranquil environment, recent results and dynamic leadership.

d'Overbroeck's College

The Swan Building, 111 Banbury Road, Oxford, Oxfordshire OX2 6JX   Tel: (01865) 310000
Fax: (01865) 552296   E-mail: mail@doverbroecks.com   Website: www.doverbroecks.com
www.gabbitas.co.uk   For entry at age 11 or 13 please contact Leckford Place School 01865 302620

Principal Mr S Cohen   **Founded** 1977
College status Independent. Co-educational
Day and Boarding 11–19 (Day only 11–16).
Boarders from 16 Entry at age 11+ and 13+ into
Leckford Place School; entry at 16+ into the
d'Overbroeck's Sixth Form
Religious denomination Non-Denominational
Member of ISA, SHMIS
Accredited by ISA, SHMIS
No of pupils 362; *(full boarding)* 122; *(day)*
240; *Senior* 120; *Sixth Form* 242; *Girls* 180;
Boys 182
Teacher:pupil ratio 1:7 **Average class size** 7
Fees per annum Leckford Place School *(day
only)* £11550; The Sixth Form *(day)* £16845;
(full boarding) £22095–£24270

The College's approach is characterized by small classes (maximum of 10 in the Sixth Form and 15 up to GCSE) and a very high level of support and encouragement that makes learning enjoyable as well as highly effective. Pastoral support is excellent. Outside of lessons there is a busy programme of sports, activities, arts, drama and music. In 2008, 51 per cent of our entries achieved grade A at A level. On average around 10 per cent of our Upper Sixth gain a place at Oxford or Cambridge. A range of scholarships are available for entry at age 11, 13 and 16.

Kingham Hill School

Kingham, Chipping Norton, Oxfordshire OX7 6TH   Tel: (01608) 658999   Fax: (01608) 658658
E-mail: admissions@kingham-hill.oxon.sch.uk
Website: www.kingham-hill.oxon.sch.uk   www.gabbitas.co.uk

Headmaster Mr N Seward MA, BEng
Registrar Mrs K A Harvey
Head of Marketing and PR Mr S King
Founded 1886
School status Independent. Co-educational
Boarding and Day 11–18. Flexi-boarding
available. Boarders from 11
Religious denomination Christian
Member of AGBIS, BSA, CReSTeD, ISBA, SHA,
SHMIS **Accredited by** ISC, SHMIS
Membership of AEGIS
Learning difficulties SNU WI/DYC DYP DYS
No of pupils 235; *(full boarding)* 168; *(day)* 67;
Senior 174; *Sixth Form* 61; *Girls* 74; *Boys* 161
Teacher:pupil ratio 1:7 **Average class size** 15
Fees per annum *(full boarding)* £18595–
£22000; *(day)* £12135–£14783
Fees SpLD per term: £1320. SpLD Sixth Form
per term: £660. ESOL per term: £1390

Kingham Hill School is a thriving mixed boarding/ day school for 250 pupils aged 11–18 years. Beautifully situated in 96 acres of beautiful Cotswold countryside it has offered many generations of students the best possible opportunity to flourish, enjoying their formative years and becoming successful, responsible and well-rounded adults.

- Christian values that permeate school life.
- Added value that enables so many to exceed all expectations.
- Family-style boarding houses and superb pastoral care.

The Manor Preparatory School

Faringdon Road, Abingdon, Oxfordshire OX13 6LN
Tel: (01235) 858462   Fax: (01235) 858458
E-mail: registrar@manorprep.org   Website: www.manorprep.org

Headmaster Mr P Heyworth MA, PGCE
Deputy Head Mrs A Stokes BA (Hons), PGCE
Founded 1907
School status Independent. Co-educational
Day Boys 2–7 Girls 2–11
Religious denomination Church of England
Member of AGBIS, IAPS, ISBA, SATIPS
Accredited by IAPS, ISC Nursery also Ofsted
accredited
Learning difficulties CA WI/DYC DYP DYS
Behavioural and emotional disorders CA
Physical and medical conditions AT CA SM
TW WA2/HEA HI VI
No of pupils 330; *(day)* 330; *Nursery* 35;
Pre-prep 101; *Prep* 194; *Girls* 309; *Boys* 21
Average class size 18
Fees per annum *(day)* £1630–£10050

including award-winning classrooms and three IT suites, set in extensive grounds. A thriving music department boasts two orchestras, four choirs, various ensembles and a jazz band. The Manor holds the 'Gold Activemark' award from Sport England for its 'commitment to promoting the benefits of physical activity and sport'.

Extra-curricular clubs and before and after school care are available. There are also sessions for pre-nursery children.

Lively, experienced staff encourages all pupils to contribute positively to the school community, to show consideration towards other people, to have a disciplined approach to work – and above all to have fun! They leave us happy, fully prepared and confident to take the next step in their education.

Renowed for academic excellence and with a broad curriculum The Manor has superb facilities,

England

The Oratory Preparatory School

Goring Heath, Reading, Oxfordshire RG8 7SF   Tel: (0118) 984 4511   Fax: (0118) 984 4806
E-mail: office@oratoryprep.co.uk   Website: www.oratoryprep.org.uk   www.gabbitas.co.uk

Headmaster Dr R J Hillier MA, PhD, PGCE
Founded 1859
School status Independent. Co-educational
Day and Boarding 3–13. Flexi-boarding
available. Boarders from 9
Religious denomination Roman Catholic
Member of AGBIS, BSA, IAPS, ISA
No of pupils 400; *(full boarding)* 20; *(weekly boarding)* 10; *(day)* 370; *Pre-prep* 115; *Prep* 285; *Girls* 150; *Boys* 250
Average class size 16
Fees per annum *(full boarding)* £15135; *(weekly)* £13935; *(day)* £3285–£10980

A Catholic preparatory school which stands in its own 60-acre estate. The OPS has an excellent record of achievement, with pupils gaining many academic, art, music, sports and all-rounder awards to The Oratory School and other major independent senior schools. Our thriving Pre-prep department was classified as 'outstanding' in a recent Ofsted inspection (Summer 2008). Our well-qualified and experienced teachers deliver a broad curriculum characterized by an unusually wide range of subjects, activities and sports and a high level of pastoral care. The OPS welcomes children of all denominations and faiths and aims to identify and develop their individual talents and gifts in all aspects of their school lives.

St Clare's, Oxford

139 Banbury Road, Oxford, Oxfordshire OX2 7AL   Tel: (01865) 552031   Fax: (01865) 513359
E-mail: admissions@stclares.ac.uk   Website: www.stclares.ac.uk   www.gabbitas.co.uk

Principal Mrs P Holloway MSc (Oxon), BSc, PGCE, Dip PM   **Founded** 1953
School status Independent Sixth Form College. Co-educational Boarding and Day 15–19. Flexi-boarding available. Boarders from 15
Religious denomination Non-Denominational
Member of English UK, CASE, CIS, IBO, ISA, LISA **Accredited by** British Council, ISA
Learning difficulties RA WI/DYP DYS
Behavioural and emotional disorders CO ST TS
Physical and medical conditions SM
No of pupils 258; *(full boarding)* 238; *(weekly boarding)* 10; *(day)* 10; *Sixth Form* 225; *Girls* 118; *Boys* 107
Teacher:pupil ratio 1:7 **Average class size** 9
Fees per annum *(full boarding)* £26449; *(weekly)* £26134; *(day)* £16355

We are the longest-established provider of the International Baccalaureate Diploma in England with a mission to advance international education and understanding. The IB Diploma is a two-year course giving access to fine universities all over the world. Our students regularly win places at Oxford, Cambridge, LSE and other leading UK universities as well as Harvard, Yale and Stanford in the USA. We also offer a Pre-IB course which provides excellent preparation for the full IB Diploma.

St Clare's is a co-educational day and boarding college occupying substantial premises in the elegant residential area of north Oxford. Over 40 different nationalities are represented of which about 15 per cent are from Britain. The atmosphere at the college is informal and friendly, encouraging personal responsibility and international friendships. Our students live in comfortable college houses under the care of a resident warden and all meals are served in the college dining room. There is also a student coffee bar, The Sugar House, which provides snacks at lunchtime and in the evening.

IB Diploma students choose six academic subjects in addition to an Extended Essay, a theory of knowledge course and a programme of physical and creative activities. There is also a mandatory programme of charitable work and service to the community. Academic subjects include the study of literature in the student's own language, a second language, subjects related to the study of individuals and societies and experimental sciences, and mathematics.

Each of our students is assigned a personal tutor who oversees welfare and progress at regular, individual weekly meetings. Our teachers are selected for their strong academic backgrounds and IB teaching experience. Many are involved in IB curriculum development and examining. We regularly assist schools who are introducing the IB and run training workshops for IB teachers from around the world.

We provide an extensive programme of social, cultural, service and sporting activities and our students are encouraged to take full advantage of the opportunities that Oxford provides. Apart from more traditional sports, our activities staff organize regular overseas trips as well as activities nearer home such as climbing in Wales, canoeing in Scotland and the popular Duke of Edinburgh Award.

Acceptance is on the basis of academic results, school reports and an interview. Scholarships are available. Almost all our students proceed to higher education in Britain or elsewhere in the world. Our two highly qualified advisers help all students with university choice, applications and interview skills as well as providing comprehensive careers advice.

England

St Edward's School

Woodstock Road, Oxford, Oxfordshire OX2 7NN   Tel: (01865) 319200   Fax: (01865) 319202
E-mail: registrar@stedwards.oxon.sch.uk   Website: www.stedwards.oxon.sch.uk

Warden Mr A Trotman MA
Registrar Ms S Munden BEd
Founded 1863
School status Independent. Co-educational
Boarding and Day 13–18
Religious denomination Church of England
Member of HMC **Accredited by** HMC
Learning difficulties SNU WI/DYC DYP DYS
Behavioural and emotional disorders CO/ADD
ADHD
Physical and medical conditions RA SM WA3/
HI IM
No of pupils 658; *(full boarding)* 506; *(day)*
152; *Sixth Form* 272; *Girls* 235; *Boys* 423
Teacher:pupil ratio 1:8
Fees per annum *(full boarding)* £27015; *(day)*
£21609

St Edward's is a distinguished and highly successful independent school situated on the outskirts of north Oxford. Largely boarding, St Edward's cares for 658 pupils, both boys and girls, aged 13 to 18.

With approximately 100 academic scholars and exhibitioners, St Edward's offers a challenging environment where every pupil has a chance to be a leader.

Academic rigour is the cornerstone of the development of the school. It has a one in eight teacher/pupil ratio and in the last five years 54 St Edward's pupils have won places to Oxbridge.

An excellent 'all round' school and a safe and reliable first choice.

Shiplake College

Henley-on-Thames, Oxfordshire RG9 4BW   Tel: (0118) 940 2455   Fax: (0118) 940 5204
E-mail: info@shiplake.org.uk   Website: www.shiplake.org.uk

Headmaster Mr A G S Davies BSc
Founded 1959
College status Independent. Day boys 11–18.
Boarding boys 13–18. Boarding and Day girls
16–18
Religious denomination Church of England
Member of AGBIS, HMC, ISBA, SHMIS
Accredited by HMC, ISC, SHMIS
Learning difficulties SNU/DYC DYP DYS
Behavioural and emotional disorders ST
Physical and medical conditions SM
No of pupils 324; *(boarding)* 223; *(day)* 101;
Girls 30; *Boys* 294
Teacher:pupil ratio 1:6 **Average class size** 15
Fees per annum *(full boarding)* £22998;
(weekly) £22998; *(day)* £15513

Shiplake College is an independent boarding and day school for boys aged 11–18 with day and boarding girls joining the Sixth Form. Just over two miles upstream of Henley-on-Thames, Shiplake College enjoys a beautiful 45-acre riverside site based around the historic Shiplake Court.

Shiplake prides itself on bringing out the best in each and every individual and we are known for our outstanding pastoral care.

We invite you to visit us for a tour of the school with an opportunity to meet pupils and staff, view our classrooms and boarding houses and enjoy a stroll around our beautiful riverside site.

Ellesmere College

Ellesmere, Shropshire SY12 9AB   Tel: (01691) 622321   Fax: (01691) 623286
E-mail: admissions.secretary@ellesmere.com   Website: www.ellesmere.com

The Headmaster Mr B J Wignall MA, FRSA, MCMI
Director of Admissions Mr P A Goodwin BEd
Founded 1894
College status Co-educational Boarding and Day 7–18. Flexi-boarding available
Religious denomination Church of England
No of pupils 612; *(full boarding)* 147; *(weekly boarding)* 87; *(day)* 378; *Girls* 211; *Boys* 401
Teacher:pupil ratio 1:8 **Average class size** 16
Fees per annum *(full boarding)* £22152; *(weekly)* £17970; *(day)* £13908

Ellesmere College is a 7–18 co-educational school, set in 144 acres of rural north Shropshire and has in recent years developed a considerable reputation for innovation. In the last 10 years, pupil numbers have grown from 320 to 620. In the Sixth Form the International Baccalaureate Diploma, introduced in September 2006, is offered alongside the traditional A levels.

An established thriving Rugby Academy with the 1st XV has retained an enviable unbeaten record over the last four years with three recent leavers gaining professional club contracts. Ellesmere has recently introduced Tennis and Cricket Academies as well as the Ellesmere College Titans, an elite swimming development programme.

Whilst aiming for academic excellence for all its pupils, an Ellesmerian education provides a broad basis for preparing young people to be successful adults. Academic, Sports and Performing Arts scholarships and bursaries are available for talented pupils.

England

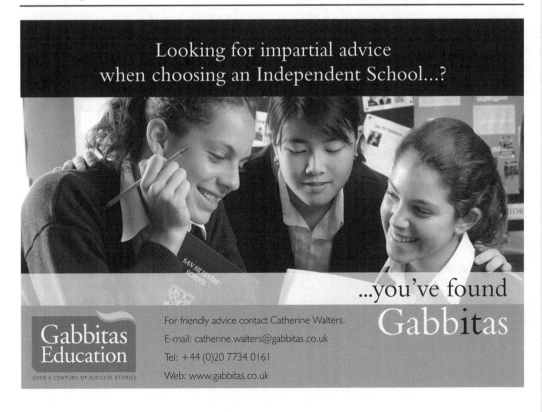

Moreton Hall School

Weston Rhyn, Oswestry, Shropshire SY11 3EW   Tel: (01691) 773671   Fax: (01691) 778552
E-mail: admin@moretonhall.com   Website: www.moretonhall.org   www.gabbitas.co.uk

The Principal Mr J Forster BA
Founded 1913
School status Independent. Girls Boarding and Day 3–18 (Boys 3–11). Boarders from 8. Safe,caring environment in north Shropshire. Excellent EFL Language Centre. New boarding accommodation
Religious denomination Non-Denominational
Member of AGBIS, BSA, GSA, SHA
Learning difficulties SNU WI/DYC DYP DYS MLD
Behavioural and emotional disorders CO ST
Physical and medical conditions IT SM TW WA3/HEA
No of pupils 353; *(full boarding)* 238; *(day)* 92; *Nursery* 29; *Pre-prep* 29; *Prep* 52; *Senior* 298; *Sixth Form* 102; *Girls* 343; *Boys* 10
Teacher:pupil ratio 1:12
Average class size 15
Fees per annum *(full boarding)* £16050–£24900; *(day)* £6900–£20100. Scholarships and bursaries are available each year

Going well beyond the National Curriculum, some 20 subjects are available at GCSE, ranging from the traditional academic subjects such as Latin and the sciences, to practical subjects such as drama, dance and physical education. Modern languages available include French, German and Spanish. A levels in history of art, human biology, business studies and theatre studies extend the range of the curriculum. Information technology is a compulsory subject up to Sixth Form, optional thereafter.

Boarding starts at the age of 8. Younger girls are housed under the supervision of resident housemistresses, resident tutors and matrons.

As pupils progress up the school, the dormitories are gradually replaced by double and single study-bedrooms. Boarding houses at Moreton are linked informally with houses at Shrewsbury School, pupils meeting regularly for musical, dramatic and social occasions. The latest Sixth Form boarding house, Rylands, was completed in 2008 and now means that all sixth formers are housed in modern, study rooms, complete with private en-suites.

Moreton Hall has recently completed an ambitious building and refurbishment programme. The new laboratories, information technology rooms and art design centre are housed within a short distance of the central classroom, careers and library complex. An exceptionally well-equipped sports centre comprising a sports hall and floodlit tennis courts and all-weather surface, along with heated, indoor swimming pool, nine-hole golf course and playing fields, are set in 100 acres of beautiful parkland at the foot of the Berwyn Hills. The school offers a wide range of sporting options, including lacrosse, netball, hockey, cricket, tennis and athletics. Sailing and riding are also popular. Moreton Enterprises, a Sixth Form managed group of companies, offers the girls real business experience. A radio station and recording studio were opened in 1997.

Girls are admitted to the senior school, normally in September, at the ages of 11–13, either by Common Entrance or by the school's entrance examination, which is held at the end of January each year. Sixth Form entrance is by interview, and numbers are limited. Girls and boys can start the primary school at 3. There is also a nursery.

A number of scholarships and bursaries are awarded to girls entering at 11, 13 and the Lower Sixth or to assist a pupil in the school to complete her education. Awards for music, drama, art and for outstanding sporting talent are made at 11+, 12+, 13+ and 16+.

Bromsgrove School

Worcester Road, Bromsgrove, Worcestershire B61 7DU   Tel: (01527) 579679   Fax: (01527) 576177
E-mail: admissions@bromsgrove-school.co.uk
Website: www.bromsgrove-school.co.uk   www.gabbitas.co.uk

Headmaster Mr C Edwards MA (Oxon)
Assistant Head Miss R Scannell BA
Founded 1553
School status Independent. Co-educational Boarding and Day 13–18. Boarders from 7
Religious denomination Church of England
Member of BSA, HMC, IAPS
Accredited by HMC, IAPS, ISC
Learning difficulties WI/DYP DYS
Behavioural and emotional disorders RA
Physical and medical conditions RA
No of pupils 741; *(full boarding)* 367; *(day)* 374; *Girls* 290; *Boys* 451
Teacher:pupil ratio 1:9 **Average class size** 20
Fees per annum *(full boarding)* £23200 pa; *(day)* £11850 pa. International boarding fee includes EAL provision: £25425 pa

Bromsgrove School, a self-contained campus near the town of Bromsgrove, is easily accessible from the national motorway network; Birmingham International airport is 35 minutes away and London Heathrow just two hours by car. The school is opportunity oriented and provides a very wide range of academic, extra-curricular and sporting activities.

Bromsgrove School, though unashamedly academic, is not as selective at 13 as its very high league table position suggests.

Entry between ages 7 and 11 is based on assessment tests and at 13 on interview and tests, or Common Entrance. Entry into the Sixth Form is dependent on results at GCSE.

England

Malvern College

College Road, Malvern, Worcestershire WR14 3DF   Tel: (01684) 581500   Fax: (01684) 581617
E-mail: registrar@malcol.org   Website: www.malcol.org   www.gabbitas.co.uk
Our Prep school can be contacted on 01684 540277 or at enquiries@thedowns.malcol.org

Headmaster Mr Antony Clark
Registrar Mrs S Jackson   **Founded** 1865
College status Independent. Co-educational
Boarding and Day 3–18. Boarders from 7
Religious denomination Church of England
Member of CASE, HMC
Accredited by HMC, ISC
Learning difficulties SNU WI/DYP DYS
Behavioural and emotional disorders RA/ADD
ADHD
Physical and medical conditions RA/EPI HEA
HI VI
No of pupils 640; *(full boarding)* 516; *(day)*
123; *Nursery* 45; *Pre-prep* 61; *Prep* 202; *Senior*
308; *Sixth Form* 332; *Girls* 276; *Boys* 364
Teacher:pupil ratio 1:8
Fees per annum *(full boarding)* £25889–
£26700; *(day)* £17163–£17697

Malvern College is set in a beautiful 250-acre campus; a safe place in which we are able to offer outstanding all-round education for pupils aged 13 to 18. Our preparatory school for pupils from 3 to 13 is located on a delightful 50-acre site nearby. We focus on academic excellence, pastoral care and achievement in all fields and are presently developing new top-class sports facilities. Malvern College is the traditional school of the future: a co-educational boarding school that maintains the finest traditions while constantly looking forward.

Malvern St James

15 Avenue Road, Great Malvern, Worcestershire WR14 3BA   Tel: (01684) 584624
Fax: (01684) 566204 E-mail: registrar@malvernstjames.co.uk Website: www.malvernstjames.co.uk

Headmistress Mrs R Hayes BA (Hons), MA
Education, PGCE, FRGS   **Founded** 1890s
School status Independent. Girls Boarding and
Day. Weekly and flexi-boarding available.
Malvern St James welcomes girls aged 4–18
Religious denomination Church of England
Member of BSA, GSA, ISBA, NAHT, SHA
Accredited by GSA
Learning difficulties SNU/DYP DYS MLD
Physical and medical conditions SM TW WA1
No of pupils 360; *(full boarding)* 168; *(weekly boarding)* 13; *(day)* 180; *Sixth Form* 127;
Girls 360
Teacher:pupil ratio 1:7.3 **Ave class size** 12–18
Fees per annum *(full boarding)* £17400–
£24420; *(weekly)* from £23520; *(day)* £6000

traditional and innovative teaching and learning styles. Academic results were impressive in 2008, with a 99 per cent pass rate at A level. An extensive extracurricular programme provides girls with the opportunity to explore new ideas, try new activities, extend boundaries and take risks.

Admission is through the schools own examination, or through Common Entrance examination. The school offers Academic Entrance Scholarships and Exhibitions, as well as Scholarships in art, music, and physical education.

Pupils at Malvern St James enjoy a range of high-quality facilities designed to enhance their learning experience. The School provides a stimulating and forward-looking curriculum using both

Moffats School

Kinlet Hall, Kinlet, Bewdley, Worcestershire DY12 3AY   Tel: (01299) 841230   Fax: (01299) 841444
E-mail: office@moffats.co.uk   Website: www.moffats.co.uk

Headmaster Mr M H Daborn MA (Cantab),
QTS   **Founded** 1934
School status Independent. Co-educational
Boarding and Day 4–13. Flexi-boarding
available. Boarders from 7
Religious denomination Church of England
Member of BSA, ISA, ISCis
Accredited by ISA, ISC
Learning difficulties WI/DYP DYS MLD
Physical and medical conditions HEA HI
No of pupils 71; *(full boarding)* 25; *(weekly
boarding)* 2; *Pre-prep* 9; *Girls* 25; *Boys* 46
Teacher:pupil ratio 1:7 **Average class size** 12
Fees per annum *(full boarding)* £13425;
(weekly) £13425; *(day)* £1000–£8415

Moffats provides a happy, safe environment valu-
ing childhood. Good manners, kindness and
respect for others are greatly valued. Small classes
ensure high attention, so that each individual,
whether a bright pupil or one needing more
assistance, progresses at the right pace, receiving
as much help as is needed.

The school's 108-acre grounds provide space
not only for daily sports but also for riding, a
popular option. The school carefully maintains a
balance between class work and other activities,
promoting cultural awareness, strengthening self-
confidence and ensuring a sense of fun. Prime
importance is given to the development of communication skills. Pupils regularly gain
distinctions in annual ESB examinations. The
school runs two choirs.

England

MAP OF THE HOME COUNTIES (NORTH)

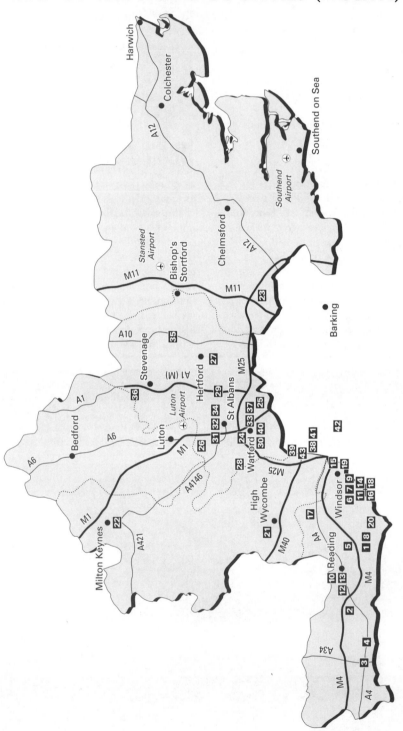

PROFILED SCHOOLS IN THE HOME COUNTIES (NORTH)

(Incorporating the counties of Bedfordshire, Berkshire, Buckinghamshire, Essex, Hertfordshire, Middlesex)

England

Bearwood College

Bearwood Road, Wokingham, Berkshire RG41 5BG   Tel: (0118) 974 8300   Fax: (0118) 977 3186
E-mail: headmaster@bearwoodcollege.co.uk
Website: www.bearwoodcollege.co.uk   www.gabbitas.co.uk   registrar@bearwoodcollege.co.uk

Headmaster Mr S Aiano MA (Cantab) PGCE, FRSA
Second Master Mr R P Ryall BA, PGCE FRGS
Academic Deputy Mr G Penlington BA, Dip Teach   **Founded** 1827
College status Independent. Co-educational Boarding and Day 11–18 (3–18 Preparatory and Senior School). Flexi-boarding available. Boarders from 11
Religious denomination Church of England
Member of BSA, SHMIS, ISBA
No of pupils 490; *(full boarding)* 71; *(weekly boarding)* 20; *(day)* 399; *Nursery* 125; *Prep* 115; *Senior (13+)* 250; *Sixth Form* 81; *Girls* 135; *Boys* 355
Teacher:pupil ratio 1:8 **Average class size** 18
Fees per annum *(full boarding)* £22020–£25380; *(weekly)* £22020–£25830; *(day)* £12555–£14790. Flexi-boarding £46 per night

Bearwood provides the best in care and education for age 3 months to 18 years through our Nursery, Pre-prep, Prep and Senior School. We welcome day pupils throughout the College and boarders from age 11. At all ages, pupils are encouraged to achieve their best, both academically and outside the classroom. Pastoral care and a supportive academic environment facilitate personal development and warm friendships. Pupils participate in an exciting programme of extra-curricular activities and outdoor pursuits. We are close to the M3 and M4, within easy reach of Heathrow and Gatwick airports, and 45 minutes from London by train.

Bradfield College

Bradfield, Reading, Berkshire RG7 6AU   Tel: (0118) 964 4510   Fax: (0118) 964 4513
E-mail: headmaster@bradfieldcollege.org.uk   Website: www.bradfieldcollege.org.uk

Head Mr P J M Roberts MA (Oxon)
Founded 1850
College status Independent. Co-educational Boarding and Day 13–18. Boarders from 13
Religious denomination Church of England
Member of BSA, HMC **Accredited by** HMC
Learning difficulties SNU WI/DYS
No of pupils 703; *(full boarding)* 589; *(day)* 114; *Sixth Form* 311; *Girls* 237; *Boys* 466
Teacher:pupil ratio 1:8 **Average class size** 16
Fees per annum *(full boarding)* £26100; *(day)* £20880

Bradfield College offers a wide selection of subjects in both the Junior and Senior schools, providing challenge and choice for all through personalized programmes of study inspired by passionate and engaging teaching. Learning extends beyond the classroom through the Athena General Studies lectures and tutorial programme including Minerva seminars for scholars.

Academic Scholarships, Dr Gray all-rounder and Sports Exhibitions, Art, DT and Music Awards are available at 13+ with entrance by Common Entrance or the Bradfield College assessment. Academic, Art and Music scholarships are available at 16+ with entrance on attainment of a minimum of 5 B grades at GCSE, Headteacher's reference and assessment if transferring from elsewhere into the college's large and vibrant Sixth Form. The college delivers an outstanding academic education, unparallelled pastoral care and a diverse range of extra-curricular activities, enabling every individual to find his or her niche.

Cheam School

Headley, Newbury, Berkshire RG19 8LD   Tel: (01635) 268381   Fax: (01635) 269345
E-mail: registrar@cheamschool.co.uk   Website: www.cheamschool.com   www.gabbitas.co.uk

Headmaster Mr M R Johnson BEd
School status Independent. Co-educational Boarding and Day 3–13. Flexi-boarding available. Boarders from 8   **Founded** 1645
Religious denomination Church of England
Member of AGBIS, BSA, IAPS, ISBA
Accredited by ISC
Learning difficulties SC SNU WI/DYP DYS MLD
Behavioural and emotional disorders CO
Physical and medical conditions RA SM WA2/ HEA
No of pupils 400; *(full boarding)* 2; *(weekly boarding)* 65; *(day)* 333; *Nursery* 26; *Pre-prep* 75; *Prep* 299; *Girls* 174; *Boys* 226
Average class size 18 maximum
Fees per annum *(full boarding)* £20535; *(weekly)* £20535; *(day)* £3990–£15210 minimum fee relates to 5 mornings per week in Nursery

Curriculum: Children are prepared in small classes (maximum 18) for Common Entrance and scholarships to all major public schools. The syllabus covers and exceeds National Curriculum requirements. Those with special needs are well catered for.

Entry requirements: By interview. One bursary awarded annually at Headmaster's discretion.

Academic and leisure facilities: Excellent facilities set in a stimulating yet secure 80-acre estate. New classroom block, music school and refurbished chapel, completed September 2001. Modern science block; dedicated IT, art and design departments; new indoor sports centre opened 2003 and sporting facilities include squash court and nine-hole golf course.

Pastoral care and boarding facilities: Each child is under the watchful eye of two house tutors and a form teacher; resident staff and matrons supervise boarders in comfortable dormitories. Separate girls' boarding accommodation. Nursery and Pre-prep on site.

Downe House

Cold Ash, Thatcham, Berkshire RG18 9JJ   Tel: (01635) 200286   Fax: (01635) 202026
E-mail: correspondence@downehouse.net   Website: www.downehouse.net   www.gabbitas.co.uk

Headmistress Mrs E McKendrick BA
Founded 1907
School status Independent. Girls Boarding and Day 11–18. Boarders from 11
Religious denomination Church of England
Member of AGBIS, BSA, GSA, ISBA
Accredited by GSA
No of pupils 567; *(full boarding)* 550; *(day)* 17; *Senior* 404; *Sixth Form* 163; *Girls* 567
Teacher:pupil ratio 1:7
Fees per annum *(full boarding)* £25968; *(day)* £18801

The school is only five miles from Newbury, with easy access to the motorway network, London and Heathrow airport. It has an excellent academic record, with nearly all pupils going on to university.

Academic and leisure facilities: Sixth Form complex with study-bedrooms. Extensive refurbishment of all boarding houses. Significant expenditure on ICT, with voicemail and e-mail for every girl. New sports hall and performing arts centre, and indoor swimming pool. One term spent in France in 12+ year.

Leith's Food and Wine Certificate is offered in the Sixth Form.

Curriculum: A wide selection of subjects is available at both GCSE and A level. Girls are also prepared for university entrance.

Entry requirements and procedures: By Common Entrance and assessment. Seven passes at grade B or above for an A level course. Scholarships at 11+, 12+, 13+ and Sixth Form.

England

Eagle House

Crowthorne Road, Sandhurst, Berkshire GU47 8PH   Tel: (01344) 772134   Fax: (01344) 779039
E-mail: info@eaglehouseschool.com   Website: www.eaglehouseschool.com

Headmaster Mr Andrew Barnard BA Hons, PGCE **Founded** 1820
School status Independent. Co-educational Day and Boarding 3–13. Flexi-boarding available. Boarders from 8
Religious denomination Church of England
Member of BSA, IAPS, NAHT, SATIPS
Accredited by IAPS, ISC
Learning difficulties CA SNU/DYP DYS
Behavioural and emotional disorders RA/ADD ADHD
Physical and medical conditions SL SM TW WA1/HEA
No of pupils 320; *(full boarding)* 18; *(weekly boarding)* 22; *(day)* 280; *Nursery* 24; *Pre-prep* 84; *Prep* 212; *Girls* 119; *Boys* 201
Teacher:pupil ratio 1:6 **Average class size** 14
Fees per annum *(full boarding)* £17400; *(weekly)* £17400; *(day)* £12975. *Pre-prep* £7800 (Rec/Year 1); £8100 (Year 2); *Nursery* £4650

At Eagle House every child is unique. From 3 to 13, girls and boys develop in a friendly, creative and expressive environment. Working closely with parents, Eagle House nurtures the individual talents of every child, so that they grow in self-esteem and confidence, through their success in academic subjects, sports, art, music and drama. The school believes in rewards and praise for good work and exemplary behaviour to encourage high standards and good citizenship.

Eagle House benefits from superb facilities and small class sizes and dedicated staff ensure that all children have the best academic start possible. The high sporting achievements of the pupils is testament to the opportunities and coaching offered by the school. A diverse activities programme, called Golden Eagle, is enjoyed by all pupils helping to give them an all-round education. With boarding opportunities from Year 3 and late-stay facilities for all children, Eagle House caters for the busy lives families lead.

Heathfield St Mary's School

London Road, Ascot, Berkshire SL5 8BQ   Tel: (01344) 898342   Fax: (01344) 890689
E-mail: registrar@heathfieldstmarys.net Website: www.heathfieldstmarys.com www.gabbitas.co.uk

Headmistress Mrs M McSwiggan MA (Surrey), BEd (Brisbane) **Founded** 1899
School status Independent. Girls Boarding 11–18. Boarders from 11
Religious denomination Christian
Member of BSA, GSA, IAPS, SHA
Accredited by GSA, IAPS, ISC
Learning difficulties CA SNU WI/DYC DYP DYS
Behavioural and emotional disorders CO ST/ADD ADHD ASP
Physical and medical conditions SM WA3/HEA
No of pupils 220; *(full boarding)* 220; *Senior* 140; *Sixth Form* 80; *Girls* 220
Teacher:pupil ratio 1:6 **Average class size** 11
Fees per annum *(full boarding)* £24300–£26094

needs of individuals, nurturing both academic and personal development to help every girl achieve her potential.

Modern teaching, sporting and leisure facilities make education a positive, exciting experience. Boarding accommodation is excellent, two thirds of the pupils having single bedrooms. We have a new performing arts centre and plans are afoot for new boarding accommodation and classrooms.

Set in spacious surroundings on the outskirts of Ascot the school is 45 minutes from London and 30 minutes from London Heathrow.

Heathfield St Mary's encourages academic success but also prepares girls for the realities of the outside world. Our philosophy is to focus on the

Licensed Victuallers' School

London Road, Ascot, Berkshire SL5 8DR   Tel: (01344) 882770   Fax: (01344) 890648
E-mail: registrar@lvs.ascot.sch.uk   Website: www.lvs.ascot.sch.uk

Head of Senior School Mr G Best BA (Hons)
Head of Junior School Mrs H Donnelly BA,
BEd (Hons)   **Founded** 1803
School status Independent. Co-educational
Boarding and Day 4–18. Boarders from 8
Religious denomination Non-Denominational
Member of AGBIS, ISA, SHMIS
Learning difficulties DYS
Physical & medical conditions SM WA2/HEA VI
No of pupils 895; *(full boarding)* 140; *(weekly boarding)* 36; *(day)* 724; *Prep* 202; *Senior* 531;
Sixth Form 162; *Girls* 370; *Boys* 525
Average class size Max 20
Fees per annum *(full boarding)* £18330–£21735; *(weekly)* £18330–£21735; *(day)*
£7155–£12375

The Licensed Victuallers' School is a unique and successful independent day and boarding school catering for over 880 pupils aged 4½ to 18.

Location: LVS is situated within easy reach of London and is readily accessible from the M3, M4 and M25 motorways, as well as Heathrow and Gatwick airports, and by train.

Facilities: The school commands a 26-acre site which includes a magnificent theatre, indoor swimming pool, sports hall and movement/dance studio, medical centre, four boarding houses and a new performing arts centre.

Our Sixth Form centre ensures that the best available resources are in place for our 150 post-16 students. The building also incorporates a new learning resource centre.

What we have to offer: The school offers a broad academic programme, a wide range of GCSE, A Level and Applied options, catering for each individual pupil's strengths. Courses, from the age of 11, are set according to ability with six to seven sets per year group in the senior school.

We have full boarding and weekly boarding facilities as well as a large number of day pupils from the local area.

Luckley-Oakfield School

Luckley Road, Wokingham, Berkshire RG40 3EU   Tel: (0118) 978 4175   Fax: (0118) 977 0305
E-mail: registrar@luckley.wokingham.sch.uk
Website: www.luckley.wokingham.sch.uk   www.gabbitas.co.uk

Headmistress Miss V A Davis BSc (Hons), ARCS
Registrar Mrs M Cope   **Founded** 1918
School status Independent. Girls Boarding and
Day 11–18. Flexi-boarding available. Boarders
from 11
Religious denomination Church of England
Member of AGBIS, BSA, GSA
Accredited by GSA
Learning difficulties WI/DYP DYS
Physical and medical conditions WA3
No of pupils 304; *(full boarding)* 30; *(weekly boarding)* 10; *(day)* 272; *Senior* 254; *Sixth Form* 50; *Girls* 304
Teacher:pupil ratio 1:8 **Average class size** 18
Fees per annum *(full boarding)* £20964;
(weekly) £19428; *(day)* £12303
Fees Fees include text books, lunch and break refreshments and most after school activities

Luckley-Oakfield encourages high aspirations, independent thinking and community spirit. Each student experiences a truly holistic education developing her academic, cultural, creative, physical and ethical dimensions. The school has high expectations for all its students and achieves excellent academic results. Students encounter rich and varied opportunities both inside and outside of the classroom. Flexi, weekly and full boarding provides a wonderful 'home from home'. Luckley-Oakfield is set in beautiful Berkshire countryside with outstanding facilities and grounds. Generous forces discounts are available.

England

The Marist Schools

Kings Road, Sunninghill, Ascot, Berkshire SL5 7PS   Tel: (01344) 626137/624291
Fax: (01344) 621566   E-mail: pa2head@marist.ascot.org.uk   Website: www.themaristschools.com

Head Mrs J A Peachey (Preparatory) and
Mr K McCloskey (Senior)
School status Girls Day 3–18
Religious denomination Roman Catholic
Learning difficulties WI
No of pupils 570; *Girls* 570
Fees per annum *(day)* £7050–£9660

The Marist Schools are based in Sunninghill, Berkshire, and offer day education for girls aged 3–18. The schools are Catholic but welcome all families supporting the schools' ethos. The schools are renowned for their successful and happy atmosphere, where pastoral care is considered paramount. Your daughter's individuality will be nurtured to develop and encourage her full potential in every area.

The Marist Schools achieve excellent academic results. In 2008 – 100 per cent of A level students passed with 83 per cent achieving A and B grades. GCSE students achieved 85 per cent A*, A and B grades, and also enjoyed a 100 per cent pass rate. The Marist Senior School is currently ranked first in the Royal Borough of Windsor & Maidenhead (source: *The Times* League Tables published 10 Jan 2008) and ranked second highest performing independent school in the UK (source: *The Daily Telegraph* League Tables published 10 Jan 2008).

The schools place a strong emphasis on extracurricular activities which help to develop important qualities such as self-confidence, individual creativity and teamwork. There is no limit to the success of Marist girls both inside and outside of the classroom.

Before and after school care is offered along with a generous sibling discount scheme. Scholarships are available for entry in Year 7 and Sixth Form.

For further information please call 01344 626137 (Preparatory) or 01344 624291 (Senior). Or please visit: www.themaristschools.com.

Padworth College

Padworth, Reading, Berkshire RG7 4NR   Tel: (0118) 983 2644   Fax: (0118) 983 4515
E-mail: info@padworth.com   Website: www.padworth.com

The Principal Mrs L Melhuish BA, MA, PGCE, NPQH   **Founded** 1963
College status Independent. Co-educational Boarding and Day 13–19. Flexi-boarding available
Religious denomination Non-Denominational
Member of English UK, BSA, ISC, SHMIS
Accredited by BAC, British Council, ISC, SHMIS
No of pupils 110; *(full boarding)* 79; *(weekly boarding)* 4; *(day)* 26; *Senior* 105; *Sixth Form* 39; *Girls* 51; *Boys* 59
Teacher:pupil ratio 1:6   **Average class size** 8
Fees per annum *(full boarding)* £20850; *(weekly)* £15900; *(day)* £9000

excellent pastoral care. Academic standards are high and nearly all students go to British universities. A significant proportion of students come from overseas creating a vibrant international community; equally a substantial number are British and many are day students. Padworth provides Year 9 Foundation and a wide range of subjects at GCSE/IGCSE and AS/A level as well as a University Access programme. In addition, the ISC provides a range of full-time short- and long-term English Language courses for overseas students of all abilities. The college's rural setting provides a peaceful and secure environment for study; yet the campus is within easy reach of the university town of Reading and just 45 minutes by road from Heathrow.

Padworth College is a co-educational boarding and day school for students aged 13–19 which brings an informal tutorial-style atmosphere to school-level education, giving individual attention in very small classes underpinned with

Papplewick School

Windsor Road, Ascot, Berkshire SL5 7LH
Tel: (01344) 621488   Fax: (01344) 874639
E-mail: hm@papplewick.org.uk
Website: www.papplewick.org.uk   www.gabbitas.co.uk

Head Mr T W Bunbury BA (Hons), PGCE
Founded 1947
School status Independent. Boys day, weekly and full boarding 7–13
Religious denomination Church of England
Member of BSA, IAPS, NAHT, SATIPS
Learning difficulties WI/DYS MLD
Behavioural and emotional disorders RA
Physical and medical conditions RA
No of pupils 190; *(full boarding)* 101; *Boys* 190
Teacher:pupil ratio 1:8
Average class size 13
Fees per annum *(full boarding)* £21150; *(day)* £16245

Curriculum: All main subjects are studied. ICT is taught throughout the school, as are art, design and technology. Outstanding teaching towards scholarships and Common Entrance passes is balanced with music, PE and a wide range of competitive sports and games. Magnificent new sports hall, music school and indoor swimming pool.

Entry requirements: Parental choice and interview followed by placing test. It is essential to register boys well in advance of their sixth birthday.

Papplewick enjoys a spacious rural location on the edge of Windsor Great Park. Convenient links with M4, M3, M25, Heathrow and Gatwick. The quality of care and the dedication of staff are outstanding and remain Papplewick's special hallmark.

Queen Anne's School

6 Henley Road, Caversham, Reading, Berkshire RG4 6DX Tel: (0118) 918 7333 Fax: (0118) 918 7310
E-mail: admissions@qas.org.uk   Website: www.qas.org.uk   www.gabbitas.co.uk

The Headmistress Mrs J Harrington
Founded 1894
School status Girls Boarding and Day 11–18. Weekly and flexi-boarding available
Religious denomination Church of England
No of pupils 320; *(full boarding)* 140; *Girls* 320
Teacher:pupil ratio 1:7.4
Average class size 16–18
Fees per annum *(full boarding)* £24585; *(flexi)* from £22095; *(day)* £16680. Overnight accommodation £35

Situated on a 35-acre campus north of Reading, with excellent road/rail links to London, Heathrow and the South East. Entry at 11+, 13+ and Sixth Form. Academic, drama, music, art, sport and Sixth Form scholarships and bursaries are available.

Facilities include: new performing arts centre, large library, art and design centre, modern languages block, ICT department and seven-laboratory science centre. Also an excellent sports centre with squash courts, climbing wall, fitness suite and indoor swimming pool. Seven boarding and day houses, including a new Sixth Form centre.

Excellent academic results, a wide range of extra-curricular activities and strong pastoral care prepare girls for university and successful careers.

England

Reading Blue Coat School

Holme Park, Sonning-on-Thames, Reading, Berkshire RG4 6SU
Tel: (0118) 944 1005   Fax: (0118) 944 2690
E-mail: vmf@blue-coat.reading.sch.uk
Website: www.blue-coat.reading.sch.uk   www.gabbitas.co.uk

Headmaster Mr M J Windsor MA, BA, PGCE
Founded 1646
School status Boys Day 11–18. Co-educational
Sixth Form
Religious denomination Church of England
Member of AGBIS, HMC, SHMIS
No of pupils 677; *Senior* 456; *Sixth Form* 221;
Girls 61; *Boys* 616

Set in 46 acres of attractive parkland including a boathouse and direct access to the Thames, Blue Coat provides a stimulating and friendly atmosphere in which each pupil can realize their full intellectual, physical and creative potential. To enable students to reach attainable goals the school provides close attention to their progress by good teaching and careful assessment.

The school sets great store by the philosophy that a good education is much more than a formal academic training consequently, while academic excellence is our goal, co-curricular activities play an important part of Blue Coat life. A wide range of sports are offered; CCF, Duke of Edinburgh Awards Scheme, Sports Leadership Award and public speaking are some of the many activities that thrive at school.

Music and drama have a strong tradition; a number of concerts and drama productions being staged regularly. Over a third of pupils play musical instruments.

St George's School

Ascot, Berkshire SL5 7DZ   Tel: (01344) 629900   Fax: (01344) 629901
E-mail: office@stgeorges-ascot.org.uk   Website: www.stgeorges-ascot.org.uk   www.gabbitas.co.uk

Headmistress Mrs C Jordan MA, PGCE
Founded 1877
School status Independent. Girls Boarding and
Day 11–18
Religious denomination Church of England
Member of GSA
Learning difficulties WI/DYC DYP DYS
Behavioural and emotional disorders RA/
ADHD ASP
Physical and medical conditions HL RA SM/
HEA VI
No of pupils 270; *(full boarding)* 117; *(day)*
153; *Girls* 270
Fees per annum *(full boarding)* £25350; *(day)*
£16440

St George's School, Ascot, is located in the Berkshire countryside. Entry is by examination and, while broadstream, the academic results are outstanding.

Boarders and day girls benefit from the caring and personal attention of a dedicated teaching and pastoral staff. The main faith is Church of England, but girls from any denomination are welcome. Extra-curricular activities are many and include music, drama, debating, voluntary service, Duke of Edinbugh's Award and photography. Sport is excellent and includes lacrosse, tennis, swimming, gymnastics, squash and fitness exercising. St George's, Ascot, is committed to the development of the individual and her talents, to the best of her ability.

St John's Beaumont

Priest Hill, Old Windsor, Windsor, Berkshire SL4 2JN   Tel: (01784) 432428   Fax: (01784) 494048
E-mail: admissions@stjohnsbeaumont.co.uk   Website: www.stjohnsbeaumont.org.uk

Headmaster Mr G Delaney BA (Hons), PGCE
School status Independent. Boys Boarding and Day 4–13. Boarders from 7   **Founded** 1888
Religious denomination Roman Catholic
Member of AGBIS, BSA, IAPS
Accredited by IAPS, ISCIT SM TW WA2
No of pupils 325; *(full boarding)* 30; *(weekly boarding)* 30; *(day)* 265; *Boys* 325
Teacher:pupil ratio 1:8 **Average class size** 17
Fees per annum *(full boarding)* £19550; *(weekly)* £16920; *(day)* £6900–£12870

St John's Beaumont is a Roman Catholic boys boarding and day preparatory school located in Old Windsor, 35 minutes from London. Set in 70 acres next to Windsor Great Park are the imposing, spacious, purpose-built premises designed by JF Bentley, architect of Westminster Cathedral.

The school has outstanding academic, creative and sporting facilities including a science, technology and art block, ICT centre, music theatre, indoor swimming pool and four floodlit tennis courts. A state-of-the-art sports complex is in construction for September 2009. Wireless technology is available in all classrooms enabling access to individual laptops. Boys are prepared for some of the country's top public schools and have won many Scholarships in recent years. There is a strong musical tradition and opportunity for a wide range of extra-curricular activities including real tennis, polo, SCUBA diving and chess.

St Mary's School, Ascot

St Mary's Road, Ascot, Berkshire SL5 9JF   Tel: (01344) 623721   Fax: (01344) 873281
E-mail: admissions@st-marys-ascot.co.uk   Website: www.st-marys-ascot.co.uk www.gabbitas.co.uk

Headmistress Mrs M Breen MSc, BSc
Founded 1885
School status Independent. Girls Boarding and Day 11–18. Boarders from 11
Religious denomination Roman Catholic
Member of BSA, GSA
Accredited by GSA
Learning difficulties WI/DYP DYS
Physical and medical conditions RA SM WA2/EPI HEA HI W
No of pupils 371; *(full boarding)* 355; *(day)* 14; *Senior* 263; *Sixth Form* 108; *Girls* 371
Teacher:pupil ratio 1:7 **Average class size** 16
Fees per annum *(full boarding)* £26610; *(day)* £18930

St Mary's School, Ascot is a Roman Catholic boarding school for girls aged 11–18 years. Entry at 11+, 13+ and 16+ is subject to the school's own entry procedure. Facilities are excellent as is our record in public examinations.

We are a friendly, stable and caring community, proud of our academic, sporting and musical achievements and dedicated to bringing out the full potential of each of our pupils. We are committed to full boarding, with spaces for a few day pupils living nearby. We offer a stimulating range of extra-curricular activities which take place in the evenings and throughout the weekend.

England

St Piran's Preparatory School

Gringer Hill, Maidenhead, Berkshire SL6 7LZ   Tel: (01628) 594302   Fax: (01628) 594301
E-mail: registrar@stpirans.co.uk   Website: www.stpirans.co.uk   www.gabbitas.co.uk

Head Master Mr J Carroll BA (Hons), BPhilEd, PGCE   **Founded** 1805
School status Independent. Co-educational Day 3–13
Religious denomination Church of England
Member of IAPS, ISBA, NAHT, SATIPS
Accredited by IAPS
Learning difficulties CA SNU/DYC DYP DYS MLD
Behavioural and emotional disorders RA/ADD ADHD ASP
Physical and medical conditions AT RA SM WA3/EPI HEA HI VI
No of pupils 375; *(day)* 375; *Nursery* 54; *Pre-prep* 112; *Prep* 178; *Senior* 31; *Girls* 150; *Boys* 225
Average class size 18
Fees per annum *(day)* £2850–£10560

Curriculum: National Curriculum subjects up to Year 8. French is offered from Reception to Year 8. German and Spanish are options for seniors.

Sport: A comprehensive range for all pupils. Facilities include a sports hall, indoor swimming pool, all-weather pitch, dance studio, music room, ICT suite and new learning resource centre.

Facilities: Excellent facilities. Fully networked ICT department, PCs and interactive whiteboards in classrooms and a new learning resource centre. We have three specialist teachers for those who need additional support. Trampolining, drama, games and crafts, among others, are activities for Year 5 to Year 8 at the end of the day.

Entry requirements: Entry is by interview, school report and, where necessary, a short assessment if entry is higher up in the school. The school has expanded to a three-form entry at age 7+.

Sunningdale School

Dry Arch Road, Sunningdale, Berkshire SL5 9PY   Tel: (01344) 620159   Fax: (01344) 873304
E-mail: headmaster@sunningdaleschool.co.uk   Website: www.sunningdaleschool.co.uk

Headmaster Mr T A C N Dawson
Founded 1874
School status Boys Boarding 8–13
Religious denomination Church of England
Member of IAPS
Accredited by IAPS
Learning difficulties SNU WI/DYC DYP DYS
No of pupils 100; *(full boarding)* 95; *Boys* 100
Teacher:pupil ratio 1:7
Average class size 11
Fees per annum *(full boarding)* £16470; *(day)* £12690

Sunningdale is a boys' prep school founded in 1874. The school retains a strong sense of tradition, allied with excellence of teaching and pastoral care; it is this vital combination that successfully prepares boys for their move onwards to some of the finest senior independent schools in the country. Sunningdale has an enviable reputation for equipping boys with good manners, confidence and outstanding academic results. A total of 10 scholarships have been awarded in the last three years which is quite an achievement for a school that is non-selective. Boys mostly go to Eton, Harrow and Stowe. There is a wide range of extra-curricular activities available including clay pigeon shooting, riding, cooking, fencing, judo and chess.

Upton House School

115 St Leonard's Road, Windsor, Berkshire SL4 3DF   Tel: (01753) 862610   Fax: (01753) 621950
E-mail: info@uptonhouse.org.uk Website: www.uptonhouse.org.uk www.gabbitas.co.uk

Headmistress Mrs M Collins BA (Hons), PGCE
Founded 1936
School status Independent. Co-educational
Day Boys 2–7 Girls 2–11
Religious denomination Church of England
Member of AHIS, IAPS, ISA, ISCis
Accredited by IAPS, ISC
Learning difficulties SNU WI/DYP DYS MLD
Behavioural and emotional disorders CA RA
ST TS/ADD AUT
Physical and medical conditions CA IT RA SM
TW/CP EPI HEA
No of pupils 250; *Nursery* 60; *Pre-prep* 110;
Prep 80; *Girls* 170; *Boys* 80
Teacher:pupil ratio 1:6 **Average class size** 17
Fees per annum *(day)* £3900–£10425

Upton House School is a thriving community of 250 children and 45 staff in the heart of historic Windsor. It is dedicated to a caring philosophy for all its children, allowing each to develop their talents and, at the same time, to learn the importance of helping others in the wider world.

A very full syllabus is offered and we take particular pride in making the whole learning process fun – with a range of extra-curricular activities, off-site visits, after-school clubs, dramatic productions, summer camps, etc.

For further information or a copy of our prospectus, please contact the Secretary, Mrs Jill Gilmour on (01753) 862610 or at info@uptonhouse.org.uk or www.uptonhouse.org.uk.

Wellington College

Duke's Ride, Crowthorne, Berkshire RG45 7PU   Tel: (01344) 444013   Fax: (01344) 444115
E-mail: admissions@wellingtoncollege.org.uk Website: www.wellingtoncollege.org.uk

Headmaster Dr A F Seldon MA, PhD, FRSA,
MBA, FRHisS
The Second Master Mr R I H B Dyer BA
Director of Admissions Mr R J W Walker MA
(Cantab) **Founded** 1853
College status Independent. Co-educational
Boarding and Day 13–18 (Co-ed Sixth Form,
fully co-ed from Sept 2006). Flexi-boarding
available. Boarders from 13
Religious denomination Church of England
Member of AGBIS, BSA, HMC, ISBA, Round
Square **Accredited by** HMC
Learning difficulties RA/DYC DYP DYS
Behavioural and emotional disorders RA/ADD
ADHD
No of pupils 844; *(full boarding)* 689; *(day)*
155; *Girls* 218; *Boys* 626
Teacher:pupil ratio 1:9 **Average class size** 16
Fees per annum *(full boarding)* £26925; *(day)*
£19215–£20175

Wellington College is one of the country's leading independent schools. A sensible priority is given to academic study (98 per cent of leavers go on to degree courses), but the highest standards are also achieved in other aspects of school life, including sport, art, technology, writing, music and drama. Extra-curricular activities are important, as they develop self-confidence and provide experience in teamwork, initiative and leadership.

Wellington provides a well-disciplined framework within which pupils have a wide range of opportunities to fulfil their personal potential.

England

Pipers Corner School

Pipers Lane, Great Kingshill, High Wycombe, Buckinghamshire HP15 6LP Tel: (01494) 718255
E-mail: theschool@piperscorner.co.uk   Website: www.piperscorner.co.uk   www.gabbitas.co.uk

Headmistress Mrs H J Ness-Gifford BA (Hons), PGCE   **Founded** 1930
School status Independent. Girls Day and Boarding 3–18. Flexi-boarding available
Religious denomination Church of England
Member of AGBIS, AHIS, BSA, GSA, ISBA
Accredited by GSA, ISC
No of pupils 514; *(full boarding)* 25; *(weekly boarding)* 9; *(day)* 480
Fees per annum *(full boarding)* £16200–£19650; *(weekly)* £15960–£19410; *(day)* £6150–£11925

At Pipers Corner there is a focus on academic excellence as girls are supported and challenged to achieve their full potential. In addition to providing a stimulating learning environment we also encourage girls to cultivate any sporting or creative talents they have through a wide range of lunch-time and after school clubs and activities. Girls enjoy the use of our excellent facilities including: swimming pool, sports hall and dance and drama studios. Academically successful, our girls progress to further study at Oxbridge and other top universities or specialist dance, drama and music colleges. The Pipers boarding community offers flexibility, freedom and peace of mind to both girls and their parents. Our safe and secure accommodation, together with our experienced house staff, provides a 'second home' environment at the heart of the school.

Swanbourne House School

Swanbourne, Milton Keynes, Buckinghamshire MK17 0HZ Tel: (01296) 720264 Fax: (01296) 728089
E-mail: office@swanbourne.org   Website: www.swanbourne.org   www.gabbitas.co.uk

Joint Heads Mr S D Goodhart BEd (Hons) and Mrs J S Goodhart BEd Cert Ed
Founded 1920
School status Independent. Co-educational Boarding and Day 3–13. Flexi-boarding available. Boarders from 7
Religious denomination Church of England
Member of BSA, IAPS, ISBA, SATIPS
Accredited by IAPS
Learning difficulties WI/DYS MLD
Behavioural and emotional disorders RA
Physical and medical conditions SM/HEA
No of pupils 413; *(full boarding)* 28; *(weekly boarding)* 21; *(day)* 364; *Nursery* 45; *Pre-prep* 123; *Prep* 275; *Girls* 188; *Boys* 225
Fees per annum *(full boarding)* £16785; *(weekly)* £16785; *(day)* £6150–£13095
Fees Sliding scale depending on age

Swanbourne House is a successful IAPS preparatory school from which academic scholarships and awards in arts/sport and music are won every year. There are many opportunities for personal development through activities, sport, the arts, holiday clubs and trips abroad. Pastoral care is our beacon and our leadership training is renowned. We have excellent facilities. London parents say we have the 'wow' factor. Come and visit, you can be assured of a warm welcome. Entry is by a familiarization day and short assessment test. Our latest inspections describe the school; boarding, spirituality, pastoral care, organization and management as outstanding.

Chigwell School

High Road, Chigwell, Essex IG7 6QF   Tel: (020) 8501 5700   Fax: (020) 8500 6232
E-mail: hm@chigwell-school.org   Website: www.chigwell-school.org   www.gabbitas.co.uk

Headmaster Mr M E Punt MA, MSC
Founded 1629
School status Co-educational Day and
Boarding 7–18. Flexi-boarding available.
Boarders from 15
Religious denomination Church of England
Member of HMC, IAPS
Accredited by HMC, IAPS, ISC
Learning difficulties RA WI/DYS
Behavioural and emotional disorders CO
Physical and medical conditions SM
No of pupils 735; *(full boarding)* 45; *(day)* 675;
Prep 338; *Senior* 377; *Sixth Form* 178;
Girls 330; *Boys* 405
Teacher:pupil ratio 1:3
Average class size 10 (Sixth Form); 20 (Junior
School)
Fees per annum *(full boarding)* £19611;
(weekly) £17493–£18567; *(day)* £8391–
£12903

The oldest major co-educational independent
school in the west Essex and east London area,
founded in 1629, set in 70 acres of green belt
while on the Central Line and bus routes, Chigwell
has a fine reputation for academic excellence and
extra-curricular achievements. In 2007 84 per
cent of A level results were either A or B grades
with 10 per cent gaining Oxbridge places and over
60 per cent reaching the leading Russell Group
universities. Excellent range of extra-curricular
activities, particular strengths in sport, drama
and music. Facilities include an outstanding
drama centre, music school and arts centre.

England

Abbot's Hill School

Bunkers Lane, Hemel Hempstead, Hertfordshire HP3 8RP
Tel: (01442) 240333   Fax: (01442) 269981
E-mail: registrar@abbotshill.herts.sch.uk   Website: www.abbotshill.herts.sch.uk

Headmistress Mrs K Lewis
Founded 1912
School status Independent. Girls Day 3–16
(Boys 3–5)
Religious denomination Church of England
Member of AHIS, GSA
Accredited by GSA, IAPS, ISC
Learning difficulties CA SNU WI/DYC DYP
DYS
Behavioural and emotional disorders CO/ASP
BESD
Physical and medical conditions IT SM/EPI
HEA HI VI
No of pupils 482; *(day)* 482; *Girls* 482
Average class size 12–18
Fees per annum *(day)* £1200–£12990

We are justly proud of our academic record but never stray from our prime objective: to educate the whole person, to achieve his or her highest personal, social and educational potential. Every pupil benefits from being known personally by the Headmistress and teaching staff in a warm and enabling environment.

A thriving, vibrant, high-achieving school, Abbot's Hill is set in 76 acres of parkland on the edge of Hemel Hempstead, Hertfordshire.

The school and its dedicated staff offer excellent facilities and a wide range of subjects and extra-curricular activities.

Aldenham School

Elstree, Hertfordshire WD6 3AJ   Tel: (01923) 858122   Fax: (01923) 854410
E-mail: enquiries@aldenham.com   Website: www.aldenham.com

Headmaster Mr J C Fowler MA
Deputy Head Mrs D E MacGinty BEd
Senior Master Mr N D Pulman MA
Founded 1597
School status Independent. Co-educational
Boarding and Day 3–18. Flexi-boarding
available. Boarders from 11
Religious denomination Church of England,
Inter-Denominational
Member of AGBIS, BSA, CASE, HMC, IAPS
Accredited by HMC, IAPS, ISA, ISC
No of pupils 700; *(boarding)* 126; *(day)* 574;
Nursery 19; *Pre-prep* 59; *Prep* 77; *Senior* 381;
Sixth Form 165; *Girls* 149; *Boys* 551
Teacher:pupil ratio 1:8
Average class size 20
Fees per annum *(boarding)* £17436–£24351;
(day) £11643–£16752

Aldenham
founded 1597

The curriculum includes the arts, sciences and humanities, music technology, business studies, drama and sports science. Personal tutors are provided.

An extensive games and activities programme includes football, hockey, basketball, squash, sailing and cricket. Strong music and drama departments stage regular productions. The Learning Support department encourages able pupils with dyslexia and dyscalculia and provides specialist English lessons for overseas students (EAL). Awards for academic potential, sport, music (including organ scholarship), art and technology are available.

Aldenham stands in a beautiful site of more than 110 acres, with modern state-of-the-art facilities.

Arts Educational School, Tring Park

Tring Park, Tring, Hertfordshire HP23 5LX   Tel: (01442) 824255   Fax: (01442) 891069
E-mail: info@aes-tring.com   Website: www.aes-tring.com

The Principal Mr S Anderson MA (Cantab)
BMus, ARCM   **Founded** 1919
School status Independent. Co-educational
Boarding and Day 8–19
Religious denomination Inter-Denominational
Member of BSA, ISA, SHA, SHMIS
Accredited by ISA, SHMIS
Learning difficulties CA WI/DYS MLD
Behavioural and emotional disorders CO
Physical and medical conditions SM WA3/HEA
No of pupils 294; *(full boarding)* 213; *(day)* 81;
Prep 13; *Senior* 153; *Sixth Form* 109; *Girls* 222;
Boys 72
Fees per annum *(full boarding)* £19005–
£26850; *(day)* £12600–£19710

Tring Park offers exciting educational opportunities for pupils who show talent in one or more of the performing arts and we are committed to ensuring that all pupils fulfil their potential. The school is set in 17 acres of attractive and secluded parkland and the main house was formerly a Rothschild Mansion.

The school accommodates 213 boarders and 81 day pupils and aims to provide an environment ideally suited to the teaching of the performing arts, combined with academic study to the highest level.

Tring Park is part of the Music and Dance Scheme, funded and administered by the DCSF, and places are awarded annually under this scheme for talented classical dancers. A number of dance and drama awards are available for the Sixth Form dance course.

Up to age 14 all pupils study dance, music and drama combined with a full and vigorous academic curriculum. The pupils all study eight or nine GCSE subjects combined with the Dance or Performance foundation course. In the Sixth Form pupils study either three or four A levels or the BTec qualification combined with the Dance, Musical Theatre or Drama Course. Academic study receives equal emphasis and the department provides a broad and balanced curriculum for all pupils. Following success in their Sixth Form examinations, many of our students proceed to higher vocational or academic studies at universities and colleges. For others, the opportunity to perform becomes a reality immediately.

For those entering the dance course, we believe in training the whole dancer in body, mind and in artistic understanding. Dancers are encouraged to fulfil their own individual potential and each pupil's progress is monitored carefully.

Sixth Form students joining the drama course will undertake an intensive and wide-ranging preparation for either direct entry into the theatre, further training at drama school or, with appropriate A levels, higher education on a relevant degree course.

The musical theatre course for Sixth Form students is designed to extend the skills of the all-round performer and to focus them in this popular entertainment area.

Throughout the school, pupils have frequent opportunities to present work in the Markova Theatre and there are regular public shows given by junior and senior pupils. The range of work undertaken provides pupils with the opportunity to become versatile and able to communicate skillfully, whatever the chosen field.

Individual appointments are made to visit the school and auditions are held on a regular basis.

Haileybury

Hertford, Hertfordshire SG13 7NU   Tel: (01992) 463353   Fax: (01992) 470663
E-mail: registrar@haileybury.com   Website: www.haileybury.com   www.gabbitas.co.uk

The Master Mr S A Westley MA
Registrar Mrs E Alexander BA   **Founded** 1862
School status Independent. Co-educational
Boarding and Day 11–18. Flexi-boarding
available. Boarders from 11
Religious denomination Church of England
Member of BSA, HMC, IBO, ISCis
Accredited by HMC, ISC
Learning difficulties RA SNU WI/DYC DYP DYS
Behavioural and emotional disorders CO/ASP
AUT
Physical and medical conditions WA2/HEA W
No of pupils 751; *(full boarding)* 496; *(day)* 255;
Senior 644; *Sixth Form* 289; *Girls* 309; *Boys* 442
Teacher:pupil ratio 1:7 **Average class size** 16
Fees per annum *(full boarding)* £16050–
£25305; *(day)* £12630–£19005

Boys and girls, mostly boarding, admitted at 11
into the Lower School, at 13 into the Main School,
and also at 16 into the Sixth Form.

Magnificent classical buildings are complemented by modern, state-of-the art developments.
Set in 500 rural acres and situated 20 miles north
of central London, Haileybury combines high
academic standards with broad-ranging excellence in art, music, drama and sport. The school
is pleased to offer the International Baccalaureate
Diploma Programme alongside A levels. Please
contact the Registrar for further details.

Haresfoot Preparatory School

Chesham Road, Berkhamsted, Hertfordshire HP4 2SZ   Tel: (01442) 872742   Fax: (01442) 872742
E-mail: haresfootschool@btconnect.com   Website: www.haresfoot.herts.sch.uk

Headteacher Mrs S Jaspal BA (QTS) (Hons)
Founded 1985
School status Independent. Co-educational
Day 0–11
Member of ISA **Accredited by** ISA
Learning difficulties CA WI/DYS SP&LD
Physical and medical conditions CA RA/IM
No of pupils 142; *(day)* 142; *Girls* 65; *Boys* 77
Average class size 15
Fees per annum *(day)* £1524–£8070

single child. Every Year
6 child is given a posi-
tion of responsibility in
their final year. Each
child plays in the
school's sports teams
and has a part in school performances, whatever
their abilities. In return, children are expected
from a young age to try their hardest, to be courteous, and to embrace new experiences.

Staff at Haresfoot know that pupils succeed when
there are high expectations of them. Exciting
lessons and activities, and a strongly nurturing
approach, help Haresfoot pupils enjoy excellent
academic success.

With a firm foundation in its Day Nursery and
Pre-School, children at Haresfoot can move
swiftly on to Haresfoot's exciting, challenging
and balanced curriculum in Key Stages 1 and 2.

Haresfoot is proud of the achievements of every

Haresfoot children perform and speak regularly
in front of others. They learn to communicate
confidently with people of all ages and to become
responsible citizens who move confidently on to a
variety of local Secondary schools (including
Buckinghamshire Grammar schools). Children
can join Haresfoot's Pre-school from rising 3
years. Younger children can join our on-site Day
Nursery, 'Happy Hares'. Wraparound care is
available for most weeks of the year for all children. Bursaries and scholarships are available.

Queenswood

Shepherds Way, Brookmans Park, Hatfield, Hertfordshire AL9 6NS
Tel: (01707) 602500   Fax: (01707) 602597
E-mail: registry@queenswood.org   Website: www.queenswood.org

Principal Mrs P Edgar BA (Hons) (London), PGCE
Founded September 1894
School status Independent. Girls Boarding and Day 11–18. Flexi-boarding available. Boarders from 11
Religious denomination Inter-Denominational
Member of BSA, GSA
Accredited by British Council, GSA, ISC
Learning difficulties WI/DYS
Behavioural and emotional disorders CO
Physical & medical conditions RA SM WA3/HI
No of pupils 411; *(full boarding)* 206; *(day)* 205; *Senior* 302; *Sixth Form* 109; *Girls* 411
Teacher:pupil ratio 1:7
Average class size 17
Fees per annum *(full boarding)* £23370–£25485; *(day)* £18015–£19680. Fees for direct Sixth Form entry carry a surcharge of £500 per term. Sibling discount available

Situated within 120 acres of Hertfordshire's finest countryside close to London, Queenswood is easily accessible by road, rail and air. We offer a well-rounded education for an integrated multi-national community of girls who live and learn together. Our well-qualified and experienced academic and pastoral staff challenge and assist the girls to develop their capabilities. We live in an environment where results matter, confidence is vital and self-belief anchors the individual.

Our extensive facilities in stimulating and safe surroundings include comfortable boarding houses, modern teaching suites, a new theatre, an arts and music centre, modern indoor pool and over 27 tennis courts. We provide a broad and balanced education to prepare young women to be part of a global community in a modern world.

The Royal Masonic School for Girls

Rickmansworth Park, Rickmansworth, Hertfordshire WD3 4HF
Tel: (01923) 773168   Fax: (01923) 896729   E-mail: admissions@royalmasonic.herts.sch.uk
Website: www.royalmasonic.herts.sch.uk   www.gabbitas.co.uk

The Headmistress Mrs D Rose MA (Cantab)
Admissions Secretary Mrs G Braiden
Founded 1788
School status Independent. Girls Day and Boarding 4–18. Flexi-boarding available. Boarders from 7
Religious denomination Non-Denominational
Member of BSA, GSA, ISBA, SHA
Accredited by GSA, ISC
No of pupils 786; *(full boarding)* 82; *(weekly boarding)* 46; *(day)* 658; *Pre-prep* 49; *Prep* 132; *Senior* 444; *Sixth Form* 161; *Girls* 786
Teacher:pupil ratio 1:11 **Average class size** 22
Fees per annum *(full boarding)* £12150–£20415; *(weekly)* £11940–£19920; *(day)* £6840–£12780. Forces discount available and sibling discount

where the highest standards prevail. The school has outstanding facilities and occupies a stunning 315-acre site, only 30 minutes from central London by underground. An impressive sports hall, indoor swimming pool, squash, tennis and netball courts, and hockey pitches maintain sporting excellence. Rickmansworth is close to the M25 with easy access to London and its airports.

Boarding pupils are cared for in well-appointed and spacious houses, with experienced, caring residential staff. Our boarding community is made up of British and overseas boarders and is well-balanced.

Admission is by the school's own entrance examination and interview. A number of generous scholarships are available.

RMS offers an exceptionally wide-ranging curriculum in a supportive and friendly environment,

St Albans High School for Girls

Townsend Avenue, St Albans, Hertfordshire AL1 3SJ   Tel: (01727) 853800   Fax: (01727) 792516
E-mail: info@stalbans-high.herts.sch.uk   Website: www.sahs.org.uk   www.gabbitas.co.uk

Headmistress Ms J C Pain MA, MA MBA, NPQH   **Founded** 1889
School status Independent. Girls Day 4–18
Religious denomination Church of England
Member of GDST, GSA **Accredited by** GSA
Learning difficulties WI/DYS MLD
Physical and medical conditions TW WA2
No of pupils 950; *(day)* 950; *Pre-prep* 123; *Prep* 187; *Senior* 469; *Sixth Form* 167; *Girls* 950
Average class size 24 (Years 7 to 9)
Fees per annum *(day)* £8745–£11115. Lunch included for infants (Years 1–2)

Curriculum: A broad and balanced academic education is provided to include National Curriculum subjects and others. Teaching methods are modern and extensive use is made of resources such as computers and audio-video equipment. Public examination results at GCSE and A level are of a consistently high standard and, for the vast majority, degree courses follow.

Entry requirements and examinations: Entry is by examination at 4, 5, 7, 11 and 16, with intermediate ages being subject to vacancies.

Academic and leisure facilities: A wide range of extra-curricular activities is offered, with sport, music and drama featuring strongly. Facilities for physical education include playing fields and a sports hall adjoining a new complex (opened Sept 2006) comprising 25-metre indoor pool, fitness suite and dance studio.

Scholarships/bursaries: Academic and music scholarships are available on entry at 11. Further academic scholarships are available at 16. Bursaries are available from Year 3 onwards.

St Albans School

Abbey Gateway, St Albans, Hertfordshire AL3 4HB   Tel: (01727) 855521   Fax: (01727) 843447
E-mail: hm@st-albans-school.org.uk   Website: www.st-albans.herts.sch.uk   www.gabbitas.co.uk

The Headmaster Mr A R Grant MA, PGCE, FRSA   **Founded** 948
School status Independent. Boys Day 11–18. Co-educational Sixth Form
Religious denomination Inter-Denominational
Member of AGBIS, HMC **Accredited by** ISC
Learning difficulties WI/DYP DYS
Behavioural and emotional disorders CO/ADHD ASP
Physical and medical conditions AT RA TW WA3/HEA HI
No of pupils 806; *Senior* 498; *Sixth Form* 274; *Girls* 34; *Boys* 772
Teacher:pupil ratio 1:9
Average class size *c.* 22 (Form size up to Y 11)
Fees per annum *(day)* £12405

The school is able to offer some assistance with fees in certain circumstances of proven need, from its own endowed bursary fund. All bursaries are means-tested. A variable number of academic scholarships worth up to 50 per cent of the annual fees are awarded on academic merit at 11+, 13+ and 16+. Scholarships for music and art are offered at 13+. Bursaries towards music tuition are awarded on the basis of an annual competition for pupils from each year in the school. Further details of all awards are available from the Head.

The school is a registered charity and aims to provide an excellent education, enabling pupils to achieve the highest standard of academic success according to ability, and to develop their character and personality so as to become caring and self-disciplined adults.

St Andrew's Montessori School

High Elms Lane, Watford, Hertfordshire WD25 0JX   Tel: (01923) 681103   Fax: (01923) 681103
E-mail: standrewsmont@hotmail.com   Website: www.standrewsmontessori.co.uk

Principal Mrs S R M O'Neill DipBA, Cert Ed, DipAMI   **Founded** 1991
School status Independent. Co-educational Day 0–11
Religious denomination Inter-Denominational AMI, MSA
Learning difficulties CA WI/DYC DYP DYS MLD SP&LD
Behavioural and emotional disorders RA/ADD ASP AUT
Physical and medical conditions AT CA DS TW WA1 WA2/HEA HI
No of pupils 70; *(day)* 70; *Nursery* 46; *Pre-prep* 12; *Prep* 12; *Girls* 30; *Boys* 40
Teacher:pupil ratio 1:3 up to 8
Average class size 10–17
Fees per annum *(day)* £1749–£7398

St Andrew's Montessori School is set in a grade II listed manor house, set in 21 acres of lawn, meadow and woodland.

Children:
- work at their own pace towards targets;
- have the love of learning instilled in them;
- are encouraged to have good behaviour;
- have opportunities to develop to their maximum potential and are encouraged to think for themselves and make decisions;
- develop self-confidence, independence and self-motivation.

St Columba's College

King Harry Lane, St Albans, Hertfordshire AL3 4AW   Tel: (01727) 855185   Fax: (01727) 892024
E-mail: admissions@st-columbas.herts.sch.uk   Website: www.stcolumbascollege.org

Head Mr D Buxton BA, MTh, MA
Director of Admissions Mr AKO Smith DLC, Cert Ed   **Founded** 1939
College status Boys Day 4–18
Religious denomination Roman Catholic
Member of HMC, IAPS, SHMIS
Accredited by HMC, IAPS, ISC
Learning difficulties WI/DYP DYS
Behavioural and emotional disorders CO ST/ADD ADHD ASP
Physical and medical conditions CA RA SM TW WA2/EPI HEA HI IM VI
No of pupils 850; *Pre-prep* 75; *Prep* 150; *Senior* 465; *Sixth Form* 160; *Boys* 850
Teacher:pupil ratio 1:10 **Average class size** 20
Fees per annum *(day)* £7920–£10017

of 850. We offer a broad, progressive education to boys from 4–18, including a Sixth Form of over 160 and no fewer than 20 subjects offered at A level. Our ethos and values are rooted within the Catholic educational tradition but our community encompasses many students of other traditions and backgrounds.

St Columba's College is unique as the only Brothers of the Sacred Heart School in the country, originally opened in 1939. The college has progressively grown over the years to its current roll

Academic standards are consistently high throughout the college, but it is the 'value added' rather than the league table position from which we derive the greater pride. We aim for every student to achieve his own best standard.

England

St Edmund's College and St Hugh's School

Old Hall Green, Ware, Hertfordshire SG11 1DS   Tel: (01920) 821504   Fax: (01920) 823011
E-mail: admissions@stedmundscollege.org Website: www.stedmundscollege.org www.gabbitas.co.uk

Headmaster Mr C P Long BA (Newcastle)
Founded 1568
College status Independent. Co-educational
Day and Boarding 3–18. Flexi-boarding
available. Boarders from 11
Religious denomination Roman Catholic
Accredited by British Council, HMC, ISC
Learning difficulties CA WI/DYP DYS
Behavioural and emotional disorders RA/ASP
Physical and medical conditions IT SM TW
WA2/EPI HEA HI VI
No of pupils 830; *(full boarding)* 97; *(weekly
boarding)* 20; *(day)* 713; *Nursery* 18; *Pre-prep*
19; *Prep* 159; *Senior* 634; *Sixth Form* 161;
Girls 305; *Boys* 525
Teacher:pupil ratio 1:9 **Average class size** 20
Fees per annum *(full boarding)* £18945–
£21660; *(weekly)* £17190–£19575; *(day)*
£8430–£13350

St Edmund's College is England's oldest Catholic

School, founded in 1568, and today provides a traditional Catholic education to over 800 students from all faiths and denominations, both from the UK and worldwide.

One of the key aspects of St Edmund's is its unique style and atmosphere, which values academic excellence and the achievement of a personal best, right through from St Hugh's, the Prep School, to Sixth Form and beyond. In addition, all students are supported by a high level of pastoral care, based on a successful house system.

Facilities included: state-of-the-art computer suites, art and design technology workshops, tennis courts and an indoor swimming pool.

St Francis' College

The Broadway, Letchworth Garden City, Hertfordshire SG6 3PJ   Tel: (01462) 670511
Fax: (01462) 682361 E-mail: enquiries@st-francis.herts.sch.uk Website: www.st-francis-herts.sch.uk

Head Mistress Miss M Hegarty BA, Hdip Ed,
DMS   **Founded** 1933
College status Girls Boarding and Day 3–18.
Flexi-boarding available. Boarders from 7
Religious denomination Christian
Accredited by GSA, ISC
Learning difficulties WI
Physical and medical conditions CA/CP HEA
HI IM VI
No of pupils 450; *(full boarding)* 25; *(weekly
boarding)* 3; *(day)* 422; *Nursery* 18; *Pre-prep*
20; *Prep* 134; *Senior* 203; *Sixth Form* 76;
Girls 450 **Average class size** up to 20
Fees per annum *(full boarding)* £17865–
£20685; *(weekly)* £14520–£17400; *(day)*
£2040–£10515

Small classes allow the girls to receive personal attention, enhancing their performance. Year after year our students achieve excellent academic results at A Level and GCSE. With a pass rate of

100 per cent at A level and 83 per cent A and B grades, the majority of the 2008 leavers gained places at their first choice university, including Oxford and Cambridge. GCSE students also gained a very impressive set of results: 99 per cent pass rate A*–C grades, with 68 per cent A* and A Grades.

While we are justifiably proud of our academic achievement, we also place great importance on the girls' development of interests and strengths through sport, music and drama, as well as enjoying a wide range of extra-curricular activities. Any visitor will notice the excellent relationships between pupils and staff and the warm and friendly atmosphere throughout the college. Class sizes are small, allowing individual attention to remain high.

A number of academic scholarships and bursaries are available. These are awarded on academic merit and financial need and are reviewed annually.

St Margaret's School

Merry Hill Road, Bushey, Hertfordshire WD23 1DT
Tel: (020) 8901 0870   Fax: (020) 8950 1677
E-mail: admissions@stmargarets.herts.sch.uk
Website: www.stmargaretsbushey.org.uk   www.gabbitas.co.uk
Visitors welcome, please contact the Admissions Secretary for an appointment

Headteacher Mrs Lynne Crighton BA (Hons)
Admissions Secretary Ms G Morris
Marketing Manager Ms M Brown
Founded 1749
School status Independent. Girls Boarding and Day 4–18. Flexi-boarding available. Boarders from 11 A thriving north London boarding and day school
Religious denomination Church of England
Member of BSA, GSA
Accredited by GSA
Learning difficulties SNU WI/DYP DYS MLD
Behavioural and emotional disorders CO/ASP
Physical and medical conditions RA SM/EPI HEA
No of pupils 443; (full boarding) 48; (weekly boarding) 10; (day) 377; Pre-prep 45; Prep 71; Senior 229; Sixth Form 98; Girls 443
Teacher:pupil ratio 1:10
Average class size 16
Fees per annum (full boarding) £22035; (weekly) £18885; (day) £8130–£12240
Fees All fees include lunch and supervised prep from Monday to Thursday for day girls

Established in 1749, St Margaret's educates girls aged 4 to 18 years. The school is set in over 70 acres of parkland yet is less than an hour from Marble Arch and Heathrow. We provide a first-class education that delivers an enviable record of success at all public examinations within a supportive, caring community that encourages lasting friendships. The original buildings have been extended and upgraded considerably in the past decade, including a £3 million sports centre, which opened in 2002. There is a wide range of sporting and cultural activities, with language exchange visits, choir, orchestra, speech and drama, ballet, judo, the Duke of Edinburgh's Award Scheme and World Challenge expeditions. A number of scholarships and bursaries are available.

England

York House School

Redheath, Sarratt Road, Croxley Green, Rickmansworth, Hertfordshire WD3 4LW
Tel: (01923) 772395   Fax: (01923) 779231
E-mail: yhsoffice@aol.com   Website: www.york-house.com   www.gabbitas.co.uk

Headmaster Mr P R MacDougall BEd (Hons)
Founded 1910
School status Independent. Boys Day 3–13
(Co-ed 2–5)
Religious denomination Church of England
Member of IAPS
Learning difficulties SNU WI/DYS
Behavioural and emotional disorders RA
No of pupils 295; *(day)* 270; *Nursery* 50;
Pre-prep 70; *Prep* 160; *Girls* 15; *Boys* 280
Teacher:pupil ratio 1:14
Average class size 15
Fees per annum *(day)* £9720
Fees Daily fee for Kindergarten

York House is a well-established, innovative and forward-looking school. Pupils are encouraged to achieve maximum potential, both academically and socially, in a happy, caring environment.

Children are encouraged to enjoy learning creativity, self-discipline and understanding of others. Music, art and drama play important roles in the school's wide curriculum, while a wide range of sports, clubs and societies round off the boys' development.

There is a multi-purpose sports hall/theatre, a library, music facilities and a state-of-the-art computer suite. A new nine-classroom block for 2- to 7-year-olds opened in 2001.

Phase III of the exciting school development plan is now complete. This excellent new building comprises large classrooms for the Junior School, design technology, art and science laboratory.

ACS Hillingdon International School

Hillingdon Court, 108 Vine Lane, Hillingdon, Middlesex UB10 0BE   Tel: (01895) 818402
Fax: (01895) 818404 E-mail: hillingdonadmissions@acs-england.co.uk Website: www.acs-england.co.uk

Head of School Mrs G Apple
Dean of Admissions Ms R Soltis
Founded 1967
School status Co-educational Day 4–18. IB
World School, (IBMYP, IB Diploma) also US
Advanced Placement (AP) & high school diploma
Religious denomination Non-Denominational
Member of CIS, IBO, IBSCA, ISA, LISA, NEASC
NEAS&C and inspected by the Independent
Schools Inspectorate on behalf of Ofsted
No of pupils 577; *(day)* 577; *Nursery* 35;
Pre-prep 193; *Prep* 242; *Senior* 107; *Girls* 283;
Boys 294
Teacher:pupil ratio 1:9 **Average class size** 15
Fees per annum *(day)* £8310–£17410

ACS Hillingdon International School ranks among
the top independent schools in the UK. Its students
have consistently achieved diploma scores well
above international results, which has led to
placements in top universities including London

School of Economics, Oxford, Imperial College
London, University College London, University of
Warwick, the School of Oriental and African
Studies and the Royal Academy of Music. Occupying an 11-acre site, ACS Hillingdon is situated
in a Grade II listed stately mansion with a modern
wing accommodating classrooms, computer labs,
an integrated IT network, libraries, cafeteria, a
gymnasium and an auditorium. The school also
has separate early-childhood pavilions and a new
music centre with a digital recording studio,
rehearsal rooms, practice studios and a computer
lab for music technology.

Heathfield School

Beaulieu Drive, Pinner, Middlesex HA5 1NB   Tel: (020) 8868 2346   Fax: (020) 8868 4405
E-mail: j.moseley@hea.gdst.net   Website: www.heathfield.gdst.net
Admissions Secretary: admissions@hea.gdst.net   Enquiries: enquiries@hea.gdst.net

Head Mistress Miss C Juett BSc (Hons), PGCE
Admissions Secretary Mrs J Smith
Founded 1900
School status Girls Day 3–18
Religious denomination Non-Denominational
Member of GDST, GSA
Learning difficulties CA WI/DYP DYS MLD
Behavioural & emotional disorders ASP
Physical & medical conditions HL RA TW WA3
No of pupils 550; *(day)* 550; *Nursery* 20;
Pre-prep 59; *Prep* 82; *Senior* 293; *Sixth
Form* 96; *Girls* 550 **Average class size** 17
Fees per annum *(day)* £6663–£11100

Heathfield was founded in 1900 and joined the
Girls' Day School Trust in 1987. We aim to promote the pursuit of academic achievement and
personal potential. We remain small so can provide a friendly, caring family atmosphere. The
school provides an all-round education, placing

a strong emphasis on extra-curricular activities.
New facilities include an indoor pool, sports hall,
library, music suite, drama studio, ICT room,
careers room, laboratories and a new dining room.
A new Sixth Form centre was opened in 2008.
Admissions are at 7+, 11+ and 16+. Entry requirements include interview and test. Subjects include
English, mathematics, biology, physics, chemistry,
Mandarin, French, Spanish, German, Latin, classical civilization, history, geography, RS, ICT, art,
music, drama and PE. Twenty-eight subjects at A
level including economics, history of art, business
studies, media studies, theatre studies, government and politics and psychology. Private
lessons in speech and drama, ballet, singing and
instruments. Heathfield has high academic standards and ranks well in the national league tables.
Over 99 per cent pass rate at GCSE and 100 per
cent at A level, on average. All Sixth Form leavers
continue to universities, including Oxbridge.

England

Northwood College

Maxwell Road, Northwood, Middlesex HA6 2YE   Tel: (01923) 825446   Fax: (01923) 836526
E-mail: admissions@northwoodcollege.co.uk   Website: www.northwoodcollege.co.uk

Head Mistress Jacqualyn Pain MA, MA, MBA
Founded 1878
College status Girls Day 3–18
Religious denomination Non-Denominational
Member of GSA, IAPS
Accredited by GSA, IAPS, ISC
Learning difficulties WI/DYP DYS
Physical and medical conditions RA/HEA HI IM VI
No of pupils 817; *Nursery* 27; *Pre-prep* 127; *Prep* 167; *Senior* 373; *Sixth Form* 123; *Girls* 817
Average class size 22–24
Fees per annum *(day)* £3334–£10975

Why choose Northwood College?

A key initiative underpinning our excellent results is our unique Thinking Skills Programme. Run throughout the school, it teaches our girls to become more independent and effective in the way they learn. Year by year, it builds their reasoning skills, improves their creativity and gives them strategies for solving problems and tackling complex decisions. It also shows them that learning is fun.

Recently described as 'a major and successful initiative' which 'makes an outstanding contribution to pupils' general education, influencing both their own and their teachers' approach to learning' (ISI Inspection Report, April 2008), it's just one of the ways in which we equip our students with skills for life.

Heads, Teachers Industry (HTI) recognized this when they awarded us 'Go4it' status earlier this year. Placing enterprise, innovation and initiative at the heart of our approach to education, we give our girls every chance to succeed.

St Catherine's School

Cross Deep, Twickenham, Middlesex TW1 4QJ   Tel: (020) 8891 2898   Fax: (020) 8744 9629
E-mail: info@stcatherineschool.co.uk   Website: www.stcatherineschool.co.uk

Headmistress Sister P Thomas BEd (Hons), MA
Founded 1914
School status Independent. Day Girls 3–16 Boys 3–7 (Sixth Form in 2010)
Religious denomination Roman Catholic
Member of GSA, ISA
Accredited by GSA, ISC
Learning difficulties WI/DYP DYS
No of pupils 354; *Girls* 350; *Boys* 4
Fees per annum *(day)* £7275–£10065

St Catherine's, Twickenham: Focus on the individual.

St Catherine's combines nearly 100 years' experience of Catholic independent education with a modern curriculum that prepares all students for success in the 21st century. We are a Catholic school, in the ecumenical tradition, where every student is a valued member of a happy community. Emphasis is placed on providing a broad education and on responsibility and the importance of respect for others. We are a small school with a strong community spirit and as such are able to focus on the individual and help every child achieve their personal best. High academic standards are maintained but without undue pressure.

In the most recent 2008 GCSE exam results the school achieved 100 per cent A*–C grades, 56 per cent A*/A grades and excellent value-added scores. The school has also recently received four excellent inspection reports for its Senior School, Early Years, After School Care and Catholic life. The Governors have recently announced that an extension for the Prep Department will open in January 2009 and that a Sixth Form centre will be opened in 2010.

The school is in the top 10 of the top 50 small schools for the last three years running in *The Sunday Times Parent Power* magazine.

St Helen's School

Eastbury Road, Northwood, Middlesex HA6 3AS   Tel: (01923) 843210   Fax: (01923) 843211
E-mail: enquiries@sthn.co.uk   Website: www.sthn.co.uk

Headteacher Mrs M Morris BA
Deputy Head Mr P Tiley BSc
Deputy Head Mrs J Parker BA   **Founded** 1899
School status Independent. Girls Day 3–18
Please note that boarding will no longer be
available from July 2009.
Religious denomination Christian
Member of GSA, IBO **Accredited by** GSA, ISC
Learning difficulties WI/DYS
Behavioural and emotional disorders CO
Physical and medical conditions AT CA SM
TW/EPI HEA HI
No of pupils 1137; *(full boarding)* 5; *(weekly
boarding)* 4; *(day)* 1128; *Nursery* 46; *Pre-prep*
177; *Prep* 258; *Senior* 484; *Sixth Form* 172;
Girls 1137
Teacher:pupil ratio 1:10 **Average class size** 21
Fees per annum *(day)* £8196–£11955

St Helen's is a highly academic school and pupils
consistently achieve outstanding results, going on
to prestigious universi-
ties of their first choice.
In the Sixth Form, girls
can study A levels or
the International Bac-
calaureate Diploma.

Staff are subject spe-
cialists who inspire and encourage pupils to learn
independently and to develop lifelong skills in a
friendly, secure and disciplined environment.
Girls study two modern foreign languages
together with Latin, and science is taught throughout as three separate subjects.

We offer excellent facilities including our new
state-of-the-art sports centre; specialist facilities
for science, design and technology, art, drama,
music and ICT; a digital, multi-media language
laboratory; an excellent library housing an extensive collection of books, ICT facilities,
newspapers and periodicals; and well-equipped
teaching rooms.

England

MAP OF LONDON

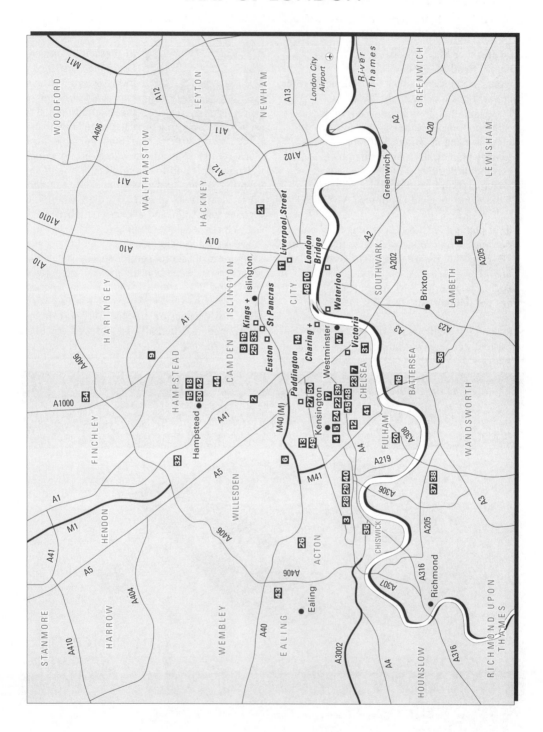

PROFILED SCHOOLS IN LONDON

England

Alleyn's School

Townley Road, Dulwich, London SE22 8SU   Tel: (020) 8557 1500   Fax: (020) 8557 1462
E-mail: registrar@alleyns.org.uk   Website: www.alleyns.org.uk

Headmaster Dr C Diggory BSc, MA, EdD, CMath, FIMA, FRSA
Senior Deputy Head Mr AR Faccinello MA
Deputy Head Mr J G Lilly BA
Founded 1619
School status Independent. Co-educational Day 4–18
Religious denomination Church of England
Member of HMC, IAPS, SHA
Accredited by HMC, IAPS
Learning difficulties WI/DYC DYP DYS
Behavioural and emotional disorders CO/ADD ASP TOU
Physical and medical conditions RA SM TW/EPI HEA HI VI
No of pupils 1181; *(day)* 1181; *Girls* 601; *Boys* 580
Teacher:pupil ratio 1:9
Average class size Juniors (under 11) 21; Seniors (11–16) 20–25; Sixth Form 12
Fees per annum *(day)* £10701–£12996

Alleyn's has been committed to providing co-educational excellence for nearly 30 years, as the best framework for boys and girls to achieve their full potential and to develop life-long skills in preparation for university, the world of work and life in general. We aim to achieve high academic success and expect high standards from all our pupils, who are cared for within a culture of strong pastoral care which promotes and values the widest possible range of co-curricular activities. Drama is very strong (National Youth Theatre was founded at Alleyn's), as is art and music. A new performing arts centre was completed in October 2008. Sport is also much valued with many county honours, but 'sport for all' is the aim.

The American School in London

1 Waverley Place, London, NW8 0NP   Tel: (020) 7449 1200   Fax: (020) 7449 1350
E-mail: admissions@asl.org   Website: www.asl.org

Head of School Mrs C R Hester
Founded 1951
School status Independent. Co-educational Day 4–18
Religious denomination Non-Denominational
Member of CASE, CIS, NAIS
Accredited by CIS, MSA (USA)
Learning difficulties WI/DYS
Behavioural and emotional disorders CO
Physical and medical conditions SM
No of pupils 1323; *Girls* 653; *Boys* 670
Fees per annum *(day)* £17100–£20920

The American School in London is a co-educational, non-profit institution which offers an outstanding American education. The curriculum leads to an American high school diploma, and a strong Advanced Placement programme enables students to enter the top universities in the USA, the UK and other countries.

The core curriculum of English, maths, science and social studies is enriched with courses in modern languages, computing, fine arts and physical education. Small classes allow teachers to focus on individuals; students are encouraged to take an active role in learning to develop the skills necessary for independent critical thinking and expression. Many extra-curricular activities, including sports, music, drama and community service, are available for students of all ages.

The American School in London welcomes students of all nationalities, including non-English speakers below the age of 10, who meet the scholastic standards. Entry is at any time throughout the year.

Arts Educational Schools London

Cone Ripman House, 14 Bath Road, Chiswick, London W4 1LY   Tel: (020) 8987 6600
Fax: (020) 8987 6601 E-mail: pupils@artsed.co.uk   Website: www.artsed.co.uk www.gabbitas.co.uk
Near Turnham Green tube station – an easy two minute walk without the need to cross major roads

Headmaster Mr O Price BEd (Hons)
Founded 1919
School status Independent (special).
Co-educational Day 11–18. Specializing in
Performing Arts with high Academic
achievement
Religious denomination Inter-Denominational
Member of ISA **Accredited by** ISA, ISC
Learning difficulties CA RA/DYS
No of pupils *(day)* 74; *Senior* 120; *Sixth
Form* 54; *Girls* 120; *Boys* 54
Average class size 15
Fees per annum *(day)* £10850
Fees No full school scholarships available

that we owe it to our
pupils to help them be
the very best that they
can be. Dancers learn
to act and sing, actors
learn to sing and
dance, musicians
learn to do more than
play their instruments
well, and everyone
has the opportunity to
be grounded in the
visual arts, languages,
humanities, sciences,

Arts Educational Schools London have been educating young performing artists since 1919, and
there is nothing quite like it in the United
Kingdom. We are small, focused, professional
and idealistic, but we are also profoundly aware

and mathematics. Excellent examination results
are a significant feature of the school. A 100 per
cent pass rate at A level has been achieved for the
past three years; while all our Year 11 pupils have
scored at least five GCSE passes at Grade C or
higher.

England

Ashbourne Independent Sixth Form College

17 Old Court Place, Kensington, London W8 4PL   Tel: (020) 7937 3858   Fax: (020) 7937 2207
E-mail: admin@ashbournecollege.co.uk Website: www.ashbournecollege.co.uk www.gabbitas.co.uk

The Principal Mr M J H Kirby BApSc (Toronto), MSc (London)
Academic Director of Studies Mr John P Wilson BSc (Oxford), PGCE
Founded 1981
College status Co-educational Day and Boarding 14–19. Boarders from 16
Religious denomination Non-Denominational
Member of CIFE **Accredited by** British Council
Learning difficulties RA WI/DYS
Behavioural and emotional disorders RA
Physical and medical conditions WA2
No of pupils 175; *(day)* 175; *Senior* 175; *Sixth Form* 175; *Girls* 90; *Boys* 85
Teacher:pupil ratio 1:6 **Average class size** 8
Fees per annum *(day)* £17100

the modern, from a Medical School Programme overseen by Professor John Foreman, FRCP, to an outstanding provision for the arts including drama, film, fashion, photography, fine art and graphics. Ashbourne achieves excellent examination results and encourages applications from ambitious students.

Wonderfully situated near Kensington Gardens, Ashbourne is a few minutes away from many of London's greatest attractions. The wide-ranging curriculum embraces both the traditional and

The importance placed on individual attention, communication and feedback is reflected in the class sizes – restricted to 10. Moreover, personal tutors have recently been introduced to support students throughout their Sixth Form studies and subsequent UCAS applications. Ashbourne believes that high expectations are the key to academic achievement, and encourages and supports students accordingly.

Ashbourne Middle School

17 Old Court Place, Kensington, London W8 4PL   Tel: (020) 7937 3858   Fax: (020) 7937 2207
E-mail: admin@ashbournecollege.co.uk Website: www.ashbournecollege.co.uk www.gabbitas.co.uk

Principal Mr M J A Kirby MSc, BApSc
Founded 1981
School status Co-educational Day 12–16
Religious denomination Non-Denominational
Member of CIFE
Accredited by BAC, British Council
No of pupils 25; *Girls* 11; *Boys* 14
Average class size 8
Fees per annum *(day)* £17100

Wonderfully situated near Kensington Gardens, Ashbourne is a few minutes away from many of London's greatest attractions.

Class sizes are restricted to a maximum of 10, reflecting the importance placed on individual attention, communication and feedback. Staff–student relations are personable and informal yet provide discipline and encourage independence and self-reliance.

Our pupils are encouraged to take nine GCSE's, mainly concentrating on traditional subjects;

however, they may also take Art and Design, ICT, Photography and Business Studies. In addition to their studies, pupils play sport and are frequently accompanied on trips to the theatre, exhibitions and museums. The college strongly encourages academic success and most students stay on for the Sixth Form.

Ashbourne believes that high expectations are the key to academic achievement, and encourages and supports students accordingly.

Bassett House School

60 Bassett Road, London W10 6JP   Tel: (020) 8969 0313   Fax: (020) 8960 9624
E-mail: info@bassetths.org.uk   Website: www.bassetths.org.uk

Head Mrs A Harris BEd (Lond), CEPLF (Caen)
Founded 1947
School status Independent. Co-educational
Day 3–11
Religious denomination Non-Denominational
Member of IAPS **Accredited by** IAPS
No of pupils *(day)* 153
Fees £5820–£12006

Bassett House School is a member of House Schools Group and has sister schools at Orchard House School in Chiswick and Prospect House School in Putney. It is situated in a large Victorian house in north Kensington, which was recently rebuilt to very high standards. Boys leave the school aged 8 for prep schools specializing in preparation for senior school examinations at 13+. Girls are prepared for senior school examinations at 11+. The school is equipped with a science and IT lab, gym/theatre and school hall, music room and art room.

Orchard House School

16 Newton Grove, Bedford Park, London W4 1LB   Tel: (020) 8742 8544   Fax: (020) 8742 8522
E-mail: info@orchardhs.org.uk   Website: www.orchardhs.org.uk

Headmistress Mrs S A B Hobbs BA (Hons) (Exeter), PGCE, MontDip
Founded 1993
School status Independent. Co-educational
Day Boys 4–8 Girls 4–11
Religious denomination Non-Denominational
Member of IAPS, ISBA
Accredited by IAPS
No of pupils 220; *Girls* 140; *Boys* 80
Fees per annum *(day)* £5820–£12006

Orchard House School is a member of House Schools Group and has sister schools at Bassett House School in Kensington and Prospect House School in Putney. It occupies a substantial Norman Shaw house in the conservation area of Bedford Park, Chiswick, with a large garden and recreational area. Boys leave the school at age 8+ for prep schools specializing in preparation for boys' senior school examinations at 13+. Girls are prepared for senior school examinations at 11+. The school has its own sports area and is equipped with a science and IT lab, music room and art room. Academic results have been strong.

Prospect House School

75 Putney Hill, London SW15 3NT   Tel: (020) 8780 0456   Fax: (020) 8780 3010
E-mail: info@prospecths.org.uk   Website: www.prospecths.org.uk

Headmistress Mrs D Barratt MEd (Newcastle)
Founded 1991
School status Co-educational Day 3–11
Religious denomination Non-Denominational
Member of IAPS **Accredited by** IAPS
No of pupils 200; *Girls* 100; *Boys* 100
Teacher:pupil ratio 1:8
Average class size 18
Fees per annum *(day)* £5640–£11694

Prospect House School is a member of House Schools Group and has sister schools at Bassett House School in Kensington and Orchard House School in Chiswick. It is based in an imposing Victorian house opposite Putney Heath. Boys and girls are prepared for examinations at senior school at 11+. The school enjoys a large garden and all-weather sports area. It is also equipped with a maths and IT lab, gym/theatre and school hall, music rooms and art room. Music is a popular key option. The school is highly staffed and equipped. Academic results have been strong.

Cameron House School

4 The Vale, Chelsea, London SW3 6AH   Tel: (020) 7352 4040   Fax: (020) 7352 2349
E-mail: info@cameronhouseschool.org Website: www.cameronhouseschool.org www.gabbitas.co.uk

The Headmistress Mrs Lucie Moore BEd (Hons)
Principal Miss Josie Cameron BSc (Hons), Dip
Ed, Cert T **Founded** 1985
School status Independent. Co-educational
Day 4–11
Religious denomination Non-Denominational
Member of CReSTeD, IAPS, NAHT, SATIPS
Accredited by IAPS, ISC
No of pupils 116; *(day)* 116; *Pre-prep* 60; *Prep*
52; *Girls* 66; *Boys* 50
Teacher:pupil ratio 1:9 **Average class size** 18
Fees per annum *(day)* £13170

Cameron House aims to produce academically
confident pupils who appreciate the virtues of
courtesy, good manners and kindness, and are
positive-minded and confident. Our highly qualified and dedicated teaching staff create a
stimulating environment in which initiative and
individual objectives can flourish.

The curriculum is broadly based and designed
to cultivate a wide range of interests, though emphasis is placed on the core curriculum. Essential disciplines are balanced with aesthetic and practical activities such as speech and drama, debating and French. The school is well equipped with its own class libraries, and a dedicated IT room with a bank of mobile laptops. Pupils discover their talents through a wide variety of optional clubs after school. Children are encouraged to join the choirs to develop singing talent. The learning process necessarily focuses on public exams. For boys these can take place at any time after the age of 8. Girls are prepared for the entrance exam to independent London day or country boarding schools.

The Cavendish School

31 Inverness Street, London NW1 7HB   Tel: (020) 7485 1958   Fax: (020) 7267 0098
E-mail: admissions@cavendish-school.co.uk
Website: www.cavendishschool.co.uk www.gabbitas.co.uk
For all enquiries please contact the Admissions Secretary, Mrs Frances Jones, as above

Headmistress Mrs T Dunbar BSc (Hons), Dip
Founded 1875
School status Independent. Girls Day 2½–11.
Boys Day 2½–7
Religious denomination Christian
Member of AGBIS, IAPS, ISBA, ISCis, NAHT,
SATIPS **Accredited by** ISC
Learning difficulties SNU WI/DYC DYP DYS
MLD
Physical and medical conditions IT SM TW/EPI
HEA
No of pupils 170; *(day)* 170; *Nursery* 25;
Pre-prep 65; *Prep* 82; *Girls* 165; *Boys* 5
Teacher:pupil ratio 1:8 **Average class size** 17
Fees per annum *(day)* £5400–£10650. Nursery
from £5400–£10050, Reception–Yr6 £10650.
All fees include lunches and outings

The Cavendish is a friendly school situated near
Regent's Park, in the heart of Camden Town with its excellent public transport links, and is academically non-selective at entry. With strong yet informal links between home, school and the local community we pride ourselves on the high level of our pastoral care and attention to each child's individual needs. We maintain manageable class sizes and high teacher--pupils ratios so that the foundations of a good education and effective study habits are laid from the beginning. Through a combination of a creative, broad and balanced curriculum, personalized learning and much specialized teaching our pupils flourish and gain entry, frequently with scholarships, to top senior schools at 11+. Our strength in music, drama, dance and art is reflected in our Artsmark Gold Award and sport is also given a high priority. Means-tested Bursaries are available for pupils into Years 4 and 5.

Channing School

Highgate, London N6 5HF   Tel: (020) 8340 2328   Fax: (020) 8341 5698
E-mail: info@channing.co.uk   Website: www.channing.co.uk

Head Mistress Mrs B Elliott MA (Cantab)
Founded 1885
School status Girls Day 4–18
Religious denomination Inter-Denominational
Member of GSA, ISCis **Accredited by** GSA
Learning difficulties WI/DYP DYS MLD
Behavioural and emotional disorders ADHD
Physical and medical conditions WA2/EPI
HI IM
No of pupils 590; *Girls* 590
Average class size 20
Fees per annum *(day)* £11430–£12390

Channing is a leading London day school for girls aged 4–18, situated in beautiful grounds in Highgate. Teaching groups are small allowing friendly, caring relationships. A level choices include ancient Greek, ICT and drama. The elegant home of the former Lord Mayor of London houses our Junior School and is notable for its happy and secure atmosphere.

Art, drama, music and sport are all strong. ICT and library facilities were extensively enhanced in 2007, and a new Sixth Form centre and performance area opened in February 2008.

Entry is by test and interview at 4, 11 and 16 and is subject to a satisfactory report from the applicant's current school. There are occasional chance vacancies.

City of London School

Queen Victoria Street, London EC4V 3AL
Tel: (020) 7489 0291   Fax: (020) 7329 6887
E-mail: headmaster@clsb.org.uk   Website: www.clsb.org.uk

Headmaster Mr D Levin B Econ, MA, FRSA
School status Boys Day 10–18
Religious denomination Non-Denominational
Member of HMC
Learning difficulties WI/DYP DYS SP&LD
Behavioural and emotional disorders CO/ADD
ADHD ASP AUT
Physical and medical conditions SL SM TW
WA2/EPI HEA HI VI
No of pupils 871; *Boys* 871
Average class size 22
Fees per annum *(day)* £12267

The ethos of this school must be such as to foster good relationships between members of the staff, the pupils themselves and between members of the staff and pupils. Bullying, harassment, victimization and discrimination will not be tolerated.

The school and its staff will act fairly in relation to the pupils and parents and we expect the same of pupils and parents in relation to the school.

The City of London School aims to welcome talented boys from a diversity of backgrounds into a tolerant, harmonious community in which they achieve the highest academic standards, make full use of their potential, and develop towards responsible adulthood.

Academic achievement is very high. In 2007 80 per cent of GCSE entries were passed at A* or A grade. At A level 94 per cent of entries were passed at A or B.

For a central London school, this is a sporty place and the school plays 12 sports competitively. There is an onsite swimming pool, sports hall, fitness suite, and a beautiful 20-acre sports ground 30 minutes' coach drive away.

England

City of London School for Girls

St Giles' Terrace, Barbican, London EC2Y 8BB   Tel: (020) 7847 5500   Fax: (020) 7638 3212
E-mail: info@clsg.org.uk   Website: www.clsg.org.uk

Headmistress Miss D Vernon BA (Hons) (Dunelm)
School status Independent. Girls Day 7–18
Religious denomination Non-Denominational
Learning difficulties WI/DYP DYS
Behavioural and emotional disorders CO
Physical and medical conditions SM TW
WA1/HEA HI IM
No of pupils 683; *Prep* 98; *Senior* 454; *Sixth
Form* 131; *Girls* 683
Fees per annum *(day)* £12375

'City' is unique: its location helps to make it so, as does the rich social and cultural blend of our pupils, which reflects the cosmopolitan character of London itself. We welcome girls from all over Greater London, offering a number of academic scholarships and bursaries in order to help maintain the diversity which we value so highly. All around us the traditions and landmarks of London's history are closely interwoven with the high-tech, dynamic culture of the City. We have galleries, museums, libraries and theatres almost on our doorstep. Our pupils have access to the very best that London has to offer.

Academic excellence is a goal for every girl here, but so too is developing individual talents and interests. We encourage girls to try their hands at new sports and activities, we play host to a wide range of eminent speakers, and girls are able to participate in a variety of performing arts and expeditions. Our programme of Community Service, participation in the Duke of Edinburgh Award Scheme and partnerships with London state schools and colleges all help the girls to develop personal responsibility and respect for others.

Visit us and you will find that City girls are articulate, confident, friendly and down to earth. They have a keen appreciation of moral values, a lively sense of purpose and a justified pride in themselves. When pupils leave us they are well equipped for fulfilling careers and success in whatever sphere they choose.

Collingham Independent GCSE and Sixth Form College

23 Collingham Gardens, London SW5 0HL   Tel: (020) 7244 7414   Fax: (020) 7370 7312
E-mail: london@collingham.co.uk   Website: www.collingham.co.uk

The Principal Mr G Hattee   **Founded** 1975
College status Independent Sixth Form College.
Co-educational Day 14–20
Religious denomination Non-Denominational
Member of CIFE
Accredited by BAC Inspected by Ofsted
Member of British Council Education-UK
Partnership
Learning difficulties RA WI/DYC DYP DYS
Physical and medical conditions AT RA WA3
No of pupils 220; *(day)* 220; *Sixth Form* 185;
Girls 105; *Boys* 115
Teacher:pupil ratio 1:3
Average class size 5
Fees per annum *(day)* £15400
Fees Fees depend on number of subjects taken

- Supportive environment
- Expert tuition

- Rigorous academic standards
- Individual learning programmes
- Small class size

David Game College

69 Notting Hill Gate, London W11 3JS   Tel: (020) 7221 6665   Fax: (020) 7243 1730
E-mail: nhg@davidgame-group.com   Website: www.davidgame-group.com

Principal Mr D Game MA, MPhil
Vice Principal Mr J Dalton BSc
Vice Principal Mr M Kahn MA
Founded 1974
College status DCSF Approved Independent
(special). Co-educational Day 15–25. Flexi-
boarding available. Boarders from 16
Accredited by BAC, British Council, DCSF
registered (DCSF 2076386)
Learning difficulties DYS
Behavioural and emotional disorders ADD
Physical and medical conditions EPI HEA
No of pupils 420; *(day)* 450; *Sixth Form* 450;
Girls 190; *Boys* 230
Teacher:pupil ratio 1:8 **Average class size** 8

David Game College is one of London's leading
independent colleges. The college specializes in
one-year intensive courses in GCSE and A level,
and has an outstanding record in preparing and
placing students at top UK universities. David
Game College also runs one of the UK's most
successful University Foundation Programmes,
which specializes in preparing international
students for university entry. The college has
excellent relations with the top universities in
the UK, in particular Imperial, LSE, UCL, Warwick
and Bath, all regularly take David Game students
for some of the most competitive degree courses.
Extensive support is provided for our students
during their studies, with small classes, close
academic monitoring and support.

England

Looking for professional one–to–one
guidance when making university and career decisions...?

...you've found
Gabbitas

Gabbitas
Education
OVER A CENTURY OF SUCCESS STORIES

For friendly advice contact Alice Murrie.
E-mail: alice.murrie@gabbitas.co.uk
Tel: +44 (0)20 7734 0161
Web: www.gabbitas.co.uk

Davies Laing and Dick

100 Marylebone Lane, London W1U 2QB
Tel: (020) 7935 8411   Fax: (020) 7935 0755
E-mail: dld@dld.org
Website: www.dld.org   www.gabbitas.co.uk
Visitors' entrance: 9 Bulstrode Street London W1U 2JD

Principal Mr David Lowe MA (Cantab), FRSA
Founded 1931
School status Independent. Co-educational
Day 14–25. Boarders from 16
Religious denomination Non-Denominational
Member of ISA
Accredited by BAC, ISA
Learning difficulties WI/DYP DYS
Behavioural and emotional disorders ADHD
ASP
Physical and medical conditions SM WA1/EPI
HEA
No of pupils 300; *(day)* 300; *Sixth Form* 270;
Girls 138; *Boys* 162
Average class size 6
Fees per annum *(day)* £2680–£18000

Davies Laing and Dick (DLD) is a co-educational London day school accepting pupils from the age of 14. There are over 300 students in the Sixth Form studying A Levels from a choice of over 40 subjects. Two thirds are doing A Levels in the normal way over a two-year period. Another large group joins DLD at the start of Upper Sixth. There are no subject restrictions at A Level. GCSE intensive courses are taught over a one-year period. The average class size is six. Supplementary lessons in English as a foreign language are taken by 6 per cent of the student body.

DLD is housed in two linked buildings in Marylebone, both are newly refurbished and very well-equipped. There are three laboratories, two IT classrooms, a library for private study with an IT annexe, an internet cafe, a GCSE study area and an 80-seat theatre which is also used to screen films. There is a recording studio and a film edit suite. Many classrooms are equipped with interactive whiteboards. Students are able to access work done in class, teachers' notes and homework assignments remotely via DLD online.

Extra-curricular activities include sport, DLD youth theatre, DLD Idol, set design, film making, the DLD house band, concerts, French club, life drawing classes, fund raising and Activities Week, which takes place at the end of June. The school day finishes at 4.40pm: most activities take place after this. Accommodation is available at International Student House (ISH) and also with host families.

While the atmosphere at DLD is more informal than in mainstream independent schools, rules regarding academic performance are strictly enforced. There are fortnightly tests in each subject and three weekly reports. Parents receive five reports each year and there are two parents' evenings.

The teaching staff are highly qualified and chosen not just for their expertise but also for their ability to relate positively to young people. The college aims to make learning interesting, active and rigorous. While clear guidelines are very important to ensure pupils establish a good working routine, the college believes strongly that pupils respond best when there is a culture of encouragement. Effort, progress, achievement and courtesy are regularly acknowledged and formally rewarded.

Devonshire House Preparatory School

2 Arkwright Road, Hampstead, London NW3 6AE
Tel: (020) 7435 1916   Fax: (020) 7431 4787
E-mail: enquiries@devonshirehouseprepschool.co.uk
Website: www.devonshirehouseschool.co.uk   www.gabbitas.co.uk

Headmistress Mrs S Alexander BA (Hons)
Founded 1989
School status Independent. Co-educational
Day Boys 2–13 Girls 2–11
Religious denomination Non-Denominational
Member of IAPS
Accredited by IAPS, ISC
Learning difficulties SC WI/DYP DYS
Behavioural and emotional disorders RA
Physical and medical conditions RA/EPI HEA
HI
No of pupils 521; *Girls* 220; *Boys* 301
Fees per annum *(day)* £6450–£12450

Curriculum: Early literacy and numeracy are very important and the traditional academic subjects form the core curriculum. Specialist teaching and the combined sciences form an increasingly important part of the timetable as the children grow older. Expression in all forms of communication is encouraged, with classes also having lessons in art, music, drama, French, and information and design technology. Much encouragement is given to pupils to help to widen their horizons and broaden their interests. The school fosters a sense of responsibility among the pupils.

Entry requirements: The offer of places is subject to availability and to an interview.

Academic and leisure facilities: The school is situated in fine premises in the heart of Hampstead with its own walled grounds. The aim is to achieve high academic standards while developing enthusiasm and initiative throughout a wide range of interests. It is considered essential to encourage pupils to develop their own individual personalities and a good sense of personal responsibility.

Scholarships: The school offers academic and music scholarships.

England

Dolphin School (Including Noah's Ark Nursery School)

106 Northcote Road, Battersea, London SW11 6QW   Tel: (020) 7924 3472   Fax: (020) 8265 8700
E-mail: admissions@dolphinschool.org.uk Website: www.dolphinschool.org.uk www.gabbitas.co.uk

Principal Mrs J Glen BA (Hons)
Head of Noah's Ark Nursery Schools Miss A Miller TTC (NZ)
Founded September 1986
School status Independent. Co-educational Day Boys 2–11 Girls 2–11
Religious denomination Christian TISCA
Learning difficulties DYP DYS
Behavioural and emotional disorders ST
Physical and medical conditions AT/HEA
No of pupils (day) 234; Nursery 112; Pre-prep 60; Prep 62; Girls 109; Boys 125
Teacher:pupil ratio 1:8 (Nursery); 1:10 (Pre-Prep); 1:15 (Prep)
Average class size 15 in Pre-prep and Prep
Fees per annum (day) £4290–£8010 £4290 annual nursery fees; £7485 annual fees Reception–Year 2; £8070 annual fees Year 3–Year 6. Weekly visits by appointment

Our aim at Dolphin School is to help your child become the best they can possibly be. School is a training ground and our small classes enable us to focus on each individual. We train children academically, giving priority to English and maths and adding hands-on science, colourful geography, history and whole-school Spanish. We train pupils in the arts with fantastic specialist teaching in a wide range of sports through dynamic coaching and a superb fixture list. Our Christian foundation gives us the impetus to develop children's character, teaching them the priority of good relationships throughout life.

Duff Miller

59 Queen's Gate, London SW7 5JP   Tel: (020) 7225 0577   Fax: (020) 7589 5155
E-mail: enqs@duffmiller.com   Website: www.duffmiller.com

Principal Mr C Denning BSc, PGCE
Vice Principal Mr C Kraft BSc, BPS
Founded 1952
School status Independent Sixth Form College. Co-educational Day 14–19
Member of CIFE
Accredited by BAC
Learning difficulties WI/DYP DYS MLD
Behavioural and emotional disorders ADD ADHD TOU
Physical and medical conditions EPI HEA VI
No of pupils 220; Girls 110; Boys 110
Teacher:pupil ratio 5.5:1
Average class size 6.5
Fees per annum (day) £4675–£15435 Examinations, special subject supplements and enrolment fee are extra

Duff Miller provides structured tuition for its students, based on the demands of their exams and closely tailored to the specific needs of the individual. What distinguishes us is an open and supportive atmosphere which encourages our students to develop on both academic and personal levels. We pride ourselves on our friendly and approachable teaching staff, who are freely available to answer questions or provide guidance and reassurance.

Small groups encourage participation and debate within the classroom, while allowing staff to focus closely on individual pupils. Duff Miller takes pride in the diversity of its pupils and in being able to meet their different needs, whether we are preparing them for medical or Oxbridge interviews or guiding them through their retakes.

Fine Arts College Hampstead

24 Lambolle Place, Hampstead, London NW3 4PG
Tel: (020) 7586 0312   Fax: (020) 7483 0355
E-mail: mail@hampsteadfinearts.com   Website: www.hampsteadfinearts.com

Principal Mr N Cochrane
Vice Principal Mr E Knox MA (Oxon), MA (Lon), Mphil, PGCE
Founded 1978
College status Independent. Co-educational Day 14–19
Religious denomination Non-Denominational
Learning difficulties DYP DYS MLD
Behavioural and emotional disorders ADD ASP AUT
Physical and medical conditions SM TW WA2
No of pupils 120; *Girls* 65; *Boys* 55
Teacher:pupil ratio 1:4
Average class size 7
Fees per annum *(day)* £5400–£14550

Fine Arts College is a specialist college in the arts and humanities for A level and GCSE. We are situated in Belsize Park and each of the three departments, A level, Art and GCSE, has its own specially designed buildings.

Fine Arts College has 120 students and is high in expectation and achievement. Classes are small to encourage discussion and maximum attention. Each student is supported by a personal tutor and has timetabled weekly meetings and fortnightly reports. The college consistently achieves excellent results with students achieving high examination passes, university and art school acceptance and success in professional careers.

We provide an excellent opportunity to study in a friendly and stimulating atmosphere: a bridge between school and university. All of our tutors are highly qualified university or art school graduates, with over 70 per cent having served as examiners, moderators or advisers for public examinations.

Francis Holland School, Regent's Park

Clarence Gate, Ivor Place, London NW1 6XR   Tel: (020) 7723 0176   Fax: (020) 7706 1522
E-mail: registrar@fhs-nw1.org.uk   Website: www.francisholland.org.uk

Headmistress Mrs V M Durham
Founded 1878
School status Independent. Girls Day 11–18
Religious denomination Church of England
Member of GSA, IAPS, ISA, SHA
Accredited by GSA, IAPS, ISA
Learning difficulties RA WI/DYP DYS MLD
Behavioural and emotional disorders RA
Physical and medical conditions RA/HI
No of pupils 433; *Girls* 433
Average class size 20
Fees per annum *(day)* £12900

Francis Holland, Regent's Park, is a happy, academic day school for girls aged 11–18. Within a friendly and supportive atmosphere, pupils achieve excellent examination results. All pupils transfer to universities, including Oxford and Cambridge. Sixth formers attend weekly lectures from visiting guest speakers. Sport, drama and music contribute strongly to the school's lively extra-curricular schedule. The school has its own swimming pool and uses Regent's Park for tennis, hockey, rounders and netball.

The Gloucester Wing opened in October 2008 providing additional classrooms, a fourth art studio and a performance area. There are two school orchestras, several choirs and a jazz band. The school runs more than 70 clubs and societies, such as history and politics, ju-jitsu, cookery, water polo, Mandarin Chinese, gymnastics and yoga.

Fulham Prep School (Prep Dept)

Prep Department, 200 Greyhound Road, London W14 9SD Tel: (020) 7386 2444 Fax: (020) 7386 2449
E-mail: prepadmin@fulhamprep.co.uk   Website: www.fulhamprep.co.uk
Pre-prep (4+–7+) based at 47A Fulham High Street, London SW6 3JJ

Principal and Head of Prep School Mrs J
Emmett
Head of Pre-prep Ms D Steven   **Founded** 1996
School status Independent. Co-educational
Day 7–13
Religious denomination Non-Denominational
Learning difficulties WI/DYC DYP DYS
Physical and medical conditions WA2
No of pupils *Pre-prep* 235; *Prep* 335; *Girls* 114;
Boys 221
Teacher:pupil ratio 1:9 **Average class size** 16
Fees per annum *(day)* £11385–£12645

FULHAM PREP SCHOOL

Curriculum: In the Pre-prep School, the curriculum, though broadly based, lays particular emphasis on the early acquisition of the traditional basic skills of reading, writing and numeracy. We do not prepare children for 7+ and 8+ exams. The curriculum in the Prep School is based on the demands of the 11+ and 13+

Common Entrance exams.

Entry requirements: The school is non-selective at the Reception stage, while entry into other years is by assessment in maths and English. Siblings of current pupils are given priority.

Academic and other facilities: Academic achievement is strong but we also put a lot of emphasis on all-round development, providing an extensive range of activities featuring sport, music, art and drama. The school has two choirs and an orchestra. A wide range of lunchtime and after-school clubs is offered each term.

Gatehouse School

Sewardstone Road, Victoria Park, London E2 9JG   Tel: (020) 8980 2978   Fax: (020) 8983 1642
E-mail: admin@gatehouseschool.co.uk   Website: www.gatehouseschool.co.uk

The Headmistress Mrs Belinda Canham JP
BA(Hons), PGCE (Froebel)
Founded 1948
School status Independent. Co-educational
Day 3–11 We have a broad access entry and
achieve places in top London independent
secondary schools
Religious denomination Christian
Learning difficulties CA SNU/DOW DYS
SP&LD
Physical and medical conditions TW
No of pupils 300; *(day)* 300; *Nursery* 50;
Pre-prep 130; *Prep* 120; *Girls* 150; *Boys* 150
Average class size 18
Fees per annum *(day)* £6300–£7740

Founded in May 1948 by Phyllis Wallbank, a
pioneer of educational development, in the

gatehouse of St Bartholomew of the Great Priory Church, West Smithfield. The school was then a pioneer of much that is now generally accepted in education.

Gatehouse's policy is: Children of any race, colour, creed, background and intellect shall be accepted as students and work side by side without streaming or any kind of segregation with the aim that each child shall get to know and love God, and to develop their own uniqueness of personality to enable them to appreciate the world and the world to appreciate them.

Gatehouse is now located in Sewardstone Road close to Victoria Park, where it continues to follow the education philosophy of Phyllis Wallbank.

Glendower Preparatory School

87 Queen's Gate, South Kensington, London SW7 5JX   Tel: (020) 7370 1927   Fax: (020) 7244 8308
E-mail: office@glendower.kensington.sch.uk   Website: www.gabbitas.co.uk

Head Mistress Mrs R Bowman BA, PGCE
Founded 1895
School status Independent. Girls Day 4–11
Girls Day only
Religious denomination Non-Denominational
Learning difficulties WI
No of pupils 182; *Girls* 182
Average class size 16
Fees per annum *(day)* £11850

Why choose Glendower for your daughter?

Our school is small in numbers, 182 pupils, aged between 4 and 11, but high in expectation and achievement. We aim to provide a stimulating environment in which each girl is valued and can enjoy developing her particular talents to the full, whether it be in art, music, sport, drama or other social activities. In the family atmosphere of Glendower, girls acquire the confidence to develop their talents to the utmost of their ability and gain the solid academic foundations necessary for competitive entry into a leading London day school or boarding school. We are a happy school!

For further details please contact the school office.

The Hampshire School

15 Manresa Road, London SW3 6LR   Tel: (020) 7584 3297   Fax: (020) 7584 9733
E-mail: hampshire@indschool.org   Website: www.ths.westminster.sch.uk
Early Years Section in 5 Wetherby Place SW7 4NX

Principal Mr A G Bray Cert Ed
Head of Early Years Miss J Scotney BSc (Hons),
PGCE   **Founded** 1928
School status Independent. Co-educational
Day 3–13
Religious denomination Inter-Denominational
Member of AHIS, ISA   **Accredited by** ISA
Learning difficulties SNU WI/DYC DYP DYS
Behavioural and emotional disorders RA
Physical and medical conditions RA
No of pupils 220; *(day)* 234; *Nursery* 78;
Pre-prep 78; *Prep* 78; *Girls* 110; *Boys* 110
Teacher:pupil ratio 1:6.4   **Ave class size** 18
Fees per annum *(day)* £7950–£11535

We give each child individual attention to ensure that they grow in confidence within a stimulating environment where they are valued as individuals.

Our dedicated and experienced staff monitor each child closely to ensure that they progress towards their full potential. We have high expectations of our children and set high standards for learning. Our results speak for themselves.

With the latest technology and resources we incorporate the best traditional methods of teaching with modern educational approaches to prepare children for the challenges of the 21st century. Every child is the centre of our focus.

We value and foster the parent–school partnership as a means of ensuring that the best possible results are achieved.

England

Hawkesdown House School

27 Edge Street, Kensington, London W8 7PN
Tel: (020) 7727 9090   Fax: (020) 7727 9988
E-mail: admin@hawkesdown.co.uk
Website: www.hawkesdown.co.uk   www.gabbitas.co.uk

Headmistress Mrs C J Leslie BA, Cert Ed
Founded 2001
School status Independent. Boys Day 3–8
Religious denomination Inter-Denominational
Member of IAPS, SATIPS
Accredited by IAPS, ISC
Learning difficulties CA WI/DYC DYP DYS
Behavioural and emotional disorders RA/
ADHD ASP
Physical and medical conditions CA/HI
No of pupils 145; *(day)* 146; *Nursery* 16;
Pre-prep 129; *Boys* 145
Teacher:pupil ratio 1:8
Average class size 17
Fees per annum *(day)* £10950–£12600

Hawkesdown House is an independent school for boys from the ages of 3 to 8. In December 2003, the Headmistress was the first Head of a free-standing pre-preparatory school to be elected to IAPS (Independent Association of Prep Schools). Early literacy and numeracy are of prime importance and the traditional academic subjects form the core curriculum. A balanced education helps all aspects of learning and a wide range of interests is encouraged. The school finds and fosters individual talents in each pupil. Boys are prepared for entry at 8 to the main London and other preparatory schools. The Headmistress places the greatest importance on matching boys happily and successfully to potential schools and spends time with parents ensuring that the transition is smooth and free of stress.

Sound and thorough early education is important for success, and also for self-confidence. The thoughtful and thorough teaching and care at Hawkesdown House ensures high academic standards and promotes initiative, kindness and courtesy. Hawkesdown is a school with fun and laughter, where boys develop their own personalities together with a sense of personal responsibility.

The school provides an excellent traditional education, with the benefits of modern technology, in a safe, happy and caring atmosphere. Many of the boys coming to the school live within walking distance and the school is an important part of the Kensington community.

There are clear expectations and the boys are encouraged by positive motivation and by the recognition and praise of their achievements, progress and effort. Individual attention and pastoral care for each of the boys is of great importance.

Hawkesdown House has a fine building in Edge Street, off Kensington Church Street.

Parents who would like further information or to visit the school and meet the Headmistress, should contact the School Office for a prospectus or an appointment.

International Community School

4 York Terrace East, Regents Park, London NW1 4PT   Tel: (020) 7935 1206   Fax: (020) 7935 7915
E-mail: admissions@ics.uk.net   Website: www.ics.uk.net

Head of School Mr P Hurd BSc, PGCSE
Director of Admissions Ms A Dabholkar BA
(Hons), MSc   **Founded** 1979
School status Co-educational Day 3–18
Religious denomination Non-Denominational
Member of English UK, CIS, IBO, LISA
Accredited by British Council, DCSF
Learning difficulties CA SC SNU/DOW DYC
DYP DYS MLD PMLD SLD SP&LD
Behavioural and emotional disorders ST/ADD
ADHD ASP AUT
No of pupils 240; *Girls* 120; *Boys* 120
Teacher:pupil ratio 1:8 **Average class size** 16
Fees per annum *(day)* £12240–£16740.
Additional fees for student support services

lum is international: IB PYP/MYP, Cambridge IGCSE's and A levels.

ICS has a strong pastoral care/welfare reputation and classes are kept to a maximum of 18 students. A large team of assistants and specialists support class teachers.

Children and faculty are from 65 countries and form a dynamic learning community.

ICS is a friendly central London school for students aged 3 to 18 years. We are a co-educational, inclusive school, specializing in teaching to different ability groups. The curricu-

The Admissions Team welcomes year-round applications.

International School of London

139 Gunnersbury Avenue, London W3 8LG
Tel: (020) 8992 5823   Fax: (020) 8993 7012
E-mail: mail@islondon.com   Website: www.ISLondon.com

Director Mr A Makarem
Founded 1972
School status Independent. Co-educational
Day Boys 3–19 Girls 3–18
Religious denomination Non-Denominational
Member of CIS, IBO, IBSCA, LISA
Accredited by CIS
Learning difficulties WI/DYS
No of pupils 342; *Girls* 149; *Boys* 193
Average class size 12
Fees per annum *(day)* £13000–£18250

The International School of London (ISL) accepts students of all nationalities from pre-school age up to the International Baccalaureate Diploma.

ISL is fully authorized to offer the IB Primary Years Programme (PYP) throughout all the primary classes, from Early childhood (3 years old) to Year 6 (10 years old). Using the PYP we

provide students with an international curriculum which focuses on developing the whole child.

The secondary curriculum follows the IB Middle Years Programme and the full IB Diploma. Comprehensive and integrated English as a Second Language programmes are available at all ages. Students can also follow courses in 20 home languages including Arabic, Danish, Dutch, German, Icelandic, Italian, Japanese, Portuguese and Spanish.

To join ISL parents will need to provide the Admissions Office with a completed application form and previous school records. Most students join ISL in September, but we admit students throughout the year, provided that we have places available.

We offer door-to-door transport covering west, central and south London.

Lansdowne College

40–44 Bark Place, London W2 4AT   Tel: (020) 7616 4400   Fax: (020) 7616 4401
E-mail: education@lansdownecollege.com Website: www.lansdownecollege.com www.gabbitas.co.uk

Principal Mr H Templeton FCCA
Vice-Principal Mr G Hunter BA, FRSA
Founded 1976
College status Independent Sixth Form College.
Co-educational Day 14–19. GCSE Department
from Year 10
Religious denomination Non-Denominational
Member of CIFE
Accredited by British Council
Learning difficulties RA/DYC DYP DYS MLD
Behavioural and emotional disorders RA/ADD
ADHD AUT
Physical and medical conditions RA WA3/EPI
HEA
No of pupils 220; *Senior* 25; *Sixth Form* 205;
Girls 108; *Boys* 112
Teacher:pupil ratio 1:7 **Average class size** 8
Fees per annum *(day)* £2900–£15500
Fees Scholarships and bursaries covering part
fees (up to an absolute maximum of 50%) are
available

Lansdowne College is housed in a modern, spacious building with excellent facilities, including a 200-seater hall, in a quiet residential road, one minute's walk from Kensington Gardens and Hyde Park.

The college is renowned for the warm, supportive atmosphere provided by our staff and students together. Our students thrive on a mixture of expert tuition, hard work and pastoral care, and, as young adults, benefit from an environment that, while maintaining academic rigour and discipline, provides a relaxed and friendly atmosphere, allowing each student to achieve his or her full potential.

At Lansdowne we offer all the subjects on the school curriculum and many others that are not. Teaching is in small groups for both A level and GCSE students. We have an expanding GCSE department and we also offer one-term and one-year A level retake courses, alongside traditional A level courses.

Latymer Prep School

LATYMER

36 Upper Mall, Hammersmith, London W6 9TA   Tel: (0845) 638 5700
Fax: (0845) 638 5732   E-mail: mlp@latymerprep.org
Website: www.latymerprep.org   www.gabbitas.co.uk

Principal Mr S P Dorrian BA
Founded 1995
School status Independent. Co-educational
Day 7–11
Religious denomination Non-Denominational
Member of IAPS, SATIPS
Accredited by ISC
Learning difficulties SNU WI/DYP DYS
Behavioural and emotional disorders CO
Physical and medical conditions WA3/IM
No of pupils *(day)* 165
Average class size 20
Fees per annum *(day)* £12105

Curriculum: Children are taught the full range of subjects following National Curriculum guidelines, but to an advanced standard. Classes are small, which allows for close monitoring and evaluation of each pupil's progress and well-being.

Entry requirements and procedures: The school is academically selective and entry to the school is by assessment in maths, English and verbal reasoning. Visits for prospective parents occur throughout the autumn term and can be arranged by telephoning the Registrar for an appointment.

Academic and leisure facilities: Academic achievement is strong, but in addition there is an extensive range of activities featuring sport, music, art and drama. The school has a large choir and its own orchestra.

The school is well resourced, sharing catering, sport and theatre facilities with the Upper School.

Sports include contact and touch rugby, soccer, cricket, tennis, hockey, gymnastics and dance. There is also a thriving swimming club (the school has its own indoor pool). Karate, chess, and a whole range of clubs take place after school.

Latymer Upper School

King Street, Hammersmith, London W6 9LR   Tel: (0845) 638 5800   Fax: (020) 8748 5212
E-mail: registrar@latymer-upper.org   Website: www.latymer-upper.org   www.gabbitas.co.uk

Head Mr P J Winter MA (Oxon)
Registrar Mrs C Sutherland-Hawes
Founded 1624
School status Independent. Co-educational
Day 11–18
Religious denomination Non-Denominational
Member of HMC **Accredited by** HMC
Learning difficulties SNU WI
Physical and medical conditions RA
No of pupils 1087; *(day)* 1087; *Sixth Form* 251;
Girls 406; *Boys* 681
Teacher:pupil ratio 1:10 **Average class size** 22
Fees per annum *(day)* £13470

Latymer Upper School has been providing education for local children since its foundation in 1624. Located in King Street, Hammersmith, Latymer is now an independent co-educational day school. A state-of-the-art Performing Arts Centre has just been opened, and a new science block, together with a library and resources centre is currently being built, and due to open in September 2008.

Means-tested scholarships, which can be up to the value of 100 per cent of the fees, are available for entry at 11+ and 16+. These are awarded on the basis of academic excellence and family circumstances. Academic scholarships, which are not means-tested, are also available but are generally not of high monetary value. Music scholarships, up to the value of 50 per cent of fees, and additional one-off entrance awards of £1,000 at time of entry in music, sport, art and drama can also be offered at 11+. Scholarships are available in music, sport, art and drama at 16+.

Lyndhurst House Preparatory School

24 Lyndhurst Gardens, Hampstead, London NW3 5NW   Tel: (020) 7435 4936
E-mail: pmg@lyndhursthouse.co.uk   Website: www.lyndhursthouse.co.uk
A large detached Victorian red-brick building with its own playground in a quiet leafy side street

Headmaster Mr A J C Reid MA (Oxon), PGCE
Founded 1952
School status Independent. Boys Day 4–13 A
small, friendly school with an intimate feel and
high expectations
Religious denomination Non-Denominational
Member of IAPS, NAHT, SATIPS
Accredited by IAPS, ISC
Learning difficulties CA WI/DYC DYP DYS
MLD
Behavioural and emotional disorders ST/
ADHD ASP AUT CB
Physical and medical conditions RA/CP HEA HI
No of pupils 150; *(day)* 150; *Pre-prep* 45; *Prep*
105; *Boys* 150
Teacher:pupil ratio 1:7.1 **Ave class size** 17
Fees per annum *(day)* £12330–£13740

Lyndhurst is a friendly and lively traditional boys' school, with its own special atmosphere and character. The environment is warm and friendly, small and familiar in feel, yet full of bustle, activity and purpose, in which every boy can find opportunities for engagement and fulfillment.

England

More House

22–24 Pont Street, Chelsea, London SW1X 0AA   Tel: (020) 7235 2855   Fax: (020) 7259 6782
E-mail: office@morehouse.org.uk   Website: www.morehouse.org.uk

Head Master Mr R Carlysle BA, MBA, PGCE, CertDys&Lit AKC, MColP   **Founded** 1953
School status Girls Day 11–18
Religious denomination Roman Catholic
Member of GSA
No of pupils 220; *Girls* 200
Teacher:pupil ratio 1:6   **Average class size** 18
Fees per annum *(day)* £13497. Includes all meals and books and certain school trips.

More House was founded in 1953 at the request of parents wanting a central London Catholic day school for their daughters. The school is a Catholic Foundation, which accepts pupils of all faiths. It is an Educational Trust with a Board of Governors drawn partly from present and past parents.

Despite our smaller size we offer a full range of academic subjects up to GCSE and A level. Girls go on to a range of prestigious universities to follow courses including medicine, law, history, art, modern languages, drama, mathematics, classics, economics and biochemistry.

Extra-curricular activities include running, swimming, fencing, choirs, orchestra, art, drama, photography, mathematics competitions, public speaking and dance. Girls are encouraged to become involved in a range of activities, although the younger girls also benefit from supervised homework after school.

Two full scholarships and smaller awards are made on entry to Year 7 and Sixth Form for academic and musical excellence. Occasional scholarships may be awarded at other levels of entry on academic grounds.

The Mulberry House School

7 Minster Road, West Hampstead, London NW2 3SD
Tel: (020) 8452 7340   Fax: (020) 8830 7015
E-mail: info@mulberryhouseschool.com
Website: www.mulberryhouseschool.com

Headteacher Ms B Lewis-Powell
School status Independent. Co-educational Day 2–8
Religious denomination Non-Denominational
Member of ISA
Accredited by ISA
Learning difficulties RA WI/DYP
Behavioural and emotional disorders RA ST
Physical and medical conditions RA SM/CP HEA HI
No of pupils *(day)* 178
Fees per annum *(day)* £7050–£13160

The Mulberry House School is an established independent school for 2–8-year-olds, offering a stimulating and caring environment that meets the needs of individuals, while preparing them for the next stage of their schooling at 4+ or 7+. Extended day, full and part-time places available. For brochures and details of Open Evenings, please telephone 020 8452 7340.

England

North Bridge House Senior School

1 Gloucester Avenue, London NW1 7AB   Tel: (020) 7267 6266   Fax: (020) 7284 2508
E-mail: seniorschool@northbridgehouse.com
Website: www.nbhseniorschool.co.uk   www.cognitaschools.co.uk

Head of Senior School Ms A Ayre
School status Co-educational Day 2½–16
Religious denomination Non-Denominational
Learning difficulties SNU/DYP DYS
No of pupils 170; *Girls* 85; *Boys* 85
Fees per annum *(day)* £3225–£11865

North Bridge House School provides a complete education for children aged 2½ to 16 years. The school comprises two Victorian villas in Hampstead and one large site by Regent's Park in Parkway.

Alongside successful academic, sporting, artistic and pastoral achievement, we emphasize an environment that encourages good manners and a strong sense of social responsibility.

Most children spend three years in the Junior school before moving on to the prep. They continue to develop their academic skills, as well as their creative and sporting abilities in a caring atmosphere, which prepares them well for their future education. Children move to the Lower Prep at Gloucester Avenue at Year 4. All classes are taught by a form teacher with specialists for music, French, PE and IT. At age 10, girls are prepared for the 11+ Common Entrance while the boys move up to the Upper Prep for Years 6– to prepare for the 13+ Common Entrance. The prep school has an outstanding record for success with pupils going on to schools such as Westminster, St Paul's, City of London, UCS, South Hampstead and North London Collegiate. The Senior school has long been achieving excellent results at GCSE with 93 per cent of pupils achieving A* to C in 2008. Our pupils have been welcomed into the Sixth Form at senior schools including Westminster, City of London, UCS, Highgate, South Hampstead, Francis Holland and Channing.

North London International School

6 Friern Barnet Lane, London N11 3LX   Tel: (020) 8920 0600   Fax: (020) 8211 4605
E-mail: admissions@wpis.org   Website: www.nlis.org

Head Mr D P Rose MA (Ed), BA, Cert Ed, LPSH
School status Co-educational Day 2–19.
Boarders from 16
Religious denomination Non-Denominational
Member of CReSTeD, IBO, LISA
Accredited by CIS, IAPS, ISA, ISC
Learning difficulties SNU/MLD
Physical and medical conditions SL
No of pupils 405; *Girls* 144; *Boys* 261
Fees per annum *(day)* £2820–£13500

North London International School provides a unique school environment where all areas of achievement are celebrated and where our students take pride in being members of a thriving school community. It is an accredited International Baccalaureate World School authorized to teach all three of the IB Programmes – Primary Years Programme (PYP), Middle Years Programme (MYP) and the Diploma programme. It combines the very best features of a traditional curriculum with opportunities for discovery, inquiry and extended learning. Children are challenged to think, learn, take risks and discover new things in a happy and caring environment. The school also encourages and enables students to become responsible and successful members of a diverse world community.

With an emphasis on individual progress and talent, the school prepares students well for life beyond school: higher education, business, family, society; wherever in the world the student might be now, or might choose to go.

Parkgate House School

80 Clapham Common North Side, London SW4 9SD   Tel: (020) 7350 2461   Fax: (020) 7738 1633
E-mail: office@parkgate-school.co.uk   Website: www.parkgate-school.co.uk

Principal Ms C Shanley   **Founded** 1987
School status Co-educational Day 2–11
Religious denomination Non-Denominational
Member of SATIPS
Learning difficulties DYC DYS
Behavioural and emotional disorders CO ST TS
Physical and medical conditions CA IT SM TW
WA2/EPI HEA
No of pupils 220; *Girls* 120; *Boys* 100
Teacher:pupil ratio 1:5 **Average class size** 18
Fees per annum *(day)* £3855–£10650

Parkgate House School is an independent school educating over 200 children aged from 2 to 11 years. Residing in an historic Georgian Grade II listed building overlooking Clapham Common, the school is supported by an impressive staff of over 40 teaching professionals.

Children receive focused attention in one of three specialized areas: the Montessori Nursery for 2 to 4 year olds; the Pre-preparatory department for those aged 4 to 7 and the Preparatory department for the 7 to 11 age range.

At any age, children enjoy an expansive, high-quality curriculum, which is further enhanced by an established after-school programme including choir, IT, drama, French, sport and horse riding.

A recent Ofsted report praised Parkgate House as 'a very good school with a friendly and welcoming atmosphere and an attractive learning environment'.

Putney Park School

11 Woodborough Road, Putney, London SW15 6PY   Tel: (020) 8788 8316   Fax: (020) 8780 2376
E-mail: office@putneypark.london.sch.uk   Website: www.putneypark.london.sch.uk

Headmistress Mrs Ruth Mann BSc (Hons),
PGCE   **Founded** 1953
School status Co-educational Day Boys 4–8
Girls 4–16
Religious denomination Church of England
Member of CReSTeD, ISA
Accredited by ISA, ISC
Learning difficulties SNU WI/DYP DYS MLD
SP&LD
Behavioural and emotional disorders RA/AUT
Physical and medical conditions RA/EPI HEA
No of pupils 269; *Prep* 163; *Senior* 106;
Girls 227; *Boys* 42
Teacher:pupil ratio 1:9 **Average class size** 18
Lower School 12 Upper School

Putney Park School, established in 1953, and now in the second generation of the Tweedie-Smith family ownership, is situated in a conservation area and consists of four delightful Edwardian houses with a welcoming, family atmosphere.

The aim of the school is to provide a sound education in a happy atmosphere.

Pupils are offered a broad curriculum to enable them to develop their creativity and individual talents to their full potential. Pupils thrive in the caring and supportive environment. The school prepares boys for entry to other schools including Colet Court and King's College, Wimbledon, at 7+ and 8+. Girls are prepared for entry to other schools, particularly Putney High, Bute House and Wimbledon High, at 7+ and 11+.

Queen's Gate School

133 Queen's Gate, Kensington, London SW7 5LE   Tel: (020) 7589 3587   Fax: (020) 7584 7691
E-mail: registrar@queensgate.org.uk   Website: www.queensgate.org.uk

Principal Mrs R M Kamaryc BA, MSc, PGCE
Founded 1891
School status Girls Day 4–18
Religious denomination Non-Denominational
Member of AGBIS, GSA **Accredited by** GSA
Learning difficulties DYC DYP DYS
Behavioural and emotional disorders RA
Physical and medical conditions RA/HEA
No of pupils (day) 436; Pre-prep 19; Prep 114;
Senior 232; Sixth Form 71; Girls 436
Teacher:pupil ratio 1:6 **Average class size** 24
Fees per annum (day) £10995–£13455

The curriculum is rich, varied, well balanced and as wide as possible during the years leading to the GCSE examinations, and is frequently reviewed to take into account new approaches. All girls sit GCSE examinations in English language, English literature, mathematics, a modern language, and a science, and have the option of taking additional subjects. Junior School: Girls enter the preliminary form aged 4 after assessment. Girls wishing to enter after this take tests in maths and English. Girls in Year 6 are required to pass the London Day Schools Consortium 11+ Examination before moving up into the Senior School. Senior School: Girls sit the London Day Schools Consortium Examination at 11+ and the school's own entrance examinations at 12+, 13+ and 16+. Sixth Form: Girls entering the Sixth Form are required to have at least six GCSE passes at Grade A or above, with at least an A grade in those subjects they wish to pursue to A2. They are expected to study four-five A/S levels and to continue three of those subjects to A2. Scholarships: One 8+ scholarship (internal), two internal Sixth Form scholarships, two Year 7 scholarships, and two 11+ scholarships.

Ravenscourt Park Preparatory School

16 Ravenscourt Avenue, London W6 0SL   Tel: (020) 8846 9153   Fax: (020) 8846 9413
E-mail: secretary@rpps.co.uk   Website: www.rpps.co.uk

Headmaster Mr R Relton
Founded 1991
School status Independent. Co-educational
Day 4–11
Religious denomination Non-Denominational
Member of IAPS
Accredited by IAPS, ISC. Please see the ISC website to read their 2007 inspection report online
Learning difficulties CA SNU WI/DYC DYP DYS MLD
Behavioural and emotional disorders CA ST
No of pupils 261; Girls 134; Boys 127
Teacher:pupil ratio 1:6 **Average class size** 18
Fees per annum (day) £11907

Founded in 1991, Ravenscourt Park Preparatory School is a co-educational independent school for children aged 4 to 11. The school provides an education of the highest quality, preparing children for transfer to the best and most selective independent schools. Parents seeking places in state or independent secondary schools at transfer age can be confident that their child will develop a range of skills and knowledge on which further specialized learning can be based.

The school ethos is quite simply to ensure that each child is happy while at school – children who are content, learn well. In order to achieve this we have developed a relaxed and attractive environment where a structured programme is designed to meet the needs of each individual. We are also fortunate to have a dedicated and talented teaching staff that is prepared to go that 'extra mile'. Finally, we understand that this is a partnership and we work closely with parents to create a trusting relationship based on mutual respect.

'I can assure parents that neither my staff nor I will spare any effort in order to make your child's years at this school happy, fulfilling and successful' – Robert Relton, Headmaster RPPS.

Redcliffe School

47 Redcliffe Gardens, London SW10 9JH   Tel: (020) 7352 9247   Fax: (020) 7352 6936
E-mail: admissions@redcliffeschool.com   Website: www.redcliffeschool.com   www.gabbitas.co.uk

Headmistress Mrs S Bourne BSc (Hons), PGCE
Founded 1948
School status Independent. Co-educational
Day Boys 3–8 Girls 3–11
Religious denomination Christian
Member of AGBIS, IAPS **Accredited by** IAPS
Learning difficulties WI/DYP DYS
Behavioural and emotional disorders RA
Physical and medical conditions RA WA3/HEA
No of pupils 122; *Nursery* 22; *Girls* 84; *Boys* 28
Average class size 12
Fees per annum *(day)* £10950
Fees Between £4200–£10950

Redcliffe School, founded in 1948, is an established and growing nursery and preparatory school situated in Chelsea and easily accessible from all parts of central and west London.

Registration information for all classes may be obtained from the School Office. Redcliffe School Trust is a registered charity (Charity No: 312716).

The Royal School, Hampstead

65 Rosslyn Hill, Hampstead, London NW3 5UD   Tel: (020) 7794 7708   Fax: (020) 7431 6741
E-mail: enquiries@royalschoolhampstead.net   Website: www.royalschoolhampstead.net
www.gabbitas.co.uk   Nursery website: www.royalschool-nursery.net

Headmistress Ms J Ebner BEd (Cantab), MA (Lon)
Founded 1855
School status Independent. Girls Day and
Boarding 3–16. Flexi-boarding available.
Boarders from 11
Religious denomination Non-Denominational
Member of AGBIS, BSA, GSA, ISA, ISBA,
NAHT, SHA
Accredited by ISA Artsmark
Learning difficulties CA SC SNU WI/DYC DYP
DYS MLD
Behavioural and emotional disorders CO/ADD
AUT BESD
Physical and medical conditions AT RA/HEA HI
No of pupils 220; *(full boarding)* 10; *(weekly*
boarding) 9; *(day)* 201; *Nursery* 14; *Pre-prep*
44; *Prep* 55; *Senior* 97; *Girls* 220
Teacher:pupil ratio 1:9 **Average class size** 13
Fees per annum *(full boarding)* £19080;
(weekly) £15870; *(day)* £7680–£9600

The Royal School, Hampstead – 'The school with a heart in the heart of Hampstead'.

The school was founded in 1855, originally for the daughters of soldiers serving in the Crimean War. Now a day and boarding school for 272 girls aged 3–16 years, with boarders from 11 years. Our Patron is HRH The Duchess of Cornwall.

The school has comfortable boarding accommodation and spacious, light classrooms with panoramic views over London.

The school's aim is 'to provide an excellent education based on individual attention to allow each girl to develop her full potential and to become a self-confident, responsible young adult with a clear sense of duty towards others'. We offer a secure and nurturing environment where the girls receive a broad-based education. Regular trips are made to art galleries and theatres, as well as annual trips to UK-based activity centres and European ski resorts. We have recently been awarded a Silver Artsmark Award and have been deemed 'a centre of excellence for art' by the examining bodies.

Pastoral care is overseen by a team of dedicated professionals and a school counsellor is available.

An experienced manager heads our boarding team and we received a good Ofsted report in November 2007. Our Learning Support Team, deemed 'outstanding' by Ofsted, meets the needs of pupils with special educational needs.

2007/2008 Results: SATs were well above the national average. At GCSE level, 99 per cent of pupils passed with 89 per cent gaining A* to C grades. Two students were ranked among the top 10 in the country for history.

Curriculum: Girls follow a balanced curriculum, including two modern languages and three sciences, leading to GCSE. The school is consistently placed among the highest positions in the value added Key Stage 3 to GCSE Performance Tables. Latin and design technology have recently been introduced to the Senior School curriculum.

Extra-curricular activities feature widely and include the Duke of Edinburgh's Award scheme, drama, art, chess, music and a wide range of games and sports. A team of peripatetic music teachers offer a wide range of individual lessons.

Boarding: The school offers a homely environment. Weekly boarding and 'flexi-boarding' can be arranged.

Entry requirements: Junior School: in-class assessment. Senior School (excluding Year 7): examinations based on maths, English and reasoning. Previous school reports required for all pupils. Entry to Year 7 is through the North London Independent Girls' Schools' Consortium (Group 1).

Bursaries and academic, music and art scholarships: Means-tested bursaries are awarded at Year 7.

England

St Benedict's School

54 Eaton Rise, Ealing, London W5 2ES   Tel: (020) 8862 2254   Fax: (020) 8862 2199
E-mail: enquiries@stbenedicts.org.uk   Website: www.stbenedicts.org.uk
Junior School contact: 5, Montpelier Avenue, Ealing, London W5 2XP   Tel: 020 8862 2054

Headmaster Mr C J Cleugh MSc, BSc
Headmaster of Junior School Mr R G Simmons BA
Founded 1902
School status Independent. Co-educational Day 3–18. The school has a unique Benedictine ethos
Religious denomination Roman Catholic
Member of HMC, IAPS
Accredited by IAPS
Learning difficulties CA SNU WI/DYP DYS
Behavioural and emotional disorders ST/ADHD ASP
Physical and medical conditions SM/HEA
No of pupils 950; *(day)* 950; *Nursery* 22; *Pre-prep* 105; *Prep* 171; *Senior* 465; *Sixth Form* 187; *Girls* 135; *Boys* 815
Teacher:pupil ratio 1:9
Average class size 18
Fees per annum *(day)* £10080–£11460

St Benedict's is proud of its uniqueness. Our mission, 'Teaching a way of living', defines us as a Benedictine school. Come and join us and experience our dynamic educational environment.

We will have high expectations of you in everything that you do. We will equip you to deal with the challenges that life in the 21st century presents, teaching you the joys of learning while enabling you to retain a moral and spiritual sensibility.

The new £6.2 million complex, open from September 2008, demonstrates the school's commitment to providing the best possible facilities for students and staff. We invite you to come and visit our school. You can be sure of a warm Benedictine welcome.

St Margaret's School

18 Kidderpore Gardens, London NW3 7SR   Tel: (020) 7435 2439   Fax: (020) 7431 1308
E-mail: principal@st-margarets.co.uk   Website: www.st-margarets.co.uk   www.gabbitas.co.uk

Headmaster Mr M R T Webster
Founded 1884
School status Independent. Girls Day 4–16
Religious denomination Church of England
Member of AGBIS, ISA
Accredited by ISA, ISC
Learning difficulties RA/DYC DYP DYS MLD
Physical and medical conditions WA3
No of pupils 137; *(day)* 137; *Prep* 55; *Senior* 82; *Girls* 137
Teacher:pupil ratio 1:7 **Average class size** 14
Fees per annum *(day)* £8778–£10116

St Margaret's offers high standards of teaching and pastoral care in small classes. Though not unduly selective in 2008 it was placed at the top of the *Sunday Times* Small Independent Schools league table. Girls are taught by specialists from Year 4, and in some subjects such as French, Music and ICT from Reception. At 16 leavers have gone to Channing, South Hampstead High, St Paul's Girls, Highgate and similar schools. Good use is made of local sports facilities and London's cultural opportunities, and within school there are a range of activities from Philosophy to Life-Skills clubs. Entrance is by assessment and viewings with the Head can be made at any time.

St Nicholas Preparatory School

23 Prince's Gate, London SW7 1PT   Tel: (020) 7225 1277   Fax: (020) 7823 7557
E-mail: info@stnicholasprep.co.uk Website: www.stnicholasprep.co.uk www.cognitaschools.co.uk

Headmaster Mr D Wilson BEd, MA Dip TEFL
Founded 1968
School status Co-educational Day 3–11
Member of NAHT
Learning difficulties SNU/DYS
Behavioural and emotional disorders ADD ASP
Physical and medical conditions WA3
No of pupils 250; *Girls* 125; *Boys* 125
Teacher:pupil ratio 1:10 **Average class size** 16
Fees per annum *(day)* £7575–£12150

At Prince's Gate, overlooking Hyde Park, Nursery and Reception classes have been in existence since 1968, offering a child-centred approach to learning using the Montessori method in classes of around 20 children. In 1998 the school developed its facilities to offer a broad-based, traditional programme of education to prepare pupils for entrance examinations to all the leading senior schools at 7+, 8+ and 11+. The school has a fully equipped science room, two networked suites of personal computers and 12 wireless laptops, an outstanding library, and also benefits from its own gymnasium and ballet floor. The academic programme is based on the National Curriculum of England and Wales, and includes a full range of sports, music and arts, providing a balanced and challenging curriculum. We take full advantage of being within walking distance of museums and other famous places of interest.

St Paul's Cathedral School

2 New Change, London EC4M 9AD
Tel: (020) 7248 5156   Fax: (020) 7329 6568
E-mail: admissions@spcs.london.sch.uk
Website: www.spcs.london.sch.uk

Head Master Mr A H Dobbin
Founded 1123
School status Co-educational Boarding and Day 4–13. Boarders from 7
Religious denomination Church of England
Member of IAPS, ISBA, ISC, NAHT
Accredited by IAPS, ISA, ISC
Learning difficulties WI
Physical and medical conditions RA SM; *(full boarding)* 31; *(day)* 196; *Pre-prep* 63; *Prep* 166
Average class size 18
Fees per annum *(full boarding)* £6336; *(day)* £10170

Governed by the Dean and Chapter, the original residential choir school now includes non-chorister day boys and girls aged 4–13.

Curriculum: A broad curriculum leads to scholarship and Common Entrance examinations at 13 and the school has an excellent record in placing pupils in senior schools of their choice, many with scholarships. A wide variety of sport and musical instrument tuition is offered. Choristers receive an outstanding choral training as members of the renowned St Paul's Cathedral Choir.

Facilities: The refurbishment of the school's facilities has provided a separate Pre-preparatory department, improved classrooms and new boarding facilities for the choristers.

Admission: Children are interviewed and tested before September entry at 4+ or 7+ years old. Voice trials and tests for choristers are held three times a year for boys of nearly 7 years and upwards.

England

Westminster School

17 Dean's Yard, Westminster, London SW1P 3PB   Tel: (020) 7963 1003   Fax: (020) 7963 1002
E-mail: registrar@westminster.org.uk   Website: www.westminster.org.uk

Head Master Dr S Spurr
School status Co-educational Boarding and
Day Boys 13–18 Girls 16–18. Boarders from 13
Religious denomination Church of England
Learning difficulties SNU WI/DYP DYS
Behavioural and emotional disorders CO/ASP
TOU
Physical and medical conditions RA SM/HEA VI
No of pupils 733; *(full boarding)* 5; *(weekly
boarding)* 166; *(day)* 562; *Girls* 126; *Boys* 607
Fees per annum *(full boarding)* £27516;
(weekly) £27516; *(day)* £19056–£20664

Situated in the heart of London next to Westminster
Abbey and the Houses of Parliament, Westminster
is one of the country's leading academic schools.
In 2008 98 per cent of A level passes were grades A
or B and over 40 per cent of leavers went on to
Oxford or Cambridge. Approximately 25 per cent
of pupils board and day pupils also benefit from the
school's boarding ethos.

13+ Entry: Boys only
Registration for entry in 2011 will remain open
until 1 July 2009.
16+ Entry: Girls and Boys
Registration for entry in 2010 will open in
June 2009.
For more information or to arrange a tour call
020 7963 1003.

Westminster Tutors

86 Old Brompton Road, London SW7 3LQ   Tel: (020) 7584 1288   Fax: (020) 7584 2637
E-mail: info@westminstertutors.co.uk   Website: www.westminstertutors.co.uk

Principal Ms V H Q L Maguire BA, MLitt
Founded 1934
School status Independent. Co-educational
Day 11–25. We tutor all ages for CE, GCSE,
A level, Oxbridge and university admissions
tests
Learning difficulties SC WI/DYP DYS MLD
Behavioural and emotional disorders RA/ASP
Physical and medical conditions AT RA/HEA
No of pupils 40; *(day)* 40; *Senior* 5; *Sixth
Form* 35; *Girls* 20; *Boys* 20
Teacher:pupil ratio 1:1 **Average class size** 2
Fees per annum *(day)* £15000–£18600. The
fees quoted are for 3 and 4 A level subjects

Westminster Tutors has been renowned for top-
flight tuition since its establishment in 1934. The
college has a friendly atmosphere and excellent
examination results in a wide range of subjects.
Small teaching groups allow tutors to pay attention to the individual needs of students, and

classes combine hard work with lively discussion.
Students have access to computers, a study room,
and a cheerful common room. We offer regular
and intensive A level and GCSE courses, and
preparation for Common Entrance. Private tuition
at all levels is available throughout the year. We
have been successfully preparing students for
entrance to top universities, including Oxford
and Cambridge, for over 70 years and we offer
preparation for all university admissions tests.

Wetherby Preparatory School

19 Pembridge Villas, London W11 3EP
Tel: (020) 7243 0243   Fax: (020) 7313 5244
E-mail: admin@wetherbyprep.co.uk
Website: www.wetherbyprep.co.uk

Head Teacher Mr N R Baker BA, PGCE
Founded 2004
School status Independent. Boys Day 8–13.
We currently have Year 4, 5, 6, 7 and 8 pupils,
having opened in September 2004
Religious denomination Christian
Learning difficulties DYS
Physical and medical conditions RA
No of pupils 103; *(day)* 103; *Prep* 103;
Boys 103
Teacher:pupil ratio 1:16
Average class size 12–18
Fees per annum *(day)* £12600

Following on with the traditions of the pre-preparatory, Wetherby School, Wetherby Preparatory has grown quickly to gain a place in the London Independent sector. Well-qualified, dedicated teachers inspire the boys in a nurturing, fun-filled environment, instilling traditional values including hard work and good manners.

The school moves to larger premises at 48 Bryanston Square, Marleybone in September 2009. Here it will be able to further develop and improve the learning environment and provision of sport, music and the arts.

Wetherby School

11 Pembridge Square, London W2 4ED   Tel: (020) 7727 9581   Fax: (020) 7221 8827
E-mail: learn@WetherbySchool.co.uk   Website: www.alphaplusgroup.co.uk

Headmaster Mr MWE Snell PGCE, BA (Hons)
Founded 1951
School status Boys Day 4–8 Wetherby
Preparatory boys 8–13, automatic entry
Pre-prep boys
Religious denomination Non-Denominational
Member of IAPS
Accredited by IAPS
Learning difficulties WI/DYP DYS
Physical and medical conditions RA/HEA
No of pupils 240; *(day)* 240; *Pre-prep* 240;
Boys 240
Teacher:pupil ratio 1:10 **Average class size** 21
Fees per annum *(day)* £12975

Wetherby School is an independent school for boys aged 4 to 8½ years. The school is based in a freehold, double-fronted listed building of the Italian Ornate style dating back to 1849. It overlooks the beautiful Pembridge Square gardens, where the boys enjoy playtime each day.

There is no test on entry; places are offered on interview with the parents and the Headmaster. Expectations of the boys are good social skills, discipline and the ability to interact with their peer group in a confident and caring manner. The school prides itself on attention to detail; each child is valued as an individual and this is implemented through a high teacher:pupil teaching ratio.

Wetherby is a traditional school; high academic standards prevail and the boys enjoy a healthy balance between this and many other curriculum activities that are offered during the school day. Sports and the arts have a particularly high profile within the school. Wetherby offers excellent facilities for IT, library, indoor gym and individual specialist teaching if required. In addition, the school is well known for the home cooked healthy lunches it provides.

The school operates a sibling policy, though early registration is advised. Please contact the Administrator's office in the first instance.

England

MAP OF THE HOME COUNTIES (SOUTH)

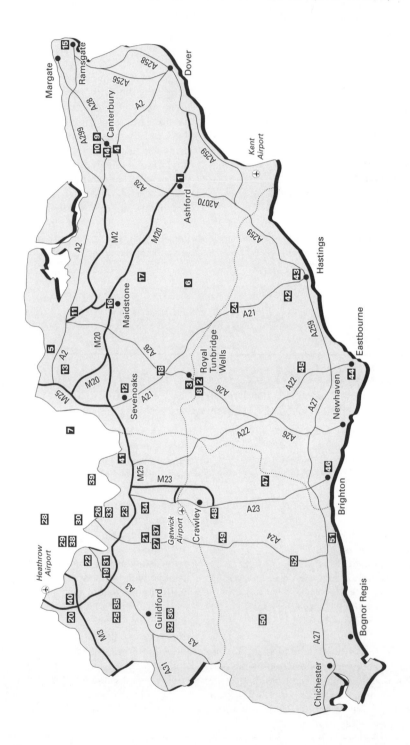

PROFILED SCHOOLS IN THE HOME COUNTIES (SOUTH)

(Incorporating the counties of Kent, Surrey, East Sussex, West Sussex)

England

Ashford School

East Hill, Ashford, Kent TN24 8PB   Tel: (01233) 739030   Fax: (01233) 665215
E-mail: registrar@ashfordschool.co.uk   Website: www.ashfordschool.co.uk

Head Mr M R Buchanan BSc Hons, Cert Ed,
NPQH, CPhys   **Founded** 1898
School status Independent. Co-educational
Day and Boarding 3–18 (Co-ed 3–11). Flexi-
boarding available. Boarders from 10
Religious denomination Inter-Denominational
Member of BSA, IAPS, SHMIS
Accredited by ISC, SHMIS
Learning difficulties CA SNU/DYP DYS MLD
Behavioural and emotional disorders CO RA/
ADHD ASP AUT
Physical and medical conditions RA SM
WA3/HEA
No of pupils 706; *(full boarding)* 115; *(weekly
boarding)* 20; *(day)* 615; *Nursery* 70; *Pre-prep*
130; *Prep* 170; *Senior* 390; *Sixth Form* 119;
Girls 475; *Boys* 231
Teacher:pupil ratio 1:10 **Average class size** 16
Fees per annum *(full boarding)* £23226–
£23823; *(weekly)* £21099; *(day)* £5640–
£13104

Ashford School is
an independent
day and boarding
school set in two
spacious, green
campuses. We
provide childcare
and education
for boys and girls
aged from 3
months to 18 years. Parents choose Ashford
School for many reasons: high achievement leading to the best universities; close attention to the
individual; an orderly, challenging and supportive
environment and a wide range of co-curricular
activities supported by energetic teachers with
extensive resources and inventive leadership.
With no lessons on Saturday there is plenty of
time to make use of school facilities or participate
in a variety of visits to London, Canterbury or even
the continent!

Beechwood Sacred Heart School

Pembury Road, Tunbridge Wells, Kent TN2 3QD   Tel: (01892) 532747   Fax: (01892) 536164
E-mail: registrar@beechwood.org.uk   Website: www.beechwood.org.uk   www.gabbitas.co.uk

Headmaster Mr N R Beesley MA (Oxon)
Founded 1915
School status Independent. Co-educational
Boarding and Day 3–18 (Boarding for Girls
only from 11). Co-educational Senior School
from September 2008
Religious denomination Roman Catholic
Member of BSA, SHMIS **Accredited by** SHMIS
Learning difficulties SNU WI/DYC DYP DYS
Behavioural and emotional disorders RA/AUT
Physical and medical conditions RA SM/EPI
HEA
No of pupils 400; *(full boarding)* 60; *(day)* 140;
Prep 200; *Senior* 200; *Sixth Form* 55; *Girls* 313;
Boys 87
Teacher:pupil ratio 1:9 **Average class size** 15
Fees per annum *(full boarding)* £21945;
(weekly) £19380; *(day)* £6285–£12945

Situated in extensive grounds, close to the centre
of Tunbridge Wells, Beechwood is a happy,

friendly school, in which high standards are maintained by expectation; pupils learn to respect and
support each other. Each individual is important,
and boys and girls quickly gain confidence, taught
in small classes by committed teachers who are
prepared to go the extra mile. A broad curriculum
and activities programme ensure that pupils are
prepared fully for life. Every year all Beechwood
pupils go on to the courses of their choice in
Higher Education.

Bell Bedgebury International School

Goudhurst, Cranbrook, Kent TN17 2SH   Tel: +44 (01580) 879100   Fax: (01580) 879102
E-mail: bedgebury@bell-centres.com   Website: www.bedgeburyschool.co.uk

Head Mr E J Squires BSc, MA, PGCE
School Administrator Ms L Jackson
School status Independent. Co-educational
Boarding and Day 12–17. Boarders from 12
International Study Centre / co-educational
international boarding school
Religious denomination Non-Denominational
Learning difficulties WI
No of pupils 43; *(full boarding)* 40; *(day)* 3;
Senior 43; *Girls* 13; *Boys* 30
Teacher:pupil ratio 1:5 **Average class size** 10
Fees per annum *(full boarding)* £22965

Bell Bedgebury International School provides the
perfect foundation for international students, aged
12–17, seeking to prepare for secondary or higher
education in the UK. Set in 220 acres of beautiful
parkland in the South of England, the school
combines outstanding English language teaching
with high-quality subject tuition and unrivalled
sports and recreational facilities.

On our Lower
School programme,
students aged 12–14
follow a broad curricu-
lum with an emphasis
on the development of
their English Language
skills. Students aged
15–17 can study on
our two-year GCSE
programme or fast-
track their studies on
our intensive one-year
GCSE course.

In addition to term-time studies we also offer
a number of intensive summer preparation programmes (pre-GCSE and pre-A level/International
Baccalaureate) designed to prepare international
students for their term time studies.

To find out more about the school and scholarships on offer visit: www.bedgeburyschool.co.uk.

CATS Canterbury

68 New Dover Road, Stafford House, Canterbury, Kent CT1 3LQ
Tel: (01227) 866540   Fax: (01227) 866550
E-mail: admissions@catscanterbury.com   Website: www.catscanterbury.com   www.ceg-uk.com

Principal Ms M L Banning BA (Hons), RSA Dip,
TEFL
Registrar Miss L Kay   **Founded** 1952
School status Independent Sixth Form College.
Co-educational Boarding and Day Boys 15–28
Girls 15–26. Boarders from 15
Religious denomination Non-Denominational
Accredited by BAC
No of pupils 180; *(full boarding)* 166; *(day)* 14;
Girls 75; *Boys* 105
Teacher:pupil ratio 1:5 **Average class size** 8
Fees per annum *(full boarding)* £18495–
£27300; *(day)* £14400–£18000

Established in 1952, CATS Canterbury remains
one of the leading international Sixth Form
schools in the UK. CATS offers the International
Baccalaureate, A levels, IB preparation, Academic English, Study Abroad and Pre Master's
Foundation programmes. We are proud of creat-

ing an environment that inspires everyone to perform their best. Our record of student success is a
matter of fact – in 2008 96 per cent of A level
students achieved A–C grades and 100 per cent of
graduating students gained a university place.

Expert teaching staff and a caring welfare team
guide students through the education system.
Tuition groups remain small and the care of a
personal tutor helps to guide, advise and support
students throughout their time at college.

England

Cobham Hall

Cobham, Gravesend, Kent DA12 3BL   Tel: +44 (0)1474 823371   Fax: +44 (0)1474 825906
E-mail: enquiries@cobhamhall.com   Website: www.cobhamhall.com   www.gabbitas.co.uk

Headmaster Mr P Mitchell BSc (Newcastle)
Registrar Mrs S Ferrers
Head of Sixth Form Mr A Pinchin MA (Cantab)
Founded 1962
School status Independent. Girls Boarding and Day 11–18. Flexi-boarding available. Boarders from 11
Religious denomination Inter-Denominational
Member of BSA, CReSTeD, GSA, Round Square
Accredited by British Council, GSA, ISC
Learning difficulties SNU WI/DYC DYP DYS
Physical and medical conditions HI
No of pupils 200; *(full boarding)* 80; *(weekly boarding)* 20; *(day)* 100; *Girls* 200
Teacher:pupil ratio 1:6 **Average class size** 15
Fees per annum *(full boarding)* £19800–£24900; *(weekly)* £19800–£24900; *(day)* £13200–£16500. Covers all boarding and tuition, meals, stationery and routine medical attention

One of Britain's leading girls' schools, Cobham Hall promotes excellence in all subjects. IB offered in Sixth Form. The majority of students proceed to higher education. Specialist help is provided for dyslexic students and our EFL department offers English language support.

The school is housed in an outstanding 16th-century mansion set in 150 acres with a purpose-built classroom block, modern boarding houses, an indoor swimming pool and sports centre.

Membership of Round Square provides the opportunity for international exchanges and education outside the classroom.

Cobham Hall is situated 25 miles from central London, with easy access to international airports.

Cranbrook School

Cranbrook, Kent TN17 3JD   Tel: (01580) 711800   Fax: (01580) 711828
E-mail: registrar@cranbrook.kent.sch.uk
Website: www.cranbrookschool.co.uk   www.gabbitas.co.uk

Headteacher Mrs A S Daly MA
Founded 1518
School status State (Voluntary-aided). Co-educational Day and Boarding 13–18. Boarders from 13 Co-educational selective boarding and day
Religious denomination Non-Denominational
Member of BSA, ISBA
Learning difficulties RA/DYP DYS
Behavioural & emotional disorders RA/ADD AUT
Physical & medical conditions RA SM/EPI HEA
No of pupils 756; *(full boarding)* 236; *(day)* 520; *Sixth Form* 320; *Girls* 354; *Boys* 402
Average class size 30
Fees per annum *(full boarding)* £8850–£9525

Cranbrook is a selective co-educational boarding and day school offering a superb all-round education at a very reasonable cost. It has a wide range of extra-curricular activities and high academic standards of 99 per cent A–C grades at GCSE and 100 per cent pass rate (67 per cent A/B grades) at A level.

Music, art and drama thrive. Many productions for music and drama are held in the theatre. Cranbrook has fine facilities for the creative arts, including a performing arts centre, a Sixth Form centre and a design/technology centre. Team and individual sports are important and the school has playing fields, a swimming pool, a sports hall and astro-turf pitches. Teams play at the highest levels locally and nationally.

Entry at 13+ is competitive and by examination. Entry at 16+ is competitive and based on school reference and GCSE grades. Boarding candidates at both 13+ and 16+ are interviewed to ensure suitability for boarding. Details from the Registrar, Cranbrook School. Cranbrook School (VA) exists to promote education in Cranbrook.

Farringtons School

Perry Street, Chislehurst, Kent BR7 6LR   Tel: (020) 8467 0256   Fax: (020) 8467 5442
E-mail: admissions@farringtons.kent.sch.uk   Website: www.farringtons.org.uk
www.gabbitas.co.uk   We are girls only in the Senior School and co-educational in the Junior School

Headmistress Mrs C E James MA
Registrar Mrs F Vail   **Founded** 1911
School status Independent. Girls Day and
Boarding 3–19. Flexi-boarding available.
Boarders from 11
Religious denomination Methodist
Member of BSA, GSA
Accredited by British Council, GSA, ISC
Learning difficulties WI/DYP DYS MLD
Behavioural and emotional disorders RA
Physical and medical conditions RA SM
WA3/EPI HEA HI VI
No of pupils 510; *(full boarding)* 46; *(weekly
boarding)* 2; *(day)* 462; *Nursery* 32; *Prep* 202;
Senior 270; *Sixth Form* 67; *Girls* 470; *Boys* 40
Average class size 16 (juniors), 20 (seniors)
Fees per annum *(full boarding)* £19800;
(weekly) £18600; *(day)* £7830–£10830

commitment to
stretch every
pupil to the
very best of his
or her ability.
    We have a
range of facil-
ities, including
a new compu-
ter suite, impressive sports hall with dance
studio and weights room, a technology centre
and a swimming pool. Our boarding facilities
have just been refurbished, giving girls comfortable study-bedrooms all freshly decorated with
new carpets, curtains and modern furniture.
    Farringtons School is situated on a beautiful 25-
acre site in a peaceful Kent village: yet it is a mere
12 miles from central London. It is also ideally
located close to airports and the M25.

Farringtons School has a wide ability intake and a

Holmewood House

Langton Green, Tunbridge Wells, Kent TN3 0EB   Tel: (01892) 860006   Fax: (01892) 863970
E-mail: registrar@holmewood.kent.sch.uk   Website: www.holmewood.kent.sch.uk

The Headmaster Mr A S R Corbett MA, PGCE
Registrar Mrs K Gwinnett BA (Hons)
Founded 1945
School status Independent. Co-educational
Day 3–13. Flexi-boarding available
Religious denomination Inter-Denominational
Member of IAPS, ISBA **Accredited by** IAPS
Learning difficulties CA SNU WI/DYP DYS
MLD
Behavioural and emotional disorders CA CO
ST TS/ASP
Physical and medical conditions CA IT SM/EPI
HEA HI VI
No of pupils 474; *(day)* 474; *Nursery* 33;
Pre-prep 138; *Prep* 303; *Girls* 193; *Boys* 281
Teacher:pupil ratio 8:1
Average class size 15
Fees per annum *(day)* £5165–£15165

child is considered unique
and will be inspired to
learn.
    The breadth of curricu-
lum, specialist teaching in
all subjects resulting in
excellent academic results,
superb facilities, a vast
range of afternoon activ-
ities, in an 'outstanding
family atmosphere'* , all
combine to make Holme-
wood one of the leading prep schools in the
country. Holmewood is 'a happy community
where pupils are confident and articulate, enthusiastic and motivated, friendly and courteous.'*
    Holmewood pupils 'clearly enjoy coming to
school and revel in the opportunities the school
provides.'* Visit us in Tunbridge Wells to see what
an inspiring place for children Holmewood truly is.
    * ISI Inspection Report, March 2007

Set in 30 acres of beautiful grounds, Holmewood
House School is a happy, busy place, where every

Junior King's School

Milner Court, Sturry, Canterbury, Kent CT2 0AY   Tel: (01227) 714000
Fax: (01227) 713171   E-mail: head@junior-kings.co.uk   Website: www.junior-kings.co.uk
For information about entry, please contact the Registrar: Mrs V A Wells (01227) 714019/714000

Headmaster Mr P M Wells BEd (Hons)
Founded 1879
School status Independent. Co-educational
Day and Boarding 3–13. Flexi-boarding
available. Boarders from 8
Religious denomination Church of England
Member of BSA, IAPS, SATIPS
Accredited by IAPS, ISC
Learning difficulties CA WI/DYC DYP DYS
MLD
Behavioural and emotional disorders CO/ADD
ADHD
Physical and medical conditions CA SM
TW/HEA HI
No of pupils 403; *(full boarding)* 54; *(weekly*
boarding) 20; *(day)* 329; *Nursery* 18; *Pre-prep*
81; *Prep* 304; *Girls* 177; *Boys* 226
Teacher:pupil ratio 1:7 **Average class size** 15
Fees per annum *(full boarding)* £18780;
(weekly) £18780; *(day)* £12450–£13780

'Encouraging life in all its fullness. . .'
The Junior King's School is a co-educational
boarding and day school with a strong Christian
ethos. It makes use of buildings which include a
medieval tithe barn and manor house, modern
purpose-built ICT suites, classrooms and laboratories, all surrounded by beautiful grounds and
gardens two miles from the centre of Canterbury.
Children from 3 to 13 lead busy and productive
lives both in and out of the classroom. Their academic studies are balanced by a large range of
sport, music, drama and art activities. They enjoy
the family atmosphere, the space and fresh air.
Boarding is at the heart of school life, with a
mixture of overseas children and weekly boarders
from London and the South East.

Kent College

Whitstable Road, Canterbury, Kent CT2 9DT   Tel: (01227) 763231/762436   Fax: (01227) 787450
E-mail: registrar@kentcollege.co.uk   Website: www.kentcollege.com   www.gabbitas.co.uk
Junior School website: www.kentcollege.com/junior

Head Master Dr D J Lamper EdD, MA, AKC
Head Master (Infant and Junior School) Mr A
Carter BEd (Hons)
Deputy Head Mr J G Waltho MA
Founded 1885
College status Independent. Co-educational
Boarding and Day 3–18. Flexi-boarding
available. Boarders from 7
Religious denomination Methodist
Member of HMC, IAPS
Accredited by HMC, IAPS, ISC
Learning difficulties SNU WI/DYP DYS SP&LD
Behavioural and emotional disorders CO
ST/ASP AUT
Physical and medical conditions AT SM
TW/HEA HI
No of pupils 645; *(full boarding)* 151; *(weekly*
boarding) 2; *(day)* 494; *Nursery* 20; *Pre-prep*
207; *Senior* 273; *Sixth Form* 160; *Girls* 272;
Boys 373

Teacher:pupil ratio 1:9 **Average class size** 15
Fees per annum *(full boarding)* £17169–
£23949; *(weekly)* £22620–£22941; *(day)*
£6405–£14187. Fees for attending the
International Study Centre are £8942 per term
(boarding)

Kent College is a
vibrant co-educa-
tional boarding
and day school,
taking children
from 3 to 18 years.
We offer full,
weekly and flexible boarding, small classes and
a broad curriculum that allows all students to fulfil
their potential. The visual and performing arts
have a high profile, as does sport, and the school
also has its own farm, and an international study
centre and dyslexic unit.

Rochester Independent College

Star Hill, Rochester, Kent ME1 1XF   Tel: (01634) 828115   Fax: (01634) 405667
E-mail: admissions@rochester-college.org Website: www.rochester-college.org www.gabbitas.co.uk

Co Principals A Brownlow MA (Hons), MPhil,
B Pain BSc (Hons), PGDiP, P Bailey HND,
PGDiP, MA
Founded 1985
College status Co-educational Day and
Boarding 11–21. Flexi-boarding available.
Boarders from 16   **Accredited by** ISA
Learning difficulties DYP DYS
Behavioural and emotional disorders RA
No of pupils 220; *(full boarding)* 60; *(day)* 120;
Senior 70; *Sixth Form* 130; *Girls* 110; *Boys* 110
Teacher:pupil ratio 1:3 **Average class size** 8
Fees per annum *(full boarding)* £24426; *(day)*
£9450–£12750. The college is committing to
holding the fees for day students until
September 2010

Rochester Independent College is a progressive
alternative to traditional private education for day
and boarding students. The focus is on examination success and progression to university in a
lively, supportive and informal atmosphere. Students achieve A level and GCSE results that often
exceed their expectations. There is no uniform, no
bells ring and everybody is on first name terms.

For many of our students the college is the first
place where they have been engaged by education and have found the freedom to be
themselves. The college is not academically
selective and direct entry is possible into any
school year.

Sevenoaks School

Sevenoaks, Kent TN13 1HU   Tel: (01732) 455133   Fax: (01732) 456143
E-mail: regist@sevenoaksschool.org Website: www.sevenoaksschool.org www.gabbitas.co.uk

Head Mrs C L Ricks MA   **Founded** 1432
Director of Admissions Mrs A M Stuart BSc
School status Independent. Co-educational
Day and Boarding 11–18. Boarders from 11
Religious denomination Inter-Denominational
Member of BSA, HMC, IBO
Accredited by HMC, ISC
Learning difficulties SNU WI/DYC DYP DYS
Behavioural and emotional disorders CO
RA/ADHD
Physical and medical conditions AT HL SL SM
TW WA1 WA2/EPI HEA HI IM VI W
No of pupils 990; *(full boarding)* 342; *(day)*
648; *Senior* 555; *Sixth Form* 435; *Girls* 517;
Boys 473
Teacher:pupil ratio 1:10 **Average class size** 15
Fees per annum *(full boarding)* £25554–
£27720; *(day)* £15936–£18102. Higher fees
shown are for direct entrants to the Sixth Form

Sevenoaks is a co-educational, independent, day
and boarding school, situated 30 minutes from
central London and Gatwick airport. Approximately one-third of the 990 students are
boarders. Pupils worldwide enter at 11, 13 or
16, taking GCSEs and the International Baccalaureate. Students proceed to major universities,
including Oxbridge and Ivy League schools with
excellent facilities for sport and co-curricular
activities. More than 50 scholarships are awarded
annually for academic excellence, art, music and
all-round ability.

England

Steephill Independent School

Castle Hill, Fawkham, Longfield, Kent DA3 7BG   Tel: (01474) 702107   Fax: (01474) 706011
E-mail: secretary@steephill.co.uk   Website: www.steephill.co.uk

Headteacher Mrs C Birtwell BSc, MBA, PGCE
Bursar Mrs Nicola Kiley   **Founded** 1935
School status Independent. Co-educational
Day 3½–11
Religious denomination Church of England
Member of ISA
Accredited by ISA Accredited by ISA
Learning difficulties CA WI/DYS MLD
Behavioural and emotional disorders RA ST
Physical and medical conditions RA TW WA2
No of pupils 118; *(day)* 118; *Nursery* 20;
Pre-prep 41; *Prep* 57; *Girls* 58; *Boys* 60
Teacher:pupil ratio 1:12 **Average class size** 14
Fees per annum *(day)* £2297

The high standards of care and teaching are reflected in the excellent academic results. Although a mixed ability school, all the children attain a very high standard with typically 80 per cent of a year group gaining a grammar school place. With just a maximum of 16 pupils in a class, each child benefits from the individual attention necessary to achieve his or her full potential. Non-academic pursuits such as sport, drama and the arts also have a very high level of importance. The School has a silver Artsmark award and its choir has won the Gravesham festival two years running. As a small school the staff, parents and children all know each other and this contributes to our happy, family atmosphere.

Steephill is situated in the beautiful Fawkham Valley countryside in a quiet lane overlooking the 13th-century village church. Our small classes bring out the best in young children, who receive all the help and encouragement they need from Steephill's qualified, dedicated teachers.

St Edmund's School Canterbury

St Thomas Hill, Canterbury, Kent CT2 8HU   Tel: (01227) 475600   Fax: (01227) 471083
E-mail: seniorschool@stedmunds.org.uk; juniorschool@stedmunds.org.uk
Website: www.stedmunds.org.uk

Headmaster Mr J M Gladwin BSc (Hons)
(Dunelm)
The Master of the Junior School Mr R G Bacon
BA (Hons) (Dunelm)
Head of the Pre-Prep School Mrs J Frampton-
Fell BA (Hons) (Kent)   **Founded** 1749
School status Independent. Co-educational
Day and Boarding 3–18. Flexi-boarding
available. Boarders from 8. Canterbury
Cathedral Choristers: 26
Religious denomination Church of England
Member of AGBIS, BSA, HMC, IAPS, ISBA,
SHA   **Accredited by** HMC, IAPS, ISC Choir
School Association
No of pupils 533; *(full boarding)* 113; *(day)*
420; *Nursery* 15; *Pre-prep* 49; *Prep* 192; *Senior*
277; *Sixth Form* 118; *Girls* 215; *Boys* 318
Teacher:pupil ratio 1:6 **Average class size** 15
Fees per annum *(full boarding)* £16818–
£24057; *(weekly)* £15324; *(day)* £11841–

£15534. Fee ranges are for Senior and Junior School, not for Pre-prep, where fees range is £3075–£8388

Creating opportunities – Realizing potential
    We are a friendly school with a creative ethos, Christian values, and a strong sense of community, pastoral care and pride. We respect and nurture each child's individuality, creating opportunities for children to fulfil their own potential, thus enabling them to become confident, sociable, well-balanced people. Because we are a small friendly school, we know our boys and girls well and we work closely with parents to create a secure and happy family atmosphere with a sense of community. We achieve strong academic performance at all levels and this is balanced with an innovative and dynamic programme of extra-curricular activities.

St Lawrence College

College Road, Ramsgate, Kent CT11 7AE   Tel: (01843) 572931   Fax: (01843) 572901
E-mail: ah@slcuk.com   Website: www.slcuk.com

Headmaster Rev C W M Aitken BA (Durham), Cert Theol, FRSA   **Founded** 1879
College status Independent. Co-educational Boarding and Day 3–18. Day from 3–18 and Boarding from 7–18
Religious denomination Church of England
Member of HMC, IAPS
Accredited by HMC, IAPS
Learning difficulties CA SNU DYC DYP DYS SP&LD
Behavioural and emotional disorders CA CO TS/ADD
Physical and medical conditions RA SM/EPI HEA HI
No of pupils 520; *(full boarding)* 214; *(day)* 306; *Nursery* 22; *Pre-prep* 49; *Prep* 114; *Senior* 218; *Sixth Form* 117; *Girls* 220; *Boys* 300
Teacher:pupil ratio 1:8 **Average class size** 15
Fees per annum *(full boarding)* £17505–£23292; *(weekly)* £17505–£23292; *(day)* £5406–£13641

Walk through the historic arch at St Lawrence College in Kent and you will immediately feel at home. The newly opened Kirby House accommodates students aged 11 and 12 in modern five-bedded dormitories with en-suite facilities. Senior students are accommodated in recently refurbished five-bedded dormitories, double and single rooms. Outstanding results are achieved by the most academic students who progress to many of the top universities. The school is also highly regarded as a centre of excellence for 'value added'. The school has excellent transport links to London and Europe.

Sutton Valence Preparatory School

Church Road, Chart Sutton, Maidstone, Kent ME17 3RF   Tel: (01622) 842117   Fax: (01622) 844201
E-mail: enquiries@svprep.svs.org.uk   Website: www.svs.org.uk

Head Mr C A Gibbs
School status Co-educational Day 3–11. Boarders from 10 Kindergarden to age 11
Religious denomination Church of England
Member of IAPS
Accredited by IAPS
Learning difficulties WI/DYS
Behavioural and emotional disorders RA
Physical and medical conditions RA
No of pupils *(Kindergarten)* 25; *Pre-prep* 116; *Prep* 224; *Girls* 166; *Boys* 365
Average class size 18
Fees per annum *(day)* £3495–£10080. Lunch £190 per term Music £205 per 10 lessons

High academic achievement goes hand in hand with a happy family atmosphere. Our children are encouraged to develop their individual talents to the full, contributing positively and enthusiastically to school life and we aim for all our pupils to be confident, articulate and well mannered.

By encouraging the children to experience a wide range of academic, sporting, musical and cultural activities, we prepare them for entrance to our senior School, Sutton Valence, or other secondary schools, both independent and maintained.

Sutton Valence School

Sutton Valence, Maidstone, Kent ME17 3HL   Tel: (01622) 845200   Fax: (01622) 844103
E-mail: enquiries@svs.org.uk   Website: www.svs.org.uk
Sutton Valence Prep School admissions: enquiries@svps.svs.org.uk   (01622) 842117

Headmaster Mr J S Davies MA St John's
Cambridge
Head of Prep School Mr C Gibbs BA (Hons),
HD Ed   **Founded** 1576
School status Independent. Co-educational
Boarding and Day 3–18. Flexi-boarding
available. Boarders from 11 Sutton Valence
School ages 11–18; Sutton Valence Prep ages
3–11
Religious denomination Church of England
Member of HMC, IAPS
Accredited by HMC, IAPS
No of pupils 915; *(full boarding)* 47; *(weekly
boarding)* 90; *(day)* 778; *Nursery* 62; *Pre-prep*
95; *Prep* 231; *Senior* 527; *Sixth Form* 147;
Girls 350; *Boys* 565
Teacher:pupil ratio 1:9
Average class size 12–18
Fees per annum *(full boarding)* £18960–
£24960; *(weekly)* £18960–£24960; *(day)*

£6990–£15780. Music tuition £205 for 10
lessons. Extra tuition £43.30 per lesson. Lunch
£190 per term

Sutton Valence pupils are expected to tackle their
academic goals with enthusiasm and commitment and to involve themselves in the wider life
of the school through our extensive extra and co-
curricular programmes.

Tonbridge School

Tonbridge, Kent TN9 1JP   Tel: (01732) 304297   Fax: (01732) 363424
E-mail: admissions@tonbridge-school.org   Website: www.tonbridge-school.co.uk   www.gabbitas.co.uk

Headmaster Mr T H P Haynes BA
Admissions Registrar Mr J S Hodgson BA
Founded 1553
School status Independent. Boys Boarding and
Day 13–18
Religious denomination Church of England
Member of BSA, HMC
Accredited by ISC
Learning difficulties SNU WI/DYP DYS
Behavioural and emotional disorders CO/
ADHD/ADD
Physical and medical conditions AT SM
WA3/HEA
No of pupils 769; *(full boarding)* 441; *(day)*
317; *Boys* 769
Teacher:pupil ratio 1:8
Fees per annum *(full boarding)* £28140; *(day)*
£20910. Substantial scholarships and bursaries
available

Tonbridge School is one of the leading boys

boarding schools in the country and highly
respected internationally. Boarders and day boys
of varying backgrounds are offered an education
remarkable both for its breadth of opportunity and
the exceptional standards routinely achieved in
all areas of school life.

We welcome you to visit Tonbridge to meet us
and see the school. For further information or for
an appointment, please contact the Admissions
Office on 01732 304297 or e-mail admissions@
tonbridge-school.org.

ACS Cobham International School

Heywood, Portsmouth Road, Cobham, Surrey KT11 1BL   Tel: (01932) 867251   Fax: (01932) 869789
E-mail: cobhamadmissions@acs-england.co.uk   Website: www.acs-england.co.uk

Head of School Mr T J Lehman
Dean of Admissions Mrs H Ayoub
Founded 1967
School status Independent. Co-educational Boarding and Day 2–18. Boarders from 12. Day, ages 2–18. Boarding, ages 12–18
Religious denomination Non-Denominational
Member of CIS, IBO, IBSCA, ISA, LISA, NEASC NEAS&C and inspected by the Independent Schools Inspectorate (ISI) on behalf of Ofsted
No of pupils 1369; *(full boarding)* 60; *(weekly boarding)* 30; *(day)* 1315; *Nursery* 188; *Pre-prep* 353; *Prep* 394; *Senior* 432; *Girls* 606; *Boys* 763
Teacher:pupil ratio 1:9 **Average class size** 15
Fees per annum *(full boarding)* £30600–£32040; *(weekly)* £26890–£28330; *(day)* £8310–£18280. £5620 for Rising 3 £8310 for full-day Pre-Kindergarten

Offering both the International Baccalaureate (IB) Diploma and American Advanced Placement (AP) courses, ACS Cobham graduates attend leading universities throughout the world. Situated on a 128-acre site, the ACS Cobham campus has excellent sports facilities with soccer and rugby fields, softball and baseball diamonds, an Olympic-sized track, tennis courts, a six-hole golf course and a sports centre with a basketball/volleyball show court, competition-class swimming pool, dance studio, fitness suite and cafeteria. A co-educational boarding house provides separate-wing accommodation for 110 students aged between 12 and 18. The school's Early Childhood programme was rated outstanding in every category in its recent ISI report.

ACS Egham International School

Woodlee, London Road (A30), Egham, Surrey TW20 0HS Tel: (01784) 430800   Fax: (01784) 430626
E-mail: eghamadmissions@acs-england.co.uk   Website: www.acs-england.co.uk

Head of School Ms M Hadley
Dean of Admissions Ms J Love   **Founded** 1967
School status Co-educational Day 2–18 IB World School, with IB Primary, Middle and IB Diploma. All graduates receive a high school diploma
Religious denomination Non-Denominational
Member of CIS, IBO, IBSCA, ISA, LISA, NEASC NEAS&C and inspected by the Independent Schools Inspectorate (ISI) on behalf of Ofsted
No of pupils 586; *(day)* 586; *Nursery* 71; *Pre-prep* 191; *Prep* 157; *Senior* 100; *Sixth Form* 67; *Girls* 284; *Boys* 302
Teacher:pupil ratio 1:9 **Average class size** 15
Fees per annum *(day)* £8310–£18050

ACS Egham International School is the UK's most successful young International Baccalaureate (IB) school. Its students have consistently achieved 100 per cent pass rates and diploma score averages well above international results. This has led to placements in top universities worldwide. Additionally, the school is one of only three schools offering the IB Primary Years Programme (PYP), the Middle Years Programme (MYP) and the IB Diploma as well as an American High School Diploma. Situated on a 20-acre site ACS Egham has students from 29 nationalities speaking 19 languages, all seeking a world-class education. With a wireless network on campus, the school operates a comprehensive information technology programme supported by extensive use of laptops and individual data technology storage units.

England

Box Hill School

Mickleham, Dorking, Surrey RH5 6EA   Tel: (01372) 373382   Fax: (01372) 363942
E-mail: enquiries@boxhillschool.org.uk   Website: www.boxhillschool.com   www.gabbitas.co.uk

Headmaster Mr M Eagers MA
Registrar Mrs K Hammond   **Founded** 1959
School status Independent. Co-educational
Boarding and Day 11–18. Flexi-boarding
available. Boarders from 11
Religious denomination Non-Denominational
Member of AGBIS, BSA, ISA, ISBA, Round
Square, SHA, SHMIS
Accredited by British Council, ISC, SHMIS
No of pupils 399; *(full boarding)* 95; *(weekly boarding)* 59; *(day)* 245; *Senior* 284; *Sixth Form* 115; *Girls* 135; *Boys* 264
Teacher:pupil ratio 1:8.5 **Average class size** 18
Fees per annum *(full boarding)* £21000–£22050; *(weekly)* £19050; *(day)* £12000–£13500. (ISC per annum) £25000

airports. It is small and friendly and places great emphasis on pastoral care so that students experience balanced academic, social and emotional growth.

Overseas students are fully integrated into social and academic life throughout the school. They enjoy social and cultural activities while being carefully guided on a course of study either in the mainstream school or in our International Study Centre.

Box Hill School is a co-educational independent day and boarding school for 11–18-year-olds located in Mickleham, Surrey, and convenient for central London, Gatwick and Heathrow

Students are well-rounded and poised to become leaders and socially responsible individuals capable of making a positive contribution to society.

Claremont Fan Court School

Claremont Drive, Esher, Surrey KT10 9LY   Tel: (01372) 467841   Fax: (01372) 471109
E-mail: jtilson@claremont.surrey.sch.uk   Website: www.claremont-school.co.uk

Principal Mrs A Stanley MA BA   **Founded** 1922
School status Co-educational Day 3–18
Religious denomination Christian Science, all
religions welcome
Member of SHMIS
Learning difficulties CA SNU/DYP DYS
Physical and medical conditions AT CA RA SL
WA2/HI IM W
No of pupils 650; *Girls* 325; *Boys* 325
Fees per annum *(day)* £3651–£12216

and developed within small classes in a happy, positive environment.

All pupils from Years 4 to Year 11 have their own laptop. This is much more than 'laptops on desks'. Each pupil in these year groups has his/her own laptop which is used both in the classroom and for work at home. The laptops are not replacing traditional teaching methods where they are shown to be effective, but are providing flexible resources that will enrich and support the students' learning experience.

Claremont Fan Court School is a co-educational school for pupils aged 3–18 years. The school is situated in the Claremont Estate, one of the premier historic sites in the country. In 1930 the school aquired the mansion and now owns 96 acres of peaceful parkland.

The school's excellent academic programme with small class sizes provide the pupils with a wide and varied curriculum. High personal expectations and moral values are established

Sport at Claremont is enhanced by a fully equipped sports centre and gymnasium. Teams compete regularly with neighbouring schools, with individuals competing at county and national levels.

Greenacre School for Girls

Sutton Lane, Banstead, Surrey SM7 3RA
Tel: (01737) 352114   Fax: (01737) 373485
E-mail: admin@greenacre.surrey.sch.uk
Website: www.greenacre.surrey.sch.uk   www.gabbitas.co.uk

Headmistress Mrs P M Wood BA
Founded 1933
School status Independent. Girls Day 3–18
Religious denomination Non-Denominational
Member of AGBIS, GSA, ISBA, SHA
Accredited by GSA
Learning difficulties WI/DYS
No of pupils 410; *Girls* 410
Fees per annum *(day)* £6300–£10800

Situated on the edge of the Banstead Downs, Greenacre School offers a clean, safe, bright and modern environment for children to learn. A balanced education is supported by a range of outstanding extra-curricular activities. Whether on the field, in the concert hall or on the stage, Greenacre children have the confidence to shine. Girls can join us at any stage – Nursery, Junior, Senior and Sixth Form. Why not come and visit the school to see what makes us so special.

Hazelwood School

Wolf's Hill, Limpsfield, Oxted, Surrey RH8 0QU   Tel: (01883) 712194   Fax: (01883) 716135
E-mail: registrar@hazelwoodschool.com   Website: www.hazelwoodschool.com
Much information about the school can be found and downloaded from our website

Head Mr Roger McDuff BEd, MA
Founded 1890
School status Independent. Co-educational Day 2–13
Religious denomination Church of England
Member of AGBIS, IAPS, NAHT
Accredited by IAPS, ISC
No of pupils 386; *(day)* 386; *Nursery* 30; *Pre-prep* 146; *Prep* 240; *Girls* 157; *Boys* 229
Teacher:pupil ratio 1:10 **Ave class size** 15–20
Fees per annum *(day)* £3825–£11865. Pre-nursery fees are £18.25 per session

stimulating, varied curriculum, in which every child has the opportunity to experience success and fulfilment and develop the self-esteem which accompanies them. The school is justifiably proud of its excellent record in gaining scholarships to senior schools; in 2007 and 2008, Hazelwood pupils achieved a record number of awards including academic, all-rounder, music, art and design and technology. The breadth of these achievements reflect the unrivalled opportunities locally that Hazelwood can offer. The natural beauty of the school's countryside location provides an apt setting for nurturing pupils through their formative years. Nonetheless, the school is conveniently located on the Surrey, Kent, Sussex borders and within minutes of the M25 junction and Oxted station.

Hazelwood is a co-educational, preparatory school affiliated to the Independent Association of Prep Schools (IAPS) and catering for all ability groups in the age range 2½ to 13. The Hazelwood mission is to 'maximize the potential of all pupils up to the age of 13' in a caring, supportive environment; Hazelwood's aim is to provide a

Hoe Bridge School

Hoe Place, Old Woking Road, Woking, Surrey GU22 8JE Tel: (01483) 760018 Fax: (01483) 757560
E-mail: enquiriesprep@hoebridgeschool.co.uk
Website: www.hoebridgeschool.co.uk www.gabbitas.co.uk

Headmaster Mr R W K Barr BEd (Oxon)
Pre-prep-Head Mrs L M Renfrew MA
School status Independent. Co-educational
Day 2–13   **Founded** 1987
Religious denomination Non-Denominational
Member of AGBIS, IAPS, ISBA
Accredited by IAPS
Learning difficulties DYP DYS
Behavioural and emotional disorders CA/ADD
Physical and medical conditions RA WA3
No of pupils 482; *Nursery* 45; *Pre-prep* 162;
Prep 275; *Girls* 145; *Boys* 337
Teacher:pupil ratio 1:10 **Average class size** 19
Fees per annum *(day)* £1620–£11640.
Including lunches

The Pre-prep department is for children aged 2½
to 7. It is an attractive purpose-built school with its
own play areas in landscaped grounds and with
its own nursery unit.

The Prep School prepares boys and girls
between the ages of 7 and 14 for scholarship
and Common Entrance requirements of all senior
independent schools. The curriculum includes
those subjects, games and activities necessary
for a child's development. The grounds afford
facilities for all games and outdoor pursuits,
including rugby, soccer, hockey, netball, basketball, cricket, athletics, tennis and swimming. It
also has four all-weather tennis courts providing
ample space for all sports.

A 17th-century mansion forms the heart of the
school but extensive architect-designed buildings
have been added. These include new laboratories, changing rooms, classrooms and a multi-
purpose sports hall. The design and music centre
set in a restored tower and stable block provides
superb facilities for art, design technology, information technology and music. ICT is networked
throughout the school.

Homefield School

Western Road, Sutton, Surrey SM1 2TE   Tel: (020) 8642 0965   Fax: (020) 8642 0965
E-mail: administration@homefield.sutton.sch.uk   Website: www.homefield.sutton.sch.uk

Head Master Mr P R Mowbray MA
(Cantab)   **Founded** 1870
School status Independent. Boys Day 2½–13
Religious denomination Non-Denominational
Member of IAPS
Accredited by IAPS, ISC
Learning difficulties WI/DYC DYP DYS MLD
Behavioural and emotional disorders RA/ADD
Physical & medical conditions SL TW WA2/HEA
No of pupils 430; *(day)* 430; *Nursery* 90;
Pre-prep 120; *Prep* 220; *Boys* 430
Teacher:pupil ratio 1:9 **Average class size** 17
Fees per annum *(day)* £3825–£8925

Rated by *The Sunday Times Parent Power* as
'Amongst the best performing schools in Great
London', Homefield is renowned for its family
atmosphere, small class sizes, the fulfilment of
individual potential, the openness of communication, the provision of specialist teaching at the
earliest opportunity and its all-round academic,
musical, dramatic and sporting achievements.
Minibus service from Wimbledon available.

Homefield is a preparatory school housed in an
extensive purpose-built complex complemented
by a two-acre adjoining playing field. A new £1.8
million development comprising two science
laboratories, a music suite, an art and DT suite
and a learning resources centre was opened in
September 2008.

Hurtwood House

Holmbury St Mary, Dorking, Surrey RH5 6NU   Tel: (01483) 279000   Fax: (01483) 267586
E-mail: info@hurtwood.net   Website: www.hurtwoodhouse.com   www.gabbitas.co.uk

The Headmaster Mr CM Jackson BEd
Founded 1970
School status Independent Sixth Form College.
Co-educational Boarding and Day 16–18.
Boarders from 16
Religious denomination Non-Denominational
Member of English UK, BSA, ISA
Accredited by BAC, British Council, ISA, ISC
Learning difficulties WI
No of pupils 300; *(full boarding)* 283; *(weekly boarding)* 283; *(day)* 12; *Sixth Form* 295; *Girls* 155; *Boys* 145
Teacher:pupil ratio 1:6 **Average class size** 10
Fees per annum *(full boarding)* £29250–£33600; *(weekly)* £29250–£33600; *(day)* £19500

Hurtwood House has the biggest and best Drama and Media Departments in England, with superb professional facilities. It is also hugely successful academically and we're top of the league tables two out of the last four years as the *best co-educational boarding school in the UK*. Uniquely, our 300 boarding students join us after GCSE, when they are ready for the fresh challenge of a Sixth Form where life is as exciting and stimulating as it is at university. Structured and secure, innovative and dynamic, Hurtwood House is one of England's most successful and exciting schools.

Kew Green Preparatory School

Layton House, Ferry Lane, Richmond, Surrey TW9 3AF   Tel: (020) 8948 5999   Fax: (020) 8948 4774
E-mail: secretary@kgps.co.uk   Website: www.kgps.co.uk

Head Mrs M Gardener PGCE
Founded 2004
School status Independent. Co-educational Day 4–11
Religious denomination Non-Denominational
Member of IAPS **Accredited by** IAPS, ISC
Learning difficulties CA SNU WI/DYC DYP DYS MLD
Behavioural and emotional disorders CA CO ST TS/ADD CB
Physical and medical conditions CA IT TW
No of pupils 280; *(day)* 280; *Prep* 280; *Girls* 140; *Boys* 140
Teacher:pupil ratio 1:7 **Average class size** 20
Fees per annum *(day)* £11907

Kew Green Preparatory School provides an education of the highest quality. Unlike many private schools, KGPS is owned by fully qualified and experienced teachers who understand that effective learning is achieved without pressure in a warm and nurturing environment. We are committed to co-education, opposed to 'cramming', and work on the basis of keeping pupils from age 4 to secondary transfer at 11 years. Within this timescale we are able to allow children to develop at their own pace while providing a rich curriculum. We strive to inculcate in our pupils a proper self-esteem and respect for others. Above all, we want our children to be clamouring at our gates every morning and to show a marked reluctance to leave at the end of the day!

Kingston Grammar School

London Road, Kingston-upon-Thames, Surrey KT2 6PY   Tel: (020) 8546 5875   Fax: (020) 8547 1499
E-mail: registar@kgs.org.uk   Website: www.kgs.org.uk   www.gabbitas.co.uk

Head Master Mr C D Baxter MA (Oxon), FRSA
Founded 1561
School status Independent. Co-educational
Day 10–18
Religious denomination Christian
Member of HMC
Learning difficulties WI/DYP DYS MLD
Behavioural and emotional disorders CO
Physical and medical conditions RA SM TW/
EPI HEA
No of pupils 802; *Prep* 24; *Senior* 560; *Sixth
Form* 218; *Girls* 340; *Boys* 462
Teacher:pupil ratio 1:9.5
Average class size 24
Fees per annum *(day)* £12687–£13029

Kingston Grammar School is proud of the out-standing achievements of its pupils academically and in sport, music, drama and a wide range of other co-curricular activities. A broad curriculum is offered to Years 7 and 8 with an option scheme in Year 9, extended in Year 10. Most pupils take 10 GCSE/IGCSEs, a number sitting mathematics and/or possibly French early. An innovative new programme for the Sixth Form, based on A levels, offers greater flexibility and is tailored to the needs of individual students.

Entry is by our own examination and interview, by Common Entrance at 13+ or GCSEs and interview at 16+. Academic, art, music and sport scholarships are available. Two 100 per cent bursaries are also available for qualifying pupils from primary schools.

Marymount International School

George Road, Kingston-upon-Thames, Surrey KT2 7PE   Tel: (020) 8949 0571   Fax: (020) 8336 2485
E-mail: admissions@marymountlondon.com
Website: www.marymountlondon.com   www.gabbitas.co.uk

Headmistress Sister K Fagan RSHM
Deputy Headmistress Dr F O'Neill PhD
Marketing and Admissions Director Mr C J
Hiscock Cert Ed, BEd, MBA
School status Independent. Girls Day and
Boarding 11–18. Flexi-boarding available.
Boarders from 11   **Founded** 1955
Religious denomination Roman Catholic
Member of CIS, GSA, IBO, LISA, SHA
Accredited by CIS, GSA, ISC, MSA (USA)
Learning difficulties RA SC SNU WI/DYC DYS
MLD
Behavioural and emotional disorders CO RA
ST TS/ADD ADHD BESD
Physical and medical conditions AT RA SM TW
WA2/HEA IM VI
No of pupils 245; *(full boarding)* 90; *(weekly
boarding)* 10; *(day)* 145; *Senior* 245; *Sixth
Form* 110; *Girls* 245
Teacher:pupil ratio 1:7   **Ave class size** 10–12

Fees per annum *(full boarding)* £26340–
£28390; *(weekly)* £25135–£27185; *(day)*
£14895–£16945. Application fee (with
Application form) £100. Confirmation fee
(Acceptance of offer) £1000

Curriculum: Celebrating 30 years of International Baccalaureate (IB) with a 100 per cent pass rate in 2008 and again, perfect scores. In 2007, two students gained maximum scores of 45 – better than 5 'A' grades at A level. A wide range of activities is provided to encourage community spirit amongst our international student body.

Parkside School

The Manor, Stoke D'Abernon, Cobham, Surrey KT11 3PX Tel: (01932) 862749 Fax: (01932) 860251
E-mail: enquiries@parkside-school.co.uk Website: www.parkside-school.co.uk

Headmaster Mr D Aylward MA, BEd (Hons),
FRSA **Founded** 1879
School status Boys Day 4–13 (Co-ed 2–4)
Religious denomination Non-Denominational
Member of AGBIS, IAPS, ISBA
Accredited by IAPS
Learning difficulties WI/DYP DYS
No of pupils 410; *Girls* 20; *Boys* 390
Teacher:pupil ratio 1:8 **Average class size** 16
Fees per annum *(day)* £786–£10950

Parkside School is a high achieving preparatory school for boys aged 4–13 and a co-educational nursery for children aged between 2½ and 4 years. In recent times, the excellence of Parkside's all-round education has seen every boy accepted by his first choice of senior school.

Set in 40 acres of beautiful grounds on the banks of the River Mole near Cobham, Surrey, Parkside was established over 125 years ago but fully prepares boys for life in the 21st century.

The warm and friendly atmosphere creates ideal conditions to develop each boy's potential through a broad-based curriculum and there is a wide range of after school activities and school trips throughout the year.

The school has an enviable sporting record and a strong musical tradition. Boys also develop their own social values of respect, compassion and generosity.

For further details on Parkside School call the Headmaster's secretary on 01932 862749 or visit www.parkside-school.co.uk.

Prior's Field School

Priorsfield Road, Godalming, Surrey GU7 2RH Tel: (01483) 810551   Fax: (01483) 810180
E-mail: registrar@priorsfieldschool.com Website: www.priorsfieldschool.com www.gabbitas.co.uk
Prior's Field is situated just south of Guildford on the A3 and within easy reach of London airports

Headmistress Mrs J Roseblade MA
Founded 1902
School status Independent. Girls Boarding and Day 11–18. Boarders from 11
Religious denomination Non-Denominational
Member of AGBIS, BSA, GSA, ISBA
Accredited by GSA, ISC
Learning difficulties DYC DYP DYS
Behavioural and emotional disorders CO/ADHD
Physical and medical conditions HL SM TW WA3/EPI HEA HI VI
No of pupils 379; *(full boarding)* 43; *(weekly boarding)* 84; *(day)* 252; *Girls* 379
Teacher:pupil ratio 1:7 **Average class size** 18
Fees per annum *(full boarding)* £21450; *(weekly)* £21450; *(day)* £13260

environment with a huge range of opportunities, activities and clubs. A tradition of high academic standards, superb pastoral care and small classes, ensures individual attention and encourages confidence and high achievement for every girl. A wide choice of A level subjects enables students to gain places at top universities including Oxbridge.

Excellent boarding facilities including single rooms for Year 10 and some en-suite rooms for Sixth Form. Scholarships available – open days and trial boarding weekends take place each term.

At Prior's Field we achieve the balance between working hard and offering a friendly, vibrant

Priory Preparatory School

Bolters Lane, Banstead, Surrey SM7 2AJ   Tel: (01737) 366920   Fax: (01737) 366921
E-mail: office@prioryprep.co.uk   Website: www.prioryprep.co.uk

Headmaster Mr G D Malcolm BEd, MA, FRSA
Founded 1921
School status Boys Day 2–13
Religious denomination Inter-Denominational
Member of IAPS, NAHT, SATIPS
Accredited by IAPS
Learning difficulties CA WI/DYC DYP DYS
MLD SP&LD
Behavioural and emotional disorders RA
Physical and medical conditions CA RA SM
TW WA3/HEA
No of pupils 160; *(day)* 160; *Boys* 160
Average class size 16
Fees per annum *(day)* £3750–£9105. Includes
lunch and many after school activities

Founded in 1921, Priory School is a preparatory
school for boys aged from 2 to 13 years. We have
approximately 180 students, with one class per
age group.

As well as being highly successful in preparing

boys for top
senior indepen-
dent schools, we
strive to provide
an environment
where each boy
is valued and
encouraged in all
aspects of his life.

We believe
that happy chil-
dren learn and grow successfully so we provide
a secure, caring and supportive community,
where boys can enjoy their childhood while preparing for the future.

Priory School provides quality teaching by
experienced and motivated staff. Our students
enjoy a broad curriculum and a wide variety of
extra-curricular activities that help them develop
into well-rounded, enthusiastic and successful
individuals.

Royal Alexandra and Albert School

Gatton Park, Reigate, Surrey RH2 0TD   Tel: (01737) 649000   Fax: (01737) 649002
E-mail: admissions@gatton-park.org.uk   Website: www.raa-school.co.uk

Headmaster Mr Paul D Spencer Ellis BA, M
Phil NPQH
Founded 1758
School status State (Voluntary-aided).
Co-educational Boarding and Day 7–18.
Boarders from 7
Religious denomination Church of England
Member of BSA, SHA, SHMIS
Accredited by SHMIS SBSA – State Boarding
Schools Association
No of pupils 780; *(full boarding)* 400
(day) 380; *Prep* 150; *Senior* 600; *Sixth Form* 30;
Girls 380; *Boys* 400
Teacher:pupil ratio 1:14.3
Average class size 24
Fees per annum *(full boarding)* £11625–
£11985; *(day)* £2670–£3810

lessons and longer holidays, and run a vast range
of sporting and other activities in the afternoons,
evenings and at weekends.

Admission is by confidential reference from the
current school and interview but is restricted to
citizens of the UK and other EU countries and
those with the right of residence in the UK.

Set in 260 acres of parkland, yet close to London, we have an excellent range of facilities
including a sports hall, riding school, indoor
swimming pool, drama studio, chapel, new music
centre and nine boarding houses.

This is a true boarding school in the sense that the
majority of pupils are boarders. We have Saturday

St Andrew's (Woking) School Trust

Church Hill House, Wilson Way, Horsell, Woking, Surrey GU21 4QW
Tel: (01483) 760943   Fax: (01483) 740314   E-mail: admin@st-andrews.woking.sch.uk
Website: www.st-andrews.woking.sch.uk   www.gabbitas.co.uk

The Headmaster Mr A K Perks MSc
Deputy Head Mrs S Marsh BEd (Hons)
Founded 1938
School status Independent. Co-educational
Day 3–13
Religious denomination Church of England
Member of IAPS **Accredited by** ISC
Learning difficulties WI/DYS
Behavioural and emotional disorders RA
Physical and medical conditions RA SM
No of pupils 296; *(day)* 296; *Nursery* 33;
Pre-prep 98; *Prep* 165; *Girls* 76; *Boys* 220
Teacher:pupil ratio 1:9 **Average class size** 14
Fees per annum *(day)* £2790–£11550

Ethos: The school's main strength lies in its determination to offer a secure, family atmosphere in which the children may thrive and develop as individuals.

Curriculum: Girls and boys are prepared for entrance exams, Common Entrance and scholarships to a wide range of senior schools, with top awards won every year. Specialist teaching facilities for all subjects including science, ICT, music and ADT. The curriculum is broad and the school places great emphasis on music, sport and the arts.

Academic and leisure activities: There is a sports hall, all-weather tennis and netball courts, heated pool and ample grounds for games. Major games are football, hockey, cricket, swimming, tennis, athletics, netball and rounders. In addition the children do rugby and cross-country.

Activities programme: Children can be supervised at school from 8am and, through our extensive after-school activities programme, until 6/6.30pm most evenings during the week.

Entry requirements: Entry test for children over 6. The school offers the possibility of scholarships and bursaries at 7+ and 11+.

St Hilary's School

Holloway Hill, Godalming, Surrey GU7 1RZ   Tel: (01483) 416551   Fax: (01483) 418325
E-mail: registrar@sthilarysschool.com   Website: www.sthilarysschool.com

The Headmistress Mrs S Bailes BA (Hons), MA,
PGCE   **Founded** 1927
School status Independent. Co-educational
Day Boys 2½–7 Girls 2½–11
Religious denomination Non-Denominational
Member of AHIS, IAPS, SATIPS
Accredited by IAPS
Learning difficulties CA SNU WI/DYP DYS
Physical and medical conditions CA HL IT/HEA
HI VI
No of pupils 288; *(day)* 288; *Nursery* 73;
Pre-prep 107; *Prep* 108; *Girls* 197; *Boys* 91
Teacher:pupil ratio 1:9 **Average class size** 16
Fees per annum *(day)* £7335–£10575

Inspection report, October 2006.

St Hilary's School develops a love of learning
'St Hilary's school provides a high quality, well-rounded education within an environment in which pupils can develop, be happy and flourish. Provision for pastoral care is outstanding, and pupils' personal development is excellent' – ISI

'Our aim is to provide a happy, secure environment and to unlock a love of learning which will last for ever,' states Headmistress Mrs Susan Bailes. The Inspectors found this aim to be fulfilled reporting: 'Learning in class is complemented by a wide range of extra-curricular activities. Pupils are well prepared for the next stage in their education. They look forward to their senior schools with confidence, both in their academic foundations and in their ability to form firm friendships with peers and positive relationships with adults.' Do visit us.

England

St Teresa's School

Effingham Hill, Dorking, Surrey RH5 6ST   Senior Tel: (01372) 452037   Fax: (01372) 450311
Prep Tel: (01372) 453456   Fax: (01372) 451562
E-mail: info@stteresas.surrey.sch.uk   Website: www.stteresasschool.com   www.gabbitas.co.uk

Head (Senior) Mrs L Falconer BSc
Head (Prep) Mrs A M Stewart MA (Hons), PGCE
Founded 1928
School status Independent. Girls Boarding and Day 2–18. Flexi-boarding available. Boarders from 8 Entrance exam to Year 7–9 in Jan each year. In 2008 100 per cent A level pass rate, 73% A–B, 100 per cent gained 5 or more A*–C GCSEs 76% A*–B
Religious denomination Roman Catholic
Member of BSA, GSA
Accredited by GSA, ISC
Learning difficulties SNU WI/DYC DYP DYS
Behavioural and emotional disorders CO/ADHD
Physical and medical conditions SM
No of pupils 518; *(full boarding)* 77; *(weekly boarding)* 13; *(day)* 273; *Senior* 362; *Sixth Form* 85; *Prep (day)* 120; *Girls* 362
Teacher:pupil ratio 1:8
Average class size 20
Fees per annum *(full boarding)* £17865–£21900; *(weekly)* £16230–£20265; *(day)* £6450–£12870

St Teresa's is a thriving girls' school situated in 48 acres of beautiful parkland in the Surrey hills, with good road and rail links to London and 45 minutes from both Heathrow and Gatwick airports. Since its establishment in 1928, the school facilities have been continually expanded and updated to high contemporary standards. A magnificent new indoor swimming pool complex opened in 2004 and a £3 million performing arts theatre hall in 2005.

St Teresa's is a community of just over 500 girls, including around 90 boarders, who enjoy first-class care in a flexible boarding system with a programme of weekend activities. Although a Catholic foundation, St Teresa's welcomes girls of all denominations and everyone is encouraged to respect one another in a happy, caring Christian environment. The school is particularly sensitive to the differing needs and latent talents of each individual girl and adopts a 'can do' attitude, stimulating, supporting and developing each girl's interests and talents.

Girls in the Preparatory School benefit from specialist subject teachers and assume responsibility in their last year through a School Council. They can take advantage of an extended day, including breakfast and homework supervision and the 19 extra-curricular activities and clubs on offer. In January 2009 they move into a brand new purpose-built premises on the extension to the senior school site.

Entrance to the Senior School is at 11+, but girls are also warmly welcomed at 12+ and 13+. Scholarships are available at all these entry points and in the Sixth Form. There are 60+ extra-curricular activities on offer and girls are encouraged to develop their life skills through the Duke of Edinburgh's Award Scheme, the Young Enterprise Scheme, World Challenge and work experience.

St Teresa's offers a very broad curriculum with 25 subjects at A level. All girls go on to higher education: many to first rank universities, including Oxbridge, others to the best art schools, drama schools and music colleges.

Surbiton High School

Surbiton Crescent, Kingston-upon-Thames, Surrey KT1 2JT Tel: (020) 8439 1309 Fax: (020) 8547 0026
E-mail: surbiton.high@church-schools.com   Website: www.surbitonhigh.com

Principal Miss A Haydon BSc (Hons), PGCE, NPQH
Registrar Mrs M Try
School status Independent. Girls Day 4–18 (Boys 4–11)
Religious denomination Church of England
Member of GSA, HMC
Accredited by GSA, HMC, IAPS
Learning difficulties RA WI/DYC DYP DYS
Behavioural and emotional disorders RA/ADD ADHD ASP
Physical and medical conditions AT BL RA
No of pupils 1234; *Prep* 233; *Senior* 668; *Sixth Form* 200; *Girls* 1101; *Boys* 133
Fees per annum *(day)* £6555–£11163

We lay the foundations of our pupils' learning by creating a happy, caring atmosphere where every child is valued and encouraged.

In 2005 we completed a major redevelopment of our main school site to provide additional purpose-built classrooms. Our extensive sports grounds at Hinchley Wood include a pavilion, all-weather tennis and netball courts and an all-weather hockey pitch.

In January 2008, Ann Haydon was appointed as the new Head of Surbiton High School replacing Dr Jennifer Longhurst. Ann, was previously Deputy Headmistress at Guildford High School, Surbiton's sister school in the United Church School Trust.

Surbiton High School provides an exemplary independent education for girls aged from 4 to 18 and, as part of our family of three schools, Surbiton Boys' Preparatory School provides a first-rate education for boys aged from 4 to 11.

Trinity School

Shirley Park, Croydon, Surrey CR9 7AT   Tel: (020) 8656 9541   Fax: (020) 8655 0522
E-mail: admissions@trinity.croydon.sch.uk   Website: www.trinity-school.org

Headmaster Mr MJ Bishop MA, MBA
School status Boys Day 10–18
Religious denomination Christian
Learning difficulties WI/DYC DYP DYS
Behavioural and emotional disorders CO/ADD ADHD ASP AUT
Physical and medical conditions SL SM WA1/HEA VI
No of pupils 890; *Boys* 890
Fees per annum *(day)* £11274

Trinity School is part of the Whitgift Foundation which allows more than half of parents to benefit from some form of financial assistance with fees. Boys are drawn from a wide catchment area with entry at 10, 11, 13 and 16.

Academic results are consistently strong at GCSE and A level with many boys gaining places at Oxbridge and other leading universities. There is a broad and balanced curriculum offering a wide choice of subjects.

Trinity's choirs and orchestras enjoy an international reputation with regular performances around the UK as well as professional engagements overseas.

Outstanding sports facilities and top level coaches, current and ex-professionals, have enabled an impressive number of pupils to be selected to compete at national and international level.

The extra-curricular provision is one of Trinity's distinctive strengths with around 100 clubs and activities on offer.

TASIS The American School in England

Coldharbour Lane, Thorpe, Surrey TW20 8TE   Tel: (01932) 565252   Fax: (01932) 564644
E-mail: ukadmissions@tasisengland.org   Website: www.tasis.com/England   www.gabbitas.co.uk
Ofsted inspected TASIS in 2008 and praised its programmes and the overall tone of the school

Headmaster Dr J A Doran PhD
Director of Admissions Mrs B Thorburn-Riseley
BSc, MSc, Dip RSA, Grad, CIPD
Founded 1976
School status Independent. Co-educational
Boarding and Day 3–18. Boarders from 14
Religious denomination Non-Denominational
Member of CASE, CIS, IBO, IBSCA, LISA,
NAIS, NEASC
Accredited by CIS. Also a member of The
Association of Boarding Schools (TABS), an
American organization, English UK and NE/SA
Learning difficulties WI
Behavioural and emotional disorders CO
Physical and medical conditions SM TW
WA2/HEA
No of pupils 750; *(full boarding)* 160; *(day)*
590; *Nursery* 20; *Pre-prep* 210; *Prep* 150;
Senior 180; *Sixth Form* 190; *Girls* 405;
Boys 345
Teacher:pupil ratio 1:8 **Average class size** 15
Fees per annum *(full boarding)* £26750; *(day)*
£5500–£17500. £95 application fee; £750 one-
time development fee

TASIS The American School in England offers its
widely respected university-preparatory curriculum to day students from ages three to 18 and to
boarding students from ages 14–18. Located on a
beautiful and historic estate 18 miles southwest of
London, TASIS England's 43-acre campus combines Georgian mansions and 17th-century
cottages with new purpose-built facilities.

The TASIS experience prepares young people
from over 50 nations to meet the challenges of a
demanding world. Small classes and over 100
dedicated, experienced teachers ensure indivi-
dualised attention and an outstanding
environment for learning.

TASIS England's excellent academic programme includes the International Baccalaureate
Diploma, Advanced Placement courses, and the
traditional high school course of study. The combination of well-equipped facilities for art, drama,
music, computers, and sports and a strong traditional academic programme has given TASIS its
valued reputation both in England and abroad.
Each year TASIS students are offered places at
some of the finest universities in the UK, USA,
Canada, Europe, and worldwide.

While academics are emphasised, extracurricular activities, community service and cultural
excursions are essential to the school's mission of
ensuring a balanced education.

TASIS England embraces three divisions: Lower
School (ages 3–10), Middle School (ages 11–13),
and Upper School (ages 14–18). Students in each
division regularly benefit from the opportunity to
work closely with visiting artists, actors, musicians
and sports professionals. The comprehensive athletics programme includes intramurals in the
Lower and Middle Schools and interscholastic
games for Junior Varsity and Varsity teams in the
Upper School.

Taking full advantage of the opportunities available in England and Europe as extensions to
classroom learning, the students enjoy numerous
field trips, weekend activities, and travel throughout the UK and abroad.

TASIS England also offers summer programmes
for day and boarding students from ages 11 to 18.
Local and international students participate in:
intensive academic courses for high school credit,
enrichment programmes, theatre workshops, ESL,
TOEFL, and SAT Review. Students enjoy extensive sports activities as well as travel opportunities, both international and within the UK.
For more information please contact Faie Gilbert,
Director of Summer Admissions. (uksummer@
tasisengland.org).

Woldingham School

Marden Park, Woldingham, Surrey CR3 7YA
Tel: (01883) 349431   Fax: (01883) 348653
E-mail: registrar@woldingham.surrey.sch.uk
Website: www.woldinghamschool.co.uk   www.gabbitas.co.uk

Headmistress Mrs Jayne Triffitt MA (Oxon)
Founded 1842
School status Independent. Girls Boarding and Day 11–18. Flexi-boarding available. Boarders from 11
Religious denomination Roman Catholic
Member of AGBIS, BSA, GSA, ISA
Accredited by GSA
Learning difficulties WI/DYC DYP DYS
Behavioural and emotional disorders RA/ADD
Physical and medical conditions SL TW WA1/ EPI HI IM W
No of pupils 516; *(full boarding)* 324; *(day)* 192; *Sixth Form* 150; *Girls* 516
Teacher:pupil ratio 1:8
Average class size 20 /fewer in Sixth Form
Fees per annum *(full boarding)* £24870; *(day)* £14985

Described as a 'hugely impressive school' and rated as one of the best independent girls schools in the UK, Woldingham School offers boarding and day tuition to girls aged 11–18. A Catholic school, welcoming girls of all faiths, Woldingham's stunning 700 acre site, just outside Caterham, provides an outstanding educational environment for its pupils. Benefiting from excellent local transport links and easy access to the M25, the school boasts an exceptional range of extra-curricular and study facilities. A consistently high standard of academic achievement places Woldingham in the first division of schools across the country.

England

Battle Abbey School

High Street, Battle, East Sussex TN33 0AD   Tel: (01424) 772385   Fax: (01424) 773573
E-mail: office@battleabbeyschool.com Website: www.battleabbeyschool.com www.gabbitas.co.uk
Situated within Battle Abbey and the site of the Battle of Hastings (1066).

Head Mr R Clark   **Founded** 1922
School status Independent. Co-educational
Boarding and Day 2–18. Flexi-boarding
available. Boarders from 11. Top school in
Sussex for GCSE in 2007. In top 58 independent
schools in the country in 2007 for GCSE
Religious denomination Non-Denominational
Member of AGBIS, SHMIS
Accredited by ISC, SHMIS
Learning difficulties CA SC WI/DYC DYP DYS
Behavioural and emotional disorders RA
ST/ADHD ASP AUT
Physical and medical conditions RA SM
WA3/HEA VI
No of pupils 370; *(full boarding)* 40; *(day)* 330;
Nursery 45; *Prep* 77; *Senior* 170; *Sixth Form* 78;
Girls 189; *Boys* 181
Teacher:pupil ratio 1:10 **Average class size** 14
Fees per annum *(full boarding)* £20790; *(day)*
£6225–£12600. Casual boarding: £37 per night

Battle Abbey School,
which occupies one
of the most famous
historical sites in the
world – that of the
1066 Battle of
Hastings – is an
independent, co-
educational school for pupils from 2 to 18. Boarders are accepted from the age of 11. The school
is large enough to encourage healthy competition
and to develop the social skills and awareness of
others, learnt by being part of a lively community,
but it is small enough to have many of the attributes of a large family. Teaching classes are small
throughout the school, allowing individual attention and the opportunity for all pupils to achieve
their maximum potential.

A new performing arts centre was opened in the
summer of 2005.

Buckswood School

Broomham Hall, Rye Road, Guestling, Hastings, East Sussex TN35 4LT
Tel: +44 (0)1424 813813   Fax: +44 (0)1424 812100
E-mail: achieve@buckswood.co.uk   Website: www.buckswood.co.uk   www.gabbitas.co.uk

Director Mr T Fish
Registrar Mr David Whitehall
School status Independent. Co-educational
Day and Boarding 10–19. Flexi-boarding
available. Boarders from 10
Religious denomination Non-Denominational
Member of English UK
Accredited by British Council
Learning difficulties DYS MLD
Physical and medical conditions AT CA/EPI
No of pupils 350; *(full boarding)* 197; *(day)*
170; *Senior* 270; *Sixth Form* 80; *Girls* 170;
Boys 180
Teacher:pupil ratio 1:8 **Average class size** 16
Fees per annum *(full boarding)* £16440–
£20790; *(weekly)* £15720; *(day)* £9735. £60
registration £800 deposit (boarding) £200
deposit (day)

A truly international educational environment

awaits your child at Buckswood. Parents select
Buckswood because they know it is a school that
contributes something special to their children's
education. Its size allows the school to preserve a
more home-like atmosphere, where the care and
welfare of students is a priority.

Buckswood follows the British curriculum, and
small classes for GCSE and A levels ensure pupils
receive more individual attention.

We have a large campus near the seaside town
of Hastings with a swimming pool, horse riding,
large sports grounds and new tennis courts –
sports and activities play an important part of a
Buckswood all-round education.

Moira House School

Upper Carlisle Road, Eastbourne, East Sussex BN20 7TE
Tel: (01323) 636800   Fax: (01323) 649720
E-mail: lyoung@moirahouse.e-sussex.sch.uk
Website: www.moirahouse.e-sussex.sch.uk/moirahouse

Head Mrs L Young
School status Girls Day and Boarding 2–11. Flexi-boarding available
Religious denomination Inter-Denominational
Learning difficulties WI
No of pupils 85; *(full boarding)* 4; *Girls* 85
Fees per annum *(full boarding)* £15540–£20670; *(weekly)* £16380–£17625; *(day)* £5460–£10290

Moira House Junior School offers a secure, caring, supportive, stimulating environment in which every child develops the confidence to achieve beyond her expectations. Each girl is encouraged to be fearless, curious, enthusiastic – in short, to be herself!

The Foundation Stage and National Curriculum are at the heart of the teaching programme, creatively developed to foster excellence throughout. As well as the core subjects, French, PE, swimming, drama and music are taught by specialists.

Teachers emphasize learning from first-hand experience. Skills, knowledge and understanding are taught in practical and relevant contexts. Those who wish may learn Mandarin from a native speaker!

Junior School pupils benefit from superb facilities.

Stop press. The Nursery, Mini MoHo, became co-educational in September and is open 50 weeks a year.

England

St Bede's School

Upper Dicker, Hailsham, East Sussex BN27 3QH   Tel: (01323) 843252   Fax: (01323) 442628
E-mail: school.office@stbedesschool.org   Website: www.stbedesschool.org   www.gabbitas.co.uk

Headmaster Mr S W Cole
Head (Prep School) Mr N Bevington
Founded 1978 and 1895
School status Independent. Co-educational
Boarding and Day 13–19. Boarders from 13
Religious denomination Inter-Denominational
Member of AGBIS, CReSTeD, HMC, IAPS,
ISCis, SHMIS
Accredited by IAPS, SHMIS
Learning difficulties SNU/DYP DYS
Behavioural and emotional disorders ADD
ADHD ASP
Physical and medical conditions SM WA2/EPI
HEA W
No of pupils 859; *(full boarding)* 343; *(day)*
517; *Girls* 317; *Boys* 542
Teacher:pupil ratio 1:8
Average class size 16 – GCSE, 12 – A Level

St Bede's is one of Britain's leading independent co-educational schools. The school is proudly and purposefully non-selective and the generous staffing ratio of 1:8 enables outstanding results to be achieved. The Senior School is located on a separate campus to the Prep School, which gives students a change of teaching staff and environment as well as the opportunity to mature.

Location: The Senior School is found at the heart of the village of Upper Dicker, based on a small country estate set in beautiful countryside. The Prep School is situated nearby on the seafront in Eastbourne. Both schools are easily accessible by road and rail from London's airports and Channel seaports. Transport to and from school can be arranged for boarders and a school bus service is available for day students.

Curriculum: St Bede's provides an extremely wide-ranging and flexible programme. In the early years at the Prep School there is a strong emphasis on literacy and numeracy as well as skills such as languages and computing. All students are prepared for Common Entrance and scholarship exams.

At the Senior School, students spend the first year following a widely based curriculum prior to

making their choice from the 30 GCSE (Key Stage 4) subjects offered. Similarly at AS and A Level, 30 subjects are offered, including media studies, theatre studies and pure and applied mathematics. The school also offers a number of other applied A Levels, a professional dance course and specialist coaching in tennis and swimming.

Facilities: Both schools have imaginatively converted and added to their original Edwardian buildings to provide excellent teaching and sporting facilities. Each site provides an indoor sports centre, indoor swimming pool, EFL centre, art, design and technology studios and an impressive computer network. In addition the Senior School has a drama studio, riding stables, a practice golf course, and ceramics and graphic design studios.

Sporting and club activities: Both schools are particularly strong in football, tennis, cricket, squash and swimming. The Prep School has a very strong games-playing tradition and encourages students of all abilities to participate in sport. At the Senior School games are organized as part of an extensive club activities programme which takes place every day. In all there are over 140 club activities, ranging from all kinds of sport and outdoor pursuits to activities within the fields of art, drama, music, journalism, science, agriculture and technology.

Scholarships and bursaries: A generous number of academic, art, music, dance, drama, and sports scholarships are available at both schools and scholarships may be awarded to those entering the Sixth Form.

St Mary's Hall

Eastern Road, Brighton, East Sussex BN2 5JF   Tel: (01273) 606061   Fax: (01273) 620782
E-mail: registrar@stmaryshall.co.uk   Website: www.stmaryshall.co.uk   www.gabbitas.co.uk

Head Mrs S M Meek MA   **Founded** 1836
School status Independent. Co-educational
Day and Boarding Boys 3–8 Girls 3–18 (Co-ed
Junior School 3–11). Flexi-boarding available.
Boarders from 11
Religious denomination Church of England
Member of AGBIS, BSA, GSA, IAPS, SHA
Accredited by GSA, ISC
Learning difficulties CA/DYS MLD
Behavioural and emotional disorders ASP
No of pupils 305; *(full boarding)* 79; *(weekly boarding)* 9; *(day)* 228; *Nursery* 17; *Pre-prep* 43; *Prep* 53; *Senior* 146; *Sixth Form* 63; *Girls* 290; *Boys* 15
Teacher:pupil ratio 1:15 average
Average class size 15
Fees per annum *(full boarding)* £15741–£20817; *(weekly)* £14985–£19956; *(day)* £5478–£12609

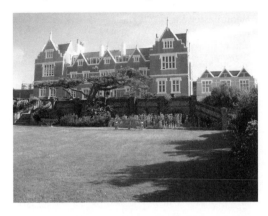

St Mary's Hall is a day and boarding school for girls aged 3–18 and boys 3–8. Established in 1836, St Mary's Hall is one of Britain's oldest schools for girls. Situated on extensive grounds overlooking the sea and within easy reach of Brighton and Hove's historic city centre, St Mary's Hall is very much a city school. The cultural buzz and artistic dynamism of Brighton and Hove make it one of the most exciting cities in Britain. London is 55 minutes away by train, Heathrow airport easily accessible, and Gatwick airport only a 40-minute drive away.

The school has over 300 students, a quarter of whom are boarders. St Mary's Hall has a long tradition of educating and caring for students of many different nationalities.

People often refer to St Mary's Hall as a 'greenhouse' rather than a 'hot house'. We nurture our students and work with their strengths, turning them into confident young adults. This is how we achieve excellent examination results, not by being highly selective. A wide range of subjects is on offer throughout the school at GCSE and A level. The majority of our A level students go on to their chosen universities including Cambridge

and Oxford. Small classes ensure that students receive personal tuition from our highly qualified staff. Teachers know each student well, which is especially valuable when preparing them for university and providing detailed references.

There are many extra-curricular opportunities, which aim to give every pupil a chance to 'shine' in some respect. Activities range from sport to the arts and include a large number of girls working towards The Duke of Edinburgh's Award at bronze, silver and gold levels.

The school has outstanding academic, creative and sporting facilities.

Our pupils come from the local community as well as from around the world. Our cultural diversity is an asset. We have an ESL Department for our overseas students. A team of talented and caring ESL specialist provides tailor-made tuition to allow a seamless integration of all nationalities into St Mary's Hall.

'The teaching of pupils with ESL is excellent,' said the Independent Schools Inspectorate.

There are two boarding houses on the school campus. Venn House accommodates our junior boarders (aged 8–15). Elliott House is our newly developed Sixth Form day centre and boarding house, which opened in September 2006. Our senior boarders are accommodated in comfortable, primarily single study-bedrooms, close to individual shower facilities. Junior boarders share bedrooms with one other student.

England

Burgess Hill School for Girls

Keymer Road, Burgess Hill, West Sussex RH15 0EG   Tel: (01444) 241050   Fax: (01444) 870314
E-mail: registrar@burgesshill-school.com   Website: www.burgesshill-school.com
www.gabbitas.co.uk   For the Junior School, please telephone 01444 233167

Headmistress Mrs A Aughwane BSc (Hons),
CertEd NPQH   **Founded** 1906
School status Independent. Girls Boarding and
Day 2–18. Flexi-boarding available. Boarders
from 11 Full boarding from Year 7, casual/flexi-
boarding available from age 7
Religious denomination Inter-Denominational
Member of BSA, GSA
Accredited by GSA
Learning difficulties RA WI/DYP DYS
Physical and medical conditions HL SM TW
WA3/HEA HI
No of pupils 674; *(full boarding)* 54; *(day)* 656;
Nursery 100; *Prep* 211; *Senior* 304; *Sixth
Form* 91; *Girls* 624; *Boys* 50
Teacher:pupil ratio 1:18
Average class size 20 max
Fees per annum *(full boarding)* £20850; *(day)*
£5730–£12000

Burgess Hill School for Girls has a happy,
challenging, supportive atmosphere, which
encourages young people to use their initiative,
be inquisitive and creative, and develop responsibility and independence.

Ours is a school in which girls flourish. The
focus is firmly on girls and the way they learn.
They develop self-esteem and confidence and go
on to make positive contribution in their chosen
professions. Burgess Hill School for Girls is constantly highly ranked nationally and regularly
leads the field in Sussex. We believe that
education for life involves much more that
academic success alone.

We do not specialize in any one area – all
subject areas and wider activities are catered for
and to extremely high standards. Girls can, and
do, strive for excellence wherever their talents lie.

Everyone is encourages to participate fully in
the many extra-curricular activities available;
great emphasis is placed on personal and social
values, consideration for others, self-discipline
and resourcefulness. We work in partnership with
parents to ensure that the girls make the most of
their talents, energy and interests to build a firm
foundation for their futures.

We are proud of our tradition in the arts. Drama
provides an active means of learning and understanding our world. The standard of music is
superb and demonstrates wide-ranging talent at
many levels. We are locally and nationally
renowned for our sporting achievements with
teams regularly winnings major tournaments in
all the sports we offer. Art, textiles and technology
also enjoy an excellent reputation.

All this is achieved in a friendly and focused
environment. Our girls work hard, play hard and
support each other in doing so. It is the norm to
approach work with diligence and commitment –
excellent attributes for a successful future.

Burgess Hill School for Girls is an outstanding
school which has high expectations of all its
pupils and upholds the best of traditions. The
achievements of our less academic students are
as important to us as those for whom academic
study is less challenging.

It is a caring community which values everyone
within it.

Burgess Hill School fees are competitive.
Entrance to either the Junior or Senior school is
by examination. Scholarships are also awarded
each year for selected year groups. Please contact
the school to find out further information.

Cottesmore School

Buchan Hill, Pease Pottage, West Sussex RH11 9AU
Tel: (01293) 520648   Fax: (01293) 614784
E-mail: office@cottesmoreschool.com
Website: www.cottesmoreschool.com   www.gabbitas.co.uk

Head Mr T F Rogerson BA, PGCE
PA to Headmaster and Registrar Miss J A Scola
Founded 1894
School status Independent. Co-educational
Day and Boarding 7–13. Flexi-boarding
available. Boarders from 7–13
Religious denomination Church of England
Member of IAPS
Accredited by IAPS, ISC
Learning difficulties CA SNU WI/DYP DYS
Behavioural and emotional disorders RA ST
Physical and medical conditions AT RA SM TW
WA3/HEA
No of pupils 150; *(full boarding)* 150; *(weekly
boarding)* 10; *(day)* 10; *Prep* 150; *Girls* 50;
Boys 100
Teacher:pupil ratio 1:9
Average class size 12
Fees per annum *(full boarding)* £17910;
(weekly) £17910; *(day)* £13440–£16119

Cottesmore is one of the UK's leading IAPS co-educational schools offering full, weekly and day boarding for children aged between 7 and 13 years. The school is situated in 35 acres of beautifully landscaped grounds in the heart of the glorious Sussex countryside, 10 minutes from Gatwick airport and less than an hour from central London. The all-round education on offer with its fun, friendships, family ethos, all contribute to making it an attractive option for today's parents and their children. At Cottesmore, apart from following the National Curriculum in all core subjects, there is a great opportunity to experience a vast number of extra activities and hobbies which are all conveniently on hand. The school has excellent facilities, including a modern purpose-built art room and state-of-the-art design technology centre, two libraries, an IT suite, theatre and music practice rooms. There is a strong musical tradition with over 80 per cent of children learning a variety of instruments; there are three choirs and a school orchestra. Within the grounds there is an indoor swimming pool, tennis and

netball courts, grass courts, a golf course, an adventure playground and extensive playing fields. Sport plays a major part in school life including rugby, football, cricket, hockey, rounders and athletics. The school has an impressive academic record: the curriculum is designed to give all children the broadest possible education, while preparing them for Scholarship or Common Entrance. We are proud of our pupils who go on to further success at the country's top public schools.

Children enjoy action-packed days from early in the morning until bedtime six days a week and although on Sunday there is plenty of free time, the children always have something to do and someone with whom to play. Play is important for children – they learn negotiation and leadership skills and how to resolve issues, as well as how to occupy their time constructively away from PSPs, MP3s and television. We place great emphasis on a healthy diet and lifestyle using fresh produce from local suppliers. Staff sit with the children and supervise table manners, as well as chatting about their day. We offer 'traditional values in a modern world'.

England

Farlington School

Strood Park, Horsham, West Sussex RH12 3PN   Tel: (01403) 254967   Fax: (01403) 272258
E-mail: office@farlingtonschool.net   Website: www.farlingtonschool.net   www.gabbitas.co.uk

Headmistress Mrs J Goyer MA
Founded 1896
School status Independent. Girls Boarding and Day 3–18. Flexi-boarding available
Religious denomination Church of England
Member of BSA, GSA, IAPS
Learning difficulties CA RA WI/DYP DYS
Behavioural and emotional disorders CO/ADHD
Physical and medical conditions CA RA TW/HEA IM W
No of pupils 480; *(full boarding)* 29; *(weekly boarding)* 9; *Nursery* 10; *Pre-prep* 45; *Prep* 125; *Senior* 250; *Sixth Form* 50; *Girls* 480
Average class size 15 (fewer in Sixth Form)
Fees per annum *(full boarding)* £15501–£18888; *(weekly)* £15120–£18507; *(day)* £5580–£11877

Curriculum: broadly-based academic curriculum. Wide range of subjects offered at GCSE; 22 subjects at A Level and AS level. Examination results 2008: 100 per cent A level pass rate; 80 per cent A to C. GCSE: 95 per cent A* to C.

Academic and leisure facilities: new sports hall, new library, new Sixth Form centre, new prep and pre-prep buildings; new computer facilities. Science building with five large laboratories, and interactive whiteboards, all-weather pitch and outdoor heated swimming pool.

Seaford College

Lavington Park, Petworth, West Sussex GU28 0NB   Tel: (01798) 867392   Fax: (01798) 867606
E-mail: seaford@clara.co.uk   Website: www.seaford.org   www.gabbitas.co.uk

The Headmaster Mr T J Mullins BA, MBA
Founded 1884
College status Independent. Co-educational
Boarding and Day 10–18. Flexi-boarding
available. Boarders from 10
Religious denomination Church of England
Member of HMC, SHMIS
Accredited by HMC, SHMIS
Learning difficulties SNU WI/DYP DYS MLD
Physical and medical conditions SL TW WA2
WA3/CP HEA W
No of pupils 551; *(full boarding)* 30; *(weekly boarding)* 103; *(day)* 418; *Senior* 423; *Sixth Form* 128; *Girls* 185; *Boys* 366
Teacher:pupil ratio 1:9   **Ave class size** 15–20
Fees per annum *(full boarding)* £17010–£22680; *(weekly)* £14925–£19200; *(day)* £12000–£14850

Seaford College was founded in 1884 and is a fully co-educational school for boarding and day pupils aged 10–18. Situated within 400 acres at the foot of the South Downs, the college is close to the historic town of Petworth and seven miles from the closest railway station. Heathrow and Gatwick airports are within an hour's drive. Pupils may board Flexi, 4-Day (Mon–Fri), weekly or full-time and a bus service collects day pupils from a wide area.

Curriculum: A wide range of subjects is offered at GCSE and A level. Ninety-six per cent of leavers go on to university.

Entry requirements and procedures: Entrance to the Junior House at 10+ and 11+ is based on a trial day and ability test. Entrance to the Senior School at 13+ is based on similar lines, along with Common Entrance examination results. Sixth Form entry is dependent on GCSE results (min requirement is 45 points, A*=8, A=7, B=6 etc) and an interview. Overseas pupils must pass an English exam set by the college and past academic achievements will also be taken into account.

Academic and leisure facilities: The college boasts an impressive and successful art, design and technology centre.

Outstanding sports facilities including six rugby pitches, an all-weather hockey pitch and a new nine-hole golf course and driving range, along with staff who have coached at international level, have helped the college gain an excellent sporting record. The hockey and rugby teams have toured Argentina, Barbados, South Africa, Australia, Canada and New Zealand and our pupils have played at county and national level.

Music and drama feature strongly in the life of the college and the chapel choir enjoys an international reputation.

Scholarships: Scholarships are offered for academic, design and technology, music (instrumental or choral), sport or art but must be accompanied by a good all-round academic standard. Value: £500. Parents who require further discount from the fees may apply for a bursary.

Bursaries: Bursaries are available to Forces' families and siblings.

Boarding facilities: Boys aged 13–18 are divided between two houses with separate boarding and day accommodation. The older boys have individual studies and the younger boys sleep in rooms of two or three. Second-year A level students are accommodated in a separate house, offering more privileges and responsibility and helping with the transition from the protection of school life to the relative freedom of university. The girls' boarding house, comprising dormitories for pre-GCSE girls, and single and twin rooms for Lower Sixth is located in the Mansion House. Dormitory facilities are provided in the Junior House for girls and boys aged 10–13.

For further information and a prospectus please contact the Admissions Secretary on 01798 867456 or e-mail jmackay@seaford.org.

England

Sompting Abbotts School

Church Lane, Sompting, West Sussex BN15 0AZ   Tel: (01903) 235960   Fax: (01903) 210045
E-mail: office@somptingabbotts.com   Website: www.somptingabbotts.com   www.gabbitas.co.uk

Principal Mrs P M Sinclair   **Founded** 1921
School status Co-educational Day and
Boarding 3–13. Flexi-boarding available.
Boarders from 8
Religious denomination Church of England
Accredited by IAPS, ISC
Learning difficulties DYS
Behavioural and emotional disorders RA
Physical and medical conditions HEA HI
No of pupils 185; *(weekly boarding)* 12;
Nursery 20; *Pre-prep* 40; *Prep* 125; *Girls* 60;
Boys 125
Teacher:pupil ratio 1:15/1:20
Average class size 20
Fees per annum *(weekly)* £10650; *(day)*
£6840–£8760. Sibling discounts: 1st 8% 2nd
10% 3rd 12%

Sompting Abbotts School is situated on the edge of
the South Downs, set in 30 acres, facing the sea
with views towards Beachy Head and the Isle of
Wight. The aim of the school is to provide a well-
balanced education in a caring environment
whilst developing the individual needs of each
child. The school has a vibrant Pre-preparatory
department, which includes lively and stimulating
nursery and reception classes. In the Preparatory
department, a well-equipped computer room and
science laboratory is enjoyed by all ages. The art
and drama departments offer wide scope for
creativity, and peripatetic teachers provide tuition
for a range of musical instruments. Weekly boarding is available for the boys from Monday
morning to Friday evening and flexi-boarding is
also available.

Windlesham House

London Road, Washington, Pulborough, West Sussex RH20 4AY
Tel: (01903) 874700   Fax: (01903) 874702
E-mail: office@windlesham.com   Website: www.windlesham.com www.gabbitas.co.uk

Headmaster Mr R Foster BEd (Hons)
Admissions Secretary Mrs S Sampson
Founded 1837
School status Independent. Co-educational
Boarding and Day 4–13 (Day pre-prep 4–7).
Boarders from 7
Religious denomination Church of England
Member of BSA, IAPS, ISBA, SATIPS
Accredited by IAPS
Learning difficulties CA SNU WI/DYC DYP
DYS MLD
Behavioural and emotional disorders CO
ST/ADD
Physical and medical conditions CA HL IT RA
SM WA3/HI
No of pupils 301; *(full boarding)* 191; *(day)*
110; *Pre-prep* 48; *Prep* 253; *Girls* 114; *Boys* 187
Teacher:pupil ratio 1:7 **Average class size** 16
Fees per annum *(full boarding)* £10890–
£18750; *(day)* £6810–£15750

Curriculum: Broad curriculum enables children to
discover and develop their personal strengths and
talents. Strong academic record and emphasis on
creative arts, drama, music and sport.

Academic/leisure facilities: Recently upgraded
science labs, ICT, dorms and classrooms. Theatre/
sports hall, swimming pool (indoor), gymnasium,
dance/drama studio, tennis courts, astro-turf
pitch, climbing wall, eight-hole golf course,
extensive playing fields and grounds (60 acres).

Boarding: This is very much a family school
with a warm, friendly, child-centred atmosphere.

MAP OF SOUTH WEST ENGLAND

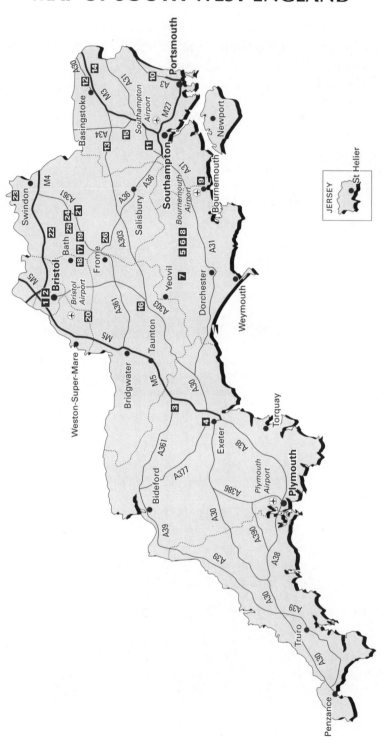

PROFILED SCHOOLS IN SOUTH WEST ENGLAND

(Incorporating the counties of Bath and North East Somerset, City of Bristol, Cornwall, Devon, Dorset, South Gloucestershire, Hampshire, Isle of Wight, Somerset, North Somerset, Wiltshire)

England

Badminton School

Westbury Road, Bristol BS9 3BA   Tel: (0117) 905 5271   Fax: (0117) 962 8963
E-mail: admissions@badminton.bristol.sch.uk   Website: www.badminton.bristol.sch.uk

The Headmistress Mrs J Scarrow BA
Director of Marketing Mrs H Lightwood BA and Dip Marketing
Director of Boarding Mrs J Dowling MA
Founded 1858
School status Girls Boarding and Day 4–18. Flexi-boarding available. Boarders from 9 Badminton is one of the top UK girls' schools and currently number 5 in the league tables
Religious denomination Non-Denominational
Member of BSA, GSA, IAPS
Accredited by GSA, IAPS
Learning difficulties RA WI/DYS
Behavioural and emotional disorders RA
Physical and medical conditions RA/HI VI
No of pupils 420; *(full boarding)* 166; *(weekly boarding)* 15; *(day)* 242; *Prep* 100; *Senior* 220; *Sixth Form* 100; *Girls* 420
Teacher:pupil ratio Depends on age of child
Average class size 14 in JS and 16 in SS
Fees per annum *(full boarding)* £16928–

£25530; *(weekly)* £16928–£25530; *(day)* £6690–£14370

Badminton School is an independent boarding, weekly boarding and day school, located on a 20-acre campus in the heart of the attractive university city of Bristol.

The school is currently ranked fifth in the national league table and around 20 per cent of girls go on to Oxford and Cambridge.

The community spirit of the school encourages girls to develop as individuals and enables them to realize their potential. By the time they leave school, the girls are confident and caring team players.

Clifton College

32 College Road, Clifton, Bristol BS8 3JH   Tel: (0117) 315 7000   Fax: (0117) 315 7101
E-mail: admissions@clifton-college.avon.sch.uk
Website: www.cliftoncollegeuk.com www.gabbitas.co.uk

Head Master Mr Mark Moore MA
Director of Admissions Mr Philip Hallworth MA, MEd   **Founded** 1862
College status Independent. Co-educational Boarding and Day 13–18. Flexi-boarding available
Religious denomination Church of England
Member of HMC
Learning difficulties CA SNU/DYC DYP DYS
Behavioural and emotional disorders CO RA/ ADD ASP
Physical and medical conditions RA WA3/HEA
No of pupils 710; *(full boarding)* 280; *(day)* 430; *Nursery* 36; *Pre-prep* 224; *Prep* 400; *Senior* 400; *Sixth Form* 310; *Girls* 270; *Boys* 440
Teacher:pupil ratio 1:8 **Average class size** 15
Fees per annum *(full boarding)* £25530; *(day)* £17220. Day Boarding for 4 nights = £22950

Clifton offers a broad and flexible curriculum with an unusually large number of subjects on offer. Entry at 13+ is by Common Entrance or ability tests. Scholarships are available at 7 (Butcombe), 11 (prep school), 13 and 16 for academic, art, music and sport. The school occupies a superb site in what has been described as 'the handsomest suburb in Europe'.

Blundell's School

Tiverton, Devon EX16 4DN   Tel: (01884) 252543   Fax: (01884) 243232
E-mail: registrars@blundells.org   Website: www.blundells.org   www.gabbitas.co.uk

Head Master Mr I R Davenport BA
Founded 1604
School status Independent. Co-educational
Boarding and Day 11–18. Flexi-boarding
available. Boarders from 11
Religious denomination Church of England
Member of BSA, HMC, ISC
Learning difficulties SNU DYS
No of pupils 570; *(full boarding)* 130; *(weekly
boarding)* 260; *(day)* 180; *Senior* 385; *Sixth
Form* 185; *Girls* 235; *Boys* 335
Teacher:pupil ratio 1:11 **Average class size** 14
Fees per annum *(full boarding)* £16365–
£24255; *(weekly)* £14790–£21345; *(day)*
£9750–£15645

Blundell's, a key West Country school, combines
balance, excellence, space and tradition to provide a unique package for 11–18-year-old day
and boarding pupils.

All traditional subjects are offered at A Level,
plus theatre studies, music, art, business studies,
psychology, photography and sports science.
Supplementary courses and lectures are also provided at all levels.

A level entry requires a minimum of five GCSEs,
interview and report from present school. At 11+
and 13+ pupils must sit Blundell's entrance test or
Common Entrance.

Examinations offered: GCSE, A level, music.
Scholarships: 11+, 13+ and Sixth Form: academic, sport, music, art and all-rounder.

Boarders are supported by a strong house structure and live in a family environment guided by
their houseparents and tutors.

Bramdean School

Richmond Lodge, Homefield Road, Heavitree, Exeter, Devon EX1 2QR   Tel: (01392) 273387
Fax: (01392) 439330   E-mail: info@bramdeanschool.com   Website: www.bramdeanschool.co.uk

Headmistress Ms D Stoneman NAHT
Soccer Coach Mr J Martin Former Barcelona
Coach FC, BSc
National Cricket Coach Mr K Brown Former
Vice-Captain MCC Lords
School status Independent. Co-educational
Day 3–18
Religious denomination Inter-Denominational
Member of NAHT **Learning difficulties** DYS
Physical and medical conditions SM/HEA
No of pupils 200; *Girls* 90; *Boys* 110
Teacher:pupil ratio 1:8 **Average class size** 18
Fees per annum *(weekly)* £10662; *(day)*
£4740–£7875. Kindergarten £1370 per term
(less grant)

Bramdean is a distinctive school established
in 1901. HMI 2007 Ofsted inspectors said,
'Academic attainment is excellent', 'Bramdean
is a distinctive school with clearly defined aims
and a well established ethos'.

Qualified graduate staff. Class sizes are kept to
a maximum of 18. Pupils progress according to
ability; this approach has culminated in pupils
achieving fine examination results over the years.
Excellent games record and facilities. The school
aims to fulfil the potential of each pupil it accepts
and supply a varied range of opportunity for a
personal success both inside and outside the
classroom.

A resident matron RGN is responsible for the
health and welfare of the pupils.

England

Bryanston School

Blandford Forum, Dorset DT11 0PX   Tel: (01258) 452411   Fax: (01258) 484661
E-mail: admissions@bryanston.co.uk   Website: www.bryanston.co.uk

Head Ms S J Thomas
School status Independent. Co-educational Boarding and Day 13–18
Religious denomination Church of England
No of pupils 662; *(full boarding)* 580; *(day)* 82; *Girls* 282; *Boys* 380
Fees per annum *(full boarding)* £26985; *(day)* £21588

Bryanston is a school which rejoices in its motto: *et nova et vetera*. We're a young enough school to have a crystal clear vision of our direction and values, much of them described by our founder in 1928, and these imbue all we do here. We are proud to teach pupils to learn, rather than treating them as so many empty vessels to be passively filled with facts. We're also clear what are the important traditions for a school: at Bryanston they are those which encourage independence, individuality, and thinking, as well as being able to learn from living in a loving community which fast becomes, and remains, a family.

Set in 400 acres of beautiful north Dorset countryside, Bryanston provides an inspiring environment in which to grow up.

Clayesmore

Iwerne Minster, Blandford Forum, Dorset DT11 8LL   Tel: (01747) 812122   Fax: (01747) 813187
E-mail: admissions@clayesmore.com   Website: www.clayesmore.com

The Headmaster Mr M G Cooke BEd (Hons), FCollP
Head of Clayesmore Prep Mr R D H Geffen BEd (Hons)   **Founded** 1896
School status Independent. Co-educational Boarding and Day 2–18. Boarders from 8. Senior School, Prep School, Pre-prep and Nursery for children aged 2½–18 years
Religious denomination Church of England
Member of CReSTeD, HMC, IAPS, SATIPS, SHMIS
Accredited by HMC, IAPS, SHMIS
Learning difficulties SNU/DYC DYS
Physical and medical conditions AT RA SM/HEA
No of pupils 640; *(full boarding)* 283; *(day)* 184; *Nursery* 31; *Pre-prep* 27; *Prep* 201; *Senior* 412; *Sixth Form* 133; *Girls* 142; *Boys* 268
Teacher:pupil ratio 1:10
Average class size 18–20
Fees per annum *(full boarding)* £16845–£25392; *(day)* £12843–£18579

An HMC school, Clayesmore has rapidly expanded in recent years and invested heavily in brand new academic buildings as well as new boarding facilities. However, amidst the quality, excellent exam results and status expected of an HMC school, Clayesmore still maintains its 'small school' family ethos. The result is a harmonious and tremendously happy atmosphere which feeds into the academic, cultural and sporting success of its pupils. Located alongside the Senior School on the same campus is the Prep School.

International College, Sherborne School

Newell Grange, Sherborne, Dorset DT9 4EZ
Tel: (01935) 814743   Fax: (01935) 816863
E-mail: reception@sherborne-ic.net
Website: www.sherborne-ic.net   www.gabbitas.co.uk   Registrar: Mrs Anne-Marie Slack

The Principal Dr C J Greenfield
Founded 1977
College status Independent. Co-educational
Boarding 11–17
Religious denomination Non-Denominational
Member of AGBIS, English UK, BSA, COBISEC,
ISA
Accredited by British Council, ISA, ISC
Founder member of British Association of
International Study Centres
Learning difficulties WI/MLD
Behavioural and emotional disorders TOU
Physical and medical conditions SM TW WA2
No of pupils 145; *(full boarding)* 145; *Girls* 50;
Boys 95
Teacher:pupil ratio 1:4
Average class size 6 students
Fees per annum *(full boarding)* £29100–
£31500. All inclusive

The International College is unique. It was established in 1977 (as the International Study Centre) to prepare boys – and later girls – from non-British educational backgrounds so that they could function successfully in traditional British boarding schools. Typically these boys and girls spend one year at the International College before moving on to a traditional British boarding school where the majority of students are British. Those students who join in Year 10 (usually around 14 or 15 years old) and start a two-year course leading towards GCSE examinations must stay at the school for the duration of the course.

The College has three major tasks:

- concentrated improvement in spoken and written English;
- academic preparation in English in the full range of curriculum subjects;
- a good introduction to British educational procedures and the British way of life.

The arrangements of the college are designed to achieve these tasks. Classes are small, usually between six and eight students to each teacher. All teachers are not only experienced specialists in their own subject, but also have additional training in teaching the English language.

Characteristics: The teaching facilities at the International College include modern classrooms, eight science laboratories, an art studio, a computer centre and a library with internet access. The College uses the extensive sporting, musical and theatre facilities at Sherborne School including a 25-metre indoor swimming pool.

The International College has gained an unrivalled reputation for providing the very best start to British independent education for children from overseas. Through a carefully supervised programme of study, students gain a sound working knowledge of the main British curriculum subjects such as mathematics, the sciences and humanities. The College has high standards of discipline and pastoral care. Most weekends there is a busy programme that ensures students are fully occupied on Saturday and Sunday.

England

Milton Abbey School

Blandford Forum, Dorset DT11 0BZ   Tel: (01258) 880484   Fax: (01258) 881194
E-mail: info@miltonabbey.co.uk   Website: www.miltonabbey.co.uk

The Headmaster Mr W J Hughes-D'Aeth BA, PGCE
Admissions Mrs D Morant BEd (Hons)
Founded 1954
School status Independent. Co-educational Boarding and Day Boys 13–18 Girls 16–18. Boarders from 13
Religious denomination Church of England
Member of CReSTeD, SHMIS
Accredited by SHMIS
Learning difficulties SC SNU WI/DYC DYP DYS
Behavioural and emotional disorders CO ST TS/ADD ADHD
Physical and medical conditions RA/HEA HI
No of pupils 230; *(full boarding)* 210; *(day)* 20; *Sixth Form* 94; *Girls* 15; *Boys* 215
Average class size 15
Fees per annum *(full boarding)* £9060; *(day)* £6800

Milton Abbey is a very personal place – a school in which everybody genuinely knows everyone. We have achieved what other, bigger schools strive in vain to achieve: an intimate community in which achievement in any area of school life is never rated more highly than quality of character. No one is overlooked. Everyone is famous.

Wentworth College

College Road, Bournemouth, Dorset BH5 2DY   Tel: (01202) 423266   Fax: (01202) 418030
E-mail: enquiries@wentworthcollege.com   Website: www.wentworthcollege.com www.gabbitas.co.uk

Executive Principal Mr H MacDonald BSc (Hons), C Chem, C Sci FRMS
Deputy Principal Miss K Castle
Founded 1871
College status Independent. Co-educational Boarding and Day 11–18. Flexi-boarding available. Boarders from 11
Religious denomination Inter-Denominational
Member of SHMIS **Accredited by** ISC, SHMIS
Learning difficulties SNU WI/DYC DYS
Physical and medical conditions AT RA WA3/ HEA
No of pupils 150; *(full boarding)* 30; *(weekly boarding)* 10; *(day)* 110; *Senior* 100; *Sixth Form* 30; *Girls* 130; *Boys* 20
Average class size 18
Fees per annum *(full boarding)* £5975; *(weekly)* £5975; *(day)* £3645

who respond to the needs of every student, helping them to reach their full potential. We aim to develop happy, confident young people who are proud of their academic success and personal achievement, and who leave equipped for adult life.

Situated in beautiful grounds on a cliff top just metres from Bournemouth's award-winning beaches and close to the New Forest, we offer well-equipped teaching and excellent sports facilities. We have a dedicated Sixth Form study centre and offer numerous extra-curricular activities.

Wentworth College provides a stimulating and caring environment with committed teachers

Bedales School

Petersfield, Hampshire GU32 2DG   Tel: (01730) 300100   Fax: (01730) 300500
E-mail: admissions@bedales.org.uk   Website: www.bedales.org.uk
Contact for admissions: Janie Jarman, Registrar (direct line 01730 711733; jjarman@bedales.org.uk)

Headmaster Mr K Budge
Founded 1893
School status Independent. Co-educational
Boarding and Day 3–18. Boarders from 8
Religious denomination Non-Denominational
Member of HMC
Learning difficulties SNU/DYP DYS
Physical and medical conditions RA SM
WA3/CP HI VI
No of pupils 732; *(boarding)* 373; *(day)* 359;
Nursery 12; *Pre-prep* 73; *Prep* 190; *Senior* 457;
Sixth Form 175; *Girls* 382; *Boys* 350
Teacher:pupil ratio 1:8
Fees per annum *(full boarding)* £18327–
£26664; *(day)* £3567–£20976

Bedales was founded as the alternative to Victorian authoritarianism. There is no uniform, everyone is on first-name terms, and our students must learn to organize their own time and methods of study, but yes – we do have rules, a timetable and a curriculum.

In effect, we start preparing students for university well before GCSE, or the new, unique and more demanding Bedales Assessed Courses that have replaced the duller GCSEs.

Bedales students characteristically develop a mind of their own, become their own person and are happy with who they are – so they go into the world with confidence.

Hampshire Collegiate School, UCST

Embley Park, Romsey, Hampshire SO51 6ZE   Tel: (01794) 512206   Fax: (01794) 518737
E-mail: info@hampshirecs.org.uk   Website: www.hampshirecs.org.uk

Principal Mr H S MacDonald
Vice Principal Mrs Teresa Rogers MA (Ed)
Founded 2005
School status Independent. Co-educational
Boarding and Day 3–18. Flexi-boarding
available. Boarders from 11
Religious denomination Church of England
Member of AGBIS, BSA, IAPS, SHA, SHMIS
Learning difficulties SNU/DYP DYS
Behavioural and emotional disorders RA/ADD
ADHD
Physical and medical conditions SM WA2/
HEA W
No of pupils 767; *(full boarding)* 30; *(weekly boarding)* 46; *Sixth Form* 70; *Girls* 367;
Boys 400
Teacher:pupil ratio 1:10 (classes) 1:15/1:20
Average class size 18 (3–16)
Fees per annum *(full boarding)* £19869–
£20271; *(day)* £7434–£12252

HCS is a 3–18 school set in 120 acres of outstanding natural beauty. ISI (2007) noted, 'Rising academic standards and very good pastoral care. Many strengths and no weaknesses'. The Senior School sets its own entry test. At GCSE a core curriculum is offered together with a choice of three separate sciences, three modern languages, humanities, creative and practical subjects. At A level 22 subjects are offered. New facilities include a new Junior School, purpose-built science and maths suites and astro-turf pitches. Scholarships available; also bursaries (HM Forces, clergy, teachers, single parents, and hardship cases).

England

Lord Wandsworth College

Long Sutton, Hook, Hampshire RG29 1TB   Tel: (01256) 862201   Fax: (01256) 860363
E-mail: info@lordwandsworth.org   Website: www.lordwandsworth.org

Headmaster Mr I G Power MA
Director of Admissions Mrs M P Hicks
Founded 1922
College status Independent. Co-educational
Boarding and Day 11–18. Flexi-boarding
available. Boarders from 11
Religious denomination Non-Denominational
Member of BSA, HMC, SHMIS
Accredited by HMC, ISC, SHMIS
Learning difficulties SNU WI/DYS
Behavioural & emotional disorders RA/ADD ASP
Physical & medical conditions RA SM/EPI HEA
No of pupils 548; *(full boarding)* 55; *(weekly
boarding)* 200; *(day)* 293; *Senior* 381; *Sixth
Form* 166; *Girls* 171; *Boys* 377
Teacher:pupil ratio 1:10 **Average class size** 19
Fees per annum *(full boarding)* £21426–
£23754; *(weekly)* £21426–£22614; *(day)*
£15999–£16854. Flexi boarding £36–£41 per
night

Lord Wandsworth College Offers:
- A safe and secure environment.
- A high level of pastoral care.
- Excellent exam results which consistently exceed individual expectations.
- Outstanding facilities for both academic and co-curricular activities.
- An unpretentious, caring, happy and relaxed atmosphere.
- A broad, balanced education.

Rookwood School

Weyhill Road, Andover, Hampshire SP10 3AL   Tel: (01264) 325900   Fax: (01264) 325909
E-mail: office@rookwood.hants.sch.uk   Website: www.rookwood.hants.sch.uk www.gabbitas.co.uk

Headmistress Mrs M P Langley BSc (Hons)
Founded 1934
School status Independent. Co-educational
Day and Boarding 3–16. Full, weekly and flexi
boarding options
Religious denomination Non-Denominational
Member of BSA, ISA, SHA **Accredited by** ISA
Learning difficulties CA WI/DYP DYS
Behavioural and emotional disorders RA/
ADHD ASP
Physical and medical conditions CA RA/HEA HI
No of pupils 360; *(full boarding)* 31; *(day)* 329;
Nursery 25; *Pre-prep* 62; *Prep* 93; *Senior* 180;
Girls 188; *Boys* 172 **Average class size** 14
Fees per annum *(full boarding)* £16500–
£19320; *(day)* £6555–£10800
Fees Day fees from Reception upwards. For
Nursery fees please contact the school
admissions office

Rookwood School was described in its latest ISI

Inspection report as an 'outstandingly happy and successful school'.

Set in eight acres of grounds, Rookwood offers a balanced, all-round education. With the Pre-prep, Prep and Senior Schools all based on the same site, pupils can begin in the Nursery and enjoy the excellent teaching, the wide range of activities and strong pastoral care right through to GCSE.

Rookwood is non-selective, yet small classes with experienced subject specialists result in high academic performance. 94 per cent of candidates gained five or more GCSEs with A*–C grades or better in 2008.

St Nicholas' School

Redfields House, Redfields Lane, Church Crookham, Fleet, Hampshire GU52 0RF
Tel: (01252) 850121   Fax: (01252) 850718   E-mail: registrar@st-nicholas.hants.sch.uk
Website: www.st-nicholas.hants.sch.uk   www.gabbitas.co.uk

Headmistress Mrs A V Whatmough BA (Hons),
Cert Ed   **Founded** 1935
School status Independent. Girls Day 3–16
(Boys 3–7). Co-educational (girls only 7–16)
independent pre-prep, prep and senior day
Religious denomination Church of England
Member of GSA, ISCis
Accredited by GSA, ISC
Learning difficulties WI/DYS
Physical and medical conditions RA/HEA
No of pupils 403; *(day)* 389; *Nursery* 36;
Pre-prep 54; *Prep* 115; *Senior* 198; *Girls* 389;
Boys 14
Teacher:pupil ratio 1:10 **Average class size** 16
Fees per annum *(day)* £3696–£10038

At St Nicholas' School we believe that the best education is a partnership between teachers, pupils and parents. By creating a supportive environment, the personal and academic potential of each pupil can be developed. Classes are small and facilities are excellent. The personal and academic progress of each individual is monitored carefully and should any help be needed, it is available. The secure base laid at St Nicholas' gives students a wide range of choice for the next stage of their education. The fact that they are welcome wherever they go is a tribute to the work of the school.

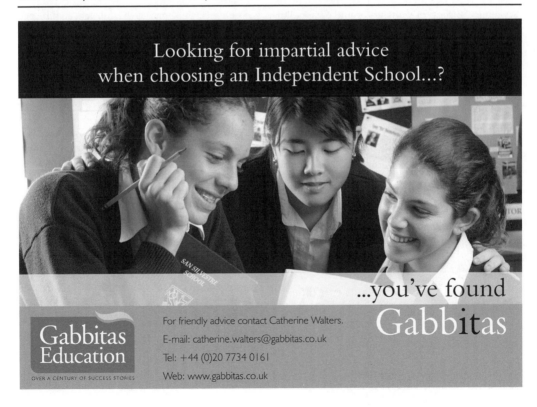
England

Winchester College

College Street, Winchester, Hampshire SO23 9NA
Tel: (01962) 621247   Fax: (01962) 621106
E-mail: admissions@wincoll.ac.uk
Website: www.winchestercollege.org   www.gabbitas.co.uk

Headmaster Dr R D Townsend MA, DPhil
Registrar Mr K M Pusey BMus, GRSM, ARMCM
Bursar Mr J E Hynam, MPhil BEd, ACP
Founded 1382
College status Independent. Boys Boarding and Day 13–18
Religious denomination Church of England
Member of AGBIS, HMC, SHA
Accredited by HMC
Learning difficulties SNU WI/DYP DYS
No of pupils 685; *(full boarding)* 681; *(day)* 4; *Senior* 406; *Sixth Form* 279; *Boys* 685
Teacher:pupil ratio 1:7
Fees per annum *(full boarding)* £27870; *(day)* £26475

Winchester College is a boarding school for boys aged 13–18. It was founded in 1382 by William of Wykeham, Bishop of Winchester and Chancellor to Richard II, and has the longest unbroken history of any school in the country. Its setting is one of unrivalled beauty and spaciousness.

Winchester enjoys an international reputation for its outstanding academic record. This can be seen not just in its excellent examination results but also in the quality of the intellectual training it provides. Nearly all of its pupils go on to good universities and about 45 each year win places at Oxford or Cambridge.

High academic standards are matched by similar achievements in music, art, drama and a wide range of sporting activities. The school has extensive playing fields and generous provision for pupils to develop their cultural and athletic interests.

Most of the boys in the school are boarders, but day boys are accepted.

Academic and music awards are offered annually to boys entering the school at age 13 and 16. Financial help with the fees is available to all candidates on a means-tested basis.

13+ academic scholarships and exhibitions: The examination of candidates for scholarships and exhibitions is held at the college in early May; about 15 scholarships and about six exhibitions are offered. Scholarships have a basic value of currently 15 per cent of the full fee. Exhibitions are also awarded on the same examination. Candidates must be under 14 and at least 12 on 1 September in the year in which they sit the examination. Entry forms, which must be returned by March, are available from the Master in College, Winchester College, College Street, Winchester SO23 9NA.

Sixth Form academic awards: The entrance examination for both awards and places takes place at the college early in the spring term. Entry forms, which must be returned by mid October the previous year, are obtainable from the Registrar (address as above).

Details of music awards can also be obtained from Winchester College Music School, Culver Road, Winchester SO23 9JF; Tel: (01962) 621122.

King's Bruton

Bruton, Somerset BA10 0ED   Tel: (01749) 814200   Fax: (01749) 813426
E-mail: registrar@kingsbruton.com   Website: www.kingsbruton.com   www.gabbitas.co.uk

Headmaster Mr N M Lashbrook BA
Founded 1519
School status Independent. Co-educational
Boarding and Day 13–18
Religious denomination Church of England
Member of CReSTeD, HMC
Accredited by HMC
Learning difficulties SNU WI/DYC DYP DYS
Behavioural and emotional disorders ADD
ADHD ASP
Physical and medical conditions RA/CP HEA VI
No of pupils 334; *(full boarding)* 226; *(day)* 96;
Senior 322; *Sixth Form* 152; *Girls* 105;
Boys 229
Teacher:pupil ratio 8:1 **Average class size** 15
Fees per annum *(full boarding)* £23910; *(day)*
£17424

The King's Senior School is situated in the small Somerset town of Bruton. Founded in the early 16th century, the school combines historic buildings with more recent development. The Preparatory School lies in 220 acres of parkland at Sparkford, eight miles away. Both schools foster a close community within which all members are given the opportunity to achieve their academic, spiritual, social, aesthetic and physical potential. The schools have a lively, purposeful and friendly atmosphere where everyone is able to flourish within a supportive and disciplined framework.

Kingswood School

Lansdown, Bath, Bath & North East Somerset BA1 5RG   Tel: (01225) 734210   Fax: (01225) 734305
E-mail: enquiries@kingswood.bath.sch.uk Website: www.kingswood.bath.sch.uk   www.gabbitas.co.uk
Contact our Admissions Office for information about scholarships and bursaries

Head Master Mr S Morris MA
Prep School Head Mr Marcus Cornah
School status Co-educational Boarding and
Day 3–18. Flexi-boarding available. Boarders
from 7   **Founded** 1748
Religious denomination Methodist
Member of BSA, HMC, IAPS, ISBA
Accredited by British Council, HMC, IAPS, ISC
Learning difficulties RA WI/DYC DYP DYS
No of pupils 971; Senior School *(full boarding)*
120; *(weekly boarding)* 41; *(day)* 485; Prep
School *(day)* 165; *(boarding)* 18 (9 boys, 9
girls); Nursery and Pre-Prep 148
Teacher:pupil ratio 1:9
Average class size 22 (Senior School)
Fees per annum *(full boarding)* £19407–
£23247; *(weekly)* £16953–£21003; *(day)*
£10425. Includes all text books, personal
accident (including dental) and personal effects
insurance

Kingswood School is set within 215 acres of beautiful parkland overlooking the world heritage city of Bath. It has been praised for its exceptional pastoral care at Inspection, and has high academic standards. Over 100 extra-curricular activities are offered, in addition to a lively and dynamic curriculum. Scholarships, Special Talent awards, HM Forces Remissions and some bursaries are available.

England

Prior Park College

Ralph Allen Drive, Bath, Bath & North East Somerset BA2 5AH
Tel: (01225) 831000   Fax: (01225) 835753
E-mail: admissions@priorpark.co.uk   Website: www.priorparkschools.co.uk   www.gabbitas.co.uk

Headmaster Dr G Mercer KSG, MA
Director of Admissions & Marketing Dr M
Ruxton BSc, Phd   **Founded** 1831
College status Independent. One of the largest
UK independent, co-educational, Catholic
boarding and day schools, 11–18 years, set in
magnificent grounds. Weekly and Flexi-boarding
available. Boarders from 13
Religious denomination Roman Catholic
Member of CIS, HMC
Accredited by CIS, HMC
Learning difficulties RA WI/DYP DYS
Physical and medical conditions SM WA3/VI
No of pupils 569; *(full boarding)* 114; *Sixth
Form* 180; *Girls* 268; *Boys* 301
Teacher:pupil ratio 1:9 **Average class size** 20
Fees per annum *(full boarding)* £22338; *(day)*
£11118–£12387. Fees include lunch and
supervised prep

Prior Park is a friendly, well-established Christian
community where an excellent work ethic mixes
seamlessly with outstanding enrichment opportunities. Positive teaching encourages excellent
academic results at GCSE and A level and 99
per cent of students go on to higher education at
good universities. Excellent facilities include the
new Mackintosh Dance studio as well as a brand
new Junior House to open in spring 2009. September 2009 will see the introduction of a new
weekly boarding fee, as well as the arrival of a
new Headmaster, Mr James Murphy-O'Connor.

The Royal High School

Lansdown Road, Bath, Bath & North East Somerset BA1 5SZ Tel: (01225) 313877 Fax: (01225) 465446
E-mail: royalhigh@bat.gdst.net   Website: www.gdst.net/royalhighbath   www.gabbitas.co.uk

Headmaster Mr J Graham-Brown BA (Hons)
M Phil
Head of Junior School Mrs Helen Fathers BA
(Hons)
School status Independent. Girls Boarding and
Day 3–18 (Boys admitted (day only) into Sixth
Form). Flexi-boarding available. Boarders from
11 (GDST school)
Religious denomination Non-Denominational
Member of GDST, GSA
Learning difficulties DYP DYS
No of pupils 835; *(full boarding)* 75; *(weekly
boarding)* 10; *(day)* 741; *Nursery* 18; *Pre-prep*
52; *Prep* 152; *Senior* 479; *Sixth Form* 175;
Girls 825; *Boys* 10
Average class size 22
Fees per annum *(full boarding)* £17445;
(weekly) £15486; *(day)* £8898

As one of the members of the Girls' Day School
Trust, we belong to an organization that is

renowned for providing a high-quality, all-round
education at an affordable cost to students of
academic promise. Our new co-educational Sixth
form college offers the International Baccalaureate Diploma as well as A levels. Recent
developments include fully refurbished boarding
accommodation, a new sports hall and astro-turf
pitches, additional ICT suites and new science
facilities. We are proud of our strong academic
tradition and our students' achievements.

Sidcot School

Oakridge Lane, Winscombe, North Somerset BS25 1PD   Tel: (01934) 843102   Fax: (01934) 844181
E-mail: admissions@sidcot.org.uk   Website: www.sidcot.org.uk   www.gabbitas.co.uk

The Headmaster Mr J Walmsley BSc
Deputy Head Mrs E Burgess BSc, BEd
School status Independent. Co-educational Boarding and Day 3–18. Flexi-boarding available   **Founded** 1699
Religious denomination Quaker
Member of BSA, IBO, ISA, ISBA, SHA, SHMIS
Accredited by ISC
Learning difficulties CA SNU/DYS
Behavioural and emotional disorders RA/ADD ADHD ASP BESD CB
Physical and medical conditions SM TW WA2/EPI HEA
No of pupils 511; *(full boarding)* 139; *(weekly boarding)* 16; *(day)* 356; *Nursery* 13; *Pre-prep* 45; *Prep* 72; *Senior* 227; *Sixth Form* 154; *Girls* 221; *Boys* 290
Teacher:pupil ratio 1:15 **Average class size** 15
Fees per annum *(full boarding)* £19800; *(weekly)* £19800; *(day)* £4875–£11850

Sidcot School is a thriving independent co-educational day and boarding school situated in 150 acres. Sidcot offers a blend of excellent traditional and state-of-the-art facilities. It is well equipped with academic facilities, a new performing and creative arts centre, learning resource and Sixth Form centre, sports hall complex with heated swimming pool, extensive playing fields and a riding centre.

Our Quaker philosophy means that we value all children whatever their abilities. Students gain excellent exam results but also develop as caring and confident individuals. Happy children learn, and small classes and good working relationships make for a positive and inclusive atmosphere. Exam results are excellent: GCSE 92 per cent of the year group gained five or more A to C grades (including maths and English); A level 99.12 per cent overall pass rate. Scholarships are available. Quaker bursaries are available for members of the Society of Friends. We welcome pupils of all faiths or none.

England

Dauntsey's School

High Street, West Lavington, Devizes, Wiltshire SN10 4HE   Tel: (01380) 814500 Fax: (01380) 814501
E-mail: information@dauntseys.wilts.sch.uk   Website: www.dauntseys.org

Head Master Mr S B Roberts MA
Registrar Mrs JH SAGERS BA   **Founded** 1542
School status Independent. Co-educational
Boarding and Day 11–18. Dauntsey's is one of
the UK's leading co-educational schools for
11–18 year olds
Religious denomination Inter-Denominational
Member of BSA, HMC
Accredited by HMC, ISC
Learning difficulties WI/DYS
Behavioural and emotional disorders CO
Physical and medical conditions SL SM TW
WA1/W
No of pupils 790; *(full boarding)* 300; *(day)*
490; *Senior* 519; *Sixth Form* 276; *Girls* 360;
Boys 430
Teacher:pupil ratio 1:9
Average class size Around 19 up to GCSE, 10–
12 in Sixth Form
Fees per annum *(full boarding)* £23850; *(day)*
£14145

Dauntsey's is a leading co-educational boarding
and day school of 780 pupils aged from 11–18.
The school is set in an estate of 160 acres on the
edge of Salisbury Plain.

The curriculum is broad and balanced and academic standards are high. In the last three years, A*
and A grades at GCSE have been over 70 per cent
and the percentage of A and B grades at A level
have been over 80 per cent. Facilities are impressive and include a superb library and study centre,
five-studio art school, science block and recently
refurbished and extended boarding houses.

Drama, music, art and sport all flourish at
Dauntsey's and the school regularly produces first
class sides in all sports. Pupils maintain and sail the
Jolie Brise, a 56' gaff cutter that won the Millen-
nium Tall Ships Race and three Fastnets. Clubs and
societies provide enrichment to academic to academic programmes and pupils choose from over
70. Please contact the Registrar for further information and to organize a visit to the school.

Grittleton House School

Grittleton, Chippenham, Wiltshire SN14 6AP   Tel: (01249) 782434   Fax: (01249) 782669
E-mail: secretary@grittletonhouseschool.org   Website: www.grittletonhouseschool.org

Headmistress Mrs C Whitney
Bursar Mr J Shipp
Founded 1951
School status Independent. Co-educational
Day 2–16
Religious denomination Non-Denominational
Learning difficulties CA/DYS
Physical and medical conditions HEA HI VI
No of pupils 315; *(day)* 315; *Nursery* 23;
Pre-prep 39; *Prep* 71; *Senior* 182; *Girls* 141;
Boys 174
Teacher:pupil ratio 1:14
Average class size 15
Fees per annum *(day)* £6150–£9270
Please note fees will be reviewed in January
2009

philosophy caters for children from nursery age to
GCSE level, in a secure and happy environment,
where the children flourish, meeting the challenges that come their way with enthusiasm.

Staff at Grittleton support, inspire – cajole when
necessary – and the pupils respond by achieving
the best possible results they can. Last year's 11th
year achieved excellent results at GCSE, and in
the Lower School SATS grades were at the highest
level. Please contact the School Secretary on
01249 782434 for a prospectus, a copy of our
recent excellent Ofsted report and any further
information you may require.

Grittleton House School is unique. Set in the
beautiful Wiltshire countryside, it offers an
unequalled chance for children to experience
the very best in education. Our 'whole school'

Prior Park Preparatory School

Calcutt Street, Cricklade, Wiltshire SN6 6BB
Tel: (01793) 750275   Fax: (01793) 750910
E-mail: officepriorparkprep@priorpark.co.uk   Website: www.priorparkschools.co.uk

Headmaster Mr G B Hobern BA Hons (London), PGCE
Founded 1946
School status Co-educational Boarding and Day 7–13. Flexi-boarding available
Religious denomination Roman Catholic
Member of BSA, CReSTeD, IAPS, ISCis
Accredited by IAPS, ISC
Learning difficulties CA SNU WI/DYC DYP DYS
Physical and medical conditions RA
No of pupils 187; *(full boarding)* 37; *(weekly boarding)* 4; *(day)* 146; *Prep* 187; *Girls* 87; *Boys* 100
Teacher:pupil ratio 1:11
Average class size 15
Fees per annum *(full boarding)* £13803–£16224; *(weekly)* £13803–£16224; *(day)* £9438–£11607. Sibling discount

School at Prior Park is fresh air, space to play and an environment where children can be children.

Just over an hour from London, based in an historic manor house on the edge of the Cotswolds, Prior Park Prep offers day, full and flexi-boarding options to suit your family's lifestyle.

The best of modern learning and facilities coupled with traditional Catholic Christian values, we are a non-selective school welcoming families from many faiths. Our pupils gain scholarships to some of the top independent senior schools in the country including our own high-achieving senior school Prior Park College in the world heritage city of Bath.

Come and try a taste of life at Prior Park. Visit on any working day or try a taster boarding evening.

St Mary's Calne

Curzon Street, Calne, Wiltshire SN11 0DF   Tel: (01249) 857200   Fax: (01249) 857207
E-mail: admissions@stmaryscalne.org   Website: www.stmaryscalne.org

Headmistress Dr H M Wright MA (Oxon), MA (Leics), EdD, FRSA   **Founded** 1873
School status Independent. Girls Boarding and Day 11–18
Religious denomination Church of England
Member of AGBIS, BSA, GSA, IAPS
Accredited by British Council, GSA, ISA
Learning difficulties SNU/DYP DYS
Behavioural and emotional disorders CO ADHD
Physical and medical conditions RA SM TW WA2 WA3 EPI HEA HI IM
No of pupils 300; *(full boarding)* 250; *(day)* 50; *Girls* 300
Teacher:pupil ratio 1:6 **Average class size** 15
Fees per annum *(full boarding)* £26400; *(day)* £18900

St Mary's Calne is one of the top achieving girls' schools in the UK, featuring regularly at the top of the school league tables. The school has a stimulating and exciting cutting-edge curriculum and prides itself on educating successful young women for the 21st century. It benefits additionally from outstanding drama and sporting facilities in a rural location which is nonetheless only just over an hour from London by train.

England

Stonar School

Cottles Park, Atworth, Melksham, Wiltshire SN12 8NT   Tel: (01225) 701740   Fax: (01225) 790830
E-mail: admissions@stonarschool.com   Website: www.stonarschool.com   www.gabbitas.co.uk

Head Mrs S Shayler BSc (Hons), MA
Founded 1895
School status Independent. Girls Boarding and Day 2–18. Flexi-boarding available. Boarders from 8
Religious denomination Inter-Denominational
Member of BSA, GSA, SHA
Accredited by GSA, ISC
Learning difficulties CA/DYC DYP DYS MLD
Behavioural and emotional disorders CA CO
Physical and medical conditions AT CA RA SM/EPI HEA VI
No of pupils 355; *(weekly boarding)* 156; *(day)* 195; *Nursery* 45; *Pre-prep* 23; *Prep* 53; *Senior* 220; *Sixth Form* 59; *Girls* 355
Teacher:pupil ratio 1:9   **Average class size** 14
Fees per annum *(full boarding)* £16350–£19050; *(weekly)* £16350–£19050; *(day)* £5550–£10800

Stonar School, set in over 80 acres of parkland within easy reach of the city of Bath, offers excellent, single-sex education for girls 2–18.

The extensive facilities include an on-site equestrian centre, swimming pool, theatre, sports hall and astro-turf as well as a purpose-built music suite and art studio. A brand new Sixth Form Centre will open in early 2009 with social centre, study rooms and seminar facilities.

Warminster School

Church Street, Warminster, Wiltshire BA12 8PJ   Tel: (01985) 210160   Fax: (01985) 210154
E-mail: admissions@warminsterschool.org.uk   Website: www.warminsterschool.org.uk

Headmaster Mr M Priestley MA (Oxon)
Admissions Registrar Mrs G Webb
Founded 1707
School status Independent. Co-educational Boarding and Day 3–19. Flexi-boarding available. Boarders from 7
Religious denomination Church of England
Member of IAPS, ISCis, SHMIS
Accredited by IAPS, ISC
Learning difficulties SNU DYC DYP DYS
Behavioural and emotional disorders CO/ADD ASP TOU
Physical and medical conditions CA SM/HEA HI
No of pupils 600; *(full boarding)* 200; *(day)* 400; *Nursery* 10; *Pre-prep* 35; *Prep* 100; *Senior* 340; *Sixth Form* 140; *Girls* 240; *Boys* 360
Teacher:pupil ratio 1:10   **Average class size** 15
Fees per annum *(full boarding)* £20640; *(weekly)* £20640; *(day)* £12084

Aims and philosophy: The school aims to provide a stimulating and caring environment in which all pupils develop as individuals and achieve their potential in as many areas as possible. We encourage our pupils to have respect for the rights and beliefs of other people, and wish to provide for them the opportunity to acquire social, academic and personal qualities which will enable them to live happy and productive lives, both within the school and as part of local, national and global communities. The school is proud of its reputation for friendliness and the close working relationship between staff and pupils.

Please telephone the school (01985 210160) to arrange a visit, and to meet the Headmaster and the Head of the Preparatory School.

3.2 Scotland

MAP OF SCOTLAND

PROFILED SCHOOLS IN SCOTLAND

(Incorporating the counties of Aberdeen City, Aberdeenshire, Angus, Argyll and Bute, East Ayrshire, North Ayrshire, South Ayrshire, Borders, City of Edinburgh, Dumfries and Galloway, East Dunbartonshire, West Dunbartonshire, Falkirk, Fife, Highland, Inverclyde, East Lothian, Midlothian, Moray, Perth and Kinross, Renfrewshire, Stirling, South Lanarkshire, West Lothian)

Map Number   **Page Number**

Scotland

Loretto School

Linkfield Road, Musselburgh, Lothian EH21 7RE   Tel: (0131) 653 4455   Fax: (0131) 653 4401
E-mail: admissions@loretto.com   Website: www.loretto.com
Junior School (0131) 653 4570 email juniorschool@loretto.com

Headmaster Mr P A Hogan PGCE, MA, FcollT, FRSA   **Founded** 1827
School status Independent. Co-educational Boarding and Day 3–18. Flexi-boarding available. Boarders from 8
Religious denomination Non-Denominational
Member of BSA, HMC, IAPS, SCIS
Accredited by British Council, HMC, IAPS, ISC
Learning difficulties SC WI/DYP DYS MLD
Behavioural and emotional disorders CO ST TS
Physical and medical conditions AT IT SM WA2/EPI HEA HI
No of pupils 530; *(full boarding)* 245; *(day)* 284; *Nursery* 30; *Pre-prep* 62; *Prep* 139; *Senior* 335; *Sixth Form* 148; *Girls* 227; *Boys* 303
Teacher:pupil ratio 1:9 **Ave class size** 10–15
Fees per annum *(full boarding)* £15975–£24450; *(day)* £3000–£16620. Flexi-boarding packages available. Weekly boarding only junior school

Loretto provides an all-round education. There is a relaxed family atmosphere and emphasis on the development of the whole person through academic study, the arts, extra-curricular and sporting activities.

GCSEs and A levels offered. 48 per cent of all A levels sat in June 2008 were at grade A and 75 per cent at grades A–B.

The school is renowned for its music, drama and art. The Loretto Golf Academy attracts talented golfers worldwide.

Merchiston Castle School

Colinton, Edinburgh, Lothian EH13 0PU   Tel: (0131) 312 2200   Fax: (0131) 441 6060
E-mail: admissions@merchiston.co.uk   Website: www.merchiston.co.uk   www.gabbitas.co.uk

Head Mr A R Hunter BA   **Founded** 1833
School status Independent. Boys Boarding and Day 8–18. Boarders from 8
Religious denomination Inter-Denominational
Member of BSA, HMC, IBSCA, ISBA, SCIS
Accredited by HMC, ISC
Learning difficulties SNU WI/DYP DYS MLD
Behavioural and emotional disorders RA/ADHD
Physical and medical conditions RA/HEA
No of pupils 453; *(full boarding)* 289; *(day)* 164; *Prep* 108; *Senior* 189; *Sixth Form* 156; *Boys* 453; **Teacher:pupil ratio** 1:9
Average class size (under 11) 15; (11–16) 16; (Sixth Form) 9
Fees per annum *(full boarding)* £15585–£23760; *(day)* £10995–£17205

GCSEs, A Levels and Highers. In 2008, 79 per cent of A level candidates gained A and B grades, while at GCSE 84 per cent of grades were awarded at A*–B; 87 per cent of pupils achieved a place at their first choice of university. Regular winners of national engineering, electronic and mathematics prizes. Sporting achievements include pupils participating at international level. Strongly featured music department with prestigious school choir and pipe band. Integral Junior department (8–12 years). Strong links with two girls' schools. Junior teaching centre, refurbished science labs, modern IT suite, music school and library. Indoor pool and sports hall. Extensive co-curricular activities. Admission though school's own exam. Scholarships and bursaries available.

Set in 100 acres of parkland Merchiston is a school renowned for academic and sporting excellence. Merchiston offers a full range of

St George's School for Girls

Garscube Terrace, Edinburgh, Lothian EH12 6BG
Tel: (0131) 311 8000   Fax: (0131) 311 8120
E-mail: admissions@st-georges.edin.sch.uk   Website: www.st-georges.edin.sch.uk

Headmistress Dr J McClure CBE, MA, Dphil, FRSA, FSA
School status Independent. Girls Day and Boarding 2–18 (Boys 2–4). Flexi-boarding available
Religious denomination Non-Denominational
Learning difficulties CA SC WI/DYC DYP DYS MLD
Behavioural and emotional disorders CO RA/ADD ASP AUT BESD
Physical and medical conditions AT BL CA HL IT SM TW WA2 WA3/EPI HEA HI IM VI
No of pupils 845; *(full boarding)* 54; *(weekly boarding)* 6; *(day)* 917; *Girls* 837; *Boys* 8
Fees per annum *(full boarding)* £16215–£20130; *(day)* £3195–£10110

St George's School for Girls was founded in 1888 by a group of women who had been denied access to university education.

Today the ethos of our founders remains – we put girls first by design and aim to give each one the confidence and competence to fulfil her potential. St George's provides a caring, stimulating and challenging environment in which girls learn and develop. Emphasis is placed on personal achievement, responsibility, diversity and on partnerships. Girls, staff and parents work cooperatively throughout. In partnership, we aim to ensure the education of St George's girls meets the needs of the outside world as well as the individual.

Academic excellence is valued and our examination results are outstanding with over 98 per cent of our girls going onto university or college. Law, science, medicine, international relations, modern languages, the arts and social sciences are favoured degree courses.

We welcome enquiries throughout the year and assessments are held to suit parental needs.

Scotland

Gordonstoun School

Elgin, Morayshire IV30 5RF   Tel: (01343) 837837   Fax: (01343) 837808
E-mail: admissions@gordonstoun.org.uk   Website: www.gordonstoun.org.uk   www.gabbitas.co.uk

The Principal Mr M C Pyper BA
Director of Admissions Mr C J Barton BEd
Head of Junior School Mr R W McVean BSc
Founded 1934
School status Independent. Co-educational Boarding and Day 8–18. Boarders from 8
Religious denomination Non-Denominational
Member of BSA, ISBA, Round Square, SCIS
Accredited by British Council
Learning difficulties SC SNU WI/DYC DYP DYS MLD
Behavioural & emotional disorders CO RA/ADD
Physical & medical conditions RA SM/HEA
No of pupils 607; *(full boarding)* 456; *(weekly boarding)* 23; *(day)* 128; *Prep* 114; *Senior* 242; *Sixth Form* 251; *Girls* 248; *Boys* 359
Teacher:pupil ratio 1:7
Fees per annum *(full boarding)* £16731–£27390; *(weekly)* £15366; *(day)* £10290–£20451. Weekly boarding available for Junior School only

Set in a magnificent estate, Gordonstoun (and its Junior School, Aberlour House), lies between the sea and mountains in beautiful countryside. It is well located for easy access to international airports as well as mainline railway stations.

The school's distinctive, holistic ethos is based on internationalism, challenge, responsibility and service and aims to prepare students to make a positive contribution to society. Offering a broad, integrated curriculum, Gordonstoun combines study for GCSE and AS/A level with sporting, creative and outdoor education, including the school's unique sail training programme, to help students encompass the school motto, *Plus est en Vous* (There is more in you).

Strathallan School

Forgandenny, Perth PH2 9EG   Tel: (01738) 812546   Fax: (01738) 812549
E-mail: admissions@strathallan.co.uk   Website: www.strathallan.co.uk

The Headmaster Mr B K Thompson MA
Founded 1913
School status Independent. Co-educational
Boarding and Day 9–18. Boarders from 9
Religious denomination Multi-Denominational
Member of AGBIS, BSA, HMC, ISBA, SCI
Accredited by British Council, HMC, ISA, ISC
SCIS
Learning difficulties SNU DYS
Behavioural and emotional disorders RA/ADD
ADHD ASP
Physical and medical conditions SM TW WA3/
EPI HEA
No of pupils 502; *(full boarding)* 326; *(day)*
176; *Sixth Form* 205; *Girls* 205; *Boys* 297
Teacher:pupil ratio 1:7 **Average class size** 13
Fees per annum *(full boarding)* £16770–
£23520; *(day)* £10470–£15960

150 acre campus in rural Perthshire, within easy reach of Scotland's airports and two hours' travel of Heathrow.

Academically excellent, over 95 per cent of pupils go on to higher education, including Oxford, Cambridge and other top universities. Strathallan aims to provide a wide range of courses using both English and Scottish qualifications.

Strathallan offers an unrivalled range of sporting and extra-curricular activities with outstanding success in sport, drama, music and art. Particular emphasis is placed on pastoral care, the positive relationship between teachers and pupils and the small class sizes. Every pupil is encouraged to develop his or her own individual talents to the full.

Strathallan School is one of Scotland's leading boarding and day schools located on a beautiful

Beaconhurst School

52 Kenilworth Road, Bridge of Allan, Stirling FK9 4RR   Tel: (01786) 832146   Fax: (01786) 833415
E-mail: secretary@beaconhurst.stirling.sch.uk   Website: www.beaconhurst.com

Headmaster Mr I W Kilpatrick BA, MEd, FRSA
School status Independent. Co-educational
Day 3–18
Religious denomination Non-Denominational
Member of HAS, IAPS, ISA, ISBA, NAHT,
WOSIS, SCIS **Accredited by** IAPS, ISA, NDNA
Learning difficulties RA WI
No of pupils 401; *(day)* 401; *Nursery* 43;
Pre-prep 140; *Prep* 40; *Senior* 156; *Sixth
Form* 22; *Girls* 196; *Boys* 205
Fees per annum *(day)* £2862–£9210

Beaconhurst is situated at the foot of the Ochils in the attractive country town of Bridge of Allan.

Its origins go back to 1919 when both the Beacon School for Girls and the Hurst Grange School for Boys were founded. The schools amalgamated in 1975 and, after a period of steady growth, the new school – Beaconhurst – embarked upon an exciting development programme, with the opening of the secondary department in 1991.

The school's administrative centre is based in a fine listed building which is surrounded by the various teaching areas. Classroom accommodation has been extended considerably over recent years to include science laboratories, modern language facilities, a purpose-built building for the Junior School, three IT suites and an expressive arts building. Most recently a sports hall, new dining hall and IT-equipped classroom block have been added to supplement existing facilities.

3.3 Schools in Continental Europe

MAP OF SCHOOLS IN CONTINENTAL EUROPE

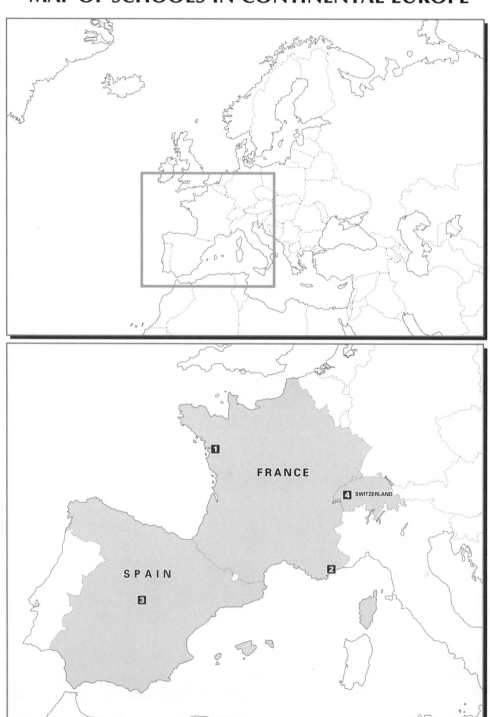

PROFILED SCHOOLS IN CONTINENTAL EUROPE

Continental Europe

Chavagnes International College

96 rue du Calvaire, 85250, Chavagnes-en-Paillers, France   Tel: (33 (0)) 51 42 39 82
Fax: (33 (0)) 51 42 39 83   E-mail: info@chavagnes.org   Website: www.chavagnes.org
Chavagnes is 40 mins from Nantes Airport, with cheap UK flights from Ryanair, Easyjet and Aer Arann

Principal Mr F D McDermott MA, MCIL, FCollT, FRSA
Chaplain Rev A Talbot BSc
Founded September 2002
College status Independent. Boys Boarding and Day 10–18. Flexi-boarding available
Religious denomination Roman Catholic Affiliated to local Catholic Education Directorate
Learning difficulties RA SC WI/MLD
Physical and medical conditions RA TW WA2/HEA IM
No of pupils 30; *(full boarding)* 26; *(weekly boarding)* 3; *(day)* 1; *Prep* 12; *Senior* 14; *Sixth Form* 4; *Boys* 30
Teacher:pupil ratio 1:3 **Average class size** 8
Fees FB from €14000 WB from €11000 DAY from €6500 (various bursaries are available)

The college provides a solid academic, cultural, spiritual and moral foundation for boys. Founded in 2002 with 10 pupils, we now have 30 and a proven track record of university entrance, including Oxbridge. All sit GCSEs and A levels. Most are British and will attend British universities. Facilities include a chapel, laboratory, theatre, library, tennis and basketball courts, computer suite, pianos, table tennis, table football and billiards. Additional activities include rowing, riding, fishing, boxing, chess, chapel choir, debating, drama, music groups and instrumental lessons.

Mougins School

615 Avenue Dr Maurice Donat, Font de l'Orme, BP 401, 06251 Mougins Cedex, France
Tel: (33 (0)) 4 93 90 15 47   Fax: (33 (0)) 4 93 75 31 40
E-mail: information@mougins-school.com Website: www.mougins-school.com www.gabbitas.co.uk

Headmaster Mr B G Hickmore
Deputy Head Ms Jane Hart
Primary School Co-ordinator Mr David Gifford
Founded 1964
School status Independent. Co-educational Day 3–18 Co-educational independent pre-prep (Reception/EY), prep (Forms 1–6), senior (Forms 7–11) and Sixth Form (Forms 12–13) day only
Religious denomination Non-Denominational
Member of COBIS
Learning difficulties CA SC WI/DYS MLD
Behavioural and emotional disorders RA/ADD AUT
Physical and medical conditions TW WA1/CP
No of pupils 459; *(day)* 459; *Nursery* 16; *Pre-prep* 20; *Prep* 152; *Senior* 204; *Sixth Form* 67; *Girls* 186; *Boys* 273
Teacher:pupil ratio 1:13 **Average class size** 22

Mougins School is situated on the Cote d'Azur, north of Cannes and west of Nice, on a purpose-built campus. Facilities include a library, three science laboratories, IT centre, two art studios, music room, performing arts centre, gymnasium, all-weather football pitch and dining room.

The school accepts students aged 3 to 18 representing over 30 nationalities. The school follows the British curriculum modified to meet the needs of an international market with examinations in IGCSE, AS and A level.

The caring family atmosphere complements the high quality of the teaching and helps to enhance the academic, cultural and physical development of our students. We offer a comprehensive education that produces excellent results, not only academically but also in the sporting and artistic domains, leading to entry to the world's leading universities.

King's College Madrid

Paseo de los Andes, 35, 28761 Soto de Vinuelas, Madrid, Spain
Tel: (+34) 918 034 800   Fax: (+34) 918 036 557
E-mail: info@kingscollege.es   Website: www.kingscollege.es   www.gabbitas.co.uk
King's College School, La Moraleja   Telephone + 34 916 585 540   Fax + 34 916 507 686

Headmaster Mr D Johnson BEd (Hons), MSc
(Oxon)   **Founded** 1969
College status Independent. Co-educational
Day and Boarding 2–18. Boarders from 13
Religious denomination Non-Denominational
Member of HMC, COBIS, BSA, NABSS
Accredited by ISC ISC, Spanish Ministry of
Education
Learning difficulties WI/DYS
Physical and medical conditions RA SM WA2
No of pupils 1880; *(full boarding)* 20; *(day)*
1860; *Prep* 1247; *Senior* 492; *Sixth Form* 141;
Girls 956; *Boys* 924
Teacher:pupil ratio 1:12.2
Average class size 25
Fees per annum *(full boarding)* €16830–
€18357; *(day)* €5454–€10476

Founded in 1969, King's College is the largest
British school in Spain and the first to have had
full UK accreditation through the Independent
Schools Inspectorate.

It is a co-educational day and boarding school
following the English National Curriculum which
prepares pupils for IGCSE and GCE A levels and
offers a wide range of subjects at both levels.
There are optional Spanish studies and preparation for Spanish university entrance examinations.

With approximately 1,880 pupils of 48 nationalities, the school has a complement of 140 fully
qualified teachers. All academic staff have British
qualifications, except the Spanish teachers and
some who teach modern languages.

The school has a reputation for high academic
standards and excellent examination results with
students going on to universities in Britain, USA,
and Spain among others. An Oxbridge preparatory group works with the most able students to
prepare university applications.

There are three King's College sites in Madrid:
the main school in Soto de Viñuelas (Pre-nursery
to Year 13), King's College School, La Moraleja
(Nursery to Year 8 in September 2009) and King's
Infant School, Chamartin (Nursery to Year 2).

The school has its own catering service and

offers three-course midday meals. There is an
optional bus service with a modern fleet of 25
vehicles covering Madrid and outlying areas for
all three school sites.

The main school offers the following facilities:

Academic facilities: Seven science laboratories,
three multimedia computer centres, two libraries,
two music rooms, art studio, etc. Recent additions
include a purpose-built Early Learning Centre, an
auditorium with seating for 350 people and a
music school for individual tuition.

Sports facilities: Gymnasium, judo room, fitness
centre, 25-metre heated indoor swimming pool,
11-a-side and 5-a-side football pitches, floodlit
multi-sports area, tennis courts, stables and riding
school.

Boarding facilities: There are boarding facilities
for boys and girls with rooms for one to two pupils
over the age of 13. At present the residence is
home to pupils from the UK, Russia, Japan as well
as students from expatriate families living in
Spain. Resident pupils enjoy access to many of
the sports facilities at the weekends and after
school.

There is a wide variety of optional activities
including: music, ballet, handicrafts, performing
arts, judo, riding, swimming and tennis.

Admission: The procedure for admission varies
according to the age of the pupil. Importance is
given to previous school records and from age 7 to
16 years candidates are required to sit entrance
tests in mathematics and English.

Continental Europe

Aiglon College

1885 Chesieres-Villars, Switzerland
Tel: (41) (0) 24 496 6126   Fax: (41) (0) 24 469 6162
E-mail: info@aiglon.ch   Website: www.aiglon.ch   www.gabbitas.co.uk

Principal Mr P J Armstrong MA, BEd (Hons), MACE
Founded 1949
College status Independent. Co-educational Day and Boarding 9–18. Boarders from 9 Co-educational independent prep, junior and senior boarding and day
Religious denomination Non-Denominational
Member of CASE, COBISEC, IAPS, NEASC, Round Square
Accredited by HMC, IAPS ECIS, NEASC, ADISR, Parents League of NY
No of pupils 378; *(day)* 65; *Pre-prep* 25; *Prep* 60; *Senior* 293; *Sixth Form* 126; *Girls* 172; *Boys* 206
Teacher:pupil ratio 1:6
Average class size 12
Fees per annum *(full boarding)* CHF 58000–CHF 73300; *(weekly)* CHF 49700; *(day)* CHF 38300–CHF 51300

Aiglon College offers a well-rounded education in a secure and friendly international community on a 25-acre campus within an Alpine ski village. It is an independent, non-profit, co-educational, international boarding school with an enrolment of over 50 nationalities. The school is registered as a charitable trust in Switzerland, the UK, USA, Netherlands and Canada. There are eight boarding houses, each with its own houseparents and tutors offering a high degree of pastoral care. The academic programme is demanding and prepares students for British GCSE and A level examinations as well as the American College Board. Courses are taught in English except in the first two years of the Junior School (ages 9–11) where the emphasis is based on French and English. The school offers an ESL (English as a Second Language) programme for all non-English speakers aged 10–14.

Facilities include a new computer centre, world languages centre, eight science laboratories, library and outstanding art and music departments. The school is also a centre for the College Board and TOEFL. Aiglon's graduates are currently enrolled in leading international universities and colleges.

Sports and expeditions form an essential component of a well-rounded approach to the development of the students' personality and character. The wide range of sports includes skiing, basketball, tennis, soccer, athletics, gymnastics, swimming and volleyball. Expeditions take place at weekends and activities include camping, climbing and skiing under expert and qualified supervision. Service and responsibility are fostered through social service and through the Round Square organization.

During vacations, Aiglon offers a summer school and a languages and snowsports programme which combine expert language tuition with fun outdoor activities. There is also a selection of winter and summer adult courses.

Part 4

Schools by Category

Schools by category

This section comprises schools listed alphabetically by category heading. Categories include *Boys Preparatory School, Catholic Boarding School, Family Atmosphere, Horse Riding and Mountain Biking Provision* and *International Sixth Form College* amongst others.

Each entry contains details, including website address and a brief description of the school's particular characteristics.

BOYS DAY AND BOARDING SCHOOL

Aldwickbury School
Wheathampstead Road
Harpenden
Herts AL5 1AD
Tel: (01582) 713022
Fax: (01582) 767696
Email:
    registrar@aldwickbury.org.uk
Web: www.aldwickbury.org.uk

A day and boarding school for boys ages 4–13 in Harpenden. Aldwickbury is renowned for polite, friendly pupils who move on to a wide range of senior schools.

BOYS DAY SCHOOL

Buckingham College Preparatory School
458 Rayners Lane
Pinner
Middlesex HA5 5DT
Fax: (020) 8868 3228
Email: office@buckprep.org
Web: www.buckprep.org

'A prestigious, well established school with small classes affording excellent pastoral care. Spectacular results at 11+ including numerous scholarships. Very strong Music and Drama departments. The school competes in all the major sports and has a wide range of optional activities after school including a Homework Club until 6.00 pm.'

BOYS PREPARATORY SCHOOL

Bickley Park School
14/24 Page Heath Lane
Bickley
Bromley
Kent BR1 2DS
Tel: (020) 8467 2195
Fax: (020) 8325 5511
Email:
    info@bickleyparkschool.co.uk
Web:
    www.bickleyparkschool.co.uk

Bickley Park provides a happy and caring environment in which all boys are helped to reach their full potential in all areas of school life.

CATHOLIC BOARDING AND DAY SCHOOL

New Hall School
Boreham
Chelmsford
Essex CM14 4UR
Tel: (01245) 467588
Fax: (01245) 464348
Email:
  registrar@newhallschool.co.uk
Web: www.newhallschool.co.uk

New Hall is one of the oldest independent Catholic schools in England. We believe a New Hall education can give you the best start in life. We know that your experience in your school days is a powerful influence on future success, in your chosen career and your personal relationships. We believe that New Hall offers a distinctive education of real quality. Accepts boys and girls aged 3–18.

CO-EDUCATIONAL CHRISTIAN SCHOOL

Hamilton College
Bothwell Road
Hamilton ML3 0AY
Tel: (01698) 282700
Fax: (01698) 281589
Email:
  admissions@hamiltoncollege.
  co.uk
Web: www.hamiltoncollege.co.uk

Hamilton College is a young dynamic co-educational Christian independent school for pupils aged 3 to 18. The vision of the College is to provide an excellent education for all pupils within a caring Christian environment.

CO-EDUCATIONAL DAY AND BOARDING SCHOOL

Great Ballard School
Eartham
Near Chichester
West Sussex PO18 0LR
Tel: (01243) 814236
Fax: (01243) 814586
Email: admin@greatballard.co.uk
Web: www.greatballard.co.uk

Friendly school with small teaching groups for children aged 2–13. Emphasis on the individual and a broad curriculum. Flexi-boarding is a popular option. Extra arts classes on a Saturday morning.

CO-EDUCATIONAL DAY SCHOOL

Bancroft's School
Tel: (020) 8505 4821
Fax: (020) 8559 0032
Email: office@bancrofts.org
Web: www.bancrofts.org

Fully co-educational, 7–18. Bancroft's is a multi-ethnic and multi-faith community. Heritage of academic excellence with outstanding sporting facilities and strong traditions in music and drama.

Cheadle Hulme School
Claremont Road
Cheadle Hulme
Cheadle
Cheshire SK8 6EF
Tel: +44 (0)161 488 3330
Fax: +44 (0)161 488 3344
Email: registrar@chschool.co.uk
Web: www.cheadlehulmeschool.
  co.uk

With high academic standards, exceptional extra-curricular opportunities and extensive facilities, Cheadle Hulme School provides an outstanding education for boys and girls aged 4 to 18.

Wellington School
Carleton Turrets
1 Craigweil Road
Ayr KA7 2XH
Tel: 01292 269321
Fax: 01292 272161
Email: info@wellingtonschool.org
Web: www.wellingtonschool.org

Excellent academic results and extracurricular provision. Small enough to treat all pupils as individuals – big enough to offer a full range of subject specialists. The school educates 590 Boys and Girls aged 3–18.

CO-EDUCATIONAL PREPARATORY DAY SCHOOL

Amesbury School
Hazel Grove
Hindhead
Surrey GU26 6BL
Tel: (01428) 604322
Fax: (01428) 607715
Web: www.amesburyschool.co.uk

Founded in 1870 Amesbury is the oldest preparatory school in the Haslemere area. The boys and girls are well rounded and interesting individuals within a system, rather than clones because of it. Accepts children aged 2–13.

Ladymede
Little Kimble
Aylesbury
Bucks HP17 0XP
Tel: (01844) 346154
Fax: (01844) 275660
Email: office@ladymede.com
Web: www.ladymedeschool.
  bucks.sch.uk

Ladymede is a small, friendly school, where an opportunity for learning is never missed, and children received an exciting education combined with sound traditional values.

CO-EDUCATIONAL PREPARATORY SCHOOL

Dame Bradbury's School
Ashdon Road
Saffron Walden
Essex CB10 2AB
Tel: (01799) 522348
Fax: (01799) 516762
Email: info@damebradburys.com
Web: www.damebradburys.com

A co-educational 3–18 school
offering a happy, stimulating
education. Our Nursery,
Reception and Late Stay were
rated 'outstanding in every
category' by Ofsted (2008).

Elm Green Preparatory School
Parsonage Lane
Little Baddow
Chelmsford
Essex CM3 4SU
Tel: (01245) 225230
Fax: (01245) 226008
Email:
    admin@elmgreen.essex.sch.uk
Web: www.elmgreenschool.co.uk

Elm Green Preparatory School is a
thriving educational community in
an idyllic woodland setting,
offering excellent academic,
sporting and musical opportunities
with outstanding pastoral care.

Hallfield School
48 Church Road
Edgbaston
Birmingham
West Midlands B15 3SJ.
Tel: (0121) 454 1496
Fax: (0121) 454 9182
Email:
    admissions@hallfield.bham.sch
Web: www.hallfieldschool.co.uk

Hallfield School is an academic
school, taking children from 3
months to 11 years. Hallfield
prepares its pupils for entrance and
scholarship examinations at 11+.

Old Vicarage School
48 Richmond Hill
Richmond
Surrey TW10 6QX
Tel: (020) 8940 0922
Fax: (020) 8948 6834
Email: office@oldvicarage-
    richmond.co.uk
Web: www.oldvicarage-
    richmond.co.uk

At the Old Vicarage we provide a
unique combination of a top
quality education in a friendly
environment with small classes of
fourteen pupils.

DAY AND NURSERY SCHOOL

Quainton Hall School
91 Hindes Road
Harrow
Middlesex HA1 1RX
Tel: (020) 8427 1304
Fax: (020) 8861 8861
Email: admin@quaintonhall.org.uk
Web: www.quaintonhall.org.uk

Quainton Hall School is an IAPS
day preparatory school and
nursery for children aged 2½ to 13
years offering a very wide range of
academic, sporting and extra-
curricular opportunities.

FAMILY ATMOSPHERE

Edenhurst Preparatory School
Westlands Avenue
Newcastle-under-Lyme
Staffordshire ST5 2PU
Tel: (01782) 619348
Fax: (01782) 662402
Email: info@edenhurst.co.uk
Web: www.edenhurst.co.uk

Edenhurst Preparatory School is a
day school for boys and girls aged
4–13 years with an onsite Day
Nursery (3 months to 4 years). The
school provides an excellent broad
education.

FULL BOARDING

Abberley Hall
Worcestershire WR6 6DD
Tel: (01299) 896275
Fax: (01299) 896875
Email: john.walker@
    abberleyhall.co.uk
Web: www.abberleyhall.co.uk

Abberley Hall is a co-educational
full boarding school for 8–13 year
olds preparing pupils for all major
public schools, providing
academic, sporting and social
grounding required for sustained
success

FULL BOARDING AND DAY SCHOOL

Ardingly College
Haywards Heath
West Sussex RH17 6SQ
Tel: (01444) 893000
Email: registrar@ardingly.com
Web: www.ardingly.com

Ardingly College is an
independent, HMC and IAPS,
school for pupils aged 2½ to 18
and is one of England's oldest,
celebrating its 150th anniversary
in 2008. Ardingly is one of the
leading co-educational boarding
and day schools in the South East
of England.

GIRLS' BOARDING

Queen Margaret's School
Escrick Park
York
North Yorkshire YO19 6EU
Tel: (01904) 728261
Fax: (01904) 728838
Email: admissions@
    queenmargaretsschool.co.uk
Web:
    www.queenmargaretsschool.
    co.uk

An independent boarding school
for girls aged 11–18 which
provides the environment and
encouragement for developing
talents. The school exists to
provide the best possible
education for girls.

GIRLS BOARDING AND DAY SCHOOL

Abbots Bromley School for Girls

Abbots Bromley
Staffordshire WS15 3BW
Tel: (01283) 840232
Fax: (01283) 840988
Email: head@abbotsbromley.net
Web: www.abbotsbromley.staffs. sch.uk

Located in a beautiful Staffordshire village, Abbots Bromley School for Girls provides a high quality all-round education for 300 girls aged 3–18.

GIRLS DAY AND BOARDING SCHOOL

Queen Mary's School

Baldersby Park
Topcliffe
Thirsk
North Yorkshire YO7 3BZ
Tel: (01845) 575000
Fax: (01845) 575001
Email: admin@queenmarys.org
Web: www.queenmarys.org

Girls Day and Boarding School for 3–16 years, co-educational Pre-prep department 3–8 years. Small school with a happy and secure family atmosphere.

GIRLS DAY SCHOOL

Brantwood School

1 Kenwood Bank
Sheffield S7 1NU
Tel: (0114) 2581747
Fax: (0114) 2581847
Email: Enquiries@ brantwoodschool.co.uk
Web: www.brantwoodschool. co.uk

Brantwood is a small and friendly school, for girls aged three to sixteen, where you can be assured that your daughter will be nurtured and encouraged to achieve her potential.

Oakfield School

Coldharbour Road
Pyrford
Woking
Surrey GU22 8SJ
Tel: (01932) 342465
Fax: (01932) 342745
Web: www.oakfieldschool.co.uk

Small classes and traditional values combine with excellent teaching to give outstanding results in core academic subjects. Co-educational pre-preparatory school 3–7 and Girls school 7–16.

HORSE RIDING AND MOUNTAIN BIKING PROVISION

Bedstone College

Bedstone
Bucknell
Shropshire SY7 0BG
Tel: (01547) 530303
Fax: (01547) 530740
Email: admissions@bedstone.org
Web: www.bedstone.org

Bedstone College is South Shropshire's leading independent, co-educational, boarding and day school catering for children 3 to 18 years. It enjoys a warm and supportive family atmosphere, where each child is encouraged to fulfil their potential.

INDEPENDENT SIXTH FORM COLLEGE

Albemarle Independent College

18 Dunraven St
Mayfair
London W1K 7FE
Tel: (020) 7409 7273
Fax: (020) 7629 9146
Email: admin@albemarle.org.uk
Web: www.albemarle.org.uk

Based in the heart of central London Albemarle is an independent sixth form college offering a wide range of GCSE and A level subjects, with an emphasis on producing excellent exam results.

INTERNATIONAL SIXTH FORM COLLEGE

Bath Academy

27 Queen Square
Bath BA1 2HX
Tel: (01225) 334577
Fax: (01225) 482414
Email: principal@bathacademy.co.uk
Web: www.bathacademy.co.uk

Bath Academy is an International College offering the University Foundation Programme, GCSE, A level and International GCSE and A level (CIE). Accommodation is available in hostels or homestay.

Part 5

Reference Section

5.1
Scholarships

The following is based on information provided by schools. The entry age, where given, is the age at which scholarships are available to pupils. Please note that for each school, not every scholarship listed is offered at all the stated entry ages. Further details of scholarships available at individual schools may be found in Part Three: School Profiles. The abbreviations are as follows:

A Art
AA Academic ability
D Drama
G Games

I Instrumental music/Choral
O All-round ability
S Science
6 Sixth Form entry

ENGLAND

BEDFORSHIRE

Bedford High School for Girls, Bedford	6 AA I O
Bedford Modern School, Bedford Entry age: 11+	A D G
Bedford Preparatory School, Bedford	AA
Bedford School, Bedford	6 AA G I
Moorlands School, Luton Entry age: 7+	A AA I O

BERKSHIRE

The Abbey School, Reading Entry age: 11+, 16+	6 AA I
The Ark School, Reading Entry age: 7	A AA I
Bearwood College, Wokingham Entry age: 11/13	6 A AA D G I O S
Bradfield College, Reading Entry age: 13+, 16+	6 A AA G I O
Brigidine School Windsor, Windsor Entry age: 11, 16	6 A AA D G I
Brockhurst and Marlston House Schools, Newbury	A AA D G I O S
Claires Court School, Maidenhead	6 A AA D G I O
Claires Court Schools, Ridgeway, Maidenhead	A AA D G I O
Claires Court Schools, The College, Maidenhead	6 A AA D G I O
Dolphin School, Reading	A AA D G I O
Downe House, Thatcham	6 A AA G I

Eagle House, Sandhurst	AA I
Elstree School, Reading Entry age: 7	AA
The Elvian School, Reading Entry age: 11+	6 A AA G I
Eton College, Windsor	6 AA I
Heathfield St Mary's School, Ascot	6 AA O
Hemdean House School, Reading	AA I O
Highfield School, Maidenhead	AA
Holme Grange School, Wokingham Entry age: 11+	AA O
Horris Hill School, Newbury	AA O
Hurst Lodge School, Ascot Entry age: various	6 A AA D I O
Langley Manor School, Slough	AA G I O
Leighton Park School, Reading Entry age: 12, 14, 17	6 A AA I O
Licensed Victuallers' School, Ascot	6 A AA G I
Long Close School, Slough Entry age: 7yrs	AA G I O
Luckley-Oakfield School, Wokingham Entry age: 11	6 A AA D G I
The Marist Senior School, Ascot Entry age: 11	6 A AA D G I O
The Oratory School, Reading Entry age: 11+, 13+	6 A AA D G I O
Padworth College, Reading Entry age: 14, 16	6 A AA
Pangbourne College, Pangbourne Entry age: 11+, 13+, 16+	6 A AA D G I O S
Papplewick School, Ascot Entry age: 7–11	A AA G I O

Queen Anne's School, Reading
Entry age: 11, 12, 13+, 16+   6 A AA D G I O
Reading Blue Coat School, Reading   A AA I
St Edward's School, Reading   AA O
St Gabriel's, Newbury
Entry age: 11, 16   6 A AA G I
St George's School, Ascot
Entry age: 11+, 16+   A AA D I
St George's School, Windsor
Entry age: 7+, 9+   AA I
St Joseph's Convent School, Reading   6 AA D G I
St Mary's School, Ascot, Ascot   6 A AA G I S
St Piran's Preparatory School, Maidenhead A AA G I O
Sunningdale School, Sunningdale   A AA D G I O
Thorngrove School, Newbury   AA G I O
Upton House School, Windsor   A AA
Wellington College, Crowthorne   6 A AA D G I O

BRISTOL

Badminton School Entry age: 11+, 13+,
16+   6 A AA I O
Bristol Cathedral School
Entry age: 11+, 13+, 16+   6 AA G I
Bristol Grammar School
Entry age: 7, 11, 13, 16   6 A AA D G I O S
Clifton College Entry age: 13+, 16+   6 A AA G I O
Clifton College Pre-Prep – Butcombe   O
Clifton College Preparatory School
Entry age: 11+   AA G I O
Clifton High School
Entry age: 11+, 13+, 16+   6 AA G I
Colston's Collegiate School   6 A AA D G I O
Colston's Girls' School   6 A AA I O S
The Downs School, Wraxall Entry age: 8+   A AA G I O
Fairfield School, Backwell   AA
Queen Elizabeth's Hospital
Entry age: 11, 13, 16   6 AA I S
The Red Maids' School Entry age: 11+,13+,
16+   6 AA G I O
Redland High School Entry age: 7, 11, 16   6 A AA I
St Ursula's High School, Westbury-on-Trym   AA
Torwood House School   O

BUCKINGHAMSHIRE

Bury Lawn School, Milton Keynes   6
Davenies School, Beaconsfield   A AA G I O
Gateway School, Great Missenden   O
Godstowe Preparatory School, High Wycombe
Entry age: 8, 11   AA
High March School, Beaconsfield Entry age: 8   AA
Ladymede, Aylesbury Entry age: 7+   AA O
Milton Keynes Preparatory School, Milton KeynesA AA G I
Pipers Corner School, High Wycombe   6 A AA D G I
St Mary's School, Gerrards Cross
Entry age: 11/16+   6 AA I
Stowe School, Buckingham
Entry age: 13, 16   6 A AA G I O
Swanbourne House School, Milton Keynes
Entry age: 11+   AA G I

Thornton College Convent of Jesus and Mary,
Milton Keynes Entry age: 11   AA
Thorpe House School, Gerrards Cross   AA
Wycombe Abbey School, High Wycombe   6 AA I

CAMBRIDGESHIRE

Bellerbys College & Embassy CES Cambridge,
Cambridge   AA O
Cambridge Centre for Sixth-form Studies,
Cambridge   6 AA O
Kimbolton School, Huntingdon   6 A AA G I O
The King's School Ely, Ely Entry age: 11+ 6 A AA D G I
The Leys School, Cambridge
Entry age: 11, 13, 16   6 A AA D G I O
MPW (Mander Portman Woodward), Cambridge 6 AA O
The Perse School, Cambridge   6 A AA I
The Perse School for Girls, Cambridge   6 I
Peterborough High School, Peterborough
Entry age: 11, 17   6 A AA I O
St Faith's, Cambridge Entry age: 7+   AA
St John's College School, Cambridge   I
St Mary's School, Cambridge   6 AA I
Sancton Wood School, Cambridge   D O

CHANNEL ISLANDS

Elizabeth College, Guernsey   I O
Ormer House Preparatory School, Alderney   AA
St George's Preparatory School, Jersey
Entry age: 7+   A AA G I O S
St Michael's Preparatory School, Jersey   AA
Victoria College, Jersey   AA I S

CHESHIRE

Abbey Gate College, Chester Entry age: 11+, 16+ 6 AA I
Abbey Gate School, Chester   AA
Alderley Edge School for Girls,
Alderley Edge   6 A AA G I
Beech Hall School, Macclesfield   O
Brabyns School, Stockport   AA
Cransley School, Northwich
Entry age: 11+   A AA G I O S
Culcheth Hall, Altrincham   AA
The Grange School, Northwich   6 AA I
Hammond School, Chester   AA D I
Hulme Hall Schools, Cheadle   AA
The King's School, Macclesfield   AA I
Merton House, Chester   AA G
Mostyn House School, South Wirral
Entry age: 7, 11   AA G O
North Cestrian Grammar School, Altrincham   AA
The Ryleys, Alderley Edge   AA O
Stockport Grammar School, Stockport Entry age: 11+   I
Terra Nova School, Holmes Chapel   A AA D G I O S

CORNWALL

The Bolitho School, Penzance
Entry age: 10+, 13+   6 A AA I O

Polwhele House School, Truro	AA I
Roselyon, Par	AA I O
St Joseph's School, Launceston	
Entry age: 7+, 11+	AA G I O
St Petroc's School, Bude Entry age: 7+	A AA D G I O S
St Piran's Preparatory School, Hayle	O
Truro High School, Truro	
Entry age: 11+, 16+	6 A AA G I
Truro School, Truro	6 A AA G I

CUMBRIA

Austin Friars St Monica's School, Carlisle	
Entry age: 11+	AA G I
Casterton School, Kirkby Lonsdale	6 A AA D G I O S
Chetwynde School, Barrow-in-Furness	6 AA G O
Harecroft Hall School, Seascale	AA
Holme Park School, Kendal Entry age: 7+	AA D G O S
Lime House School, Carlisle	AA G O
St Bees School, St Bees	6 A AA G I
Sedbergh Junior School, Sedbergh	
Entry age: 11	A AA D G I O
Sedbergh School, Sedbergh	
Entry age: 13+, 16+, 17+	6 A AA D G I O
Windermere St Anne's, Windermere	
Entry age: 11+, 13+, 16+	6 A AA D G I O

DERBYSHIRE

Derby Grammar School, Derby	6 AA G I
Derby High School, Derby Entry age: 11/16	6 AA G I O
Foremarke Hall School, Derby	A AA D G I
Mount St Mary's College, Spinkhill	
Entry age: 11+, 15+	6 AA G I O
Ockbrook School, Derby	A AA D G I
Repton School, Derby	
Entry age: 13+, 16+	6 A AA D G I O
St Wystan's School, Repton Entry age: 7+	AA

DEVON

The Abbey School, Torquay	AA O
Blundell's School, Tiverton	
Entry age: 11, 13, 16	6 A AA G I O
Bramdean School, Exeter Entry age: 7/11	AA D G I
Edgehill College, Bideford	6 A AA D G I O
Exeter Cathedral School, Exeter Entry age: 7/12+	AA I O
Exeter Junior School, Exeter Entry age: 7+	AA
Exeter School, Exeter	
Entry age: 7, 11, 12, 13	6 A AA I S
Grenville College, Bideford	
Entry age: 11, 12, 13, 16+	6 A AA D G I O
Kelly College, Tavistock	
Entry age: 11, 13, 16	6 A AA G I O
The Maynard School, Exeter	6 A G I O
Mount House School, Tavistock	AA G I
Plymouth College, Plymouth	
Entry age: 11, 13, 16	6 A AA G I
St Christophers School, Totnes	O
St Margaret's School, Exeter	6 A AA D I
St Michael's, Barnstaple	A AA D G I O
St Peter's School, Exmouth	AA G I O

St Wilfrid's School, Exeter Entry age: 7	O
Shebbear College, Beaworthy	
Entry age: 11+, 13+, 16+	6 A AA D G I O
Stoodley Knowle School, Torquay	O
Stover School, Newton Abbot	6 A AA G I O
Tower House School, Paignton	
Entry age: 11	A AA D G I O S
Trinity School, Teignmouth	6 A AA D G I O S
West Buckland Preparatory School, Barnstaple	AA O
West Buckland School, Barnstaple	6 AA G I O

DORSET

Bryanston School, Blandford Forum	
Entry age: 13, 16	6 A AA G I O S
Canford School, Wimborne	6 A AA D G I
Castle Court Preparatory School, Wimborne	AA I
Clayesmore Preparatory School,	
Blandford Forum	A AA G I O
Clayesmore, Blandford Forum	6 A AA I O
Dumpton School, Wimborne Entry age: 7	AA O
Hanford School, Blandford Forum	I
Knighton House, Blandford Forum	A AA D G I O
Leweston School, Sherborne	
Entry age: 7–13, 16	6 A AA D G I O S
Milton Abbey School, Blandford Forum	6 A AA D G I
The Park School, Bournemouth	AA I O
Port Regis School, Shaftesbury	A AA G I O
St Martin's School, Bournemouth	AA G O
St Mary's School, Shaftesbury	
Entry age: 11+, 13+, 16+	6 A AA G I
Sherborne Preparatory School, Sherborne	AA G I O
Sherborne School, Sherborne	
Entry age: 13+, 16+	6 A AA D G I
Sherborne Girls, Sherborne	6 A AA I O
Talbot Heath, Bournemouth	6 A AA D G I O
Thornlow Preparatory School, Weymouth	AA G
Uplands School, Poole Entry age: 11+, 12+, 13+	AA
Wentworth College, Bournemouth	6 A AA D G I
Yarrells School, Poole	AA I O

COUNTY DURHAM

Barnard Castle School, Barnard Castle	6 A AA G I
The Chorister School, Durham	I
Durham High School For Girls, Durham	
Entry age: 11, 16	6 A AA D G I
Durham School, Durham	
Entry age: 11–16	6 A AA G I O
Hurworth House School, Darlington	AA G O
Polam Hall, Darlington	
Entry age: 7, 11, 13, 16	6 A AA G I O
Yarm at Raventhorpe School, Darlington	O

ESSEX

Alleyn Court Preparatory School, Southend-on-Sea	
Entry age: 7	AA I O
Bancroft's School, Woodford Green	
Entry age: 11, 16	6 AA I
Brentwood School, Brentwood	
Entry age: 11, 16	6 A AA D G I O

Chigwell School, Chigwell	A AA D I O
Colchester High School, Colchester	AA
College Saint-Pierre, Leigh-on-Sea	O
Cranbrook College, Ilford	AA
Crowstone Preparatory School, Westcliff-on-Sea	O
The Daiglen School, Buckhurst Hill	AA
Dame Bradbury's School, Saffron Walden	I
Felsted Preparatory School, Felsted	AA I
Felsted School, Felsted	6 A AA D I O
Friends' School, Saffron Walden	
Entry age: 11, 13, 16	6 A AA G I
Gosfield School, Halstead	6 AA D G I O
Herington House School, Brentwood	D G I O
Holmwood House, Colchester	A AA G I O
Loyola Preparatory School, Buckhurst Hill	AA
New Hall School, Chelmsford	
Entry age: 11, 13, 16	6 A AA D I O
Park School for Girls, Ilford	AA
St Aubyn's School, Woodford Green	AA
St Hilda's School, Westcliff-on-Sea	O
St John's School, Billericay	O
St Margaret's School, Halstead Entry age: 8+	A AA G I
St Mary's School, Colchester Entry age: 11+	O
St Nicholas School, Harlow	6 A AA G I

GLOUCESTERSHIRE

Berkhampstead School, Cheltenham	AA G I
Bredon School, Tewkesbury	A AA G O
Cheltenham College, Cheltenham	
Entry age: 13, 16	6 A AA G I O S
Cheltenham College Junior School, Cheltenham	
Entry age: 11+	A AA G I
The Cheltenham Ladies' College,	
Cheltenham	6 A AA G I
Dean Close Preparatory School, Cheltenham	AA G I O
Dean Close School, Cheltenham	
Entry age: 11+, 13+, 16+	6 A AA D G I O
Hatherop Castle School, Cirencester	
Entry age: 7+	AA D G I O
The King's School, Gloucester	6 A AA D G I O
Rendcomb College, Cirencester	
Entry age: 11, 13, 16	6 A AA D G I O
The Richard Pate School, Cheltenham Entry age: 7+	AA
Rose Hill School, Wotton-under-Edge	A AA D G I O
St Edward's School Cheltenham,	
Cheltenham	6 A AA D G I
Westonbirt School, Tetbury	6 A AA D G I O S
Wycliffe, Stonehouse	6 A AA D G I O
Wycliffe Preparatory School, Stonehouse	
Entry age: 11	A AA D G I

HAMPSHIRE

Alton Convent School, Alton Entry age: 11/16	6 AA I
Ballard School, New Milton Entry age: 7	A AA G I O
Bedales School, Petersfield	6 A AA I
Boundary Oak School, Fareham	AA I
Brockwood Park School, Bramdean	O
Churchers College, Petersfield	6 AA I
Ditcham Park School, Petersfield Entry age: 11	AA I
Dunhurst (Bedales Junior School), Petersfield	I

Durlston Court, New Milton Entry age: Over 7	
in September of year of entry	A AA G I
Farnborough Hill, Farnborough	6 AA G I
The Gregg School, Southampton	A AA I
Hampshire Collegiate School UCST,	
Romsey	6 A AA D G I O S
Highfield School, Liphook	AA
Hordle Walhampton School, Lymington	AA I O
King Edward VI School, Southampton	
Entry age: 11+, 13+	6 A AA D I S
Lord Wandsworth College, Hook	
Entry age: 11+, 13+, 16+	6 A AA D G I O
Marycourt School, Gosport Entry age: 7	O
Mayville High School, Southsea	A AA D G I
Meoncross School, Fareham Entry age: 11	AA
The Pilgrims' School, Winchester	I
The Portsmouth Grammar School,	
Portsmouth	6 A AA D G I O S
Portsmouth High School GDST, Southsea	
Entry age: 11+, 13+, 16+	6 A AA D G I
Prince's Mead School, Winchester	A AA G I
Rookesbury Park School, Portsmouth	AA I
Rookwood School, Andover	AA G I
St John's College, Southsea	6 AA G I O
St Mary's College, Southampton	AA
St Neot's School, Hook	O
St Nicholas' School, Fleet Entry age: 11, 13	AA I O
St Swithun's School, Winchester	
Entry age: 11+, 13+, 16+	6 AA I
Sherborne House School, Eastleigh	A AA G I O
Sherfield School, Hook	6 A AA D G I O S
Stockton House School, Fleet	AA O
The Stroud School, Romsey	A AA D G I O
Winchester College, Winchester	
Entry age: 13, 16	6 AA I
Wykeham House School, Fareham	AA
Yateley Manor Preparatory School, Yateley	
Entry age: 7+	AA G I O

HEREFORDSHIRE

The Hereford Cathedral School, Hereford	6 A AA I
Lucton School, Leominster	
Entry age: 11, 13, 16	6 A AA D G I O S
St Richard's, Bromyard	AA

HERTFORDSHIRE

Abbot's Hill School, Hemel Hempstead	
Entry age: 11	A AA G I O
Aldenham School, Elstree	A AA G I O
Arts Educational School, Tring Park, Tring	6 D I O
Berkhamsted Collegiate Preparatory School,	
Berkhamsted	AA
Berkhamsted Collegiate School, Berkhamsted	6 A AA G I
Bishop's Stortford College, Bishop's Stortford	
Entry age: 11+, 13+, 16+	6 A AA I O
Bishop's Stortford College Junior School,	
Bishop's Stortford	A AA I
Egerton Rothesay School, Berkhamsted	
Entry age: 5+, 16+	A AA G I

Haberdashers' Aske's Boys' School, Elstree
Entry age: 11, 13   AA I
Haberdashers' Aske's School for Girls, Elstree   AA I
Haileybury, Hertford
Entry age: 11, 13, 16   6 A AA I O
Haresfoot Preparatory School, Berkhamsted   A AA D I
Heath Mount School, Hertford Entry age: 7+, 11+ A AA
Immanuel College, Bushey Entry age: 11/16   6 A AA I
Lockers Park, Hemel Hempstead   A AA G I O
The Princess Helena College, Hitchin
Entry age: 11–18   6 A AA D G I
The Purcell School, Bushey   I
Queenswood, Hatfield   6 AA D G I
The Royal Masonic School for Girls, Rickmansworth
Entry age: 7, 11, 16   6 A AA D G I O
St Albans High School for Girls, St Albans
Entry age: 11+, 13+, 16+   6 I O
St Albans School, St Albans
Entry age: 11+, 13+, 16+   6 A AA I
St Andrew's Montessori School, Watford   AA O
St Christopher School, Letchworth   6 AA
St Columba's College, St Albans
Entry age: 11+/13+   6 AA I O
St Edmund's College and St Hugh's School,
Ware   6 A AA G I O
St Francis' College, Letchworth Garden City 6 AA D G I
St Joseph's in the Park, Hertford   O
St Margaret's School, Bushey   6 A AA I O
Sherrardswood School, Welwyn   6 AA O
Stanborough School, Watford   AA G I
Westbrook Hay Preparatory School,
Hemel Hempstead Entry age: 8+   AA G O

ISLE OF MAN

King William's College, Castletown   6 A AA D G I O

ISLE OF WIGHT

Ryde School, Ryde   6 AA I

KENT

Ashford School, Ashford   6 A AA D G I O
Babington House School, Chislehurst   AA D G I O
Baston School, Bromley   AA O
Beechwood Sacred Heart School, Tunbridge Wells
Entry age: 11+, 13+   6 A AA D G I
Bell Bedgebury International School, Cranbrook   AA
Benenden School, Cranbrook
Entry age: 11, 13, 16   6 A AA G I
Bethany School, Cranbrook
Entry age: 11+, 13+, 16+   6 A AA D G I
Bickley Park School, Bromley   AA G I
Bishop Challoner RC School, Bromley
Entry age: 11+   AA I
Bromley High School GDST, Bromley
Entry age: 11/16+   6 A AA G I
Cobham Hall, Gravesend   6 A AA D G I O S
Combe Bank School, Nr Sevenoaks
Entry age: 7+   6 AA G I
Cranbrook School, Cranbrook   I

Darul Uloom London, Chislehurst   AA G O S
Derwent Lodge School for Girls, Tonbridge   AA
Dover College, Dover
Entry age: 11, 13, 16   6 A AA G I O
Duke of York's Royal Military School, Dover 6 A AA G I
Elliott Park School, Sheerness   O
Farringtons School, Chislehurst   6 A AA D G I
Fosse Bank School, Tonbridge   G
Gad's Hill School, Rochester
Entry age: 11   A AA D G I O
Haddon Dene School, Broadstairs   O
Hilden Grange School, Tonbridge   AA I
Holmewood House, Tunbridge Wells   AA
Kent College, Canterbury
Entry age: 11, 13, 16+   6 A AA G I O
Kent College Pembury, Tunbridge Wells
Entry age: 11, 13, 16   6 A AA D G I O
King's Preparatory School, Rochester   AA I
The King's School, Canterbury   6 A AA I
King's School Rochester, Rochester   6 AA I
Merton Court Preparatory School, Sidcup   AA D G I O
Northbourne Park School, Deal   A AA G I O
Rochester Independent College, Rochester 6 A AA D I O S
Sackville School, Tonbridge   6 A AA D G I
St Christopher's School, Canterbury   O
St Edmunds Junior School, Canterbury
Entry age: 11   AA G I
St Edmund's School Canterbury, Canterbury
Entry age: 11+, 13+, 16+   6 A AA D G I O
St Lawrence College Junior School, Ramsgate   AA G O
St Lawrence College, Ramsgate
Entry age: 8, 11, 13, 16   6 A AA G I O
St Michael's School, Sevenoaks Entry age: 7 AA G I O
St Ronan's School, Hawkhurst Entry age: 11   AA
Sevenoaks School, Sevenoaks
Entry age: 11+, 13+, 16+   6 A AA G I O
Solefield School, Sevenoaks   I
Spring Grove School, Ashford
Entry age: 7+   A AA D G I O S
Sutton Valence School, Maidstone
Entry age: 11+, 13+, 16+   6 A AA D G I O
Tonbridge School, Tonbridge
Entry age: 13+, 16+   6 A AA D G I
Walthamstow Hall, Sevenoaks
Entry age: 11+, 13+, 16+   6 A AA D G I
Wellesley House School, Broadstairs   AA G I
Yardley Court Preparatory School, Tonbridge   AA O

LANCASHIRE

Arnold School, Blackpool
Entry age: 11+, 16+   6 A AA D G I O
Bury Grammar School Boys, Bury   6 AA
Bury Grammar School Girls, Bury Entry age: 11   AA
Clevelands Preparatory School, Bolton   AA O
Firwood Manor Prep School, Oldham   AA O
Heathland College, Accrington   AA I
The Hulme Grammar School for Girls, Oldham   AA
King Edward VII and Queen Mary School,
Lytham St Annes Entry age: 11, 16   6 AA G I
Kingswood College Trust, Ormskirk   AA G I
Kirkham Grammar School, Preston   6 AA G I

Queen Elizabeth's Grammar School, Blackburn
    Entry age: 11+   AA S
Rossall Junior School, Fleetwood   6 A AA G I O
Rossall School, Fleetwood
    Entry age: 11, 13, 16   6 A AA G I O S
St Anne's College Grammar School,
    Lytham St Annes   6 AA
St Joseph's School, Park Hill, Burnley   I
St Mary's Hall, Stonyhurst   A AA I O
Stonyhurst College, Clitheroe
    Entry age: 13, 16   6 A AA I O
Westholme School, Blackburn   6 A AA I

LEICESTERSHIRE

Brooke House College, Market Harborough   6 AA G O
The Dixie Grammar School, Market Bosworth
    Entry age: 10, 11, 14, 16   6 A AA G I
Irwin College, Leicester Entry age: 14, 16   AA
Leicester Grammar School, Leicester   6 A AA G I O
Leicester High School For Girls, Leicester   6 AA I
Loughborough Grammar School, Loughborough
    Entry age: 10+, 11+, 13+, 16+   6 AA I
Loughborough High School, Loughborough   AA I
Ratcliffe College, Leicester
    Entry age: 11+, 13+, 16+   6 AA I
St Crispin's School, Leicester
    Entry age: 7+, 11+, 13+   AA G
Stoneygate School, Leicester   AA

LINCOLNSHIRE

Copthill School, Stamford Entry age: 11   AA
Fen School, Sleaford Entry age: 7   AA
The Grantham Preparatory School, Grantham   I
Kirkstone House School, Bourne   A AA G I O
Lincoln Minster School, Lincoln   6 A AA G I O
Maypole House School, Alford   AA O
Stamford High School, Stamford   6 A AA I O
Stamford School, Stamford   6 A AA I
Witham Hall, Bourne   AA O

NORTH EAST LINCOLNSHIRE

St James' School, Grimsby   6 AA G I O

LONDON

Abercorn School, NW8   O
Albemarle Independent College, W1K
    Entry age: 14+, 19+   AA
Alleyn's School, SE22
    Entry age: 11+, 16+   6 A AA D G I O S
Ashbourne Independent Sixth Form
    College, W8   6 A AA D G I O S
Ashbourne Middle School, W8
    Entry age: 13/16   6 A AA D O S
Barbara Speake Stage School, W3   O
Belmont (Mill Hill Preparatory School), NW7
    Entry age: 11   AA D I S
Blackheath High School GDST, SE3
    Entry age: 11+/16+   6 A AA G I

Blackheath Preparatory School, SE3   AA
Brampton College, NW4   AA
Cameron House School, SW3   AA
Channing School, N6   6 AA I
Chelsea Independent College, SW6 6 A AA D G I O S
City of London School, EC4V
    Entry age: 11+, 13+, 16+   6 AA I
City of London School for Girls, EC2Y
    Entry age: 11, 16   6 A AA D I
Colfe's School, SE12   6 A AA G I
Connaught House, W2 Entry age: 6, 8   A AA I O
David Game College, W11   AA
Davies Laing and Dick, W1U   6 AA O
Devonshire House Preparatory School, NW3   AA I
Duff Miller, SW7   6 A AA D O S
Dulwich College, SE21   6 A AA G I
Durston House, W5   AA
Ealing College Upper School, W13   6 AA
Ealing Independent College, W5   AA
Eaton House The Manor, SW4
    Entry age: 8+   A AA G I O
Eaton House The Manor Girls' School, SW4   AA G I O
Eaton Square School, SW1V   O
Emanuel School, SW11   6 A AA D G I O
Eridge House Preparatory, SW6   A AA D G
Fine Arts College Hampstead, NW3   6 O
Forest School, E17   6 A AA D G I S
Francis Holland School, Regent's Park NW1,
    NW1   6 AA I
Francis Holland School, SW1, SW1W
    Entry age: 11+, 16+   6 AA I
Fulham Prep School (Prep Dept), W14 A AA G I
The Godolphin and Latymer School, W6   I
Hall School Wimbledon, SW20   A AA D G I O
The Hampshire School, SW3   AA I O
The Hampshire Schools (The Early Years Section),
    SW7   AA I O
Hampstead Hill Pre-Preparatory & Nursery School,
    NW3   O
Harvington School, W5   D I
Hendon Preparatory School, NW4   AA G O
Highgate School, N6   AA I
Hill House International Junior School, SW1X
    Entry age: 11   A I
The Hurlingham School, SW15 Entry age: 7+   O
Ibstock Place School, SW15   6 A AA D G I O
The Italia Conti Academy of Theatre Arts, EC1M D
James Allen's Girls' School, SE22
    Entry age: 11+, 16+   6 A AA G I
Keble Preparatory School, N21
    Entry age: 11   AA G O
King's College Junior School, SW19   AA I
King's College School, SW19   6 A AA I
Knightsbridge School, SW1X   AA
Lansdowne College, W2 Entry age: 14+, 16+ 6 AA O
Latymer Prep School, W6   AA
Latymer Upper School, W6   6 A AA D G I
The Lloyd Williamson School, W10   O
Lycee Francais Charles de Gaulle, SW7   6 AA
The Lyceum, EC2A   I
Mander Portman Woodward, SW7   6 AA
Mill Hill School, NW7   6 A AA D G I O S

More House, SW1X	6 AA I
The Mount School, NW7	6 AA I
Newton Prep School, SW8	AA
Normanhurst School, E4	
Entry age: 11	AA
North Bridge House Lower Prep School, NW1	AA I
North Bridge House Senior School, NW1	I
The North London International School,	
N11	6 A AA D G I O
Notting Hill and Ealing High School GDST, W13	
Entry age: 11+, 16+	6 A AA D I O
Orchard House School, W4	AA
Palmers Green High School, N21 Entry age: 11+	AA I
Parkgate House School, SW4	AA I O
The Pointer School, SE3	AA D G O
Portland Place School, W1B	6 A AA D G I
Prospect House School, SW15	AA O
Putney High School GDST, SW15	
Entry age: 11+, 16+	6 A AA D G I S
Queen's College, W1G	6 A AA I
Queen's Gate School, SW7	6 O
Riverston School, SE12	AA G I O
The Roche School, SW18 Entry age: 7	AA
The Royal School, Hampstead, NW3	
Entry age: 7, 16	A AA I
St Augustine's Priory, W5	6 I O
St Benedict's School, W5 Entry age: 11+	AA G
St Dunstan's College, SE6	
Entry age: 11+ and Sixth Form	6 A AA D G I
St Margaret's School, NW3	AA
St Mary's School Hampstead, NW3	A AA G I
St Paul's Cathedral School, EC4M	I
St Paul's Girls' School, W6	6 A AA I
St Paul's Preparatory School, SW13	AA I
St Paul's School, SW13	6 AA I
Sinclair House School, SW6	O
South Hampstead High School, NW3	6 AA I
Southbank International School, Westminster, W1B	6
Streatham and Clapham High School, SW16	
Entry age: 11, 16	6 AA I S
Sussex House School, SW1X	I
Sydenham High School GDST, SE26	
Entry age: 11/16+	6 AA I
Sylvia Young Theatre School, NW1	
Entry age: 10–14	D I
Thomas's Preparatory School, SW11	O
University College School, NW3	AA I
Virgo Fidelis, SE19 Entry age: 7–11	AA
Welsh School of London, NW10	O
Westminster Abbey Choir School, SW1P	I
Westminster Cathedral Choir School, SW1P	I
Westminster School, SW1P	AA I
Westminster Tutors, SW7	6 AA O
Westminster Under School, SW1P Entry age: 11+	I
Willington School, SW19	AA
The White House Prep & Woodentops Kindergarten,	
SW12	AA
Wimbledon High School GDST, SW19	6 AA I S

GREATER MANCHESTER

Abbey College, Manchester	6 AA
Branwood Preparatory School, Eccles	O
Bridgewater School, Manchester Entry age: 11/16+	6 AA
Chetham's School of Music, Manchester	I
Manchester High School for Girls, Manchester	
Entry age: 11, 16	AA G I
St Bede's College, Manchester	6 AA I
William Hulme's Grammar School, Manchester	
Entry age: 11/16+	6 AA I

MERSEYSIDE

Avalon Preparatory School, Wirral Entry age: 7	AA
Birkenhead High School GDST, Wirral	6 AA I
Birkenhead School, Wirral	6 AA I
Kingsmead School, Wirral Entry age: 7/11+	AA G I
Liverpool College, Liverpool	6 A AA D G I O
Merchant Taylors' Boys' Schools, Liverpool	6 AA G
Merchant Taylors' Girls' School, Liverpool	6 AA O
Runnymede St Edward's School, Liverpool	I
St Mary's College, Liverpool	
Entry age: 11/16+	6 A AA G I
Streatham House School, Liverpool	AA
Tower College, Prescot Entry age: 7, 11	AA I

MIDDLESEX

Buckingham College Preparatory School, Pinner	AA
Buckingham College School, Harrow	6 AA
Halliford School, Shepperton	
Entry age: 11+	6 A AA D G I
Hampton School, Hampton	
Entry age: 11+, 13	A AA I O
Harrow School, Harrow on the Hill	
Entry age: 13, 16	6 A AA G I
Heathfield School, Pinner	6 AA I
The John Lyon School, Harrow	6 A AA D G I O
The Lady Eleanor Holles School, Hampton	6 AA I
Merchant Taylors' School, Northwood	6 AA I
North London Collegiate, Edgware	6 AA I
Northwood College, Northwood	
Entry age: 11+, 16+	6 A AA G I
St Catherine's School, Twickenham	
Entry age: 11	A AA G I
St David's School, Ashford	
Entry age: 11+, 16+	6 AA G I O
St Helen's School, Northwood	6 A AA D G I
St James Independent School for Boys (Senior),	
Twickenham	I
Sunflower Montessori School, Twickenham	I
Twickenham Preparatory School, Hampton	AA G I O

NORFOLK

All Saints School, Norwich	AA I
Glebe House School, Hunstanton	A AA G I O
Gresham's Preparatory School, Holt	A AA D G I O
Gresham's School, Holt	6 A AA D G I O
Hethersett Old Hall School, Norwich	6 AA G O
Langley Preparatory School & Nursery, Norwich	AA I
Langley School, Norwich	
Entry age: 11, 13, 16	6 A AA D G I O
The New Eccles Hall School, Norwich	
Entry age: 8	AA I O

Norwich High School for Girls GDST, Norwich   6 AA I
Norwich School, Norwich
   Entry age: 9+, 11+, 16+   6 A AA D G I
Sacred Heart School, Swaffham Entry age: 11+   AA
Taverham Hall Preparatory School, Norwich   AA G I
Town Close House Preparatory School, Norwich
   Entry age: 7+   AA G I
Wood Dene School, Norwich   A AA D

NORTHAMPTONSHIRE

Beachborough School, Brackley Entry age: 8–11   AA I O
Bosworth Independent College, Northampton   AA O S
Great Houghton Preparatory School,
   Northampton   A AA I
Maidwell Hall School, Northampton   A AA G I
Northampton High School, Northampton
   Entry age: 11, 13, 16   6 A AA D G I
Northamptonshire Grammar School,
   Pitsford   6 A AA D G I
Oundle School, Nr Peterborough   6 A AA D I O
Quinton House School, Northampton   6 AA O
Winchester House School, Brackley   A AA G I O

NORTHUMBERLAND

Longridge Towers School, Berwick-upon-Tweed
   Entry age: 9, 11, 13, 16   6 AA G I
Mowden Hall School, Stocksfield   AA
St Oswald's School, Alnwick   AA O

NOTTINGHAMSHIRE

Coteswood House School, Nottingham   A AA D G I O
Hollygirt School, Nottingham
   Entry age: 11+   AA I
Hollygirt School, Nottingham   AA I
Nottingham High School for Girls GDST,
   Nottingham   O
Ranby House School, Retford
   Entry age: 11+   A AA D G I O
Trent College, Nottingham   6 A AA D G I
Wellow House School, Newark   A AA G I O
Worksop College, Worksop   6 A AA G I O

OXFORDSHIRE

Abacus College, Oxford   O
Abingdon School, Abingdon   6 A AA D G I
Bloxham School, Banbury
   Entry age: 11, 13, 16   6 A AA G I O
Christ Church Cathedral School, Oxford   I
Cokethorpe School, Witney   6 A AA D G I O
Cranford House School, Wallingford   A AA D G I O
d'Overbroeck's College, Oxford   6 A AA D I S
Ferndale Preparatory School, Faringdon   AA
Headington School, Oxford
   Entry age: 11, 13, 16   6 A AA D G I
Abingdon Preparatory School, Abingdon   AA
Kingham Hill School, Chipping Norton
   Entry age: 11+, 13+   6 A AA D G I O

Leckford Place School, Oxford   A AA D I
Magdalen College School, Oxford
   Entry age: 7+, 13+, 16+   A AA G I
New College School, Oxford Entry age: 8   I
Our Lady's Abingdon School, Abingdon   6 A AA I
Oxford High School GDST, Oxford   6 A AA G I
Oxford Tutorial College, Oxford   AA
Radley College, Abingdon Entry age: 13+ 6 A AA D I O
Rye St Antony School, Oxford   6 AA O
St Andrew's, Wantage   AA
St Clare's, Oxford, Oxford Entry age: 16+   6 AA O
St Edward's School, Oxford   6 A AA D G I O
The School of St Helen & St Katharine, Abingdon 6 AA I
Shiplake College, Henley-on-Thames
   Entry age: 13+, 16+   6 A AA D G I
Sibford School, Banbury   6 A AA I
Tudor Hall School, Banbury
   Entry age: 11, 13, 16   A AA D G I
Wychwood School, Oxford   6 A AA I S
Oakham School, Oakham   6 A AA D G I S
Uppingham School, Uppingham   6 A AA I O

SHROPSHIRE

Adcote School for Girls, Shrewsbury   6 AA
Bedstone College, Bucknell   6 A AA G I O
Concord College, Shrewsbury   6 AA O S
Dower House School, Bridgnorth
   Entry age: 7, 8, 9   AA O
Ellesmere College, Ellesmere   6 A AA D G I O S
Kingsland Grange, Shrewsbury Entry age: 7–11   AA G I
Moor Park School, Ludlow   AA O
Moreton Hall School, Oswestry
   Entry age: 11+, 13+, 16+   6 A AA D G I O
The Old Hall School, Telford   AA I
Oswestry School, Oswestry
   Entry age: 9+, 11+, 13+, 16+   6 A AA G I O
Oswestry School Bellan House, Oswestry   AA I O
Packwood Haugh School, Shrewsbury   A AA G I
Prestfelde Preparatory School, Shrewsbury
   Entry age: 7+, 11+   A AA G I O
Shrewsbury High School GDST, Shrewsbury   6 AA I
Shrewsbury School, Shrewsbury   6 A AA G I O
Wrekin College, Telford
   Entry age: 11, 13, 16   6 A AA G I O

SOMERSET

All Hallows, Shepton Mallet Entry age: 11+   A I O
Bruton School for Girls, Bruton
   Entry age: 11+, 13+, 16+   6 A AA D G I O S
Chilton Cantelo School, Yeovil   O
Downside School, Bath   6 A AA G I O
Hazlegrove (King's Bruton Preparatory School),
   Yeovil   AA G I
King's Bruton, Bruton   6 A AA D G I O
King's College, Taunton   6 A AA D G I O S
King's Hall, Taunton   AA G I
Millfield Preparatory School, Glastonbury
   Entry age: 7–13   A AA G I O
Millfield School, Street
   Entry age: 13, 14, 16   6 A AA G I O

The Park School, Yeovil Entry age: 8–18+   6 A AA D I
Perrott Hill School, Crewkerne   A AA D G I O
Queen's College Junior, Pre-Prep & Nursery Schools,
    Taunton   A AA D G I O
Queen's College, Taunton   6 A AA D G I
Taunton International Study Centre (TISC), Taunton   AA
Taunton Preparatory School, Taunton
    Entry age: 11+   AA G I
Taunton School, Taunton   6 AA G I O
Wellington School, Wellington
    Entry age: 10+, 11+, 13+, 16+   6 AA I O
Wells Cathedral Junior School, Wells
    Entry age: 8–11   AA I
Wells Cathedral School, Wells
    Entry age: 11, 13, 16   6 AA I S

BATH & NORTH EAST SOMERSET

King Edward's School, Bath, Bath
    Entry age: 11–18   6 A AA D G I
Kingswood School, Bath   6 A AA D G I O
Monkton Prep , Bath   AA
Monkton Senior School, Bath   6 A AA D G I O
Paragon School, Prior Park College Junior,
    Bath   AA G I O
Prior Park College, Bath   6 A AA D G I O
The Royal High School, Bath
    Entry age: 11/16+   6 A AA D G I

NORTH SOMERSET

Sidcot School, Winscombe   6 A AA I O

STAFFORDSHIRE

Abbots Bromley School for Girls, Abbots Bromley
    Entry age: 11/16+   6 A AA D G I
Abbotsholme School, Uttoxeter
    Entry age: 11+, 13+, 16+   6 A AA D G I O
Chase Academy, Cannock
    Entry age: 3+, 18+   AA G I O
Denstone College, Uttoxeter
    Entry age: 11, 13, 16   6 A AA D G I O
Edenhurst School, Newcastle-under-Lyme   O
Lichfield Cathedral School, Lichfield
    Entry age: 7, 9, 11   A AA D G I O
Newcastle-under-Lyme School,
    Newcastle-under-Lyme   6 AA G
St Dominic's Independent Junior School,
    Stoke-on-Trent Entry age: 8+   AA
St Dominic's Priory School, Stone   6 A AA D G I O
St Dominic's School, Stafford
    Entry age: 11, 12   6 A AA D G I
Stafford Grammar School, Stafford   6 A AA D G I O
Vernon Lodge Preparatory School, Brewood   AA O
Yarlet School, Stafford Entry age: 11+   A AA D G I O

STOCKTON-ON-TEES

Teesside High School, Eaglescliffe   6 AA I
Yarm School, Yarm Entry age: 7+, 11+, 16+   6 AA I S

SUFFOLK

Amberfield School, Ipswich Entry age: 11/13+   A AA G I
Brandeston Hall, The Preparatory School for
    Framlingham College, Brandeston
    Entry age: 11+/13+   A AA D I O
Cherry Trees School, Bury St Edmunds   AA
Culford School, Bury St Edmunds   6 A AA D G I O S
Fairstead House School, Newmarket   AA
Felixstowe International College, Felixstowe   AA O
Finborough School, Stowmarket   6 A AA G I O
Framlingham College, Woodbridge   6 A AA D G I O S
Ipswich High School GDST, Ipswich
    Entry age: 11+   6 AA I
Ipswich School, Ipswich
    Entry age: 11, 13, 16   6 A AA G I O
Moreton Hall Preparatory School, Bury St Edmunds   AA I
Orwell Park, Ipswich
    Entry age: 7+   A AA I O
The Royal Hospital School, Ipswich
    Entry age: 11+   6 A AA G I O
Saint Felix School, Southwold
    Entry age: 11, 13, 16   6 A AA D G I
St Joseph's College, Ipswich   6 A AA D G I O
South Lee Preparatory School, Bury St Edmunds
    Entry age: 8+, 11+   AA O
Stoke College, Sudbury   AA I
Woodbridge School, Woodbridge   6 A AA D G I O

SURREY

Aberdour, Tadworth   AA
Amesbury, Hindhead   AA G I
Barfield School, Farnham   AA G I O
Barrow Hills School, Godalming   A AA G I
Box Hill School, Dorking   6 A AA D G I O
Cambridge Tutors College, Croydon   6 AA
Canbury School, Kingston-upon-Thames   AA O
Caterham School, Caterham   6 A AA D G I O S
Charterhouse, Godalming   6 A AA G I O
City of London Freemen's School,
    Ashtead   6 A AA D G I
Claremont Fan Court School, Esher   6 A AA D G I
Cranleigh Preparatory School, Cranleigh   AA I
Cranleigh School, Cranleigh
    Entry age: 13+, 16+   6 A AA I O
Croydon High School GDST, South Croydon   6 A AA G I
Cumnor House School, South Croydon   AA G I
Danes Hill School, Leatherhead   AA
Duke of Kent School, Guildford
    Entry age: 7+, 10+, 11+   AA G I
Dunottar School, Reigate Entry age: 11, 14, 16   6 AA I
Edgeborough, Farnham   O
Epsom College, Epsom
    Entry age: 13+, 16+   6 A AA D G I O
Essendene Lodge School, Caterham   AA O
Ewell Castle School, Epsom
    Entry age: 11+, 13+, 16+   6 A AA D G I O
Feltonfleet School, Cobham   A AA I O
Frensham Heights School, Farnham   6 A AA D G I
Greenacre School for Girls, Banstead   6 A AA D G I O
Guildford High School, Guildford   6 AA I
Hampton Court House, East Molesey   AA I

Haslemere Preparatory School,
Haslemere   A AA D G I O
Hawley Place School, Camberley
Entry age: 7, 11   A AA D G I O
The Hawthorns School, Redhill   AA I O
Hazelwood School, Oxted   AA D G I O
Hoe Bridge School, Woking Entry age: 7+   AA O
Homefield School, Sutton   A AA G I O
Hurtwood House, Dorking Entry age: 16   6 D O S
King Edward's School Witley,
Godalming   6 A AA D G I O S
Kingston Grammar School,
Kingston-upon-Thames   6 A AA G I
Kingswood House School, Epsom   AA G
Lanesborough, Guildford Entry age: 8+   I
Lingfield Notre Dame School, Lingfield
Entry age: 11+   6 AA I O
Lodge School, Purley   AA I
Lyndhurst School, Camberley   AA
Manor House School, Leatherhead
Entry age: 7+, 11+   A AA D G I
Marymount International School,
Kingston-upon-Thames Entry age: 11, 16   AA O
Milbourne Lodge School, Esher   AA
New Lodge School, Dorking   O
Notre Dame Preparatory School, Cobham   O
Notre Dame Senior School, Cobham   6 AA
Oakfield School, Woking Entry age: 7+, 11+   AA I O
Old Palace of John Whitgift School, Croydon   AA I
Prior's Field School, Godalming
Entry age: 11, 16   6 A AA D G I O
Reed's School, Cobham   6 A AA D G I O
Reigate Grammar School, Reigate   6 AA I O
Reigate St Mary's Preparatory and Choir School,
Reigate Entry age: 8+   I
Ripley Court School, Woking   A AA D G I O
Rokeby School, Kingston-upon-Thames   A AA G I
Royal Grammar School, Guildford
Entry age: 11+/13+   A AA I
Royal Russell School, Croydon
Entry age: 11+/16   6 AA D I
The Royal School, Haslemere
Entry age: 11+, 13+, 16+   6 A AA D G I O
St. Andrew's (Woking) School Trust, Woking
Entry age: 7+   A AA G I O
St Catherine's School, Guildford
Entry age: 11/16+   6 A AA G I O
St Edmund's School, Hindhead
Entry age: 7/8   A AA D G I O
St George's College, Weybridge   6 A AA I O
St Hilary's School, Godalming   A AA D I
St Ives School, Haslemere   A AA D G I O
St John's School, Leatherhead
Entry age: 13+, 16+   6 A AA G I O
St Teresa's School, Dorking   6 A AA D G I O
Seaton House School, Sutton   AA
Sir William Perkins's School, Chertsey   6 A AA I
Stowford College, Sutton Entry age: 11, 14   AA G O
Surbiton High School,
Kingston-upon-Thames   6 A AA G I
Sutton High School GDST, Sutton
Entry age: 11+, 16+   6 A AA D G I O
Tormead School, Guildford   6 A AA I

Trinity School, Croydon
Entry age: 10+, 11+, 13+, 16+   6 A AA G I O
West Dene School, Purley Entry age: 7   I
Whitgift School, South Croydon
Entry age: 10–13, 16   6 A AA D G I O
Woldingham School, Woldingham
Entry age: 11+   6 A AA D G I
Woodcote House School, Windlesham   A AA G I O
Yehudi Menuhin School, Cobham   I

EAST SUSSEX

Battle Abbey School, Battle
Entry age: 13/16+   6 A AA D G I O
Bellerbys College, Hove   6 AA
Bricklehurst Manor Preparatory, Wadhurst   AA
Brighton and Hove High School GDST, Brighton   6 AA
Brighton College, Brighton
Entry age: 13+, 16+   6 A AA D G I O
Brighton College Prep School, Brighton
Entry age: 11+   AA O
Buckswood School, Hastings   AA G I
Claremont School, St Leonards-on-Sea   A AA D G I O
Eastbourne College, Eastbourne
Entry age: 13, 16   6 A AA D G I S
The Fold School, Hove Entry age: 3+   AA I
Lancing College Preparatory School at Mowden, Hove
Entry age: 7+, 11+   AA
Lewes Old Grammar School, Lewes   6 AA I O
Moira House School, Eastbourne   O
Moira House Girls School, Eastbourne   6 AA D G I O
Newlands School, Seaford   6 A AA D G I O
Roedean School, Brighton
Entry age: 11+, 12+, 13+, 16+   6 A AA D G I S
St Andrew's School, Eastbourne   A AA D G I O
St Aubyns School, Brighton   A AA D G I O
St Bede's Prep School, Eastbourne   A AA D G I
St Bede's School, Hailsham   6 A AA D G I
St Leonards-Mayfield School, Mayfield
Entry age: 11, 13, 16   6 A AA D G I
St Mary's Hall, Brighton   6 A AA D G I
Stonelands School of Ballet & Theatre Arts, Hove   D O
Vinehall School, Robertsbridge   A AA D G I O

WEST SUSSEX

Ardingly College, Haywards Heath
Entry age: 7+, 11+, 13+ , 16+   6 A AA D G I O
Ardingly College Junior School, Haywards Heath
Entry age: 11+   A AA G I
Arundale Preparatory School, Pulborough
Entry age: 7–11   A AA G I O
Brambletye, East Grinstead Entry age: 9+   I
Burgess Hill School for Girls, Burgess Hill 6 A AA D G I O
Conifers School, Midhurst   A AA G I O
Copthorne Prep School, Copthorne   A AA D G I
Dorset House School, Pulborough   AA I
Farlington School, Horsham   6 A AA D G I O
Great Ballard School, Chichester
Entry age: 7   A AA D G I O

Great Walstead, Haywards Heath
Entry age: 7–11   AA D G I
Handcross Park School, Haywards Heath
Entry age: 7–11   AA G I O
Hurstpierpoint College, Hurstpierpoint   6 A AA D G I O
Lancing College, Lancing   6 A AA D G I O
Lavant House, Chichester Entry age: 11, 13   6 AA
Oakwood School, Chichester   AA O
Our Lady of Sion School, Worthing   6 AA
The Prebendal School, Chichester Entry age: 7   I
Seaford College, Petworth
Entry age: 10+, 11+, 13+   6 A AA G I O
Shoreham College, Shoreham-by-Sea   AA G I O
Slindon College, Arundel Entry age: 10   AA O
Stoke Brunswick, East Grinstead   AA I O
Tavistock & Summerhill School, Haywards Heath   AA
The Towers Convent School, Steyning   AA D I O
Westbourne House School, Chichester   I
Windlesham House, Pulborough   AA G I O
Worth School, Turners Hill
Entry age: 11, 13, 16   6 AA G I O

TYNE AND WEAR

Central Newcastle High School GDST,
Newcastle upon Tyne Entry age: 11+, 16+   6 AA
Dame Allan's Boys School, Newcastle upon Tyne   6 AA
Dame Allan's Girls School, Newcastle upon Tyne
Entry age: 11   6 AA I
The King's School, Tynemouth
Entry age: 11+   6 A AA I O
Newcastle School for Boys, Newcastle upon Tyne   AA
Newcastle Upon Tyne Church High School,
Newcastle upon Tyne   AA I
Sunderland High School, Sunderland   6 AA I
Westfield School, Newcastle upon Tyne   6 A AA G I O

WARWICKSHIRE

Abbotsford School, Kenilworth Entry age: 7   AA
Bilton Grange, Rugby Entry age: 8+   AA G I O
The Croft Preparatory School, Stratford-upon-Avon
Entry age: 8   AA
King's High School, Warwick, Warwick   6 AA I
The Kingsley School, Leamington Spa   6 A AA D I
Princethorpe College, Rugby
Entry age: 11/18+   6 A AA G I O
Rugby School, Rugby   6 A AA G I
Warwick School, Warwick   6 A AA I

WEST MIDLANDS

Abbey College, Birmingham   6 AA O
Al Hijrah School, Birmingham   AA
Bablake Junior School, Coventry   AA
Bablake School, Coventry   6 A AA I O
Birchfield School, Wolverhampton
Entry age: 11   A AA G I O
The Blue Coat School, Birmingham
Entry age: 7+   AA I O

Coventry Prep School, Coventry Entry age: 7+   A AA I O
Edgbaston High School for Girls, Birmingham
Entry age: 11+   6 AA G I
Elmhurst School for Dance, Birmingham   6
Eversfield Preparatory School, Solihull   AA
Highclare School, Birmingham
Entry age: 11/16+   6 A AA G I O
Hydesville Tower School, Walsall   AA G I O
King Edward VI High School for Girls, Birmingham   AA
King Edward's School, Birmingham
Entry age: 11+, 13+, 16+   6 AA I
King Henry VIII School, Coventry   6 A AA I O
Norfolk House School, Birmingham   AA
Priory School, Birmingham
Entry age: 11, 16   6 A AA D G I
The Royal Wolverhampton School,
Wolverhampton   6 A AA D G I
St George's School, Edgbaston, Birmingham
Entry age: 11+   6 AA I O
Saint Martin's School, Solihull
Entry age: 11+, 16+   6 AA I
Solihull School, Solihull   6 A AA I S
Tettenhall College, Wolverhampton
Entry age: 11   6 A AA G I O
Wolverhampton Grammar School, Wolverhampton
Entry age: 11+, 13+, 16+   6 AA I O S

WILTSHIRE

Chafyn Grove School, Salisbury   A AA D G I O
Dauntsey's School, Devizes
Entry age: 11+, 13+, 16+   6 A AA D G I O S
Godolphin Preparatory School, Salisbury   AA
The Godolphin School, Salisbury   6 A AA D G I
Grittleton House School, Chippenham   A AA D G I S
Leehurst Swan, Salisbury Entry age: 7, 11, 14   A AA G I
Leaden Hall School, Salisbury   AA
Marlborough College, Marlborough
Entry age: 13+, 16+   6 A AA G I O
Norman Court Preparatory School, Salisbury
Entry age: 7, 8, 11   A AA D G I O
Pinewood School, Shrivenham Entry age: 11+   AA O
Prior Park Preparatory School, Cricklade   AA
St Francis School, Pewsey   A AA G I O
St Mary's, Calne, Calne
Entry age: 11+, 13+, 16+   6 A AA D G I O
Salisbury Cathedral School, Salisbury
Entry age: 7, 10   A AA D G I
Sandroyd School, Salisbury   AA I O
Stonar School, Melksham   6 A AA D G I O
Warminster School, Warminster
Entry age: 7, 9, 11, 13, 16   6 A AA D G I O

WORCESTERSHIRE

Abberley Hall, Worcester Entry age: 8+   AA
The Abbey College, Malvern Wells   6 AA O S
Bromsgrove Preparatory School, Bromsgrove
Entry age: 11+   AA I O
Bromsgrove School, Bromsgrove   6 A AA D G I O
Dodderhill School, Droitwich Spa Entry age: 11+   AA I

The Downs, Malvern College Preparatory School,
   Malvern   A AA D G I O
The Elms, Malvern   AA G I O
Holy Trinity School, Kidderminster   6 AA I O S
King's Hawford, Worcester Entry age: 7+, 8+   AA
The King's School, Worcester   6 AA I
The Knoll School, Kidderminster   AA
Malvern College, Malvern   6 A AA D G I O
Malvern College Preparatory and Pre-Prep School,
   Malvern   A AA D G I O
Malvern St James, Great Malvern
   Entry age: 11+, 12+, 13+, 16+   6 A AA G I
Moffats School, Worcestershire   A AA D G I O S
Moffats School, Bewdley   A AA D G I O S
RGS The Grange, Worcester   AA
RGS Worcester & The Alice Ottley School,
   Worcester   A AA I
St Mary's Convent School, Worcester
   Entry age: 11+, 16+   6 A AA G I
Saint Michael's College, Tenbury Wells   6 AA O S
Winterfold House, Kidderminster   A AA G I O

EAST RIDING OF YORKSHIRE

Hull Collegiate School, Anlaby Entry age: 11 6 A AA G I
Pocklington School, Pocklington   6 AA I O

NORTH YORKSHIRE

Ampleforth College, York
   Entry age: 13, 16   6 A AA D G I O
Ashville College, Harrogate
   Entry age: 11–18   6 A AA D G I
Aysgarth Preparatory School, Bedale   I
Belmont Grosvenor School, Harrogate   AA
Bootham School, York
   Entry age: 11+, 13+, 16+   6 AA I O
Bramcote School, Scarborough   AA G I O
Cundall Manor School, York   AA G I
Fyling Hall School, Whitby   6 AA G I O
Giggleswick Junior School, Settle
   Entry age: 10, 11   AA G I O
Giggleswick School, Settle
   Entry age: 13, 16   6 A AA D G I O
Harrogate Ladies' College, Harrogate
   Entry age: 11+, 16+   6 AA I O
Harrogate Tutorial College, Harrogate
   Entry age: 15+   6 AA O
Lisvane, Scarborough College Junior School,
   Scarborough Entry age: 7–9   AA
Malsis School, Near Skipton   AA G I O

The Minster School, York   I
The Mount School, York   6 A AA D G I O S
Queen Ethelburga's College, York
   Entry age: 11   6 A AA D G I O S
Queen Margaret's School, York   6 A AA I O
Queen Mary's School, Thirsk   A AA I
Read School, Selby Entry age: 11+, 13+, 16+   6 AA O
Ripon Cathedral Choir School, Ripon   AA I
St Martin's Ampleforth, York Entry age: 7/12+ AA G I O
St Peter's School, York Entry age: 13/16+   6 AA I O
Scarborough College & Lisvane School,
   Scarborough   6 A AA I
Terrington Hall, York   A AA D G I O
Woodleigh School, Malton   A AA D G I

SOUTH YORKSHIRE

Birkdale School, Sheffield Entry age: 11, 16   6 AA I S
Hill House School, Doncaster   A AA G I
Rudston Preparatory School, Rotherham   AA
Sheffield High School GDST, Sheffield
   Entry age: 11, 16   6 AA I O
Westbourne School, Sheffield   AA G I O

WEST YORKSHIRE

Ackworth School, Pontefract   6 A AA I
Batley Grammar School, Batley   6
Bradford Girls' Grammar School, Bradford   I
Bradford Grammar School, Bradford Entry age: 11+   I
Bronte House School, Bradford Entry age: 9   AA
Fulneck School, Leeds   6 A AA G I O
Gateways School, Leeds Entry age: 11   6 A AA D G I
Ghyll Royd School, Ilkley Entry age: 7   AA
Hipperholme Grammar School, Halifax
   Entry age: 16+   6 AA
Huddersfield Grammar School, Huddersfield   AA I
Queen Elizabeth Grammar School, Wakefield   6 AA I
The Rastrick Independent School, Brighouse
   Entry age: 11+   O
Richmond House School, Leeds Entry age: 7/8   AA
Rishworth School, Rishworth
   Entry age: 11, 16   6 AA D G I O
Silcoates School, Wakefield Entry age: 11   AA I
The Grammar School at Leeds, Leeds
   Entry age: 11+, 16+   6 AA I
Wakefield Girls' High School, Wakefield   6 AA
Wakefield Independent School, Wakefield   AA
Wakefield Tutorial Preparatory School, Leeds   O
Woodhouse Grove School, Apperley Bridge AA D G I O

NORTHERN IRELAND

COUNTY ANTRIM

Campbell College, Belfast   A AA G I
Methodist College, Belfast   6 I

COUNTY TYRONE

The Royal School Dungannon, Dungannon
   Entry age: 11–16   AA G I

SCOTLAND

ABERDEENSHIRE

Albyn School, Aberdeen	A AA G I
International School of Aberdeen, Aberdeen	6
Robert Gordons College, Aberdeen	6 AA G I O

ANGUS

Lathallan School, Montrose	A AA D G I O

ARGYLL AND BUTE

Lomond School, Helensburgh	
Entry age: 11, 16	6 AA I

CLACKMANNANSHIRE

Dollar Academy, Dollar	A I

FIFE

St Leonards School , St Andrews	6 A AA D G I

GLASGOW

Craigholme School Entry age: 12	AA
The Glasgow Academy Entry age: 11+	6 AA
The High School of Glasgow	AA
Kelvinside Academy	6 AA

LANARKSHIRE

Hamilton College, Hamilton	AA I

LOTHIAN

Cargilfield, Edinburgh	AA I O
The Edinburgh Academy, Edinburgh	6 A AA I
Fettes College, Edinburgh	6 A AA I O

George Heriot's School, Edinburgh	
Entry age: 11+	6 A AA D G I
George Watson's College, Edinburgh	6 AA G I S
Loretto Junior School, Musselburgh	
Entry age: 10/11	A AA D G I O
Loretto School, Musselburgh	6 A AA D G I O
The Mary Erskine School, Edinburgh	6 AA I
Merchiston Castle School, Edinburgh	6 A AA I O
St Margaret's School, Edinburgh	6 A AA D G I
St Mary's Music School, Edinburgh	
Entry age: 9+	I
Stewart's Melville College, Edinburgh	6 AA I

MORAYSHIRE

Gordonstoun School, Elgin	
Entry age: 9	6 A AA D G I O

PERTH AND KINROSS

Ardvreck School, Crieff	AA
Glenalmond College, Perth	
Entry age: 12, 13, 16	6 A AA G I O
Kilgraston, Perth	6 A AA G I O
Morrison's Academy, Crieff	6 AA
Strathallan School, Perth	
Entry age: 10+, 16+	6 A AA D G I O

ROXBURGHSHIRE

St Mary's Preparatory School, Melrose	O

STIRLING

Beaconhurst School	AA

WALES

BRIDGEND

St John's School, Porthcawl	AA G O

CARDIFF

The Cardiff Academy	AA
The Cathedral School Entry age: 11	AA G I
Howell's School, Llandaff GDST	
Entry age: 11, 16	6 AA I
Kings Monkton School	6 A AA G I S

CARMARTHENSHIRE

Llandovery College, Llandovery	
Entry age: 11+, 17+	A AA D G I
St Michael's School, Llanelli	6 AA D G I O

CONWY

Lyndon Preparatory School, Colwyn Bay	6 A AA D G I O S
Rydal Penrhos Senior School, Colwyn Bay	6 AA G I
St David's College, Llandudno	
Entry age: 11	6 A AA D G I O S

DENBIGHSHIRE

Howell's School, Denbigh Entry age: 11	6 A AA D G I
Ruthin School, Ruthin Entry age: 11	6 A AA D G I O S

MONMOUTHSHIRE

Haberdashers' Monmouth School For Girls,	
Monmouth	6 AA I
Llangattock School, Monmouth	O

Monmouth School, Monmouth
  Entry age: 11, 13, 16   6 AA G I
St John's-on-the-Hill, Chepstow   A AA D G I O

NEWPORT

Rougemont School   AA

PEMBROKESHIRE

Netherwood School, Saundersfoot
  Entry age: 11, 12, 13   AA

POWYS

Christ College, Brecon
  Entry age: 11, 13, 16   6 A AA G I O S

SWANSEA

Ffynone House School Entry age: 11   6 A AA D G I
Ffynone House School   A AA D G I

SCHOOLS IN CONTINENTAL EUROPE

FRANCE

Chavagnes International College,
  Chavagnes-en-Paillers, France   6 AA I O

SPAIN

King's College Madrid, Madrid, Spain   6

5.2

Bursaries and Reserved Entrance Awards

The following is compiled from information provided by schools. For further information please contact the school direct. The abbreviations used are as follows:

E	Christian Missionary or full-time worker	FO	Foreign Office
F1	The Royal Navy	H	Financial or domestic hardship
F2	The Royal Marines	M	Medical profession
F3	The Army	T	Teaching profession
F4	The Royal Air Force	+	The Clergy

ENGLAND

BEDFORSHIRE

Bedford High School for Girls, Bedford	H
Bedford Modern School, Bedford	H
Bedford Preparatory School, Bedford	F1 F2 F3 F4 H
Dame Alice Harpur School, Bedford	H
Moorlands School, Luton	H T

BERKSHIRE

The Abbey School, Reading Entry age: 11+, 16+	H
The Ark School, Reading Entry age: 5+	H T
Bearwood College, Wokingham	+ E F1 F3 F4 H
Brigidine School Windsor, Windsor Entry age: 11	H
Brockhurst and Marlston House Schools, Newbury	+ E F1 F2 F3 F4 FO H M T
Cheam School, Newbury	H
Dolphin School, Reading	H T
Elstree School, Reading Entry age: 7	+ H T
Eton College, Windsor	H
Heathfield St Mary's School, Ascot Entry age: 11+, 13+, 16+	+ F1 F2 F3 F4 FO H
Hemdean House School, Reading Entry age: 11+	H
Highfield School, Maidenhead Entry age: 7+, 12+	H
Horris Hill School, Newbury	F1 F2 F3 F4
Hurst Lodge School, Ascot	F1 F2 F3 F4 H
Lambrook Haileybury, Bracknell	T
Leighton Park School, Reading	H
Licensed Victuallers' School, Ascot	F1 F2 F3 F4
Luckley-Oakfield School, Wokingham	F1 F2 F3 F4 H
The Oratory School, Reading Entry age: 11+, 13+	F1 F2 F3 F4 FO H T
Padworth College, Reading	H
Pangbourne College, Pangbourne	F1 F2 F3 F4 H
Queen Anne's School, Reading	+
Reading Blue Coat School, Reading	H T
St Andrew's School, Reading	+
St Gabriel's, Newbury	+
St George's School, Ascot Entry age: 11+, 16+	H
St Joseph's Convent School, Reading	H
St Michaels School, Newbury	H
St Piran's Preparatory School, Maidenhead	H T
Sunningdale School, Sunningdale	F1 F2 F3 F4 FO T
Upton House School, Windsor	H
Wellington College, Crowthorne	F1 F2 F3 F4 H
White House Preparatory School, Wokingham	+ E H

BRISTOL

Badminton School	F1 F2 F3 F4 H
Bristol Cathedral School Entry age: 11+, 13+, 16+	H
Bristol Grammar School	H
Clifton College	+ F1 F2 F3 F4 H T
Clifton College Preparatory School	+ F1 F2 F3 F4
Clifton High School Entry age: 11+, 13+, 16+	H
Colston's Collegiate School	F1 F2 F3
Colston's Girls' School	H
The Downs School, Wraxall Entry age: 8+	+ F1 F2 F3 H
Fairfield School, Backwell	H
Overndale School, Old Sodbury	H
Queen Elizabeth's Hospital Entry age: 11, 13, 16	H
The Red Maids' School	H
Redland High School Entry age: 11, 16	H
Tockington Manor School, Tockington	T

BUCKINGHAMSHIRE

Akeley Wood School, Buckingham	H
Ashfold School, Aylesbury	+ E F1 F2 F3 F4
The Beacon School, Amersham	H
Bury Lawn School, Milton Keynes	H
Caldicott School, Farnham Royal	H T
Davenies School, Beaconsfield	H
Gayhurst School, Gerrards Cross	+ E H
Godstowe Preparatory School, High Wycombe	
Entry age: 8, 11	+ F1 F2 F3 F4
High March School, Beaconsfield	H T
Ladymede, Aylesbury	F4 H
Maltman's Green School, Gerrards Cross	H
Milton Keynes Preparatory School, Milton Keynes	H
Pipers Corner School, High Wycombe	F1 F2 F3 F4
St Mary's School, Gerrards Cross	+ H
St Teresa's Catholic Independent & Nursery School,	
Princes Risborough	H
Stowe School, Buckingham	H
Swanbourne House School, Milton Keynes	
Entry age: 11+	+ F1 F2 F3 F4
Thornton College Convent of Jesus and Mary,	
Milton Keynes Entry age: 8, 11	F1 F2 F3 F4 H
Thorpe House School, Gerrards Cross	H T
Wycombe Abbey School, High Wycombe	H

CAMBRIDGESHIRE

Bellerbys College & Embassy CES Cambridge,	
Cambridge	H
Cambridge Centre for Sixth-form Studies,	
Cambridge	F1 F2 F3 F4 H
CATS Cambridge, Cambridge	H
Kimbolton School, Huntingdon	H
The King's School Ely, Ely	
Entry age: 11+	+ F1 F2 F3 F4 H
The Leys School, Cambridge	
Entry age: 11, 13, 16	+ F1 F2 F3 F4 H
Madingley Pre-Preparatory School, Cambridge	H
MPW (Mander Portman Woodward), Cambridge	H
The Perse School for Girls, Cambridge Entry age: 11	H
Peterborough High School, Peterborough	H
St John's College School, Cambridge	H
St Mary's School, Cambridge	H

Sancton Wood School, Cambridge	H T
Wisbech Grammar School, Wisbech	H

CHANNEL ISLANDS

Ormer House Preparatory School, Alderney	H
St George's Preparatory School, Jersey Entry age: 7	H T
St Michael's Preparatory School, Jersey	+ H
Victoria College, Jersey	H

CHESHIRE

Abbey Gate College, Chester Entry age: 11+, 16+	H
Abbey Gate School, Chester	H
Alderley Edge School for Girls, Alderley Edge	H
Beech Hall School, Macclesfield	+ E H T
Cheadle Hulme School, Cheadle Entry age: 11, 16	H
Culcheth Hall, Altrincham	H
The Grange School, Northwich	H
Hillcrest Grammar School, Stockport	H
Hulme Hall Schools, Cheadle	H T
The King's School, Chester Entry age: 11, 16	H
The King's School, Macclesfield	H
Mostyn House School, South Wirral Entry age: 4	H
North Cestrian Grammar School, Altrincham	H
Pownall Hall School, Wilmslow	T
The Queen's School, Chester	H
Ramillies Hall School, Cheadle	F1 F2 F3 F4
The Ryleys, Alderley Edge	H
Stockport Grammar School, Stockport Entry age: 11+	H
Terra Nova School, Holmes Chapel	+ E F1 F2 F3 F4 H
Wilmslow Preparatory School, Wilmslow	H T

CORNWALL

The Bolitho School, Penzance	
Entry age: 10+,13+	+ F1 F2 F3 F4 H
Polwhele House School, Truro	+ H T
Roselyon, Par	H
St Joseph's School, Launceston Entry age: 7+, 11+	H
St Petroc's School, Bude	+ F1 F2 F3 F4 H T
Truro High School, Truro Entry age: 11+, 16+	+ E H
Truro School Preparatory School, Truro Entry age: 7+	H
Truro School, Truro	+ H

CUMBRIA

Austin Friars St Monica's School, Carlisle	H
Casterton School, Kirkby Lonsdale	E H T
Chetwynde School, Barrow-in-Furness	+ H
Harecroft Hall School, Seascale	+ F1 F2 F3 F4 H
Hunter Hall School, Penrith	H
Lime House School, Carlisle	E F1 F2 F3 F4 FO H T
St Bees School, St Bees	+ F1 F2 F3 F4 H
St Ursulas Convent School, Wigton	H
Sedbergh Junior School, Sedbergh	F1 F2 F3 F4 H
Sedbergh School, Sedbergh	
Entry age: 13+, 16+, 17+	+ E F1 F2 F3 F4 H T
Windermere St Anne's, Windermere	
Entry age: 11+, 13+, 16+	H

DERBYSHIRE

Barlborough Hall School, Chesterfield	H
Derby Grammar School, Derby	H
Derby High School, Derby	+ H
Foremarke Hall School, Derby	F1 F2 F3 F4 H
Michael House Steiner School, Heanor	H
Mount St Mary's College, Spinkhill	
Entry age: 11+	F2 F3 F4 FO H
Repton School, Derby	
Entry age: 13+, 16+	F1 F2 F3 F4 H
S Anselm's School, Bakewell	
Entry age: 7	+ F1 F2 F3 F4 FO
St Peter & St Paul School, Chesterfield	H
St Wystan's School, Repton	H

DEVON

Blundell's School, Tiverton	
Entry age: 11, 13, 16	F1 F2 F3 F4 FO H
Bramdean School, Exeter Entry age: 7	FO H
Edgehill College, Bideford	+ E F1 F2 F3 F4 H
Emmanuel School, Exeter	H
Exeter Cathedral School, Exeter Entry age: 7+	+ H
Exeter Junior School, Exeter	H
Exeter School, Exeter Entry age: 7, 8, 11, 12, 13, 16	H
Exeter Tutorial College, Exeter	H
Grenville College, Bideford	+ F1 F2 F3 F4 H T
Kelly College, Tavistock	
Entry age: 11, 13, 16	E F1 F2 F3 F4 H T
Kelly College Preparatory School, Tavistock	F1 F2 F3 F4
The Maynard School, Exeter	H
Mount House School, Tavistock	T
Park School, Totnes	H
Plymouth College, Plymouth	H
St Christophers School, Totnes	H
St Margaret's School, Exeter	E H
St Michael's, Barnstaple	+ F1 F2 F3 F4 H T
St Wilfrid's School, Exeter	H
Sands School, Ashburton	H
Shebbear College, Beaworthy	+ E F1 F2 F3 F4 H T
Stover School, Newton Abbot	+ F1 F2 F3 F4 FO H
Tower House School, Paignton Entry age: 11	H
Trinity School, Teignmouth	F1 F2 F3 F4 H
West Buckland Preparatory School, Barnstaple	H
West Buckland School, Barnstaple	H

DORSET

Bryanston School, Blandford Forum	H
Canford School, Wimborne	H
Castle Court Preparatory School, Wimborne	+ E H
Clayesmore Preparatory School,	
Blandford Forum	+ F1 F2 F3 F4 H
Clayesmore, Blandford Forum	F1 F2 F3 F4
Dumpton School, Wimborne	H
Knighton House, Blandford Forum	F1 F2 F3 F4 H T
Leweston School, Sherborne	H
Milton Abbey School, Blandford Forum	F1 F2 F3 F4 H T
The Park School, Bournemouth	H
Port Regis School, Shaftesbury	
Entry age: 7+, 12+	F1 F2 F3 F4 T
St Martin's School, Bournemouth	+ E F1 F2 F3 F4 H T

Sherborne Preparatory School, Sherborne	F1 F2 F3 F4 H
Sherborne School, Sherborne	+ F1 F2 F3 F4 H T
Sherborne Girls, Sherborne	H
Talbot Heath, Bournemouth	H
Uplands School, Poole	H
Wentworth College, Bournemouth	+ F1 F2 F3 F4
Yarrells School, Poole	F1 F2 H

COUNTY DURHAM

Barnard Castle School, Barnard Castle	F1 F2 F3 F4
The Chorister School, Durham	+ H
Durham High School For Girls, Durham	+ H
Durham School, Durham	
Entry age: 11–18	F1 F2 F3 F4 H
Hurworth House School, Darlington	H
Polam Hall, Darlington	F1 F2 F3 F4 H T

ESSEX

Alleyn Court Preparatory School,	
Southend-on-Sea	+ H T
Bancroft's School, Woodford Green Entry age: 11	H
Brentwood School, Brentwood Entry age: 11–18	H T
Chigwell School, Chigwell	H T
Dame Bradbury's School, Saffron Walden	H
Felsted Preparatory School, Felsted	+ F1 F2 F3 F4 H
Felsted School, Felsted	F1 F2 F3 F4 H
Friends' School, Saffron Walden	F1 F3 F4
Holmwood House, Colchester	H
Littlegarth School, Colchester	H
New Hall School, Chelmsford Entry age: 11	F1 F2 F4
St Hilda's School, Westcliff-on-Sea	H
St Michael's School, Leigh-on-Sea	+ E T
St Nicholas School, Harlow	H T
Thorpe Hall School, Southend-on-Sea	H
Woodford Green Preparatory School,	
Woodford Green	H

GLOUCESTERSHIRE

Berkhampstead School, Cheltenham	H
Bredon School, Tewkesbury	F1 F2 F3 F4
Cheltenham College, Cheltenham	F1 F2 F3 F4 H
Cheltenham College Junior School,	
Cheltenham	F1 F2 F3 F4
The Cheltenham Ladies' College, Cheltenham	H
Dean Close Preparatory School,	
Cheltenham	+ E F1 F2 F3 F4 H
Dean Close School, Cheltenham	+ E F1 F2 F3 F4 H T
Hatherop Castle School, Cirencester	F1 F2 F3 F4 H
The King's School, Gloucester	H
Rendcomb College, Cirencester	F1 F2 F3 F4
Rose Hill School, Wotton-under-Edge	F1 F2 F3 F4 H T
St Edward's School Cheltenham, Cheltenham	H
The School of the Lion, Gloucester	E H
Westonbirt School, Tetbury	+ F1 F2 F3 F4 FO H T
Wycliffe, Stonehouse	F1 F2 F3 F4 H T
Wycliffe Preparatory School,	
Stonehouse	F1 F2 F3 F4 FO H T
Wynstones School, Gloucester	H

HAMPSHIRE

Ballard School, New Milton	H
Bedales School, Petersfield Entry age: 13+, 16+	H
Boundary Oak School, Fareham	F1 F2 F3 F4 H
Churchers College, Petersfield	H
Daneshill School, Basingstoke	T
Dunhurst (Bedales Junior School), Petersfield	H
Durlston Court, New Milton	H
Farleigh School, Andover	F1 F2 F3 F4 H
Farnborough Hill, Farnborough	H
Forres Sandle Manor, Fordingbridge	F1 F2 F3 F4
The Gregg School, Southampton	H
Hampshire Collegiate School UCST, Romsey	+ F1 F2 F3 F4 FO H T
Highfield School, Liphook Entry age: 7+, 12+	+ E F1 F2 F3 F4
Hordle Walhampton School, Lymington	H
King Edward VI School, Southampton Entry age: 11+, 13+	H
Mayville High School, Southsea	H T
The Pilgrims' School, Winchester	H
The Portsmouth Grammar School, Portsmouth	H T
Portsmouth High School GDST, Southsea	H
Prince's Mead School, Winchester	H
Rookesbury Park School, Portsmouth	F1 F2 F3 H
Rookwood School, Andover	H
St Neot's School, Hook Entry age: 5+	H
St Nicholas' School, Fleet	H
St Swithun's School, Winchester Entry age: 11–18	H
Salesian College, Farnborough	H
Sherborne House School, Eastleigh Entry age: 5–11	H
Stanbridge Earls School, Romsey	H
Stockton House School, Fleet	H
Winchester College, Winchester Entry age: 13, 16	H
Wykeham House School, Fareham	H

HEREFORDSHIRE

The Hereford Cathedral School, Hereford	+ F1 F2 F3 F4 H T
Lucton School, Leominster	E H
St Richard's, Bromyard	F1 F2 F3 F4

HERTFORDSHIRE

Abbot's Hill School, Hemel Hempstead	H T
Aldenham School, Elstree	H
Arts Educational School, Tring Park, Tring	H
Berkhamsted Collegiate Preparatory School, Berkhamsted	H
Berkhamsted Collegiate School, Berkhamsted	H
Bishop's Stortford College, Bishop's Stortford	F1 F2 F3 F4 H
Bishop's Stortford College Junior School, Bishop's Stortford	F1 F2 F3 F4 H
Edge Grove, Aldenham Entry age: 7+	E F1 F2 F3 F4 FO H T
Egerton Rothesay School, Berkhamsted	H
Haberdashers' Aske's Boys' School, Elstree Entry age: 11, 13	H
Haberdashers' Aske's School for Girls, Elstree	+ H
Haileybury, Hertford	H

Haresfoot Preparatory School, Berkhamsted	H
Lockers Park, Hemel Hempstead	F1 F2 F3 F4 T
The Princess Helena College, Hitchin	+ E F1 F2 F3 F4 H
The Purcell School, Bushey	H
Queenswood, Hatfield	H
Redemption Academy, Stevenage	+ E H
The Royal Masonic School for Girls, Rickmansworth Entry age: 11+	F1 F2 F3 F4 H
St Albans High School for Girls, St Albans	H
St Albans School, St Albans Entry age: 11+, 13+, 16+	H
St Andrew's Montessori School, Watford	F4 H T
St Christopher School, Letchworth	H
St Columba's College, St Albans	H
St Edmund's College and St Hugh's School, Ware	+ F1 F2 F3 F4 H T
St Francis' College, Letchworth Garden City	H
St Hilda's School, Bushey	H
St Margaret's School, Bushey	+ F1 F2 F3 F4 H
Stormont, Potters Bar	H
Westbrook Hay Preparatory School, Hemel Hempstead	H
York House School, Rickmansworth	H T

ISLE OF MAN

King William's College, Castletown	+ F1 F2 F3 F4 H T

ISLE OF WIGHT

Ryde School, Ryde	H

KENT

Ashford School, Ashford	+ F1 F2 F3 F4 H
Baston School, Bromley	H
Beechwood Sacred Heart School, Tunbridge Wells Entry age: 11+, 13+	E F1 F2 F3 F4 FO H
Benenden School, Cranbrook Entry age: 11–18	H
Bethany School, Cranbrook	+ E F1 F2 F3 F4 H
Bickley Park School, Bromley	H T
Bromley High School GDST, Bromley	H
Cobham Hall, Gravesend	E F1 F2 F3 F4 H
Combe Bank School, Nr Sevenoaks	H
Derwent Lodge School for Girls, Tonbridge	H
Dover College, Dover	F1 F2 F3 F4
Dulwich Preparatory School, Cranbrook, Cranbrook	H
Elliott Park School, Sheerness	H
Farringtons School, Chislehurst	+ E F1 F2 F3 F4
Fosse Bank School, Tonbridge	H
Gad's Hill School, Rochester	H
The Granville School, Sevenoaks	H
Hilden Grange School, Tonbridge	H
Hilden Oaks School, Tonbridge	H
Kent College, Canterbury Entry age: 11+, 13+, 16+	+ F1 F2 F3 F4 H
Kent College Pembury, Tunbridge Wells	+ F1 F2 F3 F4 H
King's Preparatory School, Rochester	+ E F1 F2 F3 F4 H
King's School Rochester, Rochester	+ F1 F2 F3 F4 H
Lorenden Preparatory School, Faversham Entry age: 7+	H

Marlborough House School, Hawkhurst   T
The Mead School, Tunbridge Wells   + E H
Merton Court Preparatory School, Sidcup   H T
Northbourne Park School, Deal   + F1 F2 F3 F4 H T
Rochester Independent College, Rochester   H
Sackville School, Tonbridge   H
St Christopher's School, Canterbury
   Entry age: 3–11   H
St Edmunds Junior School, Canterbury + F1 F2 F3 F4 FO
St Edmund's School Canterbury, Canterbury
   Entry age: 11+, 13+, 16+   + F1 F2 F3 F4 FO H
St Lawrence College Junior School,
   Ramsgate   F1 F2 F3 F4 H
St Lawrence College, Ramsgate   F1 F2 F3 F4 H T
St Michael's School, Sevenoaks   H
Sevenoaks Preparatory School, Sevenoaks   T
Sevenoaks School, Sevenoaks Entry age: 11+   H
Solefield School, Sevenoaks   H T
Sutton Valence School, Maidstone
   Entry age: 11+, 13+, 16   H
Tonbridge School, Tonbridge
   Entry age: 13+, 14+, 16+   F1 F2 F3 F4 H
Walthamstow Hall, Sevenoaks
   Entry age: 11+, 13+, 16+   + E H
Wellesley House School, Broadstairs + F1 F2 F3 F4 H T
Yardley Court Preparatory School, Tonbridge   H

LANCASHIRE

Arnold School, Blackpool   + H
Beech House School, Rochdale   H
Bolton School (Boys' Division), Bolton   H
Bolton School (Girls' Division), Bolton
   Entry age: 11, 16   H
Bury Grammar School Boys, Bury   H
Bury Grammar School Girls, Bury   H
Heathland College, Accrington   H
The Hulme Grammar School for Girls, Oldham   H
Kingswood College Trust, Ormskirk   H T
Kirkham Grammar School, Preston   H
Moorland School, Clitheroe   F1 F2 F3 F4
The Oldham Hulme Grammar School, Oldham   H
Queen Elizabeth's Grammar School, Blackburn
   Entry age: 11+   H
Rossall Junior School, Fleetwood   + F3
Rossall School, Fleetwood Entry age: 11   + F1 F2 F3
St Anne's College Grammar School,
   Lytham St Annes   F1 F2 F3 F4 FO
St Mary's Hall, Stonyhurst   H
Stonyhurst College, Clitheroe   + F1 F2 F3 F4 FO H M T

LEICESTERSHIRE

Leicester Grammar School, Leicester
   Entry age: 11,18   H
Leicester High School For Girls, Leicester   H
Loughborough Grammar School, Loughborough
   Entry age: 10–18   + F1 F2 F3 F4 H
Loughborough High School, Loughborough   H
Manor House School, Ashby-de-la-Zouch   H
Ratcliffe College, Leicester   F1 F2 F3 F4 H

St Crispin's School, Leicester
   Entry age: 3+, 7+, 13+, 16+   H
Stoneygate School, Leicester   + E H

LINCOLNSHIRE

Fen School, Sleaford Entry age: 4–5   E F1 F2 F3 F4
The Grantham Preparatory School, Grantham   H
Kirkstone House School, Bourne   H
Maypole House School, Alford   H
St Hugh's School, Woodhall Spa   F1 F2 F3 F4 T
Stamford High School, Stamford   H
Stamford School, Stamford   H
Witham Hall, Bourne   H T

NORTH EAST LINCOLNSHIRE

St James' School, Grimsby   + F1 F2 F4 FO H T

NORTH LINCOLNSHIRE

Brigg Preparatory School, Brigg   +

LONDON

Albemarle Independent College, W1K
   Entry age: 14+, 19+   H
Alleyn's School, SE22   H
The American School in London, NW8   H
Arnold House School, NW8   H
Arts Educational Schools London, W4   H
Ashbourne Independent Sixth Form College,
   W8   + FO H M T
Ashbourne Middle School, W8   + F4 FO H M T
Bales College, W10   H
Barbara Speake Stage School, W3   H
Belmont (Mill Hill Preparatory School), NW7   H
Blackheath High School GDST, SE3   H
The Cavendish School, NW1   H
Channing School, N6   H
City of London School, EC4V
   Entry age: 11+, 13+, 16+   H T
City of London School for Girls, EC2Y   H
Colfe's School, SE12   H
Collingham Independent GCSE and Sixth
   Form College, SW5   FO H T
Dallington School, EC1V   H
Davies Laing and Dick, W1U   H
Dolphin School (Including Noah's Ark
   Nursery School), SW11   + E H
Duff Miller, SW7   H M
Dulwich College, SE21 Entry age: 11, 13   H
Dulwich College Preparatory School, SE21
   Entry age: 7–8   H
Durston House, W5   H
Ealing College Upper School, W13   H
Emanuel School, SW11   H
Falkner House, SW7   H
Fine Arts College Hampstead, NW3   H
Forest School, E17   + H

Francis Holland School, SW1, SW1W	
Entry age: 11+	+ E FO H
Garden House School, SW3	H
The Godolphin and Latymer School, W6	H
The Hall School, NW3	H
Hampstead Hill Pre-Preparatory & Nursery	
School, NW3 Entry age: 4+	H
Hereward House School, NW3	+
Highgate School, N6 Entry age: 11+, 13+	H
Hill House International Junior School, SW1X	T
The Hurlingham School, SW15	H
Ibstock Place School, SW15	H
James Allen's Girls' School, SE22	H
Kerem School, N2	H
King Fahad Academy, W3	H
King's College Junior School, SW19	H
King's College School, SW19	H
Knightsbridge School, SW1X	H
Lansdowne College, W2 Entry age: 14+, 16+	H
Latymer Upper School, W6	H
Lyndhurst House Preparatory School, NW3	H
Mander Portman Woodward, SW7	FO T
Mill Hill School, NW7	H
More House, SW1X	H
Naima Jewish Preparatory School, NW6	H
The North London International School, N11	H
The Norwegian School, SW20	F1 F2 F3 F4 FO
Notting Hill and Ealing High School GDST, W13	H
Palmers Green High School, N21 Entry age: 11+	H
The Pointer School, SE3	+ E F1 F2 F3 F4 H
Putney High School GDST, SW15	H
Queen's College, W1G	H
Queen's Gate School, SW7	H
Riverston School, SE12	+ H
The Roche School, SW18	H
Royal Ballet School, WC2E	H
The Royal School, Hampstead, NW3	
Entry age: 3–18	F1 F3 F4 H
St Augustine's Priory, W5	H
St Benedict's School, W5 Entry age: 11+	H
St Dunstan's College, SE6 Entry age: 11+	
and Sixth Form	H
St James Independent Schools for Boys and	
Girls, W14	H
St James Senior Girls' School, W14	H
St James Independent Schools for Junior Boys	
and Girls, W14	H
St Johns Wood Pre-Preparatory School, NW8	H
St Margaret's School, NW3	H
St Mary's School Hampstead, NW3	H
St Paul's Cathedral School, EC4M	H
St Paul's Girls' School, W6	H
St Paul's Preparatory School, SW13	H
St Paul's School, SW13	H
Sarum Hall, NW3	H
Sinclair House School, SW6	H
South Hampstead High School, NW3	H
Streatham and Clapham High School, SW16	
Entry age: 11, 13, 16	H
Sussex House School, SW1X	+ E T
Sydenham High School GDST, SE26	H
Sylvia Young Theatre School, NW1 Entry age: 10–14	H
Thames Christian College, SW11	+ E

University College School, NW3	H
Westminster Cathedral Choir School, SW1P	H
Westminster School, SW1P	H
Westminster Tutors, SW7	H
Westminster Under School, SW1P	H
The White House Prep & Woodentops	
Kindergarten, SW12	H
Willington School, SW19	H

GREATER MANCHESTER

Abbey College, Manchester	M
Bridgewater School, Manchester Entry age: 11	H
The Manchester Grammar School, Manchester	
Entry age: 11	H
Manchester High School for Girls, Manchester	
Entry age: 11	H
Monton Prep School with Montessori Nurseries,	
Eccles	H T
St Bede's College, Manchester	H
William Hulme's Grammar School, Manchester	H
Withington Girls' School, Manchester	H

MERSEYSIDE

Avalon Preparatory School, Wirral	H
Birkenhead High School GDST, Wirral	H
Birkenhead School, Wirral	H
Highfield School, Birkenhead	H
Kingsmead School, Wirral	+ E F1 F2 F3 F4 H
Liverpool College, Liverpool	+ E F1 F2 F3 F4 H M
Merchant Taylors' Boys' Schools, Liverpool	H
Merchant Taylors' Girls' School, Liverpool	H
St Mary's College, Liverpool	H
Streatham House School, Liverpool	H
Sunnymede School, Southport	H T
Tower College, Prescot	E

MIDDLESEX

ACS Hillingdon International School, Hillingdon	H
Alpha Preparatory School, Harrow	T
Halliford School, Shepperton	H
Hampton School, Hampton Entry age: 11+, 13	H T
Harrow School, Harrow on the Hill	+ H
Heathfield School, Pinner	H
The John Lyon School, Harrow	H
The Lady Eleanor Holles School, Hampton	H
The Mall School, Twickenham	H
Merchant Taylors' School, Northwood	H
Newland House School, Twickenham	H
North London Collegiate, Edgware	H
Quainton Hall School, Harrow Entry age: 4+	+ H T
St David's School, Ashford	H
St Helen's School, Northwood	F1 F2 F3 F4 H
St James Independent School for Boys (Senior),	
Twickenham	H
Staines Preparatory School, Staines	H

NORFOLK

Beeston Hall School, Cromer	H
Glebe House School, Hunstanton	+ T
Gresham's Preparatory School, Holt	F1 F3 H T
Gresham's School, Holt	H
Hethersett Old Hall School, Norwich	+ F1 F2 F3 F4 H
Langley Preparatory School & Nursery, Norwich	F1 F2 F3 F4 H
Langley School, Norwich	
Entry age: 10+, 11+, 13+, 16+	E F1 F2 F3 F4 FO H
The New Eccles Hall School, Norwich	+ F1 F2 F3 F4 H
Norwich High School for Girls GDST, Norwich	H
Norwich School, Norwich Entry age: 11+, 12+, 16+	H
Riddlesworth Hall, Diss	F1 F2 F3 F4 H
Sacred Heart School, Swaffham	E H T
Taverham Hall Preparatory School, Norwich	+ F1 F2 F3 F4 H
Thetford Grammar School, Thetford	H
Town Close House Preparatory School, Norwich	H
Wood Dene School, Norwich	H

NORTHAMPTONSHIRE

Beachborough School, Brackley	H
Bosworth Independent College, Northampton	F1 F2 F3 F4 H
Great Houghton Preparatory School, Northampton	H
Maidwell Hall School, Northampton	F1 F2 F3 F4 H T
Northampton High School, Northampton	
Entry age: 11+	H
Northamptonshire Grammar School, Pitsford	+ H
Oundle School, Nr Peterborough	H T
Quinton House School, Northampton	H
St Peter's School, Kettering	H
Spratton Hall, Northampton	+ H T

NORTHUMBERLAND

Longridge Towers School, Berwick-upon-Tweed	F1 F2 F3 F4 H
Mowden Hall School, Stocksfield	F1 F2 F3 F4 H T
St Oswald's School, Alnwick	E H T

NOTTINGHAMSHIRE

Greenholme School, Nottingham	+ F1 F2 F3 F4
Grosvenor School, Nottingham	+ F1 F2 F3 F4
The King's School, Nottingham	H
Nottingham High School for Girls GDST, Nottingham	H
Ranby House School, Retford	
Entry age: 11+	F1 F2 F3 F4 H
Trent College, Nottingham	F1 F2 F3 F4 H
Wellow House School, Newark	H
Worksop College, Worksop	+ F1 F2 F3 F4 H

OXFORDSHIRE

Abingdon School, Abingdon	H
Bloxham School, Banbury	+ E F1 F2 F3 F4 H T
The Carrdus School, Banbury Entry age: 3–11	H T
Cherwell College, Oxford	F1 F2 F3 H
Cokethorpe School, Witney	H
Cranford House School, Wallingford	H T
Dragon School, Oxford	H
Emmanuel Christian School, Oxford Entry age: 5	H
Headington School, Oxford	
Entry age: 11+, 12+, 13+, 16+	+ F1 F2 F3 F4 H
Abingdon Preparatory School, Abingdon	H
Kingham Hill School, Chipping Norton	+ E F1 F2 F3 F4 FO H T
Magdalen College School, Oxford	H
The Manor Preparatory School, Abingdon	H
The Oratory Preparatory School, Reading	F1 F2 F3 F4 H
Our Lady's Abingdon School, Abingdon	H
Oxford High School GDST, Oxford	H
Oxford Tutorial College, Oxford	H
Radley College, Abingdon	+ H
Rye St Antony School, Oxford	F1 F2 F3 F4
St Andrew's, Wantage	H
St Clare's, Oxford, Oxford	H
St Edward's School, Oxford	+ F4
The School of St Helen & St Katharine, Abingdon	H
Shiplake College, Henley-on-Thames	H
Sibford School, Banbury	H
Wychwood School, Oxford	H
Oakham School, Oakham	H
Uppingham School, Uppingham	H

SHROPSHIRE

Adcote School for Girls, Shrewsbury	+ F1 F2 F3 F4 H
Bedstone College, Bucknell	F1 F2 F3 H
Castle House School, Newport	H
Concord College, Shrewsbury	H
Dower House School, Bridgnorth	H
Ellesmere College, Ellesmere	+ F1 F2 F3 F4 H T
Kingsland Grange, Shrewsbury	H T
Moor Park School, Ludlow	F1 F2 F3 F4 H
Moreton Hall School, Oswestry	
Entry age: 11+, 13+, 16+	E F1 F2 F3 F4 FO H T
Oswestry School, Oswestry	F1 F2 F3 F4 H T
Oswestry School Bellan House, Oswestry	+ F1 F2 F3 F4 T
Packwood Haugh School, Shrewsbury	+ F1 F2 F3 F4 H T
Prestfelde Preparatory School, Shrewsbury	+ F1 F2 F3 F4 H T
Shrewsbury High School GDST, Shrewsbury	H
Shrewsbury School, Shrewsbury	H
Wrekin College, Telford	F1 F2 F3 F4 H T

SOMERSET

All Hallows, Shepton Mallet	
Entry age: 11+	F1 F2 F3 F4 FO H
Bruton School for Girls, Bruton	F1 F2 F3 F4 H
Chard School, Chard	H
Downside School, Bath Entry age: 11+, 13+, 16+	F3 H
Hazlegrove (King's Bruton Preparatory School), Yeovil	F1 F2 F3 F4 H
King's Bruton, Bruton	+ F2 F4 H
King's College, Taunton	+ E F1 F2 F3 H

King's Hall, Taunton   + F1 F2 F3 F4
Millfield Preparatory School, Glastonbury
    Entry age: 7–13   F1 F4 H
Millfield School, Street   F1 F2 F3 F4 H
The Park School, Yeovil
    Entry age: 8–18   + E F1 F2 F3 F4
Perrott Hill School, Crewkerne   + F1 F2 F3 F4 FO H T
Queen's College Junior, Pre-Prep &
    Nursery Schools, Taunton   + F1 F2 F3 F4 H
Queen's College, Taunton   F1 F2 F3 F4 H
Taunton Preparatory School, Taunton
    Entry age: 11   + F1 F2 F3 F4 H
Taunton School, Taunton   E F1 F2 F3 F4
Wellington School, Wellington
    Entry age: 10+, 11+, 13+, 16+   F1 F2 F3 F4 H T
Wells Cathedral Junior School, Wells   + H
Wells Cathedral School, Wells   F1 F2 F3 F4 H

BATH & NORTH EAST SOMERSET

King Edward's School, Bath, Bath   H
Kingswood Preparatory School, Bath   + F1 F2 F3 F4
Kingswood School, Bath   + E F1 F2 F3 F4 FO H
Monkton Prep, Bath   E
Monkton Senior School, Bath   + E F1 F2 F3 F4 H T
Paragon School, Prior Park College Junior, Bath   H
Prior Park College, Bath   F1 F2 F3 F4 H
The Royal High School, Bath
    Entry age: 11+,16+   F1 F2 F3 F4 H

NORTH SOMERSET

Sidcot School, Winscombe   H

STAFFORDSHIRE

Abbots Bromley School for Girls,
    Abbots Bromley   + F1 F3 F4 H
Abbotsholme School, Uttoxeter   F1 F2 F3 F4
Brooklands School & Little Brooklands Nursery,
    Stafford   H
Chase Academy, Cannock   F1 F2 F3 F4 H
Denstone College, Uttoxeter   + F1 F2 F3 F4 H T
Edenhurst School, Newcastle-under-Lyme   + T
Lichfield Cathedral School, Lichfield
    Entry age: 3, 7   + F1 F2 F3 F4 H
Newcastle-under-Lyme School,
    Newcastle-under-Lyme   H
St Dominic's Priory School, Stone   H
St Dominic's School, Stafford   H
Stafford Grammar School, Stafford   H
Yarlet School, Stafford Entry age: 7   H T

STOCKTON-ON-TEES

Teesside High School, Eaglescliffe   H
Yarm School, Yarm Entry age: 7+, 11+, 16+   H

SUFFOLK

Amberfield School, Ipswich   H
Barnardiston Hall Preparatory School,
    Haverhill   + F1 F2 F3 F4
Brandeston Hall, The Preparatory School for
    Framlingham College, Brandeston   F1 F2 F3 F4 H
Culford School, Bury St Edmunds   + F1 F2 F3 F4 H
Fairstead House School, Newmarket   H
Framlingham College, Woodbridge   F1 F2 F3 F4 H
Ipswich High School GDST, Ipswich
    Entry age: 11–18   H
Ipswich School, Ipswich Entry age: 11, 13, 16 F1 F3 F4 H
Moreton Hall Preparatory School,
    Bury St Edmunds   F1 F2 F3 F4 H T
Old Buckenham Hall School, Ipswich   + E F1 F2 F3 F4
Orwell Park, Ipswich   F1 F2 F3 F4 H T
The Royal Hospital School, Ipswich
    Entry age: 11–14, 16   F1 F2 F3 F4 H
Saint Felix School, Southwold   F1 F3 F4 FO H T
St Joseph's College, Ipswich   F1 F2 F3 F4 H
Stoke College, Sudbury   H
Woodbridge School, Woodbridge   H

SURREY

Aberdour, Tadworth   H
ACS Cobham International School, Cobham   H
ACS Egham International School, Egham   H
Aldro School, Godalming   + E F1 F2 F3 F4 H
Amesbury, Hindhead   T
Barfield School, Farnham   F1 F2 F3 F4 H
Barrow Hills School, Godalming   H
Belmont School, Dorking   H
Bishopsgate School, Egham   H
Box Hill School, Dorking   + F1 F2 F3 F4 H T
Bramley School, Tadworth Entry age: 7+   H
Cambridge Tutors College, Croydon   H
Canbury School, Kingston-upon-Thames   H
Caterham Preparatory School, Caterham
    Entry age: 10+   +
Caterham School, Caterham   + F1 F2 F3 F4 FO H
Charterhouse, Godalming   H
Cranleigh School, Cranleigh   + F1 F2 F3 F4 H T
Croydon High School GDST, South Croydon   H
Drayton House School, Guildford   H
Duke of Kent School, Guildford
    Entry age: 7+, 10+, 11+   F1 F2 F3 F4
Dunottar School, Reigate   H
Edgeborough, Farnham   F1 F2 F3 F4 H
Epsom College, Epsom Entry age: 13+, 16+   M
Essendene Lodge School, Caterham   H
Ewell Castle School, Epsom   H
Feltonfleet School, Cobham   H
Frensham Heights School, Farnham   H
Glenesk School, Leatherhead   H
Greenacre School for Girls, Banstead   H
Guildford High School, Guildford
    Entry age: 11+, 16+   + H
Halstead Preparatory School, Woking   H
Haslemere Preparatory School, Haslemere   T
Hawley Place School, Camberley   H
The Hawthorns School, Redhill   + H

Hazelwood School, Oxted Entry age: 7+, 11+	H T
Hoe Bridge School, Woking	H
Holy Cross Preparatory School, Kingston-upon-Thames	H T
Homefield School, Sutton	H
King Edward's School Witley, Godalming Entry age: 11–18	+ E F1 F2 F3 F4 H T
King's House School, Richmond	H
Kingston Grammar School, Kingston-upon-Thames	H
Kingswood House School, Epsom	+ H T
Lingfield Notre Dame School, Lingfield Entry age: 11+	H
Lodge School, Purley	H
Lyndhurst School, Camberley	H
Manor House School, Leatherhead	H
Marymount International School, Kingston-upon-Thames	H
New Lodge School, Dorking	H
Notre Dame Preparatory School, Cobham	H
Oakfield School, Woking Entry age: 7	H T
Oakwood School & Nursery, Purley	H
Parkside School, Cobham	H
Prior's Field School, Godalming	F1 F2 F3 F4 H T
Priory Preparatory School, Banstead	T
Reed's School, Cobham	H
Reigate Grammar School, Reigate	H
Reigate St Mary's Preparatory and Choir School, Reigate	H
Ripley Court School, Woking Entry age: 7	H T
Royal Alexandra and Albert School, Reigate	+ H
Royal Grammar School, Guildford	H
Royal Russell School, Croydon	F1 F2 F3 F4 H
The Royal School, Haslemere Entry age: 11+, 13+, 16+	+ F1 F2 F3 F4 H T
St. Andrew's (Woking) School Trust, Woking	H
St Catherine's School, Guildford	H
St David's School, Purley	H
St Edmund's School, Hindhead	F1 F2 F3 F4 H T
St Hilary's School, Godalming	H
St Ives School, Haslemere	H
St John's School, Leatherhead Entry age: 13+, 16+	+
St Teresa's School, Dorking	F1 F2 F3 F4 H T
Shrewsbury House School, Surbiton	T
Sir William Perkins's School, Chertsey	H
Stowford College, Sutton	E H
Surbiton High School, Kingston-upon-Thames	+ H
Sutton High School GDST, Sutton Entry age: 11+, 16+	H
TASIS The American School in England, Thorpe	H
Trinity School, Croydon Entry age: 10+, 11+, 13+	H
Warlingham Park School, Croydon	H
Whitgift School, South Croydon Entry age: 10–13,16	H
Woodcote House School, Windlesham	H T
Yehudi Menuhin School, Cobham	H

EAST SUSSEX

Ashdown House School, Forest Row	+ T
Battle Abbey School, Battle	F1 F2 F3 F4 H T
Bricklehurst Manor Preparatory, Wadhurst	H
Brighton and Hove High School GDST, Brighton	H
Brighton College, Brighton	+ F3 H T
Buckswood School, Hastings	H

Eastbourne College, Eastbourne	H
The Fold School, Hove	H
Lancing College Preparatory School at Mowden, Hove	+ H
Moira House School, Eastbourne	H T
Moira House Girls School, Eastbourne	E F1 F2 F3 F4 H T
Newlands School, Seaford	F1 F2 F3 F4
Roedean School, Brighton Entry age: 11+, 12+, 13+, 16+	H
Sacred Heart R.C. Primary School, Wadhurst	H
St Andrew's School, Eastbourne	F1 F2 F3 F4
St Aubyns School, Brighton	+ H T
St Bede's Prep School, Eastbourne	F1 F2 F3 F4 H
St Christopher's School, Hove	H
St Leonards-Mayfield School, Mayfield	H
St Mary's Hall, Brighton	+ E F1 F2 F3 F4 H
Vinehall School, Robertsbridge	F1 F2 F3 F4 H

WEST SUSSEX

Ardingly College, Haywards Heath	+ H
Ardingly College Junior School, Haywards Heath	H
Arundale Preparatory School, Pulborough	H
Brambletye, East Grinstead	H
Burgess Hill School for Girls, Burgess Hill	H
Christ's Hospital, Horsham	+ F1 F2 F4 H
Conifers School, Midhurst	H T
Copthorne Prep School, Copthorne	H T
Cottesmore School, Pease Pottage	H
Dorset House School, Pulborough	+ H T
Farlington School, Horsham	+ F1 F2 F3 H
Fonthill Lodge, East Grinstead	H
Great Ballard School, Chichester	F1 F2 F3 F4
Great Walstead, Haywards Heath	+ E H T
Handcross Park School, Haywards Heath Entry age: 7–11	H T
Lancing College, Lancing	+ H
Lavant House, Chichester	H
Our Lady of Sion School, Worthing	H
Pennthorpe School, Horsham	H
The Prebendal School, Chichester Entry age: 7	H
Seaford College, Petworth Entry age: 10+, 11+, 13+	F1 F2 F3 F4 H
Shoreham College, Shoreham-by-Sea	+ H
Slindon College, Arundel Entry age: 10	F1 F2 F3 F4 H
Sompting Abbotts School, Sompting	T
Stoke Brunswick, East Grinstead	H
Tavistock & Summerhill School, Haywards Heath	H
The Towers Convent School, Steyning	H T
Windlesham House, Pulborough	F1 F2 F3 F4 FO H

TYNE AND WEAR

Central Newcastle High School GDST, Newcastle upon Tyne Entry age: 11+, 16+	H
Dame Allan's Boys School, Newcastle upon Tyne	H
Dame Allan's Girls School, Newcastle upon Tyne	H
Grindon Hall Christian School, Sunderland	+ E T
The King's School, Tynemouth Entry age: 4, 11	+ E H
Newcastle Preparatory School, Newcastle upon Tyne	H

Newcastle Upon Tyne Church High School, Newcastle upon Tyne	+
Sunderland High School, Sunderland	E H
Westfield School, Newcastle upon Tyne	H

WARWICKSHIRE

Abbotsford School, Kenilworth Entry age: 7	H
Bilton Grange, Rugby Entry age: 8+	+ F1 F2 F3 F4 H T
King's High School, Warwick, Warwick	H
The Kingsley School, Leamington Spa	H
Princethorpe College, Rugby	H
Rugby School, Rugby	H
Warwick School, Warwick	H

WEST MIDLANDS

Abbey College, Birmingham	H
Bablake Junior School, Coventry	H
Bablake School, Coventry	H
Birchfield School, Wolverhampton	F4 H T
The Blue Coat School, Birmingham	H
Edgbaston High School for Girls, Birmingham	H
Elmhurst School for Dance, Birmingham	F1 F3 F4 H
Eversfield Preparatory School, Solihull	H
Highclare School, Birmingham	H
King Edward VI High School for Girls, Birmingham	H
King Edward's School, Birmingham Entry age: 11+, 16+	H
King Henry VIII School, Coventry	H
Newbridge Preparatory School, Wolverhampton	+
Pattison College, Coventry	H
Priory School, Birmingham	H
The Royal Wolverhampton Junior School, Wolverhampton	F1 F3 H
The Royal Wolverhampton School, Wolverhampton Entry age: 11+	F1 F2 F3 F4 H
St George's School, Edgbaston, Birmingham	+ H
Solihull School, Solihull	+
Tettenhall College, Wolverhampton	+ F1 F2 F3 F4 H
West House School, Birmingham	H T
Wolverhampton Grammar School, Wolverhampton Entry age: 11+, 13+, 16+	H

WILTSHIRE

Chafyn Grove School, Salisbury	F1 F2 F3 F4 H T
Dauntsey's School, Devizes Entry age: 11+,13+,16+	H
Godolphin Preparatory School, Salisbury	F1 F2 F3 F4 H
The Godolphin School, Salisbury	F1 F2 F3 F4 H
Leaden Hall School, Salisbury	+
Marlborough College, Marlborough Entry age: 13+, 16+	+
Norman Court Preparatory School, Salisbury	F1 F2 F3 F4
Pinewood School, Shrivenham	H
Prior Park Preparatory School, Cricklade	F1 F2 F3 F4
St Francis School, Pewsey	H
St Mary's Calne, Calne	H
South Hills School, Salisbury	H

| Stonar School, Melksham | F1 F2 F3 F4 H |
| Warminster School, Warminster | F1 F2 F3 F4 H |

WORCESTERSHIRE

Abberley Hall, Worcester Entry age: 8+	F1 F2 F3 F4 H T
The Abbey College, Malvern Wells	H
Bromsgrove Preparatory School, Bromsgrove	F1 F2 F3 F4 H
Bromsgrove School, Bromsgrove	F1 F2 F3 F4 H T
The Downs, Malvern College Preparatory School, Malvern	F1 F2 F3 F4 FO H T
The Elms, Malvern	F1 F2 F3 F4 H T
King's Hawford, Worcester	+
The King's School, Worcester	H
Malvern College, Malvern	F1 F2 F3 F4 H T
Malvern College Preparatory and Pre-Prep School, Malvern	F1 F2 F3 FO
Malvern St James, Great Malvern Entry age: 11+, 12+, 13+, 16+	+ F1 F2 F3 F4 H T
Moffats School, Worcestershire	+ E F1 F2 F3 F4 FO H M T
Moffats School, Bewdley	+ E F1 F2 F3 F4 FO H M T
River School, Worcester	H
RGS Worcester & The Alice Ottley School, Worcester	H
St Mary's Convent School, Worcester Entry age: 11+, 16+	H
Winterfold House, Kidderminster	H

EAST RIDING OF YORKSHIRE

Hull Collegiate School, Anlaby Entry age: 11	H
Hymers College, Hull	H
Pocklington School, Pocklington	F1 F2 F3 F4 H

NORTH YORKSHIRE

Ampleforth College, York	H
Ashville College, Harrogate Entry age: 7	+ E F1 F2 F3 F4 H T
Aysgarth Preparatory School, Bedale	F1 F2 F3 F4 H T
Belmont Grosvenor School, Harrogate	+ F1 F2 F3 F4
Bootham School, York Entry age: 11+, 13+, 16+	H
Bramcote School, Scarborough	E F1 F2 F3 F4 FO H T
Cundall Manor School, York	F1 F2 F3 F4 FO
Giggleswick Junior School, Settle	F1 F2 F3 F4 T
Giggleswick School, Settle Entry age: 13, 16	F1 F2 F3 F4 H T
Harrogate Ladies' College, Harrogate	+ E F1 F2 F3 F4 H T
Harrogate Tutorial College, Harrogate	F1 F2 F3 F4 FO H T
Highfield Preparatory School, Harrogate	+ E F1 F2 F3 F4 T
Malsis School, Near Skipton	+ F1 F2 F3 F4 H T
The Mount School, York	H
Queen Ethelburga's College, York Entry age: 11	+ F1 F2 F3 F4 FO M T
Queen Margaret's School, York	+ F1 F2 F3
Queen Mary's School, Thirsk	+ F1 F2 F3 F4 H T
Read School, Selby Entry age: 11+, 13+, 16+	H
Ripon Cathedral Choir School, Ripon	F1 F2 F3 F4 H

St Martin's Ampleforth, York	F1 F2 F3 F4
St Peter's School, York	
Entry age: 13, 14, 16	+ F1 F2 F3 F4 H
Scarborough College & Lisvane School,	
Scarborough	F2 F3 F4 H
Terrington Hall, York	+ F1 F2 F3 F4 H T
Woodleigh School, Malton	F1 F2 F3

SOUTH YORKSHIRE

Ashdell Preparatory School, Sheffield Entry age: 4	H
Birkdale School, Sheffield	+ H
Brantwood School, Sheffield	H
Handsworth Christian School, Sheffield	H
Rudston Preparatory School, Rotherham	H T
Sheffield High School GDST, Sheffield	
Entry age: 11–18	H
Westbourne School, Sheffield	H

WEST YORKSHIRE

Ackworth School, Pontefract	H
Alcuin School, Leeds	H

Batley Grammar School, Batley	H
Bradford Girls' Grammar School, Bradford	H
Bradford Grammar School, Bradford	
Entry age: 11+, 13+, 16+	H
Bronte House School, Bradford	
Entry age: 7+, 8+	F1 F2 F3 H
The Froebelian School, Leeds	H
Fulneck School, Leeds	+ E F1 F2 F3 F4 H
Gateways School, Leeds	H
Hipperholme Grammar School, Halifax	H
Huddersfield Grammar School, Huddersfield	H
Moorlands School, Leeds	H
Queen Elizabeth Grammar School, Wakefield	H
Richmond House School, Leeds Entry age: 7/8	H T
Rishworth School, Rishworth	H
Silcoates School, Wakefield Entry age: 11	+
The Grammar School at Leeds, Leeds	
Entry age: 11+,16+	H
Wakefield Girls' High School, Wakefield	
Entry age: 11+–16+	H
Woodhouse Grove School,	
Apperley Bridge	+ F1 F2 F3 F4 H

NORTHERN IRELAND

COUNTY ANTRIM

Cabin Hill School, Belfast	F3
Methodist College, Belfast	+
Royal Belfast Academical Institution, Belfast	H

COUNTY ARMAGH

The Royal School Armagh, Armagh	+

COUNTY DOWN

The Holywood Rudolf Steiner School, Holywood	H

COUNTY LONDONDERRY

Coleraine Academical Institution, Coleraine	+ E

COUNTY TYRONE

The Royal School Dungannon, Dungannon	
Entry age: 11–16	+ E F1 F2 F3 F4

SCOTLAND

ABERDEENSHIRE

Aberdeen Waldorf School, Aberdeen	H
International School of Aberdeen, Aberdeen	H
Robert Gordons College, Aberdeen	H
St Margaret's School for Girls, Aberdeen	H

ANGUS

The High School of Dundee, Dundee	H
Lathallan School, Montrose	F1 F2 F3 F4 H

SOUTH AYRSHIRE

Wellington School, Ayr	H

FIFE

St Leonards School, St Andrews	F1 F2 F3 F4 H
Sea View Private School, Kirkcaldy	H

GLASGOW

Craigholme School Entry age: 12	H
The Glasgow Academy Entry age: 11+	+ H
The High School of Glasgow	H
Hutchesons' Grammar School	H

INVERCLYDE

St Columba's School, Kilmacolm	H

SOUTH LANARKSHIRE

Fernhill School, Glasgow   H

LOTHIAN

Belhaven Hill, Dunbar Entry age: 8+	H T
Cargilfield, Edinburgh	F1 F2 F3 F4
Clifton Hall School, Edinburgh Entry age: 3	F1 F2 F3 F4 H
The Compass School, Haddington	H
The Edinburgh Academy, Edinburgh	H
Fettes College, Edinburgh	F1 F3 F4 H T
George Heriot's School, Edinburgh	H
George Watson's College, Edinburgh	H
Loretto School, Musselburgh	F1 F2 F3 F4 H
The Mary Erskine School, Edinburgh	H
Merchiston Castle School, Edinburgh	F1 F2 F3 F4
St George's School for Girls, Edinburgh	H
St Margaret's School, Edinburgh	F1 F2 F3 F4 H
Stewart's Melville College, Edinburgh	H

MORAYSHIRE

Gordonstoun School, Elgin Entry age: 9	F1 F2 H
Rosebrae School, Elgin	H

PERTH AND KINROSS

Ardvreck School, Crieff	F1 F2 F3 F4
Craigclowan Preparatory School, Perth	H T
Glenalmond College, Perth	+ E F1 F2 F3 F4 H T
Kilgraston, Perth	F1 F2 F3 F4 H T
Morrison's Academy, Crieff	H
Queen Victoria School, Dunblane	F1 F2 F3 F4
Strathallan School, Perth	+ E F1 F2 F3 F4 FO H M T

STIRLING

Beaconhurst School   H

WALES

BRIDGEND

St John's School, Porthcawl   H

CARDIFF

The Cathedral School	H
Howell's School, Llandaff GDST	H

CARMARTHENSHIRE

Llandovery College, Llandovery Entry age: 11+, 17+	+ E F1 F2 F4 H
St Michael's School, Llanelli	H

CONWY

Lyndon Preparatory School, Colwyn Bay	E F1 F2 F3 F4 H
Rydal Penrhos Senior School, Colwyn Bay	F1 F2 F3 F4 H
St David's College, Llandudno	+ E F1 F2 F3 F4 FO H

DENBIGHSHIRE

Howell's School, Denbigh Entry age: 11	+ F1 F2 F3 F4 H T
Ruthin School, Ruthin Entry age: 5	F1 F2 F3 F4 H

GWYNEDD

Hillgrove School, Bangor   E

MONMOUTHSHIRE

Haberdashers' Monmouth School For Girls, Monmouth	F1 F2 F3 F4 H
Llangattock School, Monmouth	H
Monmouth School, Monmouth Entry age: 11, 13, 16	F1 F2 F3 F4 H T
St John's-on-the-Hill, Chepstow	F1 F2 F3 F4 H

NEWPORT

Rougemont School   H

PEMBROKESHIRE

Netherwood School, Saundersfoot   H

POWYS

Christ College, Brecon Entry age: 11+, 13+, 16	+ F1 F3 F4 H T

SWANSEA

Ffynone House School	H
Oakleigh House School	H

CONTINENTAL EUROPE

Aiglon College, Switzerland	H
Chavagnes International College, Chavagnes-en-Paillers, France	H

5.3

Specialist Schools

Schools in the directory which specialize in the theatre, dance or music are listed below. For full details about entrance requirements and the curriculum, parents are advised to contact schools direct.

Arts Schools

Arts Educational School, Tring Park, Tring
Arts Educational Schools, London W4
Barbara Speake Stage School, London W3
The Italia Conti Academy of Theatre Arts, London EC1
Pattison College, Coventry
Ravenscourt Theatre School, London W6
Sylvia Young Theatre School, London NW1

Dance Schools

Elmhurst School for Dance, Birmingham
Hammond School, Chester
Royal Ballet School, London WC2E
Stonelands School of Ballet & Theatre Arts, Hove
The Urdang Academy of Ballet, London WC2

Music Schools

Chetham's School of Music, Manchester
The Purcell School, Bushey
St Mary's Music School, Edinburgh
Yehudi Menuhin School, Cobham

5.4

Single-Sex Schools

Note: * denotes a co-educational school that educates boys and girls separately, either within a specific age range or throughout the school. For details consult the school listings in Part 2.

BOYS

ENGLAND

BEDFORDSHIRE

Bedford Preparatory School, Bedford	7–13
Bedford School, Bedford	7–18

BERKSHIRE

*Brockhurst and Marlston House Schools, Newbury	3–13
Claires Court School, Maidenhead	11–16 (Co-ed VIth Form)
Claires Court Schools, Ridgeway, Maidenhead	4–11
Crosfields School, Reading	4–13
Elstree School, Reading	3–13 (Girls 3–7)
Eton College, Windsor	13–18
Horris Hill School, Newbury	7–13
Ludgrove, Wokingham	8–13
The Oratory School, Reading	11–18
Papplewick School, Ascot	7–13
Reading Blue Coat School, Reading	11–18 (Co-ed VIth Form)
St Edward's School, Reading	4–13
St John's Beaumont, Windsor	4–13
*St Michaels School, Newbury	7–18 (Single-sex ed 13–18)
Sunningdale School, Sunningdale	8–13

BRISTOL

Queen Elizabeth's Hospital	7–18

BUCKINGHAMSHIRE

The Beacon School, Amersham	3–13
Caldicott School, Farnham Royal	7–13
Davenies School, Beaconsfield	4–13
Gayhurst School, Gerrards Cross	4–13
Kingscote Pre-Preparatory School, Gerrards Cross	3–7
Thorpe House School, Gerrards Cross	3–16

CHANNEL ISLANDS

Elizabeth College, Guernsey	2–18 (Co-ed VIth Form)
Victoria College, Jersey	11–19
Victoria College Preparatory School, Jersey	7–11

CHESHIRE

Altrincham Preparatory School, Altrincham	4–11
*The King's School, Macclesfield	3–18 (Single-sex ed 11–16)
The Ryleys, Alderley Edge	3–13
St Ambrose Preparatory School, Altrincham	4–11

DORSET

Sherborne School, Sherborne	13–18

COUNTY DURHAM

Hurworth House School, Darlington	3–18

ESSEX

*Brentwood School, Brentwood	3–18 (Single-sex ed 11–16)
Cranbrook College, Ilford	4–16
Loyola Preparatory School, Buckhurst Hill	3–11

HAMPSHIRE

The Pilgrims' School, Winchester	7–13
Salesian College, Farnborough	11–18
Winchester College, Winchester	13–18

HERTFORDSHIRE

Aldwickbury School, Harpenden	4–13

*Berkhamsted Collegiate School, Berkhamsted   11–18
  (Single-sex ed 11–16)
Haberdashers' Aske's Boys' School, Elstree   5–18
Lochinver House School, Potters Bar   4–13
Lockers Park, Hemel Hempstead   5–13
Northwood Preparatory School,
  Rickmansworth   4–13 (Girls 3–4)
St Albans School, St Albans   11–18 (Co-ed VIth Form)
St Columba's College, St Albans   4–18
York House School, Rickmansworth   3–13 (Co-ed 2–5)

KENT

Bickley Park School, Bromley   3–13
Darul Uloom London, Chislehurst   11–18
Harenc School Trust, Sidcup   3–11
The New Beacon, Sevenoaks   4–13
Solefield School, Sevenoaks   4–13
Tonbridge School, Tonbridge   13–18
Yardley Court Preparatory School, Tonbridge   7–13

LANCASHIRE

Bolton School (Boys' Division), Bolton   7–18
Bury Grammar School Boys, Bury   7–18
The Oldham Hulme Grammar School, Oldham   7–18
Tashbar School, Salford   2–11

LEICESTERSHIRE

Loughborough Grammar School, Loughborough   10–18

LINCOLNSHIRE

Stamford School, Stamford   11–18

LONDON

Al-Mizan Primary & London East Academy
  Secondary & Sixth Form, E1   7–18
*Al-Sadiq and Al-Zahra Schools, NW6   4–16
Arnold House School, NW8   5–13
Beis Hamedrash Elyon, NW11   11–14
Brondesbury College For Boys, NW6   11–16
City of London School, EC4V   10–18
Clifton Lodge Preparatory School, W5   4–13
Darul Hadis Latifiah, E2   11–19
Donhead Prep School, SW19   4–11
Dulwich College, SE21   7–18
Dulwich College Preparatory School,
  SE21   3–13 (Girls 3–5)
Durston House, W5   4–13
Eaton House School Belgravia, SW1W   4–8
Eaton House The Manor, SW4   2–13
The Falcons School for Boys, W4   3–8
*Forest School, E17   4–18 (Single-sex ed 7–16)
The Hall School, NW3   4–13
Hawkesdown House School, W8   3–8
Hereward House School, NW3   4–13
Keble Preparatory School, N21   4–13
King's College Junior School, SW19   7–13

King's College School, SW19   13–18
London East Academy, E1   7–16
London Islamic School, E1   11–16
Lubavitch House School (Junior Boys), E5   5–13
Lyndhurst House Preparatory School, NW3   4–13
Mechinah Liyeshivah Zichron Moshe, N16   11–16
North Bridge House Upper Prep School, NW1   10–13
Northcote Lodge School, SW11   8–13
Pardes Grammar Boys' School, N3   11–17
St Anthony's Preparatory School, NW3   5–13
St Paul's Preparatory School, SW13   7–13
St Paul's School, SW13   13–18
St Philip's School, SW7   7–13
Sussex House School, SW1X   8–13
Talmud Torah Bobov Primary School, N16   2–13
Tawhid Boys School, Tawhid Educational Trust,
  N16   9–16
Tower House School, SW14   4–13
University College School Junior Branch, NW3   7–11
Westminster Abbey Choir School, SW1P   8–13
Westminster Cathedral Choir School, SW1P   8–13
Westminster Under School, SW1P   7–13
Wetherby Preparatory School, W11   8–13
Wetherby School, W2   4–8
Willington School, SW19   4–13
Wimbledon Common Preparatory School, SW19   4–8
*Yesodey Hatorah Jewish School, N16   3–16
Yetev Lev Day School for Boys, N16   3–11

GREATER MANCHESTER

Al Jamiah Al Islamiyyah, Bolton   13–16
Kassim Darwish Grammar School for Boys,
  Manchester   11–16
The Manchester Grammar School, Manchester   9–18

MERSEYSIDE

Merchant Taylors' Boys' Schools, Liverpool   4–18

MIDDLESEX

Buckingham College Preparatory School, Pinner   4–11
Buckingham College School,
  Harrow   11–18 (Co-ed VIth Form)
Denmead School, Hampton   2–11 (Girls 2–7)
Halliford School, Shepperton   11–19 (Co-ed VIth Form)
Hampton School, Hampton   11–18
Harrow School, Harrow on the Hill   13–18
The John Lyon School, Harrow   11–18
The Mall School, Twickenham   4–13
Merchant Taylors' School, Northwood   11–18
St James Independent School for Boys (Senior),
  Twickenham   10–18
St John's Northwood, Northwood   3–13
*St John's Senior School, Enfield   11–18
St Martin's School, Northwood   3–13

NORTHAMPTONSHIRE

Maidwell Hall School, Northampton   7–13

NOTTINGHAMSHIRE

Al Karam Secondary School, Retford	11–16
Nottingham High Junior School, Nottingham	7–11

OXFORDSHIRE

Abingdon School, Abingdon	11–18
Christ Church Cathedral School, Oxford	3–13 (Girls 2–4)
Cothill House Preparatory School, Abingdon	8–13
Abingdon Preparatory School, Abingdon	4–13 (Girls 4–7)
Magdalen College School, Oxford	7–18
Moulsford Preparatory School, Wallingford	4–13
New College School, Oxford	4–13
Radley College, Abingdon	13–18
Summer Fields, Oxford	7–13

SHROPSHIRE

Kingsland Grange, Shrewsbury	4–13
Shrewsbury School, Shrewsbury	13–18

SURREY

Aldro School, Godalming	7–13
Charterhouse, Godalming	13–18 (Co-ed VIth Form)
Chinthurst School, Tadworth	3–13
Cranmore School, Leatherhead	3–13
Cumnor House School, South Croydon	4–13
Elmhurst School, South Croydon	4–11
Ewell Castle School, Epsom	3–18 (Co-ed 3–11)
Haslemere Preparatory School, Haslemere	2–14
Homefield School, Sutton	0–13
King's House School, Richmond	4–13
Kingswood House School, Epsom	3–13
Lanesborough, Guildford	3–13
More House School, Farnham	9–18
Parkside School, Cobham	4–13 (Co-ed 2–4)
Priory Preparatory School, Banstead	2–13
Reed's School, Cobham	11–18 (Co-ed VIth Form)
Rokeby School, Kingston-upon-Thames	4–13
Royal Grammar School, Guildford	11–18
St Edmund's School, Hindhead	2–13 (Co-ed day 2–7)
Shrewsbury House School, Surbiton	7–13
Surbiton Preparatory School, Surbiton	4–11

Trinity School, Croydon	10–18
Whitgift School, South Croydon	10–18
Woodcote House School, Windlesham	7–14

WEST SUSSEX

*Fonthill Lodge, East Grinstead	2–11 (Single-sex ed 8–11)
Slindon College, Arundel	9–16

TYNE AND WEAR

Dame Allan's Boys School, Newcastle upon Tyne	8–18 (Co-ed VIth Form)
Newcastle School for Boys, Newcastle upon Tyne	3–13
Royal Grammar School, Newcastle upon Tyne	8–18 (Co-ed VIth form)

WARWICKSHIRE

Warwick School, Warwick	7–18

WEST MIDLANDS

*Al Hijrah School, Birmingham	4–11
*Darul Uloom Islamic High School & College, Birmingham	0–0
King Edward's School, Birmingham	11–18
West House School, Birmingham	1–11 (Girls 1–4)

NORTH YORKSHIRE

Aysgarth Preparatory School, Bedale	3–13 (Co-ed day 3–8)

SOUTH YORKSHIRE

Birkdale School, Sheffield	4–18 (Co-ed VIth Form)

WEST YORKSHIRE

Ghyll Royd School, Ilkley	2–11
Olive Secondary, Bradford	11–18
Queen Elizabeth Grammar School, Wakefield	7–18

NORTHERN IRELAND

COUNTY ANTRIM

Cabin Hill School, Belfast	3–13 (Co-ed kindergarten)
Campbell College, Belfast	11–18
Royal Belfast Academical Institution, Belfast	4–18

COUNTY DOWN

Bangor Grammar School, Bangor	11–18

COUNTY LONDONDERRY

Coleraine Academical Institution, Coleraine	11–19

SCOTLAND

LOTHIAN

The Edinburgh Academy,
  Edinburgh   5–18 (Co-ed VIth Form)
Merchiston Castle School, Edinburgh   8–18

Stewart's Melville College,
  Edinburgh   12–18 (Co-ed VIth Form)

WALES

CONWY

*Rydal Penrhos Senior School,
  Colwyn Bay   11–18 (Single-sex ed 11–16)

MONMOUTHSHIRE

Monmouth School, Monmouth   7–18 (Boarding 11–18)

CONTINENTAL EUROPE

Chavagnes International College,
  Chavagnes-en-Paillers, France   10–18

GIRLS

ENGLAND

BEDFORDSHIRE

Bedford High School for Girls, Bedford   7–18
Dame Alice Harpur School, Bedford   7–18
St Andrew's School, Bedford   3–16 (Boys 3–7)

BERKSHIRE

The Abbey School, Reading   3–18
Brigidine School Windsor, Windsor   3–18 (Boys 3–7)
*Brockhurst and Marlston House Schools,
  Newbury   3–13
Claires Court Schools, The College, Maidenhead   3–16
  (Boys 3–5, co-ed VIth Form)
Downe House, Thatcham   11–18
Heathfield St Mary's School, Ascot   11–18
Highfield School, Maidenhead   3–11
Luckley-Oakfield School, Wokingham   11–18
The Marist Preparatory School, Ascot   3–11
The Marist Senior School, Ascot   11–18
Queen Anne's School, Reading   11–18
St Gabriel's, Newbury   3–18 (Boys 3–7)
St George's School, Ascot   11–18
St Joseph's Convent School, Reading   3–18
St Mary's School, Ascot, Ascot   11–18
*St Michaels School,
  Newbury   7–18 (Single-sex ed 13–18)

White House Preparatory School,
  Wokingham   2–11 (Boys 2–4)

BRISTOL

Badminton School   4–18
Colston's Girls' School   10–18
The Red Maids' School   11–18
Redland High School   3–18

BUCKINGHAMSHIRE

Godstowe Preparatory School,
  High Wycombe   3–13 (Boys 3–8)
Heatherton House School, Amersham   3–11 (Boys 2–5)
High March School, Beaconsfield   3–11 (Boys 3–5)
Maltman's Green School, Gerrards Cross   3–11
Pipers Corner School, High Wycombe   3–18
St Mary's School, Gerrards Cross   3–18
Thornton College Convent of Jesus and Mary,
  Milton Keynes   2–16 (Boys 2–4)
Wycombe Abbey School, High Wycombe   11–18

CAMBRIDGESHIRE

The Perse School for Girls, Cambridge   7–18

Peterborough High School,
  Peterborough   3–18 (Boys 3–11)
St Mary's Junior School, Cambridge   4–11
St Mary's School, Cambridge   4–18

CHANNEL ISLANDS

Beaulieu Convent School, Jersey   4–18
The Ladies' College, Guernsey   4–18

CHESHIRE

Alderley Edge School for Girls, Alderley Edge   3–18
Bowdon Preparatory School For Girls, Altrincham 2–12
Culcheth Hall, Altrincham   2–16 (Boys 2–4)
*The King's School,
  Macclesfield   3–18 (Single-sex ed 11–16)
Loreto Preparatory School, Altrincham 3–11 (Boys 4–7)
The Queen's School, Chester   4–18
Wilmslow Preparatory School, Wilmslow   2–11

CORNWALL

Truro High School, Truro   3–18 (Boys 3–5)

CUMBRIA

Casterton School, Kirkby
  Lonsdale   3–18 (Day boys 3–11)

DERBYSHIRE

Ockbrook School, Derby   3–18

DEVON

The Maynard School, Exeter   7–18
St Margaret's School, Exeter   7–18
Stoodley Knowle School, Torquay   2–18

DORSET

Hanford School, Blandford Forum   7–13
Knighton House, Blandford Forum 2–13 (Day boys 4–7)
Leweston School, Sherborne   2–18 (Boys 2–11)
St Mary's School, Shaftesbury   9–18
Sherborne Girls, Sherborne   11–18
Talbot Heath, Bournemouth   3–18 (Boys 3–7)

COUNTY DURHAM

Durham High School For Girls, Durham   3–18
Polam Hall, Darlington   4–18

ESSEX

Braeside School for Girls, Buckhurst Hill   3–16
*Brentwood School,
  Brentwood   3–18 (Single-sex ed 11–16)

Ilford Ursuline Preparatory School, Ilford   3–11
Park School for Girls, Ilford   7–18
St Hilda's School, Westcliff-on-Sea 2–16 (Boys 2–7)
St Mary's School, Colchester   4–16

GLOUCESTERSHIRE

The Cheltenham Ladies' College, Cheltenham 11–18
Gloucestershire Islamic Secondary
  School For Girls, Gloucester   11–16
Westonbirt School, Tetbury   11–18

HAMPSHIRE

Alton Convent School, Alton   2–18 (Co-ed 2–11)
Farnborough Hill, Farnborough   11–18
Portsmouth High School GDST, Southsea   3–18
St Nicholas' School, Fleet   3–16 (Boys 3–7)
St Swithun's School, Winchester   11–18
Wykeham House School, Fareham   2–16

HERTFORDSHIRE

Abbot's Hill School, Hemel Hempstead 3–16 (Boys 3–4)
*Berkhamsted Collegiate School, Berkhamsted 11–18
  (Single-sex ed 11–16)
Haberdashers' Aske's School for Girls, Elstree   4–18
The Princess Helena College, Hitchin   11–18
Queenswood, Hatfield   11–18
Rickmansworth PNEU School, Rickmansworth   3–11
The Royal Masonic School for Girls,
  Rickmansworth   4–18
St Albans High School for Girls, St Albans   4–18
St Francis' College, Letchworth Garden City   3–18
St Hilda's School, Bushey   3–11 (Boys 3–5)
St Hilda's School, Harpenden   2–11
St Margaret's School, Bushey   4–18
St Martha's Senior School, Barnet   11–18
Stormont, Potters Bar   4–11

KENT

Babington House School, Chislehurst 3–16 (Boys 3–7)
Baston School, Bromley   2–16
Bedgebury School, Cranbrook   2–18 (Boys day 2–7)
Benenden School, Cranbrook   11–18
Bromley High School GDST, Bromley   4–18
Cobham Hall, Gravesend   11–18
Combe Bank School, Nr Sevenoaks   3–18
Derwent Lodge School for Girls, Tonbridge   7–11
Farringtons School, Chislehurst   3–19
The Granville School, Sevenoaks   3–11 (Boys 3–5)
Kent College Pembury, Tunbridge Wells   3–18
Walthamstow Hall, Sevenoaks   0–18

LANCASHIRE

Bolton Muslim Girls School, Bolton   11–16
Bolton School (Girls' Division), Bolton 4–18 (Boys 4–7)
Bury Grammar School Girls, Bury   3–18 (Boys 4–7)
The Hulme Grammar School for Girls, Oldham   3–18

Islamiyah School, Blackburn	11–16
Jamea Al Kauthar, Lancaster	11–19
Markazul Uloom, Blackburn	11–19
Rochdale Girls School, Rochdale	11–16
Tauheedul Islam Girls High School, Blackburn	11–16
Westholme School, Blackburn	3–18 (Boys 3–7)

LEICESTERSHIRE

Leicester High School For Girls, Leicester	3–18
Loughborough High School, Loughborough	11–18

LINCOLNSHIRE

Stamford High School, Stamford	11–18

LONDON

*Al-Sadiq and Al-Zahra Schools, NW6	4–16
Beis Chinuch Lebanos Girls School, N4	2–16
Beis Rochel D'Satmar Girls School, N16	2–17
Beth Jacob Grammar for Girls, NW4	10–16
Blackheath High School GDST, SE3	3–18
Bute House Preparatory School for Girls, W6	4–11
The Cavendish School, NW1	2–11
Channing Junior School, N6	4–11
Channing School, N6	4–18
City of London School for Girls, EC2Y	7–18
Eaton House The Manor Girls' School, SW4	4–11
The Falcons School for Girls, W5	4–11
Falkner House, SW7	3–11 (Co-ed 3–4)
*Forest School, E17	4–18 (Single-sex ed 7–16)
Francis Holland School, Regent's Park NW1, NW1	11–18
Francis Holland School, SW1, SW1W	4–18
Glendower Preparatory School, SW7	4–11
The Godolphin and Latymer School, W6	11–18
Grange Park Preparatory School, N21	4–11
Harvington School, W5	3–16 (Boys 3–5)
Islamia Girls' School, NW6	11–16
James Allen's Girls' School, SE22	11–18
Kensington Prep School, SW6	4–11
London Jewish Girls' High School, NW4	11–16
Lubavitch House Senior School for Girls, N16	11–18
Madni Girls School, E1	12–18
More House, SW1X	11–18
The Mount School, NW7	4–18
Notting Hill and Ealing High School GDST, W13	4–18
Palmers Green High School, N21	3–16
Pembridge Hall, W2	4–11
Putney High School GDST, SW15	4–18
Queen's College, W1G	11–18
Queen's College Prep School, W1B	3–11
Queen's Gate School, SW7	4–18
Quwwatt Ul Islam Girls School, E7	4–13
The Royal School, Hampstead, NW3	3–16
St Augustine's Priory, W5	4–18
St Christopher's School, NW3	4–11
St James Senior Girls' School, W14	10–18
St Joseph's Convent School, E11	3–11
St Margaret's School, NW3	4–16
St Paul's Girls' School, W6	11–18

Sarum Hall, NW3	3–11
South Hampstead High School, NW3	4–18
Streatham and Clapham High School, SW16	3–18 (Boys 3–5)
The Study Preparatory School, SW19	4–11
Sydenham High School GDST, SE26	4–18
Tayyibah Girls School, N16	5–18
Ursuline Preparatory School, SW20	3–11 (Boys 3–7)
The Village School, NW3	4–11
*Yesodey Hatorah Jewish School, N16	3–16

GREATER MANCHESTER

Hubert Jewish High School for Girls, Salford	11–18
Manchester High School for Girls, Manchester	4–18
Manchester Islamic High School, Manchester	11–16
Withington Girls' School, Manchester	7–18

MERSEYSIDE

Birkenhead High School GDST, Wirral	3–19
Merchant Taylors' Girls' School, Liverpool	4–18 (Boys 4–7)
Streatham House School, Liverpool	2–16 (Boys 2–11)

MIDDLESEX

Heathfield School, Pinner	3–18
Jack and Jill School, Hampton	2–7 (Boys 3–5)
The Lady Eleanor Holles School, Hampton	7–18
North London Collegiate, Edgware	4–18
Northwood College, Northwood	3–18
Peterborough & St Margaret's School, Stanmore	4–16
St Catherine's School, Twickenham	3–16 (Sixth Form in 2006)
St David's School, Ashford	3–18
St Helen's School, Northwood	3–18
*St John's Senior School, Enfield	11–18

NORFOLK

Norwich High School for Girls GDST, Norwich	3–18
Thorpe House School, Norwich	3–16

NORTHAMPTONSHIRE

Northampton High School, Northampton	3–18

NOTTINGHAMSHIRE

Hollygirt School, Nottingham	3–16
Hollygirt School, Nottingham	3–16
Nottingham High School for Girls GDST, Nottingham	4–18

OXFORDSHIRE

Ash-Shifa School, Banbury	11–16
The Carrdus School, Banbury	3–11 (Boys 3–8)
Cranford House School, Wallingford	3–16 (Boys 3–7)
Headington School, Oxford	3–18 (Co-ed 3–4)

IQRA School, Oxford   10–16
Oxford High School GDST, Oxford   3–18 (Boys 4–6)
Rye St Antony School, Oxford   3–18 (Boys 3–8)
The School of St Helen & St Katharine, Abingdon   9–18
Tudor Hall School, Banbury   11–18
Wychwood School, Oxford   11–18
Kilgraston, Perth   2–18 (Boys day 2–9)

SHROPSHIRE

Moreton Hall School, Oswestry   3–18
Shrewsbury High School GDST, Shrewsbury   2–18

SOMERSET

Bruton School for Girls, Bruton   3–18

BATH & NORTH EAST SOMERSET

The Royal High School,
   Bath   3–18 (Boys admitted (day only) into Sixth Form)

STAFFORDSHIRE

Abbots Bromley School for Girls, Abbots Bromley   3–18
St Dominic's School, Stafford   2–18 (Co-ed 2–7)

SUFFOLK

Amberfield School, Ipswich   3–16 (Boys 3–7)
Ipswich High School GDST, Ipswich   3–18

SURREY

Bramley School, Tadworth   3–11
Croydon High School GDST, South Croydon   3–18
Dunottar School, Reigate   3–18
Greenacre School for Girls, Banstead   3–18
Guildford High School, Guildford   4–18
Halstead Preparatory School, Woking   3–11
Holy Cross Preparatory School,
   Kingston-upon-Thames   4–11
Laverock School, Oxted   3–11
Lodge School, Purley   2–19 (Boys 3–11)
Manor House School, Leatherhead   2–16
Marymount International School,
   Kingston-upon-Thames   11–18
Notre Dame Preparatory School,
   Cobham   2–11 (Boys 2–5)
Notre Dame Senior School, Cobham   11–18
Old Palace of John Whitgift School, Croydon   4–18
Old Vicarage School, Richmond   4–11
Prior's Field School, Godalming   11–18
Rowan Preparatory School, Esher   2–11
The Royal School, Haslemere   3–18 (Boys 2–4)
St Catherine's School, Guildford   4–18
St Ives School, Haslemere   3–11 (Boys 3–5)
St Teresa's Preparatory School, Effingham   2–11
St Teresa's School, Dorking   11–18
Seaton House School, Sutton   3–11 (Boys 3–5)

Sir William Perkins's School, Chertsey   11–18
Surbiton High School,
   Kingston-upon-Thames   4–18 (Boys 4–11)
Sutton High School GDST, Sutton   3–18
Tormead School, Guildford   4–18
Woldingham School, Woldingham   11–18

EAST SUSSEX

Brighton and Hove High School GDST, Brighton   3–18
Moira House School, Eastbourne   2–11
Moira House Girls School, Eastbourne   3–19
Roedean School, Brighton   11–18
St Leonards-Mayfield School, Mayfield   11–18

WEST SUSSEX

Burgess Hill School for Girls, Burgess Hill   2–18
Farlington School, Horsham   3–18
*Fonthill Lodge,
   East Grinstead   2–11 (Single-sex ed 8–11)
Lavant House, Chichester   3–18
The Towers Convent School, Steyning   3–16 (Boys 3–11)

TYNE AND WEAR

Central Newcastle High School GDST,
   Newcastle upon Tyne   3–18
Dame Allan's Girls School, Newcastle upon Tyne   8–18
   (Co-ed VIth Form)
Newcastle Upon Tyne Church High School,
   Newcastle upon Tyne   2–18
Westfield School, Newcastle upon Tyne   3–18

WARWICKSHIRE

King's High School, Warwick, Warwick   10–18
The Kingsley School, Leamington Spa   3–18 (Boys 2–7)

WEST MIDLANDS

*Al Hijrah School, Birmingham   4–11
Al-Burhan Grammar School, Birmingham   11–16
Birchfield Independent Girls School, Birmingham   11–16
Coventry Muslim School, Coventry   4–16
*Darul Uloom Islamic High School & College,
   Birmingham   0–0
Edgbaston High School for Girls, Birmingham   2–18
King Edward VI High School for Girls,
   Birmingham   11–18
Newbridge Preparatory School, Wolverhampton   3–11
Saint Martin's School, Solihull   3–18
Woodstock Girls' School, Birmingham   11–15

WILTSHIRE

Godolphin Preparatory School, Salisbury   3–11
The Godolphin School, Salisbury   11–18
Leaden Hall School, Salisbury   3–11 (Boys 3–4)

St Mary's Calne, Calne	11–18
Stonar School, Melksham	2–18

WORCESTERSHIRE

Dodderhill School, Droitwich Spa	3–16 (Boys 3–9)
Malvern St James, Great Malvern	5–18
St Mary's Convent School, Worcester	0–18 (Boys 2–8)

NORTH YORKSHIRE

Harrogate Ladies' College, Harrogate	10–18
Queen Margaret's School, York	11–18
Queen Mary's School, Thirsk	3–16 (Boys 3–7)

SOUTH YORKSHIRE

Ashdell Preparatory School, Sheffield	4–11
Brantwood School, Sheffield	3–16
Sheffield High School GDST, Sheffield	4–18

WEST YORKSHIRE

Bradford Girls' Grammar School, Bradford	2–18
Gateways School, Leeds	3–18 (Boys 3–7)
Islamia Girls High School, Huddersfield	11–16
Moorfield School, Ilkley	2–11
New Horizon Community School, Leeds	11–16
Wakefield Girls' High School, Wakefield	11–18

NORTHERN IRELAND

COUNTY ANTRIM

Victoria College Belfast, Belfast	4–18

SCOTLAND

ABERDEENSHIRE

St Margaret's School for Girls, Aberdeen	3–18 (Boys 3–5)

GLASGOW

Craigholme School	3–18 (Boys 3–5)

LOTHIAN

The Mary Erskine School, Edinburgh	12–18 (Co-ed VIth Form)
St George's School for Girls, Edinburgh	2–18 (Boys 2–5)
St Margaret's School, Edinburgh	1–18 (Boys 1–8)

WALES

CONWY

*Rydal Penrhos Senior School, Colwyn Bay	11–18 (Single-sex ed 11–16)

DENBIGHSHIRE

Howell's School, Denbigh	2–18

MONMOUTHSHIRE

Haberdashers' Monmouth School For Girls, Monmouth	7–18

5.5

Boarding Provision (Full, Weekly and Flexi-Boarding, Host Families)

The schools and colleges listed below offer boarding/residential accommodation. Full boarding is indicated by 'F', weekly boarding by 'W'. Many schools now offer flexi-boarding (Fl), ie pupils may board for part of the week or on an occasional basis. Please note that in some cases independent Sixth Form colleges may offer accommodation with host families (H) or in hostels. For further details please contact schools direct.

ENGLAND

BEDFORDSHIRE

Bedford High School for Girls, Bedford	F
Bedford Preparatory School, Bedford	F W Fl
Bedford School, Bedford	F W Fl
Bedford School Study Centre, Bedford	F

BERKSHIRE

Bearwood College, Wokingham	F W Fl
Bradfield College, Reading	F
Brockhurst and Marlston House Schools, Newbury	W Fl
Cheam School, Newbury	F W Fl
Downe House, Thatcham	F
Eagle House, Sandhurst	F W Fl
Elstree School, Reading	F W Fl
Eton College, Windsor	F
Heathfield St Mary's School, Ascot	F
Horris Hill School, Newbury	F
Hurst Lodge School, Ascot	W Fl
Lambrook Haileybury, Bracknell	W Fl
Leighton Park School, Reading	F W Fl
Licensed Victuallers' School, Ascot	F W
Luckley-Oakfield School, Wokingham	F W Fl
Ludgrove, Wokingham	F
The Oratory School, Reading	F
Padworth College, Reading	F W Fl
Pangbourne College, Pangbourne	F W Fl
Papplewick School, Ascot	F W
Queen Anne's School, Reading	F Fl

St Andrew's School, Reading	W Fl
St George's School, Ascot	F
St George's School, Windsor	F W Fl
St John's Beaumont, Windsor	F W
St Mary's School, Ascot, Ascot	F
St Michaels School, Newbury	F W Fl
Sunningdale School, Sunningdale	F
Wellington College, Crowthorne	F Fl

BRISTOL

Badminton School	F W Fl
Clifton College	F Fl
Clifton College Preparatory School	F W
Clifton High School	F W Fl
Colston's Collegiate School	F Fl
The Downs School, Wraxall	F W Fl
Tockington Manor School, Tockington	F Fl

BUCKINGHAMSHIRE

Ashfold School, Aylesbury	W Fl
Caldicott School, Farnham Royal	F
Godstowe Preparatory School, High Wycombe	F W
Pipers Corner School, High Wycombe	F W Fl
Stowe School, Buckingham	F
Swanbourne House School, Milton Keynes	F W Fl
Thornton College Convent of Jesus and Mary, Milton Keynes	F W Fl
Wycombe Abbey School, High Wycombe	F

CAMBRIDGESHIRE

Bellerbys College & Embassy CES Cambridge, Cambridge	F
Cambridge Centre for Sixth-form Studies, Cambridge	F W Fl
CATS Cambridge, Cambridge	F H
Kimbolton School, Huntingdon	F Fl
The King's School Ely, Ely	F W Fl
The Leys School, Cambridge	F
MPW (Mander Portman Woodward), Cambridge	Fl
Peterborough High School, Peterborough	F W Fl
St Andrew's, Cambridge	Fl
St John's College School, Cambridge	F Fl
St Mary's School, Cambridge	F W H

CHESHIRE

Hammond School, Chester	F W
Terra Nova School, Holmes Chapel	W Fl

CORNWALL

The Bolitho School, Penzance	F W Fl
Polwhele House School, Truro	W Fl
Truro High School, Truro	F W Fl
Truro School, Truro	F Fl

CUMBRIA

Casterton School, Kirkby Lonsdale	F Fl
Harecroft Hall School, Seascale	F W Fl
Holme Park School, Kendal	Fl
Lime House School, Carlisle	F W
St Bees School, St Bees	F W Fl
Sedbergh Junior School, Sedbergh	F W Fl
Sedbergh School, Sedbergh	F
Windermere St Anne's, Windermere	F W Fl

DERBYSHIRE

Foremarke Hall School, Derby	F W Fl
Mount St Mary's College, Spinkhill	F W Fl
Ockbrook School, Derby	F W Fl
Repton School, Derby	F
S Anselm's School, Bakewell	F

DEVON

Blundell's School, Tiverton	F W Fl
Edgehill College, Bideford	F W Fl
Exeter Cathedral School, Exeter	F W Fl
Grenville College, Bideford	F W
Kelly College, Tavistock	F W Fl
Kelly College Preparatory School, Tavistock	F W Fl
Mount House School, Tavistock	F W
Plymouth College, Plymouth	F W
St Peter's School, Exmouth	W Fl
Shebbear College, Beaworthy	F W Fl
Stover School, Newton Abbot	F W Fl H
Trinity School, Teignmouth	F W H
West Buckland Preparatory School, Barnstaple	F Fl
West Buckland School, Barnstaple	F W Fl

DORSET

Bryanston School, Blandford Forum	F
Canford School, Wimborne	F
Clayesmore Preparatory School, Blandford Forum	F W Fl
Clayesmore, Blandford Forum	F W
Hanford School, Blandford Forum	F
International College, Sherborne School, Sherborne	F
Knighton House, Blandford Forum	F W Fl
Leweston School, Sherborne	F W Fl
Milton Abbey School, Blandford Forum	F
Port Regis School, Shaftesbury	F W
St Mary's School, Shaftesbury	F
Sherborne Preparatory School, Sherborne	F W Fl
Sherborne School, Sherborne	F
Sherborne Girls, Sherborne	F
Talbot Heath, Bournemouth	F W Fl
Wentworth College, Bournemouth	F W Fl

COUNTY DURHAM

Barnard Castle School, Barnard Castle	F W Fl
The Chorister School, Durham	F W Fl
Durham School, Durham	F W Fl
Polam Hall, Darlington	F W Fl

ESSEX

Brentwood School, Brentwood	F W
Chigwell School, Chigwell	F W Fl
Felsted Preparatory School, Felsted	W Fl
Felsted School, Felsted	F Fl
Friends' School, Saffron Walden	F W Fl
Gosfield School, Halstead	F Fl
Holmwood House, Colchester	W Fl
New Hall School, Chelmsford	F Fl

GLOUCESTERSHIRE

Beaudesert Park School, Stroud	W Fl
Bredon School, Tewkesbury	F W Fl
Cheltenham College, Cheltenham	F
Cheltenham College Junior School, Cheltenham	F W Fl
The Cheltenham Ladies' College, Cheltenham	F
Dean Close Preparatory School, Cheltenham	F Fl
Dean Close School, Cheltenham	F
Hatherop Castle School, Cirencester	F W Fl
Rendcomb College, Cirencester	F W Fl
Westonbirt School, Tetbury	F W Fl
Wycliffe, Stonehouse	F Fl H
Wycliffe Preparatory School, Stonehouse	F W
Wynstones School, Gloucester	F W Fl H

HAMPSHIRE

Bedales School, Petersfield	F
Boundary Oak School, Fareham	W Fl
Brockwood Park School, Bramdean	F
Dunhurst (Bedales Junior School), Petersfield	F Fl
Farleigh School, Andover	F W Fl
Forres Sandle Manor, Fordingbridge	F W Fl

Hampshire Collegiate School UCST, Romsey	F W Fl
Highfield School, Liphook	F
Hordle Walhampton School, Lymington	F W
Lord Wandsworth College, Hook	F W Fl
Moyles Court School, Ringwood	F
The Pilgrims' School, Winchester	F W
Rookesbury Park School, Portsmouth	F W Fl
Rookwood School, Andover	F W Fl
St John's College, Southsea	F Fl
St Neot's School, Hook	W Fl
St Swithun's School, Winchester	F W
Stanbridge Earls School, Romsey	F
Twyford School, Winchester	W Fl H
Winchester College, Winchester	F

HEREFORDSHIRE

Lucton School, Leominster	F W Fl
St Richard's, Bromyard	F W Fl

HERTFORDSHIRE

Aldenham School, Elstree	F W Fl
Aldwickbury School, Harpenden	W Fl
Arts Educational School, Tring Park, Tring	F
Beechwood Park School, St Albans	W Fl
Berkhamsted Collegiate School, Berkhamsted	F W Fl
Bishop's Stortford College, Bishop's Stortford	F W Fl
Bishop's Stortford College Junior School, Bishop's Stortford	F W Fl
Edge Grove, Aldenham	F Fl
Haileybury, Hertford	F Fl
Heath Mount School, Hertford	W Fl
Lockers Park, Hemel Hempstead	F Fl
The Princess Helena College, Hitchin	F W Fl
The Purcell School, Bushey	F
Queenswood, Hatfield	F Fl
The Royal Masonic School for Girls, Rickmansworth	F W Fl
St Christopher School, Letchworth	F W Fl
St Edmund's College and St Hugh's School, Ware	F W Fl
St Francis' College, Letchworth Garden City	F W Fl
St Margaret's School, Bushey	F W Fl
Stanborough School, Watford	F W Fl

ISLE OF MAN

King William's College, Castletown	F W

ISLE OF WIGHT

Ryde School, Ryde	F W Fl

KENT

Ashford School, Ashford	F W Fl
Bedgebury School, Cranbrook	F W
Beechwood Sacred Heart School, Tunbridge Wells	F W Fl
Bell Bedgebury International School, Cranbrook	F

Benenden School, Cranbrook	F
Bethany School, Cranbrook	F W
CATS Canterbury, Canterbury	F H
Cobham Hall, Gravesend	F W Fl
Cranbrook School, Cranbrook	F
Darul Uloom London, Chislehurst	F
Dover College, Dover	F W Fl
Duke of York's Royal Military School, Dover	F
Dulwich Preparatory School, Cranbrook, Cranbrook	W Fl
Farringtons School, Chislehurst	F W Fl
Junior King's School, Canterbury	F W Fl
Kent College, Canterbury	F W Fl
Kent College Infant & Junior School, Canterbury	F W Fl
Kent College Pembury, Tunbridge Wells	F W Fl
King's Preparatory School, Rochester	F W Fl
The King's School, Canterbury	F
King's School Rochester, Rochester	F W
Marlborough House School, Hawkhurst	Fl
Northbourne Park School, Deal	F W Fl
Rochester Independent College, Rochester	F Fl
St Edmunds Junior School, Canterbury	F Fl
St Edmund's School Canterbury, Canterbury	F W Fl
St Lawrence College Junior School, Ramsgate	F W Fl
St Lawrence College, Ramsgate	F
St Ronan's School, Hawkhurst	Fl
Sevenoaks School, Sevenoaks	F
Sutton Valence School, Maidstone	F W Fl
Tonbridge School, Tonbridge	F W
Wellesley House School, Broadstairs	F W

LANCASHIRE

Jamea Al Kauthar, Lancaster	F
Kirkham Grammar School, Preston	F W Fl
Moorland School, Clitheroe	F W Fl
Rossall Junior School, Fleetwood	F Fl
Rossall School, Fleetwood	F Fl
Rossall School International Study Centre, Fleetwood	F
St Anne's College Grammar School, Lytham St Annes	F W Fl H
St Mary's Hall, Stonyhurst	F W Fl
Stonyhurst College, Clitheroe	F W

LEICESTERSHIRE

Brooke House College, Market Harborough	F W Fl H
Irwin College, Leicester	F
Loughborough Grammar School, Loughborough	F W Fl
Ratcliffe College, Leicester	F W Fl

LINCOLNSHIRE

Lincoln Minster School, Lincoln	F W Fl
St Hugh's School, Woodhall Spa	F W
Stamford High School, Stamford	F W Fl
Stamford Junior School, Stamford	F W Fl
Stamford School, Stamford	F W Fl
Witham Hall, Bourne	F W Fl

NORTH EAST LINCOLNSHIRE

St. James' School, Grimsby	F W Fl

LONDON

Ashbourne Independent Sixth Form College, W8	F
Bales College	
Dulwich College, SE21	F W
Dulwich College Preparatory School, SE21	W
King's College Madrid, Madrid, Spain	F
Mill Hill School, NW7	F
Royal Ballet School, WC2E	F
The Royal School, Hampstead, NW3	F W Fl
St Paul's Cathedral School, EC4M	F
St Paul's School, SW13	F W Fl
Sylvia Young Theatre School, NW1	F W H
Westminster Abbey Choir School, SW1P	F Fl
Westminster Cathedral Choir School, SW1P	F
Westminster School, SW1P	F W

GREATER MANCHESTER

Chetham's School of Music, Manchester	F

MERSEYSIDE

Arden College, Southport	
Clarence High School, Formby	
Kingsmead School, Wirral	F W Fl

MIDDLESEX

Harrow School, Harrow on the Hill	F
St David's School, Ashford	F W Fl
St James Independent School for Boys (Senior), Twickenham	W

NORFOLK

Beeston Hall School, Cromer	F
Glebe House School, Hunstanton	W Fl
Gresham's Preparatory School, Holt	F W Fl
Gresham's School, Holt	F W
Hethersett Old Hall School, Norwich	F W Fl
Langley School, Norwich	F W
The New Eccles Hall School, Norwich	F W Fl
Riddlesworth Hall, Diss	F W Fl
Sacred Heart School, Swaffham	F W Fl
Taverham Hall Preparatory School, Norwich	W Fl

NORTHAMPTONSHIRE

Beachborough School, Brackley	Fl
Bosworth Independent College, Northampton	F W H
Maidwell Hall School, Northampton	F W
Oundle School, Nr Peterborough	F
Winchester House School, Brackley	F W Fl

NORTHUMBERLAND

Longridge Towers School, Berwick-upon-Tweed	F W Fl
Mowden Hall School, Stocksfield	F W

NOTTINGHAMSHIRE

Al Karam Secondary School, Retford	F Fl
Ranby House School, Retford	F W Fl
Trent College, Nottingham	W Fl
Wellow House School, Newark	W Fl
Worksop College, Worksop	F W Fl

OXFORDSHIRE

Abacus College, Oxford	F
Abingdon School, Abingdon	F W
Bloxham School, Banbury	F W Fl
Cherwell College, Oxford	F W H
Cothill House Preparatory School, Abingdon	F
d'Overbroeck's College, Oxford	F H
Dragon School, Oxford	F
Greene's Tutorial College, Oxford	F W Fl H
Headington School, Oxford	F W Fl
Kingham Hill School, Chipping Norton	F W Fl
Moulsford Preparatory School, Wallingford	W
The Oratory Preparatory School, Reading	F W Fl
Oxford Tutorial College, Oxford	H
Radley College, Abingdon	F
Rye St Antony School, Oxford	F W Fl
St Clare's, Oxford, Oxford	F W Fl
St Edward's School, Oxford	F
St Hugh's School, Faringdon	W Fl
Shiplake College, Henley-on-Thames	F W
Sibford School, Banbury	F W Fl
Summer Fields, Oxford	F
Tudor Hall School, Banbury	F
Wychwood School, Oxford	F W Fl

RUTLAND

Oakham School, Oakham	F
Uppingham School, Uppingham	F

SHROPSHIRE

Adcote School for Girls, Shrewsbury	F W Fl H
Bedstone College, Bucknell	F
Concord College, Shrewsbury	F
Ellesmere College, Ellesmere	F W Fl
Moor Park School, Ludlow	F W Fl
Moreton Hall School, Oswestry	F H
Oswestry School, Oswestry	F W Fl
Packwood Haugh School, Shrewsbury	F
Prestfelde Preparatory School, Shrewsbury	W Fl
Shrewsbury School, Shrewsbury	F
Wrekin College, Telford	F Fl

SOMERSET

All Hallows, Shepton Mallet	F Fl
Bruton School for Girls, Bruton	F W Fl
Chilton Cantelo School, Yeovil	F Fl

Downside School, Bath	F W
Hazlegrove (King's Bruton Preparatory School), Yeovil	F W Fl
King's Bruton, Bruton	F
King's College, Taunton	F
King's Hall, Taunton	F W Fl
Millfield Preparatory School, Glastonbury	F
Millfield School, Street	F
The Park School, Yeovil	F W H
Perrott Hill School, Crewkerne	F W Fl
Queen's College Junior, Pre-Prep & Nursery Schools, Taunton	F W
Queen's College, Taunton	F Fl
Taunton International Study Centre (TISC), Taunton	F
Taunton Preparatory School, Taunton	F Fl
Taunton School, Taunton	F
Wellington School, Wellington	F W Fl
Wells Cathedral Junior School, Wells	F W Fl
Wells Cathedral School, Wells	F Fl

BATH & NORTH EAST SOMERSET

Bath Academy, Bath	F Fl H
Kingswood Preparatory School, Bath	F W Fl
Kingswood School, Bath	F W Fl
Monkton Prep , Bath	F W Fl
Monkton Senior School, Bath	F W Fl
Prior Park College, Bath	F W Fl
The Royal High School, Bath	F W Fl

NORTH SOMERSET

Sidcot School, Winscombe	F W Fl

STAFFORDSHIRE

Abbots Bromley School for Girls, Abbots Bromley	F W Fl
Abbotsholme School, Uttoxeter	F W Fl
Chase Academy, Cannock	F
Denstone College, Uttoxeter	F W Fl
Lichfield Cathedral School, Lichfield	F W Fl
St Bede's School, Stafford	F W Fl
Yarlet School, Stafford	Fl

SUFFOLK

Alexanders International School, Woodbridge	
Barnardiston Hall Preparatory School, Haverhill	F W Fl
Brandeston Hall, The Preparatory School for Framlingham College, Brandeston	F W Fl
Culford School, Bury St Edmunds	F W Fl
Felixstowe International College, Felixstowe	F
Finborough School, Stowmarket	F W Fl
Framlingham College, Woodbridge	F W Fl
Ipswich School, Ipswich	F W Fl
Moreton Hall Preparatory School, Bury St Edmunds	F W Fl
Old Buckenham Hall School, Ipswich	F W
Orwell Park, Ipswich	F W Fl
The Royal Hospital School, Ipswich	F W Fl

Saint Felix School, Southwold	F W Fl
St Joseph's College, Ipswich	F W Fl H
Stoke College, Sudbury	W Fl
Summerhill School, Leiston	Fl
Woodbridge School, Woodbridge	F W Fl

SURREY

ACS Cobham International School, Cobham	F W
Aldro School, Godalming	F
Belmont School, Dorking	W Fl
Bishopsgate School, Egham	W Fl
Box Hill School, Dorking	F W Fl
Cambridge Tutors College, Croydon	H
Caterham School, Caterham	F W Fl
Charterhouse, Godalming	F
City of London Freemen's School, Ashtead	F W Fl
Cranleigh Preparatory School, Cranleigh	
Cranleigh School, Cranleigh	F
Duke of Kent School, Guildford	F W Fl
Edgeborough, Farnham	W Fl
Epsom College, Epsom	F W
Feltonfleet School, Cobham	W Fl
Frensham Heights School, Farnham	F Fl
Hall Grove School, Bagshot	W Fl
Hurtwood House, Dorking	F W
King Edward's School Witley, Godalming	F Fl
Marymount International School, Kingston-upon-Thames	F W Fl H
More House School, Farnham	
Prior's Field School, Godalming	F W
Reed's School, Cobham	F
Royal Alexandra and Albert School, Reigate	F
Royal Ballet School, Richmond	
Royal Russell School, Croydon	F W Fl
The Royal School, Haslemere	F Fl
St Catherine's School, Guildford	F W Fl
St Edmund's School, Hindhead	W Fl
St John's School, Leatherhead	F
St Teresa's Preparatory School, Effingham	F W Fl
St Teresa's School, Dorking	F W Fl
TASIS The American School in England, Thorpe	F
Woldingham School, Woldingham	F W Fl
Woodcote House School, Windlesham	
Yehudi Menuhin School, Cobham	F Fl

EAST SUSSEX

Ashdown House School, Forest Row	F
Battle Abbey School, Battle	F W Fl
Bellerbys College, Hove	F
Brighton College, Brighton	F W
Buckswood School, Hastings	F W Fl
Eastbourne College, Eastbourne	F
Greenfields School, Forest Row	F W Fl
Michael Hall (Steiner Waldorf School), Forest Row	F W Fl H
Moira House School, Eastbourne	F W Fl
Moira House Girls School, Eastbourne	F W Fl
Newlands School, Seaford	F W
Roedean School, Brighton	Fl
St Andrew's School, Eastbourne	F W Fl

St Aubyns School, Brighton	W Fl
St Bede's Prep School, Eastbourne	F W Fl
St Bede's School, Hailsham	F W
St Leonards-Mayfield School, Mayfield	F W Fl
St Mary's Hall, Brighton	F W Fl
Stonelands School of Ballet & Theatre Arts, Hove	F Fl
Vinehall School, Robertsbridge	F Fl

WEST SUSSEX

Ardingly College, Haywards Heath	F W Fl
Ardingly College Junior School, Haywards Heath	Fl
Brambletye, East Grinstead	F
Burgess Hill School for Girls, Burgess Hill	F Fl
Christ's Hospital, Horsham	F
Copthorne Prep School, Copthorne	W Fl
Cottesmore School, Pease Pottage	F W Fl
Cumnor House School, Haywards Heath	F Fl
Dorset House School, Pulborough	W Fl
Farlington School, Horsham	F W Fl
Great Ballard School, Chichester	W Fl
Great Walstead, Haywards Heath	W Fl
Handcross Park School, Haywards Heath	W Fl
Hurstpierpoint College, Hurstpierpoint	F W Fl
Lancing College, Lancing	F Fl
Lavant House, Chichester	F W Fl
The Prebendal School, Chichester	F W Fl
Seaford College, Petworth	F W Fl
Slindon College, Arundel	F W Fl
Sompting Abbotts School, Sompting	W Fl
Stoke Brunswick, East Grinstead	W Fl
The Towers Convent School, Steyning	F W Fl
Westbourne House School, Chichester	F Fl
Windlesham House, Pulborough	F
Worth School, Turners Hill	F

WARWICKSHIRE

Bilton Grange, Rugby	F W Fl
Rugby School, Rugby	F
Warwick School, Warwick	F W Fl

WEST MIDLANDS

Birchfield School, Wolverhampton	W
Darul Uloom Islamic High School & College, Birmingham	F
Elmhurst School for Dance, Birmingham	F
The Royal Wolverhampton Junior School, Wolverhampton	F
The Royal Wolverhampton School, Wolverhampton	F W Fl
Tettenhall College, Wolverhampton	F W Fl

WILTSHIRE

Appleford School, Salisbury	F W
Chafyn Grove School, Salisbury	F W Fl
Dauntsey's School, Devizes	F
The Godolphin School, Salisbury	F Fl
Leaden Hall School, Salisbury	F Fl

Marlborough College, Marlborough	F
Norman Court Preparatory School, Salisbury	F W Fl
Pinewood School, Shrivenham	F W Fl
Prior Park Preparatory School, Cricklade	F W Fl
St Mary's Calne, Calne	F
Salisbury Cathedral School, Salisbury	F Fl
Sandroyd School, Salisbury	F
Stonar School, Melksham	F W Fl H
Warminster School, Warminster	F W Fl

WORCESTERSHIRE

Abberley Hall, Worcester	F Fl
The Abbey College, Malvern Wells	Fl
Bromsgrove Preparatory School, Bromsgrove	F W Fl
Bromsgrove School, Bromsgrove	F
The Downs, Malvern College Preparatory School, Malvern	F W Fl
The Elms, Malvern	F Fl
Malvern College, Malvern	F
Malvern College Preparatory and Pre-Prep School, Malvern	F Fl
Malvern St James, Great Malvern	F W Fl
Moffats School, Worcestershire	F W Fl
Moffats School, Bewdley	F W Fl
Saint Michael's College, Tenbury Wells	F H

EAST RIDING OF YORKSHIRE

Pocklington School, Pocklington	F W

NORTH YORKSHIRE

Ampleforth College, York	F
Ashville College, Harrogate	F W Fl
Aysgarth Preparatory School, Bedale	F W Fl
Bootham School, York	F W Fl
Bramcote School, Scarborough	F W Fl
Cundall Manor School, York	F
Fyling Hall School, Whitby	F W
Giggleswick Junior School, Settle	F Fl
Giggleswick School, Settle	F
Harrogate Ladies' College, Harrogate	F W Fl
Harrogate Tutorial College, Harrogate	F W Fl H
Highfield Preparatory School, Harrogate	F W Fl
Lisvane, Scarborough College Junior School, Scarborough	F W
Malsis School, Near Skipton	F
The Mount School, York	F W Fl
Queen Ethelburga's College, York	F
Queen Margaret's School, York	F W
Queen Mary's School, Thirsk	F W Fl
Read School, Selby	F W Fl
Ripon Cathedral Choir School, Ripon	F W Fl
St Martin's Ampleforth, York	F Fl
St Peter's School, York	F
Scarborough College & Lisvane School, Scarborough	F W Fl
Terrington Hall, York	F W Fl
Woodleigh School, Malton	F W Fl

WEST YORKSHIRE

Ackworth School, Pontefract	F W Fl
Bronte House School, Bradford	F W Fl
Fulneck School, Leeds	F W Fl
Rishworth School, Rishworth	F W Fl
Woodhouse Grove School, Apperley Bridge	F W Fl

NORTHERN IRELAND

COUNTY ANTRIM

Cabin Hill School, Belfast	Fl
Campbell College, Belfast	F W Fl
Methodist College, Belfast	F
Victoria College Belfast, Belfast	F W Fl

COUNTY ARMAGH

The Royal School Armagh, Armagh	F W Fl

COUNTY DOWN

Rockport School, Holywood	W Fl

COUNTY TYRONE

The Royal School Dungannon, Dungannon	F W Fl

SCOTLAND

ANGUS

Lathallan School, Montrose	W Fl

ARGYLL AND BUTE

Lomond School, Helensburgh	F H

CLACKMANNANSHIRE

Dollar Academy, Dollar	F W Fl

DUMFRIES & GALLOWAY

Cademuir International School, Thornhill	F

FIFE

St Leonards School , St Andrews	F W Fl

LOTHIAN

Basil Paterson Tutorial College, Edinburgh	H
Belhaven Hill, Dunbar	F
Cargilfield, Edinburgh	F W Fl
The Edinburgh Academy, Edinburgh	Fl

Fettes College, Edinburgh	F
Loretto Junior School, Musselburgh	F W Fl
Loretto School, Musselburgh	F W Fl
The Mary Erskine School, Edinburgh	F W
Merchiston Castle School, Edinburgh	F
St George's School for Girls, Edinburgh	F W Fl
St Mary's Music School, Edinburgh	F
Stewart's Melville College, Edinburgh	F W Fl

MORAYSHIRE

Gordonstoun School, Elgin	F W

PERTH AND KINROSS

Ardvreck School, Crieff	F
Glenalmond College, Perth	F
Kilgraston, Perth	F W Fl
Queen Victoria School, Dunblane	F
Strathallan School, Perth	F

ROXBURGHSHIRE

St Mary's Preparatory School, Melrose	W Fl

WALES

CARDIFF

Westbourne School	

CARMARTHENSHIRE

Llandovery College, Llandovery	F W Fl

CONWY

Lyndon Preparatory School, Colwyn Bay	F W Fl
Rydal Penrhos Senior School, Colwyn Bay	F Fl
St David's College, Llandudno	F W Fl

DENBIGHSHIRE

Howell's School, Denbigh	F W Fl
Ruthin School, Ruthin	F W Fl

MONMOUTHSHIRE

Haberdashers' Monmouth School For Girls, Monmouth	F W Fl
Monmouth School, Monmouth	F W Fl
St John's-on-the-Hill, Chepstow	F W Fl

PEMBROKESHIRE

Netherwood School, Saundersfoot	F W Fl

POWYS

Christ College, Brecon	F W Fl

CONTINENTAL EUROPE

Aiglon College, Switzerland	F W	Chavagnes International College, Chavagnes-en-Paillers, France	F W Fl

5.6
Religious Affiliation

The following index lists all schools specifying a particular denomination. However, it should be noted that this is intended as a guide only and that many of the schools listed also welcome children of other faiths. Schools which claim to be non- or inter-denominational are not listed. Parents should check precise details with individual schools. A full list of each school's entries elsewhere in the book is given in the main index at the back.

BUDDHIST
Dharma School, Brighton

CHRISTIAN
Alderley Edge School for Girls, Alderley Edge
Aldro School, Godalming
All Saints School, Norwich
Amberfield School, Ipswich
Ardvreck School, Crieff
The Ark School, Reading
Arnold Lodge School, Leamington Spa
Ashdell Preparatory School, Sheffield
Ashfold School, Aylesbury
Avon House, Woodford Green
Avondale School, Salisbury
Bangor Independent Christian School, Bangor
Barnsley Christian School, Barnsley
Benedict House Preparatory School, Sidcup
Berkhamsted Collegiate Preparatory School, Berkhamsted
Berkhamsted Collegiate School, Berkhamsted
Blundell's Preparatory School, Tiverton
Bowbrook House School, Pershore
Bradford Christian School, Bradford
The Branch Christian School, Heckmondwike
Bromley High School GDST, Bromley
Broomwood Hall School, SW12
Brownberrie School, Leeds
Carmel Christian School
Castle Court Preparatory School, Wimborne
Castle House School, Newport
Caterham Preparatory School, Caterham
The Cavendish School, NW1

Cedars School, Aldermaston
Chard School, Chard
Chase Academy, Cannock
Christ the King School, Sale
Clifton Lodge Preparatory School, W5
The Crescent School, Rugby
The Daiglen School, Buckhurst Hill
Dale House School, Batley
Dame Alice Harpur School, Bedford
Danes Hill School, Leatherhead
Darvell School, Robertsbridge
Dean Close School, Cheltenham
Derby Grammar School, Derby
Derwent Lodge School for Girls, Tonbridge
Ditcham Park School, Petersfield
Dolphin School (Including Noah's Ark Nursery School), SW11
The Dolphin School, Exmouth
Dower House School, Bridgnorth
Downham Prep School and Montessori Nursery, Kings Lynn
The Downs, Malvern College Preparatory School, Malvern
East London Christian Choir School, E8
Egerton Rothesay School, Berkhamsted
Emmanuel Christian School, Oxford
Emmanuel Christian School, Blackpool
Emmanuel School, Exeter
Emmanuel School, Walsall
Emmanuel School, Derby
Emmaus School, Trowbridge
Eversfield Preparatory School, Solihull
Exeter Junior School, Exeter
Exeter School, Exeter
Filgrave School, Newport Pagnell

Fosse Bank School, Tonbridge
Francis House Preparatory School, Tring
The Froebelian School, Leeds
Fulneck School, Leeds
Gatehouse School, E2
Gateway Christian School, Ilkeston
Ghyll Royd School, Ilkley
Glenarm College, Ilford
Godolphin Preparatory School, Salisbury
Gracefield Preparatory School, Fishponds
Grangewood Independent School, E7
Great Walstead, Haywards Heath
Grey House Preparatory School, Hook
Guildford High School, Guildford
Hamilton College, Hamilton
Handsworth Christian School, Sheffield
Haslemere Preparatory School, Haslemere
Heath House Preparatory School, SE3
Heathfield St Mary's School, Ascot
Herne Hill School, SE24
Heswall Preparatory School, Wirral
Hillgrove School, Bangor
Holy Trinity School, Kidderminster
Howell's School, Denbigh
Hydesville Tower School, Walsall
Jack and Jill School, Hampton
Abingdon Preparatory School, Abingdon
King of Kings School, Manchester
The King's School, Nottingham
King's School, Plymouth
The King's School Senior, Eastleigh
Ffynone House School
The King's School, Primary, Witney
Kingham Hill School, Chipping Norton
Kings Primary School, Southampton
The King's School, Harpenden
Kingsmead School, Wirral
Kingston Grammar School, Kingston-upon-Thames
Knighton House, Blandford Forum
Lady Barn House School, Cheadle
Lambs Christian School, Birmingham
Langley Manor School, Slough
Leicester Grammar School, Leicester
Lightcliffe Preparatory, Halifax
Lighthouse Christian School, Manchester
Lingfield Notre Dame School, Lingfield
Lisvane, Scarborough College Junior School, Scarborough
Locksley Christian School, Manby
Lorenden Preparatory School, Faversham
Lucton School, Leominster
The Lyceum, EC2A
Mannafields Christian School, Edinburgh
Maranatha Christian School, Swindon
Maypole House School, Alford
The Mead School, Tunbridge Wells
Meadowpark Nursery & Pre-Prep School, Cricklade
Monton Prep School with Montessori Nurseries, Eccles
Mountjoy House School, Huddersfield
New Life Christian School, Croydon
Norfolk House Preparatory & Kids Corner Nursery, Sandbach
Norfolk House School, Birmingham
Norwich School, Norwich

Paragon Christian Academy, E5
The Park School, Yeovil
Plymouth College, Plymouth
The Pointer School, SE3
The Portsmouth Grammar School, Portsmouth
The Potters House School, Bury
Priory School, Shanklin
Prospect School, Bristol
The Rastrick Independent School, Brighouse
Red House School, Norton
Redcliffe School, SW10
Regius Christian School, Edinburgh
Richmond House School, Leeds
Rickmansworth PNEU School, Rickmansworth
River School, Worcester
Roundstone Preparatory School, Trowbridge
The Royal Hospital School, Ipswich
St Aubyn's School, Woodford Green
St Christophers School, Totnes
St David's College, Llandudno
St Dominic's School, Stafford
St Francis' College, Letchworth Garden City
St George's School, Edgbaston, Birmingham
St Helen's College, Hillingdon
St Helen's School, Northwood
St Hilda's School, Westcliff-on-Sea
St Ia School, St Ives
St John's Senior School, Enfield
St Joseph's College, Ipswich
St Mary's Preparatory School, Lincoln
St Matthews School, Northampton
St Michael's School, Leigh-on-Sea
St Oswald's School, Alnwick
Sceptre School, Dunstable
The School of the Lion, Gloucester
Sedbergh Junior School, Sedbergh
Sefton Park School, Stoke Poges
Sherborne Preparatory School, Sherborne
Somerhill Pre-Preparatory School, Tonbridge
South Hills School, Salisbury
Springfield Christian School, SE6
St Swithun's Junior School, Winchester
Stonehouse Nursery School, Leyland
Stoneygate College, Leicester
Stowford College, Sutton
Sunflower Montessori School, Twickenham
Sunninghill Preparatory School, Dorchester
Tabernacle School, W11
Thames Christian College, SW11
The Terrace School, Leamington Spa
Thomas's Kindergarten, SW1W
Thomas's Preparatory School, W8
Thorpe Hall School, Southend-on-Sea
Trent College, Nottingham
Trinity School, Croydon
Trinity School, Stalybridge
Twickenham Preparatory School, Hampton
Uplands School, Poole
Victoria College, Jersey
Wakefield Tutorial Preparatory School, Leeds
Warlingham Park School, Croydon
Warwick Preparatory School, Warwick
West Buckland School, Barnstaple

Weston Green School, Thames Ditton
Wetherby Preparatory School, W11
White House Preparatory School, Wokingham
Wickham Court School, West Wickham
Windmill House School, Uppingham
Woodford Green Preparatory School, Woodford Green
Worksop College, Worksop
Yardley Court Preparatory School, Tonbridge
Yarm School, Yarm

CHRISTIAN SCIENCE

Claremont Fan Court School, Esher
Haberdashers' Aske's School for Girls, Elstree

CHURCH IN WALES

Albemarle Independent College, W1K
The Cathedral School
Christ College, Brecon
Ffynone House School
Llandovery College, Llandovery
Monmouth School, Monmouth

CHURCH OF ENGLAND

Abbey Gate College, Chester
Abbey Gate School, Chester
The Abbey School, Reading
The Abbey, Woodbridge
Abbot's Hill School, Hemel Hempstead
Abbots Bromley School for Girls, Abbots Bromley
Abbotsbury School, Newton Abbot
Abingdon School, Abingdon
Acorn School, Nailsworth
Adcote School for Girls, Shrewsbury
Airthrie School, Cheltenham
Aldenham School, Elstree
Aldwickbury School, Harpenden
Alleyn Court Preparatory School, Southend-on-Sea
Alleyn's School, SE22
Amesbury, Hindhead
Ardingly College, Haywards Heath
Ardingly College Junior School, Haywards Heath
Arnold House School, NW8
Ashdown House School, Forest Row
Aysgarth Preparatory School, Bedale
Ballard School, New Milton
Bancroft's School, Woodford Green
Barfield School, Farnham
Barnardiston Hall Preparatory School, Haverhill
Baston School, Bromley
Beachborough School, Brackley
The Beacon School, Amersham
Bearwood College, Wokingham
Beaudesert Park School, Stroud
Bedford Preparatory School, Bedford
Bedford School, Bedford
Bedstone College, Bucknell
Beech Hall School, Macclesfield
Beechenhurst Preparatory School, Liverpool
Beechwood Park School, St Albans

Beeston Hall School, Cromer
Belmont School, Dorking
Benenden School, Cranbrook
Berkhampstead School, Cheltenham
Bethany School, Cranbrook
Bilton Grange, Rugby
Birchfield School, Wolverhampton
Bloxham School, Banbury
The Blue Coat School, Birmingham
Blundell's School, Tiverton
Bodiam Manor School, Robertsbridge
The Bolitho School, Penzance
Bradfield College, Reading
Brambletye, East Grinstead
Bramcote School, Scarborough
Brandeston Hall, The Preparatory School for Framlingham
    College, Brandeston
Bredon School, Tewkesbury
Brentwood School, Brentwood
Brigg Preparatory School, Brigg
Brighton College, Brighton
Brighton College Pre-preparatory School, Brighton
Brighton College Prep School, Brighton
Bristol Cathedral School
Broadwater Manor School, Worthing
Brockhurst & Marlston House Pre-Preparatory School,
    Thatcham
Brockhurst and Marlston House Schools, Newbury
Bromsgrove Pre-preparatory and Nursery School,
    Bromsgrove
Bromsgrove Preparatory School, Bromsgrove
Bromsgrove School, Bromsgrove
Bronte School, Gravesend
Broomfield House School, Richmond
Bryanston School, Blandford Forum
Buckingham College Preparatory School, Pinner
Burys Court School and Moon Hall College, Reigate
Caldicott School, Farnham Royal
Canford School, Wimborne
Casterton School, Kirkby Lonsdale
Chafyn Grove School, Salisbury
Chandlings Manor School, Oxford
Charterhouse, Godalming
Cheam School, Newbury
Cheltenham College, Cheltenham
Cheltenham College Junior School, Cheltenham
Chigwell School, Chigwell
Chilton Cantelo School, Yeovil
The Chorister School, Durham
Christ Church Cathedral School, Oxford
Christ's Hospital, Horsham
Claremont School, St Leonards-on-Sea
Clayesmore Preparatory School, Blandford Forum
Clayesmore, Blandford Forum
Clifton College
Clifton College Preparatory School
Colfe's School, SE12
Colston's Collegiate School
Conifers School, Midhurst
Conway Preparatory School, Boston
Coopersale Hall School, Epping
Copthorne Prep School, Copthorne
Cothill House Preparatory School, Abingdon

Cottesmore School, Pease Pottage
Coventry Prep School, Coventry
Cranford House School, Wallingford
Cranleigh Preparatory School, Cranleigh
Cranleigh School, Cranleigh
The Croft Preparatory School, Stratford-upon-Avon
Cumnor House School, South Croydon
Cumnor House School, Haywards Heath
Cundall Manor School, York
Dair House School Trust Ltd, Farnham Royal
Daneshill School, Basingstoke
Dean Close Preparatory School, Cheltenham
Deepdene School, Hove
Denmead School, Hampton
Denstone College, Uttoxeter
Derby High School, Derby
The Dormer House PNEU School, Moreton-in-Marsh
Dorset House School, Pulborough
Dover College, Dover
Downe House, Thatcham
The Downs School, Wraxall
Duke of York's Royal Military School, Dover
Dulwich College, SE21
Dulwich College Preparatory School, SE21
Dulwich Preparatory School, Cranbrook, Cranbrook
Dumpton School, Wimborne
Duncombe School, Hertford
Durham High School For Girls, Durham
Durham School, Durham
Durlston Court, New Milton
Eagle House, Sandhurst
Eastbourne College, Eastbourne
Edenhurst School, Newcastle-under-Lyme
Edge Grove, Aldenham
Edgeborough, Farnham
Elizabeth College, Guernsey
Ellesmere College, Ellesmere
Elmhurst School for Dance, Birmingham
The Elms, Malvern
Elstree School, Reading
The Elvian School, Reading
Emanuel School, SW11
Epsom College, Epsom
Eton College, Windsor
Eton End PNEU, Slough
Ewell Castle School, Epsom
Exeter Cathedral School, Exeter
Fairfield School, Backwell
Fairholme Preparatory School, St Asaph
Farlington School, Horsham
Felixstowe International College, Felixstowe
Felsted Preparatory School, Felsted
Felsted School, Felsted
Feltonfleet School, Cobham
Fen School, Sleaford
Fonthill Lodge, East Grinstead
Foremarke Hall School, Derby
Forest School, E17
Forres Sandle Manor, Fordingbridge
Framlingham College, Woodbridge
Francis Holland School, Regent's Park NW1, NW1
Francis Holland School, SW1, SW1W
Gayhurst School, Gerrards Cross

Giggleswick School, Settle
Glebe House School, Hunstanton
The Godolphin School, Salisbury
Godstowe Preparatory School, High Wycombe
Great Ballard School, Chichester
Grenville College, Bideford
Gresham's Preparatory School, Holt
Gresham's School, Holt
Haberdashers' Aske's Boys' School, Elstree
Haileybury, Hertford
The Hall School, NW3
Hallfield School, Birmingham
Halstead Preparatory School, Woking
Hammond School, Chester
Hampshire Collegiate School UCST, Romsey
Handcross Park School, Haywards Heath
Hanford School, Blandford Forum
Harrogate Ladies' College, Harrogate
Harrow School, Harrow on the Hill
Hatherop Castle School, Cirencester
Hazelwood School, Oxted
Hazlegrove (King's Bruton Preparatory School), Yeovil
Headington School, Oxford
Heath House Preparatory School, SE3
Heath Mount School, Hertford
Heathland College, Accrington
The Hereford Cathedral Junior School, Hereford
The Hereford Cathedral School, Hereford
Hethersett Old Hall School, Norwich
Highfield Preparatory School, Harrogate
Highfield School, Liphook
Highgate School, N6
Hilden Grange School, Tonbridge
Hilden Oaks School, Tonbridge
Holme Grange School, Wokingham
Holme Park School, Kendal
Hordle Walhampton School, Lymington
Hull Collegiate School, Anlaby
The Hurlingham School, SW15
Hurstpierpoint College, Hurstpierpoint
Innellan House School, Pinner
Ipswich School, Ipswich
James Allen's Girls' School, SE22
James Allen's Preparatory School, SE22
Junior King's School, Canterbury
Kelly College, Tavistock
Kelly College Preparatory School, Tavistock
King Edward's School, Birmingham
King William's College, Castletown
King's Bruton, Bruton
King's College, Taunton
King's College Junior School, SW19
King's College School, SW19
King's Hall, Taunton
King's Hawford, Worcester
King's Preparatory School, Rochester
The King's School, Canterbury
The King's School, Chester
The King's School, Gloucester
The King's School, Macclesfield
The King's School, Worcester
The King's School Ely, Ely
King's School Rochester, Rochester

Kingscote Pre-Preparatory School, Gerrards Cross
Kingshott School, Hitchin
Kingsland Grange, Shrewsbury
The Kingsley School, Leamington Spa
The Knoll School, Kidderminster
The Lady Eleanor Holles School, Hampton
Lambrook Haileybury, Bracknell
Lancing College, Lancing
Lancing College Preparatory School at Mowden, Hove
Lanesborough, Guildford
Lavant House, Chichester
Laxton Junior School, Nr Peterborough
Leicester Grammar Junior School, Leicester
Leicester Grammar School, Leicester
Leicester High School For Girls, Leicester
Lichfield Cathedral School, Lichfield
Liverpool College, Liverpool
Lockers Park, Hemel Hempstead
Luckley-Oakfield School, Wokingham
Ludgrove, Wokingham
Maidwell Hall School, Northampton
Malsis School, Near Skipton
Malvern College, Malvern
Malvern College Preparatory and Pre-Prep School,
    Malvern
Malvern St James, Great Malvern
The Manor Preparatory School, Abingdon
Marlborough College, Marlborough
Marlborough House School, Hawkhurst
Meadowbrook Montessori School, Bracknell
Merchant Taylors' School, Northwood
Merton Court Preparatory School, Sidcup
Merton House, Chester
Micklefield School, Reigate
Milbourne Lodge School, Esher
Milton Abbey School, Blandford Forum
The Minster School, York
Moffats School, Worcestershire
Moffats School, Bewdley
Monkton Prep , Bath
Monkton Senior School, Bath
Moorland School, Clitheroe
Morley Hall Preparatory School, Derby
Moulsford Preparatory School, Wallingford
Mount House School, Tavistock
Mowden Hall School, Stocksfield
Netherwood School, Saundersfoot
The New Beacon, Sevenoaks
New College School, Oxford
New Lodge School, Dorking
New School, Exeter
Newcastle Upon Tyne Church High School,
    Newcastle upon Tyne
Norman Court Preparatory School, Salisbury
Northampton High School, Northampton
Northbourne Park School, Deal
Northcote Lodge School, SW11
Northwood Preparatory School, Rickmansworth
Oakham School, Oakham
Oakwood School, Chichester
Old Buckenham Hall School, Ipswich
The Old Hall School, Telford
Old Palace of John Whitgift School, Croydon

The Old School, Beccles
Old Vicarage School, Richmond
Orley Farm School, Harrow
Oswestry School Bellan House, Oswestry
Oundle School, Nr Peterborough
Packwood Haugh School, Shrewsbury
Pangbourne College, Pangbourne
Papplewick School, Ascot
Park Hill School, Kingston-upon-Thames
Peaslake School, Guildford
Pennthorpe School, Horsham
Perrott Hill School, Crewkerne
Peterborough & St Margaret's School, Stanmore
Peterborough High School, Peterborough
Pilgrims Pre-Preparatory School, Bedford
The Pilgrims' School, Winchester
Pinewood School, Shrivenham
Pipers Corner School, High Wycombe
Plumtree School, Nottingham
Pocklington School, Pocklington
The Prebendal School, Chichester
Prebendal School (Northgate House), Chichester
Prestfelde Preparatory School, Shrewsbury
Prince's Mead School, Winchester
The Princess Helena College, Hitchin
Putney Park School, SW15
Quainton Hall School, Harrow
Queen Anne's School, Reading
Queen Ethelburga's College, York
Queen Margaret's School, York
Queen Mary's School, Thirsk
Queen's College, W1G
Queen's College Prep School, W1B
Querns Westonbirt School, Tetbury
Radley College, Abingdon
Ranby House School, Retford
Rathvilly School, Birmingham
Ravenscourt Theatre School, W6
Read School, Selby
Reading Blue Coat School, Reading
Reddiford, Pinner
Reed's School, Cobham
Reigate St Mary's Preparatory and Choir School, Reigate
Rendcomb College, Cirencester
Repton School, Derby
Riddlesworth Hall, Diss
Ripon Cathedral Choir School, Ripon
Rishworth School, Rishworth
Rock Hall School, Alnwick
Roedean School, Brighton
Rose Hill School, Wotton-under-Edge
Roselyon, Par
Rossall Junior School, Fleetwood
Rossall School, Fleetwood
Rosslyn School, Birmingham
Roxeth Mead School, Harrow on the Hill
Royal Alexandra and Albert School, Reigate
Royal Russell School, Croydon
The Royal School, Haslemere
The Royal Wolverhampton Junior School,
    Wolverhampton
The Royal Wolverhampton School, Wolverhampton
Rugby School, Rugby

Rushmoor School, Bedford
Russell House School, Sevenoaks
Ryde School, Ryde
Sackville School, Tonbridge
Saddleworth Preparatory School, Oldham
St Agnes PNEU School, Leeds
St Albans High School for Girls, St Albans
St Andrew's School, Eastbourne
St Andrew's School, Reading
St Andrew's (Woking) School Trust, Woking
S Anselm's School, Bakewell
St Aubyns School, Brighton
St Bees School, St Bees
St Catherine's School, Guildford
St Christopher's School, Epsom
St Christopher's School, Hove
St David's School, Purley
St Dunstan's College, SE6
St Edmunds Junior School, Canterbury
St Edmund's School Canterbury, Canterbury
St Edmund's School, Hindhead
St Edward's School, Oxford
St Francis School, Pewsey
St Gabriel's, Newbury
St George's School, Ascot
St George's School, Windsor
St Hilda's School, Harpenden
St Hilda's School, Wakefield
St Hugh's School, Woodhall Spa
St Hugh's School, Faringdon
St Ives School, Haslemere
St. James' School, Grimsby
St John's College School, Cambridge
St John's Northwood, Northwood
St John's School, Leatherhead
St John's-on-the-Hill, Chepstow
St Lawrence College Junior School, Ramsgate
St Lawrence College, Ramsgate
St Margaret's School, Halstead
St Margaret's School, NW3
St Margaret's School, Bushey
St Margaret's School, Exeter
St Martin's School, Bournemouth
St Martin's School, Northwood
St Mary's Calne, Calne
St Mary's Hall, Brighton
St Mary's School, Gerrards Cross
St Michael's, Barnstaple
St Michael's School, Sevenoaks
St Michael's School, Leigh-on-Sea
St Neot's School, Hook
St Nicholas' School, Fleet
St Paul's Cathedral School, EC4M
St Paul's Preparatory School, SW13
St Paul's School, SW13
St Peter's School, Kettering
St Peter's School, York
St Petroc's School, Bude
St Piran's Preparatory School, Maidenhead
St Ronan's School, Hawkhurst
St Swithun's School, Winchester
St Wilfrid's School, Exeter
St Wystan's School, Repton

Salisbury Cathedral School, Salisbury
Sancton Wood School, Cambridge
Sandroyd School, Salisbury
Sarum Hall, NW3
The School of St Helen & St Katharine, Abingdon
Seaford College, Petworth
Sedbergh School, Sedbergh
Sherborne Preparatory School, Sherborne
Sherborne School, Sherborne
Sherborne Girls, Sherborne
Shernold School, Maidstone
Sherrardswood School, Welwyn
Shiplake College, Henley-on-Thames
Shoreham College, Shoreham-by-Sea
Shrewsbury House School, Surbiton
Shrewsbury School, Shrewsbury
Slapton Pre-Preparatory School, Towcester
Smallwood Manor Preparatory School, Uttoxeter
Snaresbrook College Preparatory School, E18
Solefield School, Sevenoaks
Solihull School, Solihull
Sompting Abbotts School, Sompting
Spratton Hall, Northampton
Stamford High School, Stamford
Stamford Junior School, Stamford
Stamford School, Stamford
Steephill Independent School, Longfield
Stepping Stones Nursery and Pre-Preparatory School,
   Marlborough
Stoke Brunswick, East Grinstead
Stoneygate School, Leicester
Stourbridge House School, Warminster
Stover School, Newton Abbot
Stowe School, Buckingham
The Stroud School, Romsey
The Study School, New Malden
Summer Fields, Oxford
Sunderland High School, Sunderland
Sunningdale School, Sunningdale
Surbiton High School, Kingston-upon-Thames
Surbiton Preparatory School, Surbiton
Sussex House School, SW1X
Sutton Valence Preparatory School, Maidstone
Sutton Valence School, Maidstone
Swanbourne House School, Milton Keynes
Talbot Heath, Bournemouth
Taverham Hall Preparatory School, Norwich
Thomas's Kindergarten, Battersea, SW11
Thomas's Preparatory School, SW11
Thomas's Preparatory School Clapham, SW11
Thorpe House School, Gerrards Cross
Tockington Manor School, Tockington
Tonbridge School, Tonbridge
Town Close House Preparatory School, Norwich
Trevor Roberts School, NW3
Truro High School, Truro
Tudor Hall School, Banbury
Twyford School, Winchester
Uppingham School, Uppingham
Upton House School, Windsor
Vinehall School, Robertsbridge
Wakefield Independent School, Wakefield
Warminster School, Warminster

Warwick School, Warwick
Wellesley House School, Broadstairs
Wellington College, Crowthorne
Wellington School, Wellington
Wells Cathedral Junior School, Wells
Wells Cathedral School, Wells
West Buckland Preparatory School, Barnstaple
Westbourne House School, Chichester
Westbrook Hay Preparatory School, Hemel Hempstead
Westminster Abbey Choir School, SW1P
Westminster School, SW1P
Westminster Under School, SW1P
Westonbirt School, Tetbury
Widford Lodge, Chelmsford
Winchester College, Winchester
Winchester House School, Brackley
Windlesham House, Pulborough
Windrush Valley School, Chipping Norton
Wisbech Grammar School, Wisbech
Witham Hall, Bourne
Wood Dene School, Norwich
Woodbridge School, Woodbridge
Woodleigh School, Malton
Worksop College, Worksop
Wrekin College, Telford
Wycombe Abbey School, High Wycombe
Wykeham House School, Fareham
Yateley Manor Preparatory School, Yateley
York House School, Rickmansworth
Yorston Lodge School, Knutsford

CHURCH OF SCOTLAND

The Glasgow Academy

EPISCOPELIAN

Glenalmond College, Perth
Hemdean House School, Reading

GREEK ORTHODOX

Knightsbridge School, SW1X

JEWISH

Akiva School, N3
Beis Hamedrash Elyon, NW11
Beis Rochel D'Satmar Girls School, N16
Hubert Jewish High School for Girls, Salford
Immanuel College, Bushey
Kerem School, N2
London Jewish Girls' High School, NW4
Lubavitch House School (Junior Boys), E5
Lubavitch House Senior School for Girls, N16
Mechinah Liyeshivah Zichron Moshe, N16
Naima Jewish Preparatory School, NW6
OYH Primary School, NW4
Pardes Grammar Boys' School, N3
Talmud Torah Bobov Primary School, N16

Tashbar School, Salford
Yesodey Hatorah Jewish School, N16
Yetev Lev Day School for Boys, N16

METHODIST

Ashville College, Harrogate
Bronte House School, Bradford
Culford School, Bury St Edmunds
Edgehill College, Bideford
Farringtons School, Chislehurst
Kent College, Canterbury
Kent College Infant & Junior School, Canterbury
Kent College Pembury, Tunbridge Wells
Kingswood Preparatory School, Bath
Kingswood School, Bath
The Leys School, Cambridge
Lyndon Preparatory School, Colwyn Bay
Queen's College Junior, Pre-Prep & Nursery Schools, Taunton
Queen's College, Taunton
Rydal Penrhos Senior School, Colwyn Bay
St Crispin's School, Leicester
Shebbear College, Beaworthy
Truro School Preparatory School, Truro
Truro School, Truro
Woodhouse Grove School, Apperley Bridge

MUSLIM

Abu Bakr Independent School, Walsall
Al Hijrah School, Birmingham
Al Karam Secondary School, Retford
Al-Burhan Grammar School, Birmingham
Al-Mizan Primary & London East Academy Secondary & Sixth Form, E1
Al-Muntada Islamic School, SW6
Balham Preparatory School, SW12
Birchfield Independent Girls School, Birmingham
Bolton Muslim Girls School, Bolton
Brondesbury College For Boys, NW6
Coventry Muslim School, Coventry
Darul Hadis Latifiah, E2
Darul Uloom Islamic High School & College, Birmingham
Date Valley School, Mitcham
Gloucestershire Islamic Secondary School For Girls, Gloucester
IQRA School, Oxford
Islamia Girls High School, Huddersfield
Islamia Girls' School, NW6
Islamic Shakhsiyah Foundation, N15
Islamiyah School, Blackburn
Jamahiriya School, SW3
Jamea Al Kauthar, Lancaster
Jamiah Madaniyah Primary School, Forest Gate
King Fahad Academy, W3
London East Academy, E1
London Islamic School, E1
Madni Girls School, E1
Manchester Islamic High School, Manchester
Markazul Uloom, Blackburn
New Horizon Community School, Leeds

Noor Ul Islam Primary School, E10
Quwwatt Ul Islam Girls School, E7
Rawdha Tul Uloom, Blackburn
Rochdale Girls School, Rochdale
Tawhid Boys School, Tawhid Educational Trust, N16
Tayyibah Girls School, N16
Tiny Tots Pre- School, Leicester

QUAKER

Ackworth School, Pontefract
Bootham School, York
Friends' School, Saffron Walden
Leighton Park School, Reading
The Mount School, York
Sibford School, Banbury
Sidcot School, Winscombe
Tregelles, York

ROMAN CATHOLIC

All Hallows, Shepton Mallet
Alton Convent School, Alton
Ampleforth College, York
Austin Friars St Monica's School, Carlisle
Barlborough Hall School, Chesterfield
Barrow Hills School, Godalming
Beechwood Sacred Heart School, Tunbridge Wells
Bishop Challoner RC School, Bromley
Brigidine School Windsor, Windsor
Bury Catholic Preparatory School, Bury
Carleton House Preparatory School, Liverpool
Chavagnes International College, Chavagnes-en-Paillers, France
Claires Court Schools, The College, Maidenhead
Combe Bank School, Nr Sevenoaks
Convent of Mercy, Guernsey
Crackley Hall School, Kenilworth
Cranmore School, Leatherhead
Donhead Prep School, SW19
Downside School, Bath
Farleigh School, Andover
Farnborough Hill, Farnborough
FCJ Primary School, Jersey
Fernhill School, Glasgow
Grace Dieu Manor School, Leicester
Holy Cross Preparatory School, Kingston-upon-Thames
Ilford Ursuline Preparatory School, Ilford
Kilgraston, Perth
Laleham Lea School, Purley
Leweston School, Sherborne
Loreto Preparatory School, Altrincham
Loyola Preparatory School, Buckhurst Hill
The Marist Preparatory School, Ascot
The Marist Senior School, Ascot
Marymount International School, Kingston-upon-Thames
Moor Park School, Ludlow
More House, SW1X
More House School, Farnham
Moreton Hall Preparatory School, Bury St Edmunds
Mount St Mary's College, Spinkhill

Mylnhurst Preparatory School & Nursery, Sheffield
New Hall School, Chelmsford
Notre Dame Preparatory School, Cobham
Notre Dame Preparatory School, Norwich
Notre Dame Senior School, Cobham
Oakhill College, Clitheroe
Oakwood School & Nursery, Purley
The Oratory Preparatory School, Reading
The Oratory School, Reading
Our Lady's Convent Junior School, Abingdon
Our Lady's Convent School, Loughborough
Our Lady's Abingdon Senior School, Abingdon
Our Lady's Preparatory School, Crowthorne
Princethorpe College, Rugby
Prior Park College, Bath
Prior Park Preparatory School, Cricklade
Priory School, Birmingham
Ratcliffe College, Leicester
Redcourt- St Anselms, Prenton
Runnymede St Edward's School, Liverpool
Rye St Antony School, Oxford
Sacred Heart School, Swaffham
Sacred Heart RC Primary School, Wadhurst
St Aloysius' College, Glasgow
St Ambrose Preparatory School, Altrincham
St Anthony's Preparatory School, NW3
St Anthonys School, Cinderford
St Augustine's Priory, W5
St Bede's College, Manchester
St Bede's School, Stafford
St Benedict's Junior School, W5
St Benedict's School, W5
St Bernard's Preparatory School, Slough
St Catherine's Preparatory School, Stockport
St Catherine's School, Twickenham
St Christina's RC Preparatory School, NW8
St Columba's College, St Albans
St Dominic's Priory School, Stone
St Edmund's College and St Hugh's School, Ware
St Edward's School Cheltenham, Cheltenham
St George's College, Weybridge
St George's College Junior School, Weybridge
St Gerard's School, Bangor
St John's Beaumont, Windsor
St John's College, Southsea
St Joseph's Convent, Chesterfield
St Joseph's Convent School, E11
St Joseph's Convent School, Reading
St Joseph's Preparatory School, Stoke-on-Trent
St Joseph's School, Nottingham
St Joseph's School, Park Hill, Burnley
St Leonards-Mayfield School, Mayfield
St Margaret's School, Midhurst
St Martha's Senior School, Barnet
St Martin's Ampleforth, York
St Mary's College, Liverpool
St Mary's College, Southampton
St Mary's Convent School, Worcester
St Mary's Hall, Stonyhurst
St Mary's Hare Park School, Romford
St Mary's Junior School, Cambridge
St Mary's School, Cambridge
St Mary's School, Shaftesbury

St Mary's School, Ascot, Ascot
St Mary's School Hampstead, NW3
St Michaels School, Newbury
St Philip's School, SW7
St Philomena's Preparatory School, Frinton-on-Sea
St Pius X Preparatory School, Preston
St Richard's, Bromyard
St Teresa's Catholic Independent & Nursery School,
    Princes Risborough
St Teresa's Preparatory School, Effingham
St Teresa's School, Dorking
St Thomas Garnet's School, Bournemouth
St Ursula's High School, Westbury-on-Trym
St Winefride's Convent School, Shrewsbury
Salesian College, Farnborough
Sinclair House School, SW6
Stella Maris Junior School, Stockport
Stonyhurst College, Clitheroe
Thornton College Convent of Jesus and Mary,
    Milton Keynes
The Towers Convent School, Steyning
Ursuline Preparatory School, SW20
Ursuline Preparatory School, Brentwood

Virgo Fidelis, SE19
Vita Et Pax School, N14
Westminster Cathedral Choir School, SW1P
Winterfold House, Kidderminster
Woldingham School, Woldingham
Worth School, Turners Hill

SEVENTH DAY ADVENTIST

Dudley House School, Grantham
Fletewood School, Plymouth
Hyland House, E17
Newbold School, Bracknell
Stanborough School, Watford

UNITED REFORMED CHURCH

Caterham School, Caterham
The Firs School, Chester
Silcoates School, Wakefield
Sunny Hill House School, Wakefield

5.7

Schools Registered with CReSTeD (Council for the Registration of Schools Teaching Dyslexic Pupils)

Registered charity number 1052103
Information provided by CReSTeD

CReSTeD (the Council for the Registration of Schools Teaching Dyslexic Pupils) produces a twice yearly register of schools that provide for dyslexic children. The aim is to help parents and those who advise them to choose a school that has been approved to published criteria. CReSTeD was established in 1989 – its main supporters are the British Dyslexia Association and Dyslexia Action. Schools wishing to be included in the Register are visited by a CReSTeD consultant whose report is considered by the CReSTeD Council before registration can be finalized.

Consulting the Register should enable parents to decide which schools they wish to approach for further information. Dyslexic students have a variety of difficulties and so have a wide range of special needs. An equally wide range of teaching approaches is necessary. CReSTeD has therefore grouped schools together under four broad categories, which are designed to help parents match their child's needs to an appropriate philosophy and provision.

The four categories of the schools are described below:

SPECIALIST PROVISION SCHOOLS – SP

The school is established primarily to teach pupils with dyslexia. The curriculum and timetable are designed to meet specific needs in a holistic, coordinated manner with a significant number of staff qualified in teaching dyslexic pupils.

DYSLEXIA UNIT – DU

The school has a designated unit or centre that provides specialist tuition on a small group or individual basis, according to need. The unit or centre is an adequately resourced teaching area under the management of a senior specialist teacher, who coordinates the work of other specialist teachers and ensures ongoing liaison with all mainstream teachers. This senior specialist teacher will probably have head of department status, and will certainly have significant input into the curriculum design and delivery.

SPECIALIST CLASSES – SC

Schools where dyslexic pupils are taught in separate classes within the school for some lessons, most probably English and Mathematics. These are taught by teachers with qualifications in teaching dyslexic pupils. These teachers are deemed responsible for communicating with the pupils' other subject teachers.

WITHDRAWAL SYSTEMS – WS

Schools where dyslexic pupils are withdrawn from appropriately selected lessons for specialist tuition from a teacher qualified in teaching dyslexic pupils. There is ongoing communication between mainstream and specialist teachers.

Note: **Qualified** means holding a BDA-recognized qualification in the teaching of dyslexic pupils.

The list below includes those schools registered with CReSTeD which are listed elsewhere in this Guide. For a full list of schools registered with CReSTeD, including specialist schools and maintained schools, contact CReSTeD on 01242 604852 or by email at admin@crested.org.uk, or by writing to The Administrator, CReSTeD, Greygarth, Littleworth, Winchcombe, Cheltenham, GL54 5BT. Alternatively, visit the website at www.crested.org.uk.

SPECIALIST PROVISION SCHOOLS

Abingdon House School, London W8
Appleford School, Salisbury
Brown's School, Orpington
Calder House School, Bath
The Dominie, London SW11
East Court School, Ramsgate
Edington & Shapwick School, Bridgewater
Fairley House School, London SW1P
Frewen College, Rye
Knowl Hill School, Pirbright
Mark College, Highbridge
The Moat School, Fulham
Moon Hall School, Dorking
More House School, Farnham
Northease Manor School, Lewes
Nunnykirk Centre for Dyslexia, Morpeth
The Old Rectory School, Ipswich
Stanbridge Earls School, Romsey
Sunnydown School, Caterham

Trinity School, Rochester
The Unicorn School, Abingdon

DYSLEXIA UNIT

Avon House, Woodford Green
Barnardiston Hall, Havershill
Bethany School, Cranbrook
Bloxham School, Banbury
Bredon School, Tewkesbury
Centre Academy, Battersea SW11
Clayesmore Preparatory School, Blandford Forum
Clayesmore, Blandford Forum
Clifton College Preparatory School
Cobham Hall, Gravesend
Danes Hill School, Leatherhead
Ellesmere College, Ellesmere
Finborough School, Stowmarket
Fulneck School, Pudsey
Grenville College, Bideford

Hazlegrove (King's Bruton Preparatory School), Yeovil
Holmwood House, Colchester
Hordle Walhampton School, Lymington
King's Bruton, Bruton
Kingham Hill School, Chipping Norton
Kingswood College Trust, Ormskirk
Kingswood House School, Epsom
Lime House School, Carlisle
Malvern St James, Great Malvern
Mayville High School, Southsea
Monkton Combe School, Bath
Mostyn House School, South Wirral
Moyles Court School, Ringwood
Newlands School, Seaford
Ramillies Hall School, Cheadle
Riddlesworth Hall, Diss
St Bees School, St Bees
St David's College, Llandudno
Sibford School, Banbury
Slindon College, Arundel
Stowford College, Sutton
Tettenhall College, Wolverhampton

Wycliffe, Stonehouse
Wycliffe Preparatory School, Stonehouse

SPECIALIST CLASSES
Bruern Abbey School, Chesterton
St Crispin's School, Leicester

WITHDRAWAL SYSTEM
Dover College, Dover
Kilgraston, Perth
King's School, Rochester
Milton Abbey School, Blandford Forum
Prior Park Preparatory School, Cricklade
Putney Park School, Putney
The Royal Wolverhampton School
Thames Christian College, SW11
Woodleigh School, Malton
Woodside Park International School, N11
Ysgol Rhydygors, Carmarthen

5.8
Provision for English as a Foreign Language

This index is intended as a general guide only and is compiled upon the basis of information given to Gabbitas by schools. Parents should note that there are wide variations in provision and are advised to contact individual schools for further details.

Schools listed below with a 'U' have a dedicated English language unit or offer intensive initial tuition for students whose first language is not English. Schools with no 'U' displayed offer one-to-one English language tuition, or arrange this tuition, according to need, for students whose first language is not English.

Parents may also wish to refer to the list of International Study Centres on page 32.

ENGLAND

BEDFORDSHIRE

Acorn School, Bedford
Bedford High School for Girls, Bedford
Bedford School, Bedford

BERKSHIRE

The Ark School, Reading
Bearwood College, Wokingham   U
Bradfield College, Reading   U
Brockhurst & Marlston House Pre-Preparatory School, Thatcham
Brockhurst and Marlston House Schools, Newbury
Cedars School, Aldermaston
Cheam School, Newbury
Claires Court School, Maidenhead
Claires Court Schools, Ridgeway, Maidenhead
Claires Court Schools, The College, Maidenhead
Dolphin School, Reading
Eagle House, Sandhurst
Elstree School, Reading
The Elvian School, Reading
Heathfield St Mary's School, Ascot
Highfield School, Maidenhead
Holme Grange School, Wokingham
Horris Hill School, Newbury

Hurst Lodge School, Ascot
Leighton Park School, Reading   U
Licensed Victuallers' School, Ascot
Luckley-Oakfield School, Wokingham
The Oratory School, Reading   U
Padworth College, Reading   U
Papplewick School, Ascot
Queen Anne's School, Reading
St Gabriel's, Newbury
St George's School, Ascot
St John's Beaumont, Windsor   U
St Joseph's Convent School, Reading
St Piran's Preparatory School, Maidenhead
Sunningdale School, Sunningdale
Upton House School, Windsor
Waverley School, Wokingham
White House Preparatory School, Wokingham
Winbury School, Maidenhead

BRISTOL

Badminton School
Clifton College   U
Clifton College Preparatory School   U
The Downs School, Wraxall
Gracefield Preparatory School, Fishponds

Queen Elizabeth's Hospital
St Ursula's High School, Westbury-on-Trym   U
Tockington Manor School, Tockington   U
Torwood House School

BUCKINGHAMSHIRE

Akeley Wood School, Buckingham
Bury Lawn School, Milton Keynes
Caldicott School, Farnham Royal
Godstowe Preparatory School, High Wycombe   U
Grove Independent School, Milton Keynes
High March School, Beaconsfield
Ladymede, Aylesbury
Maltman's Green School, Gerrards Cross
Milton Keynes Preparatory School, Milton Keynes
Pipers Corner School, High Wycombe
Stowe School, Buckingham   U
Swanbourne House School, Milton Keynes
Thornton College Convent of Jesus and Mary,
    Milton Keynes
Thorpe House School, Gerrards Cross
Wycombe Abbey School, High Wycombe

CAMBRIDGESHIRE

Bellerbys College & Embassy CES Cambridge,
    Cambridge   U
Cambridge Centre for Sixth-form Studies, Cambridge
CATS Cambridge, Cambridge   U
Kimbolton School, Huntingdon
The King's School Ely, Ely   U
The Leys School, Cambridge   U
Madingley Pre-Preparatory School, Cambridge
MPW (Mander Portman Woodward), Cambridge   U
Peterborough High School, Peterborough   U
St Mary's School, Cambridge   U
Sancton Wood School, Cambridge

CHANNEL ISLANDS

St George's Preparatory School, Jersey

CHESHIRE

Abbey Gate School, Chester
Beech Hall School, Macclesfield
Cransley School, Northwich
Culcheth Hall, Altrincham
The Firs School, Chester
Forest Park School, Sale
Hale Preparatory School, Altrincham   U
Loreto Preparatory School, Altrincham
Mostyn House School, South Wirral   U
The Queen's School, Chester
The Ryleys, Alderley Edge
Terra Nova School, Holmes Chapel

CORNWALL

The Bolitho School, Penzance   U
St Ia School, St Ives

CUMBRIA

Chetwynde School, Barrow-in-Furness
Harecroft Hall School, Seascale
Holme Park School, Kendal
Lime House School, Carlisle   U
St Bees School, St Bees   U
Sedbergh School, Sedbergh   U
Windermere St Anne's, Windermere   U

DERBYSHIRE

Derby High School, Derby
Foremarke Hall School, Derby
Mount St Mary's College, Spinkhill   U
Repton School, Derby   U
S Anselm's School, Bakewell

DEVON

Blundell's School, Tiverton
Bramdean School, Exeter
Edgehill College, Bideford   U
Exeter Cathedral School, Exeter
Exeter Tutorial College, Exeter   U
Grenville College, Bideford   U
Kelly College, Tavistock   U
The Maynard School, Exeter
Mount House School, Tavistock
Plymouth College, Plymouth   U
Plymouth College Junior School, Plymouth
Shebbear College, Beaworthy   U
Stover School, Newton Abbot   U
Tower House School, Paignton
Trinity School, Teignmouth   U
West Buckland School, Barnstaple   U

DORSET

Bryanston School, Blandford Forum
Claddesmore Preparatory School, Blandford Forum
Claddesmore, Blandford Forum
International College, Sherborne School, Sherborne U
Knighton House, Blandford Forum
Leweston School, Sherborne
Milton Abbey School, Blandford Forum
Port Regis School, Shaftesbury   U
St Mary's School, Shaftesbury
Sherborne Preparatory School, Sherborne
Sherborne School, Sherborne
Sherborne Girls, Sherborne   U
Talbot Heath, Bournemouth
Wentworth College, Bournemouth   U
Yarrells School, Poole

COUNTY DURHAM

Durham High School For Girls, Durham
Durham School, Durham
Polam Hall, Darlington   U

ESSEX

Brentwood School, Brentwood	U
Chigwell School, Chigwell	U
College Saint-Pierre, Leigh-on-Sea	
Elm Green Preparatory School, Chelmsford	U
Felsted Preparatory School, Felsted	
Felsted School, Felsted	U
Friends' School, Saffron Walden	U
New Hall School, Chelmsford	U
Oaklands School, Loughton	
St John's School, Billericay	
St Mary's School, Colchester	
Thorpe Hall School, Southend-on-Sea	

GLOUCESTERSHIRE

Bredon School, Tewkesbury	U
Cheltenham College, Cheltenham	
Cheltenham College Junior School, Cheltenham	
The Cheltenham Ladies' College, Cheltenham	
Dean Close Preparatory School, Cheltenham	U
Dean Close School, Cheltenham	U
Hatherop Castle School, Cirencester	
The King's School, Gloucester	
Rendcomb College, Cirencester	
Rose Hill School, Wotton-under-Edge	
Westonbirt School, Tetbury	U
Wycliffe, Stonehouse	U
Wycliffe Preparatory School, Stonehouse	U
Wynstones School, Gloucester	

SOUTH GLOUCESTERSHIRE

Silverhill School, Winterbourne

HAMPSHIRE

Bedales School, Petersfield	
Brockwood Park School, Bramdean	U
Forres Sandle Manor, Fordingbridge	
Glenhurst School, Havant	
Hampshire Collegiate School UCST, Romsey	
Highfield School, Liphook	
Hordle Walhampton School, Lymington	
Lord Wandsworth College, Hook	
Mayville High School, Southsea	U
Rookesbury Park School, Portsmouth	
Rookwood School, Andover	
St John's College, Southsea	
St Mary's College, Southampton	
St Nicholas' School, Fleet	
Sherborne House School, Eastleigh	
Stanbridge Earls School, Romsey	
Twyford School, Winchester	
Woodhill School, Chandler's Ford	
Wykeham House School, Fareham	

HEREFORDSHIRE

Lucton School, Leominster
St Richard's, Bromyard

HERTFORDSHIRE

Aldenham School, Elstree	
Arts Educational School, Tring Park, Tring	
Berkhamsted Collegiate School, Berkhamsted	U
Bishop's Stortford College, Bishop's Stortford	
Bishop's Stortford College Junior School, Bishop's Stortford	
Egerton Rothesay School, Berkhamsted	
Haileybury, Hertford	
The King's School, Harpenden	
Lockers Park, Hemel Hempstead	
The Princess Helena College, Hitchin	
Queenswood, Hatfield	U
The Royal Masonic School for Girls, Rickmansworth	
St Andrew's Montessori School, Watford	
St Christopher School, Letchworth	
St Edmund's College and St Hugh's School, Ware	U
St Francis' College, Letchworth Garden City	U
St Margaret's School, Bushey	
Stanborough School, Watford	U

ISLE OF MAN

King William's College, Castletown

ISLE OF WIGHT

Ryde School, Ryde

KENT

Ashford School, Ashford	
Bedgebury School, Cranbrook	U
Beechwood Sacred Heart School, Tunbridge Wells	U
Bell Bedgebury International School, Cranbrook	U
Benenden School, Cranbrook	
Bethany School, Cranbrook	U
Bromley High School GDST, Bromley	
Cobham Hall, Gravesend	U
Dover College, Dover	U
Dulwich Preparatory School, Cranbrook, Cranbrook	
Farringtons School, Chislehurst	U
Harenc School Trust, Sidcup	
Holmewood House, Tunbridge Wells	
Junior King's School, Canterbury	U
Kent College, Canterbury	U
Kent College Infant & Junior School, Canterbury	U
Kent College Pembury, Tunbridge Wells	
King's School Rochester, Rochester	
Northbourne Park School, Deal	U
Rochester Independent College, Rochester	U
St Christopher's School, Canterbury	U
St Edmunds Junior School, Canterbury	
St Edmund's School Canterbury, Canterbury	
St Lawrence College Junior School, Ramsgate	
St Lawrence College, Ramsgate	U
St Michael's School, Sevenoaks	
Sevenoaks School, Sevenoaks	
Sutton Valence School, Maidstone	
Tonbridge School, Tonbridge	
Walthamstow Hall, Sevenoaks	
Wellesley House School, Broadstairs	
West Lodge Preparatory School, Sidcup	

LANCASHIRE

Bolton School (Girls' Division), Bolton
Clevelands Preparatory School, Bolton
Kingswood College Trust, Ormskirk
Kirkham Grammar School, Preston
Langdale Preparatory School, Blackpool
Moorland School, Clitheroe
Rossall School, Fleetwood   U
Rossall School International Study Centre, Fleetwood   U
St Anne's College Grammar School, Lytham St Annes   U
St Mary's Hall, Stonyhurst   U
Stonyhurst College, Clitheroe   U
The Bennett House School, Chorley

LEICESTERSHIRE

Brooke House College, Market Harborough   U
Grace Dieu Manor School, Leicester
Irwin College, Leicester   U
Leicester Grammar School, Leicester   U
Our Lady's Convent School, Loughborough
Ratcliffe College, Leicester   U
St Crispin's School, Leicester

LINCOLNSHIRE

Copthill School, Stamford
Kirkstone House School, Bourne
Stamford High School, Stamford
Stamford Junior School, Stamford
Stamford School, Stamford

NORTH EAST LINCOLNSHIRE

St James' School, Grimsby   U

LONDON

Albemarle Independent College, W1K   U
The American School in London, NW8   U
Ashbourne Independent Sixth Form College, W8
Ashbourne Middle School, W8
Aston House School, W5
Bales College, W10
Brampton College, NW4   U
Cameron House School, SW3
Chelsea Independent College, SW6   U
Collingham Independent GCSE and Sixth Form
   College, SW5
Connaught House, W2
David Game College, W11   U
Davies Laing and Dick, W1U   U
Donhead Prep School, SW19
Duff Miller, SW7
Ealing Independent College, W5
Eaton House School Belgravia, SW1W
Eaton House The Manor, SW4
Eaton House The Vale, SW7
Eaton Square School, SW1V
Finton House School, SW17
Gatehouse School, E2
Francis Holland School, SW1, SW1W

Hall School Wimbledon, SW20
The Hampshire School, SW3
Heath House Preparatory School, SE3
Heathside Preparatory School, NW3
Hendon Preparatory School, NW4   U
Hill House International Junior School, SW1X   U
International Community School, NW1   U
International School of London, W3   U
Islamia Girls' School, NW6
Knightsbridge School, SW1X
Lansdowne College, W2
Lion House School, SW15
The Lloyd Williamson School, W10
Mander Portman Woodward, SW7   U
Mill Hill School, NW7
The Mount School, NW7   U
North Bridge House Senior School, NW1
North Bridge House Upper Prep School, NW1
North London International School
Orchard House School, W4   U
Parkgate House School, SW4
Portland Place School, W1B   U
Primrose Independent School, N5
Putney Park School, SW15
Ravenscourt Park Preparatory School, W6
River House Montessori School, E14
Riverston School, SE12
The Roche School, SW18
The Rowans School, SW20
The Royal School, Hampstead, NW3
St Augustine's Priory, W5
St Johns Wood Pre-Preparatory School, NW8
St Margaret's School, NW3
St Martin's, NW7
St Mary's School Hampstead, NW3
St Olave's Preparatory School, SE9
St Paul's Preparatory School, SW13
Southbank International School, Kensington, W11   U
Southbank International School, Hampstead, NW3   U
Southbank International School, Westminster, W1B   U
The Study Preparatory School, SW19
Thames Christian College, SW11   U
Thomas's Fulham, SW6
Thomas's Preparatory School, W8   U
Welsh School of London, NW10
Westminster Tutors, SW7
Wetherby Preparatory School, W11
The White House Prep & Woodentops Kindergarten,
   SW12
Willington School, SW19

GREATER MANCHESTER

Clarendon Cottage School, Eccles
St Bede's College, Manchester
Withington Girls' School, Manchester

MERSEYSIDE

Kingsmead School, Wirral   U
Liverpool College, Liverpool
Merchant Taylors' Girls' School, Liverpool

MIDDLESEX

ACS Hillingdon International School, Hillingdon   U
Denmead School, Hampton
Halliford School, Shepperton
Harrow School, Harrow on the Hill
Little Eden & Eden High SDA, Brentford
The Mall School, Twickenham
St Catherine's School, Twickenham
St Christopher's School, Wembley
St David's School, Ashford   U
St Helen's School, Northwood
St Martin's School, Northwood
Staines Preparatory School, Staines

NORFOLK

Beeston Hall School, Cromer
Gresham's Preparatory School, Holt
Gresham's School, Holt
Hethersett Old Hall School, Norwich   U
Langley School, Norwich   U
The New Eccles Hall School, Norwich   U
Norwich High School for Girls GDST, Norwich
Notre Dame Preparatory School, Norwich
Riddlesworth Hall, Diss   U
St Nicholas House Kindergarten & Prep School,
    North Walsham   U
Taverham Hall Preparatory School, Norwich   U

NORTHAMPTONSHIRE

Bosworth Independent College, Northampton   U
Maidwell Hall School, Northampton
Northamptonshire Grammar School, Pitsford
Oundle School, Nr Peterborough
Quinton House School, Northampton

NORTHUMBERLAND

Longridge Towers School, Berwick-upon-Tweed

NOTTINGHAMSHIRE

Attenborough Preparatory School, Nottingham
Dagfa House School, Nottingham
Greenholme School, Nottingham
Ranby House School, Retford
Wellow House School, Newark

OXFORDSHIRE

Abacus College, Oxford   U
Abingdon School, Abingdon
Bloxham School, Banbury   U
Cherwell College, Oxford
Christ Church Cathedral School, Oxford
Cokethorpe School, Witney
Cothill House Preparatory School, Abingdon
Cranford House School, Wallingford
d'Overbroeck's College, Oxford   U
Greene's Tutorial College, Oxford
Headington School, Oxford

IQRA School, Oxford   U
Abingdon Preparatory School, Abingdon
Kingham Hill School, Chipping Norton   U
Leckford Place School, Oxford
The Manor Preparatory School, Abingdon
New College School, Oxford
Our Lady's Abingdon School, Abingdon
Oxford Tutorial College, Oxford   U
Rye St Antony School, Oxford
St Clare's, Oxford, Oxford   U
St Edward's School, Oxford
The School of St Helen & St Katharine, Abingdon
Shiplake College, Henley-on-Thames
Sibford School, Banbury   U
Summer Fields, Oxford

SHROPSHIRE

Adcote School for Girls, Shrewsbury
Bedstone College, Bucknell   U
Dower House School, Bridgnorth
Ellesmere College, Ellesmere   U
Kingsland Grange, Shrewsbury
Moor Park School, Ludlow
Moreton Hall School, Oswestry   U
Oswestry School, Oswestry   U
Packwood Haugh School, Shrewsbury
Prestfelde Preparatory School, Shrewsbury
St Winefride's Convent School, Shrewsbury
Shrewsbury School, Shrewsbury
Wrekin College, Telford

SOMERSET

All Hallows, Shepton Mallet
Bruton School for Girls, Bruton   U
Chilton Cantelo School, Yeovil
Downside School, Bath
Hazlegrove (King's Bruton Preparatory School), Yeovil
King's Bruton, Bruton
King's College, Taunton
King's Hall, Taunton
Millfield Preparatory School, Glastonbury   U
Millfield School, Street   U
The Park School, Yeovil
Perrott Hill School, Crewkerne
Queen's College Junior, Pre-Prep & Nursery Schools,
    Taunton
Queen's College, Taunton   U
Taunton International Study Centre (TISC), Taunton   U
Taunton Preparatory School, Taunton   U
Taunton School, Taunton   U
Wellington School, Wellington   U
Wells Cathedral School, Wells   U

BATH & NORTH EAST SOMERSET

Bath Academy, Bath   U
Kingswood Preparatory School, Bath
Kingswood School, Bath   U
Monkton Senior School, Bath   U
Prior Park College, Bath
The Royal High School, Bath

NORTH SOMERSET

Sidcot School, Winscombe   U

STAFFORDSHIRE

Abbots Bromley School for Girls, Abbots Bromley
Denstone College, Uttoxeter
Lichfield Cathedral School, Lichfield
St Bede's School, Stafford   U
St Dominic's School, Stafford

SUFFOLK

The Abbey, Woodbridge   U
Brandeston Hall, The Preparatory School for
   Framlingham College, Brandeston   U
Culford School, Bury St Edmunds
Felixstowe International College, Felixstowe   U
Framlingham College, Woodbridge   U
Ipswich School, Ipswich
Moreton Hall Preparatory School, Bury St Edmunds
Old Buckenham Hall School, Ipswich   U
Orwell Park, Ipswich
The Royal Hospital School, Ipswich   U
Saint Felix School, Southwold
St Joseph's College, Ipswich   U
Summerhill School, Leiston   U
Woodbridge School, Woodbridge   U

SURREY

Aberdour, Tadworth
ACS Cobham International School, Cobham   U
ACS Egham International School, Egham   U
Aldro School, Godalming
Amesbury, Hindhead
Box Hill School, Dorking   U
Cambridge Tutors College, Croydon   U
Canbury School, Kingston-upon-Thames   U
Caterham School, Caterham
Charterhouse, Godalming
Chinthurst School, Tadworth
City of London Freemen's School, Ashtead
Cranleigh School, Cranleigh
Croydon High School GDST, South Croydon
Epsom College, Epsom
Ewell Castle School, Epsom
Feltonfleet School, Cobham
Frensham Heights School, Farnham   U
Grantchester House, Esher
Greenacre School for Girls, Banstead
Hampton Court House, East Molesey
Hawley Place School, Camberley
Hurtwood House, Dorking   U
Kew Green Preparatory School, Richmond   U
King Edward's School Witley, Godalming   U
King's House School, Richmond
Kingswood House School, Epsom
Lodge School, Purley
Longacre School, Guildford
Marymount International School,
   Kingston-upon-Thames   U
New Lodge School, Dorking

Notre Dame Preparatory School, Cobham
Old Palace of John Whitgift School, Croydon
Park Hill School, Kingston-upon-Thames   U
Prins Willem-Alexander School, Woking   U
Prior's Field School, Godalming
Priory Preparatory School, Banstead
Reigate St Mary's Preparatory and Choir School,
   Reigate
Royal Ballet School, Richmond
Royal Russell School, Croydon   U
The Royal School, Haslemere   U
St Catherine's School, Guildford
St David's School, Purley
St Hilary's School, Godalming
St John's School, Leatherhead   U
St Teresa's School, Dorking   U
Stowford College, Sutton
Surbiton High School, Kingston-upon-Thames
Surbiton Preparatory School, Surbiton
Sutton High School GDST, Sutton
TASIS The American School in England, Thorpe   U
Westbury House School, New Malden
Woldingham School, Woldingham   U
Woodcote House School, Windlesham
Yehudi Menuhin School, Cobham   U

EAST SUSSEX

Ashdown House School, Forest Row
Battle Abbey School, Battle   U
Brighton College, Brighton   U
Brighton College Pre-preparatory School, Brighton
Brighton Steiner School Limited, Brighton
Buckswood School, Hastings   U
Eastbourne College, Eastbourne   U
Greenfields School, Forest Row   U
Lancing College Preparatory School at Mowden, Hove
Michael Hall (Steiner Waldorf School), Forest Row   U
Moira House School, Eastbourne
Moira House Girls School, Eastbourne   U
Newlands School, Seaford   U
Roedean School, Brighton   U
St Andrew's School, Eastbourne   U
St Aubyns School, Brighton
St Leonards-Mayfield School, Mayfield   U
St Mary's Hall, Brighton   U
Stonelands School of Ballet & Theatre Arts, Hove
Vinehall School, Robertsbridge   U

WEST SUSSEX

Ardingly College Junior School, Haywards Heath
Arundale Preparatory School, Pulborough
Brambletye, East Grinstead
Burgess Hill School for Girls, Burgess Hill
Cottesmore School, Pease Pottage
Dorset House School, Pulborough
Farlington School, Horsham   U
Great Ballard School, Chichester
Hurstpierpoint College, Hurstpierpoint
Lavant House, Chichester
Seaford College, Petworth

Slindon College, Arundel
The Towers Convent School, Steyning
Windlesham House, Pulborough   U
Worth School, Turners Hill

TYNE AND WEAR

Central Newcastle High School GDST,
   Newcastle upon Tyne
Grindon Hall Christian School, Sunderland   U
The King's School, Tynemouth
Sunderland High School, Sunderland
Westfield School, Newcastle upon Tyne

WARWICKSHIRE

Abbotsford School, Kenilworth   U
Arnold Lodge School, Leamington Spa
Bilton Grange, Rugby
The Kingsley School, Leamington Spa
Princethorpe College, Rugby
Rugby School, Rugby

WEST MIDLANDS

Birchfield School, Wolverhampton
The Blue Coat School, Birmingham
Coventry Prep School, Coventry
Eversfield Preparatory School, Solihull
Highclare School, Birmingham
Mander Portman Woodward, Birmingham
Priory School, Birmingham
The Royal Wolverhampton School, Wolverhampton   U
St George's School, Edgbaston, Birmingham
Tettenhall College, Wolverhampton   U

WILTSHIRE

Chafyn Grove School, Salisbury
Dauntsey's School, Devizes
Grittleton House School, Chippenham
Norman Court Preparatory School, Salisbury
Prior Park Preparatory School, Cricklade
St Margaret's Preparatory School, Calne
Sandroyd School, Salisbury
Stonar School, Melksham
Warminster School, Warminster   U

WORCESTERSHIRE

Abberley Hall, Worcester   U
Bowbrook House School, Pershore
Bromsgrove Preparatory School, Bromsgrove   U
Bromsgrove School, Bromsgrove   U

The Downs, Malvern College Preparatory School, Malvern
Malvern College, Malvern   U
Malvern College Preparatory and Pre-Prep School,
   Malvern
Malvern St James, Great Malvern   U
Moffats School, Worcestershire
Moffats School, Bewdley
Saint Michael's College, Tenbury Wells   U
Winterfold House, Kidderminster

EAST RIDING OF YORKSHIRE

Pocklington School, Pocklington

NORTH YORKSHIRE

Ampleforth College, York
Ashville College, Harrogate
Bootham School, York
Brackenfield School, Harrogate
Bramcote School, Scarborough
Fyling Hall School, Whitby
Giggleswick Junior School, Settle
Giggleswick School, Settle
Harrogate Ladies' College, Harrogate   U
Harrogate Tutorial College, Harrogate   U
The Mount School, York   U
Queen Ethelburga's College, York   U
Queen Margaret's School, York
Read School, Selby
St Martin's Ampleforth, York
Scarborough College & Lisvane School, Scarborough
Terrington Hall, York
Woodleigh School, Malton

SOUTH YORKSHIRE

Ashdell Preparatory School, Sheffield
Sheffield High School GDST, Sheffield

WEST YORKSHIRE

Ackworth School, Pontefract   U
Batley Grammar School, Batley
Dale House School, Batley   U
Fulneck School, Leeds   U
Gateways School, Leeds
New Horizon Community School, Leeds
The Rastrick Independent School, Brighouse
Richmond House School, Leeds
Rishworth School, Rishworth   U
Woodhouse Grove School, Apperley Bridge   U

NORTHERN IRELAND

COUNTY ANTRIM

Victoria College Belfast, Belfast

COUNTY ARMAGH

The Royal School Armagh, Armagh   U

COUNTY DOWN

The Holywood Rudolf Steiner School, Holywood
Rockport School, Holywood

COUNTY TYRONE

The Royal School Dungannon, Dungannon   U

SCOTLAND

ABERDEENSHIRE

International School of Aberdeen, Aberdeen   U
St Margaret's School for Girls, Aberdeen

FIFE

St Leonards School , St Andrews

GLASGOW

Hutchesons' Grammar School

LOTHIAN

Basil Paterson Tutorial College, Edinburgh   U
Belhaven Hill, Dunbar   U
The Edinburgh Rudolf Steiner School, Edinburgh   U
Fettes College, Edinburgh   U

George Watson's College, Edinburgh
Loretto Junior School, Musselburgh   U
Loretto School, Musselburgh   U
Merchiston Castle School, Edinburgh   U
St George's School for Girls, Edinburgh   U
St Serf's School, Edinburgh

MORAYSHIRE

Gordonstoun School, Elgin

PERTH AND KINROSS

Craigclowan Preparatory School, Perth
Glenalmond College, Perth
Kilgraston, Perth   U
Morrison's Academy, Crieff
Strathallan School, Perth   U

WALES

BRIDGEND

St Clare's School, Porthcawl

CARDIFF

The Cardiff Academy
Kings Monkton School
Westbourne School   U

CARMARTHENSHIRE

Llandovery College, Llandovery   U

CONWY

Lyndon Preparatory School, Colwyn Bay
Rydal Penrhos Senior School, Colwyn Bay   U
St David's College, Llandudno

DENBIGHSHIRE

Howell's School, Denbigh   U
Ruthin School, Ruthin   U

MONMOUTHSHIRE

Monmouth School, Monmouth
St John's-on-the-Hill, Chepstow

PEMBROKESHIRE

Netherwood School, Saundersfoot

POWYS

Christ College, Brecon   U

CONTINENTAL EUROPE

Aiglon College, Switzerland   U
Chavagnes International College,
   Chavagnes-en-Paillers, France

Mougins School, France   U

5.9

Schools in Membership of the Constituent Associations of the Independent Schools Council

The schools listed below are all in membership of the Independent Schools Council in the UK. Please note that ISC-accredited special schools and overseas schools are not included. The constituent associations of the ISC include:

Association of Governing Bodies of Independent Schools (AGBIS)
The Girls' Schools Association (GSA)
The Headmasters' and Headmistresses' Conference (HMC)
The Independent Association of Prep Schools (IAPS)
The Independent Schools Association (ISA)
The Independent Schools' Bursars Association (ISBA)
The Society of Headmasters and Headmistresses of Independent Schools (SHMIS)

Further information about ISC can be found in Part 1.1.

ENGLAND

BEDFORDSHIRE

Bedford High School, Bedford
Bedford Modern School, Bedford
Bedford Preparatory School, Bedford
Bedford School, Bedford
Dame Alice Harpur School, Bedford
Moorlands School, Luton
Pilgrims Pre-Preparatory School, Bedford
Rushmoor School, Bedford
St Andrew's School, Bedford

BERKSHIRE

The Abbey School, Reading
Bearwood College, Wokingham
Bradfield College, Reading
Brigidine School Windsor, Windsor

Brockhurst and Marlston House Schools, Newbury
Cheam School, Newbury
Crosfields School, Reading
Dolphin School, Reading
Downe House, Thatcham
Eagle House, Sandhurst
Elstree School, Reading
The Elvian School, Reading
Eton College, Windsor
Eton End PNEU, Slough
Heathfield St Mary's School, Ascot
Hemdean House School, Reading
Herries School, Maidenhead
Highfield School, Maidenhead
The Highlands School, Reading
Holme Grange School, Wokingham
Horris Hill School, Newbury
Hurst Lodge School, Ascot

Lambrook Haileybury, Bracknell
Leighton Park School, Reading
Licensed Victuallers' School, Ascot
Luckley-Oakfield School, Wokingham
Ludgrove, Wokingham
The Marist Preparatory School, Ascot
The Marist Senior School, Ascot
The Oratory Preparatory School, Reading
The Oratory School, Reading
Pangbourne College, Pangbourne
Papplewick School, Ascot
Queen Anne's School, Reading
Reading Blue Coat School, Reading
Ridgeway School, Maidenhead
St Andrew's School, Reading
St Bernard's Preparatory School, Slough
St Edward's School, Reading
St Gabriel's School, Newbury
St George's School, Ascot
St John's Beaumont, Windsor
St Joseph's Convent School, Reading
St Mary's School, Ascot
St Piran's Preparatory School, Maidenhead
Sunningdale School, Sunningdale
Upton House School, Windsor
Waverley School, Wokingham
Wellington College, Crowthorne
White House Preparatory School, Wokingham
Winbury School, Maidenhead

BRISTOL

Badminton School, Bristol
Bristol Grammar School, Bristol
Clifton College, Bristol
Clifton College Preparatory School, Bristol
Clifton College Pre-Prep–Butcombe, Bristol
Clifton High School, Bristol
Colston's Collegiate School, Bristol
Colston's Girls' School, Bristol
Colston's Lower School, Bristol
The Downs School, Bristol
Fairfield School, Backwell
Queen Elizabeth's Hospital, Bristol
The Red Maids' School, Bristol
Redland High School, Bristol
St Ursula's High School, Bristol
Tockington Manor School, Bristol

BUCKINGHAMSHIRE

Ashfold School, Aylesbury
The Beacon School, Amersham
Bury Lawn School, Milton Keynes
Caldicott School, Farnham Royal
Chesham Preparatory School, Chesham
Crown House School, High Wycombe
Dair House School Trust Ltd, Farnham Royal
Davenies School, Beaconsfield
Gateway School, Great Missenden
Gayhurst School, Gerrards Cross
Godstowe Preparatory School, High Wycombe

Heatherton House School, Amersham
High March School, Beaconsfield
Kingscote Pre-Preparatory School, Gerrards Cross
Ladymede, Aylesbury
Maltman's Green School, Gerrards Cross
Milton Keynes Preparatory School, Milton Keynes
Pipers Corner School, High Wycombe
St Mary's School, Gerrards Cross
St Teresa's Catholic Independent & Nursery School,
    Princes Risborough
Stowe School, Buckingham
Swanbourne House School, Milton Keynes
Thornton College Convent of Jesus and Mary,
    Milton Keynes
Thorpe House School, Gerrards Cross
Wycombe Abbey School, High Wycombe

CAMBRIDGESHIRE

CATS Cambridge
Cambridge Centre for Sixth-form Studies, Cambridge
Kimbolton School, Huntingdon
The King's School Ely, Ely
The Leys School, Cambridge
The Perse School, Cambridge
The Perse School for Girls, Cambridge
Peterborough High School, Peterborough
St Colette's School, Cambridge
St Faith's, Cambridge
St John's College School, Cambridge
St Mary's Junior School, Cambridge
St Mary's School, Cambridge
Whitehall School, Huntingdon
Wisbech Grammar School, Wisbech

CHANNEL ISLANDS

Elizabeth College, Guernsey
The Ladies' College, Guernsey
St Michael's Preparatory School, Jersey
Victoria College, Jersey
Victoria College Preparatory School, Jersey

CHESHIRE

Abbey Gate College, Chester
Abbey Gate School, Chester
Alderley Edge School for Girls, Alderley Edge
Beech Hall School, Macclesfield
Cransley School, Northwich
The Firs School, Chester
The Grange School, Northwich
Hammond School, Chester
The King's School, Chester
The King's School, Macclesfield
Lady Barn House School, Cheadle
Loreto Preparatory School, Altrincham
Mostyn House School, South Wirral
Pownall Hall School, Wilmslow
The Queen's School, Chester
Ramillies Hall School, Cheadle
The Ryleys, Alderley Edge

Terra Nova School, Holmes Chapel
Wilmslow Preparatory School, Wilmslow

CORNWALL

The Bolitho School, Penzance
Polwhele House School, Truro
Roselyon, Par
St Joseph's School, Launceston
St Piran's Preparatory School, Hayle
Truro High School, Truro
Truro School, Truro

COUNTY DURHAM

Barnard Castle School, Barnard Castle
The Chorister School, Durham
Durham High School For Girls, Durham
Durham School, Durham
Polam Hall, Darlington

CUMBRIA

Austin Friars St Monica's School, Carlisle
Casterton School, Kirkby Lonsdale
Chetwynde School, Barrow-in-Furness
Hunter Hall School, Penrith
Lime House School, Carlisle
St Bees School, St Bees
Sedbergh School, Sedbergh
Windermere St Anne's, Windermere

DERBYSHIRE

Derby Grammar School, Derby
Derby High School, Derby
Foremarke Hall School, Derby
Mount St Mary's College, Spinkhill
Ockbrook School, Derby
Repton School, Derby
St Anselm's School, Bakewell
St Peter and St Paul School, Chesterfield
St Wystan's School, Repton

DEVON

Blundell's Preparatory School, Tiverton
Blundell's School, Tiverton
Edgehill College, Bideford
Exeter Cathedral School, Exeter
Exeter School, Exeter
Grenville College, Bideford
Kelly College, Tavistock
Kelly College Preparatory School, Tavistock
Manor House School, Honiton
The Maynard School, Exeter
Mount House School, Tavistock
Plymouth College, Plymouth
St Dunstan's Abbey, Plymouth
St John's School, Sidmouth
St Margaret's School, Exeter

St Michael's, Barnstaple
St Peter's School, Exmouth
Shebbear College, Beaworthy
St Dunstan's Abbey-Plymouth College Junior School,
    Plymouth
Stover School, Newton Abbot
Trinity School, Teignmouth
West Buckland School, Barnstaple

DORSET

Bryanston School, Blandford Forum
Canford School, Wimborne
Castle Court Preparatory School, Wimborne
Clayesmore Preparatory School, Blandford Forum
Clayesmore, Blandford Forum
Dumpton School, Wimborne
Hanford School, Blandford Forum
International College, Sherborne School, Sherborne
Knighton House, Blandford Forum
Milton Abbey School, Blandford Forum
The Park School, Bournemouth
Port Regis School, Shaftesbury
St Antony's Leweston Schools, Sherborne
St Mary's School, Shaftesbury
Sherborne Preparatory School, Sherborne
Sherborne School, Sherborne
Sherborne School for Girls, Sherborne
Sunninghill Preparatory School, Dorchester
Talbot Heath, Bournemouth
Thornlow Preparatory School, Weymouth
Uplands School, Poole
Wentworth College, Bournemouth
Yarrells School, Poole

ESSEX

Alleyn Court Preparatory School, Southend-on-Sea
Bancroft's School, Woodford Green
Braeside School for Girls, Buckhurst Hill
Brentwood School, Brentwood
Chigwell School, Chigwell
Colchester High School, Colchester
Coopersale Hall School, Epping
Cranbrook College, Ilford
Crowstone Preparatory School, Westcliff-on-Sea
The Daiglen School, Buckhurst Hill
Dame Bradbury's School, Saffron Walden
Elm Green Preparatory School, Chelmsford
Felsted Preparatory School, Felsted
Felsted School, Felsted
Friends' School, Saffron Walden
Gidea Park College, Romford
Gosfield School, Halstead
Heathcote School, Chelmsford
Holmwood House, Colchester
Littlegarth School, Colchester
Loyola Preparatory School, Buckhurst Hill
Maldon Court Preparatory School, Maldon
New Hall School, Chelmsford
Oaklands School, Loughton
Park School for Girls, Ilford

St Anne's Preparatory School, Chelmsford
St Aubyn's School, Woodford Green
St Cedd's School, Chelmsford
St Hilda's School, Westcliff-on-Sea
St John's School, Billericay
St Margaret's School, Halstead
St Mary's School, Colchester
St Michael's School, Leigh-on-Sea
St Nicholas School, Harlow
St Philomena's Preparatory School, Frinton-on-Sea
Thorpe Hall School, Southend-on-Sea
Ursuline Preparatory School, Brentwood
Widford Lodge, Chelmsford
Woodford Green Preparatory School, Woodford Green
Woodlands Schools, Brentwood

GLOUCESTERSHIRE

Beaudesert Park School, Stroud
Berkhampstead School, Cheltenham
Bredon School, Tewkesbury
Cheltenham College, Cheltenham
Cheltenham College Junior School, Cheltenham
The Cheltenham Ladies' College, Cheltenham
Dean Close Preparatory School, Cheltenham
Dean Close School, Cheltenham
Hatherop Castle School, Cirencester
The King's School, Gloucester
Rendcomb College, Cirencester
The Richard Pate School, Cheltenham
Rose Hill School, Wotton-under-Edge
St Edward's School, Cheltenham
Westonbirt School, Tetbury
Wycliffe, Stonehouse
Wycliffe Preparatory School, Stonehouse

HAMPSHIRE

Alton Convent School, Alton
Ballard School, New Milton
Bedales School, Petersfield
Boundary Oak School, Fareham
Churchers College, Petersfield
Daneshill School, Basingstoke
Ditcham Park School, Petersfield
Dunhurst (Bedales Junior School), Petersfield
Durlston Court, New Milton
Farleigh School, Andover
Farnborough Hill, Farnborough
Forres Sandle Manor, Fordingbridge
The Gregg School, Southampton
Hampshire Collegiate School UCST, Romsey
Highfield School, Liphook
Hordle Walhampton School, Lymington
King Edward VI School, Southampton
Lord Wandsworth College, Hook
Mayville High School, Southsea
Moyles Court School, Ringwood
The Pilgrims' School, Winchester
The Portsmouth Grammar School, Portsmouth
Portsmouth High School GDST, Southsea
Prince's Mead School, Winchester

Rookesbury Park School, Portsmouth
Rookwood School, Andover
St John's College, Southsea
St Neot's School, Hook
St Nicholas' School, Fleet
St Swithun's School, Winchester
St Winifred's School, Southampton
Salesian College, Farnborough
Sherborne House School, Eastleigh
Sherfield School, Hook
Stanbridge Earls School, Romsey
The Stroud School, Romsey
Twyford School, Winchester
West Hill Park, Fareham
Winchester College, Winchester
Wykeham House School, Fareham
Yateley Manor Preparatory School, Yateley

HEREFORDSHIRE

The Hereford Cathedral Junior School, Hereford
The Hereford Cathedral School, Hereford
Lucton School, Leominster
St Richard's, Bromyard

HERTFORDSHIRE

Abbot's Hill School, Hemel Hempstead
Aldenham School, Elstree
Aldwickbury School, Harpenden
Arts Educational School, Tring Park, Tring
Beechwood Park School, St Albans
Berkhamsted Collegiate Preparatory School, Berkhamsted
Berkhamsted Collegiate School, Berkhamsted
Bishop's Stortford College, Bishop's Stortford
CKHR Immanuel College, Bushey
Edge Grove, Aldenham
Egerton Rothesay School, Berkhamsted
Francis House, Tring
Haberdashers' Aske's Boys' School, Elstree
Haberdashers' Aske's School for Girls, Elstree
Haileybury, Hertford
Haresfoot Preparatory School, Berkhamsted
Heath Mount School, Hertford
Howe Green House School, Bishop's Stortford
Immanuel College, Bushey
Kingshott School, Hitchin
Lochinver House School, Potters Bar
Lockers Park, Hemel Hempstead
Manor Lodge School, Radlett
Northwood Preparatory School, Rickmansworth
The Princess Helena College, Hitchin
The Purcell School, Bushey
Queenswood, Hatfield
Rickmansworth PNEU School, Rickmansworth
The Royal Masonic School for Girls, Rickmansworth
St Albans High School for Girls, St Albans
St Albans School, St Albans
St Christopher School, Letchworth
St Columba's College, St Albans
St Edmund's College and St Hugh's School, Ware
St Francis' College, Letchworth Garden City

St Hilda's School, Bushey
St Hilda's School, Harpenden
St Margaret's School, Bushey
Sherrardswood School, Welwyn
Stanborough School, Watford
Stormont, Potters Bar
Westbrook Hay Preparatory School, Hemel Hempstead
York House School, Rickmansworth

ISLE OF MAN

The Buchan School, Castletown
King William's College, Castletown

ISLE OF WIGHT

Ryde School, Ryde

KENT

Ashford School, Ashford
Beechwood Sacred Heart School, Tunbridge Wells
Benenden School, Cranbrook
Bethany School, Cranbrook
Bickley Park School, Bromley
Bronte School, Gravesend
Cobham Hall, Gravesend
Combe Bank School, Nr Sevenoaks
Derwent Lodge School for Girls, Tonbridge
Dover College, Dover
Duke of York's Royal Military School, Dover
Dulwich Preparatory School, Cranbrook, Cranbrook
Farringtons School, Chislehurst
Gad's Hill School, Rochester
The Granville School, Sevenoaks
Harenc School Trust, Sidcup
Hilden Grange School, Tonbridge
Hilden Oaks School, Tonbridge
Holmewood House, Tunbridge Wells
Junior King's School, Canterbury
The Junior School, St Lawrence College, Ramsgate
Kent College, Canterbury
Kent College Infant & Junior School, Canterbury
Kent College Pembury, Tunbridge Wells
King's Preparatory School, Rochester
The King's School, Canterbury
King's School Rochester, Rochester
Marlborough House School, Hawkhurst
The New Beacon, Sevenoaks
Northbourne Park School, Deal
Rose Hill School, Tunbridge Wells
Russell House School, Sevenoaks
Sackville School, Tonbridge
St Edmunds Junior School, Canterbury
St Edmund's School, Canterbury
St Lawrence College, Ramsgate
St Michael's School, Sevenoaks
St Ronan's School, Hawkhurst
Sevenoaks Preparatory School, Sevenoaks
Sevenoaks School, Sevenoaks
Solefield School, Sevenoaks
Spring Grove School, Ashford

Steephill Independent School, Longfield
Sutton Valence Preparatory School, Maidstone
Sutton Valence School, Maidstone
Tonbridge School, Tonbridge
Walthamstow Hall, Sevenoaks
Wellesley House School, Broadstairs
Yardley Court, Tonbridge

LANCASHIRE

Arnold School, Blackpool
Highfield Priory School, Preston
The Hulme Grammar School for Girls, Oldham
King Edward VII and Queen Mary School,
    Lytham St Annes
Kingswood College Trust, Ormskirk
Kirkham Grammar School, Preston
The Oldham Hulme Grammar School, Oldham
Queen Elizabeth's Grammar School, Blackburn
Rossall Junior School, Fleetwood
Rossall School, Fleetwood
St Joseph's Convent School, Burnley
St Mary's Hall, Stonyhurst
St Pius X Preparatory School, Preston
Stonyhurst College, Clitheroe
Westholme School, Blackburn

LEICESTERSHIRE

The Dixie Grammar School, Market Bosworth
Fairfield Preparatory School, Loughborough
Grace Dieu Manor School, Leicester
Leicester Grammar School, Leicester
Leicester High School For Girls, Leicester
Leicester Montessori Grammar School, Leicester
Loughborough Grammar School, Loughborough
Loughborough High School, Loughborough
Manor House School, Ashby-de-la-Zouch
Our Lady's Convent School, Loughborough
PNEU School, Loughborough
Ratcliffe College, Leicester
Stoneygate School, Leicester

LINCOLNSHIRE

Ayscoughfee Hall School, Spalding
Copthill School, Stamford
Kirkstone House School, Bourne
Lincoln Minster School, Lincoln
St Hugh's School, Woodhall Spa
Stamford High School, Stamford
Stamford Junior School, Stamford
Stamford School, Stamford
Witham Hall, Bourne

NORTH EAST LINCOLNSHIRE

St James' School, Grimsby
St Martin's Preparatory School, Grimsby

NORTH LINCOLNSHIRE

Brigg Preparatory School, Brigg

LONDON

Abercorn School, NW8
Abingdon House School, W8
Alleyn's School, SE22
Arnold House School, NW8
Arts Educational Schools, W4
Avenue House School, W13
Bassett House School, W10
Belmont (Mill Hill Preparatory School), NW7
Blackheath High School GDST, SE3
Broomwood Hall School, SW12
Bute House Preparatory School for Girls, W6
Cameron House School, SW3
The Cavendish School, NW1
Channing School, N6
City of London School, EC4V
City of London School for Girls, EC2Y
Colfe's School, SE12
Devonshire House Preparatory School, NW3
Dulwich College, SE21
Dulwich College Preparatory School, SE21
Durston House, W5
Eltham College, SE9
Emanuel School, SW11
Falkner House, SW7
Finton House School, SW17
Forest School, E17
Francis Holland School, Regent's Park NW1
Francis Holland School, SW1W
Garden House School, SW3
Gatehouse School, E2
Glendower Preparatory School, SW7
The Godolphin and Latymer School, W6
Grange Park Preparatory School, N21
Grangewood Independent School, E7
The Hall School, NW3
The Hampshire Schools (Kensington Gardens), W2
The Hampshire Schools (Knightsbridge Under School), SW7
The Hampshire Schools (Knightsbridge Upper School), SW7
Harvington School, W5
Hawkesdown House School, W8
Hereward House School, NW3
Ibstock Place School, SW15
The Italia Conti Academy of Theatre Arts, EC1M
James Allen's Girls' School, SE22
James Allen's Preparatory School, SE22
Keble Preparatory School, N21
Kensington Prep School, SW6
The King Alfred School, NW11
King's College Junior School, SW19
King's College School, SW19
Latymer Prep School, W6
Latymer Upper School, W6
Lyndhurst House Preparatory School, NW3
Mander Portman Woodward, SW7
Mill Hill School, NW7
More House, SW1X

The Mount School, NW7
Naima Jewish Preparatory School, NW6
Newton Prep School, SW8
Norland Place School, W11
Normanhurst School, E4
Northcote Lodge School, SW11
Notting Hill and Ealing High School GDST, W13
Oakfield Preparatory School, SE21
Orchard House School, W4
Palmers Green High School, N21
Pembridge Hall, W2
Portland Place School, W1B
Prospect House School, SW15
Putney High School GDST, SW15
Putney Park School, SW15
Queen's College, W1G
Queen's Gate School, SW7
Ravenscourt Park Preparatory School, W6
Redcliffe School, SW10
Riverston School, SE12
Rosemead Preparatory School, SE21
The Royal School, Hampstead, NW3
St Anthony's Preparatory School, NW3
St Benedict's School, W5
St Christina's RC Preparatory School, NW8
St Christopher's School, NW3
St Dunstan's College, SE6
St James Independent School for Boys and Girls, W14
St James Independent School for Girls (Juniors), W14
St James Independent School for Senior Girls, W14
St Margaret's School, NW3
St Mary's School Hampstead, NW3
St Olave's Preparatory School, SE9
St Paul's Cathedral School, EC4M
St Paul's Girls' School, W6
St Paul's Preparatory School, SW13
St Paul's School, SW13
Salcombe Preparatory School, N14
Sarum Hall, NW3
Snaresbrook College Preparatory School, E18
South Hampstead High School, NW3
Southbank International School, Hampstead, NW3
Southbank International School, Kensington, W11
Streatham and Clapham High School, SW16
The Study Preparatory School, SW19
Sussex House School, SW1X
The Swaminarayan School, NW10
Sydenham High School GDST, SE26
Sylvia Young Theatre School, NW1
Tower House School, SW14
Trevor Roberts School, NW3
University College School, NW3
University College School Junior Branch, NW3
Virgo Fidelis, SE19
Vita Et Pax School, N14
Westminster Abbey Choir School, SW1P
Westminster Cathedral Choir School, SW1P
Westminster School, SW1P
Westminster Under School, SW1P
Wimbledon High School GDST, SW19
Woodside Park International School, N11

GREATER MANCHESTER

Abbotsford Preparatory School, Manchester
Bridgewater School, Manchester
Chetham's School of Music, Manchester
The Manchester Grammar School, Manchester
Manchester High School for Girls, Manchester
Moor Allerton School, Manchester
St Bede's College, Manchester
William Hulme's Grammar School, Manchester
Withington Girls' School, Manchester

MERSEYSIDE

The Belvedere School GDST, Liverpool
Birkenhead High School GDST, Wirral
Birkenhead School, Wirral
Carleton House Preparatory School, Liverpool
Kingsmead School, Wirral
Liverpool College, Liverpool
Merchant Taylors' School, Liverpool
Merchant Taylors' Girls' School, Liverpool
Prenton Preparatory School, Wirral
Runnymede St Edward's School, Liverpool
St Mary's College, Liverpool
Sunnymede School, Southport
Tower College, Prescot

MIDDLESEX

ACS Hillingdon International School, Hillingdon
Alpha Preparatory School, Harrow
Ashton House School, Isleworth
Buckingham College School, Harrow
Denmead School, Hampton
Halliford School, Shepperton
Hampton School, Hampton
Harrow School, Harrow on the Hill
Heathfield School, Pinner
Innellan House School, Pinner
The John Lyon School, Harrow
The Lady Eleanor Holles School, Hampton
The Mall School, Twickenham
Merchant Taylors' School, Northwood
Newland House School, Twickenham
North London Collegiate, Edgware
Northwood College, Northwood
Orley Farm School, Harrow
Peterborough & St Margaret's School, Stanmore
Quainton Hall School, Harrow
Reddiford, Pinner
St Catherine's School, Twickenham
St Christopher's School, Wembley
St David's School, Ashford
St Helen's College, Hillingdon
St Helen's School, Northwood
St James Independent School for Boys (Senior),
    Twickenham
St John's Northwood, Northwood
St Martin's School, Northwood
Staines Preparatory School, Staines
Twickenham Preparatory School, Hampton

NORFOLK

Beeston Hall School, Cromer
Glebe House School, Hunstanton
Gresham's Preparatory School, Holt
Gresham's School, Holt
Hethersett Old Hall School, Norwich
Langley Preparatory School & Nursery, Norwich
Langley School, Norwich
The New Eccles Hall School, Norwich
Norwich High School for Girls GDST, Norwich
Norwich School, Norwich
Notre Dame Preparatory School, Norwich
Riddlesworth Hall, Diss
Sacred Heart Convent School, Swaffham
St Christopher's School, Norwich
St Nicholas House Kindergarten & Prep School,
    North Walsham
Taverham Hall Preparatory, Norwich
Thetford Grammar School, Thetford
Thorpe House School, Norwich
Town Close House Preparatory School, Norwich

NORTHAMPTONSHIRE

Beachborough School, Brackley
Great Houghton Preparatory School, Northampton
Laxton Junior School, Nr Peterborough
Maidwell Hall School, Northampton
Northampton High School, Northampton
Northamptonshire Grammar School, Pitsford
Oundle School, Nr Peterborough
St Peter's School, Kettering
Spratton Hall, Northampton
Winchester House School, Brackley

NORTHUMBERLAND

Longridge Towers School, Berwick-upon-Tweed
Mowden Hall School, Stocksfield

NOTTINGHAMSHIRE

Bramcote Lorne School, Retford
Dagfa House School, Nottingham
Greenholme School, Nottingham
Grosvenor School, Nottingham
Highfields School, Newark
Hollygirt School, Nottingham
Nottingham High Junior School, Nottingham
Nottingham High School, Nottingham
Nottingham High School for Girls GDST, Nottingham
Plumtree School, Nottingham
Ranby House School, Retford
St Joseph's School, Nottingham
Salterford House School, Nottingham
Trent College, Nottingham
Wellow House School, Newark
Worksop College, Worksop

OXFORDSHIRE

Abingdon School, Abingdon
Bloxham School, Banbury
Bruern Abbey School, Chesterton
The Carrdus School, Banbury
Chandlings Manor School, Oxford
Christ Church Cathedral School, Oxford
Cokethorpe School, Witney
Cothill House Preparatory School, Abingdon
Cranford House School, Wallingford
d'Overbroeck's College, Oxford
Dragon School, Oxford
Ferndale Preparatory School, Faringdon
Headington School, Oxford
Kingham Hill School, Chipping Norton
Magdalen College School, Oxford
The Manor Preparatory School, Abingdon
Moulsford Preparatory School, Wallingford
New College School, Oxford
Our Lady's Convent Senior School, Abingdon
Oxford High School GDST, Oxford
Radley College, Abingdon
Rupert House, Henley-on-Thames
Rye St Antony School, Oxford
St Edward's School, Oxford
St Hugh's School, Faringdon
St John's Priory School, Banbury
St Mary's School, Henley-on-Thames
St Mary's School, Wantage
The School of St Helen & St Katharine, Abingdon
Shiplake College, Henley-on-Thames
Sibford School, Banbury
Summer Fields, Oxford
Tudor Hall School, Banbury
Windrush Valley School, Chipping Norton
Wychwood School, Oxford

RUTLAND

Brooke Priory School, Oakham
Oakham School, Oakham
Uppingham School, Uppingham

SHROPSHIRE

Adcote School for Girls, Shrewsbury
Bedstone College, Bucknell
Castle House School, Newport
Concord College, Shrewsbury
Ellesmere College, Ellesmere
Moor Park School, Ludlow
Moreton Hall School, Oswestry
The Old Hall School, Telford
Oswestry School, Oswestry
Packwood Haugh School, Shrewsbury
Prestfelde Preparatory School, Shrewsbury
St Winefride's Convent School, Shrewsbury
Shrewsbury High School GDST, Shrewsbury
Shrewsbury School, Shrewsbury
Wrekin College, Telford

SOMERSET

All Hallows, Shepton Mallet
Bruton School for Girls, Bruton
Chilton Cantelo School, Yeovil
Downside School, Bath
Hazlegrove (King's Bruton Preparatory School), Yeovil
King's College, Taunton
King's Hall, Taunton
King's Bruton, Bruton
Millfield Preparatory School, Glastonbury
Millfield School, Street
The Park School, Yeovil
Perrott Hill School, Crewkerne
Queen's College, Taunton
Queen's College Junior, Pre-Prep & Nursery Schools, Taunton
Taunton Preparatory School, Taunton
Taunton School, Taunton
Wellington School, Wellington
Wells Cathedral Junior School, Wells
Wells Cathedral School, Wells

BATH & NORTH EAST SOMERSET

King Edward's School, Bath
Kingswood Preparatory School, Bath
Kingswood School, Bath
Monkton Combe Junior School, Bath
Monkton Combe School, Bath
Paragon School, Bath
Prior Park College, Bath
The Royal High School, Bath

NORTH SOMERSET

Sidcot School, Winscombe

STAFFORDSHIRE

Abbots Bromley School for Girls, Abbots Bromley
Abbotsholme School, Uttoxeter
Brooklands School, Stafford
Chase Academy, Cannock
Denstone College, Uttoxeter
Edenhurst School, Newcastle-under-Lyme
Lichfield Cathedral School, Lichfield
Newcastle-under-Lyme School, Newcastle-under-Lyme
St Bede's School, Stafford
St Dominic's Priory School, Stone
St Dominic's School, Stafford
St Joseph's Preparatory School, Stoke-on-Trent
Smallwood Manor Preparatory School, Uttoxeter
Stafford Grammar School, Stafford
Vernon Lodge Preparatory School, Brewood
Yarlet School, Stafford

STOCKTON-ON-TEES

Red House School, Norton
Teesside High School, Eaglescliffe

SUFFOLK

The Abbey, Woodbridge
Amberfield School, Ipswich
Barnardiston Hall Preparatory School, Haverhill
Cherry Trees School, Bury St Edmunds
Culford School, Bury St Edmunds
Fairstead House School, Newmarket
Finborough School, Stowmarket
Framlingham College, Woodbridge
Framlingham College Preparatory School, Brandeston
Ipswich High School GDST, Ipswich
Ipswich Preparatory School, Ipswich
Ipswich School, Ipswich
Moreton Hall Preparatory School, Bury St Edmunds
Old Buckenham Hall School, Ipswich
The Old School, Beccles
Orwell Park, Ipswich
Royal Hospital School, Ipswich
Saint Felix Schools, Southwold
St Joseph's College, Ipswich
South Lee Preparatory School, Bury St Edmunds
Stoke College, Sudbury
Woodbridge School, Woodbridge

SURREY

Aberdour, Tadworth
ACS Cobham International School, Cobham
ACS Egham International School, Egham
Aldro School, Godalming
Amesbury, Hindhead
Barfield School, Farnham
Barrow Hills School, Godalming
Belmont School, Dorking
Bishopsgate School, Egham
Box Hill School, Dorking
Bramley School, Tadworth
Canbury School, Kingston-upon-Thames
Caterham Preparatory School, Caterham
Caterham School, Caterham
Charterhouse, Godalming
Chinthurst School, Tadworth
City of London Freemen's School, Ashtead
Claremont Fan Court School, Esher
Coworth-Flexlands School, Woking
Cranleigh Preparatory School, Cranleigh
Cranleigh School, Cranleigh
Cranmore School, Leatherhead
Cumnor House School, South Croydon
Danes Hill Preparatory School, Leatherhead
Duke of Kent School, Ewhurst
Dunottar School, Reigate
Edgeborough, Farnham
Epsom College, Epsom
Ewell Castle School, Epsom
Feltonfleet School, Cobham
Frensham Heights School, Farnham
Glenesk School, Leatherhead
Greenacre School for Girls, Banstead
Greenfield School, Woking
Guildford High School, Guildford

Hall Grove School, Bagshot
Halstead Preparatory School, Woking
Haslemere Preparatory School, Haslemere
Hawley Place School, Camberley
The Hawthorns School, Redhill
Hazelwood School, Oxted
Hoe Bridge School, Woking
Homefield School, Sutton
Hurtwood House, Dorking
Kew College, Richmond
King Edward's School Witley, Godalming
King's House School, Richmond
Kingston Grammar School, Kingston-upon-Thames
Kingswood House School, Epsom
Lanesborough, Guildford
Laverock School, Oxted
Lingfield Notre Dame School, Lingfield
Longacre School, Guildford
Lyndhurst School, Camberley
Manor House School, Leatherhead
Marymount International School, Kingston-upon-Thames
Micklefield School, Reigate
Milbourne Lodge School, Esher
More House School, Farnham
Notre Dame Preparatory School, Cobham
Notre Dame Senior School, Cobham
Oakhyrst Grange School, Caterham
Parkside School, Cobham
Prior's Field School, Godalming
Priory School, Banstead
Reed's School, Cobham
Reigate Grammar School, Reigate
Reigate St Mary's Preparatory and Choir School, Reigate
Ripley Court School, Woking
Rowan Preparatory School, Esher
Royal Grammar School, Guildford
The Royal School, Haslemere
Rydes Hill Preparatory School, Guildford
St Andrew's (Woking) School Trust, Woking
St Catherine's School, Guildford
St Christopher's School, Epsom
St David's School, Purley
St Edmund's School, Hindhead
St George's College, Weybridge
St George's College Junior School, Weybridge
St Hilary's School, Godalming
St Ives School, Haslemere
St John's School, Leatherhead
St Teresa's Preparatory School, Effingham
St Teresa's School, Dorking
Seaton House School, Sutton
Shrewsbury House School, Surbiton
Sir William Perkins's School, Chertsey
The Study School, New Malden
Surbiton High School, Kingston-upon-Thames
Surbiton Preparatory School, Surbiton
Sutton High School GDST, Sutton
Tormead School, Guildford
Wispers School for Girls, Haslemere
Woldingham School, Woldingham
Woodcote House School, Windlesham
Yehudi Menuhin School, Cobham

EAST SUSSEX

Ashdown House School, Forest Row
Battle Abbey School, Battle
Bodiam Manor School, Robertsbridge
Bricklehurst Manor Preparatory, Wadhurst
Brighton and Hove High School GDST, Brighton
Brighton College, Brighton
Brighton College Prep School, Brighton
Eastbourne College, Eastbourne
Greenfields School, Forest Row
Lancing College Preparatory School at Mowden, Hove
Lewes Old Grammar School, Lewes
Moira House Girls School, Eastbourne
Mowden School, Hove
Newlands Manor School, Seaford
Newlands Preparatory School, Seaford
Roedean School, Brighton
St Andrew's School, Eastbourne
St Aubyns School, Brighton
St Bede's Prep School, Eastbourne
St Bede's School, Hailsham
St Leonards-Mayfield School, Mayfield
St Mary's Hall, Brighton
Sacred Heart School, Wadhurst
Skippers Hill Manor Preparatory School, Mayfield
Vinehall School, Robertsbridge

WEST SUSSEX

Ardingly College, Haywards Heath
Ardingly College Junior School, Haywards Heath
Arundale Preparatory School, Pulborough
Brambletye, East Grinstead
Broadwater Manor School, Worthing
Burgess Hill School for Girls, Burgess Hill
Christ's Hospital, Horsham
Copthorne Prep School, Copthorne
Cottesmore School, Pease Pottage
Cumnor House School, Haywards Heath
Dorset House School, Pulborough
Farlington School, Horsham
Fonthill Lodge, East Grinstead
Great Ballard School, Chichester
Great Walstead, Haywards Heath
Handcross Park School, Haywards Heath
Hurstpierpoint College, Hurstpierpoint
Lancing College, Lancing
Lavant House, Chichester
Oakwood School, Chichester
Our Lady of Sion School, Worthing
Pennthorpe School, Horsham
The Prebendal School, Chichester
St Margaret's School Convent of Mercy, Midhurst
Seaford College, Petworth
Shoreham College, Shoreham-by-Sea
Slindon College, Arundel
Sompting Abbotts School, Sompting
Stoke Brunswick, East Grinstead
The Towers Convent School, Steyning

Westbourne House School, Chichester
Windlesham House, Pulborough
Worth School, Turners Hill

TYNE AND WEAR

Argyle House School, Sunderland
Central Newcastle High School GDST,
    Newcastle upon Tyne
Dame Allan's Boys School, Newcastle upon Tyne
Dame Allan's Girls School, Newcastle upon Tyne
The King's School, Tynemouth
La Sagesse School, Newcastle upon Tyne
Newcastle Preparatory School, Newcastle upon Tyne
Newcastle Upon Tyne Church High School,
    Newcastle upon Tyne
Newlands School, Newcastle upon Tyne
Royal Grammar School, Newcastle upon Tyne
Sunderland High School, Sunderland
Westfield School, Newcastle upon Tyne

WARWICKSHIRE

Abbotsford School, Kenilworth
Arnold Lodge School, Leamington Spa
Bilton Grange, Rugby
The Crescent School, Rugby
The King's High School for Girls, Warwick
The Kingsley School, Leamington Spa
Princethorpe College, Rugby
Rugby School, Rugby
Stratford Preparatory School, Stratford-upon-Avon
Twycross House School, Atherstone
Warwick Preparatory School, Warwick
Warwick School, Warwick

WEST MIDLANDS

Bablake School, Coventry
The Blue Coat School, Birmingham
Coventry Prep School, Coventry
Crackley Hall School, Kenilworth
Davenport Lodge School, Coventry
Edgbaston High School for Girls, Birmingham
Elmhurst School for Dance, Birmingham
Eversfield Preparatory School, Solihull
Hallfield School, Birmingham
Highclare School, Birmingham
King Edward VI High School for Girls, Birmingham
King Edward's School, Birmingham
King Henry VIII School, Coventry
Mayfield Preparatory School, Walsall
Newbridge Preparatory School, Wolverhampton
Norfolk House School, Birmingham
Priory School, Birmingham
The Royal Wolverhampton Junior School,
    Wolverhampton
The Royal Wolverhampton School, Wolverhampton
Ruckleigh School, Solihull
St George's School, Edgbaston, Birmingham

St Martin's School, Solihull
Solihull School, Solihull
Tettenhall College, Wolverhampton
West House School, Birmingham
Wolverhampton Grammar School, Wolverhampton

WILTSHIRE

Appleford School, Salisbury
Chafyn Grove School, Salisbury
Dauntsey's School, Devizes
The Godolphin School, Salisbury
Heywood Preparatory School, Corsham
Leaden Hall School, Salisbury
Marlborough College, Marlborough
Pinewood School, Shrivenham
Prior Park Preparatory School, Cricklade
St Francis School, Pewsey
St Margaret's Preparatory School, Calne
St Mary's Calne, Calne
Salisbury Cathedral School, Salisbury
Sandroyd School, Salisbury
Stonar School, Melksham
Warminster School, Warminster

WORCESTERSHIRE

Abberley Hall, Worcester
The Alice Ottley School, Worcester
Bowbrook House School, Pershore
Bromsgrove Preparatory School, Bromsgrove
Bromsgrove School, Bromsgrove
Dodderhill School, Droitwich Spa
The Downs School, Malvern
The Elms, Malvern
Heathfield School, Kidderminster
Holy Trinity School, Kidderminster
King's Hawford, Worcester
The King's School, Worcester
The Knoll School, Kidderminster
Malvern College, Malvern
Malvern College Preparatory and Pre-Prep School, Malvern
Malvern Girls' College, Malvern
Moffats School, Bewdley
Royal Grammar School Worcester, Worcester
St James's School, Malvern
St Mary's Convent School, Worcester
Winterfold House, Kidderminster

EAST RIDING OF YORKSHIRE

Hull Collegiate School, Anlaby
Hymers College, Hull
Pocklington School, Pocklington

NORTH YORKSHIRE

Ampleforth College, York
Ashville College, Harrogate

Aysgarth Preparatory School, Bedale
Bootham School, York
Bramcote School, Scarborough
Catteral Hall School, Settle
Clifton Preparatory School, York
Fyling Hall School, Whitby
Giggleswick School, Settle
Harrogate Ladies' College, Harrogate
Lisvane, Scarborough College Junior School, Scarborough
Malsis School, Nr Skipton
The Minster School, York
The Mount School, York
Queen Ethelburga's College, York
Queen Margaret's School, York
Queen Mary's School, Thirsk
Read School, Selby
Ripon Cathedral Choir School, Ripon
St Martin's Ampleforth, York
St Olave's School (Junior of St Peter's), York
St Peter's School, York
Scarborough College & Lisvane School, Scarborough
Terrington Hall, York

SOUTH YORKSHIRE

Ashdell Preparatory School, Sheffield
Birkdale School, Sheffield
Brantwood School, Sheffield
Hill House St Mary's School, Doncaster
Mylnhurst RC School & Nursery, Sheffield
Rudston Preparatory School, Rotherham
Sheffield High School GDST, Sheffield
Westbourne School, Sheffield

WEST YORKSHIRE

Ackworth School, Pontefract
Batley Grammar School, Batley
Bradford Girls' Grammar School, Bradford
Bradford Grammar School, Bradford
Bronte House School, Bradford
Cliff School, Wakefield
Dale House School, Batley
The Froebelian School, Leeds
Fulneck School, Pudsey
Gateways School, Leeds
The Gleddings School, Halifax
Hipperholme Grammar School, Halifax
Lady Lane Park School, Bingley
Moorfield School, Ilkley
Moorlands School, Leeds
Queen Elizabeth Grammar School, Wakefield
The Rastrick Independent School, Brighouse
Richmond House School, Leeds
Rishworth School, Rishworth
Silcoates School, Wakefield
Sunny Hill House School, Wakefield
Wakefield Girls' High School, Wakefield
Westville House Preparatory School, Ilkley
Woodhouse Grove School, Apperley Bridge

NORTHERN IRELAND

COUNTY ANTRIM

Belfast Royal Academy, Belfast
Campbell College, Belfast
Methodist College, Belfast
Royal Belfast Academical Institution, Belfast

COUNTY DOWN

Bangor Grammar School, Bangor
Rockport School, Holywood

COUNTY FERMANAGH

Portora Royal School, Enniskillen

COUNTY LONDONDERRY

Coleraine Academical Institution, Coleraine

COUNTY TYRONE

The Royal School Dungannon, Dungannon

SCOTLAND

ABERDEENSHIRE

Robert Gordons College, Aberdeen
St Margaret's School for Girls, Aberdeen

ANGUS

The High School of Dundee, Dundee
Lathallan School, Montrose

ARGYLL AND BUTE

Lomond School, Helensburgh

CLACKMANNANSHIRE

Dollar Academy, Dollar

FIFE

St Leonards School & VIth Form College, St Andrews

GLASGOW

Craigholme School, Glasgow
The Glasgow Academy, Glasgow
The High School of Glasgow, Glasgow
Hutchesons' Grammar School, Glasgow
Kelvinside Academy, Glasgow
St Aloysius Junior School, Glasgow

LOTHIAN

Belhaven Hill, Dunbar
Cargilfield, Edinburgh
Clifton Hall School, Edinburgh

The Edinburgh Academy, Edinburgh
Fettes College, Edinburgh
George Heriot's School, Edinburgh
George Watson's College, Edinburgh
Loretto School, Musselburgh
The Mary Erskine School, Edinburgh
Merchiston Castle School, Edinburgh
St George's School for Girls, Edinburgh
St Margaret's School, Edinburgh
Stewart's Melville College, Edinburgh

MORAYSHIRE

Gordonstoun School, Elgin

PERTH AND KINROSS

Ardvreck School, Crieff
Craigclowan Preparatory School, Perth
Glenalmond College, Perth
Kilgraston, Perth
Morrison's Academy, Crieff
Strathallan School, Perth

RENFREWSHIRE

St Columba's School, Kilmacolm

ROXBURGHSHIRE

St Mary's Preparatory School, Melrose

STIRLING

Beaconhurst School, Bridge of Allan

WALES

CARDIFF

The Cathedral School, Cardiff
Howell's School, Llandaff GDST, Cardiff
Kings Monkton School, Cardiff
St John's College, Old St Mellors
Westbourne School, Cardiff

CARMARTHENSHIRE

Llandovery College, Llandovery
St Michael's School, Llanelli

CONWY

Lyndon Preparatory School, Colwyn Bay
Rydal Penrhos Senior School, Colwyn Bay
St David's College, Llandudno

DENBIGHSHIRE

Howell's School, Denbigh
Ruthin School, Ruthin

GWYNEDD

St Gerard's School, Bangor

MONMOUTHSHIRE

Haberdashers' Monmouth School For Girls,
    Monmouth
Monmouth School, Monmouth
St John's-on-the-Hill, Chepstow

NEWPORT

Rougemont School, Newport

POWYS

Christ College, Brecon

5.10

Educational Associations and Useful Addresses

The Allied Schools
Cross House
38 High Street
Banbury
Oxon OX16 5ET
Tel: (01295) 256441
Fax: (01295) 275350
E-mail: z.foard@alliedschools.org.uk
Website: www.alliedschools.org.uk
General Manager: Michael Porter BA, MSc

The organization provides management, financial, helpline and other support services to member schools, as well as operating a communications network between school governors, heads, bursars and other staff for the exchange of information and ideas. The Allied Schools include:

Barnardiston Hall
Harrogate Ladies' College
Stowe
Wrekin Old Hall Trust

Canford School
Riddlesworth Hall
Westonbirt School

The Association for the Education and Guardianship of International Students (AEGIS)
Tel/Fax: (01453) 755160
E-mail: secretary@aegisuk.net
Website: www.aegisuk.net
Secretary: Janet Bowman
Registered Charity No. 1111 384

The Association promotes best and legal practice in all areas of guardianship and the care of international students, under 18 years of age, at school or college in the United Kingdom. All members, including school members, are required to adhere to the AEGIS Code of Practice and undertake to follow guidelines on caring for international students.

Guardianship organizations are admitted to membership after a successful accreditation inspection.

Association of Governing Bodies of Independent Schools (AGBIS)
Renshaw Barns
Upper Woodford
Salisbury
Wiltshire SP4 6FA
Tel: (01722) 782900
Fax: (05601) 264801
E-mail: gensec@agbis.org.uk
Website: www.agbis.org.uk
General Secretary: Brigadier S Rutter-Jerome

The aim of the Association is to advance education in independent schools, to promote good governance and administration in independent schools and to encourage co-operation between their governing bodies. For details please contact the General Secretary.

Association of Heads of Independent Schools
St Nicholas School
Redfields House, Redfields Lane
Church Crookham
Fleet
Hampshire GU52 0RF
Honorary Secretary: Mrs A V Whatmough

Membership of AHIS is open to the Heads of girls' independent secondary schools and girls' co-educational junior independent schools which are accredited by the Independent Schools Council (see below).

Association of Nursery Training Colleges
The Chiltern College
16 Peppard Road
Caversham
Reading RG4 8JZ
Tel: (0118) 9471847

Provides information and advice on careers in childcare, as nannies and nursery workers. Also gives information on Diplomas, National Vocational Qualifications (NVQs) and Montessori training in childcare and education offered at Chiltern College in Reading (www.chilterncollege.com), the Norland College in Bath (www.norland.co.uk) and the Montessori Centre International, whose headquarters are in London (www.montessori.ac.uk).

Association of School and College Leaders (ASCL)
130 Regent Road
Leicester LE1 7PG
Tel: (0116) 299 1122
Fax: (0116) 299 1123
E-mail: info@ascl.org.uk
Website: www.ascl.org.uk
General Secretary: J E Dunford

ASCL is the only professional association and trade union in Britain to speak exclusively for secondary school and college leaders, in both the independent and mainstream sectors.

The Association has nearly 13,000 members including heads, deputy heads, assistant heads, bursars and business managers and others with school/college responsibility.

ASCL has strong ties with the Headmasters' Conference and Girls' School Association and their members are automatically part of ASCL.

Benefits of ASCL membership include access to legal support and advice, a telephone hotline for guidance on urgent issues, personal support from regional field officers, regular publications and guidance on courses and conferences, and pension advice.

Association of Tutors
Sunnycroft
63 King Edward Road
Northampton NN1 5LY
Tel: (01604) 624171
Fax: (01604) 624718
Website: www.tutor.co.uk
Secretary: Dr D J Cornelius

The professional body for independent private tutors. Members provide advice and individual tuition to students at all levels of education. The tutoring may be supplementary to full course provision or may be on a full course basis.

Boarding Schools' Association (BSA)
Grosvenor Gardens House
35–37 Grosvenor Gardens
London SW1W 0BS
Tel: (020) 7798 1580
Fax: (020) 7798 1581
E-mail: bsa@boarding.org.uk
Website: www.boarding.org.uk
National Director: Hilary Moriarty

The BSA has the twin objectives of promoting boarding education and developing quality boarding through high standards of pastoral care and boarding facilities.

A school can join the BSA only if it is a member of one of the constituent associations of the Independent Schools Council or, for state-maintained boarding schools, a member of SBSA (the State Boarding Schools Association). These two bodies require member schools to be regularly inspected by the Independent Schools Inspectorate (ISA) or OFSTED. Parents and prospective pupils choosing a boarding school can therefore be assured that BSA member schools are committed to providing the best possible boarding environment for their pupils.

For further information about the BSA Professional Development Programme please contact:

Alex Thompson BSc (Hons) PGCE DipEd
BSA Director of Training
7 Millbrook
Shady Bower
Salisbury SP1 1NH
E-mail: training@boarding.org.uk

British Accreditation Council
The Chief Executive
44 Bedford Row
London WC1R 4LL
Tel: (020) 7447 2554
Fax: (020) 7447 2555
E-mail: info@the-bac.org
Website: www.the-bac.org

BAC is a registered charity organization which was established in 1984 to act as the national accrediting body for independent further and higher education. A college accredited by BAC undergoes a thorough inspection every four years, which is followed up with an interim visit after two years. Accreditation means that a BAC college has achieved a satisfactory standard in the areas of *health and safety provision, administration and staffing, the management of quality, student welfare* and *teaching and learning.* BAC also attempts to take action to intercede for students if a conflict arises between the student and the accredited college.

At present BAC accredits over 230 colleges in the UK and more than 25 overseas in 11 different countries: the Czech Republic, France, Spain, Pakistan, United Arab Emirates, Bulgaria, Greece, India, Mauritius, Germany and Switzerland.

British Association for Early Childhood Education (Early Education)
111 City View House
463 Bethnal Green Road
London E2 9QY
Tel: (020) 7739 7594
Fax: (020) 7613 5330

A charitable association which advises on the care and education of young children from birth to 8 years. The Association also publishes booklets and organizes conferences for those interested in early childhood education.

British Dyslexia Association
Unit 8 Bracknell Beeches
Old Bracknell Lane
Bracknell RG12 7BW
Fax: (0118) 935 1927
E-mail: helpline@bdadyslexia.org.uk
Website: www.bdadyslexia.org.uk
(Helpline/Information Service 10am–4pm Monday–Friday (5pm–7pm) also Wednesdays.

Charity offering information and help to dyslexic people, their families, professionals and employees.

Children's Education Advisory Service
Trenchard Lines
Upavon
Pewsey
Wilts SN9 6BE
Tel: (01980) 618244
E-mail: enquiries@ceas.detsa.gov.uk

To support Service families and entitled civilians in obtaining appropriate educational facilities for their children and to provide high quality, impartial advice on all aspects of education worldwide.

Choir Schools Association
Wolvesey
College Street
Winchester SO23 9ND
Tel: (01962) 890530
Fax: (01962) 869978
E-mail: info@choirschools.org.uk
Administrator: Susan Rees

An association of schools educating cathedral and collegiate boy and girl choristers. Membership comprises the following schools:

Ampleforth College, Ampleforth, North Yorkshire
Bristol Cathedral School, Bristol
The Cathedral School, Llandaff
Chetham's School of Music, Manchester
The Chorister School, Durham
Christ Church Cathedral School, Oxford
Exeter Cathedral School, Exeter
Hereford Cathedral Junior School, Hereford
King's College School, Cambridge

King's Preparatory School, Rochester
The King's School, Ely
The King's School, Gloucester
The King's School, Worcester
Lanesborough, Guildford
Lichfield Cathedral School, Lichfield
Lincoln Minster School, Lincoln
Magdalen College School, Oxford
The Minster School, Southwell
The Minster School, York
New College School, Oxford
Norwich School, Norwich
The Pilgrim's School, Winchester
Polwhele House, Truro
The Prebendal School, Chichester
Reigate St Mary's Preparatory and Choir
    School, Reigate

Ripon Cathedral Choir School, Ripon
Runnymede St Edward's School, Liverpool
St Edmunds Junior School, Canterbury
St George's School, Windsor
St James's School, Grimsby
St John's College, Cardiff
St John's College School, Cambridge
St Mary's Music School, Edinburgh
St Paul's Cathedral School, London EC4
Salisbury Cathedral School, Salisbury
Wells Cathedral School, Wells
Westminster Abbey Choir School,
    London SW1
Westminster Cathedral Choir School,
    London SW1

Associate Members
City of London School, EC4V
The King's School, Peterborough
The Oratory School, Reading
Portsmouth Grammar School, Portsmouth
Queen Elizabeth Grammar School, Wakefield
St Cedd's School, Chelmsford
St Edward's College, Liverpool
Warwick School, Warwick

Council for Independent Education (CIFE)
1 Knightsbridge Green
London SW1X 7NW
Tel: (020) 8767 8666
E-mail: enquiries@cife.org.uk
Website: www.cife.org.uk

CIFE, founded in 1973, is a professional association for independent colleges of further education which specialize in preparing students for GCSEs, A and AS levels and university entrance. In addition, some colleges offer English language tuition for students from abroad. The Association promotes good practice and adherence to strict standards of professional conduct and ethical propriety. Full membership is open to colleges which have been accredited either by the British Accreditation Council (BAC) or by the Independent Schools Council. All CIFE colleges, of which there are currently 17 spread throughout England, with concentrations in London, Oxford and Cambridge, have to abide by exacting codes of conduct and practice; and the character and presentation of their published exam results are subject to formal validation by the BACS. Further information and a list of colleges are available from the Secretary.

CReSTeD (Council for the Registration of Schools Teaching Dyslexic Pupils)
Registered Charity No: 1052103
Greygarth, Littleworth
Winchcombe
Cheltenham GL54 5BT
Tel: (01242) 604 852
E-mail: admin@crested.org.uk
Website: www.crested.org.uk
Chairman: Brendan Wignall

The CReSTeD Register is to help parents and those who advise them to choose schools for children with SpLD (dyslexia). Its main supporters are the British Dyslexia Association and Dyslexia Action who, with others, established CReSTeD to produce an authoritative list of schools, both maintained and independent, which have been through an established registration procedure, including a visit by the CReSTeD selected consultant.

Department for Children, Schools and Families
Sanctuary Buildings
Great Smith Street
London SW1P 3BT
Tel: (08700) 000 2288
Fax: (01928) 794 248
E-mail: info@dcsf.gsi.gov.uk
Website: www.dcsf.gov.uk

The Dyslexia Institute: National Training and Resources Centre
Park House, Wick Road
Egham
Surrey TW20 0HH
Tel: (01784) 222300
Fax: (01784) 222333
E-mail: info@dyslexiaaction.org.uk
Website: www.dyslexiaaction.org.uk
Registered Charity No. 268502

Dyslexia Action is a national charity and the UK's leading provider of services and support for people with dyslexia and literacy difficulties. We specialize in assessment, teaching and training. We also develop and distribute teaching materials and undertake research.

Dyslexia Action is committed to improving public policy and practice. We partner with schools, LEAs, colleges, universities, employers, voluntary sector organizations and government to improve the quality and quantity of help for people with dyslexia and specific learning difficulties.

Our services are available through our 26 centres and 160 teaching locations around the UK. Over half a million people benefit from our work each year.

Gabbitas Educational Consultants
Carrington House
126–130 Regent Street
London W1B 5EE
Tel: (020) 7734 0161
Fax: (020) 7437 1764
E-mail: market@gabbitas.co.uk
Website: www.gabbitas.co.uk

Gabbitas offers independent, expert advice on all stages of education and careers:

- choice of independent schools and colleges;
- educational assessment services for parents concerned about their child's progress at school;
- Sixth Form options – A and AS level, International Baccalaureate and vocational courses;
- university and degree choices and UCAS applications;
- alternatives to university;
- careers assessment and guidance;
- extensive guidance for overseas students transferring into the British system;
- specialist services, including guardianship, for overseas students attending UK boarding schools.

Gabbitas also provides a full range of services for schools, including the appointment of Heads and staff as well as consultancy on any aspect of school management and development.

The Girls' Day School Trust (GDST)
100 Rochester Row
London SW1P 1JP
Tel: (020) 7393 6666
Fax: (020) 7393 6789
E-mail: info@wes.gdst.net
Website: www.gdst.net
The GDST is a registered Charity (No. 306983).

The GDST is one of the largest, longest-established and most successful groups of independent schools in the UK, with 4,000 staff and 20,000 students. As a charity that owns and runs a family of 29 schools in England and Wales, it reinvests all its income for the benefit of the pupils. With a long history of pioneering innovation in the education of girls, the GDST now also educates boys in some of its schools; has two co-educational Sixth Form Colleges; and is developing a selective group of prep schools, some of which are co-educational.

The wide-ranging curricular and extra-curricular opportunities available in GDST schools encourage creativity, articulate self-expression and enterprise in students who are prepared to participate fully in the challenges of 21st-century life.

Schools

The Belvedere Academy, Liverpool
Birkenhead High School, Birkenhead
Blackheath High School, London SE3
Brighton and Hove High School, Sussex
Bromley High School, Kent
Central Newcastle High School,
 Newcastle-upon-Tyne
Croydon High School, Croydon
Great Houghton Prep School,
 Northampton
The Hamlets Prep School, Liverpool
Heathfield School, Pinner
Hilden Grange School, Tonbridge, Kent
Howell's School, Llandaff, Cardiff
Ipswich High School, Suffolk
Kensington Preparatory School,
 London SW6
Northampton High School, Northampton

Norwich High School for Girls, Norfolk
Notting Hill & Ealing High School,
 London W13
Nottingham High School for Girls,
 Nottingham
Oxford High School, Oxford
Portsmouth High School, Hampshire
Putney High School, London SW15
Royal High School, Bath
Sheffield High School, Sheffield
Shrewsbury High School, Shropshire
South Hampstead High School,
 London NW3
Streatham & Clapham High School,
 London SW16
Sutton High School, Surrey
Sydenham High School, London SE26
Wimbledon High School, London SW19

All GDST schools are non-denominational day schools, and The Royal High School, Bath, also takes boarders. The GDST's small group of prep schools – Great Houghton, The Hamlets, Hilden Grange and Kensington – prepare pupils for entry to other schools at 11 or 13. All other schools in the group offer an 'all-through' education, catering for pupils from ages 3 or 4 to 18, with thriving Sixth Forms and, in many cases, nursery classes too.

Howell's School in Cardiff and the Royal High School in Bath have a co-educational Sixth Form College and, in a new initiative, The Belvedere School in Liverpool has transferred from the independent sector to Academy status and opened as The Belvedere Academy in September 2007.

The Girls' Schools Association (GSA)
130 Regent Road
Leicester LE1 7PG
Tel: (0116) 254 1619
Fax: (0116) 255 3792
E-mail: office@gsa.uk.com
President: Mrs Jill Berry
Executive Director: Ms Sheila Cooper

The GSA exists to represent the 200 schools whose Heads are in membership. Its direct aim is to promote excellence in the education of girls. This is achieved through a clear understanding of the individual potential of girls and young women. Over 110,000 pupils are educated in schools which cover day and boarding, large and small, city and country, academically elite and broad-based education. Scholarships and bursaries are available in most schools.

The Headmasters' and Headmistresses' Conference (HMC)
12 The Point
Rockingham Road
Market Harborough
Leicestershire LE16 7QU
Tel: (01858) 469 059
Fax: (01858) 469 532
Membership Secretary: R V Peel
Secretary: G H Lucas

The Headmasters' and Headmistresses' Conference (HMC) represents the headteachers of some 250 leading independent schools in the United Kingdom and the Republic of Ireland.

IAPS (The Independent Association of Prep Schools)
11 Waterloo Place
Leamington Spa
Warwickshire CV32 5LA
Tel: (01926) 887833
Fax: (01926) 888014
E-mail: iaps@iaps.org.uk
Chief Executive: David Hanson

IAPS is the main professional association for Heads of independent preparatory and junior schools in the UK and overseas. There are some 600 schools whose Heads are in membership, accommodating over 130,000 children.

The Independent Schools Association (ISA)
Boys' British School
East Street
Saffron Walden
Essex CB10 1LS
Tel: (01799) 523619
Secretary: Mrs Jane Le Poidevin

There are approximately 300 schools in membership of ISA. These are all schools which have been accredited by the Independent Schools Council Inspection Service. This and the requirement that the school should be good of its kind are the criteria for membership. ISA represents schools with pupils throughout the age range. The majority of schools are day schools, but a significant number also have boarders. Membership of the Association enables Heads to receive support from the Association in a number of ways and enables pupils to take part in many events organized by ISA.

The Independent Schools' Bursars Association (ISBA)
Unit 11–12, Manor Farm
Cliddesden, Basingstoke
Hants RG25 2JB
Tel: (01256) 330369
Fax: (01256) 330376
E-mail: office@theisba.org.uk
Website: www.theisba.org.uk
General Secretary: Mr Jonathan Cook

The ISBA, with over 900 schools in membership, aims to support and advance financial and operational performance in schools. The Association deals with Ministers, civil servants, the media, the general public, a wide range of professional advisers and suppliers, and schools at a number of different levels including governors, heads and bursars. It works closely with the Independent Schools Council (ISC) and its other seven associations together with the Independent Schools Inspectorate (ISI) and the Boarding Schools Association (BSA). The ISBA's staff and Secretariat provide help and advice, seek to keep ahead of regulatory change and promote the sharing of best practice.

The Independent Schools Careers Organisation (ISCO)
ISCO is the independent schools careers service from The Inspiring Futures Foundation.

ISCO c/o Inspiring Futures
St George's House
Knoll Road
Camberley
Surrey GU15 3SY
Tel: (01276) 687525
E-mail: helpline@inspiringfutures.org.uk
Websites: www.isco.org.uk; www.inspiringfutures.org.uk; www.myfuturewise.org.uk; www.expandinghorizons.info; www.careerscope.org.uk

ISCO, part of Inspiring Futures, is a not-for-profit organization established to help young people make informed decisions about higher education and career choices. It provides support to schools through its ISCO Membership and Information Service schemes and direct help and guidance to young people and their parents through the Futurewise scheme. This provides a range of career and higher education services, online and face-to-face, from enrolment to age 23. Services are delivered across the UK and internationally through a network of professionally qualified Regional Directors and Regional Advisers. Operations are supported centrally to ensure that up-to-date information is provided to members of the schemes through a range of resources, online services and the termly *Careerscope* magazine. The Expanding Horizons team organizes a range of unique development and career preparation opportunities for young people including InterActives, Insight courses and GAP year fairs.

Independent Schools Council (ISC)

St Vincent House
30 Orange Street
London WC2H 7HH
Tel: (020) 7766 7070
Fax: (020) 7766 7071
Chief Executive: David Lyscom

ISC is the umbrella body for the following associations:

The Association of Governing Bodies of Independent Schools (AGBIS), (COBIS)
The Girls' Schools Association (GSA)
The Headmasters' and Headmistresses' Conference (HMC)
The Independent Association of Prep Schools (IAPS)
The Independent Schools' Association (ISA)
The Independent Schools' Bursars Association (ISBA)
The Society of Headmasters and Headmistresses of Independent Schools (SHMIS), (COBIS)

The total membership of ISC comprises about 1,300 schools which are accredited by ISC and inspected on a six-year cycle by the Independent Schools Inspectorate (ISI) under arrangements agreed by the DCSF and OFSTED. ISC deals with matters of policy and other issues common to its members and when required speaks collectively on their behalf. It represents its members in discussions with the Department for Children, Schools and Families and with other organizations, and represents the collective view of members on independent education.

Independent Schools Examinations Board

Jordan House, Christchurch Road
New Milton
Hants BH25 6QJ
Tel: (01425) 621111
Fax: (01425) 620044
E-mail: enquiries@iseb.co.uk
Website: iseb.co.uk

Details of the Common Entrance examinations (see the section on Examinations and Qualifications) are available from the General Secretary at the address above.

The Round Square Schools
Braemar Lodge
Castle Hill, Hartley, Dartford
Kent DA3 7BH
Tel: (0147) 470 6927
Fax: (01737) 217133
E-mail: jane@roundsquare.org
Secretary: Mrs J Howson

An international group of schools which follow the principles of Kurt Hahn, founder of the Salem School in Germany and Gordonstoun in Scotland. There are now over 50 member schools in more than 12 countries: Australia, Canada, England, France, Germany, India, Japan, Kenya, Oman, Scotland, South Africa, Switzerland, Thailand and the United States. Member schools arrange regular exchange visits for pupils and undertake aid projects in India, Kenya, Eastern Europe and Thailand. All member schools uphold the five principles of outdoor adventure, community service, education for democracy, international understanding and environmental conservation. UK member schools are as follows:

Abbotsholme, Uttoxeter (Co-ed)
Box Hill, Dorking (Co-ed)
Cobham Hall, Gravesend (Girls')
Gordonstoun, Elgin (Co-ed)

Wellington College, Crowthorne
    (Boys', Girls in Sixth Form)
Westfield, Newcastle upon Tyne (Girls')
Windermere St Anne's (Co-ed)

SATIPS
Professional Support and Training for Staff in Independent Schools
Cherry Trees, Stebbing
Great Dunmow
Essex CM6 3ST
Tel/Fax: (01371) 856823
E-mail: admin@satips.com
Website: www.satips.com
General Secretary: Andrew Davis
Administrator: Mrs P M Harrison

SATIPS – founded in 1952 – is a source of professional support and encouragement for staff in preparatory and other schools. We are now one of the foremost providers of subject-based and cross-curricular INSET courses for prep school and other staff. SATIPS is a registered charity. In 1993 the Society widened its appeal by changing its emphasis from purely preparatory school teachers to any school staff, especially those in independent schools. In particular, teachers who have pupils in Key Stages 1, 2 and 3 will find the membership of SATIPS useful: we are particularly interested in making contact with colleagues in the maintained sector. The Society publishes 19 Broadsheets each term in all subject areas and runs conferences (mostly one-day) at various venues during the year. We offer school and individual membership.

The Society of Headmasters and Headmistresses of Independent Schools (SHMIS)
12 The Point
Rockingham
Roth Market Harborough
Leicestershire LE16 7QU
Tel: (01572) 755426
Fax: (01572) 756234
E-mail: gensec@shmis.org.uk
Website: www.shmis.org.uk
General Secretary: David Richardson

A society of some 105 schools, most of which are co-educational, day and boarding, and all of which educate children up to the age of 18.

Steiner Waldorf Schools Fellowship
Kidbrooke Park
Forest Row
East Sussex RH18 5JA
Tel: (01342) 822115
Fax: (01342) 826004
E-mail: info@swsf.org.uk
Website: www.steinerwaldorf.org.uk
Chairman: Christopher Clouder

The Steiner Waldorf Schools Fellowship represents the 32 autonomous Steiner Waldorf Schools and 45 Early Years Centres in the UK and Eire. There are now over 890 schools worldwide. Key characteristics of the education include: careful balance in the artistic, practical and intellectual content of the international Steiner Waldorf curriculum; co-educational from 3 to 19 years. Shared Steiner Waldorf curriculum for all pupils. GCSE and A Level examinations. A broad education based on Steiner's approach to the holistic nature of the human being. Co-operative school management – usually a variable parent payment scheme. Steiner Waldorf education is rapidly gaining in popularity all over the world.

Woodard Schools (The Woodard Corporation)
High Street
Abbots Bromley
Rugeley
Staffordshire WS15 3BW
Tel: (01283) 840120

The Woodard Corporation has 40 schools throughout the country, including 17 Affiliated schools. All have an Anglican foundation and together they form the largest independent group of Church Schools in England and Wales.

Member Schools

Southern Region

Ardingly College, Haywards Heath
Ardingly College Junior School,
    Haywards Heath
Bloxham School, Banbury
Hurstpierpoint College, Hassocks
Hurstpierpoint Junior School, Hassocks
Lancing College, Lancing
Lancing College Preparatory School at
    Mowden, Hove

Midland Region

Abbots Bromley School for Girls,
    Rugeley
Denstone College, Uttoxeter
Ellesmere College, Ellesmere
Prestfelde, Shrewsbury
Ranby House, Retford

Smallwood Manor Preparatory,
    Uttoxeter
Worksop College, Worksop

Eastern Region

Peterborough High School, Peterborough
St James's School, Grimsby

Western Region

The Cathedral School, Llandaff
Grenville College, Bideford
King's College, Taunton
King's Hall School, Taunton
St Margaret's School, Exeter

Northern Region

The King's School, Tynemouth
Queen Mary's School, Thirsk

Affiliated Schools

Alderley Edge School for Girls, Alderley Edge
Bishop of Hereford's Bluecoat School, Tupsley (Voluntary Aided)
Bishop Stopford School, Kettering (Voluntary Aided)
Bishop's Blue Coat Church of England High School, Chester (Voluntary Aided)
Bolitho School, Penzance
Crompton House Church of England School, Oldham (Maintained)
Derby High School, Derby
The King's School, Wolverhampton (Maintained)
Saint George's Church of England School, Gravesend
St Michael's London and All Angels (Academy)
St Olaves Grammar School, Orpington (Voluntary Aided)
St Peter's Church of England High School, Stoke on Trent (Voluntary Aided)
St Peter's Collegiate School, Wolverhampton (Voluntary Aided)
St Saviour's and St Olave's Church of England School, Southwark (Maintained)
St Wilfred's Church of England High School and Technology College, Blackburn
    (Voluntary Aided)

5.11
Glossary of Abbreviations

ABRSM	Associated Board of the Royal Schools of Music
ADD	Attention Deficit Disorder
ADISR	Association des Directeurs d'Instituts de la Suisse Romande
AEB	Associated Examining Board
AGBIS	Association of Governing Bodies of Independent Schools
AHIS	Association of Heads of Independent Schools
ASCL	Association of School and College Leaders
AICE	Advanced International Certificate of Education
ANTC	Association of Nursery Training Colleges
ARCS	Accreditation, Review and Consultancy Service
AVDEP	Association Vaudoise des Ecoles Privees
BACIFHE	British Accreditation Council for Independent Further and Higher Education
BAGA	British Amateur Gymnastics Association
BAYS	British Association for the Advancement of Science
BHS	British Horse Society
BSA	Boarding Schools Association
CAE	Cambridge Certificate in Advanced English
CASE	Council for Advancement and Support of Education
CEE	Common Entrance Examination
CIFE	Council for Independent Further Education
COBIS	Council of British International Schools
CReSTeD	Council for the Registration of Schools Teaching Dyslexic Pupils
CSA	Choir Schools Association
DCSF	Department for Children, Schools and Families
ECIS	European Council for International Schools
EFL	English as a Foreign Language
ESL	English as a Second Language
ESOL	English for Speakers of Other Languages
EUK	English UK, language teaching association
FCE	Cambridge First Certificate in English

FOBISSEA	Federation of British International Schools in South-East Asia
FSEP	Federation Suisse des Ecoles Privees
GBA	Governing Bodies Association
GBGSA	Governing Bodies of Girls' Schools Association
GDST	Girls' Day School Trust
GSA	Girls' Schools Association
HAS	Head Teachers' Association of Scotland
HMC	Headmasters' and Headmistresses' Conference
IAPS	Independent Association of Prep Schools
IB	International Baccalaureate
IBO	International Baccalaureate Organisation
IBSCA	International Baccalaureate Schools and Colleges Association
IBTA	Independent Business Training Organisation
ICG	Independent Colleges Group
IGCSE	International General Certificate of Secondary Education
ISA	Independent Schools Association
ISBA	Independent Schools Bursars' Association
ISC	Independent Schools Council (formerly Independent Schools Joint Council or ISJC)
ISCIS	Independent Schools Council Information Service (formerly ISIS)
ISCO	Independent Schools Careers Organisation
ISI	Independent Schools Inspectorate
ISIS	Independent Schools Information Service
LAMDA	London Academy of Music and Dramatic Art
LISA	London International Schools Association
MSA	Middle States Association of Colleges and Schools (USA)
NABSS	National Association of British Schools in Spain
NAHT	National Association of Head Teachers
NAIS	National Association of Independent Schools
NE/SA	Near East/South Asia
NEAB	Northern Examinations and Assessment Board
NEASC	New England Association of Schools and Colleges
OFSTED	Office for Standards in Education
OUDLE	University of Oxford Delegacy of Local Examinations
PET	Cambridge Preliminary English Test
PSE	Personal and Social Education
RSA CLAIT	Computer Literacy and Information Technology
SATIPS	Society of Assistants Teaching in Preparatory Schools
SCIS	Scottish Council of Independent Schools
SGS	Scottish Girls' Schools
SHMIS	Society of Headmasters and Headmistresses of Independent Schools
SpLD	Specific Learning Difficulties
STABIS	State Boarding Schools Information Service
WJEC	Welsh Joint Education Committee

Abbreviations used to denote Special Needs provision in the profiles section are as follows:

Special needs support provided (independent mainstream schools)

Learning difficulties

CA   Some children with special needs receive help from classroom assistants

RA   There are currently very limited facilities for pupils with learning difficulties but reasonable adjustments can be made if necessary

SC   Some children with special needs are taught in separate classes for specific subjects

SNU   School has a dedicated Special Needs Unit, which provides specialist tuition on a one-to-one or small group basis by appropriately qualified teachers

WI   There is no dedicated Special Needs Unit but some children with special needs are withdrawn individually from certain lessons for one-to-one tuition

Behavioural disorders/emotional and behavioural difficulties/challenging behaviour

CA   Some children with behavioural problems receive help from classroom assistants

CO   Trained counsellors available for pupils

RA   There are currently very limited facilities for pupils with behavioural disorders but reasonable adjustments can be made if necessary

ST   Behaviour management strategies identified in school's behaviour management policy

TS   Staff trained in behaviour management available

Physical impairments/medical conditions

AT   Adapted timetable for children with health problems

BL   Materials can be provided in Braille

CA   Some children receive help from classroom assistants

DS   Signing by staff and pupils

HL   Hearing loops available

IT   Specialist IT provision available

RA   There are currently very limited facilities for pupils with physical impairments or medical conditions but reasonable adjustments can be made if necessary

SL   Stairlifts

SM   Staff with medical training available

TW   Accessible toilet and washing facilities

W   School has wheelchair access (unspecified)

WA1 School is fully wheelchair accessible

WA2 Main teaching areas are wheelchair accessible

WA3 No permanent access for wheelchairs; temporary ramps available

Special needs

ADD	Attention Deficit Disorder
ADHD	Attention Deficit/Hyperactivity Disorder
ASD	Autistic Spectrum Disorder
ASP	Asperger's Syndrome
BESD	Behavioural, Emotional and Social Disorders
CB	Challenging Behaviour
CP	Cerebral Palsy
DOW	Down's Syndrome
DYC	Dyscalculia
DYP	Dyspraxia
DYS	Dyslexia
EPI	Epilepsy
HEA	Health Problems (eg heart defect, asthma)
HI	Hearing Impairment
IM	Impaired Mobility
MLD	Moderate Learning Difficulties
PMLD	Profound and Multiple Learning Difficulties
SLD	Severe Learning Difficulties
SP&LD	Speech and Language Difficulties
TOU	Tourette's Syndrome
VI	Visual Impairment
WU	Wheelchair User

5.12
Further Reading

Schools and Further Education

Schools for Special Needs: A complete guide
14th Edition: Gabbitas Educational Consultants
*The definitive guide to special needs education in the UK
£19.99   Paperback   ISBN 978 0 7494 5086 1   697 pages   2008

How to Pass Secondary School Selection Tests
Contains over 600 Practice Questions
Mike Bryon
*Ideal for 11+ common entrance & SATS
£8.99   Paperback   ISBN 978 0 7494 4217 0   224 pages   2004

Everything You Need to Know about Going to University
3rd Edition: Sally Longson
"comprehensive resource to help you make the right choices" – Mandy Telford, former National President, National Union of Students,
£9.99   Paperback   ISBN 978 0 7494 3985 9   192 pages   2003

Educational Reference

British Qualifications
A complete guide to professional, vocational & academic qualifications in the United Kingdom
39th Edition
"The single best one-volume reference on British educational awards in print" – *World Education News & Reviews*
£48.00   Paperback   ISBN 978 0 7494 5342 8   1104 pages   2008
£70.00   Hardback   ISBN 978 0 7494 5343 5   1104 pages   2008

British Vocational Qualifications
A directory of vocational qualifications available in the United Kingdom
10th Edition
"Splendid. . . Every imaginable accessible procedure is packed into its pages" – *New Statesman*
£40.00   Paperback   ISBN 978 0 7494 5074 8   464 pages   2008

Careers

The A–Z of Careers & Jobs
16th Edition: Susan Hodgson published in association with *The Times*
"The perfect starting point for students and school leavers" – *Education & Training*
£14.99   Paperback   ISBN 978 0 7494 5510 1   480 pages   2009

Also available:

Careers & Jobs in IT David Yardley   £7.99   Paperback   ISBN 978 0 7494 4245 X   144 pages   2004
Careers & Jobs in the Police Service   Kim Clabby   £7.99   Paperback   ISBN 978 0 7494 4204 2   112 pages   2004
Careers & Jobs in Travel & Tourism   Verité Reily Collins   £7.99   Paperback   ISBN 978 0 7494 4205 0   112 pages   2004

What Next after School?
All you need to know about work, travel & study
7th Edition: Elizabeth Holmes, published in association with *The Times*
"A wealth of practical information about the world of work, training and higher-education" – *Evening Standard*
£7.99   Paperback   ISBN 978 0 7494 5401 2   400 pages   2008

What Next after University?
Work, travel, education & life with a degree
2nd Edition: Simon Kent, published in association with *The Times*
"Covers everything from basic work, travel and education options and graduate recruitment tests to finding a home and personal finance" – *Girl About Town*
£8.99   Paperback   ISBN 978 0 7494 4251 4   320 pages   2004

Job Applications

Great Answers to Tough Interview Questions
7th Edition: Martin Yate
"The best book on job-hunting." – *Financial Times*
£8.99   Paperback   ISBN 978 0 7494 5196 7   240 pages   2008

Ultimate CV
Write the perfect CV and get that job
Martin Yate
*Over 100 samples of job-winning CVs
£9.99   Paperback   ISBN 0 978 0 7494 5327 5   2008

Ultimate Job Search Letters
Write the perfect letter and get that job
Martin Yate
£9.99   Paperback   ISBN 978 0 7494 5328 2   2008

Readymade Job Search Letters
Every type of letter for getting the job you want
3rd Edition: Lynn Williams, published in association with *The Times*
"The first book I've seen which specifically deals with letters. . . . A really useful resource" – *Phoenix Journal*, Keele University
£8.99   Paperback   ISBN 978 0 7494 5322 0   224 pages   2008

Readymade CVs
Sample CVs for every type of job
3rd Edition: Lynn Williams, published in association with *The Times*
"A resource book offering several ways to design your CV for a multitude of needs" – *All About Money Making*
£8.99   Paperback   ISBN 978 0 7494 5323 7   224 pages   2008

Property

The Complete Guide to Buying & Selling Property
How to get the best deal on your home
2nd Edition: Sarah O'Grady
Published in association with the *Daily Express*
"Valuable, no-nonsense information" – *Ideal Home*
£8.99   Paperback   ISBN 978 0 7494 4194 4   240 pages   2004

The Complete Guide to Renovating & Improving Your Property
2nd Edition: Liz Hodgkinson
"Focuses on major renovation work, from obtaining planning permission to employing and managing contractors" – *What Mortgage*
£10.99   Paperback   ISBN 978 0 7494 4870 7   224 pages   2007

Also available:

The Complete Guide to Buying Property Abroad
7th Edition: Liz Hodgkinson
£12.99 Paperback ISBN 978 0 7494 5240 7   320 pages 2008

The Complete Guide to Buying Property in France
4th Edition: Charles Davey
£10.99   Paperback   ISBN 978 0 7494 4646 8   304 pages   2006

The Complete Guide to Buying Property in Italy
Barbara McMahon
£9.99   Paperback   ISBN 978 0 4794 4151 7   224 pages   2004

The Complete Guide to Buying Property in Portugal
Colin Barrow
£9.99   Paperback   ISBN 978 0 7494 4303 0   240 pages   2005

The Complete Guide to Buying Property in Spain
Charles Davey
£9.99 Paperback   ISBN 978 0 7494 4056 5   208 pages   2004

Personal Finance

A Complete Guide to Family Finance
Essential advice on everything from student loans to inheritance tax
Roderick Millar: published in association with the *Daily Express*
*Comprehensive and practical advice on everything you need to know about saving, investing and insuring for the future.
£12.99   Paperback   ISBN 978 0 7494 4203 3   368 pages   2004

How the Stock Market Works
A beginner's guide to investment
2nd Edition: Michael Beckett
"Not just for investors, but for anyone who wishes to understand our financial system" – Neil Collins, City Editor, *Daily Telegraph*
£8.99   Paperback   ISBN 978 0 7494 4190 6   208 pages   2004

How to Write Your Will
18th Edition: Marlene Garsia
"A practical and easy-to-read guide" – *Pensions World*
£9.99   Paperback   ISBN 978 0 7494 5325 1   240 pages   2008

Relocation

Working Abroad
The complete guide to overseas employment
29th Edition: Jonathan Reuvid
"Anyone involved in working abroad will quickly come to look upon this as their bible" – *Personnel Today*
£12.99   Paperback   ISBN 978 0 7494 5057 1   320 pages   2008

Kogan Page publishes books on Business, Management, Marketing, HR, Training, Careers and Testing, Personal Finance, Property and more.

Visit our website for our full online catalogue:
www.koganpage.com

5.13
Main Index

C

D

G

Maria Montessori School Hampstead, London
   NW3   143
Maria Montessori School, Exeter   97
The Marist Preparatory School, Ascot   75, 298, 451,
   471, 485
The Marist Senior School, Ascot   75, 298, 421, 451,
   471, 485
Mark College, Highbridge   474
Markazul Uloom, Blackburn   129, 453, 470
Marlborough College, Marlborough   217, 431,
   444, 461, 468, 494
Marlborough House School, Hawkhurst   125, 439,
   458, 468, 488
The Mary Erskine School, Edinburgh   238, 433,
   446, 455, 462, 495
Marycourt School, Gosport   112, 424
Marymount International School, Kingston-upon-
   Thames   196, 364, 430, 443, 454, 460, 471, 481,
   492
Mayfield Preparatory School, Walsall   215, 493
The Maynard School, Exeter   97, 423, 437, 452,
   477, 486
Maypole House School, Alford   135, 426, 439, 465
Mayville High School, Southsea   114, 424, 438,
   475, 478, 487
The Mead School, Tunbridge Wells   128, 439, 465
Meadowbrook Montessori School, Bracknell   75,
   468
Meadowpark Nursery & Pre-Prep School,
   Cricklade   216, 465
Mechinah Liyeshivah Zichron Moshe, London
   N16   141, 449, 470
Meoncross School, Fareham   111, 424
Merchant Taylors' Boys' Schools, Liverpool   162,
   427, 440, 449
Merchant Taylors' Girls' School, Liverpool   163,
   427, 440, 453, 479, 490
Merchant Taylors' School, Liverpool   490
Merchant Taylors' School, Northwood   166, 427,
   440, 449, 468, 490
Merchiston Castle School, Edinburgh   239, 402,
   433, 446, 451, 462, 483, 495
The Merlin School, London SW15   153
Merton Court Preparatory School, Sidcup   127,
   425, 439, 468
Merton House, Chester   90, 422, 468
Methodist College, Belfast   230, 432, 445, 462, 495
Michael Hall (Steiner Waldorf School), Forest
   Row   203, 460, 481
Michael House Steiner School, Heanor   95, 437
Micklefield School, Reigate   198, 468, 492
Milbourne Lodge School, Esher   193, 430, 468, 492

Mill Hill School, London NW7   145, 426, 440, 459,
   479, 489
The Mill School, Devizes   217
Millfield Preparatory School, Glastonbury   181,
   428, 442, 460, 480, 491
Millfield School, Street   181, 428, 442, 460, 480,
   491
Milton Abbey School, Blandford Forum   100, 388,
   423, 437, 457, 468, 475, 477, 486
Milton Keynes Preparatory School, Milton
   Keynes   84, 422, 436, 477, 485
Milverton House School, Nuneaton   211
The Minster School, York   224, 432, 468, 494
The Moat School, Fulham   474
Moffats School, Bewdley   219, 291, 432, 444, 461,
   468, 482, 494
Moira House Girls School, Eastbourne   203, 430,
   443, 454, 460, 481, 493
Moira House School, Eastbourne   203, 373, 430,
   443, 454, 460, 481
Monkton Combe Junior School, Bath   491
Monkton Combe School, Bath   475, 491
Monkton Prep, Bath   184, 429, 442, 460, 468
Monkton Senior School, Bath   184, 429, 442, 460,
   468, 480
Monmouth School, Monmouth   247, 434, 446,
   451, 463, 466, 483, 496
The Montessori House, London N10   141
Monton Prep School with Montessori Nurseries,
   Eccles   160, 440, 465
Moon Hall School, Dorking   474
Moor Allerton School, Manchester   161, 490
Moor Park School, Ludlow   179, 428, 441, 459,
   471, 480, 491
Moorfield School, Ilkley   227, 455, 494
Moorland School, Clitheroe   130, 439, 458, 468,
   479
Moorlands School, Leeds   228, 445, 494
Moorlands School, Luton   74, 421, 435, 484
More House School, Farnham   194, 450, 460, 471,
   474, 492
More House, London SW1   149, 338, 427, 440,
   453, 471, 489
Moreton Hall Preparatory School, Bury St
   Edmunds   187, 429, 442, 460, 471, 481, 492
Moreton Hall School, Oswestry   179, 288, 428,
   441, 454, 459, 480, 491
Morley Hall Preparatory School, Derby   95, 468
Morrison's Academy, Crieff   433, 446, 483, 495
Mostyn House School, South Wirral   91, 422, 436,
   475, 477, 485
Mougins School, France   250, 410, 483

T

W

XYZ